T0190368

Dirk Fahland · Chiara Ghidini ·
Jörg Becker · Marlon Dumas (Eds.)

Business Process Management

18th International Conference, BPM 2020
Seville, Spain, September 13–18, 2020
Proceedings

 Springer

Editors
Dirk Fahland 🆔
Eindhoven University of Technology
Eindhoven, The Netherlands

Chiara Ghidini 🆔
FBK-irst
Trento, Italy

Jörg Becker 🆔
University of Münster
Münster, Germany

Marlon Dumas 🆔
University of Tartu
Tartu, Estonia

ISSN 0302-9743   ISSN 1611-3349   (electronic)
Lecture Notes in Computer Science
ISBN 978-3-030-58665-2   ISBN 978-3-030-58666-9   (eBook)
https://doi.org/10.1007/978-3-030-58666-9

LNCS Sublibrary: SL3 – Information Systems and Applications, incl. Internet/Web, and HCI

This Springer imprint is published by the registered company Springer Nature Switzerland AG
The registered company address is: Gewerbestrasse 11, 6330 Cham, Switzerland

Preface

The year 2020 will be remembered as the time when many business processes were turned upside down as a result of the COVID-19 pandemic. The process of organizing and hosting conferences was one of them. The 18th International Conference on Business Process Management (BPM 2020) was no exception. Under the leadership of the general chairs, Manuel Resinas and Antonio Ruiz Cortés, from University of Seville, Spain, BPM 2020 became the first edition in the BPM conference series to be held online.

The World Health Organization declared COVID-19 a global pandemic on March 12, 2020, just four days before the deadline for paper submissions. As many countries entered into lock-down, the BPM research community displayed an exemplary level of resilience and flexibility. Despite the disruptions caused by the lock-down, the conference received 138 full paper submissions, which is comparable to the number of submissions on a regular year.

As in previous editions, the BPM 2020 conference was structured into three tracks, corresponding to the three traditional communities of the conference series: the foundations track (computer science), the engineering track (information systems engineering), and the management track (information systems management). Out of the 138 submissions, 32 came into the foundations track, 50 into the engineering track, and 56 into the management track. Following initial verification of each paper leading to some desk-rejections, 125 submissions made it to the review process (respectively 28, 45, and 52 across the three tracks).

The tracks cover not only different phenomena of interest and research methods, but also apply different evaluation criteria. Accordingly, each track had a dedicated track chair and Program Committee. The foundations track was chaired by Dirk Fahland, the engineering track by Chiara Ghidini, and the management track by Jörg Becker. Marlon Dumas acted as consolidation chair. Each paper was reviewed by at least three Program Committee members and a Senior Program Committee member who triggered and moderated scientific discussions that were summarized in a meta-review. In the end, we accepted 27 papers to the main conference (acceptance rate 19.5%). Moreover, 19 submissions appeared in the BPM Forum, published in a separate volume of the Springer LNBIP series.

The accepted papers cover a wide range of topics, from multiple perspectives. Alongside already well-established topics such as business process modeling, process mining, process redesign, BPM maturity, and stakeholder management, we witnessed a notable increase in submissions related to predictive process monitoring and robotic process automation, in line with ongoing industry developments.

The topics of the conference are also reflected by the keynote speakers. Avigdor Gal, from Technion, Israel, spoke about process mining, specifically reflecting on the ongoing move in this field from small data to big data. Rama Akkiraju from IBM, USA, exposed her vision of how AI techniques will transform the DNA of business processes and the challenges that this transformation raises for researchers and practitioners. Finally, Jan vom Brocke led a reflection into the meaning of process science and how the BPM research community needs to take the next step in embracing its multidisciplinary nature by conceptualizing processes in a way that is independent from a single discipline's perspective.

This year, the conference made a step towards embracing the principles of Open Science, including reproducibility and replicability. The evaluation form for research papers included an item asking reviewers if the artifacts (prototypes, interview protocols, questionnaires) and the datasets used in or produced by the empirical evaluation reported in the paper, are available in a suitable form. Authors were asked to include in their paper a link to one or more repositories where reviewers could find the research artifacts associated with the paper. We are thankful to the authors for embracing these principles as reflected by the large proportion of papers that have permanent links to artifacts.

Organizing a scientific conference is a complex process involving many roles and countless interactions. The pivot from a physical conference to an online conference added to this complexity. We thank all our colleagues involved for their exemplary work. The workshop chairs attracted seven workshops, the tutorial chairs attracted five tutorials, the industry chairs organized an exciting industry forum, the doctoral consortium chairs allowed PhD students to benefit from the advice of experienced researchers, and the demo chairs expanded the scope of the demonstrations track in order to host not only tool demonstrations, but also presentations of resources of interest to the community, such as datasets and benchmarks. Weaving across all these tracks, the publicity chairs energetically mobilized the BPM research community despite the challenging times, while the proceedings chair, Bedilia Estrada, professionally interacted with Springer and with the authors to seamlessly prepare the conference and forum proceedings, as well as the other proceedings associated with the conference.

The members of the tracks' Program Committees and Senior Program Committees deserve particular acknowledgment for their dedication and commitment. We are grateful for the help and expertise of sub-reviewers, who provided valuable feedback during the reviewing process and engaged in deep discussions at times. BPM 2020 had a dedicated process to consolidate paper acceptance across tracks. During the very intensive weeks of this phase, many Senior Program Committee members evaluated additional papers and were engaged in additional discussions. Special thanks go to these colleagues, who were instrumental during this crucial phase of the reviewing process. We also thank our sponsors: Signavio (Platinum), Celonis (Platinum), AuraPortal (Gold), DCR Solutions (Gold), Papyrus (Silver), Springer, and University of Seville.

Finally, we applaud the Organizing Committee, including Adela del Río Ortega, Amador Durán, Alfonso Márquez, Bedilia Estrada, and Beatriz Bernárdez who, together with the general chairs, sacrificed a tremendous amount of time to overcome the challenges of switching from a physical to an online conference. The BPM research community is forever grateful for their effort.

September 2020

Dirk Fahland
Chiara Ghidini
Jörg Becker
Marlon Dumas

In Memoriam of Florian Daniel

Fabio Casati[1], Stefano Ceri[2], and Marco Montali[3]

[1] Servicenow, Inc., USA
[2] Politecnico di Milano, Italy
[3] Free University of Bozen-Bolzano, Italy

Florian Daniel recently passed away, at the age of 42. He was not only a passionate, frank, enthusiastic person, but also a brilliant, sharp, thoughtful colleague. He was a multifaceted, talented researcher who contributed to advance the state of the art in several areas of research, including that of Business Process Management. In this *In Memoriam* we briefly recall the scientific career of Florian, as well as his impact and service to the BPM community. We then include some memories from colleagues who had the chance, and the pleasure, to work with him. Those who loved or knew him will for sure find some of his most distinctive traits. Those who did not will learn about a role model who inspired, and will inspire, many of us.

1 Academic Life and Impact in BPM

Florian's career as a student was at Politecnico di Milano, where he obtained his master degree cum laude in 2003 and his PhD in 2007; then, after a short period as post doc, he moved to Trento. During his PhD, advised by Stefano Ceri, Florian was extremely prolific: by 2008, Florian had produced 11 journal papers and 22 conference papers, setting an outstanding record of productivity. What is most impressive, Florian managed to collaborate with over 50 scholars – besides Stefano Ceri and Fabio Casati who had been mentoring him in Milano and Trento, he started working with scholars who have been work companions throughout his life, including Maristella Matera, Boualem Benatallah, and Sven Casteleyn; in 2008 he produced the first of many works with Cinzia Cappiello, much loved partner in life.

In his early years, Florian's interests covered several aspects, but with a very coherent approach. Topics included web applications, web services, process modeling, and mashups; the research contribution made them well founded and sound, but also simple, clear, and easy to use and compose. Throughout his very productive career, thanks to his acute and brilliant mindset, Florian's work has been able to mix formal elegance and abstraction with pragmatics and engineering. He left Milano for Trento,

We are deeply thankful to Chiara Ghidini and Marlon Dumas for having supported this initiative, and to the many colleagues who contributed to this *In Memoriam* by sharing their experiences, thoughts, and feelings.

but he continuously collaborated within an international network rooted in Milano and Trento but encompassing a huge number of collaborators worldwide. In Trento, he worked with Fabio to advise dozens of PhD students, lead EU and industrial projects, and write grants. In summary, as a post doc, he was already doing the kind of work expected from a professor, and was doing so brilliantly. He was always incredibly helpful and supportive with the students as well as brilliant and prolific in research. Besides Milano and Trento, his affiliations included HP in Palo Alto, the University of Alicante, UNSW in Sydney, PUCRS in Porto Alegre, TPU in Tomsk, UNIST in Korea, and USI in Lugano – a sign of his ability to create collaborations around the world.

Florian was active in the BPM conference and community since the time he joined the University of Trento, both as author and organizer. As for service to the community, he acted as program chair of the BPM 2013 conference, held in Beijing. He was workshop chair twice: at BPM 2011 in Clermont-Ferrand and at BPM 2018 in Sydney. He also served as Program Committee (PC) member and Senior PC member in several editions of the conference. Research wise, he contributed to advancing the state of the art in BPM along several research directions, all oriented towards enriching process models and systems with computational and human intelligence. Particularly interesting is how Florian was able to intertwine processes with mashups and crowdsourcing. In this respect, we like to remember his work on distributed orchestration of user interfaces [1], on crowd-based mining of process patterns [2], and on micro-task crowdsourcing [3].

The approach in [1] brings forward the notion of distributed orchestration for user interfaces. Specifically, the paper presents a novel component-based model, language, and system for orchestrating complex processes that include human tasks, which in turn require dedicated, end user-tailored interfaces. Well-known research challenges related to process and service orchestration, and composition is consequently lifted to the much more challenging case where humans are part of the picture.

In [2] a complementary perspective is adopted: instead of studying how to better support humans during the execution of processes, the paper investigates how humans can be effective when mining specifications, a task that is usually ascribed to machines. The type of specification considered in the paper is that of model patterns, to be extracted from a repository of mashup (or process) models. Notably, an extensive experimental evaluation leads to the conclusion that a complex task such as that of model pattern mining can be effectively crowdsourced, obtaining patterns that are rich in domain knowledge especially in the case where the input repository is small.

Finally, [3] proposes an extension of BPMN to properly account for crowdsourcing processes where different tasks and multiple actors (machines, individual humans, and the crowd) are integrated. The notion of multi-instance task in BPMN is conceptually extended towards that of crowd task. But the paper does not limit itself to modeling: it also shows how to enrich standard BPMN engines with crowdsourcing platforms, resolving the impedance mismatch between the process orchestration flow and the flow of information produced by the crowd.

All in all, the three papers are exemplar witnesses of Florian's passion in research: the intersection between processes, user interfaces, and people.

2   Memories from Colleagues

We have collected some memories, impressions, thoughts, anecdotes about Florian from various colleagues active in the BPM community, and who had the chance to know Florian and to work with him.

Barbara Pernici. I met Florian many years ago during his PhD at Politecnico di Milano where he attended a PhD course. At that time, I came to know about his brilliant mind and, on the side, how passionate he was about brewing beer. Many years later he talked to me about possible student projects, about supporting recipes, and beer production with very sophisticated workflows. He was so passionate about it and several groups of students enjoyed working on those projects enjoying his very rigorous technical approach in research. He was a special and dedicated teacher and he was able to transmit his passion to all his students who loved him a lot. I will always remember how brilliant, gentle, and original he was.

Gigi Plebani. Florian was first of all a friend then a colleague. Literally. We started spending time together when we were PhD students and then postdocs at Politecnico. After his period in Trento, when he was came back to Milan, I was really happy for him and for Cinzia to really start living together and also to have more opportunities to talk with him about everything: life, running, beers, and eventually work. Yep, even though I knew Florian for 15 years, it was only last year that we had the chance to work together when we started to investigate on the relationship between business processes and blockchains. Thus, I had the possibility to see how the same kindness, determination, and method he used to face any type of issues in life, he also used to apply to his research works. It was great to work together with the students of Alta Scuola Politecnica, to share ideas with him, and together, make those ideas grow. In many situations, we did not have the same opinion, but he was always open to understand the others' standpoint and we had the opportunity to make our positions more aligned. Thanks Florian, it was a pleasure to know you. I learned a lot from you, as a man and as a researcher. Everyone can appreciate your contribution to research, but only I can appreciate your contribution to my life.

Wil van der Aalst. Florian was an amazing person: smart, funny, and social. He was an active and highly respected member of the BPM community for many years. Next to his seminal contribution to the Business Process Management (BPM) field, he worked on web engineering, service-oriented computing, blockchain, and crowdsourcing. Florian is well-known for his work on mashup development, context-aware web applications, service composition, and crowdsourcing. He was also active in organizing various events within our community. He was able to connect different fields and

Fig. 1. Florian was one of the PC chairs of the successful BMP 2013 conference in Beijing.

Fig. 2. There as always time to socialize with fellow BPM-ers.

communities. He was also one of the program chairs of the International Business Process Management conference in Beijing in 2013 and workshop chair of BPM 2011 and 2018. I vividly remember a trip to Rifugio Maranza (a mountain hut close to Povo).[1] He was always able to create a positive atmosphere where people matter most. In his last email to me he wrote: "Sure... mountains in Milano... not good. But with good weather I can see them in the distance :-) ... There is beer too in Milano :-)." This is the way that I would like to remember him.

---

[1] A note from Marco: I was also there. We organized a visit to Florian and Fabio in Povo. Florian had the idea to meet in the woods instead of the department. This transformed what could have been a standard research meeting into one of the most striking memories I have, not just about Florian, but about my research life in general.

Fig. 3. During presentations in one of the main tracks and demo session at BPM 2012, Tallinn, Estonia.

Frank Leymann. I met Florian the first time more than a decade ago in 2008 in context of the EU project COMPAS. This project was about compliance by design, and one of the focus areas was compliance of business processes. My team worked on the modeling side, how to specify corresponding compliance rules as process fragments, while Florian (part of Fabio's group) worked on how to assess compliance during runtime and present it properly on a dashboard. Very soon it became clear to me that Florian was exceptional, both, as a scientist as well as a human. We soon became friends: besides joint cooperations, we had several joint dinners and drank "one or two" beers (well, it's mandatory to mention "beer" when remembering Florian). He was very passionate about his work, and he was able to explain his ideas very clearly and vividly. Because of this, I was always very pleased when he accepted invitations to my institute to discuss and present his ideas to a broader community. But also via mail, we were exchanging ideas and joint publications resulted. For example, in the area of blockchains, a language to describe smart contracts and a mechanism to actually locate them has been designed. In our last work, we were focusing on function as a service – which we are finishing in his spirit. We wanted to meet in Milano in September to begin an exchange on quantum computing to see what we could jointly contribute to this area. Then, we planned to finally realize a long delayed idea: a joint hiking tour in Tuscany, having "one or two" glasses of – well not beer – wine together. It turned out that we delayed this event for too long …

Boualem Benatallah. I have known Florian since 2006. Florian was both a friend and a colleague. We have collaborated intensively in the area of web services and mashups, quality control in crowdsourcing, and more recently on conversational bots. Multiple times, Florian visited UNSW for one or two months joint research periods. I also visited him in Politecnico di Milano. We planned to meet in Milano this September to continue working on our recent collaborative work. We co-authored several research papers and jointly supervised students. I will always remember his positive, collaborative, and constructive attitude. I also enjoyed our social meetings and friendship. Florian was a highly respected member of the research community and a wonderful colleague and friend. He will be remembered by his outstanding scholarly achievements and research contributions to the research community and also services to the university and community.

Carlos Rodriguez. Florian was a wonderful person, academic and professional. I was very lucky to have him not only as a co-advisor during my PhD studies at the University of Trento, but also as a colleague and friend. As an advisor he taught our cohort the best professionalism and guided us in navigating the research world in a rigorous and systematic manner. In the area of BPM, we explored research problems in the context of business process compliance, crowdsourcing for BPM, and extraction of process progression information from transactional databases. As a colleague and friend, he was always happy to collaborate in projects, discuss ideas, and talk about life, where he would always bring in not only smart ideas and wisdom, but also passion and fun. On the latter, I just cannot emphasize enough how much fun it was to work and share time together with Florian. Even during the toughest deadlines and research challenges, Florian would always crack a joke or tell an anecdote that made us laugh and brought fun to our meetings. And, of course, outside work, we would always find some time to enjoy his amazing craft beers. I will always remember him as a true mentor and wonderful colleague and friend.

Stefano Ceri. Florian was one of my PhD students, he has always been appreciated by colleagues and friends for his frank character, his kindness and humanity, and also his ironic style, he was always able to surprise us with his keen observations. Activity with Florian went beyond the end of his PhD, we communicated perhaps more after graduation. I remember long conversations while attending a conference in Shanghai, we discussed a lot about research and what is important in life. During those days, he questioned some of my beliefs, and these dialogues started meditations that were important to me. He appericated scientific merit and independent thinking, thanks to these he was always able to live and work outside the box. When he won a researcher (RTB) position in Milan, he had publications warranting a full professorship; what's more important, he was a mature and independent thinker, as is clear from his production and overwhelming number of collaborations. Florian leaves our department with an immense void.

Fabio Casati. Florian has been, and is, a close friend, a colleague, and an inspiration to me for many years. I will never forget the many lessons that he gave by example – never with the intent to teach. Many of them had to do with how you approach any problem with the care and passion it deserves, without hidden goals but only with the objective of doing the best he could in solving a problem and being as helpful as possible for those affected, be it the occasional lecture, the work on a project deliverable, a small research effort with a bachelor student, and on and on. As I said many times for the last 10 years, he would have been my choice for full professorship since three years into his post doc tenure. Everywhere he went, in whatever environment, he would just make that place a better one. He was the friend and colleague anybody would want to have, and when he left Trento, although he moved only two hours away, it felt like losing a part of me. To this day, I still think about how he would behave in a given situation, and this helps me figure out the right course of action. Florian, I am sure you are happy and drinking (and probably a bit drunk) wherever you are. We miss you.

References

1. Daniel, F., Soi, S., Tranquillini, S., Casati, F., Heng, C., Yan, L.: From people to services to UI: distributed orchestration of user interfaces. In: Hull, R., Mendling, J., Tai, S. (eds.) BPM 2010. LNCS, vol. 6336, pp. 310–326. Springer, Heidelberg (2010). https://doi.org/10.1007/978-3-642-15618-2_22
2. Rodríguez, C., Daniel, F., Casati, F.: Crowd-based mining of reusable process model patterns. In: Sadiq, S., Soffer, P., Völzer, H. (eds.) BPM 2014. LNCS, vol. 8659, pp. 51–66. Springer, Cham (2014). https://doi.org/10.1007/978-3-319-10172-9_4
3. Tranquillini, S., Daniel, F., Kucherbaev, P., Casati, F.: BPMN task instance streaming for efficient micro-task crowdsourcing processes. In: Motahari-Nezhad, H., Recker, J., Weidlich, M. (eds.) BPM 2016. LNCS, vol. 9253, pp. 333–349. Springer, Cham (2015). https://doi.org/10.1007/978-3-319-23063-4_23

Organization

The 18th International Conference on Business Process Management (BPM 2020) was organized by the Research Group of Applied Software Engineering (ISA Group) at the University of Seville, Spain, with the collaboration of SCORE Lab and the Instituto de Investigación en Ingeniería Informática (I3US). It took place online due to the restrictions imposed because of the COVID-19 pandemic. Originally, it was going to take place in Seville, Spain.

Steering Committee

Mathias Weske (Chair)	HPI, University of Potsdam, Germany
Boualem Benatallah	University of New South Wales, Australia
Jörg Desel	Fernuniversität in Hagen, Germany
Shazia Sadiq	The University of Queensland, Australia
Marlon Dumas	University of Tartu, Estonia
Wil van der Aalst	RWTH Aachen University, Germany
Jan Mendling	Vienna University of Economics and Business, Austria
Barbara Weber	University of St. Gallen, Switzerland
Stefanie Rinderle-Ma	University of Vienna, Austria
Manfred Reichert	Ulm University, Germany
Michael Rosemann	Queensland University of Technology, Australia

Executive Committee

General Chairs

Manuel Resinas	University of Seville, Spain
Antonio Ruiz-Cortés	University of Seville, Spain

Main Conference Program Chairs

Dirk Fahland (Track Chair, Track I)	Eindhoven University of Technology, The Netherlands
Chiara Ghidini (Track Chair, Track II)	Fondazione Bruno Kessler-IRST, Italy
Jörg Becker (Track Chair, Track III)	University of Münster, ERCIS, Germany
Marlon Dumas (Consolidation)	University of Tartu, Estonia

Workshop Chairs

Henrik Leopold	Kühne Logistics University, Germany
Adela del Río Ortega	University of Seville, Spain
Flavia Maria Santoro	Rio de Janeiro State University, Brazil

Demonstration and Resources Chairs

Marco Comuzzi	Ulsan National Institute of Science and Technology, South Korea
Claudio Di Ciccio	Sapienza University of Rome, Italy
Luise Pufahl	Technische Universität Berlin, Germany

Industry Forum Chairs

Gero Decker	Signavio, Germany
Manuel Lama	Universidade de Santiago de Compostela, Spain
Pedro Robledo	ABPMP Spain, Spain

Blockchain Forum Chairs

José María García	University of Seville, Spain
Agnes Koschmider	Kiel University, Germany
Jan Mendling	Vienna University of Economics and Business, Austria
Giovanni Meroni	Politecnico di Milano, Italy

RPA Forum Chairs

Aleksandre Asatiani	University of Gothenburg, Sweden
Nina Helander	Tampere University, Finland
Andrés Jiménez-Ramírez	University of Seville, Spain
Hajo A. Reijers	Utrecht University, The Netherlands

Doctoral Consortium Chairs

Félix García	University of Castilla-La Mancha, Spain
Manfred Reichert	Ulm University, Germany
Jan vom Brocke	University of Liechtenstein, Liechtenstein

Tutorial Chairs

Josep Carmona	Universitat Politècnica de Catalunya, Spain
Hajo A. Reijers	Utrecht University, The Netherlands
Minseok Song	Pohang University of Science and Technology, South Korea

Panel Chairs

Ernest Teniente	Universitat Politècnica de Catalunya, Spain
Mathias Weidlich	Humboldt-Universität zu Berlin, Germany

BPM Dissertation Award Chair

Jan Mendling   Vienna University of Economics and Business, Austria

Organizing Committees Chairs

Adela del Río Ortega   University of Seville, Spain
Amador Durán   University of Seville, Spain

Publicity Chairs

Cristina Cabanillas   University of Seville, Spain
Artem Polyvyanyy   The University of Melbourne, Australia
Kate Revoredo   Vienna University of Economics and Business, Austria
Armin Stein   University of Münster, Germany

Web Chair

Alfonso Márquez   University of Seville, Spain

Proceedings Chair

Bedilia Estrada-Torres   University of Seville, Spain

Supporting Staff Coordination Chair

Beatriz Bernárdez   University of Seville, Spain

Track I – Foundations

Senior Program Committee

Florian Daniel   Politecnico di Milano, Italy
Jörg Desel   Fernuniversität in Hagen, Germany
Chiara Di Francescomarino   Fondazione Bruno Kessler-IRST, Italy
Thomas Hildebrandt   University of Copenhagen, Denmark
Fabrizio Maria Maggi   Free University of Bozen-Bolzano, Italy
Marco Montali   Free University of Bozen-Bolzano, Italy
John Mylopoulos   University of Toronto, Canada
Oscar Pastor Lopez   Universitat Politècnica de València, Spain
Artem Polyvyanyy   The University of Melbourne, Australia
Manfred Reichert   Ulm University, Germany
Arthur Ter Hofstede   Queensland University of Technology, Australia
Hagen Voelzer   IBM Research, Switzerland
Mathias Weske   HPI, University of Potsdam, Germany

Program Committee

Lars Ackermann   University of Bayreuth, Germany
Daniel Amyot   University of Ottawa, Canada
Ahmed Awad   University of Tartu, Estonia

Irene Barba	University of Seville, Spain
Søren Debois	IT University of Copenhagen, Denmark
Claudio Di Ciccio	Sapienza University of Rome, Italy
Rik Eshuis	Eindhoven University of Technology, The Netherlands
Peter Fettke	German Research Center for Artificial Inteilligence (DFKI), Saarland University, Germany
Hans-Georg Fill	University of Fribourg, Switzerland
Luciano García-Bañuelos	Tecnológico de Monterrey, Mexico
María Teresa Gómez López	University of Seville, Spain
Guido Governatori	Data61, CSIRO, Australia
Gianluigi Greco	University of Calabria, Italy
Richard Hull	New York University, USA
Jetty Kleijn	LIACS, Leiden University, The Netherlands
Sander J. J. Leemans	Queensland University of Technology, Australia
Irina Lomazova	National Research University Higher School of Economics, Russia
Xixi Lu	Utrecht University, The Netherlands
Andrea Marrella	Sapienza University of Rome, Italy
Werner Nutt	Free University of Bozen-Bolzano, Italy
Wolfgang Reisig	Humboldt-Universität zu Berlin, Germany
Daniel Ritter	SAP, Germany
Andrey Rivkin	Free University of Bozen-Bolzano, Italy
Stefan Schönig	University of Regensburg, Germany
Arik Senderovich	University of Toronto, Canada
Tijs Slaats	University of Copenhagen, Denmark
Ernest Teniente	Universitat Politècnica de Catalunya, Spain
Sebastian Uchitel	University of Buenos Aires, Argentina, and Imperial College London, UK
Roman Vaculín	IBM Research, USA
Jan Martijn van der Werf	Utrecht University, The Netherlands
Francesca Zerbato	University of Verona, Italy

Track II – Engineering

Senior Program Committee

Andrea Burattin	Technical University of Denmark, Denmark
Josep Carmona	Universitat Politècnica de Catalunya, Spain
Remco Dijkman	Eindhoven University of Technology, The Netherlands
Avigdor Gal	Technion - Israel Institute of Technology, Israel
Marcello La Rosa	The University of Melbourne, Australia
Jorge Munoz-Gama	Pontificia Universidad Católica de Chile, Chile
Luise Pufahl	Technische Universität Berlin, Germany
Hajo A. Reijers	Utrecht University, The Netherlands
Stefanie Rinderle-Ma	University of Vienna, Austria
Pnina Soffer	University of Haifa, Israel

Wil van der Aalst   RWTH Aachen University, Germany
Boudewijn van Dongen   Eindhoven University of Technology, The Netherlands
Ingo Weber   Technische Universität Berlin, Germany
Matthias Weidlich   Humboldt-Universität zu Berlin, Germany

Program Committee

Marco Aiello   University of Stuttgart, Germany
Abel Armas Cervantes   The University of Melbourne, Australia
Boualem Benatallah   University of New South Wales, Australia
Cristina Cabanillas   University of Seville, Spain
Fabio Casati   ServiceNow, USA
Massimiliano de Leoni   University of Padua, Italy
Jochen De Weerdt   Katholieke Universiteit Leuven, Belgium
Joerg Evermann   Memorial University of Newfoundland, Canada
Walid Gaaloul   Télécom SudParis, France
Daniela Grigori   Laboratoire LAMSADE, Paris Dauphine University,
                                        France
Georg Grossmann   University of South Australia, Australia
Anna Kalenkova   The University of Melbourne, Australia
Dimka Karastoyanova   University of Groningen, The Netherlands
Agnes Koschmider   Karlsruhe Institute of Technology, Germany
Henrik Leopold   Kühne Logistics University, Germany
Felix Mannhardt   SINTEF Digital, Norway
Elisa Marengo   Free University of Bozen-Bolzano, Italy
Jan Mendling   Vienna University of Economics and Business, Austria
Rabeb Mizouni   Khalifa University, UAE
Hye-Young Paik   University of New South Wales, Australia
Cesare Pautasso   University of Lugano, Switzerland
Pierluigi Plebani   Politecnico di Milano, Italy
Pascal Poizat   Université Paris Nanterre, LIP6, France
Barbara Re   University of Camerino, Italy
Manuel Resinas   University of Seville, Spain
Shazia Sadiq   The University of Queensland, Australia
Marcos Sepúlveda   Pontificia Universidad Católica de Chile, Chile
Natalia Sidorova   Eindhoven University of Technology, The Netherlands
Nick van Beest   Data61, CSIRO, Australia
Han van der Aa   Humboldt-Universität zu Berlin, Germany
Sebastiaan J. van Zelst   Fraunhofer FIT, Germany
Barbara Weber   University of St. Gallen, Switzerland
Moe Thandar Wynn   Queensland University of Technology, Australia
Nicola Zannone   Eindhoven University of Technology, The Netherlands

Track III – Management

Senior Program Committee

Daniel Beverungen	Universität Paderborn, Germany
Adela del Río Ortega	University of Seville, Spain
Patrick Delfmann	Universität Koblenz-Landau, Germany
Paul Grefen	Eindhoven University of Technology, The Netherlands
Susanne Leist	University of Regensburg, Germany
Peter Loos	IWi at DFKI, Saarland University, Germany
Martin Matzner	Friedrich-Alexander-Universität Erlangen-Nürnberg, Germany
Jan Recker	University of Cologne, Germany
Maximilian Roeglinger	FIM Research Center Finance & Information Management, Germany
Michael Rosemann	Queensland University of Technology, Australia
Flavia Maria Santoro	Rio de Janeiro State University, Brazil
Peter Trkman	University of Ljubljana, Slovenia
Amy van Looy	Ghent University, Belgium
Jan Vom Brocke	University of Liechtenstein, Liechtenstein

Program Committee

Wasana Bandara	Queensland University of Technology, Australia
Alessio Maria Braccini	University of Tuscia, Italy
Friedrich Chasin	Universität Münster, Germany
Ann-Kristin Cordes	Universität Münster, Germany
Rod Dilnutt	The University of Melbourne, Australia
Michael Fellmann	University of Rostock, Germany
Elgar Fleisch	ETH Zurich, Switzerland
Frederik Gailly	Ghent University, Belgium
Bernd Heinrich	Universität Regensburg, Germany
Mojca Indihar Štemberger	University of Ljubljana, Slovenia
Christian Janiesch	Julius-Maximilians-Universität Würzburg, Germany
Peter Kawalek	Loughborough University, UK
Ralf Knackstedt	University of Hildesheim, Germany
John Krogstie	Norwegian University of Science and Technology, Norway
Michael Leyer	University of Rostock, Germany
Alexander Mädche	Karlsruhe Institute of Technology, Germany
Monika Malinova	Wirtschaftsuniversität Wien, Austria
Fredrik Milani	University of Tartu, Estonia
Juergen Moormann	Frankfurt School of Finance & Management, Germany
Markus Nüttgens	University of Hamburg, Germany
Sven Overhage	University of Bamberg, Germany
Ralf Plattfaut	Fachhochschule Südwestfalen, Germany
Geert Poels	Ghent University, Belgium

Jens Pöppelbuß	University of Bochum, Germany
Hans-Peter Rauer	Universität Münster, Germany
Dennis M. Riehle	Universität Münster, Germany
Stefan Sackmann	University of Halle-Wittenberg, Germany
Werner Schmidt	Technische Hochschule Ingolstadt Business School, Germany
Theresa Schmiedel	University of Applied Sciences and Arts Northwestern Switzerland, Switzerland
Minseok Song	Pohang University of Science and Technology, South Korea
Oktay Türetken	Eindhoven University of Technology, The Netherlands
Jan Vanthienen	Katholieke Universiteit Leuven, Belgium
Axel Winkelmann	Julius-Maximilians-Universität Würzburg, Germany

Additional Reviewers

Mehdi Acheli
Ivo Benke
Yevgen Bogodistov
Silvano Colombo Tosatto
Jasper Feine
Rick Gilsing
Sebastian Halsbenning
Markus Heuchert
Benedikt Hoffmeister
Felix Härer
Florian Johannsen
Julian Koch
Safak Korkut
Ingo Kregel
Martin Käppel
Fabienne Lambusch
Susanne Leist

Jonas Lutz
Hugo-Andrés López
Steven Mertens
Miguel Meza
Roman Nesterov
Xavier Oriol
Nadine Ostern
Guido Perscheid
Michael Poppe
Tim Rietz
Lorenzo Rossi
Alexander Schiller
Fatemeh Shafiee
Peyman Toreini
Michael Trampler
Jonas Wanner
Anna Wilbik

Abstracts of Keynotes

Process Minding: Closing the Big Data Gap

Avigdor Gal[1(✉)] and Arik Senderovich[2]

[1] Technion – Israel Institute of Technology, Technion City, 82000 Haifa, Israel
avigal@technion.ac.il
[2] University of Toronto, Toronto, Canada
arik.senderovich@utoronto.ca
http://ie.technion.ac.il/~avigal
https://ischool.utoronto.ca/profile/arik-senderovich/

Abstract. The discipline of process mining was inaugurated in the BPM community. It flourished in a world of small(er) data, with roots in the communities of software engineering and databases and applications mainly in organizational and management settings. The introduction of big data, with its volume, velocity, variety, and veracity, and the big strides in data science research and practice pose new challenges to this research field. The paper positions process mining along modern data life cycle, highlighting the challenges and suggesting directions in which data science disciplines (*e.g.*, machine learning) may interact with a renewed process mining agenda.

Characterizing Machine Learning Processes: A Maturity Framework

Rama Akkiraju[✉], Vibha Sinha, Anbang Xu, Jalal Mahmud,
Pritam Gundecha, Zhe Liu, Xiaotong Liu, and John Schumacher

IBM Watson, IBM Almaden Research Center, San Jose, CA, USA
{akkiraju,vibha.sinha,anbangxu,jumahmud,psgundec,
liuzh,Xiaotong.Liu,jfs}@us.ibm.com

Abstract. Academic literature on machine learning modeling fails to address how to make machine learning models work for enterprises. For example, existing machine learning processes cannot address how to define business use cases for an AI application, how to convert business requirements from product managers into data requirements for data scientists, and how to continuously improve AI applications in term of accuracy and fairness, how to customize general purpose machine learning models with industry, domain, and use case specific data to make them more accurate for specific situations etc. Making AI work for enterprises requires special considerations, tools, methods and processes. In this paper we present a maturity framework for machine learning model lifecycle management for enterprises. Our framework is a re-interpretation of the software Capability Maturity Model (CMM) for machine learning model development process. We present a set of best practices from authors' personal experience of building large scale real-world machine learning models to help organizations achieve higher levels of maturity independent of their starting point.

Keywords: Machine learning models · Maturity model · Maturity framework · AI model life cycle management

Towards Process Science: Embracing Interdisciplinary Research Opportunities in the Digital Age

Jan vom Brocke

Hilti Chair of Business Process Management, University of Liechtenstein,
Vaduz, Liechtenstein
jan.vom.brocke@uni.li

As process researchers, we live in exciting times. Processes are deeply interwoven with digital technologies, such as the Internet of Things, machine learning, distributed ledger technology combined with data analytics, among many others. Processes move beyond organizational boundaries and become independent entities of their own. Processes deliver and connect various services, such as health care, mobility, investments, education, and other important economic and societal services, while organizations such as hospitals, public transport, banks, and universities, only contribute specific shares in form of services to such processes. In essence, we see that processes (not organizations or applications) are becoming the prime phenomena of interest in the digital age. While the growing importance of process is fascinating, we need to ask: Are we prepared to fully embrace the new role of process within our research field? We see a central challenge ahead. We need to conceptualize processes independent of a single discipline's perspective but integrate contributions from various disciplinary fields. This is because processes are socio-technical by nature and, thus, they entail numerous aspects of different kinds. This is evident through contributions by well-established research disciplines, such as computer science, management science, and information systems research, which have developed distinct views on processes. With processes growing outside organizations and application systems, a plethora of additional disciplines will gain increasing importance, too, such as psychology, engineering, architecture, law, ethics, and others. This is exciting because such contributions – when brought together – will greatly advance our understanding of processes. However, we need a platform to integrate and synthesize those various contributions, and given the joint focus is process, we shall call this effort "process science". We envision process science as a new scientific field, which is based on three key pillars.

1. Interdisciplinary at its core. Process science is an inter disciplinary field that uses various scientific methods to generate knowledge about the development, implementation, and management of processes. Thereby, it draws on insights from various fields and aims to advance our understanding of how processes create value in diverse contexts and settings. These fields include organization science, information systems research, organizational design, computer science, psychology and neuroscience, ethics, among many others.

2. Continuous engagement in and between research and practice. The field of process science aims to develop a shared language among these disciplines in order to direct their attention towards shared phenomena. In order to think about processes in truly novel ways, we need to acknowledge and synthesize assumptions of individual fields. In our view, the term "process science" marks a new beginning for process research, where we develop common assumptions, a core terminology, joint research questions, as well as innovative ways to engage with practice to continuously update and further develop an emerging research agenda.
3. Creating impact by design. By integrating and synthesizing insights from various disciplines, process science aims to develop a prescriptive understanding of how processes can be designed and managed in context. Certainly, the competences we have developed in the field of BPM will play a key role to translate interdisciplinary perspectives into a prescriptive science about processes. The challenge is now how these different assumptions can be brought together under a unified vision of process science, design, and management.

To give an example, one big contribution process science can make is to advance our understanding of change and the adaptability of processes. In times, when change is the "new normal", the adaptability of processes becomes a crucial skill of the future. How can we organize for a spectrum of emerging changes where desired future states can hardly be anticipated? What are appropriate approaches when pre-defined to-be processes cannot be an option? How can we conceptualize, measure, and predict change? How can we allow for sufficient adaptability in the design and management of processes? Clearly, such solutions need contributions from various different perspectives, including technological infrastructures but also governance structures, skill sets, and cultural values to increase the adaptation capabilities of processes. The BPM community has the theories, methods, and tools to make such contributions. However, to get at the core of these phenomena, we need to equally embrace views and theories from other fields. This is what a joint effort in process science can deliver. This talk will sketch out the field of process science. The aim is to conceptualize essential elements of process science, provide examples for research projects, and stimulate a discourse on the establishment of process science as an interdisciplinary field both for research and practice. I invite all people with an interest in processes to be part of establishing process science to advance both theory and practice. It will be great to – on occasion of the BPM Conference 2020 – jointly bring process science to life and to decide on a few important operational next steps.

Abstracts of Tutorials

Queue Mining: Process Mining Meets Queueing Theory

Avigdor Gal[1], Arik Senderovich[2], and Matthias Weidlich[3]

[1] Technion – Israel Institute of Technology
avigal@ie.technion.ac.il
[2] University of Toronto
arik.senderovich@utoronto.ca
[3] Humboldt-Universität zu Berlin
matthias.weidlich@hu-berlin.de

Abstract. The tutorial will expose the audience to queue mining, which is a set of novel data-driven techniques used for modeling and analyzing complex resource-driven environments. Queue mining was born from the synergy between process mining [1] and queueing theory [2]. From automated discovery [3], through conformance checking [4], to predictive monitoring [5], process mining plays a key role in modern process-oriented data analysis. Historically, process mining has mainly focused on the single-case perspective, while in reality, performance of processes is highly influenced from correlations between running cases. Queueing theory, in turn, is a well-established paradigm in operations research that addresses this gap. It revolves around processes that exhibit scarce resources and highly correlated cases that compete for these resources.

In the first part of the tutorial, we shall present a high-level overview of queue mining methodologies. Specifically, we will discuss a range of queue mining methods that involve predictive monitoring in various queueing settings, conformance checking in queue-driven systems, and a generalized congestion-driven approach for predicting remaining times and analyzing bottlenecks. Subsequently, we shall demonstrate the usefulness of queue mining in real-life applications coming from three service domains: call centers, public transportation, and healthcare. We will conclude the tutorial with a discussion of novel research directions that involve queue mining and its extensions into other evolving fields.

We believe that the tutorial will attract both researchers and practitioners in the area of process management and mining, who are interested in performance analysis, predictive monitoring, and operations management.

References

1. van der Aalst, W.M.P.: Process Mining - Data Science in Action, Second Edition. Springer (2016)
2. Bolch, G., Greiner, S., de Meer, H., Trivedi, K.S.: Queueing Networks and Markov Chains - Modeling and Performance Evaluation with Computer Science Applications, Second Edition. Wiley (2006)

3. Augusto, A. et al.: Automated discovery of process models from event logs: Review and benchmark. IEEE Trans. Knowl. Data Eng. **31**(4), 686–705 (2019)
4. Carmona, J., van Dongen, B.F., Solti, A., Weidlich, M.: Conformance Checking - Relating Processes and Models. Springer (2018)
5. Teinemaa, I., Dumas, M., Rosa, M.L., Maggi, F.M.: Outcome-oriented predictive process monitoring: Review and benchmark. TKDD **13**(2), 17:1–17:57 (2019)

Driving Digitalization on the Shopfloor Through Flexible Process Technology

Stefanie Rinderle-Ma

Faculty of Computer Science, University of Vienna, Austria
stefanie.rinderle-ma@univie.ac.at

Abstract. The current crisis shows that digitalization has become more crucial than ever. We believe that process technology constitutes the vehicle to drive digital transformation throughout all application domains. In this tutorial, we reflect on the opportunities of process technology in more "physical" environments such as industrial manufacturing with machines, sensors, and manual work.

For this, the tutorial discusses and combines questions in the areas of flexible process technology, Internet of Things (IoT), and industrial manufacturing processes. Specifically, the goals of the tutorial are to

- Show how process technology can be used to foster the digital transformation in industrial manufacturing.
- Discuss challenges and possible solutions at the interface of BPM and IoT.
- Explain challenges and requirements on process flexibility.
- Outline how process flexibility can be provided from the system side.
- Outline prospects of the contextualized collection of manufacturing data.

The tutorial is outlined as follows: a) introduction into flexible process technology, b) introduction to a real-world industrial manufacturing case, c) solution based on the secure manufacturing orchestration platform centurio.work [1, 2] which is already applied in several real-world industrial settings, and d) benefits of a process-oriented solution such as vertical and horizontal integration as well as contextualized data collection and integration of the activities of the employees. The tutorial features a mix of presentation and interactive parts, including a demonstration of centurio.work and exercises with the Cloud Process Execution Engine CPEE (http://www.cpee.org/).

Keywords: Digital transformation · Process technology · Shopfloor · Process flexibility · Internet of Things

References

1. Mangler, J., Pauker, F., Rinderle-Ma, S., Ehrendorfer, M.: Centurio.work – Industry 4.0 integration assessment and evolution, Industry Forum at BPM, pp. 106–117, CEUR 2428 (2019)
2. Pauker, F., Mangler, J., Rinderle-Ma, S., Pollak, C.: Centurio.work – Modular Secure Manufacturing Orchestration, Industrial Track at BPM, pp. 164–171, CEUR 2196 (2018)

Predictive Process Monitoring: From Theory to Practice

Chiara Di Francescomarino[1] ⓘ, Chiara Ghidini[1] ⓘ,
Fabrizio Maria Maggi[1] ⓘ, and Williams Rizzi[2] ⓘ

[1] FBK-IRST, Trento, Italy
{dfmchiara,ghidini,wrizzi}@fbk.eu
[2] Free University of Bozen-Bolzano, Bolzano, Italy
maggi@inf.unibz.it

Abstract. Predictive process monitoring is a branch of process mining that aims at predicting, at runtime, the future development of ongoing cases of a process [1]. Predictions related to the future of an ongoing process execution can pertain to numeric measures of interest (e.g., the completion time), to categorical outcomes (e.g., whether a given predicate will be fulfilled or violated), or to the sequence of future activities (and related payloads). Recently, different approaches have been proposed in the literature in order to provide predictions on the outcome, the remaining time, the required resources as well as the remaining activities of an ongoing execution, by leveraging information related to control flow and data contained in event logs recording information about process executions. The approaches can be of a different nature and some of them also provide users with support in tasks such as parameter tuning. The interested reader can refer to recent surveys such as [2–4]. This tutorial aims at (i) providing an introduction on predictive process monitoring, including an overview on how to move within the large number of approaches and techniques available; (ii) introducing the current research challenges and advanced topics; and (iii) providing an overview on how to use the existing instruments and tools, with particular emphasis on the Nirdizati tool [5].

References

1. Maggi, F.M., Di Francescomarino, C., Dumas, M., Ghidini, C.: Predictive monitoring of business processes. In: Jarke, M. et al. (eds.) Advanced Information Systems Engineering. CAiSE 2014. LNCS, vol. 8484, pp. 457–472. Springer, Cham (2014). https://doi.org/10.1007/978-3-319-07881-6_31
2. Di Francescomarino, C., Ghidini, C., Maggi, F.M., Milani, F.: Predictive Process Monitoring Methods: Which One Suits Me Best?. In: Weske, M., Montali, M., Weber, I., vom Brocke., J. (eds.) BPM 2018. LNCS, vol. 11080, pp. 462–479. Springer, Cham (2018). https://doi.org/10.1007/978-3-319-98648-7_27
3. Verenich, I., Dumas, M., La Rosa, M., Maggi, F.M., Teinemaa, I.: Survey and cross-benchmark comparison of remaining time prediction methods in business process monitoring. ACM Trans. Intell. Syst. Technol. **10**(4), 34:1–34:34 (2019)

4. Teinemaa, I., Dumas, M., La Rosa, M., Maggi, F.M.: Outcome-oriented predictive process monitoring: Review and benchmark. ACM Trans. Knowl. Discov. Data **13**(2), 17:1–17:57 (2019)
5. Rizzi, W., Simonetto, L., Di Francescomarino, C., Ghidini, C., Kasekamp, T., Maggi, F.M.: Nirdizati 2.0: Newfeatures and redesigned backend. In: Proceedings of the Dissertation Award, Doctoral Consortium, and Demonstration Track at BPM 2019. CEUR Workshop Proceedings, vol. 2420, pp. 154–158 (2019)

Business Process Analysis Using Scripting Languages

Gert Janssenswillen[1] and Sebastiaan J. van Zelst[2,3]

[1] Hasselt University, Belgium
gert.janssenswillen@uhasselt.be
[2] Fraunhofer Institute for Applied Information Technology, Germany
sebastiaan.van.zelst@fit.fraunhofer.de
[3] RWTH Aachen University, Germany

Abstract. During the recent decade, various (commercial) software solutions have been developed that support the semi-automated analysis of business processes, i.e., known as process mining solutions. Examples include, and are not limited to, Celonis, Disco, ProcessGold, and myInvenio on the commercial side, and ProM, Apromore, and RapidProM on the open-source/academic side. More recently, several process mining techniques have been developed in the context of scripting languages, e.g., Python, R, etc. The advantage of using scripting languages, which are often interpreted, with regards to compiled programming languages, include flexibility, rapid prototyping, portability, etc. In this tutorial, we focus on two, recently developed software libraries, i.e., PM4Py and bupaR, developed for python and R respectively. We sketch the main functions of the two libraries and compare their strengths and weaknesses. For both libraries, importing event data will be discussed. In the context of PM4Py, we furthermore focus on applying process discovery and conformance checking. In the context of bupaR, we focus more on visualization of event data for descriptive and exploratory analysis, as well as declarative conformance checking. This tutorial is intended for academics, data scientists, software scientists and process (intelligence) consultants, and might additionally be interesting for process owners and department heads/managers. We also aim to discuss the applicability and limitations of scripting languages for the development of novel enterprise-grade process mining technologies.

Keywords: Process mining · Python · R · PM4Py · bupaR

Information Systems Modeling
Playing with the Interplay Between Data and Processes

Artem Polyvyanyy[1] and Jan Martijn E. M. van der Werf[2]

[1] School of Computing and Information Systems, The University of Melbourne,
Parkville, VIC, 3010, Australia
artem.polyvyanyy@unimelb.edu.au
[2] Department of Information and Computing Science, Utrecht University,
The Netherlands
j.m.e.m.vanderwerf@uu.nl

Abstract. Data and processes go hand-in-hand in information systems but are often modeled, validated, and verified separately in the systems' design phases. Designers of information systems often proceed by ensuring that database tables satisfy normal forms, and process models capturing the dynamics of the intended information manipulations are deadlock and livelock free. However, such an approach is not sufficient, as perfect data and process designs assessed in isolation can, indeed, induce faults when combined in the end system.

In this tutorial, we demonstrate our recent approach to modeling and verification of models of information systems in three parts. Firstly, we present our Information Systems Modeling Language (ISML) for describing information and process constraints and the interplay between these two types of constraints [1, 2]. Secondly, we demonstrate Information Systems Modeling Suite (ISM Suite) [3], an integrated environment for developing, simulating, and analyzing models of information systems described in ISML, released under an open-source license.[1] In this part, using our tools, we show several example pitfalls at the level of information and process interplay. Finally, we discuss current and future research directions that aim at strengthening the theoretical foundations and practical aspects of our approach to the design of information systems.

References

1. van der Werf, J.M.E.M., Polyvyanyy, A.: An assignment on information system modeling. In: Daniel, F., Sheng, Q., Motahari, H. (eds.) BPM 2018. LNBIP, vol. 342, pp. 553–566. Springer, Cham (2019). https://doi.org/10.1007/978-3-030-11641-5_44

---

[1] see: http://www.informationsystem.org/ismsuite/.

2. Polyvyanyy, A., van der Werf, J.M.E.M., Overbeek, S., Brouwers, R.: Information systems modeling: language, verification, and tool support. In: Giorgini, P., Weber, B. (eds.) CAiSE 2019. LNCS, vol. 11483, pp. 194–212. Springer, Cham (2019). https://doi.org/10.1007/978-3-030-21290-2_13
3. van der Werf, J.M.E.M., Polyvyanyy, A.: The information systems modeling suite. In: Janicki, R., Sidorova, N., Chatain, T. (eds.) PETRI NETS 2020. LNCS, vol. 12152, pp. 414–425. Springer, Cham (2020). https://doi.org/10.1007/978-3-030-51831-8_22

Contents

Management

Keynotes

Process Minding: Closing the Big Data Gap

Avigdor Gal[1]($\boxtimes$) and Arik Senderovich[2]

[1] Technion – Israel Institute of Technology, Technion City, 82000 Haifa, Israel
avigal@technion.ac.il
[2] University of Toronto, Toronto, Canada
arik.senderovich@utoronto.ca
http://ie.technion.ac.il/~avigal,
https://ischool.utoronto.ca/profile/arik-senderovich/

Abstract. The discipline of process mining was inaugurated in the BPM community. It flourished in a world of small(er) data, with roots in the communities of software engineering and databases and applications mainly in organizational and management settings. The introduction of big data, with its volume, velocity, variety, and veracity, and the big strides in data science research and practice pose new challenges to this research field. The paper positions process mining along modern data life cycle, highlighting the challenges and suggesting directions in which data science disciplines (*e.g.*, machine learning) may interact with a renewed process mining agenda.

1 Introduction

The rapidly growing research field of process mining [1] offers techniques that focus on data that is generated from some (possibly unknown) process. Using process mining, event data is transformed into processes to be observed, analyzed, and improved. The mining techniques vary from discovery of models through conformance checking [2] to process enhancement via, *e.g.* predictive monitoring [3].

The origins of process mining research is in an organizational setting, with motivating applications in process-aware information systems [4]. Such systems use an explicit notion of a process and provide support to run processes whose footprints are recorded in an information system from which event logs can be easily created. The data market has seen a major change in the past decade, challenged by the need to handle large volumes of data, arriving at high velocity from a variety of sources, which demonstrate varying levels of veracity. This challenging setting, often referred to as *big data*, renders many existing techniques, especially those that are human-intensive, obsolete. As processes are mined from data, any change in the data market requires re-evaluating the tools that are used for process mining.

In the challenging arena of data science, the science of dealing with big data, we offer in this paper an analysis of the role process mining can play and the

© Springer Nature Switzerland AG 2020
D. Fahland et al. (Eds.): BPM 2020, LNCS 12168, pp. 3–16, 2020.
https://doi.org/10.1007/978-3-030-58666-9_1

directions to be taken by researchers to affect and be affected by research in the affiliated fields of data science, such as databases and machine learning. We observe that the discipline of process mining was inaugurated in a world of small(er) data and its sample set of applications was very different from the set of applications that drive other data oriented research disciplines. We also observe that these differences, and the fact that the process mining community has evolved in relative isolation from other data science communities offer both challenges and opportunities that will be discussed in the remainder of the paper.

We first introduce, as a background, a common framework for data science, detailing the characteristics of big data and the data life cycle (Sect. 2). We then offer views on discovery (Sect. 3), conformance checking (Sect. 4), and enhancement via process perspectives (Sect. 5) in light of contemporary data ecosystem. We conclude in Sect. 6 with a survival guide to the young researcher in the data science academic jungle.

2 Data Science and Process Mining

In this section, we offer a brief introduction to big data and data science. We start with characterization of big data (Sect. 2.1), followed by an overview of data life cycle (Sect. 2.2). An illustration of the coverage of data science is given in Table 1, using a matrix visualization. Such a visualization can assist in connecting the terminology of process mining with that of data science yet it is meant to offer a loose intuition when needed rather than a thorough mapping. We conclude the section with the positioning of process mining in the context of the data science matrix (Sect. 2.3), emphasizing the role process mining can play in the field of explainable AI [5].

2.1 Big Data Characteristics Are Process Mining Challenges

Big data is commonly characterized via a set of "V"s, out of which four became mostly prominent. Big data is characterized by *volumes* of data to be gathered, managed, and analyzed. *Velocity* involves the rapid arrival of new data items and also the notion of change in states of artifacts. Big data *variety* refers to the availability of multiple heterogeneous data sources. The fourth "V", *veracity*, involves the truthfulness and reliability of the data to be integrated.

Data volume was not an issue for process mining when initiated. The logs that served for the first works on process discovery were rather small. For example, the first BPI challenge[1] uses "a real-life log, taken from a Dutch Academic Hospital. This log contains some 150,000 events in over 1100 cases" and it did not take much to create a "spaghetti" model from an activity log. A few years later, Senderovich *et al.* experimented on another medical dataset, with RTLS data taken from an American hospital, with approximately 240,000 events per year [6]. In 2014, a smart city dataset, which was used in a task that analyzed bus routes as processes contained over 1 million events per day for a period of one month (approximately 30 million events) [7].

---

[1] https://www.win.tue.nl/bpi/doku.php?id=2011:challenge.

Table 1. Data Science Matrix. The matrix entries identify links of process mining terminology to the data science ecosystem. Discovery, conformance, and enhancement are all data science activities and as such, require the full data cycle and may be challenged by any of the big data characteristics.

	Gathering	Managing	Analyzing	Explaining
Volume	Sensors		Incremental discovery	Filtering
				Aggregation
Velocity			Concept drift	
			Event stream discovery	
Variety	Log creation	Perspectives		
Veracity		Log merging		

Data velocity has been a main focus of process mining, not due to the speed of event arrival (after all, registering a new child in a Dutch municipality does not have to be done in a matter of seconds) but due to the inherent notion of change, which is common to data velocity and the understanding of the nature of a process. A recent evidence on the impact data velocity has on process mining can be seen with a line of research into concept drift where "real-world processes are subject to continuous change" [8]. The need to deal with concept drift in process mining can serve as evidence to the changing type of processes that the community work with, aligned with the change of dynamics in the data world. The specific use-case that was proposed by Maisenbacher and Weidlich [8] was that of health insurance claims [9] (rather than Dutch municipalities), yet keeping loyal to Dutch meticulous recording of events, other works (such as [10]) analyzed concept drifts of Dutch installation services company. Another process mining challenge, related to both volume and velocity, involves event stream-based process discovery [11], where a discovery algorithm needs to elicit process models from streams of events without assuming an existence of an event log (due to size and frequency of arriving data).

As for data variety, the initial assumption for process mining has been that data comes from an information system, which implies that it underwent a cleaning process. Only later came additional perspectives [12] and with them, naturally, the challenges of data integration.

Finally, modern applications replace the traditional usage of well-curated information systems with crude raw data that comes from multiple sensors so variety is high and veracity is low. Veracity depends on many factors, including source reliability and the additional processing sensor data undergo along the way. As an example, consider RTLS data in a hospital that uses the whereabout of patients to understand the inter-relationships between various activities patients perform as part of a hospital treatment process. The noisy nature of RTLS devices may provide false or missing indications. In addition, if a processing system assumes that patients always stay in their last recorded position, additional uncertainty regarding the correctness of the reported locations may be injected into the log.

2.2   Data Life Cycle... and More Challenges

The process of handling big data can be described using a data life cycle, with four main steps, namely *gathering, managing, analyzing,* and *explaining*. In the first step, data is gathered from multiple sources. Then, in the management step it is integrated, stored, and prepared for analysis using multiple database methods. Analysis is performed using algorithmic solutions, typically machine learning and data mining. The results of the analysis are then shared with stake holders, resulting in new questions that require more data to be gathered, and so the cycle begins anew. Henceforth, we shall refer to disciplines that orbit the data life cycle as data science disciplines, with examples being process mining itself, machine learning, data mining, databases, statistics, and visual analytics.

As part of data gathering, process mining uses a log, which requires at least three elements, namely case identifier (who?), activity name (what?), and a timestamp (when?). These three elements enable the creation of a *trace*, constructing a sequence (using the timestamp) of related activities (through the case identifier) that is recorded in the log. Such a log calls for preprocessing that may be far from trivial when data arrives in a raw form from multiple data sources. Also, an important aspect of the gathering step is to understand which additional process perspectives should be added or deduced from the log.

An important component of data management is data integration. Process mining has mostly enjoyed the privilege of using rather clean logs, such as logs that arrive from a centralized-managed process aware information systems. Big data offer multitude of opportunities to combine data from multiple resources and enrich the logs to allow better discovery, conformance, and enhancement. However, with such opportunities, comes much uncertainty regarding the correct way to combine the data in a way that will contribute to process understanding.

The process mining discipline has provided multitude of tools for analyzing process data from the control-flow perspective. In addition, methods for mining concrete perspectives, such as the queueing perspective were also introduced [13]. Other communities, such as machine learning and data mining, also offer tools to generate models from data. The machine learning community, in particular, saw an amazingly increasing interest in the past few years. From a small community, focused on designing efficient and effective algorithms that immitate human learning from evidence, machine learning turned in matter of weeks to be the center piece of the latest technology evolution with impact on all walks of life.

Finally, explainability (with the latest buzzword *explainable AI*) encompasses a set of means to enhance explainability of models, many of which draw on the research field of high dimension visualization. Processes can naturally be visualized by means of graphs and many of the tools that were developed for process mining are accompanied by useful visualization tools [14] and explainability techniques [15]. New generation of visualization tools that can enhance visual analytics and highlight appropriate model properties are yet to be developed.

The cycle of data begins a new once the results of previous analysis were introduced and duely explained to stakeholders, leading to new questions that may require gathering more data. In the context of process mining, for example, once predictive monitoring kicks into place, data should be continuously gathered to understand the impact of such monitoring on the process.

2.3   I Get Big Data, Now What?

The connection between process mining and data science is obvious and was discussed before, *e.g.*, [16] and several blogs.[2] However, what we see as a community is not all that obvious for other communities in the data science realm and this paper focuses on how to get our gospel heard.

There is one element of process mining that positions it at the heart of the future discussion of other data science disciplines such as databases, data mining, and machine learning. It is not the ability to analyze timestamped data (although many brilliant algorithms were suggested in the community), nor is it the ability to utilize state-of-the-art machine learning algorithms when analyzing such data (although many excellent works did just that). As a discipline that evolved from the human-rich interaction discipline of BPM, process mining researchers have always taken as given the human-in-the-loop approach. As a result, researchers were always seeking better ways to explain discovered processes to humans. Also, the community has developed a rich literature to allow humans to compare between the discovered processes and their own understanding of it. Moreover, researchers of this community know how to make use of human expertise when performing data analytics. Therefore, we argue that this community is well positioned to lead the new trends of explainable AI, interpretability of machine learning, and embedding expert knowledge in machine learning. We shall provide examples of how process mining can influence those trends.

To become an influential player in the broader field of data science, process mining must build on the strengths mention above while creating bridges to other disciplines. In this paper, we show three such bridges. First, we relate process discovery to explainability of machine learning algorithms. Next, we suggest directions to position conformance checking in the world of algorithms evaluation. Lastly, we demonstrate, via a successful direction of queue mining, how to build on human knowledge as encoded in the academic literature in embedding process perspectives into supervised machine learning.

3   Process Discovery

Perhaps the most significant avenue of research in the process mining community aims at automated discovery of process models from data streams emitted by complex systems for individual cases [17]. One reason for the centrality of the

---

[2] https://tinyurl.com/yadduec4, https://tinyurl.com/ybtxrl53.

discovery process in process mining is its tight link with the field of BPM where a main goal is the "(re-)design of individual business processes" [18]. In this section we analyze process discovery as a machine learning task (Sect. 3.1). We then focus on discovery as an algorithmic explainability tool (Sect. 3.2).

3.1 Discovery as a Machine Learning Task

Discovery has all the characteristics of a machine learning task. It uses sample or training data (log) to create a mathematical model (process, typically a Petri net). The outcome of a discovery process can be used for classification (is this a regular loan request or a mortgage?), clustering (are these traces similar?), and prediction (how long will I stay in the emergency room?)

Viewing process discovery through the lens of machine learning provides us with some interesting observations. To start with, consider the difference between supervised and unsupervised learning. In a supervised setting, the algorithm learns using labeled data, offering a way to evaluate its accuracy on training data. In an unsupervised setting, data is unlabeled and the algorithm needs to use some prior knowledge about "good" and "bad" behavior to generate a model. So, is a process discovery algorithm supervised or unsupervised? it seems to be a little bit of both. The log that is used for training provides activity labels and together with the case ID and the timestamp allows an algorithm to understand which activity proceeds which other activity. This, however, may be insufficient to understand complex structures such as parallel execution. For that, the algorithm requires to apply techniques of unsupervised learning, *e.g.*, by interpreting certain patterns across cases (samples) as representing parallel execution [17]. We note here that process mining demonstrates also characteristics of semi-supervised learning. In particular, most process mining algorithms are driven by the ability of the model to parse positive examples (those examples that appear in the log).

Challenges may arise when all we have are low level events that cannot be directly correlated to activity labels. For example, events that provide GPS locations or mouse movement on a screen. Here, we lose the benefit of knowing the *what* while keeping knowledge about *who* and *when*. We can fill the gap using, well, machine learning. For example, we can cluster low level events together based on patterns in the raw data and create a log that is ready for discovery [19–21] or simply develop a new discovery algorithm for exactly such data [22]. Imagine next that we lose, in turn, the *who* and the *when*. Where does that lead us? to what extent can process discovery help us there?

3.2 Discovery Is the New Explanability

Evaluation of a model that is trained from examples is multi-facet and depends on the task at hand. In machine learning, evaluation differs between binary problems (such as classification) and problems with numerical outcomes (such as regression). For binary problems, evaluation is based on the confusion matrix and many measures (*e.g.*, accuracy, precision, recall, f-measure) use a combination of true positives, true negatives, false positives, and false negatives. For regression-based models, measures are based on variance computation, with measures such as Mean Squared Error (MSE), Root Mean Squared Error (RMSE), and Median Relative Absolute Error (MdRAE).

For process mining, there are four common evaluation measures that quantify the quality of discovered models:

Fitness indicates how much of the observed behavior is captured by ("fits") the process model. Fitness essentially computes the number of true positives out of the total number of traces (true positives + false negatives) and thus is equivalent to recall.

Precision measures to what extent a discovered model identifies behaviors beyond those that are present in the log. Therefore, the number of true positives is divided by the total number of traces that the discovered model admits (true positives + false positives).

Generalization measures the ability of a discovered model to generalize beyond the behaviors the data allows. Similar measures are discussed in the machine learning literature, when discussing the risks of overfitting.

Simplicity assesses to what extent the discovered model is simple. This measure does not have a common mathematical definition and is sometimes measured by the representation spatial properties, *e.g.*, the number of crossing edges [23].

Clearly, the first two measures are aligned with the evaluation of binary problems in machine learning and the third is of growing interest, recalling that many efforts are devoted to prove algorithms' generalization (including in transfer learning) and that empirical results are to show generalization error. The fourth measure, that of simplicity, fits nicely with notions of explainability and interpretability, which became mandatory ingredients in any machine learning-based solution [5].

Explainability and interpretability are often used interchangeably despite their varying roles in presenting the outcome of machine learning solutions. Interpretability is about the extent to which a cause and effect can be observed within a system. Therefore, considering control flow, when the discovered model shows that activity A is followed by activity B, the user is offered a causal relationship between the two activities. When adding a time perspective, interpretability may be added in a form that would allow, for example to understand **that** at time $14 : 05$ the process should execute activity A. Explainability is the extent to which the internal mechanisms of a system can be explained in human terms. For example, it can be used to explain that the execution of activity A **is** time dependent.

In the context of process discovery, a realization of interpretability is in the form of decision and constraint annotations. Explainability was recently discussed when context-aware process trees were introduced [24]. All-in-all, process discovery has a lot to offer in terms of both interpretability and explainability. The natural graphical representations of processes (and in particular trees) offer opportunities to create self-explainable process models.

Process discovery does not make use of regression measures. Rather, it makes use of non-binary measures by using data replay and counting the number of misfit movements in the log and the process for each trace [25]. In this context, works such as the one proposed by Sagi and Gal [26] offer interesting directions for extending the non-binary evaluation research of process discovery by assigning different relative emphasis on commonality vs. differences [27] among traces.

4 Conformance and the Changing Role of Humans

Machine learning has developed tools for model fitting to test to what extent the model generalizes from the data on which it was trained. A model that is well-fitted produces more accurate outcomes, a model that is overfitted matches the data too closely, and a model that is underfitted does not match closely enough. The notion of model fitting is captured well in the evaluation measures discussed in Sect. 3.2.

Conformance checking offers, beyond a fitness evaluation between a model and a trace, also a more general notion, that of model comparison. While in the machine learning literature the use of model comparison is mainly in comparing performance (and hence fitness to the data is sufficient), process mining also focuses on the differences between models, one of which is human created while the other is revealed from the data [28]. Identifying the equivalent to conformance checking in main stream machine learning is even harder than that of the discovery process. There, at least, it is clear what is the parallel mechanism to discovery that works in machine learning, although the end goal is mostly very different. With conformance checking, a machine learning researcher is most likely to wonder why there is a need to compare two models at all if not for understanding which one yields better results.

Equipped with our understanding that process mining is about human-in-the-loop, we can gain two main insights on where conformance checking may contribute best to the machine learning literature. Machine learning, as a discipline, was thrown into the heart of general audience interest, portrayed as AI (recall your favorite sci-fi movie, ours is the Matrix trilogy). As such, it offers a great promise to areas such as medicine, smart cities, and more. However, algorithms do not just find their way into sensitive systems in hospitals, banks, and city control rooms. Rather, they need to face an obstacle named the human decision maker, and to do that they need to show how their outcome fit a mental model of a human decision maker for solving the same problem.

The first research direction has to do with the way explainability is performed. Machine learning algorithms generate models that are at times functionally black boxes and it is impossible to understand their inner workings. A question that may be raised is to what extent we trust the model and the data from which it is created. When embeddings (of words but not only) become a common method in building learning models, machine learning literature seeks new methods to interpret the algorithm results, see for example LIME [29]. We should not, however, stop there. Once an interpretable model is created, it can be fine tuned to fit human decision maker's mental model by creating minor modifications, along the lines of the generalized conformance checking framework of Rogge-Solti *et al.* [28].

Another place where humans and machines can interact around models is when tuning hyper parameters. Consider a very simple case, where a human expert trains a clustering model using k-means, where $k = 2$. Setting the k value follows the expert understanding of the world she aims at modeling. The algorithm may reveal that while for $k = 2$ the algorithm fitness is poor, revising the hyper parameter to a larger k value yields better results. Negotiating the hyper parameters when starting from the expert mental model helps in reaching a consensus between the human expert and the algorithm on the best tuning. It is worth noting that tuning hyper parameters lies currently in the realm of machine learning experts, those that build a model for end users. We argue here that hyper parameter tuning should be part of a human-in-the-loop approach, where the human is in face the domain expert, rather than the machine learning expert. Conformance checking, with its multitude of techniques to interpret alignments and its multi-dimensional quality assessment, is an entryway to perform judicial hyper parameter tuning in machine learning algorithms, especially when those hyper parameters can be associated with a real-world meaning that can be interpreted by domain experts.

5   From Model Enhancement Through Perspectives to Feature Engineering and Model Adaptation

Process enhancement is "the extension or improvement of an existing process model using information about the actual process recorded in some event log" [16]. Process extension, "a form of process enhancement where apriori model is extended with a new aspect or perspective", [16] is often brought up when enhancement is discussed. Big data brought with it an opportunity to integrate (part of the management stage in the data life cycle) additional data (recall data variety) to an existing log. The process mining community, which devoted much effort to mining the control flow of processes from data, focused its enhancement efforts on identifying contextual data that can identify new process perspectives (*e.g.*, time, resources, and costs).

With plenty of data from which contextual information can be derived, two questions come to mind, namely *how to choose a perspective?* and *how to select data for better enhancement?* These questions point to a common practice in machine learning, that of feature engineering. Feature engineering is commonly known as "the process of using domain knowledge to extract features from raw data via data mining techniques. These features can be used to improve the performance of machine learning algorithms."[3]

Domain knowledge brings up again the human-in-the-loop. Clearly, the visualization tools that were developed over the years for process discovery can

---

[3] https://tinyurl.com/y9l6njyh.

become handy when gathering domain knowledge for additional perspectives. Moreover, domain knowledge does not have to be gathered directly from human experts. Rather, seeking domain expertise in the relevant scientific literature provides a good starting point for developing a feature set for a perspective.

To illustrate a possible approach that combines process enhancement with expert knowledge for creating a focused set of features to create a perspective, consider queue mining [12], which enhanced a log with a queueing perspective to extract congestions from process data.

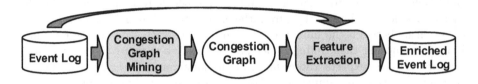

Fig. 1. Our solution to generate congestion features.

Feature engineering using a model-driven approach to automatically generate congestion-related features, as illustrated in Fig. 1, was proposed by Senderovich *et al.* [30]. Given an event log, the first step mines congestion graphs, graphical representations of the dynamics observed in a system. These dynamic graphs represent the flow of entities in terms of events and are labeled with performance information that is extracted from the event log. Extraction of such performance information is grounded in some general assumptions on the system dynamics. For congestion graphs it is a state representation of an underlying queueing system. Finally, a transformation function is created to encode the labels of a congestion graph into respective features. This feature creation yields an enriched event log, which can be used as input for a supervised learning method.

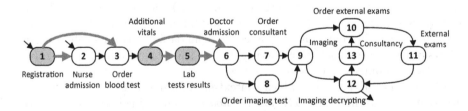

Fig. 2. Main treatment events and flows; events and flows of important features are highlighted.

One of the advantages of discovering congestion graphs is the ability to move from prediction to explainability. Providing insights as to the most important features and root-causes for delays in the system is a crucial step when optimizing processes. We demonstrate this by considering the congestion graph in Fig. 2 and show how the features obtained from congestion graphs provide insights into the root-causes of delays.

Feature importance was evaluated by ranking features according to their role in the prediction task. Specifically, methods like gradient boosting enable the ranking of features in correspondence to their predictive power [31]. For example, the most dominant feature for the healthcare process in Fig. 2 based on the congestion graph are the number of patients who entered reception. This implies that a greater arrival volume has an impact on time prediction, as it results in delays. The second feature, corresponds to the elapsed time since lab results are ready (i.e., blood work). This feature is highly predictive as the next step after lab is typically the visit to the physician. Hence, an important feature is the time in queue for the physician.

To summarize, the example illustrates a feasible mechanism to generate features for a new perspective using domain knowledge that is extracted from the scientific literature. Existing approaches in process mining can offer ways to interpret feature importance and provide insights on the domain. Mined information can then serve for explainability analysis and understanding the process beyond the specific prediction goal.

6   Conclusions

The world is buzzing with new opportunities that were made possible due to a set of technologies, from cheap sensors and Iot, to cloud computing, to better interfaces. Data science finds new applications in healthcare logistics, luggage handling systems, software analysis, smart maintenance, Web site analytics, customer journey, and more.

The surge of interest in machine learning and AI technologies for daily activities has found those communities unprepared. Almost instantly, a purely academic discipline, with minimal connection to the commercial world, has found itself in the eye of a storm, with more and more application domain demand to be upgraded with the shining new algorithmic solutions.

The process mining community, has always been ready to this wave of demand. With its tight connection to the BPM community, process mining grew with the constant need to explain its output to human experts. Methods in process discovery, conformance checking, and process enhancement, were always designed with the end user in mind.

The time is ripe for the community of process mining to go out of its comfort zone and contribute, not just for what was traditionally promoted in the community but also become part of the recent trend of explainable AI. To do so, we provide a quick survival guide to the young (and young in spirit) process mining researcher when entering the data science academic jungle:

– Know your stuff well: whether you offer the use of a process discovery algorithm, a conformance checking multi-dimensional evaluation measure, or a new perspective make sure you know it inside out. Going out to the wilderness you will meet many new terms and concepts, some may be mapped clearly to your own research but you should be able to see the wood for the trees.

– Identify the gap in literature when it comes to human-in-the-loop. The wider the gap the higher are the chances your bag of tricks will fit in nicely. However, the jungle of data science literature is such that you may have to wedge your work in. Make sure you prepare well to defend your position when the natives come running wildly at you.

– Establish an inter-disciplinary team. Join forces with open-minded researchers in the data science disciplines (AI, ML, DM, or DB). Remember that research should be seen to be done.

With such a guide at hand and with a little bit of courage, process mining will become the new explainable AI in no time.

> *Little friends may prove great friends.*
> – Aesop

Acknowledgement. We thank Matthias Weidlich and Roee Shraga for fruitful discussions.

References

1. van der Aalst, W.M.P.: Process Mining: Discovery. Conformance and Enhancement of Business Processes. Springer, Heidelberg (2011). https://doi.org/10.1007/978-3-642-19345-3

2. Carmona, J., van Dongen, B., Solti, A., Weidlich, M.: Conformance Checking. Springer, Heidelberg (2018). https://doi.org/10.1007/978-3-319-99414-7

3. Maggi, F.M., Di Francescomarino, C., Dumas, M., Ghidini, C.: Predictive monitoring of business processes. In: Jarke, M., et al. (eds.) CAiSE 2014. LNCS, vol. 8484, pp. 457–472. Springer, Cham (2014). https://doi.org/10.1007/978-3-319-07881-6_31

4. Dumas, M., Van der Aalst, W.M., Ter Hofstede, H.: Process-Aware Information Systems: Bridging People and Software Through Process Technology. Wiley, Hoboken (2005)

5. Došilović, F.K., Brčić, M., Hlupić, N.: Explainable artificial intelligence: a survey. In: 2018 41st International Convention on Information and Communication Technology, Electronics and Microelectronics (MIPRO), pp. 0210–0215. IEEE (2018)

6. Senderovich, A., et al.: Data-driven performance analysis of scheduled processes. In: Motahari-Nezhad, H.R., Recker, J., Weidlich, M. (eds.) BPM 2015. LNCS, vol. 9253, pp. 35–52. Springer, Cham (2015). https://doi.org/10.1007/978-3-319-23063-4_3

7. Gal, A., Mandelbaum, A., Schnitzler, F., Senderovich, A., Weidlich, M.: Traveling time prediction in scheduled transportation with journey segments. Inf. Syst. **64**, 266–280 (2017)

8. Maisenbacher, M., Weidlich, M.: Handling concept drift in predictive process monitoring. In: 2017 IEEE International Conference on Services Computing (SCC), pp. 1–8. IEEE (2017)

9. Bose, R.J.C., Van Der Aalst, W.M., Žliobaitė, I., Pechenizkiy, M.: Dealing with concept drifts in process mining. IEEE Trans. Neural Netw. Learn. Syst. **25**(1), 154–171 (2013)
10. Spenrath, Y., Hassani, M.: Ensemble-based prediction of business processes bottlenecks with recurrent concept drifts. In: EDBT/ICDT Workshops (2019)
11. van Zelst, S.J., van Dongen, B.F., van der Aalst, W.M.P.: Event stream-based process discovery using abstract representations. Knowl. Inf. Syst. **54**(2), 407–435 (2017). https://doi.org/10.1007/s10115-017-1060-2
12. Senderovich, A.: Queue mining: service perspectives in process mining. Ph.D. dissertation, Technion-Israel Institute of Technology (2017)
13. Senderovich, A., Weidlich, M., Gal, A., Mandelbaum, A.: Queue mining – predicting delays in service processes. In: Jarke, M., et al. (eds.) CAiSE 2014. LNCS, vol. 8484, pp. 42–57. Springer, Cham (2014). https://doi.org/10.1007/978-3-319-07881-6_4
14. van Dongen, B.F., Adriansyah, A.: Process mining: fuzzy clustering and performance visualization. In: Rinderle-Ma, S., Sadiq, S., Leymann, F. (eds.) BPM 2009. LNBIP, vol. 43, pp. 158–169. Springer, Heidelberg (2010). https://doi.org/10.1007/978-3-642-12186-9_15
15. Senderovich, A., Shleyfman, A., Weidlich, M., Gal, A., Mandelbaum, A.: To aggregate or to eliminate? Optimal model simplification for improved process performance prediction. Inf. Syst. **78**, 96–111 (2018)
16. Van Der Aalst, W.: Data science in action. In: van der Aalst, W. (ed.) Process Mining, pp. 3–23. Springer, Heidelberg (2016). https://doi.org/10.1007/978-3-662-49851-4_1
17. Augusto, A., et al.: Automated discovery of process models from event logs: review and benchmark. IEEE Trans. Knowl. Data Eng. **31**(4), 686–705 (2018)
18. Vom Brocke, J., Rosemann, M.: Handbook on Business Process Management 1: Introduction, Methods, and Information Systems. Springer, Heidelberg (2014). https://doi.org/10.1007/978-3-642-45100-3
19. Lu, X., et al.: Semi-supervised log pattern detection and exploration using event concurrence and contextual information. In: Panetto, H., et al. (eds.) OTM 2017. LNCS, vol. 10573, pp. 154–174. Springer, Cham (2017). https://doi.org/10.1007/978-3-319-69462-7_11
20. Senderovich, A., Rogge-Solti, A., Gal, A., Mendling, J., Mandelbaum, A.: The ROAD from sensor data to process instances via interaction mining. In: Nurcan, S., Soffer, P., Bajec, M., Eder, J. (eds.) CAiSE 2016. LNCS, vol. 9694, pp. 257–273. Springer, Cham (2016). https://doi.org/10.1007/978-3-319-39696-5_16
21. Mannhardt, F., de Leoni, M., Reijers, H.A., van der Aalst, W.M.P., Toussaint, P.J.: From low-level events to activities - a pattern-based approach. In: La Rosa, M., Loos, P., Pastor, O. (eds.) BPM 2016. LNCS, vol. 9850, pp. 125–141. Springer, Cham (2016). https://doi.org/10.1007/978-3-319-45348-4_8
22. Günther, C.W., van der Aalst, W.M.: Mining activity clusters from low-level event logs. Beta, Research School for Operations Management and Logistics (2006)
23. De San Pedro, J., Carmona, J., Cortadella, J.: Log-based simplification of process models. In: Motahari-Nezhad, H.R., Recker, J., Weidlich, M. (eds.) BPM 2015. LNCS, vol. 9253, pp. 457–474. Springer, Cham (2015). https://doi.org/10.1007/978-3-319-23063-4_30
24. Shraga, R., Gal, A., Schumacher, D., Senderovich, A., Weidlich, M.: Process discovery with context-aware process trees. Inf. Syst. 101533 (2020)

25. Van der Aalst, W., Adriansyah, A., van Dongen, B.: Replaying history on process models for conformance checking and performance analysis. Wiley Interdiscip. Rev.: Data Min. Knowl. Discov. **2**(2), 182–192 (2012)
26. Sagi, T., Gal, A.: Non-binary evaluation measures for big data integration. VLDB J. **27**(1), 105–126 (2017). https://doi.org/10.1007/s00778-017-0489-y
27. Lin, D., et al.: An information-theoretic definition of similarity. Icml **98**, 296–304 (1998)
28. Rogge-Solti, A., Senderovich, A., Weidlich, M., Mendling, J., Gal, A.: In log and model we trust? A generalized conformance checking framework. In: La Rosa, M., Loos, P., Pastor, O. (eds.) BPM 2016. LNCS, vol. 9850, pp. 179–196. Springer, Cham (2016). https://doi.org/10.1007/978-3-319-45348-4_11
29. Ribeiro, M.T., Singh, S., Guestrin, C.: "Why should I trust you?" Explaining the predictions of any classifier. In: Proceedings of the 22nd ACM SIGKDD International Conference on Knowledge Discovery and Data Mining, pp. 1135–1144 (2016)
30. Senderovich, A., Beck, J.C., Gal, A., Weidlich, M.: Congestion graphs for automated time predictions. In: Proceedings of the AAAI Conference on Artificial Intelligence, vol. 33, pp. 4854–4861 (2019)
31. Pan, F., Converse, T., Ahn, D., Salvetti, F., Donato, G.: Feature selection for ranking using boosted trees. In: Proceedings of the 18th ACM Conference on Information and Knowledge Management, pp. 2025–2028 (2009)

Characterizing Machine Learning Processes: A Maturity Framework

Rama Akkiraju[✉], Vibha Sinha, Anbang Xu, Jalal Mahmud, Pritam Gundecha,
Zhe Liu, Xiaotong Liu, and John Schumacher

IBM Watson, IBM Almaden Research Center, San Jose, CA, USA
{akkiraju,vibha.sinha,anbangxu,jumahmud,psgundec,liuzh,
Xiaotong.Liu,jfs}@us.ibm.com

Abstract. Academic literature on machine learning modeling fails to address how to make machine learning models work for enterprises. For example, existing machine learning processes cannot address how to define business use cases for an AI application, how to convert business requirements from product managers into data requirements for data scientists, and how to continuously improve AI applications in term of accuracy and fairness, how to customize general purpose machine learning models with industry, domain, and use case specific data to make them more accurate for specific situations etc. Making AI work for enterprises requires special considerations, tools, methods and processes. In this paper we present a maturity framework for machine learning model lifecycle management for enterprises. Our framework is a re-interpretation of the software Capability Maturity Model (CMM) for machine learning model development process. We present a set of best practices from authors' personal experience of building large scale real-world machine learning models to help organizations achieve higher levels of maturity independent of their starting point.

Keywords: Machine learning models · Maturity model · Maturity framework · AI model life cycle management

1 Introduction

Software and Services development has gone through various phases of maturity in the past few decades. The community has evolved lifecycle management theories and practices to disseminate best practices to developers, companies and consultants alike. For example, in software field, Software Development Life Cycle (SDLC) Management, capability maturity models (CMM) Application Life Cycle Management (ALM), Product Life Cycle Management (PLM) models prescribe systematic theories and practical guidance for developing products in general, and software products in particular. Information Technology Infrastructure Library (ITIL) organization presents a set of detailed practices for IT Services management (ITSM) by aligning IT services with business objectives. All these practices provide useful guidance for developers in systematically building software and services assets. However, these methods fall short in managing

© Springer Nature Switzerland AG 2020
D. Fahland et al. (Eds.): BPM 2020, LNCS 12168, pp. 17–31, 2020.
https://doi.org/10.1007/978-3-030-58666-9_2

a new breed of software services being developed rapidly in the industry. These are software services built with machine learnt models.

We are well into the era of Artificial Intelligence (AI), spurred by algorithmic, and computational advances, the availability of the latest algorithms in various software libraries, Cloud technologies, and the desire of companies to unleash insights from the vast amounts of untapped unstructured data lying in their enterprises. Companies are actively exploring and deploying trial versions of AI-enabled applications such as chat bots, personal digital assistants, doctors' assistants, radiology assistants, legal assistants, health and wellness coaches in their enterprises. Powering these applications are the AI building block services such as conversation enabling service, speech-to-text and text to speech, image recognition service, language translation and natural language understanding services that detect entities, relations, keywords, concepts, sentiments and emotions in text. Several of these services are machine learnt, if not all. As more and more machine learnt services make their way into software applications, which themselves are part of business processes, robust life cycle management of these machine learnt models becomes critical for ensuring the integrity of business processes that rely on them. We argue that two reasons necessitate a new maturity framework for machine learning models. First, the lifecycle of machine learning models is significantly different from that of the traditional software and therefore a reinterpretation of the software capability maturity model (CMM) maturity framework for building and managing the lifecycle of machine learning models is called for. Second, building machine learning models that work for enterprises requires solutions to a very different set of problems than the academic literature on machine learning typically focuses on. We explain these two reasons below a bit more in detail.

1.1 Traditional Software Development vs. Machine Learning Model Development

While traditional software applications are deterministic, machine learning models are probabilistic. Machine learning models learn from data. They need to be trained while traditional software applications are programmed to behave as per the requirements and specifications. As a result, traditional software applications are always accurate barring defects, whereas machine learning models typically need multiple iterations of improvements to achieve acceptable levels of accuracy, and it may or may not be possible to achieve 100% accuracy. Data in traditional software applications tends to be transactional in nature and mostly of structured type whereas data for machine learning models can be structured, or unstructured. Unstructured data can further come in multiple forms such as text, audio, video and images. In addition, data management in machine learning pipeline has multiple stages, namely data acquisition, data annotation, data preparation, data quality checking, data sampling, data augmentation steps – each involving their own life cycles thereby necessitating a whole new set of processes and tools. Machine learning models have to deal with fairness, trust, transparency, explainability that traditional software doesn't have to deal with. Machine learning pipeline has a whole new set of roles such as data managers, data annotators, data scientists, fairness testers etc. in addition to traditional software engineering roles. While one has to deal with code versioning and code diff functions in traditional software application development, machine learning models bring interesting twists with training data and testing data diffs and model diffs. A full version of compare and contrast is the sole subject of a different paper under preparation.

All these new aspects in machine learning model lifecycle need explication, disciplined management and optimization lest organizations end up with chaotic, poor quality models thereby leaving a trail of dissatisfied customers.

1.2 Making Machine Learning and AI Work for Enterprises

Making AI work for enterprises requires special considerations, tools, methods and processes. This necessitates a new maturity framework for machine learning models.

To address these problems, based on our own experience of building practical, large-scale, real-world, machine learning models, we present a new interpretation of CMM maturity framework for managing the lifecycle of machine learnt models. To the best of our knowledge, this is the first of its kind.

In this paper we use machine learning model and AI model synonymously, although we understand that machine learning models are only a type of AI models.

2 Related Work

Our work is related to software maturity model [1], Big data maturity models [3, 4, 6, 7], and knowledge discovery process.

Humphrey proposed capability maturity model (CMM) for Software [1]. He described five levels of process maturity for Software: initial, repeatable, defined, managed, optimizing. An organization's maturity is considered initial when there is no control of the process and no orderly progress of process improvement is possible. An organization can reach repeatable level when it has achieved a stable process with repeatable level of statistical control by initiating rigid project management of commitments, cost, schedule and changes. Defined level can be attained when the organization has defined the process to ensure consistent implementation and provide a basis for better understanding of the process. An organization attains a managed level when it has initiated comprehensive process measurements beyond those of cost and schedule performance. An organization reaches optimizing level when the organization has a foundation for continuous improvement and optimization of the process. Our work is inspired by such process maturity definitions. In our work, we propose a set of required processes for organizations building machine learning models.

3 Machine Learning Model Lifecycle

In this section we describe the AI Service development lifecycle, along with roles involved in each. AI lifecycle include: data pipeline, feature pipeline, train pipeline, test pipeline, deployment pipeline, and continuous improvement pipeline. Each step is an iterative and requires continuous improvements in itself. This iterative process is illustrated in Fig. 1. A brief introduction to each step is given in this section. The sections that follow provide deep-dives and maturity assessment questionnaire.

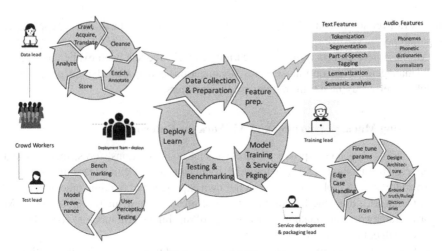

Fig. 1. AI model lifecycle

3.1   Model Goal Setting and Product Management

A product manager kicks off the AI model development process by setting goals for the AI model i.e., what must it be good at, creates test cases and minimum required thresholds upon which the models' quality and runtime performance targets are to be measured. This person also defines thresholds for model competitiveness and the associated levels. A product manager must set goals for an AI model considering the current state as well as achievable levels with stretch targets. The goals must apply not only the model quality and runtime metrics but also to the process by which the models are built so that the outcomes are predictable, consistent and repeatable.

3.2   Content Management Strategy

A content manager is responsible for proactively identifying suitable training data sources from public and private legal sources, checking the legality of data, establishing governance process around data, data vendor contract negotiations, pricing, data budget management and data lineage management.

3.3   Data Pipeline

Data collection and preparation is a key step in training an AI model. In this step, an AI Service Data Lead leads the efforts around data collection and labeled data preparation. The model needs to see enough instances of each kind that you are trying to detect/predict. For example, a Sentiment Analyzer service needs to see enough instances of positive, negative and neutral sentiment samples in order to learn to classify them correctly. This stage of data collection and ground truth preparation involves many activities such as identifying right type of data in right distributions, sampling the data so as to guide the model performance, enriching the data via labeling, storing the lineage of the data, checking the quality of the labeled and prepared data, establishing specific metrics for measuring the quality of the data, storing and analyzing the data. This step may also involve augmenting the training data via data synthesis techniques or with adversarial examples to enhance the robustness of models. Each step is iterative in itself and goes through multiple iterations before the data is readied for training.

3.4 Feature Preparation

This step involves preparing the features from the collected data to initiate the training models. The actual preparation steps depend on the type of AI service being developed. Figure 1 shows the preparatory steps involved in text processing and audio signal processing for building natural language understanding (NLU) and speech-to-text type of services. Typically, these include, developing tokenizers, sentence segmentation capabilities, part-of-speech taggers, lemmatization, syntactic parsing capabilities etc. In the case of audio data, these things include developing phonetic dictionaries, text normalizers etc. These assets and services once prepared are then used in training algorithms. Typically, a Training Lead works closely with the Data Lead to prepare these assets.

3.5 Model Training

A Training Lead leads this activity. A Training Lead makes decisions about what algorithms to experiment with the prepared data and the feature assets that are prepared. This includes making decisions about what frameworks to use (TensorFlow/Pytorch/Keras etc.), if neural nets are involved, how many hidden layers and the specific activation functions at each layer etc. A Training Lead then trains the models, after making the train/dev/test set splits on labeled data and runs multiple experiments before finally making the model selection. Throughout the training process, Training Lead makes many decisions on the various hyper parameters and strives to optimize the network/architecture of the training algorithm to achieve best results. A Training Lead also conducts error analysis on failed training and dev/cross-validation cases and optimizes the model to reduce those errors. A Training Lead does not have access to the test cases.

3.6 Testing and Benchmarking

A Test Lead leads the testing and benchmarking activity. Finalized model is tested against multiple datasets that are collected. The model is also tested against various competitor services, if accessible, and applicable. Comparing the quality and run-time performance of the model with competitor's services and all known competing AI models to establish its quality for each model version is a critical aspect of testing phase. As noted earlier, a test lead is also responsible for conducting detailed and thorough error analysis on the failed test cases and sharing the observations and patterns with the Training Lead so as to help improve the AI model in future iterations.

3.7 Model Deployment

This is the step where critical decisions are made by the Deployment Lead on the deployment configuration of the model. In Software-as-a-Service (SaaS) services, this often involves, infrastructure components, memory, disk, CPUs/GPUs, and number of pods needed based on the expected demand. Very often as part of deployment, significant engineering might be required to make the feature extraction steps production-grade and wrap the trained model into a software package that can be invoked from the larger business application.

3.8 AI Operations Management

Any AI Service's lifecycle hardly ends when the first model is deployed for the first time by following the steps described above. Each AI model has to continuously improve overtime by learning from the mistakes it makes. With each iteration, with each feedback loop, with each new model version, the model continuously evolves. Managing these iterations that lead to continuous learning of AI services is what we call as AI Operations, and is a joint activity between the operations, data and training team.

Deployment team is responsible for logging the payloads of AI models, and managing the governance of payload data with help of Data Lead. During continuous improvement cycle, the new incoming data is included by Train Lead to re-do training process and prepare a model that is more accurate for the data it is being used for. The payload data is also used to detect and address aspects such as biases, errors, model drifts, misalignments and explainability.

In the following sections we elaborate on each of these pipeline stages. In Appendix A we present a small snippet of our maturity framework. A more detailed maturity framework could not be attached due to space limitations but will be made available via company website.

4   Data Pipeline

Given input data X, A machine learning model approximates a mapping function f to predict an output value y such that $f(X) = y$. Training machine learning models is a data intensive effort. Training data must have enough representation of the world that the model wants to approximate. Real-world data is often messy and must be cleaned and prepared to make it usable for training AI models. Since data plays a pivotal role in AI, managing the data pipeline effectively, and aligning data curation efforts with the business goals and requirements can be key differentiators for organizations. Below, we describe some strategies for managing one's data pipelines effectively.

4.1   Define Data Requirements According to Business Needs

Mature organizations aspiring to produce high quality AI models start with defining goals for their AI models. A model product manager must first define the scope, purpose and expected minimum quality thresholds for an AI model. In organizations just starting with machine learning, this strategic job is left to data scientists responsible for training. While data scientists do their best to build a good model, it is not their job or role to define what it must be good at. For example, asking data scientists to 'build a world-class face recognition AI model' is too broad and vague. A more specific and focused goal would look like this: 'build a face recognition service that can detect male, female genders, these specified age groups, and these specified subset of races, and ethnicities, which are defined in the requirements document (the requirements document may point to a more specific taxonomy of races and ethnicities to be detected from a neutral entity such as the United Nations Race and Ethnicity taxonomy) with at least 90% accuracy on 'these' given specific test datasets where 'these' test datasets were carefully crafted by the product management team to have an even distribution of all the genders, age groups, specific races, and ethnicities for which the model is supposed do well. That is a specific, focused and measurable goal that a data scientist can build a model for. Such a focused goal is also non-disputable. If the business purpose and goal is not clear, organizations have to deal with poor performance and unfairness claims once the model goes into production where users may complain that the face recognition is biased and doesn't recognize faces of certain races and ethnicities. Such a specific goal also sets specific objectives for data and training leads in collecting the right kind of data and setting right type of train, and dev splits respectively while building the model. This way, instead of shooting in the dark, an organization managing a mature data pipeline can convert high-level business goals (e.g. target industries, domains, scenario and etc.) into specific data requirements.

4.2 Define a Data Acquisition Strategy

A mature data pipeline should be able to consider the time and cost of data curation and correlate and quantify the performance gains of AI models with the curated data. This way, an organization can justify the data curation efforts while maximizing performance gains for their AI solutions.

4.3 Apply Data Selection to Select Suitable Training Data

The goal of data selection is to select representative, unbiased and diverse data. This is a funneling process. Data cleansing and data selection both reduce data as the result of processing. Therefore, in order to achieve desired quantities of representative data, organizations may have to be prepared to collect more data than they may end up using. If data selection is not done, on the other hand, i) models may end up with undesirable biases as proper representation may not be achieved ii) organizations may have to pay for labeling data that may or may not be useful, adding to the costs and iii) too much unselected data may unnecessarily add to the processing time and computational capacity requirements of the machine learning process. Therefore, it is critical to apply appropriate sampling techniques in order to generate quality training data sets in reasonable sizes.

4.4 Create Data Annotation Guidelines to Achieve Consistency with Data Labeling

In general, the more the available annotated data, the better the model performs. However, labeling data can be difficult and expensive. To deliver high-quality annotated data in an efficient way, an organization should consider the following three aspects: (i) create unambiguous definitions for terms, prepare clear annotation guidelines and continuously refine the guidelines and definitions with user feedback. A mature pipeline should support a rapid feedback loop between data scientists and data annotators, (ii) use a combination of internal team of annotators and external crowd workers to get data annotated at scale, (iii) use machine learning to pre-annotate data that human annotators can validate. This can greatly speed up the human annotation process.

4.5 Augment Data Using Synthetic Techniques as Applicable

In machine learning algorithms, there is often a need to synthetically augment data, to increase the amount of training data to cover scenarios where real data might be difficult to get by. For example, in the case of audio data for training a Speech-to-Text model, a given set of audio files can be augmented by superposition of noise tracks, echoes, reverberations etc. Also, rate, pitch modulation can be performed on audio files to synthesize additional data. In the case of image recognition modeling, an image can be tilted, rotated, and colors changed to generate additional training data. As a best practice, we recommend organizations to have a strategy and develop a pipeline for data augmentation and align the augmented data

5 Feature Pipeline

The success or failure of the machine learning algorithms is intimately tied to how the data is represented. In this section, we present some best practices for managing the feature pipeline:

5.1 Keep Your Options Open During Feature Selection

Researchers have explored different types of training algorithms that aim to exploit different types of feature representations. These feature representations can be grouped into 3 types, (1) raw-features (2) expert-designed features and (3) latent-features. Characters, pixels or audio waves are prime example of raw features. Raw features require minimal pre-processing and transformations to data before being fed to the training algorithms. From engineering point-of-view, it has resulted in much simpler training and testing pipelines. However, this comes at the cost of need for large amounts of data for training. Other extreme to using raw features is using expert-designed features. Experts often bring domain knowledge to create these features. However, applying learning from one domain to other is often the Achilles heel for such algorithms. The over-dependence on expert users is often seen as a limitation in terms of time and cost. In the last decade, in particular with image and speech applications, state-of-the-art models have often used lower-level features than expert-level features. Recent advancement of deep-learning algorithms made a consistent case for third type of features known as latent-features. These features typically come from unsupervised pre-trained models. Intuitively, these features compress the high-quality information that goes beyond explicitly created features. Success of Word embeddings is a primary example of usefulness of latent features. Recent advancement in GPU technologies fueled the possibility of training complex unsupervised models at a much faster-rate. Hence, unsupervised deep-learning based techniques are consistently providing much better latent features in varieties of applications that deal with texts, audios, images, and videos. The main drawback of these features is that it's very hard to explain them. Hence, building the explainable model using latent features is an open research problem. A mature organization implementing machine learning pipeline should always keep the option of using all types of features and be aware of which features make more sense for a given task.

5.2 Understand Performance Tradeoffs with Feature Processing

If feature-pipeline has to support real-world applications, then often response time of the model in production environment becomes a bottleneck in addition to the effectiveness of features. Hence, understanding the trade-offs between response times and model quality is necessary. Since most of these trade-offs are influenced by the available training datasets at the time, these trade-offs need be revisited when underlying datasets, training algorithms or requirements change significantly. To better generalize a machine learning service, organizations often collect datasets from various sources. Features are key to understanding the differences between these sources. Since collecting high-quality datasets is costly, powerful feature analysis provide clues on when to collect and how to diversify data for the training algorithms.

5.3 Master the Art of Feature Representation

Preparing features for a given task often requires creativity. Many-a-times organization needs task-specific features to build the best model. For example, in text analysis, it's important to pay attention to how sentences are getting tokenized. Successful tokenizer segments emoticons, slangs, abbreviations to improve the overall perception of the sentiment analysis system. Organizations often need to be flexible to modify or even re-write the tokenizer to keep the task specific features. Similarly, for effective speech recognition system, creating language or even dialect specific phonetic dictionaries have shown to have better generalization with less amount of labeled data.

6 Train Pipeline

We present some best practices from our own experience of training large scale AI models deployed to production.

6.1 From Experimentation to Production: Design Your Compute Strategy

The train step in an AI project often starts with a single data scientist working on developing a model that learns the input and output relationship from the training data. In quest of implementing the best model, the data scientist experiments with multiple algorithms, frameworks, and configurations. While, initially, it might be sufficient to run these experiments on a local machine or couple of servers, very soon the number of experiments that need to be executed starts getting constrained by available compute.

Furthermore, often special compute is required for running specific machine learning algorithms e.g. for deep learning GPUs are preferred. Speech training requires large amount of storage when compared to storage required for running training on text data. Hence, a scalable infrastructure strategy is needed to support training needs. It is better to plan for such compute needs as soon as the initial experiments and approach shows promise.

6.2 Data and Model Versioning for Efficient Collaboration and Experimentation

As the initial train experiments start showing promise, the data science team also grows. In order to support collaboration, coordination and reuse in a growing team version management of models become imperative. However, it is no longer just train and feature extraction code that needs to be versioned, but also the training data, along with experiment settings so any of the train experiments can be reproduced.

6.3 Modularizing Train Code and Plan for Train to Serve Handoff Management

Modularizing train code, so it becomes easy to plug in different components, is another productivity booster. A data scientist might have started off with a monolithic piece of code where data pre-processing, feature engineering, training code are all inter-twined. However, this soon becomes a problem as data science team would need to experiment with different machine learning approaches, different features, different data pre-processing steps, with different team members focusing on different pieces, and different frameworks being used for each.

While data scientists focus on building the most accurate model, the engineering team focuses on the nonfunctional aspects such as run-time performance, capacity planning, and scaling approach. Often at this step, the serve and train pipelines start differing as train is an offline process, and test is an online one. Long times to productize an AI model is a big challenge many AI projects face. As organizations mature there is increased demand for experimentation-production parity because of use of standardized frameworks, development of common pre-processing, feature engineering packages and so on. Therefore, closer collaboration between data scientists and engineers to arrive at shared understanding of nonfunctional serve requirements also helps close the gap between train and serve code.

6.4 AI Models Are Rarely Perfect on Day-One. Plan for Continuous Improvements

AI models are not static, they need to improve or adjust to data over time. In order to improve the model, it is important to have access to data that is representative of real data the model is getting used on. In traditional software projects, limited exception and error logging is done in production. The main reason for logging is to help developers debug any production issues that might arise. However, in AI implementations it is important to have a strategy to collect payloads, as they are the real examples of data the model is being used for. Payload data needs to be brought back into the train pipeline to improve the model. Once more training data is available data scientists are again required to go through the data through train pipeline to arrive at improved model, followed by engineering team who needs to optimize for performance and deploy. This makes model improvement a recurring and continuous process.

6.5 Automate the Train Pipeline

Having automated training pipelines can help significantly reduce the time a data scientist has to spend in improving model. When new training data comes in, the train pipeline would be executed, and as part of this, multiple experiments are auto executed. Data scientists can then select the best model and push it for deployment. Best practices and tooling for continuous integration and delivery from traditional software development life cycle (SDLC) can help reduce engineering time spent in deploying a new model.

Organizations that rely on AI models as part of their daily operations have made significant progress in maturing their train pipelines. New tools to manage train and serve pipeline are regularly being released in market, e.g. version manage AI projects, integrated environments to build and run AI models.

7 Test Pipeline

Testing is an investigation process conducted to derive insights about the quality of the machine learning models under test. Here, we share some of the best practices in testing based on our experience.

7.1 Be Prepared to Iterate Between Train and Test

While we often have lots of choices to learn and apply various machine learning algorithms on our data sets, selecting the final best model out of many good working models is a challenging and time-consuming task. In practice, train data scientists and testers often work together to compare the performance of models generated with different algorithm parameters before deciding which parameters to use; they may also compare performance of the models using different feature-based representations to ensure the selected features are improving the models as expected.

7.2 Testing Is not just a One-Time Build Activity. It Is Continuous Throughout an AI Model's Lifecycle. Keep the Test Datasets Updated

In AI services, there is a notion of continuously improving the accuracy of the models as more data becomes available either via continuous data acquisition process or from payload data. While each iteration of the machine learning model can be tested on the same set of standard datasets it can be unfair to test systems on only one set when the newer models have 'seen more of the world' via more training data. As more and more training data is added from different sources, testing should be an iterative and dynamic process wherein test cases are continuously updated to improve the test coverage to represent the new world they live in. This makes comparing models from one version to another difficult. There is no perfect solution for this. We have noted that maintaining old and new test cases and testing model versions on all test cases each time gives a comprehensive view of the quality of the current and past models.

7.3 Whose Side Is the Real 'Truth'? Sometimes Machine Learning Models Are Both Right and Wrong!

The 'ground-truth' can be different for different people in certain domains. For example, what appears as a complaint to some may appear as a neutral statement to others. Therefore, user acceptance testing of AI-based services may depend on individual user perceptions. Special user perception testing needs to be instituted in addition to conventional performance testing in cases where ground truth can be ambiguous. As the predictions of models from one version to another can often be different, such user perception testing has to be done continuously to allow testers to select the best user perceived model in some cases.

7.4 Adversarial and Long Tail Testing for Robustness

A mature organization needs to do proactive testing for understanding and guiding effective AI model testing to ensure their robustness. Proactive testing differs from conventional testing metrics in two aspects. First, it extends the coverage of the testing dataset by dynamically collecting supplementary data. Second, AI developers can collect additional data belonging to certain categories to target corner cases. To create failed cases at scale, adversarial sample has attracted attention in machine learning communities in recent years. For example, different perturbation strategies (e.g., insertion, deletion, and replacement) have been proposed to evade DNN-based text classifiers.

8 Model Fairness, Trust, Transparency, Error Analysis and Monitoring

8.1 Set Proper Goals for AI Models to Mitigate Undesirable Biases and Start with Test Cases

Statistical machine learning models rely on biases in data to learn patterns. Therefore, the concept of data bias by itself is not bad. What people mean, when they say biases is 'undesirable biases'. We argue that undesirable biases creep in because of lack of discipline in setting proper goals for the AI models. Proper goals can be set for AI models by preparing test cases upfront and setting specific objectives on what is expected of the model. As noted in the data requirements section, asking data scientists to 'build a world-class face recognition AI model' is too broad, vague and leads to unanticipated biases. A more specific and focused goal such as: 'build a face recognition service that can detect male/female genders, with pre-defind specific age groups, and these specific subset of races, and ethnicities in the requirements document (which is grounded in a standard taxonomy from a neutral organization such as the United Nations Race and Ethnicity taxonomy)) with at least 90% accuracy on 'these' given specific test datasets' where 'these' test datasets were carefully crafted by the product management ream to have an even distribution of all the genders, age groups, specific races, and ethnicities for which the model is supposed do well. That is a specific, focused and measurable goal that a data scientist can build a model for. Such a focused goal is also non-disputable, measurable and tested for biases. It is this lack of specificity that leads to undesirable biases.

8.2 Declare Your Biases to Establish Trust

Rarely do organization have unlimited budgets and time to collect representative samples to prepare most comprehensive datasets that can avoid undesirable biases completely. One can, at best, mitigate biases with careful planning. Therefore, we'd argue that it is more practical for a machine learning model to declare its biases than to pretend that it is unbiased or that it can ever be fully unbiased. That is, product managers must declare what the model is trained on. That way, the consumers of the model know exactly what they are getting. This establishes trust in AI models. This is akin to having nutrition labels on processed and packaged foods. People can judge based on the contents, whether a particular snack item is right for them or not. While not all machine learning model builders may have the incentive to declare the secrets of their ingredients, it may be required in some regulated industries.

8.3 Do We Always Need Full Explainability? Let the Use Case Drive the Needs and Select Machine Learning Algorithms Accordingly

We still don't know why and how certain medicines work in human body and yet patients rarely question when a doctor prescribes a medicine. They inherently the trust the doctor to give them the best treatment and trust their choice of medicine. Citing such analogies, some argue whether full explainability may not be always needed. Whether or not the medical analogy is appropriate for a business domain, one thing is clear. Some use cases demand full transparency while others are more forgiving. For example, a sentiment prediction model which aims to predict consumer sentiments against products from social media data may not need the same level of transparency as a loan approval AI model which is subject to auditability. Therefore, based on the use case and need, AI model development team must set transparency goals ahead of time. A data scientist training an AI model can use these requirements in making the right kind of AI model that might offer more explainability or not.

8.4 Diagnose Errors at Scale

Traditionally, error analysis is often manually performed on fixed datasets at a small scale. This cannot capture errors made by AI models in practice. A mature error analysis process should enable data scientists to systemically analyze a large number of "unseen" errors and develop an in-depth understanding of the types of errors, distribution of errors, and sources of errors in the model.

8.5 Error Validation and Categorization

A mature error analysis process should be able to validate and correct mislabeled data during testing. Compared with traditional methods such as Confusion Matrix, a mature process for an organization should provide deeper insights into when an AI model fails, how it fails and why. Creating a user-defined taxonomy of errors and prioritizing them based not only on the severity of errors but also on the business value of fixing those errors is critical to maximizing time and resources spent in improving AI models.

8.6 Version Models and Manage Their Lineage to Better Understand Model Behavior Over Time

An organization may have multiple versions of a machine learning model. A mature organization needs to maintain different versions in a data-store. They should also keep the lineage of training data used to building such models. In addition, they should be able to run automated tests to understand the difference between such models using well defined metrics, and test sets. With each version, they should track whether model quality is improving for such test sets.

In conclusion, we have presented a set of best practices applicable to building and managing the life cycle of machine learning models. Appendix A contains snippets of our framework for select stages of the pipeline. We are unable to publish the full framework in this paper due to space limitations. However, we intend to make it available on our company website for reference.

9 Conclusions and Discussion

In this paper we argued that traditional software development lifecycle methodologies fall short when managing AI models as AI lifecycle management has many differences from traditional software development lifecycle. We presented a re-interpretation of software capability maturity model (CMM) for AI mode lifecycle management.

We argued that AI models need to be robust (R), accurate (A), continuously improving (C), explainable (E), fair (F), accountable (A), transparent (T), and secure (S). When put together, they form a pneumonic 'RACE your FACTS' – as an easy way to remember. We have presented various best practices and a maturity assessment framework (Appendix A) for addressing these topics.

Implementing these best practices requires many innovations, tools and techniques. So much AI is needed throughout the AI lifecycle management to build and management AI models. We are excited about the research and innovation possibilities and frontiers that this offers. A journey informed by best practices and maturity awareness is the best way to get there.

Appendix A

A snippet of our Machine Learning Maturity Framework is attached below. A more detailed one could not be attached due to space limitations but will be made available upon request or posted on the company website shortly.

Capability	Detailed Capability	Role	Initial	Repeatable	Defined	Managed	Optimizing
AI Model Goal Setting	Target Scope and Purpose	Offering Manager	* Scope is unclear - goal is set in statements as vague as 'build world-class models'. For what, for which industries, for whom, for which type of data is not enunciated.	* Qualitative goal setting. Build models with 90% accuracy on Sentiment analysis for any type of data. No idea if 90% is achievable or not. * Qualitative scope and targets. Still lacks clarity and formality.	* Acknowledgement of the importance of scope clarity across the organization. * Some clarity starts to emerge on use cases, industries, and users needs and perspectives are taken.	* Proactively scopes the model goals and targets after each iteration and adjusts and communicates model purpose to clients and users. * All parties have a clear understanding of what to expect of the model.	* Model's purpose, goals are clearly stated. Methods, automation tools are in place to measure and monitor the model metrics. * Explicitly declares what training data the model is built with and declares known biases with clients to establish trust. * As much clarity as what the model isn't meant to do as there is clarity on what the model is meant to do.
Data Pipeline Management	Data Annotation	Data Manager	* Have initial annotation guidelines.	* Have consistent annotation procedures across annotation teams.	* Have a process to define the difficulty of the annotation tasks and split the tasks between subject-matter experts and non-expert workers for data annotation accordingly.	* have a routine feedback loop between data scientists and data annotators. * Have machine learning methods in the pre-annotation process to reduce the human annotation efforts. * Manage the workload between the human annotation and machine annotation.	* Have a process to optimize the cost and annotation outcome. * update annotation guidelines and produces timely and appropriately based on new requirements from AI models
Feature Preparation Pipeline	Externalized feature processing pipeline	Train Lead	* Feature processing pipeline is not designed as an independent module. Part of feature processing appears in the data pre-processing preparation. * Train and test pipelines might not be following exact same steps or order to generate features	* Feature processing is an independent module, but not externalized separately. Hence, same feature processing module code is repeated in train and test pipelines.	* Feature processing module is externalized and shared between train and test. Hence code maintenance is extremely efficient. * The cost of the externalization on the response time is not considered	* The cost of the externalization on the reponse time is thoroughly understood. * However, externalization cost may have come at the cost of removing the important features.	* Alternative strategies have been employed, including efficient and faster implementation of feature extraction module, to make sure that cost of externalization is minimal.
Train Pipeline Management	Modularizing Train code	Train Lead	* Left to data scientist	* Have basic guidelines for data scientist to create separate modules for feature engineering, training.	* Data science team publishes, discusses best practices.	* Train code and model pipeline review process established.	* Shared repository of reusable feature extraction modules, and training frameworks. * Data scientists routinely experiment with different feature sets, training modules to build better models.
Test Pipeline management	Test Metrics and Goals	Test Lead	* No metrics or goals were set for testing.	* Only test on summary metrics such as Precision, Recall, Accuracy, F-measure. * Goal is set to merely improve the accuracy of the model.	* Multiple test goals are manually created by test lead. * Multiple test metrics are manually selected by test lead.	* Test goals are created to address specific concerns of the model * Test metrics are defined and refined for a variety of coverage.	* Test goals are created and customized for domain-specific problem with high market viability * Test metrics reflect the domain and scope of where the model will be deployed
Model Quality, Performance and Model Management	Quality metrics measurement	Quality Assurance Lead	* non-existent	* Manually looking at model output for few test cases and assessing for goodness	* Well defined metric set for measuring model quality	* Automated means established to measure model quality using well defined metric	* Tools developed to measure model quality using well defined metric.
Model Error Analysis	Error Categorization	Quality Assurance Lead	* Have single-score metrics such as precision and recall	* Have traditional error categorization methods such as Confusion Matrix	* Have a process to define the testing covering of cxing datasets. * Have a process to define model user-defined error taxonomy.	* Have an automated process to categorize errors into severity levels can help an organization to prioritize their efforts to address critical errors in their AI applications	* Have an optimized process to prioritize errors in terms of user-defined error types, data-driven metrics, and error severity. * Have a process to automate the classification of errors into the user-defined error types. * Categorize Errors based on data-specific features. For example, for a text-based model (e.g. Nature Language Understanding), errors made by the model can be categorized based on text topics, sentence length, and etc.)
Model Fairness & Trust	Undesirable bias awareness	AI Operations Manager	* Not aware of the existence of any type of bias.	* Only aware the existence of a set of pre-defined explicit bias (e.g. gender, age, race). * Do not aware of the existence of explicit bias out side of the pre-defined list, as well as implicit bias.	* Aware the existence of a broad set of explicit bias, not just limited to the pre-defined list. * Do not aware of the existence of implicit bias.	* Aware the existence of both explicit and implicit biases.	* Aware the existence of both explicit and implicit biases. * Being able to automatically quantify the risks of bias exposure, and to inform the stakeholders accordingly.
Model Transparency	Awareness of Explainability of algorithmic choices	AI Operations Manager	* Not aware the importance and necessity of model explainability	* Aware the importance and necessity of model explainability.	* Aware the importance and necessity of model explainability. * Provide only some global level interpretation of the model (e.g. training information, underlying algorithms, performance description).	* Provide both global level (e.g. training information, underlying algorithms, performance description) and local level (contributing features regarding one specific case interpretation of the model. * Being able to adjust the model interpretations based on the different background of end users (e.g. technical vs. non-technical, novice vs. expert).	* Allow users to interact with the model interpretation and to flag attributes that they think the model learned incorrectly. * Being able to adjust the model according to the user's feedback. * Allow users to appeal to certain model prediction.

References

1. Humphrey, W.S.: Characterizing the software process: a maturity framework. IEEE Softw. **5**(2), 73–79 (1988)
2. Braun, H.T.: Evaluation of big data maturity models–a benchmarking study to support big data maturity assessment in organizations (2015)
3. Halper, F., Krishnan, K.: TDWi big data maturity model guide. Interpreting your assessment score. TDWI Research **1**, 16 (2013)
4. Nott, C.: A maturity model for big data and analytics. IBM (2015). https://www.ibm.com/developerworks/community/blogs/bigdataanalytics/entry/A_maturity_model_for_big_data_and_analytics?lang=en_us
5. Schmarzo, B.: Big data business model maturity index guide. Dell EMC (2016). https://infocus.dellemc.com/william_schmarzo/big-data-business-model-maturity-index-guide/
6. Dhanuka, V.: Hortonworks big data maturity model. Hortonworks (2017). http://hortonworks.com/wp-content/uploads/2016/04/Hortonworks-Big-Data-Maturity-Assessment.pdf
7. El-Darwiche, B., Koch, V., Meer, D., Shehadi, R.T., Tohme, W.: Big data maturity: an action plan for policymakers and executives. Glob. Inf. Technol. Rep. **43**, 51 (2014)

Foundations

Extending Temporal Business Constraints with Uncertainty

Fabrizio Maria Maggi[1]([✉]), Marco Montali[1], Rafael Peñaloza[2], and Anti Alman[3]

[1] Free University of Bozen-Bolzano, Bolzano, Italy
{maggi,montali}@inf.unibz.it
[2] University of Milano-Bicocca, Milan, Italy
rafael.penaloza@unimib.it
[3] University of Tartu, Tartu, Estonia
anti.alman@ut.ee

Abstract. Temporal business constraints have been extensively adopted to declaratively capture the acceptable courses of execution in a business process. However, traditionally, constraints are interpreted logically in a crisp way: a process execution trace conforms with a constraint model if all the constraints therein are satisfied. This is too restrictive when one wants to capture best practices, constraints involving uncontrollable activities, and exceptional but still conforming behaviors. This calls for the extension of business constraints with uncertainty. In this paper, we tackle this timely and important challenge, relying on recent results on probabilistic temporal logics over finite traces. Specifically, our contribution is threefold. First, we delve into the conceptual meaning of probabilistic constraints and their semantics. Second, we argue that probabilistic constraints can be discovered from event data using existing techniques for declarative process discovery. Third, we study how to monitor probabilistic constraints, where constraints and their combinations may be in multiple monitoring states at the same time, though with different probabilities.

Keywords: Declarative process models · Temporal logics · Process mining · Probabilistic process monitoring · Probabilistic conformance checking

1 Introduction

A key functionality that any process-aware information system should support is that of *monitoring* [12]. Monitoring concerns the ability to verify at runtime whether an actual process execution conforms to a prescriptive business process model. This runtime form of conformance checking is instrumental to detect, and then suitably handle, deviations appearing in ongoing process instances [14].

A common way of representing monitoring requirements that capture the expected behavior prescribed by a process model is by using declarative, business constraints. Many studies demonstrated that, in several settings, business

© Springer Nature Switzerland AG 2020
D. Fahland et al. (Eds.): BPM 2020, LNCS 12168, pp. 35–54, 2020.
https://doi.org/10.1007/978-3-030-58666-9_3

constraints can be formalized in terms of temporal logic rules [19]. Within this paradigm, the *Declare* constraint-based process modeling language [21] has been introduced as a front-end language to specify business constraints based on Linear Temporal Logic over finite traces (LTL$_f$) [2]. The advantage of this approach is that the automata-theoretic characterization of LTL$_f$ is based on standard, finite-state automata. These can be exploited to provide advanced monitoring facilities where the state of constraints is determined in a sophisticated way by combining the events collected at runtime with the possible, future continuations [1,16], in turn enabling the early detection of conflicting constraints [17].

In a variety of application domains, business constraints are inherently *uncertain*. This is clearly the case for constraints which: *(i)* capture best practices that have to be followed by default, that is, in most, but not necessarily all, cases; *(ii)* link controllable activities to activities that are under the responsibility of uncontrollable, external stakeholders; *(iii)* should hold in exceptional but still conforming courses of execution. Uncertainty is intrinsically present also when business constraints are discovered from event data. It is then very surprising that only very few approaches incorporate uncertainty as a first-class citizen. This is the case not just when the prescriptive behavior to be monitored is expressed as a set of business constraints, but also when a more conventional imperative approach is adopted [11].

It is well known that combining uncertainty with temporal logics is extremely challenging. This is due to the interplay of temporal operators and uncertainty, which becomes especially tricky considering that, usually, temporal logics are interpreted over infinite traces. The resulting, combined logics then come with semantic or syntactic restrictions (see, e.g., [8,20]). To tackle these issues, the probabilistic temporal logic over finite traces PLTL$_f$, and its fragment PLTL$_f^0$, have been recently proposed in [15]. Since these logics are defined over finite traces, they are the natural candidate to enrich existing constraint-based process modeling approaches with uncertainty.

In this paper, we indeed employ PLTL$_f^0$ to achieve this goal. Specifically, we exploit the fact that PLTL$_f^0$ handles time and probabilities in a way that naturally matches with the notion of conformance: a constraint φ holds with probability p if, by considering all the traces contained in a log, φ is satisfied by a fraction p of all the traces contained therein. Based on this observation, we provide a threefold contribution.

First, we exploit PLTL$_f^0$ to introduce *probabilistic constraints* and delve into their semantics and conceptual meaning; notably, our semantics is based on the already established notion of stochastic language [11]. We then show how probabilistic constraints can be used to naturally lift the Declare language to its probabilistic version ProbDeclare. Second, we observe that probabilistic Declare constraints can be discovered off-the-shelf using already existing techniques for declarative process discovery [7,9,13,22], with strong guarantees on the consistency of the generated models. In fact, the discovered constraints are for sure (probabilistically) consistent, without incurring in the notorious consistency issues experienced when the discovered constraints are interpreted in a crisp way [4,5]. Third, we study how to monitor probabilistic constraints, where constraints and their combinations may be in multiple monitoring states at the same time, though with different associated probabilities. This is based on the fact that a single ProbDeclare model gives raise to multiple scenarios, each with its own distinct probability, where some of the constraints are expected to be satisfied, and the others to be violated. Specifically, we show how to lift existing automata-theoretic monitoring techniques to this more sophisticated probabilistic setting, and report on a proof-of-concept implementation of the resulting framework.

The paper is structured as follows. After preliminary notions introduced in Sect. 2, we introduce the syntax and semantics of probabilistic constraints in Sect. 3. In Sect. 4, we discuss how ProbDeclare constraints can be discovered from event data using existing techniques. In Sect. 5, we show how to monitor probabilistic constraints, and report on the corresponding implementation. In Sect. 6, we conclude the paper and spell out directions for future work.

2   Preliminaries

We consider a finite alphabet Σ of atomic activities. A *trace* τ over Σ is a finite sequence $a_1 \ldots a_n$ of activities, where $a_i \in \Sigma$ for $i \in \{1, \ldots, n\}$. The *length* of trace τ is denoted by $length(\tau)$. We use notation $\tau(i)$ to select the activity a_i present in position (also called instant) i of τ, and Σ^* for the (infinite) set of all possible traces over Σ. A *log* over Σ is a finite multiset of traces over Σ.

We recall next syntax and semantics of LTL$_f$ [1,2], and its application in the context of Declare [18,21]. Consistently with the BPM literature, we make the simplifying assumption that formulae are evaluated on sequences where, at each point in time, only one proposition is true, matching the notion of trace defined above.

LTL Over Finite Traces. LTL$_f$ has exactly the same syntax of standard LTL, but, differently from LTL, it interprets formulae over finite traces, as defined above. An LTL$_f$ formula φ over Σ is built by extending propositional logic with temporal operators:

$$\varphi ::= a \mid \neg\varphi \mid \varphi_1 \vee \varphi_2 \mid \bigcirc\varphi \mid \varphi_1 \,\mathcal{U}\, \varphi_2 \quad \text{where } a \in \Sigma.$$

A formula φ is evaluated over a trace τ in a valid instant i of τ, such that $1 \leq i \leq length(\tau)$. Specifically, we inductively define that φ *holds at instant i of* τ, written $\tau, i \models \varphi$, as:

- $\tau, i \models a$ for $a \in \Sigma$ iff $\tau(i) = a$;
- $\tau, i \models \neg\varphi$ iff $\tau, i \not\models \varphi$;
- $\tau, i \models \varphi_1 \vee \varphi_2$ iff $\tau, i \models \varphi_1$ or $\tau, i \models \varphi_2$;
- $\tau, i \models \bigcirc\varphi$ iff $i < length(\tau)$ and $\tau, i+1 \models \varphi$;
- $\tau, i \models \varphi_1 \,\mathcal{U}\, \varphi_2$ iff for some j such that $i \leq j \leq length(\tau)$, we have $\tau, j \models \varphi_2$ and for every k such that $i \leq k < j$, we have $\tau, k \models \varphi_1$.

Table 1. Some Declare templates, with their LTL$_f$ and graphical representations.

TEMPLATE	NOTATION	TEMPLATE	NOTATION
existence(a): $\Diamond$a	1..* [a]	absence(a) $\neg\Diamond$a	0 [a]
existence2(a) $\Diamond$(a $\wedge$ $\bigcirc\Diamond$a)	2..* [a]	absence2(a) $\neg\Diamond$(a $\wedge$ $\bigcirc\Diamond$a)	0..1 [a]
response(a, b) $\Box$(a $\rightarrow$ $\bigcirc\Diamond$b)	[a] ●→ [b]	precedence(a, b) $\neg$b$\mathcal{W}$a	[a] →●→ [b]
resp $-$ existence(a, b) $\Diamond$a $\rightarrow$ $\Diamond$b	[a] ●— [b]	not $-$ coexistence(a, b) $\neg$($\Diamond$a $\wedge$ $\Diamond$b)	[a] ●‖‖● [b]

Intuitively, $\bigcirc$ denotes the *next state* operator, and $\bigcirc\varphi$ holds if there exists a next instant (i.e., the current instant does not correspond to the end of the trace), and, in the next instant, φ holds. Operator $\mathcal{U}$ instead is the *until* operator, and $\varphi_1\mathcal{U}\varphi_2$ holds if φ_1 holds now and continues to hold until eventually, in a future instant, φ_2 holds.

From these operators, we can derive the usual boolean operators $\wedge$ and $\rightarrow$, the two formulae *true* and *false*, as well as additional temporal operators. We consider, in particular, the following three: *(i)* (eventually) $\Diamond\varphi = true\,\mathcal{U}\varphi$ is true, if there is a future state where φ holds; *(ii)* (globally) $\Box\varphi = \neg\Diamond\neg\varphi$ is true, if now and in all future states φ holds; *(iii)* (weak until) $\varphi_1\mathcal{W}\varphi_2 = \varphi_1\mathcal{U}\varphi_2 \vee \Box\varphi_1$ relaxes the until operator by admitting the possibility that φ_2 never becomes true, in this case by requiring that φ_1 holds now and in all future states. We write $\tau \models \varphi$ as a shortcut notation for $\tau, 0 \models \varphi$, and say that formula φ is *satisfiable*, if there exists a trace τ such that $\tau \models \varphi$.

Example 1. The LTL$_f$ formula $\Box$(close $\rightarrow$ $\bigcirc\Diamond$accept) (called *response* in Declare) models that, whenever an order is closed, then it is eventually accepted. ◁

Every LTL$_f$ formula φ can be translated into a corresponding standard finite-state automaton $\mathcal{A}_\varphi$ that accepts all and only those finite traces that satisfy φ [1,2]. Although the complexity of reasoning with LTL$_f$ is the same as that of LTL, finite-state automata are much easier to manipulate in comparison with the Büchi automata used when formulae are interpreted over infinite traces. This is the main reason why LTL$_f$ has been extensively and successfully adopted within BPM to capture constraint-based, declarative processes, in particular providing the formal basis of *Declare*.

Declare is a constraint-based process modeling language based on LTL$_f$. Declare models a process by fixing a set of activities, and defining a set of *temporal constraints* over them, accepting every execution trace that satisfies all constraints. Constraints are specified via pre-defined LTL$_f$ templates, which come with a corresponding graphical representation (see Table 1 for the Declare templates we use in this paper). For the sake of generality, in this paper, we consider arbitrary LTL_f formulae as constraints. However, in the examples, we consider formulae whose templates can be represented graphically in Declare. Automata-based techniques for LTL_f have been adopted in Declare to tackle fundamental tasks within the lifecycle of Declare processes, such as consistency checking [19,21], enactment and monitoring [1,16,21], and discovery support [13].

3 Probabilistic Constraints and ProbDeclare

We now lift LTL_f constraints to their *probabilistic* version. As done in Sect. 2, we assume a fixed finite set Σ of activities.

Definition 1. *A probabilistic constraint over Σ is a triple $\langle \varphi, \bowtie, p \rangle$, where: (i) φ, the constraint formula, is an LTL_f formula over Σ; (ii) $\bowtie \in \{=, \neq, \leq, \geq, < , >\}$ is the probability operator; (iii) p, the constraint probability, is a rational value in $[0, 1]$.*   ◁

We use the compact notation $\langle \varphi, p \rangle$ for the probabilistic constraint $\langle \varphi, =, p \rangle$. A probabilistic constraint is interpreted over an event log, where traces have probabilities attached. Formally, we borrow the notion of *stochastic language* from [11].

Definition 2. *A stochastic language over Σ is a function $\rho : \Sigma^* \to [0, 1]$ that maps every trace over Σ onto a corresponding probability, so that $\sum_{\tau \in \Sigma^*} \rho(\tau) = 1$.*   ◁

An event log can be easily turned into a corresponding stochastic language through normalization of the trace quantities, in particular by dividing the number of occurrences of each trace by the total number of traces in the log [11]. Similarly, a stochastic language can be turned into a corresponding event log by considering only the traces with non-zero probabilities.

Example 2. Consider the following traces over $\Sigma = \{$close, accept, nop$\}$: *(i)* $\tau_1 = \langle$close, accept$\rangle$; *(ii)* $\tau_2 = \langle$close, accept, close, nop, accept$\rangle$; *(iii)* $\tau_3 = \langle$close, accept, close, nop$\rangle$; *(iv)* $\tau_4 = \langle$close, nop$\rangle$. Log $\mathcal{L} = \{\tau_1^{50}, \tau_2^{30}, \tau_3^{10}, \tau_4^{10}\}$ corresponds to the stochastic language ρ defined as follows: *(i)* $\rho(\tau_1) = 0.5$; *(ii)* $\rho(\tau_2) = 0.3$; *(iii)* $\rho(\tau_3) = 0.1$; *(iv)* $\rho(\tau_4) = 0.1$; *(v)* ρ is 0 for any other trace in Σ^*.   ◁

We say that a stochastic language ρ *satisfies* a probabilistic constraint $C = \langle \varphi, \bowtie, p \rangle$, written $\rho \models C$, iff $\sum_{\tau \in \Sigma^*, \tau \models \varphi} \rho(\tau) \bowtie p$. In other words, we first obtain all the traces that satisfy φ in the classical LTL_f sense. We then use ρ to sum up the overall probability associated to such traces. We finally check whether the so-obtained number n is so that the comparison expression $n \bowtie p$ is true. Constraint $C = \langle \varphi, \bowtie, p \rangle$ is *plausible* if $p \neq 0$ and it is logically plausible, that is, $\rho \models C$ for some stochastic language ρ. This latter requirements simply means that φ is satisfiable in the classical LTL_f sense.

Thanks to the correspondence between stochastic languages and event logs, we can define an analogous notion of satisfaction for event logs. With a slight abuse of notation, we use the same notation $\mathcal{L} \models C$ to indicate that event log $\mathcal{L}$ satisfies C. The resulting semantics naturally leads to interpret the constraint probability as a frequency, that is, as the fraction of conforming vs nonconforming traces contained in a log.

Example 3. The log $\mathcal{L}$ from Example 2 satisfies the probabilistic constraint $C_{ca} = \langle \Box(\texttt{close} \rightarrow \bigcirc\Diamond\texttt{accept}), 0.8 \rangle$. In fact, $\Box(\texttt{close} \rightarrow \bigcirc\Diamond\texttt{accept})$ is satisfied[1] by traces τ_1 and τ_2, whose overall probability is $0.5 + 0.3 = 0.8$.   ◁

This statistical interpretation of probabilities is central in the context of this paper, and leads to the following key observation: ρ *satisfies* $C = \langle \varphi, p \rangle$ iff it satisfies $\overline{C} = \langle \neg\varphi, 1 - p \rangle$. This reflects the intuition that, whenever φ holds in a fraction p of traces from an event log, then $\neg\varphi$ must hold in the complementary fraction $1 - p$ of traces from that log. Conversely, an unknown execution trace τ will satisfy φ with probability p, and will violate φ (i.e., satisfy $\neg\varphi$) with probability $1 - p$. This can be extended to the other probability operators in the natural way, taking into account that $\leq$ should be replaced by its dual $\geq$ (and vice-versa). Hence, we can interpret φ and $\neg\varphi$ as two alternative, *possible scenarios*, each coming with its own probability (respectively, p and $1 - p$). Whether such possible scenarios are indeed plausible depends, in turn, on their logical consistency (a plausible scenario must be logically satisfiable, that is, have at least one conforming trace) and associated probability (a plausible scenario must have a non-zero probability). A probabilistic constraint of the form $\langle \varphi, 1 \rangle$ with φ satisfiable gives raise to a single possible world, where all traces in the log satisfy φ.

Example 4. Consider constraint C_{ca} from Example 3, modeling that, in 80% of the process traces, it is true that, whenever an order is closed, then it is eventually accepted. This is equivalent to assert that, in 20% of the traces, the response is violated, i.e., there exists an instant where the order is closed and not accepted afterward. Given an unknown trace τ, there is then 0.8 chance that τ will satisfy the response formula $\Box(\texttt{close} \rightarrow \bigcirc\Diamond\texttt{accept})$, and 0.2 that τ will violate such a formula (i.e., satisfy its negation $\Diamond(\texttt{close} \wedge \neg\bigcirc\Diamond\texttt{accept})$).   ◁

3.1   Probabilistic Declare

We now consider probabilistic declarative process models including multiple probabilistic constraints at once. We lift Declare to its probabilistic version Prob-Declare.

Definition 3. *A ProbDeclare model is a pair* $\langle \Sigma, \mathcal{C} \rangle$, *where* Σ *is a set of activities and* $\mathcal{C}$ *is a set of probabilistic constraints.*   ◁

---

[1] Recall that a response constraint is satisfied if *every* execution of the source is followed by the execution of the target.

A stochastic language ρ over Σ satisfies a ProbDeclare model $\langle \Sigma, \mathcal{C} \rangle$ if it satisfies every probabilistic constraint $C \in \mathcal{C}$. It is interesting to note that, since $C = \langle \varphi, p \rangle$ and $\overline{C} = \langle \neg \varphi, 1 - p \rangle$ are equivalent, in ProbDeclare the distinction between existence and absence templates (cf. the first two lines of Table 1) gets blurred. In fact, $\langle \text{existence(a)}, p \rangle$ corresponds to $\langle \Diamond a, p \rangle$. In turn, $\langle \Diamond a, p \rangle$ is semantically equivalent to $\langle \neg \Diamond a, 1 - p \rangle$, which corresponds to $\langle \text{absence}(a), 1 - p \rangle$. The same line of reasoning applies to the existence2 and absence2 templates. All such constraints have in fact to be interpreted as the *probability of (repeated) occurrence* for a given activity.

Example 5. A small ProbDeclare model is shown on the left-hand side of Fig. 1, where only the equality operator is used for the various probabilities. Crisp constraints with probability 1 are shown in dark blue, and genuine probabilistic constraints are shown in light blue, with probability values attached. The model expresses that each order is at some point closed, and, whenever this happens, there is probability 0.8 that it will be eventually accepted, and probability 0.3 that it will be eventually refused. Note that the sum of these probabilities exceeds 1, and, consequently, in a small fraction of traces, there will be an acceptance and also a rejection (capturing the fact that a previous decision on a closed order was subverted later on). On the other hand, there is a sensible amount of traces where the order will be eventually accepted, but not refused, given the fact that the probability of the response constraint connecting close order to refuse order is only of 0.3. In 90% of the cases, it is asserted that acceptance and rejection are mutually exclusive. Finally, accepting/rejecting an order can only occur if the order was closed.   ◁

We remark that ProbDeclare models and stochastic languages have a direct correspondence to the PLTL_f^0 logic and its interpretations (as defined in [15]). Specifically, a constraint of the form $\langle \varphi, \bowtie, p \rangle$ corresponds to the PLTL_f^0 formula $\odot_{\bowtie p} \varphi$. PLTL_f^0 is a fragment of PLTL_f, also defined in [15]. Models of PLTL_f formulae are finite trees where nodes are propositional assignments, and edges carry probabilities, with the condition that the sum of the probabilities on the edges that depart from the same node add up to 1. A stochastic language ρ can then be easily represented as a PLTL_f model. This can be done by creating a tree where the root has as many outgoing edges as the number of traces in ρ. Each edge gets the probability that ρ associates to the corresponding trace. Then each edge continues into a single branch where nodes sequentially encode the events of the trace, and where edges all have probability 1. Due to this direct correspondence, we get that reasoning on ProbDeclare models (e.g., to check for satisfiability) can be carried out in PSPACE, thus yielding the same complexity of LTL_f. This does not yet give a concrete technique to actually carry out reasoning and, more in general, understand how different probabilistic constraints and their probabilities interact with each other. This is answered in the next section, again taking advantage from the fact that, thanks to the correspondence with the PLTL_f framework in [15], all the techniques presented next are formally correct.

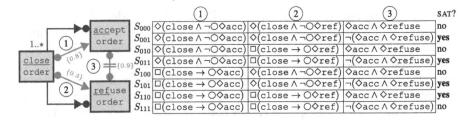

Fig. 1. A ProbDeclare model, with 8 constraint scenarios, out of which only 4 are logically plausible. Recall that each scenario implicitly contains also the three constraint formulae derived from the three constraints with probability 1.

3.2   Constraints Scenarios and Their Probabilities

Since a ProbDeclare model contains multiple probabilistic constraints, we have to consider that, probabilistically, a trace may satisfy or violate each of the constraints contained in the model, thus yielding multiple possible worlds, each one defining which constraints are satisfied, and which violated. E.g., in Fig. 1, we may have a trace containing close order followed by accept order and refuse order, thus violating the not − coexistence constraint relating acceptance and refusal. This is indeed possible in 10% of the traces. More in general, consider a ProbDeclare model $M = \langle \Sigma, \{\langle \varphi_1, p_1 \rangle, \ldots, \langle \varphi_n, p_n \rangle\} \rangle$. Each constraint formula φ_i is satisfied by a trace with probability p_i, and violated with probability $1 - p_i$. Hence, a model of this form implicitly yields, potentially, 2^n possible worlds resulting from all possible choices of which constraints formulae are satisfied, and which are violated (recall that violating a formula means satisfying its negation). We call such possible worlds *constraint scenarios*. The key point is to understand which scenarios are plausible, and with which overall probability, starting from the "local" probabilities attached to each single constraint. Overall, a set of constraint scenarios with their corresponding probabilities can be seen as a sort of *canonical stochastic language* that provides a uniform representation of all stochastic languages that satisfy the ProbDeclare model under study.

Example 6. If a constraint has probability 1, we do not need to consider the two alternatives, since every trace will need to satisfy its formula. An alternative way of reading this is to notice that the negated constraint would, in this case, have probability 0. Hence, to identify a scenario, we proceed as follows. We consider the $m \leq n$ constrains with probability different than 1, and fix an order over them. Then, a scenario is defined by a number between 0 and 2^{m-1}, whose corresponding binary representation defines which constraint formulae are satisfied, and which violated: specifically, for constraint formula φ_i of index i, if the bit in position $i-1$ is 1, then the scenario contains φ_i, if instead that bit is 0, then the scenario contains $\neg \varphi_i$. The overall formula describing a scenario is then simply the conjunction of all such formulae, together with all the formulae of constraints with probability 1. Clearly, each execution trace belongs to one and only one constraint scenario: it does so when it satisfies the conjunctive formula associated to that scenario. We say that a scenario is *logically plausible*, if such a conjunctive LTL_f formula is satisfiable in the LTL_f sense: if it is not, then the scenario has to be discarded, since no trace will ever belong to it.

Figure 1 shows a ProbDeclare model with 6 constraints, three of which are crisp constraints with probability 1, while the other three are genuinely probabilistic. Circled numbers represent the ordering of such constraints. 8 possible constraint scenarios are induced, each enforcing the satisfaction of the three crisp constraints, while picking the satisfaction or violation of the three constraints response(close, acc), response(close, ref), and not − coexistence(acc, ref). Logically speaking, we have to consider 6 different formulae: □(close → ○◇acc) and its negation ◇(close ∧ ¬○◇acc) (similarly for response(close,ref)), as well as ¬(◇acc ∧ ◇refuse) and its negation ◇acc ∧ ◇refuse. The resulting scenarios are reported in the same figure, using the naming conventions introduced before. E.g., scenario S_{101} is the scenario that satisfies response(close, acc) and not − coexistence(acc, ref), but violates response(close, ref).

By checking the LTL_f satisfiability of the conjunction of the formulae entailed by a given scenario, we can see whether the scenario is logically plausible. In Fig. 1, only 4 scenarios are actually logically plausible. For example, S_{111} is *not* logically plausible. In fact, it requires that the order is closed (due to the crisp 1..* constraint on close order) and, consequently, that the order is eventually accepted and refused (due to the two response constraints attached to close order, which in this scenario must be both satisfied); however, the presence of both an acceptance and a refusal violates the not − coexistence constraint linking such two activities, contradicting the requirement that also this constraint must be satisfied in this scenario. S_{101} is logically plausible: it is satisfied by the trace where an order is closed and then accepted. All in all, we have 4 logically plausible scenarios: *(i)* S_{001}, where an order is closed and later not accepted nor refused; *(ii)* S_{011}, where an order is closed and later refused (and not accepted); *(iii)* S_{101}, where an order is closed and later accepted (and not refused); *(iv)* S_{110}, where an order is closed and later accepted and refused.   ◁

While it is clear that a logically implausible scenario should correspond to probability 0, are all logically plausible scenarios really plausible when the actual probabilities are taken into account? By looking at Fig. 1, one can notice that scenario S_{001} is logically plausible: it describes traces where an order is closed but not accepted nor refused. As we will see, however, this cannot happen given the probabilities of 0.8 and 0.3 attached to response(close, acc) and response(close, ref). More in general, what is the probability of a constraint scenario, i.e., the fraction of traces in a log that belong to that scenario? Is it possible to assign probabilities to scenarios, while respecting the probabilities attached to the constraints? The latter question points out that a ProbDeclare model may be *unsatisfiable* (in a probabilistic sense), if there is no way to properly lift the probabilities attached to constraints to corresponding probabilities of the scenarios induced by those constraints. To answer these questions, we resort to the technique in [15]. We associate each scenario to a probability variable, keeping the same naming convention. E.g., scenario S_{001} corresponds to variable x_{001}. More in general, for a ProbDeclare model $M = \langle \Sigma, \{\langle \varphi_1, \bowtie_1, p_1 \rangle, \ldots, \langle \varphi_n, \bowtie_n, p_n \rangle\}\rangle$, we construct the system $\mathcal{L}_M$ of inequalities using probability variables x_i, with i ranging from 0 to 2^n (in boolean):

$$x_i \geq 0 \qquad 0 \leq i < 2^n$$
$$\sum_{i=0}^{2^n-1} x_i = 1$$
$$\sum_{j\text{th position is }1} x_i \bowtie_j p_j \qquad 0 \leq j < n$$
$$x_i = 0 \qquad \text{if scenario } S_i \text{ is logically implausible}$$

The first two lines guarantee that we assign a non-negative value to each variable, and that their sum is 1. We can see these assignments as probabilities, having the guarantee that all scenarios together cover the full probability spectrum. The third line verifies the probability associated to each constraint in M. In particular, it constructs one (in)equality per constraint $\langle \varphi_j, \bowtie_j, p_j \rangle$ in M, ensuring that all the variables that correspond to scenarios making φ_j true should all together yield a probability that is $\bowtie_j p_i$. The last line enforces that logically implausible scenarios get assigned probability 0. This shows how logical and probabilistic reasoning come together in $\mathcal{L}_M$.

We can use this system of inequalities to check whether a given ProbDeclare model is *satisfiable*: M is satisfiable if and only if $\mathcal{L}_M$ admits a solution. In fact, solving $\mathcal{L}_M$ corresponds to verifying whether the class of all possible traces can be divided in such a way that the proportions required by the probabilistic constraints in the different scenarios are satisfied. This, in turn, witnesses that there must be at least one logically plausible scenario that gets a non-zero probability. Checking whether $\mathcal{L}_M$ admits a solution can be done in PSPACE in the size of M, if we calculate the size as the length of the LTL$_f$ formulae appearing therein [15].

Example 7. Consider the ProbDeclare model M containing two constraints:

1. existence(close)=$\Diamond$close with probability $= 0.1$;
2. response(close,accept)=$\Box$(close $\rightarrow$ $\bigcirc\Diamond$acc) with probability $= 0.8$.

M indicates that only 10% of the traces contain that the order is closed, and that 80% of the traces are so that, whenever an order is closed, it is eventually accepted. This model is inconsistent. Intuitively, the fact that, in 80% of the traces, whenever an order is closed, it is eventually accepted, is equivalent to say that, in 20% of the traces, we violate such a response constraint, i.e., we have that an order is closed but then not accepted. All such traces satisfy the existence constraint over the close order activity, and, consequently, the probability of such a constraint must be at least 0.2. However, this is contradicted by the first constraint of M, which imposes that such a probability is 0.1.

We now show how this is detected formally. M yields 4 constraint scenarios:

$S_{00} = \{\neg\Diamond\text{close}, \Diamond(\text{close} \wedge \neg\bigcirc\Diamond\text{acc})\}$ $S_{01} = \{\neg\Diamond\text{close}, \Box(\text{close} \rightarrow \bigcirc\Diamond\text{acc})\}$
$S_{10} = \{\Diamond\text{close}, \Diamond(\text{close} \wedge \neg\bigcirc\Diamond\text{acc})\}$ $S_{11} = \{\Diamond\text{close}, \Box(\text{close} \rightarrow \bigcirc\Diamond\text{acc})\}$

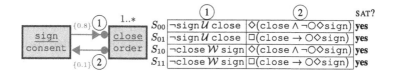

Fig. 2. A ProbDeclare model and its 4 constraint scenarios.

Scenario S_{00} is logically implausible: it requires and forbids that the order is closed; the other scenarios are instead all logically plausible. Hence, the equations of $\mathcal{L}_M$ are:

$$x_{00} + x_{01} + x_{10} + x_{11} = 1$$
$$x_{10} + x_{11} = 0.1$$
$$x_{01} \quad + x_{11} = 0.8$$
$$x_{00} \quad = 0$$

The equations yield $x_{10} = 0.2$, $x_{01} = 0.9$, and $x_{11} = -0.1$. This is an inconsistent probability assignment, and witnesses that it is not possible to properly assign suitable fractions of traces to the various constraint scenarios.   ◁

When $\mathcal{L}_M$ is solvable, M is satisfiable. In addition, the solutions of $\mathcal{L}_M$ tell us what is the probability (or range of probabilities) for each constraint scenario. If a logically plausible scenario admits a probability that is strictly > 0, then it is actually *plausible* also in probabilistic terms. Contrariwise, a logically plausible scenario that gets assigned a probability that is forcefully 0 is actually *implausible*. This witnesses in fact that, due to the probabilities attached to the various constraints in M, the fraction of traces belonging to it must be 0.

Example 8. Consider the ProbDeclare model in Fig. 1. Its system of inequalities is so that $x_{000} = x_{010} = x_{100} = x_{111} = 0$, since the corresponding constraint scenarios are logically implausible. For the logically plausible scenarios, we instead get the following equalities, once the variables above are removed (being them all equal to 0):

$$x_{001} + x_{011} + x_{101} + x_{110} = 1$$
$$x_{101} + x_{110} = 0.8$$
$$x_{011} \quad + x_{110} = 0.3$$
$$x_{001} + x_{011} + x_{101} \quad = 0.9$$

It is easy to see that this system of equations admits only one solution: $x_{001} = 0$, $x_{011} = 0.2$, $x_{101} = 0.7$, $x_{110} = 0.1$. This solution witnesses that scenario S_{001} is implausible, and that the most plausible scenario, holding in 70% of cases, is actually S_{101}, namely the one where after the order is closed, it is eventually accepted, and not refused. In addition, the solution tells us that there are other two outlier scenarios: the first, holding in 20% of cases, is the one where, after the order is closed, it is eventually refused (and not accepted); the second, holding in 10% of cases, is the one where a closed order is accepted and refused.   ◁

In general, the system $\mathcal{L}_M$ of inequalities for a ProbDeclare model M may have more than one solution. If this is the case, we can attach to each constraint scenario a probability interval, whose extreme values are calculated by minimizing and maximizing its corresponding variable over $\mathcal{L}_M$. Since these intervals are computed by analyzing each variable in isolation, not all the combinations of values residing in such intervals are actually consistent (which would entail yielding an overall probability of 1). Still, for sure these intervals contain probability values that are overall consistent, and, in addition, they provide a good indicator of which are the most (and less) plausible scenarios. We illustrate this in the next example.

Example 9. Consider the ProbDeclare model in Fig. 2. It comes with 4 constraint scenarios, obtained by considering the two constraint formulae precedence (sign,close) $= \neg$close $\mathcal{W}$ sign and response(close,sign) $= \square$(close $\rightarrow$ $\bigcirc\Diamond$sign), as well as their respective negated formulae $\neg$sign $\mathcal{U}$ close and $\Diamond$(close $\wedge \neg\bigcirc\Diamond$sign). All such scenarios are logically plausible, and hence the equations of the system are:

$$
\begin{aligned}
x_{00} + x_{01} + x_{10} + x_{11} &= 1 \\
x_{10} + x_{11} &= 0.8 \\
x_{01} \qquad\quad + x_{11} &= 0.1
\end{aligned}
$$

This system admits multiple solutions. In fact, by calculating the minimum and maximum values for the 4 variables, we get that: *(i)* scenario S_{00}, where the order is closed but consent is not signed, comes with probability interval $[0, 0.1]$; *(ii)* scenario S_{01}, where the order is closed and consent is signed afterward, comes with probability interval $[0, 0.1]$; *(iii)* scenario S_{10}, where the order is closed after having signed consent, comes with probability interval $[0.7, 0.8]$; *(iv)* scenario S_{11}, where the order is closed and consent is signed at least twice (once before, and once afterward), comes with probability interval $[0.1, 0.2]$.   ◁

4   Discovering ProbDeclare Models from Event Logs

We now show that ProbDeclare models can be discovered from event data using, off-the-shelf, already existing techniques, with a quite interesting guarantee: that the discovered model is always consistent. We use the standard notation $[\cdot]$ for multisets, and use superscript numbers to identify the multiplicity of an element in the multiset.

A plethora of different algorithms have been devised to discover Declare models from event data [7,9,13,22]. In general, the vast majority of these algorithms adopt the following approach to discovery: (1) Candidate constraints are generated by analyzing the activities contained in the log. (2) For each constraint, its *support* is computed as the fraction of traces in the log where the constraint holds. (3) Candidate constraints are filtered, retaining only those whose support exceeds a given threshold. (4) Further filters (e.g., considering the "relevance" of a constraint [6]) are applied. (5) The overall model is checked for satisfiability, operating with different strategies if it is not; this is necessary since constraints with high support, but less than 1, may actually conflict with each other [4,5]. In this procedure, the notion of support is formalized as follows.

Definition 4. *The* support *of an* LTL_f *constraint* φ *in an event log* $\mathcal{L} = [\tau_1, \ldots, \tau_n]$ *is* $supp_{\mathcal{L}}(\varphi) = \frac{|\mathcal{L}_\varphi|}{|\mathcal{L}|}$, *where* $\mathcal{L}_\varphi = [\tau \in \mathcal{L} \mid \tau \models \varphi]$. ◁

We can adopt this approach off-the-shelf to discover ProbDeclare constraints: *we just use the constraint support as its associated probability, with operator* $=$. In other words, if φ is discovered with support p, we turn it into the probabilistic constraint $\langle \varphi, p \rangle$. When doing so, we can also relax step (3), e.g., to retain constraints with a very low support, implying that their negated versions have a very high support.

Example 10. Consider $\mathcal{L} = [\langle \mathsf{close}, \mathsf{acc} \rangle^7, \langle \mathsf{close}, \mathsf{ref} \rangle^2, \langle \mathsf{close}, \mathsf{acc}, \mathsf{ref} \rangle^1]$, capturing the evolution of 10 orders, 7 of which have been closed and then accepted, 2 of which have been closed and then refused, and 1 of which has been closed, then accepted, then refused. The support of constraint response(close,acc) is $8/10 = 0.8$, witnessing that 8 traces satisfy such a constraint, whereas 2 violate it. This corresponds exactly to the interpretation of probability 0.8 for the probabilistic response(close,acc) constraint in Fig. 1. More in general, the entire ProbDeclare model of Fig. 1 can be discovered from $\mathcal{L}$. ◁

A second key observation is that once this procedure is used to discover ProbDeclare constraints, step (5) is unnecessary: the overall discovered model is in fact guaranteed to be satisfiable (in our probabilistic sense).

Theorem 1. *Let* Σ *be a set of activities,* $\mathcal{L}$ *an event log over* Σ, *and* $\mathcal{C} = \{\langle \varphi_1, p_1 \rangle, \ldots, \langle \varphi_n, p_n \rangle\}$ *a set of probabilistic constraints, such that for each* $i \in \{1, \ldots, n\}$, $p_i = supp_{\mathcal{L}}(\varphi_i)$. *The ProbDeclare model* $\langle \Sigma, \mathcal{C} \rangle$ *is satisfiable.* ◁

Proof. Technically, $\langle \Sigma, \mathcal{C} \rangle$ is satisfiable if its corresponding $PLTL_f^0$ formula $\Phi := \{\odot_{p_1}\varphi_1, \ldots, \odot_{p_n}\varphi_n\}$ is satisfiable. To show this, we simply use $\mathcal{L}$ to build a model of Φ. For every set $I \subseteq \{1, \ldots, n\}$, let φ_I be the LTL_f formula $\varphi_I := \bigwedge_{i \in I} \varphi_i \wedge \bigwedge_{i \notin I} \neg\varphi_i$, and let $\mathcal{L}_I$ be the sublog of $\mathcal{L}$ containing all the traces that satisfy φ_I. Note that the sublogs $\mathcal{L}_I$ form a partition of $\mathcal{L}$; that is, every trace appears in exactly one such $\mathcal{L}_I$. For each I such that $\mathcal{L}_I$ is not empty, choose a representative $t_I \in \mathcal{L}_I$ and let $p_I := \frac{|\mathcal{L}_I|}{|\mathcal{L}|}$ be the fraction of traces that belong to $\mathcal{L}_I$. We build a stochastic language ρ by setting $\rho(t_I) = p_I$ for each I such that $\mathcal{L}_I \neq \emptyset$ and $\rho(\tau) = 0$ for all other traces. We need to show that ρ satisfies $\mathcal{C}$. Consider a constraint $\langle \varphi, p \rangle \in \mathcal{C}$; we need to show that $\sum_{\tau \models \varphi} \rho(\tau) = p$. Note that by construction, $\sum_{\tau \models \varphi} \rho(\tau) = \sum_{t_I \models \varphi} p_I$ and since $\mathcal{L}_I$ form a partition, the latter is, in fact, the fraction of traces that satisfy φ. On the other hand, p is also the support of φ; that is, the proportion of traces satisfying φ. Hence, both values are equal, and ρ satisfies the ProbDeclare model. ⊣

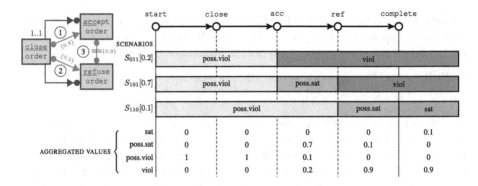

SCENARIOS	start	close	acc	ref	complete
$S_{011}[0.2]$	poss.viol		viol		
$S_{101}[0.7]$	poss.viol		poss.sat	viol	
$S_{110}[0.1]$	poss.viol			poss.sat	sat

AGGREGATED VALUES					
sat	0	0	0	0	0.1
poss.sat	0	0	0.7	0.1	0
poss.viol	1	1	0.1	0	0
viol	0	0	0.2	0.9	0.9

Fig. 3. Result computed by monitoring the ProbDeclare model on the top left against the trace ⟨close, acc, ref⟩, which conforms to the outlier constraint scenario where the two response constraints are satisfied, while the not − coexistence one is violated.

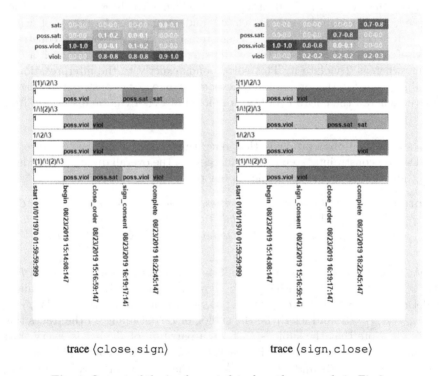

trace ⟨close, sign⟩   trace ⟨sign, close⟩

Fig. 4. Output of the implemented tool on the example in Fig.2.

By this theorem, probabilistic constraints can be discovered in a *purely local* way, having the guarantee that they will never conflict with each other. Obviously, non-local filters can still prove useful to prune implied constraints and select the most relevant ones. Also, note that the probabilities of the discovered constraints can be easily adjusted when new traces are added to the log, by incrementally recomputing the support values after checking how many new traces satisfy the various constraints.

There are many open questions that deserve a dedicated investigation, such as: when do we stop the discovery procedure, now that every constraint can be retained, irrespectively of its support? What is the impact of retaining constraints with various degrees of support in terms of over/under-fitting? How to learn constraints with probability operators different from just equality? And how does this impact generalization?

5   Monitoring Probabilistic Constraints

In Sect. 3.2, we have shown how we can take a ProbDeclare model and generate its constraint scenarios, together with their corresponding probability intervals. We now describe how this technique can be directly turned into an operational probabilistic monitoring and conformance checking framework.

Let $M = \langle \Sigma, \mathcal{C} \rangle$ be a ProbDeclare model with n probabilistic constraints. For simplicity, we do not distinguish between crisp and genuinely probabilistic constraints, nor prune away implausible scenarios: the produced monitoring results do not change, but obviously our implementation, presented at the end of this section, takes into account these aspects for optimization reasons. M generates 2^n constraint scenarios. As discussed in Sect. 3.2, each scenario S comes with a corresponding characteristic LTL_f formula, which amounts to the conjunction of positive and negated constraints in $\mathcal{C}$, where the decision of which ones are taken positive and which negative is defined by the scenario itself. We denote such a formula by $formula(S)$. For example, if $\mathcal{C} = \{\langle \varphi_1, p_1 \rangle, \langle \varphi_2, p_2 \rangle, \langle \varphi_3, p_3 \rangle\}$, then $formula(S_{101}) = \varphi_1 \wedge \neg\varphi_2 \wedge \varphi_3$. In addition, if M is satisfiable, and hence $\mathcal{L}_M$ is solvable, each scenario S comes with its own probability. More specifically, we have to consider the case where multiple (possibly infinite) solutions exist for $\mathcal{L}_M$. There are various possibilities to handle this case. We tackle it by resorting to a quite direct approach: for each scenario S, we solve $\mathcal{L}_M$ twice by respectively imposing, as an additional constraint, that the probability variable for S has to be *minimized/maximized*. This, in turn, yields a probability interval for S, which we denote by $prob(S)$. From Example 9, we have, e.g., that $prob(S_{10}) = [0.7, 0.8]$. More sophisticated ways to extract probabilities from $\mathcal{L}_M$ can be investigated.

5.1   Prefix Monitoring

A very direct form of monitoring consists in checking whether a partial trace, that is, the prefix of a full trace whose continuation is yet to be determined, *conforms* to a given ProbDeclare model M. This amounts to a *probabilistic version of conformance checking* that can be tackled as follows. We fix an order over the constraints in M, and precompute the probability intervals of the scenarios induced by M. At runtime, we consider the current prefix τ and, for every formula φ of each probabilistic constraint $\langle \varphi, \bowtie, p \rangle \in M$ considered in isolation, we output 1 if $\tau \models \varphi$, and 0 otherwise. One effective way to do this check is to precompute the finite-state automaton that recognizes all and only the finite traces accepted by φ [1], then checking at runtime whether τ is recognized by that automaton. The automaton can be determinized upfront, making in turn possible to perform this check incrementally. The overall, so-produced output, interpreted as an array of bits, matches exactly one and only one scenario of M. If the scenario has probability 0, then τ is not conforming to M, whereas if the scenario has a proper probability (interval), then τ conforms to M, and the actual probability value can be used to understand whether τ represents a common or an outlier behavior - that is, coupling "conformance" with an estimation of the degree of "conformism". This approach comes with a main limitation though: it does not reason on the possible future continuations of the current prefix. This is particularly limiting in a probabilistic setting: monitoring a prefix makes it impossible to understand if and how its matching scenario will change as new events are acquired.

5.2   Full Monitoring

We now show how prefix monitoring can be further developed into full monitoring of prefixes and their possible continuations in our probabilistic setting. In this case, we cannot consider anymore the constraints in isolation, but we have to reason at the level of scenarios. Notice that most of the computational burden is at design time, whereas, at runtime, we incur simply in the cost of incrementally recognizing a growing prefix on a fixed set of deterministic finite-state automata, which is computationally lightweight.

To handle full monitoring, first notice that the characteristic formula of a scenario is in standard LTL$_f$, and so we can construct a *scenario monitor* by recasting well-known automata-theoretic techniques [1,16]. Specifically, given an LTL$_f$ formula φ over a set Σ of activities, and a partial trace τ representing an ongoing process execution, a monitor outputs one of the four following truth values:

- τ *(permanently) satisfies* φ, if φ is currently satisfied ($\tau \models \varphi$), and φ stays satisfied no matter how the execution continues, that is, for every possible continuation trace τ' over Σ, we have $\tau \cdot \tau' \models \varphi$ (the $\cdot$ operator denotes the concatenation of two traces);
- τ *possibly satisfies* φ, if φ is currently satisfied ($\tau \models \varphi$), but φ may become violated in the future, that is, there exists a continuation trace τ' over Σ such that $\tau \cdot \tau' \not\models \varphi$;
- τ *possibly violates* φ, if φ is currently violated ($\tau \not\models \varphi$), but φ may become satisfied in the future, that is, there exists a continuation trace τ' over Σ such that $\tau \cdot \tau' \models \varphi$;
- τ *(permanently) violates* φ, if φ is currently violated ($\tau \not\models \varphi$), and φ stays violated no matter how the execution continues, that is, for every possible continuation trace τ' over Σ, we have $\tau \cdot \tau' \not\models \varphi$.

This is used as follows. For each plausible scenario S over M, we construct the monitor for S.[2] We then track the evolution of a running trace by delivering its events to *all* such monitors in parallel, returning the truth values they produce. As pointed out in Sect. 5.1, at runtime we do not always know to which scenario the trace will belong to once completed. However, we can again combine logical and probabilistic reasoning to obtain a meaningful feedback.

A first key observation is that, for every partial trace, at most one scenario can turn out to be permanently or temporarily satisfied. Call this scenario S. In the first case, this verdict is irrevocable, and also implies that all other scenarios are permanently violated. This witnesses that no matter how the execution continues, the resulting trace will for sure belong to S. We then return immediately that the trace is conforming, and also return $prob(S)$ to give an indication about the degree of conformism of the trace (see above). In the second case, the verdict may instead change as the execution unfolds, but would collapse to the previous case if the execution terminates, which is communicated to the monitors by a special *complete* event.

A second key observation is that multiple scenarios may be at the same time temporarily or permanently violated. For this reason, we need to aggregate in some way the probabilities of the scenarios that produce the same truth value to have an indication of the overall probability associated with that value. Having this aggregated probability is useful to have sophisticated feedback about the monitored trace. For example, the aggregated probability for permanently violated scenarios is useful as it can never decrease over time: it is possible that new scenarios become permanently violated, but those that already are will never switch to a different truth value. So a high value associated to permanent violation can be interpreted as a clear indication that the monitored trace will turn out to be either a conforming outlier or not conforming at all. At the same time, the aggregated value of permanent violation can be used as a conditional probability, when one is interested in understanding what is the probability that a trace will end up in a given scenario. The extreme values of the *aggregated probability interval* for temporary/permanent violations are computed using the system of inequalities $\mathcal{L}_M$. In particular, this is done by adding a constraint that minimizes/maximizes the sum of the probability variables associated to the scenarios that produce that truth value.

Example 11. Consider the ProbDeclare model in Fig. 1 with its three plausible scenarios (recall that four scenarios are logically plausible there, but one of those has probability 0, so only three remains to be monitored). Figure 3 shows the result produced when monitoring a trace that at some point appears to belong to the most plausible scenario, but in the end turns out to conform to the least plausible one. From the image, we can also clearly see that the trace consisting only of a close order activity would be judged as non-conforming, as it would violate all scenarios.   ◁

---

[2] Implausible scenarios are irrelevant: they produce an output that is associated to probability 0.

This probabilistic monitoring technique has been fully implemented.[3] For solving systems of inequalities, we use the LP solver[4]. The implementation comes with various optimizations. First, scenarios are computed by directly imposing that crisp constraints with probability 1 must hold in their positive form in all scenarios. Second, only plausible scenarios are retained for monitoring. Third, the results obtained by minimizing and maximizing for aggregate probability variables are cached, to avoid solving multiple times the same problem. Figure 4 shows the output of the implemented monitoring tool on the example in Fig. 2 and for two different traces.[5] Here, the aggregated probability intervals are shown with a dark gray or light gray background depending on whether their midpoint is closer to 1 or to 0, respectively. The first trace (on the left) is classified as belonging to scenario S_{01} and is an outlier because this scenario has low probability (corresponding to a probability interval of $prob(S_{01}) = [0.0, 0.1]$). The second trace (on the right) is classified as belonging to the highly plausible scenario S_{10} (corresponding to a probability interval of $prob(S_{10}) = [0.7, 0.8]$).

6   Conclusion

In this paper, we have introduced the notion of probabilistic business constraint and demonstrated how this notion affects the outcomes of standard process monitoring (and mining) approaches based on Declare, when standard Declare is replaced by its probabilistic counterpart. We have introduced a framework for monitoring a trace with respect to a set of probabilistic constraints. The framework classifies completed traces as violating a given probabilistic model or as belonging to a certain constraint scenario (i.e., satisfying a certain combination of probabilistic constraints). Technically, our approach seamlessly handles more sophisticated logics for specifying constraints, only requiring that they have a corresponding automata-theoretic characterization. Thus, for example, regular expressions or LDL_f [1] can be used in place of LTL_f, as well as $FO\text{-}LTL_f$ [3].

For future work, we plan to better investigate the influence of probabilistic constraints on the state-of-the-art techniques for declarative process mining. In addition, as it has been shown in the paper, very sophisticated monitoring feedbacks can be extracted, but their interpretation is not at all straightforward. A dedicated study focused on end user-tailored feedbacks is needed. Last but not least, we plan to relate, and possibly integrate, the declarative approach presented in this paper with recent advancements in stochastic conformance checking on imperative process models [10]. Note that, if we extend our approach with probabilities within constraints (ending up in the full logic studied in [15]), we have to manipulate more sophisticated automata that are reminiscent of the stochastic automata used in [10]. At the same time, the entropy-based approach brought forward in [10] could be used in our setting to measure the "distance"

---

[3] https://bitbucket.org/fmmaggi/probabilisticmonitor/src/master/.

[4] http://lpsolve.sourceforge.net/5.5/.

[5] In the screenshots, 1 and 2 represent the probabilistic constraints labeled with 1 and 2 in Fig. 2, whereas 3 represents the crisp constraint in the same example.

between a set of probabilistic constraints and an event log whose trace frequencies are not fully aligned to what prescribed by the probabilistic constraints.

Acknowledgments. This work has been supported by the Estonian Research Council (project PRG887).

References

1. De Giacomo, G., De Masellis, R., Grasso, M., Maggi, F.M., Montali, M.: Monitoring business metaconstraints Based on LTL and LDL for finite traces. In: Sadiq, S., Soffer, P., Völzer, H. (eds.) BPM 2014. LNCS, vol. 8659, pp. 1–17. Springer, Cham (2014). https://doi.org/10.1007/978-3-319-10172-9_1
2. De Giacomo, G., Vardi, M.Y.: Linear temporal logic and linear dynamic logic on finite traces. In: Proceedings of the 23rd International Joint Conference on Artificial Intelligence, IJCAI 2013, Beijing, China, 3–9 August 2013, pp. 854–860 (2013). http://www.aaai.org/ocs/index.php/IJCAI/IJCAI13/paper/view/6997
3. De Masellis, R., Maggi, F.M., Montali, M.: Monitoring data-aware business constraints with finite state automata. In: International Conference on Software and Systems Process 2014, ICSSP 2014, Nanjing, China, 26–28 May 2014, pp. 134–143 (2014). https://doi.org/10.1145/2600821.2600835
4. Di Ciccio, C., Maggi, F.M., Montali, M., Mendling, J.: Ensuring model consistency in declarative process discovery. In: Motahari-Nezhad, H.R., Recker, J., Weidlich, M. (eds.) BPM 2015. LNCS, vol. 9253, pp. 144–159. Springer, Cham (2015). https://doi.org/10.1007/978-3-319-23063-4_9
5. Di Ciccio, C., Maggi, F.M., Montali, M., Mendling, J.: Resolving inconsistencies and redundancies in declarative process models. Inf. Syst. **64**, 425–446 (2017). https://doi.org/10.1016/j.is.2016.09.005
6. Di Ciccio, C., Maggi, F.M., Montali, M., Mendling, J.: On the relevance of a business constraint to an event log. Inf. Syst. **78**, 144–161 (2018). https://doi.org/10.1016/j.is.2018.01.011
7. Di Ciccio, C., Mecella, M.: On the discovery of declarative control flows for artful processes. ACM Trans. Manag. Inf. Syst. **5**(4), 24:1–24:37 (2015). https://doi.org/10.1145/2629447
8. Kovtunova, A., Peñaloza, R.: Cutting diamonds: a temporal logic with probabilistic distributions. In: Principles of Knowledge Representation and Reasoning: Proceedings of the Sixteenth International Conference, KR 2018, Tempe, Arizona, 30 October–2 November 2018, pp. 561–570 (2018). https://aaai.org/ocs/index.php/KR/KR18/paper/view/18037
9. Lamma, E., Mello, P., Montali, M., Riguzzi, F., Storari, S.: Inducing declarative logic-based models from labeled traces. In: Alonso, G., Dadam, P., Rosemann, M. (eds.) BPM 2007. LNCS, vol. 4714, pp. 344–359. Springer, Heidelberg (2007). https://doi.org/10.1007/978-3-540-75183-0_25
10. Leemans, S.J.J., Polyvyanyy, A.: Stochastic-aware conformance checking: an entropy-based approach. In: Dustdar, S., Yu, E., Salinesi, C., Rieu, D., Pant, V. (eds.) CAiSE 2020. LNCS, vol. 12127, pp. 217–233. Springer, Cham (2020). https://doi.org/10.1007/978-3-030-49435-3_14
11. Leemans, S.J.J., Syring, A.F., van der Aalst, W.M.P.: Earth movers' stochastic conformance checking. In: Hildebrandt, T., van Dongen, B.F., Röglinger, M., Mendling, J. (eds.) BPM 2019. LNBIP, vol. 360, pp. 127–143. Springer, Cham (2019). https://doi.org/10.1007/978-3-030-26643-1_8

12. Ly, L.T., Maggi, F.M., Montali, M., Rinderle-Ma, S., van der Aalst, W.M.P.: Compliance monitoring in business processes: functionalities, application, and tool-support. Inf. Syst. **54**, 209–234 (2015). https://doi.org/10.1016/j.is.2015.02.007
13. Maggi, F.M., Bose, R.P.J.C., van der Aalst, W.M.P.: Efficient discovery of under-standable declarative process models from event logs. In: Ralyté, J., Franch, X., Brinkkemper, S., Wrycza, S. (eds.) CAiSE 2012. LNCS, vol. 7328, pp. 270–285. Springer, Heidelberg (2012). https://doi.org/10.1007/978-3-642-31095-9_18
14. Maggi, F.M., Montali, M., van der Aalst, W.M.P.: An operational decision support framework for monitoring business constraints. In: de Lara, J., Zisman, A. (eds.) FASE 2012. LNCS, vol. 7212, pp. 146–162. Springer, Heidelberg (2012). https://doi.org/10.1007/978-3-642-28872-2_11
15. Maggi, F.M., Montali, M., Peñaloza, R.: Temporal logics over finite traces with uncertainty. In: The Thirty-Fourth AAAI Conference on Artificial Intelligence, AAAI 2020, The Thirty-Second Innovative Applications of Artificial Intelligence Conference, IAAI 2020, The Tenth AAAI Symposium on Educational Advances in Artificial Intelligence, EAAI 2020, New York, NY, USA, 7–12 February 2020, pp. 10218–10225 (2020). https://aaai.org/ojs/index.php/AAAI/article/view/6583
16. Maggi, F.M., Montali, M., Westergaard, M., van der Aalst, W.M.P.: Monitoring business constraints with linear temporal logic: an approach based on colored automata. In: Rinderle-Ma, S., Toumani, F., Wolf, K. (eds.) BPM 2011. LNCS, vol. 6896, pp. 132–147. Springer, Heidelberg (2011). https://doi.org/10.1007/978-3-642-23059-2_13
17. Maggi, F.M., Westergaard, M., Montali, M., van der Aalst, W.M.P.: Runtime ver-ification of LTL-based declarative process models. In: Khurshid, S., Sen, K. (eds.) RV 2011. LNCS, vol. 7186, pp. 131–146. Springer, Heidelberg (2012). https://doi.org/10.1007/978-3-642-29860-8_11
18. Montali, M.: Specification and Verification of Declarative Open Interaction Models: a Logic-Based Approach. LNBIP, vol. 56. Springer, Heidelberg (2010). https://doi.org/10.1007/978-3-642-14538-4
19. Montali, M., Pesic, M., van der Aalst, W.M.P., Chesani, F., Mello, P., Storari, S.: Declarative specification and verification of service choreographies. ACM Trans. Web **4**(1), 3:1–3:62 (2010). https://doi.org/10.1145/1658373.1658376
20. Ognjanovic, Z.: Discrete linear-time probabilistic logics: completeness, decidability and complexity. J. Log. Comput. **16**(2), 257–285 (2006). https://doi.org/10.1093/logcom/exi077
21. Pesic, M., Schonenberg, H., van der Aalst, W.M.P.: Declare: full support for loosely-structured processes. In: 11th IEEE International Enterprise Distributed Object Computing Conference (EDOC 2007), 15–19 October 2007, Annapolis, Maryland, USA, pp. 287–300. IEEE Computer Society (2007). https://doi.org/10.1109/EDOC.2007.14
22. Schönig, S., Rogge-Solti, A., Cabanillas, C., Jablonski, S., Mendling, J.: Efficient and customisable declarative process mining with SQL. In: Nurcan, S., Soffer, P., Bajec, M., Eder, J. (eds.) CAiSE 2016. LNCS, vol. 9694, pp. 290–305. Springer, Cham (2016). https://doi.org/10.1007/978-3-319-39696-5_18

Petri Nets with Parameterised Data
Modelling and Verification

Silvio Ghilardi[1], Alessandro Gianola[2,3], Marco Montali[2],
and Andrey Rivkin[2(✉)]

[1] Dipartimento di Matematica, Università degli Studi di Milano, Milan, Italy
silvio.ghilardi@unimi.it
[2] Faculty of Computer Science, Free University of Bozen-Bolzano, Bolzano, Italy
{gianola,montali,rivkin}@inf.unibz.it
[3] CSE Department, University of California San Diego (UCSD),
San Diego, CA, USA
agianola@eng.ucsd.edu

Abstract. During the last decade, various approaches have been put
forward to integrate business processes with different types of data. Each
of these approaches reflects specific demands in the whole process-data
integration spectrum. One particularly important point is the capability of these approaches to flexibly accommodate processes with multiple
cases that need to co-evolve. In this work, we introduce and study an
extension of coloured Petri nets, called catalog-nets, providing two key
features to capture this type of processes. On the one hand, net transitions are equipped with guards that simultaneously inspect the content
of tokens and query facts stored in a read-only, persistent database. On
the other hand, such transitions can inject data into tokens by extracting
relevant values from the database or by generating genuinely fresh ones.
We systematically encode catalog-nets into one of the reference frameworks for the (parameterised) verification of data and processes. We show
that fresh-value injection is a particularly complex feature to handle, and
discuss strategies to tame it. Finally, we discuss how catalog-nets relate
to well-known formalisms in this area.

1 Introduction

The integration of control flow and data has become one of the most prominently investigated topics in BPM [25]. Taking into account data when working
with processes is crucial to properly understand which courses of execution are
allowed [11], to account for decisions [5], and to explicitly accommodate business policies and constraints [13]. Hence, considering how a process manipulates
underlying volatile and persistent data, and how such data influence the possible
courses of execution within the process, is central to understand and improve
how organisations, and their underlying information systems, operate throughout the entire BPM lifecycle: from modelling and verification [10,18] to enactment [19,21] and mining [2]. Each of such approaches reflects specific demands
in the whole process-data integration spectrum. One key point is the capability

© Springer Nature Switzerland AG 2020
D. Fahland et al. (Eds.): BPM 2020, LNCS 12168, pp. 55–74, 2020.
https://doi.org/10.1007/978-3-030-58666-9_4

of these approaches to accommodate processes with multiple co-evolving case objects [4,14]. Several modelling paradigms have adopted to tackle this and other important features: data-/artifact-centric approaches [10,18], declarative languages based on temporal constraints [4], and imperative, Petri net-based notations [14,22,24].

With an interest in (formal) modelling and verification, in this paper we concentrate on the latter stream, taking advantage from the long-standing tradition of adopting Petri nets as the main backbone to formalise processes expressed in front-end notations such as BPMN, EPCs, and UML activity diagrams. In particular, we investigate for the first time the combination of two different, key requirements in the modelling and analysis of data-aware processes. On the one hand, we support the creation of fresh (case) objects during the execution of the process, and the ability to model their (co-)evolution using guards and updates. Examples of such objects are orders and their orderlines in an order-to-cash process. On the other hand, we handle read-only, persistent data that can be accessed and injected in the objects manipulated by the process. Examples of read-only data are the catalog of product types and the list of customers in an order-to-cash process. Importantly, read-only data have to be considered in a *parameterised* way. This means that the overall process is expected to operate as desired in a robust way, irrespectively of the actual configuration of such data.

While the first requirement is commonly tackled by the most recent and sophisticated approaches for integrating data within Petri nets [14,22,24], the latter has been extensively investigated in the data-centric spectrum [9,12], but only recently ported to more conventional, imperative processes with the simplifying assumptions that the process control-flow is block-structured (and thus 1-bounded in the Petri net sense) [7].

In this work, we reconcile these two themes in an extension of coloured Petri nets (CPNs) called *catalog-nets* (CLog-nets). On the one hand, in CLog-net transitions are equipped with guards that simultaneously inspect the content of tokens and query facts stored in a read-only, persistent database. On the other hand, such transitions can inject data into tokens by extracting relevant values from the database or by generating genuinely fresh ones. We systematically encode CLog-nets into the most recent version of MCMT [1,16], one of the few model checkers natively supporting the (parameterised) verification of data and processes [6,8,9]. We show that fresh-value injection is a particularly complex feature to handle, and discuss strategies to tame it. We then stress that, thanks to this encoding, a relevant fragment of the model can be readily verified using MCMT, and that verification of the whole model is within reach with a minor implementation effort. Finally, we discuss how catalog nets provide a unifying approach for some of the most sophisticated formalisms in this area, highlighting differences and commonalities.

2   The CLog-net Formal Model

Conceptually, a CLog-net integrates two key components. The first is a read-only persistent data storage, called *catalog*, to account for read-only, parameterised data. The second is a variant of CPN, called ν-CPN [23], to model the process backbone. Places carry tuples of data objects and can be used to represent: *(i)* states of (interrelated) case objects, *(ii)* read-write relations, *(iii)* read-only relations whose extension is fixed (and consequently not subject to parameterisation), *(iv)* resources. As in [14,23,24], the net employs ν-variables (first studied in the context of ν-PNs [26]) to inject fresh data (such as object identifiers). A distinguishing feature of CLog-nets is that transitions can have guards that inspect and retrieve data objects from the read-only, catalog.

Catalog. We consider a *type domain* $\mathfrak{D}$ as a finite set of pairwise disjoint data types accounting for the different types of objects in the domain. Each type $\mathcal{D} \in \mathfrak{D}$ comes with its own (possibly infinite) *value domain* $\Delta_{\mathcal{D}}$, and with an equality operator $=_{\mathcal{D}}$. When clear from the context, we simplify the notation and use $=$ in place of $=_{\mathcal{D}}$. $R(a_1 : \mathcal{D}_1, \ldots, a_n : \mathcal{D}_n)$ is a $\mathfrak{D}$-*typed relation schema*, where R is a relation name and $a_i : \mathcal{D}_i$ indicates the i-th attribute of R together with its data type. When no ambiguity arises, we omit relation attributes and/or their data types. A $\mathfrak{D}$-*typed catalog (schema)* $\mathcal{R}_{\mathfrak{D}}$ is a finite set of $\mathfrak{D}$-typed relation schemas. A $\mathfrak{D}$-*typed catalog instance Cat* over $\mathcal{R}_{\mathfrak{D}}$ is a finite set of facts $R(\mathsf{o}_1, \ldots, \mathsf{o}_n)$, where $R \in \mathcal{R}_{\mathfrak{D}}$ and $\mathsf{o}_i \in \Delta_{\mathcal{D}_i}$, for $i \in \{1, \ldots, n\}$.

We adopt two types of *constraints* in the catalog relations. First, we assume the first attribute of every relation $R \in \mathcal{R}_{\mathfrak{D}}$ to be its *primary key*, denoted as $\text{PK}(R)$. Also, a type of such attribute should be different from the types of other primary key attributes. Then, for any $R, S \in \mathcal{R}_{\mathfrak{D}}$, $R.a \to S.id$ defines that the projection $R.a$ is a *foreign key* referencing $S.id$, where $\text{PK}(S) = id$, $\text{PK}(R) \neq a$ and $\text{type}(id) = \text{type}(a)$. While the given setting with constraints may seem a bit restrictive, it is the one adopted in the most sophisticated settings where parameterisation of read-only data is tackled [9,12].

Example 1. Consider a simple catalog of an order-to-delivery scenario, containing two relation schemas. Relation schema $ProdCat(p : \texttt{ProdType})$ indicates the product types (e.g., vegetables, furniture) available in the organisation catalogue of products. Relation schema $Comp(c : \texttt{CId}, p : \texttt{ProdType}, t : \texttt{TruckType})$ captures the compatibility between products and truck types used to deliver orders; e.g. one may specify that vegetables are compatible only with types of trucks that have a refrigerator. ◁

Catalog Queries. We fix a countably infinite set $\mathcal{V}_{\mathfrak{D}}$ of typed variables with a *variable typing function* $\texttt{type} : \mathcal{V}_{\mathfrak{D}} \to \mathfrak{D}$. Such function can be easily extended to account for sets, tuples and multisets of variables as well as constants. As query language we opt for the union of conjunctive queries with inequalities and atomic negations that can be specified in terms of first-order (FO) logic extended with types. This corresponds to widely investigated SQL select-project-join queries with filters, and unions thereof.

A *conjunctive query (CQ) with atomic negation* Q over $\mathcal{R}_{\mathfrak{D}}$ has the form

$$Q ::= \varphi \mid R(x_1, \ldots, x_n) \mid \neg R(x_1, \ldots, x_n) \mid Q_1 \wedge Q_2 \mid \exists x.Q,$$

where *(i)* $R(\mathcal{D}_1, \ldots, \mathcal{D}_n) \in \mathcal{R}_{\mathfrak{D}}$, $x \in \mathcal{V}_{\mathfrak{D}}$ and each x_i is either a variable of type $\mathcal{D}_i$ or a constant from $\Delta_{\mathcal{D}_i}$; *(ii)* $\varphi ::= y_1 = y_2 \mid \neg\varphi \mid \varphi \wedge \varphi \mid \top$ is a *condition*, s.t. y_i is either a variable of type $\mathcal{D}$ or a constant from $\Delta_{\mathcal{D}}$. $\mathtt{CQ}_{\mathfrak{D}}^{\neg}$ denotes the set of all such conjunctive queries, and *Free*(Q) the set of all free variables (i.e., those not occurring in the scope of quantifiers) of query Q. $\mathcal{C}_{\mathfrak{D}}$ denotes the set of all possible conditions, *Vars*(Q) the set of all variables in Q, and *Const*(Q) the set of all constants in Q. Finally, $\mathtt{UCQ}_{\mathfrak{D}}^{\neg}$ denotes the set off all *unions of conjunctive queries* over $\mathcal{R}_{\mathfrak{D}}$. Each query $Q \in \mathtt{UCQ}_{\mathfrak{D}}^{\neg}$ has the form $Q = \bigwedge_{i=1}^{n} Q_i$, with $Q_i \in \mathtt{CQ}_{\mathfrak{D}}^{\neg}$.

A *substitution* for a set $X = \{x_1, \ldots, x_n\}$ of typed variables is a function $\theta : X \to \Delta_{\mathfrak{D}}$, such that $\theta(x) \in \Delta_{\mathtt{type}(x)}$ for every $x \in X$. An empty substitution is denoted as $\langle\rangle$. A *substitution θ for a query Q*, denoted as $Q\theta$, is a substitution for variables in *Free*(Q). An *answer to a query Q* in a catalog instance *Cat* is a set of substitutions $ans(Q, Cat) = \{\theta : Free(Q) \to Val(Cat) \mid Cat, \models \theta Q\}$, where *Val*(Cat) denotes the set of all constants occurring in *Cat* and $\models$ denotes standard FO entailment.

Example 2. Consider the catalog of Example 1. Query *ProdCat*(p) retrieves the product types p present in the catalog, whereas given a product type value veg, query $\exists c. Comp(c, \mathsf{veg}, t)$ returns the truck types t compatible with veg.   ◁

CLog-nets. We first fix some standard notions related to *multisets*. Given a set A, the *set of multisets* over A, written $A^{\oplus}$, is the set of mappings of the form $m : A \to \mathbb{N}$. Given a multiset $S \in A^{\oplus}$ and an element $a \in A$, $S(a) \in \mathbb{N}$ denotes the number of times a appears in S. We write $a^n \in S$ if $S(a) = n$. The support of S is the set of elements that appear in S at least once: $supp(S) = \{a \in A \mid S(a) > 0\}$. We also consider the usual operations on multisets. Given $S_1, S_2 \in A^{\oplus}$: *(i)* $S_1 \subseteq S_2$ (resp., $S_1 \subset S_2$) if $S_1(a) \le S_2(a)$ (resp., $S_1(a) < S_2(a)$) for each $a \in A$; *(ii)* $S_1 + S_2 = \{a^n \mid a \in A \text{ and } n = S_1(a) + S_2(a)\}$; *(iii)* if $S_1 \subseteq S_2$, $S_2 - S_1 = \{a^n \mid a \in A \text{ and } n = S_2(a) - S_1(a)\}$; *(iv)* given a number $k \in \mathbb{N}$, $k \cdot S_1 = \{a^{kn} \mid a^n \in S_1\}$; *(v)* $|m| = \sum_{a \in A} m(a)$. A multiset over A is called empty (denoted as $\emptyset^{\oplus}$) iff $\emptyset^{\oplus}(a) = 0$ for every $a \in A$.

We now define CLog-nets, extending ν-CPNs [23] with the ability of querying a read-only catalog. As in CPNs, each CLog-net place has a color type, which corresponds to a data type or to the cartesian product of multiple data types from $\mathfrak{D}$. Tokens in places are referenced via *inscriptions* – tuples of variables and constants. We denote by Ω_A the set of all possible inscriptions over a set A and, with slight abuse of notation, use *Vars*(ω) (resp., *Const*(ω)) to denote the set of variables (resp., constants) of $\omega \in \Omega_A$. To account for fresh external inputs, we employ the well-known mechanism of ν-Petri nets [26] and introduce a countably infinite set $\Upsilon_{\mathfrak{D}}$ of $\mathfrak{D}$-typed *fresh variables*, where for every $\nu \in \Upsilon_{\mathfrak{D}}$, we have that $\Delta_{\mathtt{type}(\nu)}$ is countably infinite (this provides an unlimited supply of fresh values). We fix a countably infinite set of $\mathfrak{D}$-typed variable $\mathcal{X}_{\mathfrak{D}} = \mathcal{V}_{\mathfrak{D}} \uplus \Upsilon_{\mathfrak{D}}$ as the disjoint union of "normal" ($\mathcal{V}_{\mathfrak{D}}$) and fresh ($\Upsilon_{\mathfrak{D}}$) variables.

Definition 1. *A $\mathfrak{D}$-typed CLog-net $\mathcal{N}$ over a catalog schema $\mathcal{R}_{\mathfrak{D}}$ is a tuple* $(\mathfrak{D}, \mathcal{R}_{\mathfrak{D}}, P, T, F_{in}, F_{out}, \mathtt{color}, \mathtt{guard})$, *where:*

1. P and T are finite sets of places and transitions, s.t. $P \cap T = \emptyset$;
2. color $: P \to \wp(\mathfrak{D})$ is a place typing function;
3. $F_{in} : P \times T \to \Omega_{\mathcal{V}_{\mathfrak{D}}}^{\oplus}$ is an input flow, s.t. $\text{type}(F_{in}(p,t)) = \text{color}(p)$ for every $(p,t) \in P \times T$;
4. $F_{out} : T \times P \to \Omega_{\mathcal{X}_{\mathfrak{D}} \cup \Delta_{\mathfrak{D}}}^{\oplus}$ is an output flow, s.t. $\text{type}(F_{out}(t,p)) = \text{color}(p)$ for every $(t,p) \in T \times P$;
5. guard $: T \to \{Q \wedge \varphi \mid Q \in \text{UCQ}_{\mathfrak{D}}^{\neg}, \varphi \in \mathcal{C}_{\mathfrak{D}}\}$ is a partial guard assignment function, s.t., for every $\text{guard}(t) = Q \wedge \varphi$ and $t \in T$, the following holds:
   (a) $\text{Vars}(\varphi) \subseteq \text{InVars}(t)$, where $\text{InVars}(t) = \cup_{p \in P} \text{Vars}(F_{in}(p,t))$;
   (b) $\text{OutVars}(t) \setminus (\text{InVars}(t) \cup \Upsilon_{\mathfrak{D}}) \subseteq \text{Free}(Q)$ and $\text{Free}(Q) \cap \text{Vars}(t) = \emptyset$, where $\text{OutVars}(t) = \cup_{p \in P} \text{Vars}(F_{out}(t,p))$ and $\text{Vars}(t) = \text{InVars}(t) \cup \text{OutVars}(t)$.   ◁

Here, the role of guards is twofold. On the one hand, similarly, for example, to CPNs, guards are used to impose *conditions* (using φ) on tokens flowing through the net. On the other hand, a guard of transition t may also *query* (using Q) the catalog in order to propagate some data into the net. The acquired data may be still filtered by using $\text{InVars}(t)$. Note that in condition *(b)* of the guard definition we specify that there are some variables (excluding the fresh ones) in the outgoing arc inscriptions that do not appear in $\text{InVars}(t)$ and that are used by Q to insert data from the catalog. Moreover, it is required that all free variables of Q must coincide with the variables of inscriptions on outgoing and incoming arcs of a transition it is assigned to. In what follows, we shall define arc inscriptions as $k \cdot \omega$, where $k \in \mathbb{N}$ and $\omega \in \Omega_A$ (for some set A).

Semantics. The execution semantics of a CLog-net is similar to the one of CPNs. Thus, as a first step we introduce the standard notion of net marking. Formally, a *marking* of a CLog-net $N = (\mathfrak{D}, \mathcal{R}_{\mathfrak{D}}, P, T, F_{in}, F_{out}, \text{color}, \text{guard})$ is a function $m : P \to \Omega_{\mathfrak{D}}^{\oplus}$, so that $m(p) \in \Delta_{\text{color}(p)}^{\oplus}$ for every $p \in P$. We write $\langle N, m, Cat \rangle$ to denote CLog-net N marked with m, and equipped with a read-only catalog instance Cat over $\mathcal{R}_{\mathfrak{D}}$.

The firing of a transition t in a marking is defined w.r.t. a so-called *binding* for t defined as $\sigma : \text{Vars}(t) \to \Delta_{\mathfrak{D}}$. Note that, when applied to (multisets of) tuples, σ is applied to every variable singularly. For example, given $\sigma = \{x \mapsto 1, y \mapsto a\}$, its application to a multiset of tuples $\omega = \{\langle x, y \rangle^2, \langle x, b \rangle\}$ results in $\sigma(\omega) = \{\langle 1, a \rangle^2, \langle x, b \rangle\}$.

Definition 2. *A transition* $t \in T$ *is* enabled *in a marking* m *and a fixed catalog instance* Cat, *written* $m[t\rangle_{Cat}$, *if there exists binding* σ *satisfying the following: (i)* $\sigma(F_{in}(p,t)) \subseteq m(p)$, *for every* $p \in P$; $\sigma(\text{guard}(t))$ *is true; (ii)* $\sigma(x) \notin Val(m) \cup Val(Cat)$, *for every* $x \in \Upsilon_{\mathfrak{D}} \cap \text{OutVars}(t)$;[1] *(iii)* $\sigma(x) \in ans(Q, Cat)$ *for* $x \in \text{OutVars}(t) \setminus (\Upsilon_{\mathfrak{D}} \cup \text{InVars}(t)) \cap \text{Vars}(Q)$ *and query* Q *from* $\text{guard}(t)$. ◁

---

[1] Here, with slight abuse of notation, we define by $Val(m)$ the set of all values appearing in m.

Essentially, a transition is enabled with a binding σ if the binding selects data objects carried by tokens from the input places and the read-only catalog instance, so that the data they carry make the guard attached to the transition true.

When a transition t is enabled, it may fire. Next we define what are the effects of firing a transition with some binding σ.

Definition 3. *Let* $\langle N, m, Cat \rangle$ *be a marked CLog-net, and* $t \in T$ *a transition enabled in* m *and* Cat *with some binding* σ. *Then,* t *may fire producing a new marking* m', *with* $m'(p) = m(p) - \sigma(F_{in}(p,t)) + \sigma(F_{out}(t,p))$ *for every* $p \in P$. *We denote this as* $m[t\rangle_{Cat} m'$ *and assume that the definition is inductively extended to sequences* $\tau \in T^*$. ◁

For $\langle N, m_0, Cat \rangle$ we use $\mathcal{M}(N) = \{m \mid \exists \tau \in T.m_0[\tau\rangle_{Cat} m\}$ to denote the set of all markings of N reachable from its initial marking m_0.

We close with an example that illustrates all the main features of CLog-nets.

Given $b \in \mathbb{N}$, a marked CLog-net $\langle N, m_0, Cat \rangle$ is called *bounded with bound* b if $|m(p)| \leq b$, for every marking $m \in \mathcal{M}(N)$ and every place $p \in P_c$. Unboundedness in CLog-nets can arise due to various reasons: classical unbounded generation of tokens, but also uncontrollable emission of fresh values with ν-variables or replication of data values from the catalog via queries in transition guards. Notice that Definition 3 does not involve the catalog, which is in fact fixed throughout the execution.

Execution Semantics. The execution semantics of a marked CLog-net $\langle N, m_0, Cat \rangle$ is defined in terms of a possibly infinite-state transition system in which states are labeled by reachable markings and each arc (or transition) corresponds to the firing of a transition in N with a given binding. The transition system captures all possible executions of the net, by interpreting concurrency as interleaving. Due to space limitations, the formal definition of how this transition system is induced can be found in [15].

As pointed out before, we are interested in analysing a CLog-net irrespectively of the actual content of the catalog. Hence, in the following when we mention a (catalog-parameterised) marked net $\langle N, m_0 \rangle$ without specifying how the catalog is instantiated, we actually implicitly mean the *infinite set of marked nets* $\langle N, m_0, Cat \rangle$ for every possible instance Cat defined over the catalog schema of N.

Example 3. Starting from the catalog in Example 1, Fig. 1 shows a simple, yet sophisticated example of CLog-net capturing the following order-to-delivery process. Orders can be created by executing the new order transition, which uses a ν-variable to generate a fresh order identifier. A so-created, working order can be populated with items, whose type is selected from those available in the catalog relation *ProdCat*. Each item then carries its product type and owning order. When an order contains at least one item, it can be paid. Items added to an order can be removed or loaded in a compatible truck. The set of available trucks, indicating their plate numbers and types, is contained in a dedicated *pool*

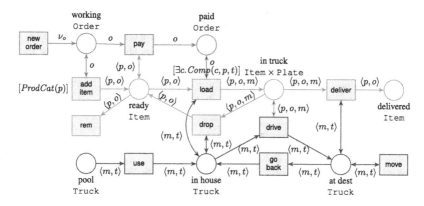

Fig. 1. A CLog-net (its catalog is in Example 1). In the picture, `Item` and `Truck` are compact representations for `ProdType × Order` and `Plate × TruckType` respectively. The top blue part refers to orders, the central orange part to items, and the bottom violet part to delivery trucks.

place. Trucks can be borrowed from the pool and placed in house. An item can be loaded into a truck if its owning order has been paid, the truck is in house, and the truck type and product type of the item are compatible according to the *Comp* relation in the catalog. Items (possibly from different orders) can be loaded in a truck, and while the truck is in house, they can be dropped, which makes them ready to be loaded again. A truck can be driven for delivery if it contains at least one loaded item. Once the truck is at its destination, some items may be delivered (this is simply modelled non-deterministically). The truck can then either move, or go back in house. ◁

Example 3 shows various key aspects related to modelling data-aware processes with multiple case objects using CLog-nets. First of all, whenever an object is involved in a many-to-one relation from the "many" side, it then becomes responsible of carrying the object to which it is related. This can be clearly seen in the example, where each item carries a reference to its owning order and, once loaded into a truck, a reference to the truck plate number. Secondly, the three object types involved in the example show three different modelling patterns for their creation. Unboundedly many orders can be genuinely created using a ν-variable to generate their (fresh) identifiers. The (finite) set of trucks available in the domain is instead fixed in the initial marking, by populating the *pool* place. The CLog-net shows that such trucks are used as resources that can change state but are never destroyed nor created. Finally, the case of items is particularly interesting. Items in fact can be arbitrarily created and destroyed. However, their creation is not modelled using an explicit ν-variable, but is instead simply obtained by the add item transition with the usual token-creation mechanism, in which the product type is taken from the catalog using the query assigned to add item. Thanks to the multiset semantics of Petri nets, it is still possible to create multiple items having the same product type and owning order. However, it is not possible to track the evolution of a specific item, since there is no explicit identifier carried by item tokens. This is not a limitation in this example, since items are not referenced by other objects present in the net (which is instead the case for orders and trucks). All in all, this shows that ν-variables are only necessary when the CLog-net needs to handle the arbitrary creation of objects that are referenced by other objects.

3   From CLog-nets to MCMT

We now report on the encoding of CLog-nets into the verification language supported by the MCMT model checker, showing that the various modelling constructs of CLog-nets have a direct counterpart in MCMT, and in turn enabling formal analysis.

MCMT is founded on the theory of *array-based systems* [1,16], an umbrella term used to refer to *infinite-state transition systems* specified using a declarative, logic-based formalism by which arrays are manipulated via logical updates. An array-based system is represented using a multi-sorted theory with two kinds of sorts: one for the indexes of arrays, and the other for the elements stored therein. Since the content of an array changes over time, it is referred to by a function variable, whose interpretation in a state is that of a total function mapping indexes to elements (applying the function to an index denotes the classical *read* array operation). We adopt here the module of MCMT called "database-driven mode", which supports the representation of read-only databases.

Specifically, we show how to encode a CLog-net $\langle N, m_0 \rangle$, where $N = (\mathfrak{D}, \mathcal{R}_\mathfrak{D}, P, T, F_{in}, F_{out}, \texttt{color}, \texttt{guard})$ into (data-driven) MCMT specification. The translation is split into two phases. First, we tackle the type domain and catalog. Then, we present a step-wise encoding of the CLog-net places and transitions into arrays.

Data and Schema Translation. We start by describing how to translate static data-related components. Let $\mathfrak{D} = \{\mathcal{D}_1, \ldots, \mathcal{D}_{n_d}\}$. Each data type $\mathcal{D}_i$ is encoded in MCMT with declaration :smt (define-type Di). For each declared type $\mathcal{D}$ MCMT implicitly generates a special NULL constant indicating an empty/undefined value of $\mathcal{D}$.

To represent the catalog relations of $\mathcal{R}_\mathfrak{D} = \{R_1, \ldots, R_{n_r}\}$ in MCMT, we proceed as follows. Recall that in catalog every relation schema has $n + 1$ typed attributes among which some may be foreign keys referencing other relations, its first attribute is a primary key, and, finally, primary keys of different relation schemas have different types. With these conditions at hand, we adopt the functional characterisation of read-only databases studied in [9]. For every relation $R_i(id, A_1, \ldots, A_n)$ with $\text{PK}(R) = \{id\}$, we introduce unary functions that correctly reference each attribute of R_i using its primary key. More specifically, for every A_j $(j = 1, \ldots, n)$ we create a function $f_{R_i, A_j} : \Delta_{\texttt{type}(id)} \to \Delta_{\texttt{type}A_j}$. If A_j is referencing an identifier of some other relation S (i.e., $R_i.A_j \to S.id$), then f_{R_i, A_j} represents the foreign key referencing to S. Note that in this case the types of A_j and $S.id$ should coincide. In MCMT, assuming that D_Ri.id = type(id)

and $D\_Aj = \text{type}(A_j)$, this is captured using statement `:smt (define Ri_Aj`
`::(-> D_Ri.id D_Aj))`.

All the constants appearing in the net specification must be properly defined.
Let $C = \{v_1, \ldots, v_{n_c}\}$ be the set of all constants appearing in N. C is defined
as $\bigcup_{t \in T} Const(\text{guard}(t)) \cup supp(m_0) \cup \bigcup_{t \in T, p \in P} Const(F_{out}(t, p))$. Then, every
constant $v_i \in C$ of type $\mathcal{D}$ is declared in MCMT as `:smt (define vi ::D)`.

The code section needed to make MCMT aware of the fact that these elements have been declared to describe a read-only database schema is depicted in Listing 1.1 (notice that the last declaration is required when using MCMT in the database-driven mode).

Listing 1.1.	Listing 1.2.
| ```
: db_driven
: db_sorts  D1 ,... , Dnd
: db_functions
       R1_A1 ,... , Rnr_Ak
: db_constants  v1 ,... , vnc
: db_relations   // leave empty
``` | ```
: initial
: var  x
: cnj  init_p1
       ...
       init_pn
``` |

Places. Given that, during the net execution, every place may store unboundedly many tokens, we need to ensure a potentially infinite provision of values to places p using unbounded arrays. To this end, every place $p \in P$ with $\text{color}(p) = \mathcal{D}_1 \times \ldots \times \mathcal{D}_k$ is going to be represented as a combination of arrays $p_1, \ldots, p_k$, where a special index type $\mathbf{P_{ind}}$ (disjoint from all other types) with domain $\Delta_{P_{ind}}$ is used as the array index sort and $\mathcal{D}_1, \ldots, \mathcal{D}_k$ account for the respective target sorts of the arrays.[2] In MCMT, this is declared as `:local p_1 D1 ... :local p_k Dk`. Then, intuitively, we associate to the j-th token $(v_1, \ldots, v_k) \in m(p)$ an element $j \in \Delta_{P_{ind}}$ and a tuple $(j, p_1[j], \ldots, p_k[j])$, where $p_1[j] = v_1, \ldots, p_k[j] = v_k$. Here, j is an *"implicit identifier"* of this tuple in $m(p)$. Using this intuition and assuming that there are in total n control places, we represent the initial marking m_0 in two steps (a direct declaration is not possible due to the language restrictions of MCMT). First, we symbolically declare that all places are by default empty using the MCMT initialisation statement from Listing 1.2. There, `cnj` represents a conjunction of atomic equations that, for ease of reading, we organized in blocks, where each $init\_p_i$ specifies for place $p_i \in P$ with $\text{color}(p_i) = \mathcal{D}_1 \times \ldots \times \mathcal{D}_k$ that it contains no tokens. This is done by explicitly "nullifying" all component of each possible token in p_i, written in MCMT as `(= pi_1[x] NULL_D1)(= pi_2[x] NULL_D2)...(= pi_k[x] NULL_DK)`. The initial marking is then injected with a dedicated MCMT code that populates the place arrays, initialised as empty, with records representing tokens therein. Due to the lack of space, this code is provided in [15].

Transition Enablement and Firing. We now show how to check for transition enablement and compute the effect of a transition firing in MCMT. To this

---

[2] MCMT has only one index sort, but, as shown in [15], there is no loss of generality in doing that.

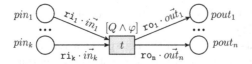

Fig. 2. A generic CLog-net transition ($\mathtt{ri}_j$ and $\mathtt{ro}_j$ are natural numbers)

end, we consider the generic, prototypical CLog-net transition $t \in T$ depicted in Fig. 2. The enablement of this transition is subject to the following conditions: *(FC1)* there is a binding σ that correctly matches tokens in the places to the corresponding inscriptions on the input arcs (i.e., each place pin_i provides enough tokens required by a corresponding inscription $F(pin_i, t) = \vec{in_i}$), and that computes new and possibly *fresh* values that are pairwise distinct from each other as well as from all other values in the marking; *(FC2)* the guard $\mathtt{guard}(t)$ is satisfied under the selected binding. In MCMT, t is captured with a transition statement consisting of a guard G and an update U as in Listing 1.3.

Listing 1.3.	Listing 1.4.
`:transition`	`:numcases NC`
`:var x,x1,...,xK,y1,...,yN`	`...`
`:var j`	`:case (= j i)`
`:guard G`	`:val `$v_{1,i}$
`... U ...`	`...`
	`:val `$v_{k,i}$
	`...`

Here every $\mathtt{x}$ (resp., $\mathtt{y}$) represents an existentially quantified index variable corresponding to variables in the incoming inscriptions (resp., outgoing inscriptions), $\mathtt{K} = \sum_{j \in \{1,...,k\}} \mathtt{ri}_j$, $\mathtt{N} = \sum_{j \in \{1,...,n\}} \mathtt{ro}_j$ and $\mathtt{j}$ is a universally quantified variable, that will be used for computing bindings of ν-variables and updates. In the following we are going to elaborate on the construction of the MCMT transition statement. We start by discussing the structure of G which in MCMT is represented as a conjunction of atoms or negated atoms and, intuitively, addresses all the conditions stated above.

First, to construct a binding that meets condition *(FC1)*, we need to make sure that every place contains enough of tokens that match a corresponding arc inscription. Using the array-based representation, for every place pin_i with $F_{in}(pin_i, t) = \mathtt{ri}_i \cdot \vec{in_i}$ and $|\mathtt{color}(pin_i)| = k$, we can check this with a formula

$$\psi_{pin_i} := \exists \mathbf{x_1}, \ldots, \mathbf{x_{ri_i}}. \bigwedge_{\substack{j_1, j_2 \in \{\mathbf{x_1},...,\mathbf{x_{ri_i}}\}, j_1 \neq j_2, \\ l \in \{1,...,k\}}} pin_{i,l}[j_1] = pin_{i,l}[j_2] \wedge \bigwedge_{l \in \{1,...,k\}} pin_{i,l}[\mathbf{x_1}] \neq \mathtt{NULL\_D}_l$$

Given that variables representing existentially quantified index variables are already defined, in MCMT this is encoded as conjunctions of atoms (= pini_l[j_1] pini_l[j_2]) and atoms not(= pini_l[x1] NULL_Dl), where NULL_Dl is a special null constant of type of elements stored in pini_l. All such conjunctions, for all input places of t, should be appended to G.

We now define the condition that selects proper indexes in the output places so as to fill them with the tokens generated upon transition firing. To this end, we need to make sure that all the q declared arrays a_w of the system[3] (including the arrays $pout_i$ corresponding to the output places of t) contain no values in the slots marked by y index variables. This is represented using a formula

$$\psi_{pout_i} := \exists \mathbf{y}_1, \ldots, \mathbf{y}_{ri_i} . \bigwedge_{j \in \{\mathbf{y}_1, \ldots, \mathbf{y}_{ri_j}\}, w \in \{1, \ldots q\}} a_w[j] = \text{NULL\_D}_w,$$

which is encoded in MCMT similarly to the case of ψ_{pin_i}.

Moreover, when constructing a binding, we have to take into account the case of arc inscriptions causing implicit "joins" between the net marking and data retrieved from the catalog. This happens when there are some variables in the input flow that coincide with variables of Q, i.e., $Vars(F_{in}(pin_j, t)) \cap Vars(Q) \neq \emptyset$. For ease of presentation, denote the set of such variables as $\mathbf{s} = \{s_1, \ldots, s_r\}$ and introduce a function π that returns the position of a variable in a tuple or relation. E.g., $\pi(\langle x, y, z \rangle, y) = 2$, and $\pi(R, B) = 3$ in $R(id, A, B, E)$. Then, for every relation R in Q we generate a formula

$$\psi_R := \bigwedge_{j \in \{1, \ldots, k\}, s \in (\mathbf{s} \cap Vars(R))} pin_{j, \pi(\vec{in}_j, s)}[\mathbf{x}] = f_{R, A_{\pi(R, s)}}(id)$$

This formula guarantees that values provided by a constructed binding respect the aforementioned case for some index $\mathbf{x}$ (that has to coincide with one of the index variables from ψ_{pin_j}) and identifier id. In MCMT this is encoded as a conjunction of atoms (= (R_Ai id) pinj_l[x]), where i = $\pi(R, s)$ and l = $\pi(\vec{in}_j, s)$. As in the previous case, all such formulas are appended to G.

We now incorporate the encoding of condition (FC2). Every variable z of Q with type(z) = D has to be declared in MCMT as :eevar z D. We call an extended guard a guard $Q^e \wedge \varphi^e$ in which every relation R has been substituted with its functional counterpart and every variable z in φ has been substituted with a "reference" to a corresponding array pin_j that z uses as a value provider for its bindings. More specifically, every relation $R/n + 1$ that appears in Q as $R(id, z_1, \ldots, z_n)$ is be replaced by conjunction $id \neq \text{NULL\_D} \wedge f_{R, A_1}(id) = z_1 \wedge \ldots \wedge f_{R, A_n}(id) = z_n$, where D = type($id$). In MCMT, this is written as (not (= id NULL_D)) $expr_1 \ldots expr_n$ (id should be declared using :eevar as well). Here, every $expr_i$ corresponds to an atomic equality from above and is specified in MCMT in three different ways based on the nature of z_i. Let us assume that z_i has

---

[3] This is a technicality of MCMT, as explained in [15], since MCMT has only one index sort.

been declared before as :eevar z_i D. If z_i appears in a corresponding incoming transition inscription, then $expr_i$ is defined as (= (R_Ai id) pin_j[x]) (= z_i pin_j[x]), where i-th attribute of R coincides with the j-th variable in the inscription $F_{in}(pin, t)$. If z_i is a variable bound by an existential quantifier in Q, then $expr_i$ in MCMT is going to look as (= (R_Ai id) zi). Finally, if z_i is a variable in an outgoing inscription used for propagating data from the catalog (as discussed in condition *(1)*), then $expr_i$ is simply defined with the following statement: (= (R_Ai id) z_i), where Di is the type of z_i.

Variables in φ are substituted with their array counterparts. In particular, every variable $z \in Vars(\varphi)$ is substituted with pinj_i[x], where i = $\pi(\vec{in}_j, z)$. Given that φ is represented as a conjunction of variables, its representation in MCMT together with the aforementioned substitution is trivial. To finish the construction of G, we append to it the MCMT version of $Q^e \wedge \varphi^e$.

We come back to condition *(FC1)* and show how bindings are generated for ν-variables of the output flow of t. In MCMT we use a special universal guard :uguard (to be inserted right after the :guard entry) that, for every variable $\nu \in \Upsilon_{\mathfrak{D}} \cap (OutVars(t) \setminus Vars(\vec{out}_j))$ previously declared using :eevar nu D, and for arrays $p_1, \ldots, p_k$ with target sort D, consists of expression (not(=nu p_1[j]))...(not(=nu p_k[j])) for all p. This encodes "local" freshness for ν-variables, which suffice for our goal.

After a binding has been generated and the guard of t has been checked, a new marking is generated by assigning corresponding tokens to the outgoing places and by removing tokens from the incoming ones. Note that, while the tokens are populated by assigning their values to respective arrays, the token deletion happens by nullifying (i.e., assigning special NULL constants) entries in the arrays of the input places. All these operations are specified in the special update part of the transition statement U and are captured in MCMT as depicted in Listing 1.4. There, the transition runs through NC cases. All the following cases go over the indexes y1,..., yN that correspond to tokens that have to be added to places. More specifically, for every place $pout \in P$ such that $|color(pout)| = k$, we add an i-th token to it by putting a value $v_{r,i}$ in i-th place of every r-th component array of $pout$. This $v_{r,i}$ can either be a ν-variable nu from the universal guard, or a value coming from a place pin specified as pin[xm] (from some x input index variable) or a value from some of the relations specified as (R_Ai id). Note that id should be also declared as :eevar id D_Ri.id, where type(id) = D_Ri.id. Every :val v statement follows the order in which all the local and global variables have been defined, and, for array variables a and every every case (= j i), such statement stands for a simple assignment $a[i]$:= v.

Implementation Status. The provided translation is fully compliant with the concrete specification language MCMT. The current implementation has however a limitation on the number of supported index variables in each MCMT transition statement. Specifically, two existentially quantified and one universally quantified variables are currently supported. This has to be taken into account if one wants to run the model checker on the result produced by translating a CLog-net, and possibly requires to rewrite the net (if possible) into one that does not exceed the supported number of index variables. What can be actually rewritten (and how) is beyond the scope of this paper.

In addition, notice that this limitation is not dictated by algorithmic nor theoretical limitations, but is a mere characteristic of the current implementation, and comes from the fact that the wide range of systems verified so far with MCMT never required to simultaneously quantify on many array indexes. There is an ongoing implementation effort for a new version of MCMT that supports arbitrarily many quantified index variables, and consequently concrete model checking of the full CLog-net model is within reach. Currently, we do not have a software prototype that encodes the translation, but this section indicates exactly how this should be implemented.

4   Parameterised Verification

Thanks to the encoding of CLog-nets into (the database-driven module of) MCMT, we can handle the parameterised verification of safety properties over CLog-nets, and study crucial properties such as soundness, completeness, and termination by relating CLog-nets with the foundational framework underlying such an MCMT module [8,9].

This amounts to verifying whether it is true that *all* the reachable states of a marked CLog-net satisfy a desired condition, *independently from the content of the catalog*. As customary in this setting, this form of verification is tackled in a converse way, by formulating an *unsafe condition*, and by checking whether there exists an instance of the catalog such that the CLog-net can evolve the initial marking to a state where the unsafe condition holds. Technically, given a property ψ capturing an unsafe condition and a marked CLog-net $\langle N, m_0 \rangle$, we say that $\langle N, m_0 \rangle$ is *unsafe* w.r.t. ψ if there exists a catalog instance Cat for N such that the marked CLog-net with fixed catalog $\langle N, m_0, Cat \rangle$ can reach a configuration where ψ holds.

With a slight abuse of notation, we interchangeably use the term CLog-net to denote the input net or its MCMT encoding. We start by defining (unsafety) properties, in a way that again guarantees a direct encoding into the MCMT model checker. For space limitations, we refer to the translation of properties over CLog-nets in [15].

Definition 4. *A property over CLog-net N is a formula of the form $\exists \vec{y}.\psi(\vec{y})$, where $\psi(\vec{y})$ is a quantifier-free query that additionally contains atomic predicates $[p \geq c]$ and $[p(x_1, \ldots, x_n) \geq c]$, where p is a place name from N, $c \in \mathbb{N}$, and $Vars(\psi) = Y_P$, with Y_P being the set of variables appearing in the atomic predicates $[p(x_1, \ldots, x_n) \geq c]$.* ◁

Here, $[p \geq c]$ specifies that in place p there are at least c tokens. Similarly, $[p(x_1, \ldots, x_n) \geq c]$ indicates that in place p there are at least c tokens carrying the tuple $\langle x_1, \ldots, x_n \rangle$ of data objects. A property may also mention relations from the catalog, provided that all variables used therein also appear in atoms that inspect places.

This can be seen as a language to express *data-aware coverability properties* of a CLog-net, possibly relating tokens with the content of the catalog. Focusing on covered markings as opposed as fully-specified reachable markings is customary in data-aware Petri nets or, more in general, well-structured transition systems (such as ν-PNs [26]).

Example 4. Consider the CLog-net of Example 3, with an initial marking that populates the *pool* place with available trucks. Property $\exists p, o.[delivered(p, o) \geq 1] \wedge [working(o) \geq 1]$ captures the undesired situation where a delivery occurs for an item that belongs to a working (i.e., not yet paid) order. This can never happen, irrespectively of the content of the net catalog: items can be delivered only if they have been loaded in a compatible truck, which is possible only if the order of the loaded item is *paid*.   ◁

In the remainder of the section, we focus on the key properties of soundness and completeness of the backward reachability procedure encoded in MCMT, which can be used to handle the parameterised verification problem for CLog-nets defined above.[4] We call this procedure BREACH, and in our context we assume it takes as input a marked CLog-net and an (undesired) property ψ, returning UNSAFE if there exists an instance of the catalog so that the net can evolve from the initial marking to a configuration that satisfies ψ, and SAFE otherwise. For details on the procedure itself, refer to [9,16]. We characterise the (meta-)properties of this procedure as follows.

Definition 5. *Given a marked CLog-net $\langle N, m_0 \rangle$ and a property ψ, BREACH is: (i) sound if, whenever it terminates, it produces a correct answer; (ii) partially sound if a SAFE result it returns is always correct; (iii) complete (w.r.t. unsafety) if, whenever $\langle N, m_0 \rangle$ is UNSAFE with respect to ψ, then BREACH detects it and returns UNSAFE.*   ◁

In general, BREACH is not guaranteed to terminate (which is not surprising given the expressiveness of the framework and the type of parameterised verification tackled).

As we have seen in Sect. 3, the encoding of fresh variables requires to employ a limited form of universal quantification. This feature goes beyond the foundational framework for (data-driven) MCMT [9], which in fact does not explicitly consider fresh data injection. It is known from previous works (see, e.g., [3]) that when universal quantification over the indexes of an array is employed, BREACH cannot guarantee that all the indexes are considered, leading to potentially spurious situations in which some indexes are simply "disregarded" when exploring the state space. This may wrongly classify a SAFE case as being UNSAFE, due to spurious exploration of the state space, similarly to what happens in lossy systems. By combining [9] and [3], we then obtain:

Theorem 1. BREACH *is partially sound and complete for marked CLog-nets.*   ◁

---

[4] *Backward reachability* is not *marking reachability*. We consider reachability of a configuration satisfying a property that captures the covering of a data-aware marking.

Fortunately, MCMT is equipped with techniques [3] for debugging the returned result, and tame partial soundness. In fact, MCMT warns when the produced result is provably correct, or *may* have been produced due to a spurious state-space exploration.

A key point is then how to tame partial soundness towards recovering full soundness and completeness We obtain this by either assuming that the CLog-net of interest does not employ at all fresh variables, or is bounded.

Conservative CLog-nets are CLog-nets that do not employ ν-variables in arc inscriptions. It turns out that such nets are fully compatible with the foundational framework in [9], and consequently inherit all the properties established there. In particular, we obtain that BREACH is a semi-decision procedure.

Theorem 2. BREACH *is sound and complete for marked, conservative CLog-nets.*   ◁

One may wonder whether studying conservative nets is meaningful. We argue in favour of this by considering modelling techniques to "remove" fresh variables present in the net. The first technique is to ensure that ν-variables are used only when necessary. As we have extensively discussed at the end of Sect. 2, this is the case only for objects that are referenced by other objects. This happens when an object type participates on the "one" side of a many-to-one relationship, or for one of the two end points of a one-to-one relationship. The second technique is to limit the scope of verification by singling out only one (or a bunch of) "prototypical" object(s) of a given type. This is, e.g., what happens when checking soundness of workflow nets, where only the evolution of a single case from the input to the output place is studied.

Example 5. We can turn the CLog-net of Example 3 into a conservative one by removing the **new order** transition, and by ensuring that in the initial marking one or more order tokens are inserted into the *working* place. This allows one to verify how these orders co-evolve in the net. A detected issue carries over the general setting where orders can be arbitrarily created.   ◁

A third technique is to remove the part of the CLog-net with the fresh objects creation, assuming instead that such objects are all "pre-created" and then listed in a read-only, catalog relation. This is more powerful than the first technique from above: now verification considers all possible configurations of such objects as described by the catalog schema. In fact, using this technique on Example 3 we can turn the CLog-net into a conservative CLog-net that mimics exactly the behaviour of the original one.

Example 6. We make the CLog-net from Example 3 conservative in a way that reconstructs the original, arbitrary order creation. To do so we extend the catalog with a unary relation schema *CrOrder* accounting for (pre-)created orders. Then, we modify the **new order** transition: we substitute the ν-variable ν_o with a normal variable o, and we link this variable to the catalog, by adding as a guard a query *CrOrder(o)*. This modified **new order** transition extracts an order from the catalog and making it *working*. Since in the original CLog-net the creation of orders is unconstrained, it is irrelevant for verification if all the orders involved in an execution are created on-the-fly, or all created at the very beginning. Paired with the fact that the modified CLog-net is analysed for all possible catalog instances, i.e., all possible sets of pre-created orders, this tells us that the original and modified nets capture the same relevant behaviours. ◁

Bounded CLog-nets. An orthogonal approach is to study what happens if the CLog-net of interest is bounded (for a given bound). In this case, we can "compile away" fresh-object creation by introducing a place that contains, in the initial marking, enough provision of pre-defined objects. This effectively transforms the CLog-net into a conservative one, and so Theorem 2 applies. If we consider a boudned CLog-net and its catalog is acyclic (i.e., its foreign keys cannot form referential cycles where a table directly or indirectly refers to itself), then it is possible to show using the results from [9] that verifying safety of conservative CLog-nets becomes decidable.

Several modelling strategies can be adopted to turn an unbounded CLog-net into a bounded one. We illustrate two strategies in the context of our running example.

Example 7. Consider again the CLog-net of Example 3. It has two sources of unboundedness: the creation of orders, and the addition of items to working orders. The first can be tackled by introducing suitable resource places. E.g., we can impose that each order is controlled by a manager and can be created only when there is an idle manager not working on any other order. This makes the overall amount of orders unbounded over time, but bounded in each marking by the number of resources. Items creation can be bounded by imposing, conceptually, that each order cannot contain more than a maximum number of items. This amounts to impose a maximum multiplicity on the "many" side of each one-to-many relation implicitly present in the CLog-net.   ◁

5   Comparison to Other Models

We comment on how the CLog-nets relate to the most recent data-aware Petri net-based models, arguing that they provide an interesting mix of their main features.

DB-nets. CLog-nets in their full generality match with an expressive fragment of the DB-net model [22]. DB-nets combine a control-flow component based on CPNs with fresh value injection a là ν-PNs with an underlying read-write persistent storage consisting of a relational database with full-fledged constraints. Special "view" places in the net are used to inspect the content of the underlying database, while transitions are equipped with database update operations.

In CLog-nets, the catalog accounts for a persistent storage solely used in a "read-only" modality, thus making the concept of view places rather unnecessary. More specifically, given that the persistent storage can never be changed but only queried for extracting data relevant for running cases, the queries from view places in DB-nets have been relocated to transition guards of CLog-nets. While CLog-nets do not come with an explicit, updatable persistent storage, they can still *employ places and suitably defined subnets to capture read-write relations and their manipulation.* In particular, as shown in [23], read-write relations queried using $\text{UCQ}_{\overline{\mathcal{D}}}$ queries can be directly encoded with special places and transitions at the net level. The same applies to CLog-nets.

While verification of DB-nets has only been studied in the bounded case, CLog-nets are formally analysed here without imposing boundedness, and parametrically w.r.t. read-only relations. In addition, the MCMT encoding provided here constitutes the first attempt to make this type of nets practically verifiable.

PNIDs. The net component of our CLog-nets model is equivalent to the formalism of Petri nets with identifiers (PNIDs [17]) without inhibitor arcs. Interestingly, PNIDs without inhibitor arcs form the formal basis of the *Information Systems Modelling Language* (ISML) defined in [24]. In ISML, PNIDs are paired with special CRUD operations to define how relevant facts are manipulated. Such relevant facts are structured according to a conceptual data model specified in ORM, which imposes structural, first-order constraints over such facts. This sophistication only permits to formally analyse the resulting formalism by bounding the PNID markings and the number of objects and facts relating them. The main focus of ISML is in fact more on modelling and enactment. CLog-nets can be hence seen as a natural "verification" counterpart of ISML, where the data component is structured relationally and does not come with the sophisticated constraints of ORM, but where parameterised verification is practically possible.

Proclets. CLog-nets can be seen as a sort of *explicit data* version of (a relevant fragment of) Proclets [14]. Proclets handle multiple objects by separating their respective subnets, and by implicitly retaining their mutual one-to-one and one-to-many relations through the notion of correlation set. In Fig. 1, that would require to separate the subnets of orders, items, and trucks, relating them with two special one-to-many channels indicating that multiple items belong to the same order and loaded in the same truck.

A correlation set is established when one or multiple objects $o_1, \ldots, o_n$ are co-created, all being related to the same object o of a different type (cf. the creation of multiple items for the same order in our running example). In Proclets, this correlation set is implicitly reconstructed by inspecting the concurrent histories of such different objects. Correlation sets are then used to formalise two sophisticated forms of synchronisation. In the *equal* synchronisation, o flows through a transition t_1 while, simultaneously, *all* objects $o_1, \ldots, o_n$ flow through another transition t_2. In the *subset* synchronisation, the same happens but only requiring a subset of $o_1, \ldots, o_n$ to synchronise.

Interestingly, CLog-nets can encode correlation sets and the subset synchronisation semantics. A correlation set is explicitly maintained in the net by imposing that the tokens carrying $o_1, \ldots, o_n$ also carry a reference to o. This is what happens for items in our running example: they explicitly carry a reference to the order they belong to. Subset synchronisation is encoded via a properly crafted subnet. Intuitively, this subnet works as follows. First, a lock place is inserted in the CLog-net so as to indicate when the net is operating in a normal mode or is instead executing a synchronisation phase. When the lock is taken, some objects in $o_1, \ldots, o_n$ are nondeterministically picked and moved through their transition t_2. The lock is then released, simultaneously moving o through its transition t_1. Thanks to this approach, a Proclet with subset synchronisation points can be encoded into a corresponding CLog-net, providing for the first time a practical approach to verification. This does not carry over Proclets with equal synchronisation, which would allow us to capture, in our running example, sophisticated mechanisms like ensuring that when a truck moves to its destination, *all* items contained therein are delivered. Equal synchronisation can only be captured in CLog-nets by introducing a data-aware variant of wholeplace operation, which we aim to study in the future.

6   Conclusions

We have brought forward an integrated model of processes and data founded on CPN that balances between modelling power and the possibility of carrying sophisticated forms of verification parameterised on read-only, immutable relational data. We have approached the problem of verification not only foundationally, but also showing a direct encoding into MCMT, one of the most well-established model checkers for the verification of infinite-state dynamic systems. We have also shown that this model directly relates to some of the most sophisticate models studied in this spectrum, attempting at unifying their features in a single approach. Given that MCMT is based on Satisfiability Modulo Theories (SMT), our approach naturally lends itself to be extended with numerical data types and arithmetics. We also want to study the impact of introducing wholeplace operations, essential to capture the most sophisticated syhncronization semantics defined for Proclets [14]. At the same time, we are currently defining a benchmark for data-aware processes, systematically translating the artifact systems benchmark defined in [20] into corresponding imperative data-aware formalisms, including CLog-nets.

Acknowledgments. This work has been partially supported by the UNIBZ projects VERBA and DACOMAN.

References

1. MCMT: Model checker modulo theories. http://users.mat.unimi.it/users/ghilardi/mcmt/. Accessed 15 June 2020
2. Aalst, W.M.P.: Object-centric process mining: dealing with divergence and convergence in event data. In: Ölveczky, P.C., Salaün, G. (eds.) SEFM 2019. LNCS, vol. 11724, pp. 3–25. Springer, Cham (2019). https://doi.org/10.1007/978-3-030-30446-1_1

3. Alberti, F., Ghilardi, S., Pagani, E., Ranise, S., Rossi, G.P.: Universal guards, relativization of quantifiers, and failure models in model checking modulo theories. J. Satisf. Boolean Model. Comput. **8**(1/2), 29–61 (2012)
4. Artale, A., Kovtunova, A., Montali, M., van der Aalst, W.M.P.: Modeling and reasoning over declarative data-aware processes with object-centric behavioral constraints. In: Hildebrandt, T., van Dongen, B.F., Röglinger, M., Mendling, J. (eds.) BPM 2019. LNCS, vol. 11675, pp. 139–156. Springer, Cham (2019). https://doi.org/10.1007/978-3-030-26619-6_11
5. Batoulis, K., Haarmann, S., Weske, M.: Various notions of soundness for decision-aware business processes. In: Mayr, H.C., Guizzardi, G., Ma, H., Pastor, O. (eds.) ER 2017. LNCS, vol. 10650, pp. 403–418. Springer, Cham (2017). https://doi.org/10.1007/978-3-319-69904-2_31
6. Calvanese, D., Ghilardi, S., Gianola, A., Montali, M., Rivkin, A.: Verification of data-aware processes via array-based systems (extended version). Technical report arXiv:1806.11459 (2018)
7. Calvanese, D., Ghilardi, S., Gianola, A., Montali, M., Rivkin, A.: Formal modeling and SMT-based parameterized verification of data-aware BPMN. In: Hildebrandt, T., van Dongen, B.F., Röglinger, M., Mendling, J. (eds.) BPM 2019. LNCS, vol. 11675, pp. 157–175. Springer, Cham (2019). https://doi.org/10.1007/978-3-030-26619-6_12
8. Calvanese, D., Ghilardi, S., Gianola, A., Montali, M., Rivkin, A.: From model completeness to verification of data aware processes. In: Lutz, C., Sattler, U., Tinelli, C., Turhan, A.-Y., Wolter, F. (eds.) Description Logic, Theory Combination, and All That. LNCS, vol. 11560, pp. 212–239. Springer, Cham (2019). https://doi.org/10.1007/978-3-030-22102-7_10
9. Calvanese, D., Ghilardi, S., Gianola, A., Montali, M., Rivkin, A.: SMT-based verification of data-aware processes: a model-theoretic approach. Math. Struct. Comput. Sci. **30**(3), 271–313 (2020)
10. Calvanese, D., De Giacomo, G., Montali, M.: Foundations of data aware process analysis: a database theory perspective. In: Proceedings of PODS, pp. 1–12. ACM (2013)
11. De Masellis, R., Di Francescomarino, C., Ghidini, C., Montali, M., Tessaris, S.: Add data into business process verification: bridging the gap between theory and practice. In: Singh, S.P., Markovitch, S. (eds.) Proceedings of AAAI, pp. 1091–1099 (2017)
12. Deutsch, A., Li, Y., Vianu, V.: Verification of hierarchical artifact systems. In: Proceedings of PODS, pp. 179–194. ACM (2016)
13. Dumas, M.: On the convergence of data and process engineering. In: Eder, J., Bielikova, M., Tjoa, A.M. (eds.) ADBIS 2011. LNCS, vol. 6909, pp. 19–26. Springer, Heidelberg (2011). https://doi.org/10.1007/978-3-642-23737-9_2
14. Fahland, D.: Describing behavior of processes with many-to-many interactions. In: Donatelli, S., Haar, S. (eds.) PETRI NETS 2019. LNCS, vol. 11522, pp. 3–24. Springer, Cham (2019). https://doi.org/10.1007/978-3-030-21571-2_1
15. Ghilardi, S., Gianola, A., Montali, M., Rivkin, A.: Petri nets with parameterised data: modelling and verification (extended version). Technical report arXiv:2006.06630 (2020)
16. Ghilardi, S., Ranise, S.: Backward reachability of array-based systems by SMT solving: termination and invariant synthesis. Log. Methods Comput. Sci. **6**(4), 1–46 (2010)

17. van Hee, K.M., Sidorova, N., Voorhoeve, M., van der Werf, J.M.E.M.: Generation of database transactions with petri nets. Fundamenta Informaticae **93**(1–3), 171–184 (2009)
18. Hull, R.: Artifact-centric business process models: brief survey of research results and challenges. In: Meersman, R., Tari, Z. (eds.) OTM 2008. LNCS, vol. 5332, pp. 1152–1163. Springer, Heidelberg (2008). https://doi.org/10.1007/978-3-540-88873-4_17
19. Künzle, V., Weber, B., Reichert, M.: Object-aware business processes: fundamental requirements and their support in existing approaches. Int. J. Inf. Syst. Model. Des. **2**(2), 19–46 (2011)
20. Li, Y., Deutsch, A., Vianu, V.: VERIFAS: a practical verifier for artifact systems. PVLDB **11**(3), 283–296 (2017)
21. Meyer, A., Pufahl, L., Fahland, D., Weske, M.: Modeling and enacting complex data dependencies in business processes. In: Daniel, F., Wang, J., Weber, B. (eds.) BPM 2013. LNCS, vol. 8094, pp. 171–186. Springer, Heidelberg (2013). https://doi.org/10.1007/978-3-642-40176-3_14
22. Montali, M., Rivkin, A.: DB-Nets: on the marriage of colored petri nets and relational databases. Trans. Petri Nets Other Models Concurr. **28**(4), 91–118 (2017)
23. Montali, M., Rivkin, A.: From DB-nets to coloured petri nets with priorities. In: Donatelli, S., Haar, S. (eds.) PETRI NETS 2019. LNCS, vol. 11522, pp. 449–469. Springer, Cham (2019). https://doi.org/10.1007/978-3-030-21571-2_24
24. Polyvyanyy, A., van der Werf, J.M.E.M., Overbeek, S., Brouwers, R.: Information systems modeling: language, verification, and tool support. In: Giorgini, P., Weber, B. (eds.) CAiSE 2019. LNCS, vol. 11483, pp. 194–212. Springer, Cham (2019). https://doi.org/10.1007/978-3-030-21290-2_13
25. Reichert, M.: Process and data: two sides of the same coin? In: Meersman, R., et al. (eds.) OTM 2012. LNCS, vol. 7565, pp. 2–19. Springer, Heidelberg (2012). https://doi.org/10.1007/978-3-642-33606-5_2
26. Rosa-Velardo, F., de Frutos-Escrig, D.: Decidability and complexity of petri nets with unordered data. Theoret. Comput. Sci. **412**(34), 4439–4451 (2011)

Socially-Aware Business Process Redesign

Arik Senderovich[1]([✉]), Joop J. Schippers[2], and Hajo A. Reijers[3]

[1] Faculty of Information, University of Toronto, Toronto, Canada
arik.senderovich@utoronto.ca
[2] School of Economics, Utrecht University, Utrecht, The Netherlands
j.j.schippers@uu.nl
[3] Department of Information and Computing Sciences, Utrecht University,
Utrecht, The Netherlands
h.a.reijers@uu.nl

Abstract. Existing techniques for the redesign of business processes are mostly concerned with optimizing efficiency and productivity, but do not take social considerations into account. In this paper, we represent social business process redesign (SBPR) as a constrained optimization problem (COP). Assuming a workforce of human and computer resources, SBPR considers two types of decisions: (1) how to allocate tasks among this workforce and (2) which skills it should acquire. The latter decision can be used to control for the amount of automation (by setting an upper bound), which may ensure, for example, that disadvantaged workers are included. We discuss scenarios inspired by real-world considerations where the COP representation of SBPR can be used as a decision support tool. Furthermore, we present an extensive computational analysis that demonstrates the applicability of our COP-based solution to large SBPR instances, as well as a detailed analysis of the factors that influence the performance of the approach. Our work shows that it is feasible to incorporate multiple considerations into redesign decision making, while providing meaningful insights into the trade-offs involved.

1 Introduction

Socially responsible organizations look beyond shareholder interests to shape their business practices. By taking into account the interests of a broader group of stakeholders (or even society as a whole), they could become even more successful in attracting and retaining highly skilled, quality employees [1] and may enjoy a higher corporate performance than their traditional competitors [2]. The adoption of social responsibility principles in itself can also be seen as a sign of moral development of humanity, which accelerates as societies climb the stages of human empowerment [3].

In this paper, we aim to contribute to widening the conventional focus of Business Process Management (BPM) such that it can also guide and inspire socially responsible organizations. As such, it is congruent with other attempts to look beyond the traditional scope of the BPM discipline. Notably, *Green BPM* calls for a consideration of the environmental consequences of business process endeavors [4], while *Social BPM* emphasizes a better user engagement to overcome adoption issues [5].

© Springer Nature Switzerland AG 2020
D. Fahland et al. (Eds.): BPM 2020, LNCS 12168, pp. 75–92, 2020.
https://doi.org/10.1007/978-3-030-58666-9_5

Our particular focus is on the development of a technique that supports *process redesign*, one of the prime phases of the BPM life-cycle. This phase is eminently concerned with achieving economic benefits through its focus on efficiency and cost reduction. We introduce a novel dimension to include in redesign initiatives, namely *social responsibility*. That is, the process of decision making and process change will not only be driven by economic motives, but will also comprise social considerations. We shall refer to socially responsible redesign initiatives as Socially-aware Business Process Redesign (SBPR).

Our motivation for SBPR is rooted in a number of dilemmas that executives today face when redesigning business processes. First of all, numerous automation opportunities may exist that could be pursued to improve the efficiency of a business process. But how can automation be balanced with the social objectives of providing meaningful jobs to society and job security to employees? Secondly, executives may realize that a diverse representation of employees is righteous, social, and ethical. What is more difficult to establish is whether they can afford to train such a new workforce and how the inclusion of disadvantaged employees may affect business performance. While the management of a process-centered organization will know its processes, the activities that those processes are composed of, and the skills that are required to execute those activities, it lacks the tools to decide on how to redesign its processes while balancing productivity and social objectives.

In this work, we set to develop a decision support tool that facilitates SBPR. To this end, we formulate an SBPR problem as a constrained optimization problem (COP). The COP considers two types of decisions: (1) decisions that allocate activities to roles (classical redesign decisions) and (2) decisions on training existing or new roles to acquire new skills. The objective of our COP is to maximize efficiency, while limiting a pre-defined social budget. A *social budget* can be seen as a compensation sum, which is for example agreed upon with labor unions when a reorganization happens. The social budget is spent whenever an 'unsocial' decision is made, e.g., automating a task by moving it away from a human resource to a machine-based role.

Against this background, the main contribution of our work is threefold:

1. Formulating the social business process redesign (SBPR) problem as a constrained optimization problem and proving its computational complexity (Sect. 3).
2. Presenting an extensive computational analysis of the COP that shows its relevance to large SBPR instances and provides insights into problem characteristics (Sect. 4).
3. Demonstrating how decision-making with SBPR could take place in real-life settings by exploring the impact of various social policies on the associated COP (Sect. 5).

We will now first provide the background for the redesign dilemmas that we mentioned.

2   Background

In this section, we describe how recent technological developments fundamentally change the workplace. In addition, companies become increasingly aware of their social responsibilities. These elements create dilemmas for executives, which we will describe in more detail here. This section is a stepping stone towards the formulation of the optimization problem in Sect. 3.

2.1 Automation

In the past 15 years, the opinion on what human tasks can be automated has radically changed.[1] Since computers excel at following exact procedures designed by programmers, this was believed to mean that computers can only be made to perform tasks that humans have thoroughly understood and meticulously codified (see e.g. [6]).

Advances in digital technology, in particular in machine learning, are such that a much wider range of tasks are now susceptible to automation [7]. The self-driving car has become a threat to the drivers of taxis, buses, and trucks. Language translation is available to anyone with internet access. Algorithmic approaches have proved more accurate than medical specialists for a range of diagnosis tasks. Journalistic text writing can now be automated to some extent, as can personal financial advice [8]. Robotic Process Automation (RPA) is a technology that can be applied to perform some activities better and faster than human employees can [9]. So, more than ever before, *companies can improve their productivity by automating tasks hitherto performed by human workers.*

2.2 Training

Automation is, however, not the only approach to performance improvement. By investing in human capital, notably on-the-job training, workers can become more productive [10]. Training can also be used to let employees handle new technologies, e.g. AI. A third type of training is concerned with increasing the employability of people. For example, a recent analysis of German data suggests that training can be effective to move people to jobs at lower risk of automation (i.e., *requalification*) [11].

The majority of modern studies of developed economies indicate that automation and computerisation are at this point the main factors shaping the task composition of jobs. In addition, a recent study shows that the growth of non-routine cognitive tasks in Central and Eastern Europe is mostly driven by workforce up-skilling [12]. In the United States, companies like Amazon, Walmart, and AT&T just announced massive training programs for their own workers [13]. These developments show *that companies are actively looking into training as an additional way to improve their productivity.*

2.3 Inclusion

The motives of companies to invest in requalifying their existing workforce can also be explained by other than economic interests. A recent McKinsey report states that thirty-eight percent of the responding executives in a survey, coming from all world regions, cited the desire to "align with our organization's mission and values" as a key reason for initiating training programs [14]. In a similar vein, at the 2017 World Economic Forum in Davos, 80% of CEOs who were investing heavily in artificial intelligence also publicly pledged to retain and retrain existing employees (ibid). This shows that companies do realize that taking care of their workforce is a "social good".

---

[1] Automating a task is not the same as completely automating an *occupation* or *job*. Most human jobs involve a range of tasks.

One aspect of being a socially responsible employer is to extend hiring practices towards "nontraditional talent pools" [14]. The insight is growing that company practices to attain new employees might be biased against anyone on such bases as race, gender, sexual orientation, disability and other physical, cultural, and social attributes. An overarching concern among employers has been that the costs associated with hiring disadvantaged people, notably the disabled, will outweigh the benefits [15]. These perceived concerns with costs include the provision of expensive accommodations, decreased employee productivity, and increased supervisory time. While these are often exaggerated and a full cost-benefit analysis might also want to take into account workers' long time loyalty to the firm and the positive effects on the company's public image, an empirical study that compared a range of factors did find that the productivity (speed and accuracy) of employees with a disability are significantly lower than that of non-disabled employees [16]. In other words, *companies who want to hire responsibly, may need to account for some performance loss.*

In summary, we discussed in this section (1) that automation has become a ubiquitous instrument for productivity enhancement; (2) that training of the workforce is a further approach to productivity enhancement, with additional social benefits; (3) that other socially responsible practices, in particular the hiring of disadvantaged employees, may be costly or even negatively affect performance. This characterizes the dilemma of interest for us: how can organizations that wish to redesign their business processes balance automation, training, and hiring practices when they pursue productivity objectives as well as socially responsible outcomes? To address these questions, we need to formulate the decision problem in more precise terms, which is the focus of the next section.

3   The Problem of Social Business Process Redesign

In this section we formulate the social business process redesign (SBPR) problem as a constrained optimization problem (COP). The COP can then be used as a decision support tool for social redesign. As a running example, we shall consider the automation of the outpatient clinic process described in Fig. 1. Patients arrive at the front desk and register with the clerk. Next, their vital signs and basic lab tests are collected by the nurse. The nurse then sequences the patients according to their level of urgency and sends them to the medical doctor, who examines and treats each patient. After treatment, patients continue for a check-out with the clerk. We aim at redesigning the process such that several activities will be allocated to an automated resource.

In what follows, we start by presenting the input parameters of the SBPR problem, followed by a definition of the decision variables and the COP formulation. Subsequently, we apply the approach to our running example and conclude the section with a discussion on setting SBPR parameters.

3.1   Input Parameters

We start by describing the input parameters to the SBPR problem. Let $\mathcal{A}$ be the set of activities to be (re-)allocated to a set of resource types $\mathcal{R}$. In the as-is model presented in Fig. 1 there are 7 activities performed by 3 resource types, which we denote

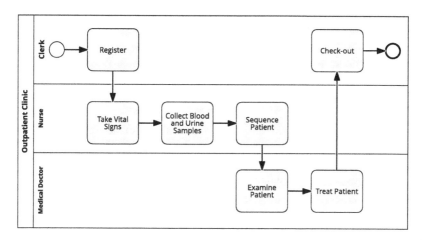

Fig. 1. An outpatient hospital treatment process.

by $C, N, M \in \mathcal{R}$ for Clerk, Nurse, and Medical Doctor, respectively. In our model, a resource type $r \in \mathcal{R}$ can execute an activity $a \in \mathcal{A}$ if and only if the resource type possesses the skill required to execute the activity. Returning to the process in Fig. 1, resource type 'Clerk' must possess the relevant skill 'Clerkship', which is required for executing 'Register' and 'Check-out'. Formally, we denote by $\mathcal{S}$ the set of skills that resource types are required to learn in order to perform the various activities. In our running example, we consider 6 skills, namely 'Clerkship', 'Vital Signs', 'Lab Tests', 'Patient Sequencing', 'Examine', and 'Treat', which we denote by $s_1, \ldots, s_6$, respectively (e.g., s_1 denotes 'Clerkship'). We assume that an activity a requires exactly one skill, which we denote by $s(a) \in \mathcal{S}$. For example, activity 'Take Vital Signs' requires s_2, which is the 'Vital Signs' skills.

We model skill acquisition using a directed acyclic skill graph $\mathcal{G}(\mathcal{S}, E)$ with its vertices being skills and its edges $E \subseteq \mathcal{S} \times \mathcal{S}$ corresponding to precedence relation between skills. For example, an edge $(s_1, s_2) \in E$ implies that one must acquire skill s_1 prior to acquiring skill s_2. By definition, a skill may have more than a single predecessor. Furthermore, we assume that a single universal skill graph exists, meaning that the clerk can learn skills that are currently possessed by nurses. We assume that the skill graph is given to us as an input. Note that our definition of a skill graph is inspired by *career paths graphs* defined in [17]. In practice, one can elicit a skill graph using existing documentation and other types of organisational data.

Figure 2 demonstrates a possible skill graph that corresponds to our running example. Note that the graph in all three figures remains the same, while the skills possessed by the different resource types are different. The as-is set of skills possessed by the resource types is defined using a coloring function $\sigma : \mathcal{R} \to 2^{\mathcal{S}}$ that maps resource types to their current sets of skills. The three different coloring functions presented in Fig. 2 correspond to the current skills of the three resource types in our running example. Note that since $(s_1, s_2) \in E$ we get that $s_1 \in \sigma(N)$, which means that a nurse can

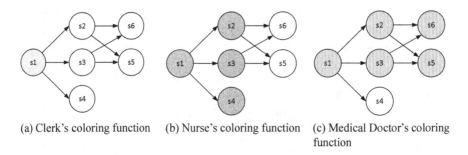

(a) Clerk's coloring function   (b) Nurse's coloring function   (c) Medical Doctor's coloring function

Fig. 2. Skills graph with 3 different coloring functions of the three resource types

also perform clerkship-related activities. The as-is coloring function of every resource is assumed to be known.

3.2   Decision Variables

Having defined the inputs to the problem, we are now ready to introduce the decision variables of SBPR. The first decision that we must make in order to solve the redesign problem is allocating activities to resource types. We denote by $x_{a,r} \in \{0,1\}$ the decision variable that equals to 1 if activity a is assigned to resource type r. This is a 'classical' redesign decision, which must be considered in any BPR initiative. In this work, we assume that an activity must be allocated to exactly one resource type. The cost of allocating activity a to resource type r is denoted by $w_{a,r}$. In practice, these costs may correspond to full-time equivalent (FTE) number of resource type r (per year) that we require to perform activity a. The quantity can be scaled by the wages of the different resource types.

Another decision that we allow in SBPR is for resource types to learn new skills. Formally, we denote by $y_{s,r} \in \{0,1\}$ the decision variable of whether resource type r acquires skill s. Skill acquisition is associated with a learning cost $l_{s,r}$, which corresponds to various expenses related to training, hiring, and programming (in case the new resource type is a computer). In the running example, we may decide that nurses should be up-skilled to perform examinations and treatments. This skill acquisition may be expensive, yet it may pay off overall due to savings in activity allocation costs. The learning costs can also be used to specify that not all skills can be acquired by each resource type. Note that one of the strengths of our SBPR formulation is the symmetric treatment of human resources and computers. Both are treated as resource types that can be allocated to activities and trained to acquire new skills.

3.3   Objective Function and Constraints

To represent the aforementioned trade-offs between the two types of costs (activity allocation and learning), the objective function of our redesign problem minimizes the following expression:

$$\min_{x,y} \sum_{a \in \mathcal{A}} \sum_{r \in \mathcal{R}} w_{a,r} x_{a,r} + \sum_{r \in \mathcal{R}} \sum_{s \in \mathcal{S}} l_{s,r} y_{s,r}. \tag{1}$$

The first term represents the total costs of assigning activities to resource types. The second term corresponds to the total cost of resource type r learning skill s. We assume that each activity must be assigned to exactly one resource type. This corresponds to a set of constraints, $\sum_{r \in \mathcal{R}} x_{a,r} = 1, \forall a \in \mathcal{A}$. Since we aim at *social* redesign, we define the social cost that we incur when assigning activity a to resource type r as $c_{a,r}$ and assume that a social budget b_r is set by the organization for every resource type r. The budget is an upper bound on the total cost of 'unsocial' decisions made with respect to resource type r. For example, if resource A is an RPA tool, allocating many activities to A will result in high usage of the social budget. In practice, the social costs and budgets are based on a company's social policy. Companies that aim at limiting the scale of automation would assign higher costs to automating certain activities, while setting lower social budgets for computerised resources. Furthermore, organizations that target inclusion would assign higher social costs and lower social budgets to advantaged resources, compared to their disadvantaged colleagues. To represent the relation between social costs and social budgets, we add the following set of constraints to our redesign problem:

$$\sum_{a \in \mathcal{A}} c_{a,r} x_{a,r} \le b_r, \forall r \in \mathcal{R}. \tag{2}$$

In addition, for each activity a and resource type r for which $x_{a,r} = 1$, either $s(a)$ is already in the existing skills of the resource type, i.e., $s(a) \in \sigma(r)$, or we train r to obtain skill $s(a)$. Formally, we add the constraints:

$$(x_{a,r} = 1 \wedge s(a) \notin \sigma(r)) \rightarrow (y_{s(a),r} = 1), \forall a \in \mathcal{A}, r \in \mathcal{R}. \tag{3}$$

Lastly, a skill s can be obtained only if all its predecessor skills $s' : (s', s) \in E$ were obtained. This yields the following constraints:

$$y_{s,r} = 1 \rightarrow \forall (s', s) \in E(y_{s',r} = 1 \vee s' \in \sigma(r)), \forall s \in \mathcal{S}, r \in \mathcal{R}. \tag{4}$$

Given the above objective function and the set of constraints, the SBPR problem can be written as the following constrained optimization problem (COP):

$$
\begin{aligned}
\min_{x,y} \quad & \sum_{a \in \mathcal{A}} \sum_{r \in \mathcal{R}} w_{a,r} x_{a,r} + \sum_{r \in \mathcal{R}} \sum_{s \in \mathcal{S}} l_{s,r} y_{s,r} \\
\text{s.t.} \quad & \sum_{a \in \mathcal{A}} c_{a,r} x_{a,r} \le b_r, && \forall r \in \mathcal{R} \\
& \sum_{r \in \mathcal{R}} x_{a,r} = 1 && \forall a \in \mathcal{A} \\
& (x_{a,r} = 1 \wedge s(a) \notin \sigma(r)) \rightarrow (y_{s(a),r} = 1) && \forall a \in \mathcal{A}, r \in \mathcal{R}, \\
& y_{s,r} = 1 \rightarrow \forall (s', s) \in E \ (y_{s',r} = 1 \vee s' \in \sigma(r)) && \forall s \in \mathcal{S}, r \in \mathcal{R}, \\
& x_{a,r} \in \{0,1\}, y_{s,r} \in \{0,1\} && \forall s \in \mathcal{S}, \forall r \in \mathcal{R}, \forall a \in \mathcal{A}.
\end{aligned} \tag{5}
$$

The COP in Eq. (5) can be solved using standard constraint solvers. The following result states the computational complexity of the SBPR.

Theorem 1. *The SBPR problem defined in Eq. (5) is $\mathcal{NP}$-complete.*

Proof. We show by reduction into the *generalized assignment problem* (GAP), which is known to be $\mathcal{NP}$-hard [18]. For a special case of the problem when $\forall s, r(l_{s,r} = 0 \wedge s \in \sigma(r))$, i.e., each learning cost is zero and each resource type has all skills, we get that the objective function comprises only the first expression and the two implication constraints are satisfied. The latter stems from the fact that the first implication

$$(x_{a,r} = 1 \wedge s(a) \notin \sigma(r)) \rightarrow (y_{s(a),r} = 1)$$

always holds, since $s(a) \in \sigma(r)$ for any activity. The second implication has a true right-hand side regardless whether $y_{s,r} = 1$ or not. Removing the two implication constraints and the second objective term turns the problem into an instance of the GAP [18]. Hence, we get that the GAP is a special case of SBPR, which makes SBPR at least as hard as the GAP, namely at least $\mathcal{NP}$-hard. Since the SBPR can be formulated as a mixed-integer programming using the constraint reformulation in [19], we get that SBPR's computational complexity is at most $\mathcal{NP}$-hard. Therefore, the complexity of SBPR is $\mathcal{NP}$-complete.   □

This appears to be a discouraging result for the general formulation of the SBPR. However, our experiments show that for some variants of large problems (1000 activities, 500 resource types, 100 skills) the run time is a matter of seconds when using a constrained solver. In our computational analysis of SBPR (Sect. 4) we pinpoint the conditions that make the problem intractable.

3.4 Applying SBPR to the Running Example

To show how SBPR can be applied in practice, we instantiate the running example in Fig. 1. We use the activities and resources as depicted in the BPMN diagram. Moreover, we consider the skill graph in Fig. 2. Next, we add a new resource type, which is an RPA tool that can be trained to perform clerkship (acquire skill s_1). Therefore, the new resource set is now $\mathcal{R} = \{C, N, M, A\}$ with C, N, M being Clerk, Nurse, and Medical Doctor, as before, and A being the RPA solution. The activities that must be allocated remain as before. We set the parameters of the model as follows:

- The weights $w_{a,r}$ are set such that the RPA tool receives $w_{a,A} = 0$ for each activity (assuming that once the tool is trained and deployed, its costs are 0). The other weights are set according to the yearly salary that the human resources receive. We assume that weights are dependent only on resources (and not the activities) and set $w_{a,C} = 1, w_{a,N} = 3, w_{a,M} = 9, \forall a \in \mathcal{A}$. Note that we do not assume that some of the activities cannot be automated.
- The social cost $c_{a,r}$ is set to be 0 for human resource types and $c_{a,A} = 1$ for the proposed RPA solution.

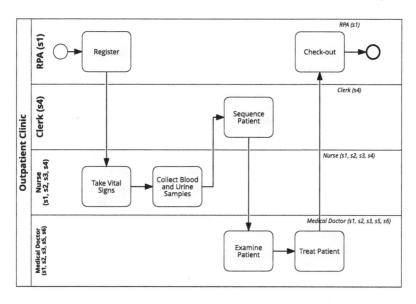

Fig. 3. SBPR result for the outpatient hospital treatment process.

- The social budget is set to be equal to the number of activities for human resources ($b_r = 7$), since we do not wish to limit the number of activities that they can perform. On the other hand, we set $b_r = 2$ for our RPA tool, implying that we allow computerisation of at most two activities.
- The learning costs $l_{s,r}$ are set to be high for human resource types ($l_{s,r} = 10000$), except for the clerk who is allowed to up-skill and learn the sequencing of patients ($l_{C,s_4} = 1$). In alternative scenarios, one may wish to up-skill nurses to perform some of the medical doctor's activities. For the RPA tool, A, we set the learning cost of clerkship and sequencing to be low, $l_{A,s_1}, l_{A,s_4} = 1$, while setting the costs to learn other skills (e.g., 'Treat' and 'Examine') to be high ($l_{A,s} = 10000, \forall s \neq s_1, s_4$).

Figure 3 presents the resulting redesigned process model that stems from a solution of the COP. Note that the acquired skills are embedded into the name of the corresponding resource types for each lane. We observe that the clerk resource type was trained to perform the 'Sequence Patient' activity, while the RPA tool was trained for the 'Register' and 'Check-out' activities. The 'Sequence Patient' activity was not chosen to be computerised, since performing 3 activities is outside the social budget of the RPA. Without a social element in the re-design initiative, the clerks would remain without any activity assignments and their role would become obsolete.

Lastly, note that the as-is solution is also a feasible solution to the problem. However, it is suboptimal, since it yields an objective value of 29, while the optimal value is 27. The difference of 2 units may well be substantial if we consider a unit to be the wage of a full-time equivalent position. Without the social consideration, we could achieve an objective value of 26, which stems from the infeasible solution of automating patient sequencing.

3.5 Setting SBPR Inputs

In this part, we generalize from a specific application of our approach to setting SBPR input parameters in realistic settings. We start by an observation that a key distinction in how we set the various input parameters comes from their origin.

The set of weights, $w_{a,r}$, the learning costs $l_{r,s}$, and the skill graph (including the as-is coloring functions) are *exogenous* to the SBPR problem. These exogenous parameters can be estimated using organizational data. For example, the weights $w_{a,r}$ can be computed as the number of FTEs of resource type $r \in \mathcal{R}$ that were historically required to perform activity $a \in \mathcal{A}$. Similarly, one can assess past costs of training using the total manpower required to acquire a skill s for resource type r. The skill graph and the coloring functions can be derived from employee training guidelines, professional curricula, and other organisational documents.

Conversely, social costs and resource budgets are *endogenous*, since they represent organisational policies concerning social responsibility. Clearly, by setting all social costs $c_{a,r}$ to be 0, an organization would be stating that they do not wish to be socially responsible for the distribution of work. The SBPR would then collapse into a simple task to resource allocation problem. We shall demonstrate the implications of setting different social policies on the corresponding SBPR implementations in Sect. 5, but will perform a computation analysis of the SBPR first.

4   Computational Analysis of SBPR

In this part, we describe a thorough computational analysis, which we conducted using synthetically generated instances of SBPR. To demonstrate the applicability of the COP, we measure the run-time of solving SBPR to optimality as function of various controlled variables (e.g., number of activities, number of skills, and ratio between activities and resources). We shall first describe our experimental design, followed by the main results and insights gathered from the evaluation.

4.1   Experimental Design

In this part, we discuss the experimental setting that we used for our empirical analysis. Below, we provide the methods we used to generate input parameters, control for the computational complexity of the SBPR problem, the controlled and uncontrolled variables, and details on the implementation of our approach.

Generating Input Parameters. In Theorem 1, we proved that the GAP is a special case of SBPR. Hence, for our experiment we used well-established GAP problem instances to create instances of SBPR. Specifically, we generated sets of parameters from previous work that analyzed the GAP's computational complexity [20]:

- Allocation coefficients $w_{a,r}$ were sampled from a discrete uniform distribution $U[15, 25]$,

– Social cost coefficients $c_{a,r}$ were sampled from $U[0, 25]$, thus allowing for some activities to have 0 social cost (i.e., they can be fully automated).

In addition, we created skills sets of sizes $10, 50, 100$, randomly assigning the skills required to perform the activities by setting $s(a), \forall a \in \mathcal{A}$. We created random skill graphs with random initial coloring functions (σ) and sampled learning coefficients ($l_{s,r}$) from uniform distribution $U[5, 25]$.

Controlling for Computational Complexity. In order to control for the hardness of the SBPR (as it depends on the hardness of the GAP), we have used a well-known result that the computational complexity of the GAP depends mainly on the ratio between the left-hand side (LHS) and the right-hand side (RHS) of the constraints in Eq. (2) [20]. Specifically, the LHS expression, $\sum_{a \in \mathcal{A}} c_{a,r} x_{a,r}$, corresponds to the demand for the budget expressed in the RHS. We shall refer to the LHS as the *social pressure* on a resource. One can show that the GAP becomes hard when the mean total social pressure approaches the total social budget [20], i.e., $\frac{1}{|\mathcal{R}|} \sum_{r \in \mathcal{R}} \sum_{a \in \mathcal{A}} c_{a,r} \approx \sum_{r \in \mathcal{R}} b_r$. In GAP experiments, one typically sets the budget b_r using a parameter ρ by setting:

$$b_r = \frac{\rho}{|\mathcal{R}|} \sum_{a \in \mathcal{A}} c_{a,r}. \tag{6}$$

When ρ decreases, the social pressure per resource increases (and with it the computational complexity of the GAP), and vice versa. Therefore, ρ can be thought of as the *inverse* social pressure. In the literature, ρ is often set to be 0.8, which is a value known to be generating hard instances. Similarly, to control for the hardness of the SBPR problem, we vary the values of ρ between 0.5 and 0.99. SBPR problems with $\rho < 0.5$ were often found to be infeasible. So, in the final experiments we used 0.5 as the lowest value for ρ.

Controlled and Uncontrolled Variables. Below, we summarize the values of the controlled variables in the randomly generated SBPR instances:

– The number of activities $|\mathcal{A}|$ varied in $\{100, 250, 500, 750, 1000\}$,
– Activity to resource type ratio $\frac{|\mathcal{A}|}{|\mathcal{R}|}$ was set to be $2, 5, 10$ (with 2 meaning that there are 2 times more activities than resource types),
– The number of skills $|\mathcal{S}|$ was set to be in $\{10, 50, 100\}$,
– Social pressure per resource, ρ, received values in $\{0.5, 0.8, 0.9, 0.95, 0.99\}$.

The uncontrolled variable was the run-time (in seconds), which is defined as the time until a feasible solution was proven to be optimal. The experimental setting led to 675 randomly generated SBPR instances, which served as the data points for the statistical analysis provided in Sect. 4.2.

Implementation Details. We implemented the SBPR problem using Minizinc [21], a constraint modeling language that works with a plethora of solvers. The batch optimization of all instances was conducted using the *pymzn* Minizinc wrapper for Python[2]. The experiments were conducted on a Dell Inspiron Intel machine with i7-8565U CPU @

---

[2] http://paolodragone.com/pymzn/.

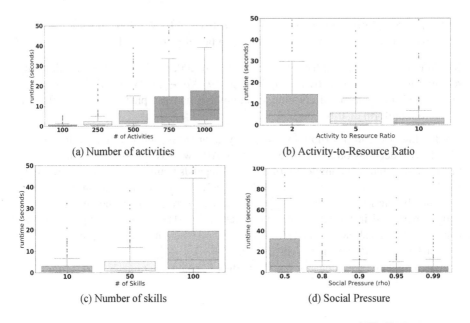

Fig. 4. Run-time as function of the main effects.

1.80 GHZ, 16 GB of RAM, and 512 GB of SSD external memory. The problem definition in Minizinc and the code that generates instances and solves them to optimality are
available online[3].

4.2 Main Results and Empirical Insights

We treat the controlled variables as categorical factors that influence the run-time. We
performed an analysis of variance (ANOVA) for the run-time across the four controlled
factors, namely the number of activities, the activity-to-resource ratio, the number of
skills, and the inverse social pressure. The main effects of the controlled variables and
the interactions between those variables were found to have a statistically significant
influence on the run-time. Below, we provide a graphical exploration of both the main
effects and significant three-way interactions.

The four box plots in Fig. 4 present the run-time as function of the main effects. The
lines crossing the box plots correspond to the median run-time per level and box limits
correspond to the 5th and the 95th percentiles, respectively. According to the main
effects, the run-time grows with the number of activities and the number of skills; it
decreases as the activity-to-resource ratio increases and as the social pressure becomes
smaller (ρ increases).

We turn to present two significant interactions between our controlled variables. We
first examine the three-way interaction between social pressure, activities, and ratios.
Figure 5 presents an interaction plot. The points represent the median values, while the

---

[3] https://bit.ly/2Q2H18R.

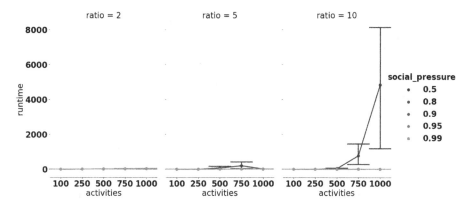

Fig. 5. Three-way interaction: activities, social pressure and ratio.

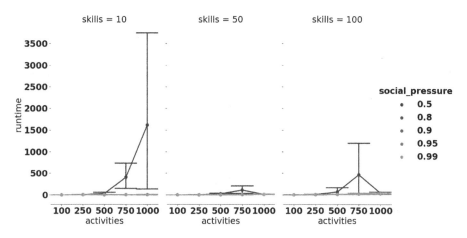

Fig. 6. Three-way interaction: activities, social pressure and skills.

intervals correspond to the upper and lower 5% quantiles, as in Fig. 4. Surprisingly, we observe that the run-time does not increase significantly as function of the number of activities nor the social pressure, as long as the activity-to-resource ratio is 2 or 5. When the ratio becomes 10, we have scarce resources and run-time increases exponentially. Therefore, unlike what we see in the main effect of activity-to-resource ratio, the computational complexity increases exponentially with the ratio when the social pressure is kept high ($\rho = 0.5$).

This phenomenon can be explained by reduced flexibility when assigning jobs to a scarce amount of resource types with limited social budgets. For example, if an RPA tool has met its budget due to high social pressure, having less alternative human resources leaves less options to distribute the remaining social pressure. Conversely, having more resource types available (per activity), turns the problem of finding a different allocation for the activities into an easy one, regardless of the absolute number of activities.

Next, we continue by presenting the three-way interaction between the number of skills, the number of activities, and the social pressure (Fig. 6). We observe that as the numbers of activities grow and with the increase of social pressure, having less skills increases the run-time exponentially. In other words, when less skills are present, resources are limited in learning and re-qualifying. Therefore, when the social pressure and the number of activities per resource increase, we cannot use learning as an alternative solution to allocating activities. This leads to a higher computational complexity, essentially turning the SBPR problem into a GAP.

These observations imply that in settings where the social pressure is high compared to the social budget, the approach is efficient only in with high number of skills and low activity-to-resource ratios. Otherwise, using the COP to find optimal allocation and re-qualification decisions can become impractical for large instances. This may be partly countered by choosing a different level of granularity of skills and resource types when using the COP.

5   SBPR-Based Decision Making

In this part, we present considerations related to social policies of organisations that wish to apply our approach. Specifically, we discuss the question *how different social policies would influence SBPR-based decision making?* To answer the question, we provide three settings in which we demonstrate how different organizational policies impact the resulting SBPR problems and their corresponding redesign solutions.

Across all settings, we shall assume the existence of two special resource types, $m, d \in \mathcal{R}$, that correspond to a computerised resource type m (e.g., an RPA tool) and a disadvantaged employee group d [4]. We shall denote the set of all other resource types by $\mathcal{R}^-$, i.e., $\mathcal{R}^- = \mathcal{R} \setminus \{m, d\}$. We shall assume that $|\mathcal{R}^-| > 0$, which implies that there is at least a single advantaged human resource type. For the analysis, we shall assume that the weights are ordered as follows:

$$w_{a,m} < w_{a,r} < w_{a,d}, \forall r \in \mathcal{R}^-, \forall a \in \mathcal{A},$$

which implies that computerisation is always more economic to implement than to hire humans, and that inclusion is always less beneficial (from a strictly short-term, economic perspective) than hiring advantaged humans.

Setting 1: Limiting Automation. Learning Costs are Negligible. In this setting, we assume that the learning costs are negligible compared to the operational weights $w_{a,r}$, i.e., $l_{s,r} = 0, \forall s, r$. Furthermore, we assume that the decision makers only strive to limit automation. Therefore, they set $c_{a,m} = 1$ and $c_{a,r} = 0, \forall r \neq m$. The automation budget is set to be $|\mathcal{A}| > b_m > 0$ while the budget for human resource types $b_r, \forall r \neq m$ is set large enough to be considered infinite. Since the learning costs are negligible, we can train any resource type to perform any activity. Hence, there is always a feasible solution, regardless of the initial coloring functions (we can always train one of the

---

[4] One can easily generalize the applicability analysis that follows to sets of M automation types and D disadvantaged employee types.

human resource types to perform all activities). Since $w_{a,m} < w_{a,r}, \forall r \neq m$, an optimal solution will always allocate exactly b_m of the activities to resource m. Moreover, it will allocate to m the first b_m activities with respect to an order by $w_{a,r} - w_{a,m}$. Lastly, the solution will assign the rest of the activities to advantaged human resources ($r \neq d$), since $w_{a,d} > w_{a,r}, r \neq d$.

In this setting, the social policy neglects inclusion, because the social cost of assigning an activity to *any* human resource is set to 0.

Setting 2: Still Limiting Only Automation. Learning Costs are Non-negligible. As a policy, the organization is only limiting automation by setting the social costs and budgets as described in Setting 1. Since learning costs are non-zero, it may be beneficial to train disadvantaged resources and assign them to newly learned tasks, compared to learning new skills and assigning activities to advantaged human resource types (e.g., due to a government program)[5]. In this setting, we may achieve inclusion indirectly, depending on the values of exogenous parameters.

Setting 3: Automation and Inclusion via Training. In the last setting, we assume that policy makers aim at both inclusion and automation. By setting social costs and budgets properly, it can be guaranteed that for any values of exogenous parameters that allow training of disadvantaged employees, at least some portion of the activities in $\mathcal{A}$ will be allocated to resource type d. We demonstrate this point by setting the social costs such that $c_{a,d} = 0, c_{a,r} = 1$ and $c_{a,m} > c_{a,r}, \forall r \in \mathcal{R}^-$. This means that assigning disadvantaged resources does not consume any social budget, while assigning advantaged humans and computers to tasks will result in non-negative consumption of the social budget (clearly, higher social costs are assigned to computerized tasks). Furthermore, the social budgets are set to satisfy,

$$b_m + \sum_{r \in \mathcal{R}^-} b_r < \sum_{a \in \mathcal{A}} c_{a,m} + \sum_{r \in \mathcal{R}^-} c_{a,r},$$

implying that at least a single activity must be assigned to d. This shows that the COP can be effectively used to guarantee inclusion via training, while limiting automation.

By providing the three *special cases* of setting social policies, we have shown that one can gain insights into the types of choices that the user of our approach must take before applying it in a real-life setting. Furthermore, we demonstrated how the COP representation of SBPR can be useful in supporting decisions in a model-based fashion, thus replacing the need of speculating regarding potential outcomes of setting social policies. Having said the above, configuring parameter values for the underlying redesign problem (setting costs, budgets and weights) is problem-specific. It will also require additional information that must be based on data coming from the application. Therefore, parameter configuration is out of scope for the current work.

6 Conclusion

This work is the first attempt to methodologically include socially responsible practices into the redesign of business processes. Specifically, we provided three main

---

[5] Counter-intuitively, some automation procedures can be extremely costly, while training disadvantaged employees could be sponsored by the government and thus have negligible costs.

motivations for socially-aware redesign, namely automation, training, and inclusion. To support decision making we formulated social business process redesign (SBPR) as a constrained optimization problem (COP). The resulting COP allows managers to make efficient and socially responsible decisions in complex organisational settings. We have proven that the computational complexity of the SBPR problem is $\mathcal{NP}$-complete and conducted a computational study of our approach to show that it is applicable to large redesign problems. Moreover, we provided a detailed factor analysis of variables that influence the computational complexity of SBPR. Lastly, we demonstrated the impact of organisational policies on the COP and the resulting redesign solutions in real-life scenarios.

Our work paves the way for follow-up research, but has already some practical implications. To start with the latter, we can imagine that our formulation of SBPR can help organizations to make it explicit for themselves what the objective function of their redesign initiative is. We demonstrated that both traditional, efficiency-oriented objectives *and* less traditional objectives, including social or sustainable goals, can be integrated into one and the same redesign initiative. Furthermore, our discussion of the effect of different social policies on SBPR-based decision making (see Sect. 5) shows how tangible support for redesign decisions can be generated. In more concrete terms, we have shown how a range of policies can be mapped onto the characteristics of SBPR to reveal the *nature* of the feasible redesign actions. While the insights that we generated in this way may appear straightforward to the reader, it is our impression that this should be attributed to *hindsight bias* – it is very difficult to foresee these without conducting a quantitative analysis, such as presented in this work.

In future work, we aim at expanding our SBPR model to take into account second-order effects. Specifically, over-qualification may sometimes lead to productivity loss [22], which the current model does not account for. Similarly, the effects of learning decisions may pan out differently for human resources compared to computer resources; productivity growth through AI, for example, may cover multiple years. This would require reformulating SBPR as a dynamic program, taking into account decisions made over a finite time horizon. These decisions must be jointly optimal for every time point, since resource-to-activity and learning decisions at time t influence the corresponding decisions at times $t + 1, t + 2, \ldots$.

Our model also assumes that an activity may be carried out by a single resource, which is rather strict. It is quite likely that hybrid man-machine teams will become more attractive over time to allocate activities to. The immediate influence of multi-resource activities on our model is at least two-fold. Firstly, we would need to relax the single-activity per resource constraint and consider sets of resources as indices of the decision variable. Secondly, the speedup or slowdown effect of having multiple resources performing a task (compared to a single resource) must be taken into account via the objective function by increasing or decreasing the weights of the allocations. While this may incur more 'unsocial decisions', this development may also benefit individual employees who will be freed of heavy, unhealthy, or dangerous parts of their jobs. This multi-faceted impact also underlines how important it is to advance tools that will help managers to make difficult redesign decisions.

Changing the model to accommodate for additional considerations, such as employee safety and time-dependent redesign, is possible given the expressiveness of constrained optimization problems. However, such changes will require encoding additional features into the model, which may result in a further increase of the computational complexity of SBPR.

References

1. Greening, D.W., Turban, D.B.: Corporate social performance as a competitive advantage in attracting a quality workforce. Bus. Soc. **39**(3), 254–280 (2000)
2. Wang, H., Choi, J.: A new look at the corporate social-financial performance relationship: the moderating roles of temporal and interdomain consistency in corporate social performance. J. Manag. **39**(2), 416–441 (2013)
3. Brieger, S.A., Terjesen, S.A., Hechavarría, D.M., Welzel, C.: Prosociality in business: a human empowerment framework. J. Bus. Ethics **159**(2), 361–380 (2019)
4. Couckuyt, D., Van Looy, A.: Green BPM as a business-oriented discipline: a systematic mapping study and research agenda. Sustainability **11**(15), 4200 (2019)
5. Suša Vugec, D., Tomičić-Pupek, K., Vukšić, V.B.: Social business process management in practice: overcoming the limitations of the traditional business process management. Int. J. Eng. Bus. Manag. **10**, 1847979017750927 (2018)
6. Autor, D.H., Levy, F., Murnane, R.J.: The skill content of recent technological change: an empirical exploration. Q. J. Econ. **118**(4), 1279–1333 (2003)
7. Brynjolfsson, E., McAfee, A.: The Second Machine Age: Work, Progress, and Prosperity in a Time of Brilliant Technologies. WW Norton & Company, New York (2014)
8. Frey, C.B., Osborne, M.A.: The future of employment: how susceptible are jobs to computerisation? Technol. Forecast. Soc. Change **114**, 254–280 (2017)
9. Syed, R., et al.: Robotic process automation: contemporary themes and challenges. Comput. Ind. **115**, 103162 (2020)
10. Becker, G.S.: Human Capital: A Theoretical and Empirical Analysis, with Special Reference to Education, 3rd edn. University of Chicago Press, Chicago (1993)
11. Nedelkoska, L., Quintini, G.: Automation, skills use and training. OECD Social, Employment and Migration Working Papers, No. 202 (2018)
12. Hardy, W., Keister, R., Lewandowski, P.: Technology or upskilling. Trends Task (2016, working paper)
13. Casselman, B., Satariano, A.: Amazon's Latest Experiment: Retraining its Work Force. The New York Times, 11 July 2019 (2019)
14. Illanes, P., Lund, S., Mourshed, M., Rutherford, S., Tyreman, M.: Retraining and reskilling workers in the age of automation. McKinsey Glob. Inst. **29** (2018)
15. Hernandez, B., Keys, C., Balcazar, F.: Employer attitudes toward workers with disabilities and their ADA employment rights: a literature review. J. Rehabil. **66**(4), 4–16 (2000)
16. Graffam, J., Smith, K., Shinkfield, A., Polzin, U.: Employer benefits and costs of employing a person with a disability. J. Vocat. Rehab. **17**(4), 251–263 (2002)
17. Shirani, A.: Upskilling and retraining in data analytics: a skill-adjacency analysis for career paths. Issues Inf. Syst. **20**(4), 65–74 (2019)
18. Fisher, M.L., Jaikumar, R., Van Wassenhove, L.N.: A multiplier adjustment method for the generalized assignment problem. Manag. Sci. **32**(9), 1095–1103 (1986)
19. Plastria, F.: Formulating logical implications in combinatorial optimisation. Eur. J. Oper. Res. **140**(2), 338–353 (2002)

20. Cattrysse, D.G., Salomon, M., Van Wassenhove, L.N.: A set partitioning heuristic for the generalized assignment problem. Eur. J. Oper. Res. **72**(1), 167–174 (1994)
21. Nethercote, N., Stuckey, P.J., Becket, R., Brand, S., Duck, G.J., Tack, G.: MiniZinc: towards a standard CP modelling language. In: Bessière, C. (ed.) CP 2007. LNCS, vol. 4741, pp. 529–543. Springer, Heidelberg (2007). https://doi.org/10.1007/978-3-540-74970-7_38
22. Tsang, M.C., Rumberger, R.W., Levin, H.M.: The impact of surplus schooling on worker productivity. Ind. Relat.: J. Econ. Soc. **30**(2), 209–228 (1991)

Incentive Alignment of Business Processes

Tobias Heindel$^{(\boxtimes)}$ and Ingo Weber

Chair of Software and Business Engineering, Technische Universitaet Berlin, Berlin,
Germany
{heindel,ingo.weber}@tu-berlin.de

Abstract. Many definitions of business processes refer to business goals,
value creation, profits, etc. Nevertheless, the focus of formal methods
research on business processes lies on the correctness of the execution
semantics of models w.r.t. properties like deadlock freedom, liveness, or
completion guarantees. However, the question of whether participants
are *interested* in working towards completion – or in participating in the
process at all – has not been addressed as of yet.

In this work, we investigate whether inter-organizational business processes give participants incentives for achieving the business goals: in
short, whether *incentives are aligned* within the process. In particular,
fair behavior should pay off and efficient completion of tasks should be
rewarded. We propose a game-theoretic approach that relies on algorithms for solving stochastic games from the machine learning community. We describe a method for checking incentive alignment of process
models with utility annotations for tasks, which can be used for *a priori*
analysis of inter-organizational business processes. Last but not least, we
show that the soundness property is a special case of incentive alignment.

Keywords: Inter-organizational business processes · Incentive
alignment · Collaboration · Choreography

1 Introduction

Many definitions of what a business process is refer to business goals [29] or
value creation [7], but whether process participants are actually incentivized to
contribute to a process has not been addressed as yet. For *intra*-organizational
processes, this question is less relevant; motivation to contribute is often based
on loyalty, bonuses if the organization performs well, or simply that tasks in a
process are part of one's job. Instead, economic modeling of intra-organizational
processes often focuses on cost, e.g. in activity-based costing [12], which can be
assessed using model checking tools [9] or simulation [5].

For *inter*-organizational business processes, such indirect motivation cannot
be assumed. A prime example of misaligned incentives was the $2.5B write-off
in Cisco's supply chain in April 2001 [20]: success of the overall supply chain
was grossly misaligned with the incentives of individual participants. (This happened despite the availability of several game theoretic approaches for analyzing

© Springer Nature Switzerland AG 2020
D. Fahland et al. (Eds.): BPM 2020, LNCS 12168, pp. 93–110, 2020.
https://doi.org/10.1007/978-3-030-58666-9_6

incentive structures for the case of supply chains [4].) Furthermore, modeling incentives accurately is actually possible in cross-organizational processes, e.g., based on contracts and agreed-upon prices. With the advent of *blockchain* technology [30], it is possible to execute cross-organizational business processes or choreographies as smart contracts [18,28]. The blockchain serves as a neutral, participant-independent computational infrastructure, and as such enables collaboration across organizations even in situations characterized by a *lack of trust* between participants [28]. However, as there is no central role for oversight, it is important that incentives are properly designed in such situations, e.g., to avoid unintended –possibly devastating– results, like those encountered by Cisco. In fact, a main goal of the Ethereum blockchain is, according to its founder Vitalik Buterin, to create "a better world by aligning incentives"[1].

In this paper, we present a framework for incentive alignment of inter-organizational business processes based on game theory. We consider BPMN models with suitable annotation concerning the utility[2] of activities, very much in the spirit of activity-based costing (ABC) [12, Chapter 5]. In short, fair behavior should pay off and participants should be rewarded for efficient completion of process instances. In more detail, we shall consider BPMN models as stochastic games [24] and formalize incentive alignment as "good" equilibria of the resulting game. Which equilibria are the desirable ones depends on the business goals w.r.t. which we want align incentives. In the present paper, we focus on *proper completion* and *liveness* of activities. Interestingly, the soundness property [2] will be rediscovered as the special case of incentive alignment within a single organization that rewards completion of every activity.

The overall contribution of the paper is a framework for incentive alignment of business process models, particularly in inter-organizational settings. Our approach is based on game theory and inspired by advances on the solution of stochastic games from the machine learning community, which has developed algorithms for the practical computation of Nash [22] and correlated equilibria [16,17]. The framework focuses on checking incentive alignment as an *a priori* analysis of business processes specified as BPMN models with activity-based utility annotations. Specifically, we:

1. describe a principled method for translating BPMN-models with activity-based costs to stochastic games [24]
2. propose a notion of incentive alignment that we prove to be a conservative extension of Van der Aalst's soundness property [2],
3. illustrate the approach with a simplified order-to-cash (O2C) process.

We pick up the idea of incentive alignment for supply chains [4] and set out to apply it in the realm of inter-organizational business processes. From a technical point of view, we are interested in extending the model checking tools for cost analysis [9] for BPMN process models to proper collaborations, which we model as stochastic games [24]. This is analogous to how the model checker

---

[1] https://www.ikiguide.com/ethereum/, accessed 8-3-2020.
[2] We shall use utility functions in the sense of von Neumann and Morgenstern [19].

PRISM has been extended from Markov decision processes to games [14]. We keep the connection with established concepts from the business process management community by showing that incentive alignment is a conservative extension of the soundness property (see Theorem 1). Our approach hinges on algorithms [16,22] for solving the underlying stochastic games of BPMN process models, which are sufficient for checking incentive alignment.

The remainder of the paper is structured as follows. We introduce concepts and notations in Sect. 2. On this basis, we formulate two versions of incentive alignment in Sect. 3. Finally, we draw conclusions in Sect. 4. The proof of the main theorem can be found in the extended version [8].

2   Game Theoretic Concepts and the Petri Net Tool Chest

We now introduce the prerequisite concepts for stochastic games [24] and elementary net systems [23]. The main benefit of using a game theoretic approach is a short list of candidate definitions of equilibrium, which make precise the idea of a "good strategy" for rational actors that compete as players of a game. We shall require the following two properties of an equilibrium: (1) no player can benefit from unilateral deviation from the "agreed" strategy and (2) players have the possibility to base their moves on information from a single (trusted) mediator. The specific instance that we shall use are *correlated equilibria* [3,10] as studied by Solan and Vieille [25].[3] We take ample space to review the latter two concepts, followed by a short summary of the background on Petri nets.

We use the following basic concepts and notation. The cardinality and the powerset of a set M are denoted by $|M|$ and $\wp M$, respectively. The set of real numbers is denoted by $\mathbb{R}$ and $[0,1] \subseteq \mathbb{R}$ is the unit interval. A probability distribution over a finite or countably infinite set M is a function $p \colon M \to [0,1]$ whose values are non-negative and sum up to 1, in symbols $\sum_{m \in M} p(m) = 1$. The set of all probability distributions over a set M is denoted by $\Delta(M)$.

2.1   Stochastic Games, Strategies, Equilibria

We proceed by reviewing core concepts and central results for stochastic games [24], introducing notation alongside; we shall use examples to illustrate the most important concepts. The presentation is intended to be self-contained such that no additional references should be necessary. However, the interested reader might want to consult standard references or additional material, e.g., textbooks [15,21], handbook articles [11], and surveys [26]. We start with the central notion.

Definition 1 (Stochastic game). *A stochastic game G is a quintuple $G = \langle N, S, A, q, u \rangle$ that consists of*

---

[3] Nash equilibria are a special case, which however have drawbacks that motivate Aumann's work on the more general correlated equilibria [3,10].

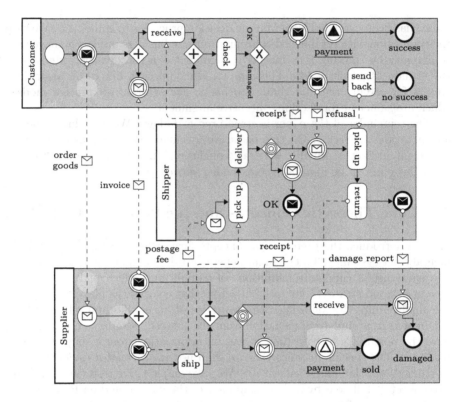

Fig. 1. A simplified order-to-cash process

- *a finite set of* players $N = \{1, \ldots, |N|\}$ *(ranged over by* i, j, i_n, *etc.);*
- *a finite set of* states S *(ranged over by* s, s', s_n, *etc.);*
- *a finite, non-empty set of* action profiles $A = \prod_{i=1}^{|N|} A^i$ *(ranged over by* a, a_n, *etc.), which is the Cartesian product of a player-indexed family* $\{A^i\}_{i \in N}$ *of sets* A^i, *each of which contains the* actions *of the respective player (ranged over by* a^i, a_n^i, *etc.);*
- *a non-empty set of* available actions $A^i(s) \subseteq A^i$, *for each state* $s \in S$ *and player* i;
- *probability distributions* $q(\cdot \mid s, a) \in \Delta(S)$, *for each state* $s \in S$ *and every action profile* $a \in A$, *which map each state* $s' \in S$ *to* $q(s' \mid s, a)$, *the transition probability from state* s *to state* s' *under the action profile* a; *and*
- *the payoff vectors* $u(s, a) = \langle u^1(s, a), \ldots, u^{|N|}(s, a) \rangle$, *for each state* $s \in S$ *and every action profile* $a = \langle a^1, \ldots, a^{|N|} \rangle \in A$.

Note that players always have some action(s) available, possibly just a dedicated idle action, see e.g. [13].

The BPMN model of Fig. 1 can be understood as a stochastic game played by a shipper, a customer, and a supplier. Abstracting from data, precise timings, and similar semantic aspects, a state of the game is a state of an instance of the process, which is represented as a token marking of the BPMN model. The actions of each player are the activities and events in the respective pool, e.g., the *ship* task, which *Supplier* performs after receiving an order from the *Customer* and payment of the postage fee to *Shipper*. Action profiles are combinations of actions that can (or must) be executed concurrently. For example, sending the order and receiving the order after the start of the collaboration may be performed synchronously (e.g., via telephone). The available actions of a player in a given state are the tasks or events in the respective pool that can be executed or happen next – plus the idle action. The transition probabilities for available actions in this BPMN process are all 1, such that if players choose to execute certain tasks next, they will be able to do so if the chosen activities are actually available actions. As a consequence, all other transition probabilities are 0.

One important piece of information that we have to add to a BPMN model via annotations is the utility of tasks and events. In analogy to the ABC method, which attributes a cost to every task, we shall assume that each task has a certain utility for every role – and be it just zero. Utility annotations are the basis for the subsequent analysis of incentive alignment, vastly generalizing cost minimization. Note that, in general, it is non-trivial to chose utility functions, especially in competitive situations. However, the O2C process comes with natural candidates for utilities, e.g., postage fees can be looked up from one's favorite carrier, the cost for gas, maintenance, and personnel for shipping is fairly predictable, and finally there is the profit for selling a good.

A single instance of the O2C process exhibits the phenomenon that *Customer* has no incentive to pay. However, we want to stress that – very much for the same reason – *Shipper* would not have any good reason to perform delivery, once the postage fee is paid. Thus, besides the single instance scenario, we shall consider an unbounded number of repetitions of the process, but only one active process instance at each point in time.[4] In the repeating variant, the rational reason for the shipper to deliver (and return damaged goods) is expected revenue from future process instances.

One distinguishing feature of the O2C collaboration is that participants do not have to make any joint decisions. Let us illustrate the point with another example. Alice and Bob are co-founders of a company, which is running so smoothly that it suffices when, any day of the week, only one of them is going to work.

Alice suggests that their secretary Mrs. Medina could help them out by rolling a 10-sided die each morning and notifying them about who is going to go to work that day, dependent on whether the outcome is smaller or larger than six. This elaborate process (as shown in Fig. 2), lets Bob work 60% and Alice 40% of the days, respectively. Alice's reasoning behind it is the observation that Alice is 50% more efficient than Bob when it comes to generating revenue, as indicated by the amount of $ signs in the process.

In game theoretic terminology, Mrs. Medina is taking the role of a common source of randomness that is independent of the state of the game and does not

---

[4] We leave the very interesting situation of interleaved execution of several process instances for future work.

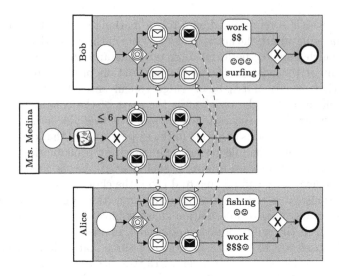

Fig. 2. The *To work or not to work?* collaboration

need to observe the actions of the players. The specific formal notion that we shall use is that of an *autonomous correlation device* [25, Definition 2.1].

Definition 2 (Autonomous correlation device). *An* autonomous correlation device *is a family of pairs* $\mathcal{D} = \left\{ \langle \{M_n^i\}_{i \in N}, d_n \rangle \right\}_{n \in \mathbb{N}}$ *(that is indexed over natural numbers $n \in \mathbb{N}$) each of which consists of*

- *a family of finite sets of* signals M_n^i, *(additionally) indexed over players; and*
- *a function d_n that maps lists of signal vectors $\langle \underline{x}_1, \ldots, \underline{x}_{n-1} \rangle \in \prod_{k=1}^{n-1} \mathcal{M}_k$ to probability distributions $d_n \langle \underline{x}_1, \ldots, \underline{x}_{n-1} \rangle \in \Delta(\mathcal{M}_n)$ over the Cartesian product $\mathcal{M}_n = \prod_{i=1}^{|N|} M_n^i$ of all signal sets M_n^i.*

We shall refer to operators of autonomous correlation devices as *mediators*, which guide the actions of players during the game.

Each correlation device for a game induces an extended game, which proceeds in *stages*. In general, given a game and an autonomous correlation device, the n-th stage begins with the mediator drawing a signal vector $\underline{x}_n \in \mathcal{M}_n = \prod_{i=1}^{|N|} M_n^i$ according to the device distribution $d_n \langle \underline{x}_1, \ldots, \underline{x}_{n-1} \rangle$ – e.g., Mrs. Medina rolling the die – and sending the components to the respective players – the sending of messages to Bob and Alice (in one order or the other). Then, each player i chooses an available action a_n^i. This choice can be based on the respective component $\underline{x}_n^i$ of the signal vector $\underline{x}_n \in \mathcal{M}_n$, information about previous states s_k of the game G, and moves a_k^j of (other) players from the history.[5] After all players made their choice, we obtain an action profile $a_n = \langle a_n^1, \ldots, a_n^{|N|} \rangle$.

---

[5] In the present paper, we only consider games of perfect information, which is suitable for business processes in a single organization or which are monitored on a blockchain.

While playing the extended game described above, each player makes observations about the state and the actions of players; the role of the mediator is special insofar as it does not need and is also not expected to observe the run of the game. The "local" observations of each player are the basis of their strategies.

Definition 3 (Observation, strategy, strategy profile). *An* observation at stage n *by player* i *is a tuple* $h = \langle s_1, \underline{x}_1^i, a_1, \ldots, s_{n-1}, \underline{x}_{n-1}^i, a_{n-1}, s_n, \underline{x}_n^i \rangle$ *with*

- *one state* s_k, *signal* $\underline{x}_k^i$, *and action profile* a_k, *for each number* $k < n$,
- *the* current *state* s_n, *also denoted by* s_h, *and*
- *the* current *signal* $\underline{x}_n^i$.

The set of all observations is denoted by $H_n^i(\mathcal{D})$. *The union* $H^i(\mathcal{D}) = \bigcup_{n \in \mathbb{N}} H_n^i(\mathcal{D})$ *of observations at any stage is the set of* observations *of player* i. *A* strategy *is a map* $\sigma^i \colon H^i(\mathcal{D}) \to \Delta(A^i)$ *from observations to probability distributions over actions that are available at the current state of histories, i.e.,* $\sigma_h^i(a^i) = 0$ *if* $a^i \notin A^i(s_h)$, *for all histories* $h \in H^i(\mathcal{D})$. *A* strategy profile *is a player-indexed family of strategies* $\{\sigma^i\}_{i \in N}$.

Thus, each of the players observes the history of other players, including the possibility of punishing other players for not heeding the advice of the mediator. This is possible since signals might give (indirect) information concerning the (mis-)behavior of players in the past, as remarked by Solan and Vieille [25, p. 370]: by revealing information about proposed actions of previous rounds, players can check for themselves whether some player has ignored some signal of the mediator.

The data of a game, a correlation device, and a strategy profile induce probabilities for finite plays of the game, which in turn determine the expected utility of playing the strategy. Formally, an autonomous correlation device and a strategy profile with strategies for every player yield a probabilistic trajectory of a sequence of "global" states, signal vectors of all players, and complete action profiles, dubbed *history*. The formal details are as follows.

Definition 4 (History and its probability). *A* history at stage n *is a tuple* $h = \langle s_1, \underline{x}_1, a_1, \ldots, s_{n-1}, \underline{x}_{n-1}, a_{n-1}, s_n, \underline{x}_n \rangle$ *that consists of*

- *one state* s_k, *signal vector* $\underline{x}_k$, *and action profile* a_k, *for each number* $k < n$,
- *the* current *state* s_n, *often denoted by* s_h, *and*
- *the* current *signal vector* $\underline{x}_n$.

The set of all histories at state n *is denoted by* $H_n(\mathcal{D})$. *The union* $H(\mathcal{D}) = \bigcup_{n \in \mathbb{N}} H_n(\mathcal{D})$ *of histories at arbitrary stages is the set of* finite histories. *The probability of a finite history* $h = \langle s_1, \underline{x}_1, a_1, \ldots, s_{n-1}, \underline{x}_{n-1}, a_{n-1}, s_n, \underline{x}_n \rangle$ *in the context of a correlation device* $\mathcal{D}$, *an initial state* s, *and a strategy profile* σ *is defined as follows, by recursion over the length of histories.*

$$n = 1 \colon \mathbf{P}_{\mathcal{D}, s, \sigma}(\langle s_1, \underline{x}_1 \rangle) = \begin{cases} 0 & \text{if } s \neq s_1 \\ d_1 \langle \rangle (\underline{x}_1) & \text{otherwise} \end{cases}$$

$n > 1$: $\mathbf{P}_{\mathcal{D},s,\sigma}(\langle \hbar, a_{n-1}, s_n, \underline{x}_n \rangle) = \underbrace{p_{\langle \hbar \rangle}(a_{n-1})}_{\prod_{i \in N} \sigma^i_{\langle \hbar \rangle}(a^i_{n-1})} q(s_n \mid s_{n-1}, a_{n-1}) \underbrace{p_{d_{n-1}}(\underline{x}_n)}_{d_{n-1}\langle \underline{x}_1, \ldots, \underline{x}_{n-1} \rangle(\underline{x}_n)}$

Again, note that the autonomous correlation device does not "inspect" the states of a history, in the sense that the distributions over signal vectors d_n are *not* parameterized over *states* from the history, but only over previously drawn *signal vectors* – whence the name.

Definition 5 (Mean expected payoff). *The* mean expected payoff *of player i for stage n is* $\bar{\gamma}^i_n(\mathcal{D}, s, \sigma) = \sum_{h \in H_{n+1}(\mathcal{D})} \frac{\mathbf{P}_{\mathcal{D},s,\sigma}(h)}{n} \sum_{k=1}^{n} u^i(s_k, a_k)$ *where $h = \langle s_1, \underline{x}_1, a_1, \ldots a_n, s_{n+1}, \underline{x}_{n+1} \rangle$.*

At this point, we can address the question of what a good strategy profile is and fill in all the details of the idea that an equilibrium is a strategy profile that does not give players any good reason to deviate unilaterally. We shall tip our hats to game theory and use the notation (π^i, σ^{-i}) for the strategy profile which is obtained by "overwriting" the single strategy σ^i of player i with a strategy π^i (which might, but does not have to be different); thus, the expression '(π^i, σ^{-i})' denotes the unique strategy subject to equations $(\pi^i, \sigma^{-i})^i = \pi^i$ and $(\pi^i, \sigma^{-i})^j = \sigma^j$ (for $i \neq j$).

Definition 6 (Autonomous correlated ε-equilibrium). *Given a positive real $\varepsilon > 0$, an* autonomous correlated ε-equilibrium *is a pair $\langle \mathcal{D}, \sigma^* \rangle$, which consists of an autonomous correlation device $\mathcal{D}$ and a strategy profile σ^* for which there exists a natural number $n_0 \in \mathbb{N}$ such that for any alternative strategy σ^i of any player i, the following inequality holds, for all $n \geq n_0$ and all states $s \in S$.*

$$\bar{\gamma}^i_n(\mathcal{D}, s, \sigma^*) \geq \bar{\gamma}^i_n\left(\mathcal{D}, s, (\sigma^i, \sigma^{*-i})\right) - \varepsilon \tag{1}$$

Thus, a strategy is an autonomous correlated ε-equilibrium if the benefits that one might reap in the long run by unilateral deviation from the strategy are negligible as ε can be arbitrarily small. In fact, other players will have ways to punish deviation from the equilibrium [25, § 3.2].

2.2   Petri Nets and Their Operational Semantics

We shall use the definitions concerning Petri nets that have become established in the area of business processes management [2].

Definition 7 (Petri net, marking, and marked Petri net). *A* Petri net *is a triple $\mathcal{N} = (P, T, F)$ that consists of*

- *a finite set of* places *P;*
- *a finite set of* transitions *T that is disjoint from places, i.e., $T \cap P = \varnothing$; and*
- *a finite set of* arcs *$F \subseteq (P \times T) \cup (T \times P)$ (a.k.a. the* flow relation*).*

An input place *(resp.* output place*) of a transition* $t \in T$ *is a place* $p \in P$ *s.t.* $(p, t) \in F$ *(resp.* $(t, p) \in F$*). The* pre-set $^{\bullet}t$ *(resp.* post-set $t^{\bullet}$*) of a transition* $t \in T$ *is the set of all input places (resp. output places), i.e.,*

$$^{\bullet}t = \{p \in P \mid p \text{ is an input place of } t\} \quad t^{\bullet} = \{p \in P \mid p \text{ is an output place of } t\}.$$

A marking *of a Petri net* $\mathcal{N}$ *is a multiset of places* m*, i.e., a function* $m : P \to \mathbb{N}$ *that assigns to each place* $p \in P$ *a non-negative integer* $m(p) \geq 0$*. A* marked Petri net *is a tuple* $\mathcal{N} = (P, T, F, m_0)$ *whose first three components* (P, T, F) *are a Petri net and whose last component* m_0 *is the* initial marking*, which is a marking of the latter Petri net.*

One essential feature of Petri nets is the ability to execute several transitions concurrently – possibly several occurrences of one and the same transition. However, we shall only encounter situations in which a set of transitions fires. To avoid proliferation of terminology, we shall use the general term *step*. We fix a Petri net $\mathcal{N} = (P, T, F)$ for the remainder of the section.

Definition 8 (Step, step transition, reachable marking). *A* step *in the net* $\mathcal{N}$ *is a set of transitions* $\underline{t} \subseteq T$*. The* transition relation *of a step* $\underline{t} \subseteq T$ *relates a marking* m *to another marking* m'*, in symbols* $m \; [\underline{t}\rangle \; m'$*, if the following two conditions are satisfied, for every place* $p \in P$*.*

1. $m(p) \geq |\{t \in \underline{t} \mid p \in {}^{\bullet}t\}|$
2. $m'(p) = m(p) - |\{t \in \underline{t} \mid p \in {}^{\bullet}t\}| + |\{t \in \underline{t} \mid p \in t^{\bullet}\}|$

We write $m \; [\rangle \; m'$ *if* $m \; [\underline{t}\rangle \; m'$ *holds for some step* $\underline{t}$ *and denote the reflexive transitive closure of the relation* $[\rangle$ *by* $[\rangle^{*}$*. A marking* m' *is* reachable *in a marked Petri net* $\mathcal{N} = (P, T, F, m_0)$ *if* $m_0 \; [\rangle^{*} \; m'$ *holds, in the net* (P, T, F)*.*

For a transition $t \in T$, we write $m \; [t\rangle \; m'$ instead of $m \; [\{t\}\rangle \; m'$. Thus the empty step is always fireable, i.e., for each marking m, we have an "idle" step $m \; [\varnothing\rangle \; m$.

Recall that a marked Petri net $\mathcal{N} = (P, T, F, m_0)$ is *safe* if all reachable markings m' have at most one token in any place, i.e., if they satisfy $m'(p) \leq 1$, for all $p \in P$. Thus, a marking m corresponds to a set $\hat{m} \subseteq P$ satisfying $p \in \hat{m}$ iff $m(p) > 0$; for convenience, we shall identity a safe marking m with its set of places $\hat{m}$. The main focus will be on Petri nets that are safe and *extended free choice*, i.e., if the pre-sets of two transitions have a place in common, the pre-sets coincide. Also, recall that the *conflict relation*, denoted by $\#$, relates two transitions if their pre-sets intersect, i.e., $t \# t'$ if $^{\bullet}t \cap {}^{\bullet}t' \neq \varnothing$, for $t, t' \in T$; for extended free choice nets, the conflict relation is an equivalence relation. We call a marked Petri net an *elementary net system* [23] if all pre-sets and post-sets of transitions are non-empty and every place is input or output to some transition. The latter encompass the following class of Petri nets that is highly relevant to formal methods research of business processes.

Definition 9 (Workflow net (WF-net)). *A Petri net* $\mathcal{N} = (P, T, F)$ *is a* Workflow net *or* WF-net*, for short, if*

1. *there are unique places $i, o \in P$ such that i is not an output place of any transition and o is not an input place of any transition and*
2. *if we add a new transition t^* and the two arcs $(o, t^*), (t^*, i)$, the resulting directed graph $(P \cup T \cup \{t^*\}, F \cup \{(o, t^*), (t^*, i)\})$ is strongly connected.*

Finally, let us recall the soundness property [1]. A Workflow net is

sound if and only if the following three requirements are satisfied: (1) *option to complete*: for each case it is always still possible to reach the state which just marks place *end*, (2) *proper completion*: if place *end* is marked all other places are empty for a given case, and (3) *no dead transitions*: it should be possible to execute an arbitrary activity by following the appropriate route

where *end* is place o, *each case* means every marking reachable from the initial marking $\{i\}$, *state* means marking, *marked* means marked by a reachable marking, *activity* means *transition*, and *following the appropriate route* means after executing the appropriate firing sequence.

3   Incentive Alignment

Soundness of business processes in the sense of Van der Aalst [2] implies termination if transitions are governed by a strongly fair scheduler [1]; indeed, such a scheduler fits the intra-organizational setting. However, as discussed for the O2C process model, unfair scheduling practices could arise in the inter-organizational setting if undesired behavior yields higher profits. We consider incentive alignment to rule out scenarios that lure actors into counterproductive behavior. We even can check whether all activities in a given BPMN model with utility annotations are relevant and profitable.

As BPMN models have established Petri net semantics [6], it suffices to consider the latter for the game theoretic aspects of incentive alignment. As a preparatory step, we extend Petri nets with utility functions as pioneered by von Neumann and Morgenstern [19]. Then we describe two ways to associate a stochastic game to a Petri net with transition-based utilities: the first game retains the state space and the principal design choice concerns transition probabilities; the second game is the restarting version of the first game. Finally, we define incentive alignment in formally based on stochastic games and show that the soundness property for Workflows nets [2] can be "rediscovered" as a special case of incentive alignment; in other words, the original meaning of soundness is conserved, and thus we extend soundness conservatively in our framework for incentive alignment.

3.1   Petri Nets with Utility and Role Annotations

We assume that costs (respectively profits) are incurred (resp. gained) per task and that, in particular, utility functions do not depend on the state. Note that the game theoretic results do not require this assumption; however, this assumption does not only avoid clutter, but also retains the spirit of the ABC method [12] and is in line with the work of Herbert and Sharp [9].

Definition 10 (Petri net with transition payoffs and roles). *For a set of roles* $\mathcal{R}$, *a Petri net with transition payoffs and roles is a triple* $(\mathcal{N}, u, \rho)$ *where*

- $\mathcal{N} = (P, T, F, m_0)$ *is a marked Petri net with initial marking* m_0,
- $u \colon \mathcal{R} \to T \to \mathbb{R}$ *is a utility function, and*
- $\rho \colon T \rightharpoonup \mathcal{R}$ *is a partial function, assigning at most one role to each transition.*

The utility $u^i(\underline{t})$ *of a step* $\underline{t} \subseteq T$ *is the sum of the utilities of its elements, i.e.,* $u^i(\underline{t}) = \sum_{t \in \underline{t}} u^i(t)$, *for each role* $i \in \mathcal{R}$.

As a consequence of the definition, the idle step has zero utility. We have included the possibility that some of the transitions are .not controlled by any of the roles (of a BPMN model) by using a partial function from transitions to roles; we take a leaf out of the game theorist's book and attribute the missing role to *nature*.

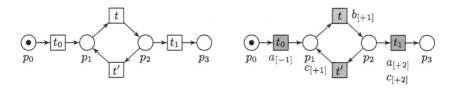

Fig. 3. Extending Petri nets with role and utility annotations

Figure 3 displays a Petri net on the left. The names of the places $p_1, \ldots, p_4$ will be convenient later. In the same figure on the right, we have added annotations that carry information concerning roles, costs, and profits in the form of lists of role-utility pairs next to transitions. E.g., the transition t_0 is assigned to role a and firing t_0 results in utility -1 for a, i.e., one unit of cost. The first role in each list denotes responsibility for the transition and we have omitted entries with zero utility. We also have colored transitions with the same color as the role assigned to it. If we play the token game for Petri nets as usual, each firing sequence gives cumulative utilities for each one of the roles; each transition gives an immediate reward. These rewards will influence the choice between actions that are performed by roles as made precise in the next subsection.

There are natural translations from BPMN models with payoff annotations for activities to Petri nets with payoffs and roles (relative to any of the established Petri net semantics for models in BPMN [6]). If pools are used, we take one role per pool and each task is assigned to its enclosing pool; for pairs of sending and receiving tasks or events, the sender is responsible for the transition to be taken. The only subtle point concerns the role of nature. When should we blame nature for the data on which choices are based? The answer depends on the application at hand. For instance, let us consider the O2C model of Fig. 1: whether or not the goods will be damaged during shipment is only partially within the control of the shipper; thus, we shall blame nature for any damage or praise her if everything went well against all odds. In a first approximation, we simply let nature determine whether goods will arrive unscathed.

3.2   Single Process Instances and the Base Game with Fair Conflicts

We now describe how each Petri net with transition payoffs and roles gives rise to a stochastic game, based on two design choices: each role can execute only one (enabled) transition at a time and conflicts are resolved in a probabilistically fair manner. For example, for the net on the right in Fig. 3, we take four states p_0, p_1, p_2, p_3, one for each reachable marking. The Petri net does not prescribe what should happen if roles a and c both try to fire transitions t_1 and t' simultaneously if the game is in state p_2. The simplest probabilistically fair solution consists of flipping a coin; depending on the outcome, the game continues in state p_1 or in state p_3. For the general case, let us fix a safe, extended free-choice net $(\mathcal{N}, u, \rho)$ with payoffs and roles whose initial marking is m_0 where the marked net $\mathcal{N}$ is an elementary net system (e.g., a WF-net).

Definition 11 (The base game with fair conflicts). *Let $\mathcal{X} \subseteq \wp T$ be the partitioning of the set of transitions into equivalence classes of the conflict relation on the set of transitions, i.e., $\mathcal{X} = \{\{t' \in T \mid t' \mathrel{\#} t\} \mid t \in T\}$; its members are called* conflict sets. *Given a safe marking $m \subseteq P$ and a step $\underline{t} \subseteq T$, a maximal m-enabled sub-step is a step $\underline{t}'$ that is enabled at the marking m, is contained in the step $\underline{t}$, and contains one transition of each conflict set that has a non-empty intersection with the step, i.e., such that all three of $m\,[\underline{t}'\rangle$, $\underline{t}' \subseteq \underline{t}$ and $|\underline{t}'| = |\{X \in \mathcal{X} \mid \underline{t} \cap X \neq \varnothing\}|$ hold. We write $\underline{t}' \sqsubseteq_m \underline{t}$ if the step $\underline{t}'$ is a maximal m-enabled sub-step of the step $\underline{t}$.*

The base game with fair conflicts *$\langle N, S, A, q, u\rangle$ of the net $(\mathcal{N}, u, \rho)$ is defined as follows.*

- *The set of players $N := \mathcal{R} \cup \{\bot\}$ is the set of roles and nature, $\bot \notin \mathcal{R}$.*
- *The state space S is the set of reachable markings, i.e., $S = \{m' \mid m_0\,[\rangle^* m'\}$.*
- *The action set of an individual player i is $A^i := \{\varnothing\} \cup \{\{t\} \mid t \in T, \rho(t) = i\}$, which consists of the empty set and possibly singletons of transitions, where $\rho(t) = \bot$ if $\rho(t)$ is not defined. We identify an action profile $a \in A = \prod_{i=1}^{|N|} A^i$ with the union of its components $a \equiv \bigcup_{i \in N} a^i$.*
- *In a given state m, the available actions of player i are the enabled transitions, i.e., $A^i(m) = \{\{t\} \in A^i \mid m\,[t\rangle\}$.*
- *$q(m' \mid m, \underline{t}) = \sum_{\underline{t}' \sqsubseteq_m \underline{t} \text{ s.t. } m[\underline{t}'\rangle m'} \prod_{X \in \mathcal{X} \text{ s.t. } \underline{t} \cap X \neq \varnothing} \frac{1}{|\underline{t} \cap X|}$*
- *$u^i(m, \underline{t}) = \sum_{t \in \underline{t}} u^i(t)$ if $i \in \mathcal{R}$ and $u^\bot(m, \underline{t}) = 0$, for all $\underline{t} \subseteq T$, and $m \subseteq P$.*

Let us summarize the stochastic game of a given Petri net with transition payoffs and roles. The stochastic game has the same state space as the Petri net, i.e., the set of reachable markings. The available actions for each player at a given marking are the enabled transitions that are assigned to the player, plus the "idle" step. Each step comes with a state-independent payoff, which sums up the utilities of each single transition, for each player i. In particular, if all players chose to idle, the corresponding action profile is the empty step $\varnothing$, which gives 0 payoff. The transition probabilities implement the idea that all transitions of an action profile get a fair chance to fire, even if the step contains conflicting transitions. Let us highlight the following two points for a fixed marking and step: (1) given a maximal enabled sub-step, we roll a fair "die" for each conflict set where the "die" has one "side" for each transition in the conflict set that also belongs to the sub-step (unless the "die" has zero sides); (2) there might be several choices of maximal enabled sub-steps that lead to the same marking. In the definition of transition probabilities, the second point is captured by summation over maximal enabled sub-steps of the step and the first point corresponds to a product of probabilities for each outcome of "rolling" one of the "dice".

We want to emphasize that if additional information about transition probabilities are known, it should be incorporated. In a similar vein, one can adapt the approach of Herbert and Sharp [9], which extends the BPMN language with probability annotations for choices. However, as we are mainly interested in *a priori* analysis, our approach might be preferable since it avoids arbitrary parameter guessing. The most important design choice that we have made concerns the role of nature, which we consider as absolutely neutral; it is not even concerned with progress of the system as it does not benefit from transitions being fired.

Now, let us consider once more the O2C process. If the process reaches the state in which customer's next step is payment, there is no incentive for paying. Instead, customer can choose to idle, *ad infinitum*. In fact, this strategy yields maximum payoff for the customer. The BPMN-model does not give any means for punishing customer's payment inertia. However, even earlier there is no incentive for shipper to pick up the goods. Incentives in the single instance scenario can be fixed, e.g., by adding escrow. However, in the present paper, we shall give yet a different perspective: we repeat the process indefinitely.

3.3   Restarting the Game for Multiple Process Instances

The single instance game from Definition 11 has one major drawback. It allows to analyze only a single instance of a business process. We shall now consider a variation of the stochastic game, which addresses the case of multiple instances in the simplest form. The idea is the same as the one for looping versions of Workflow nets that have been considered in the literature, e.g., to relate soundness with liveness [1, Lemma 5.1]: we simply restart the game in the initial state whenever we reach a final marking.

Definition 12 (Restart game). *A safe marking $m \subseteq P$ is* final *if it does not intersect with any pre-set, i.e., if $m \cap {}^\bullet t = \varnothing$, for all transitions $t \in T$; we write $m \downarrow$ if the marking m is final, and $m \not\downarrow$ if not. Let $\langle N, S, A, q, u \rangle$ be the base game with fair conflicts of the net $(\mathcal{N}, u, \rho)$. The* restart game *of the net $(\mathcal{N}, u, \rho)$ is the game $\langle N, \mathring{S}, \mathring{A}, \mathring{q}, u \rangle$ with*

$$- \mathring{S} = S \setminus \{m'' \subseteq P \mid m'' \downarrow\};$$

$$- \mathring{q}(m' \mid m, \underline{t}) = \begin{cases} q(m' \mid m, \underline{t}) & \text{if } m' \neq m_0 \\ q(m_0 \mid m, \underline{t}) + \sum_{m'' \downarrow} q(m'' \mid m, \underline{t}) & \text{if } m' = m_0 \end{cases}$$

for all $m, m' \in \mathring{S}$; and the available actions restricted to $\mathring{S} \subseteq S$, i.e., $\mathring{A}^i(s) = A^i(s)$, for $s \in \mathring{S}$.

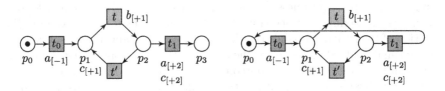

Fig. 4. Restarting process example

For WF-nets, the variation amounts to identifying the final place with the initial place. The passage to the restart game is illustrated in Fig. 4. The restart game of our example is drastically different from the base game. Player c will be better off "cooperating" and never choosing the action t', but instead idly reaping benefits by letting players a and b do the work. As a consequence, the transition t' will probably never occur since the responsible role has no interest in executing it. Thus, if we assume that the process *may* restart, the net from Fig. 3 is an example where incentives are aligned w.r.t. completion but not with full liveness.

3.4   Incentive Alignment w.r.t. Proper Completion and Full Liveness

We now formalize the idea that participants want to expect benefits from taking part in a collaboration if agents behave rationally – the standard assumption of game theory. The proposed definition of incentive alignment is in principle of qualitative nature, but it hinges on quantitative information, namely the expected utility for each of the business partners of an inter-organizational process.

Let us consider a Petri net with payoffs $(\mathcal{N}, u, \rho)$, e.g., the Petri net semantics of a BPMN model. Incentive alignment amounts to existence of equilibrium strategies in the associated restart game $\langle N, \mathring{S}, \mathring{A}, \mathring{q}, u \rangle$ (as per Definition 12) that eventually will lead to positive utility for every participating player. The full details are as follows.

Definition 13 (Incentive alignment w.r.t. completion and full liveness). *Given an autonomous correlation device $\mathcal{D}$, a correlated strategy profile σ is eventually positive if there exists a natural number $\bar{n} \in \mathbb{N}$ such that, for all larger natural numbers $n > \bar{n}$, the expected payoff of every player is positive, i.e., for all $i \in N$, $\bar{\gamma}_n^i(\mathcal{D}, m_0, \sigma) > 0$. Incentives in the net $(\mathcal{N}, u, \rho)$ are aligned with*

- proper completion *if, for every positive real $\varepsilon > 0$, there exist an autonomous correlation device $\mathcal{D}$ and an eventually positive correlated ε-equilibrium strategy profile σ of the restart game $\langle N, \mathring{S}, \mathring{A}, \mathring{q}, u \rangle$ such that, for every natural number $\bar{n} \in \mathbb{N}$, there exists a history $h \in H_n(\mathcal{D})$ at stage $n > \bar{n}$ with current state $s_h = m_0$ that has non-zero probability, i.e., $\mathbf{P}_{\mathcal{D}, m_0, \sigma}(h) > 0$;*
- full liveness *if, for every positive real $\varepsilon > 0$, there exist an autonomous correlation device $\mathcal{D}$ and an eventually positive correlated ε-equilibrium strategy profile σ of the restart game $\langle N, \mathring{S}, \mathring{A}, \mathring{q}, u \rangle$ such that, for every transition $t \in T$, for every reachable marking m', and for every natural number $\bar{n} \in \mathbb{N}$, there exists a history $h = \langle m', \underline{x}_1, a_1, \ldots, s_{n-1}, \underline{x}_{n-1}, a_{n-1}, s_n, \underline{x}_n \rangle \in H_n(\mathcal{D})$ at stage $n > \bar{n}$ with $t \in a_{n-1}$ and $\mathbf{P}_{\mathcal{D}, m', \sigma}(h) > 0$.*

Both variations of incentive alignment ensure that all participants can expect to gain profits on average, eventually; moreover, something "good" will always be possible in the future where something "good" is either restart of the game (upon completion) or additional occurrences of every transition.

There are several interesting consequences. First, incentive alignment w.r.t. full liveness implies incentive alignment w.r.t. proper completion, for the case of safe, conflict-free elementary net systems where the initial marking is only reachable via the empty transition sequence; this applies in particular to Workflow nets. Next, note that incentive alignment w.r.t. full liveness implies the soundness property for safe, free-choice Workflow nets. The main insight is that correlated equilibria cover a very special case of strongly fair schedulers, not only for the case of a single player. However, we can even obtain a characterization of soundness in terms of incentive alignment w.r.t. full liveness.

Theorem 1 (Characterization of the soundness property). *Let $\mathcal{N}$ be a Workflow net that is safe and extended free-choice; let $(\mathcal{N}, \rho \colon T \to \{\Sigma\}, \underline{1})$ be the net with transition payoffs and roles where Σ is a unique role, $\rho \colon T \to \{\Sigma\}$ is the unique total role assignment function, and $\underline{1}$ is the constant utility-1 function. The soundness property holds for the Workflow net $\mathcal{N}$ if, and only if, we have incentive alignment w.r.t. full liveness in $(\mathcal{N}, \rho \colon T \to \{\Sigma\}, \underline{1})$.*

The full proof can be found in the extended version [8, Appendix A]. However, let us outline the main proof ideas. The first observations is that, w.l.o.g., schedulers that witness soundness of a WF-net can be assumed to be stochastic; in fact, truly random scheduling is strongly fair (with probability 1). Somewhat more detailed, if a WF-net is sound, the scheduler is the only player and scheduling the next best random transition at every point in time yields maximum payoff for the single player. Now, the random choice of a transition at each point in time is the simplest example of an equilibrium strategy (profile); moreover, no matter what the current reachable state of the net, any transition will occur again with non-zero probability, by soundness of the net.

Conversely, incentive alignment w.r.t. strong liveness entails that the unique player – which we might want to think of as the scheduler – will follow a strategy that will eventually fire a transition of the "next instance" of the "process". In particular, we always will have an occurrence of an *initial* transition by which we mean a transition that consumes the unique token from the initial marking. After firing an initial transition (of which there will be one by the structure of the net) we are in a state that does not allow us to fire another initial transition. However, strong liveness entails that it has to occur with non-zero probability again if we follow a witnessing equilibrium strategy (profile). Thus, with probability 1, the "current instance" of the "process" will complete such that we will again be able to fire an initial transition.

Finally, the reader may wonder why we consider the restarting game. First, let us emphasize that the restart *games* are merely a means to an end to reason about incentive alignment of BPMN models with suitable utility annotations by use of their execution semantics, i.e., Petri nets with transition payoffs and roles. If these Petri nets do not have any cycles, one could formalize the idea of incentive alignment using finite extensive form games for which correlated equilibria have been studied as well [27]. However, this alternative approach is only natural for BPMN models *without cycles*. In the present paper we have opted for a general approach, which does not impose the rather strong restriction on nets to be acyclic. Notably, while we work with restart *games*, we derive them from *arbitrary* free-choice safe elementary net systems – i.e., without assuming that the input nets are restarting. The restart game is used to check whether incentives are aligned in the original Petri net with transition payoffs and roles.

4   Conclusions and Future Work

We have described a game theoretic perspective on incentive alignment of inter-organizational business processes. It applies to BPMN collaboration models that have annotations for activity-based utilities for all roles. The main theoretical result is that incentive alignment is a conservative extension of the soundness property, which means that we have described a uniform framework that applies the same principles to intra- and inter-organizational business processes. We have illustrated incentive alignment for the example of the order-to-cash process and an additional example that is tailored to illustrate the game theoretic element of mediators.

The natural next step is the implementation of a tool chain that takes a BPMN collaboration model with annotations, transforms it into a Petri net with transition payoffs and roles, which in turn is analyzed concerning incentive alignment, e.g., using algorithms for solving stochastic games [17]. A very challenging venue for future theoretical work is the extension to the analysis of interleaved execution of several instances of a process.

Acknowledgments. We would like to thank the anonymous referees for their detailed comments and suggestions on a previous version of this paper.

References

1. Van der Aalst, W.M.P., Van Hee, K.M., ter Hofstede, A.H.M., et al.: Soundness of workflow nets: classification, decidability, and analysis. Formal Asp. Comp. **23**(3), 333–363 (2011)

2. Aalst, W.M.P.: Verification of workflow nets. In: Azéma, P., Balbo, G. (eds.) ICATPN 1997. LNCS, vol. 1248, pp. 407–426. Springer, Heidelberg (1997). https://doi.org/10.1007/3-540-63139-9_48

3. Aumann, R.J.: Subjectivity and correlation in randomized strategies. J. Math. Econ. **1**(1), 67–96 (1974)

4. Cachon, G.P., Netessine, S.: Game theory in supply chain analysis. In: Simchi-Levi, D., Wu, S.D., Shen, Z.J. (eds.) Handbook of Quantitative Supply Chain Analysis, pp. 13–65. Springer, Heidelberg (2004). https://doi.org/10.1007/978-1-4020-7953-5_2

5. Cartelli, V., Di Modica, G., Manni, D., Tomarchio, O.: A cost-object model for activity based costing simulation of business processes. In: European Modelling Symposium (2014)

6. Dijkman, R.M., Dumas, M., Ouyang, C.: Semantics and analysis of business process models in BPMN. Inf. Softw. Technol. **50**(12), 1281–1294 (2008)

7. Dumas, M., Rosa, M.L., Mendling, J., Reijers, H.A.: Fundamentals of Business Process Management, 2nd edn. Springer, Heidelberg (2018). https://doi.org/10.1007/978-3-662-56509-4

8. Heindel, T., Weber, I.: Incentive alignment of business processes: a game theoretic approach (2020). arXiv e-print 2006.06504

9. Herbert, L., Sharp, R.: Using stochastic model checking to provision complex business services. In: IEEE International Symposium High-Assurance Systems Engineering (2012)

10. Aumann, R.J.: Correlated equilibrium as an expression of Bayesian rationality. Econometrica **55**(1), 1–18 (1987)

11. Jaśkiewicz, A., Nowak, A.S.: Non-zero-sum stochastic games. In: Basar, T., Zaccour, G. (eds.) Handbook of Dynamic Game Theory, pp. 1–64. Springer, Heidelberg (2017). https://doi.org/10.1007/978-3-319-27335-8_8-2

12. Kaplan, R., Atkinson, A.: Advanced Management Accounting, 3rd edn. Prentice Hall (1998)

13. Kwiatkowska, M., Norman, G., Parker, D., Santos, G.: Automated verification of concurrent stochastic games. In: McIver, A., Horvath, A. (eds.) QEST 2018. LNCS, vol. 11024, pp. 223–239. Springer, Cham (2018). https://doi.org/10.1007/978-3-319-99154-2_14

14. Kwiatkowska, M., Parker, D., Wiltsche, C.: PRISM-Games 2.0: a tool for multi-objective strategy synthesis for stochastic games. In: Chechik, M., Raskin, J.-F. (eds.) TACAS 2016. LNCS, vol. 9636, pp. 560–566. Springer, Heidelberg (2016). https://doi.org/10.1007/978-3-662-49674-9_35

15. Leyton-Brown, K., Shoham, Y.: Essentials of game theory: a concise multidisciplinary introduction. Synthesis Lect. AI ML **2**(1), 1–88 (2008)

16. MacDermed, L., Isbell, C.L.: Solving stochastic games. In: Conference on Neural Information Processing Systems, pp. 1186–1194 (2009)

17. MacDermed, L., Narayan, K.S., Isbell, C.L., Weiss, L.: Quick polytope approximation of all correlated equilibria in stochastic games. In: AAAI Conference (2011)

18. Mendling, J., Weber, I., Van der Aalst, W.M.P., et al.: Blockchains for business process management - challenges and opportunities. ACM Trans. Manag. Inf. Syst. (TMIS) **9**(1), 4:1–4:16 (2018)

19. Morgenstern, O., von Neumann, J.: Theory of games and economic behavior. Princeton University Press (1953)

20. Narayanan, V., Raman, A.: Aligning incentives in supply chains. Harvard Bus. Rev. 82, 94–102, 149 (2004)

21. Osborne, M.J., Rubinstein, A.: A Course in Game Theory. MIT Press, Cambridge (1994)
22. Prasad, H.L., LA, P., Bhatnagar, S.: Two-timescale algorithms for learning Nash equilibria in general-sum stochastic games. In: International Conference on Autonomous Agents and Multiagent Systems (2015)
23. Rozenberg, G., Engelfriet, J.: Elementary net systems. In: Reisig, W., Rozenberg, G. (eds.) ACPN 1996. LNCS, vol. 1491, pp. 12–121. Springer, Heidelberg (1998). https://doi.org/10.1007/3-540-65306-6_14
24. Shapley, L.S.: Stochastic games. Proc. Natl. Acad. Sci. **39**(10), 1095–1100 (1953)
25. Solan, E., Vieille, N.: Correlated equilibrium in stochastic games. Games Econ. Behav. **38**(2), 362–399 (2002)
26. Solan, E., Vieille, N.: Stochastic games. Proc. Natl. Acad. Sci. **112**(45), 13743–13746 (2015)
27. von Stengel, B., Forges, F.: Extensive-form correlated equilibrium: definition and computational complexity. Math. Oper. Res. **33**, 1002–1022 (2008)
28. Weber, I., Xu, X., Riveret, R., Governatori, G., Ponomarev, A., Mendling, J.: Untrusted business process monitoring and execution using blockchain. In: La Rosa, M., Loos, P., Pastor, O. (eds.) BPM 2016. LNCS, vol. 9850, pp. 329–347. Springer, Cham (2016). https://doi.org/10.1007/978-3-319-45348-4_19
29. Weske, M.: Business Process Management - Concepts, Languages, Architectures, 3rd edn. Springer, Heidelberg (2019)
30. Xu, X., Weber, I., Staples, M.: Architecture for Blockchain Applications. Springer, Cham (2019). https://doi.org/10.1007/978-3-030-03035-3

PRIPEL: Privacy-Preserving Event Log Publishing Including Contextual Information

Stephan A. Fahrenkrog-Petersen[1]([⊠]), Han van der Aa[2], and Matthias Weidlich[1]

[1] Humboldt-Universität zu Berlin, Berlin, Germany
{stephan.fahrenkrog-petersen,matthias.weidlich}@hu-berlin.de
[2] University of Mannheim, Mannheim, Germany
han@informatik.uni-mannheim.de

Abstract. Event logs capture the execution of business processes in terms of executed activities and their execution context. Since logs contain potentially sensitive information about the individuals involved in the process, they should be pre-processed before being published to preserve the individuals' privacy. However, existing techniques for such pre-processing are limited to a process' control-flow and neglect contextual information, such as attribute values and durations. This thus precludes any form of process analysis that involves contextual factors. To bridge this gap, we introduce PRIPEL, a framework for privacy-aware event log publishing. Compared to existing work, PRIPEL takes a fundamentally different angle and ensures privacy on the level of individual cases instead of the complete log. This way, contextual information as well as the long tail process behaviour are preserved, which enables the application of a rich set of process analysis techniques. We demonstrate the feasibility of our framework in a case study with a real-world event log.

Keywords: Process mining · Privacy-preserving data publishing · Privacy-preserving data mining

1 Introduction

Process Mining [34] enables the analysis of business processes based on event logs that are recorded by information systems. Events in these logs represent the executions of activities as part of a case, including contextual information, as illustrated for the handling of patients in an emergency room in Table 1. Such rich event logs do not only enable discovery of a model of a process' control-flow, see [1], but provide the starting point for multi-dimensional analysis that incorporates the impact of the context on process execution. An example is the prediction of the remaining wait time of a patient based on temporal information (e.g., arrival in night hours), patient characteristics (e.g., age and sex), and activity outcomes (e.g., dispensed drugs) [23]. The inclusion of such contextual information provides a means for a fine-granular separation of classes of cases in

© Springer Nature Switzerland AG 2020
D. Fahland et al. (Eds.): BPM 2020, LNCS 12168, pp. 111–128, 2020.
https://doi.org/10.1007/978-3-030-58666-9_7

Table 1. Event log example

Patient ID	Activity	Timestamp	Payload
2200	Registration	03/03/19 23:40:32	{Age: 37, Sex: M, Arrival: Ambulance}
2200	Triage	03/05/17 00:47:12	{HIV-Positive: True}
2200	Surgery	03/05/17 02:22:17	{Operator: House}
...	...	...	...
2201	Registration	03/05/17 00:01:02	{Age: 67, Sex: F, Arrival: Check-In}
2201	Antibiotics	03/05/17 00:15:16	{Drug: Cephalexin}
...	...	...	...

the analysis. Since the separation is largely independent of the frequency of the respective trace variants, analysis is not limited to cases that represent common behaviour, but includes cases that denote unusual process executions.

Event logs, particularly those that include contextual information, may contain sensitive data related to individuals involved in process execution [26]. Even when explicit pointers to personal information, such as employee names, are pseudonymised or omitted from event logs, they remain susceptible to re-identification attacks [13]. Such attacks still allow personal data of specific individuals to be identified based on the contents of an event log [36]. Consequently, publishing an event log without respective consent violates regulations such as the GDPR, given that this regulation prohibits processing of personal data for such secondary purposes [35]. This calls for the design of methods targeted specifically to protect the privacy of individuals in event logs. Existing approaches for privacy-preserving process mining [12,25] emphasise the control-flow dimension, though. They lack the ability to preserve contextual information, such as timestamps and attribute values, which prevents any fine-granular analysis that incorporates the specifics of different classes of cases. However, aggregations of contextual information in the spirit of k-anonymity, see [12], are not suited to overcome this limitation. Such aggregations lead to a loss of the long tail process behaviour, i.e., infrequent traces of cases that are uncommon and, hence, of particular importance for any analysis (e.g., due to exceptional runtime characteristics). The only existing anonymisation approach that incorporates contextual information [31] achieves this using homomorphic encryption. As such, it fails to provide protection based on any well-established privacy guarantee.

To overcome these gaps, this paper introduces *PRIPEL*, a framework for privacy-preserving event log publishing that incorporates contextual information. Our idea is to ensure differential privacy of an event log on the basis of individual cases rather than on the whole log. To this end, the PRIPEL framework exploits the maxim of parallel composition of differential privacy. Based on a differentially private selection of activity sequences, contextual information from the original log is integrated through a sequence enrichment step. Subsequently, the integrated contextual information is anonymised following the principle of local differential privacy. Ensuring privacy on the level of individual cases is a fundamentally different angle, which enables us to overcome the aforementioned limitations of existing work. PRIPEL is the first approach to ensure differential privacy not only for the control-flow, but also for contextual information in event logs, while preserving large parts of the long tail process behaviour.

Since differential privacy ensures that personal data belonging to specific individuals can not longer be identified, the anonymisation achieved by PRIPEL is in line with the requirements imposed by the GDPR [10,14].

We demonstrate the feasibility of our approach through a case study in the healthcare domain. Applying PRIPEL to a real-world event log of Sepsis cases from a hospital, we show that the anonymisation preserves utility on the level of event-, trace-, and log-specific characteristics.

The remainder is structured as follows. In Sect. 2, we provide background in terms of an event log model and privacy guarantees. In Sect. 3, we introduce the PRIPEL framework. We present a proof-of-concept in Sect. 4, including an implementation and a case study. We discuss our results and reflect on limitations in Sect. 5, before we review related work in Sect. 6 and conclude in Sect. 7.

2   Background

This section presents essential definitions and background information. In particular, Sect. 2.1 presents the event log model we employ in the paper. Subsequently, Sect. 2.2 defines the foundations of local differential privacy, followed by an introduction to differential privacy mechanisms in Sect. 2.3.

2.1   Event Log Model

We adopt an event model that builds upon a set of *activities* $\mathcal{A}$. An *event* recorded by an information system, denoted by e, is assumed to be related to the execution of one of these activities, which is written as $e.a \in \mathcal{A}$. By $\mathcal{E}$, we denote the universe of all events. Each event further carries information on its execution context, such as the data consumed or produced during the execution of an activity. This payload is defined by a set of data attributes $\mathcal{D} = \{D_1, \ldots, D_p\}$ with $\mathrm{dom}(D_i)$ as the domain of attribute D_i, $1 \leq i \leq p$. We write $e.D$ for the value of attribute D of an event e. For example, an event representing the activity *'Antibiotics'* may be associated with the *'Drug'* attribute that reflects the prescribed medication, see Table 1. Each event e further comes with a timestamp, denoted by $e.ts$, that models the time of execution of the respective activity according to some totally ordered time domain.

A single execution of a process, i.e., a case, is represented by a *trace*. This is a sequence $\xi = \langle e_1, \ldots, e_n \rangle$ of events $e_i \in \mathcal{E}$, $1 \leq i \leq n$, such that no event occurs in more than one trace and the events are ordered by their timestamps. We adopt a standard notation for sequences, i.e., $\xi(i) = e_i$ for the i-th element and $|\xi| = n$ for the length. For two distinct traces $\xi = \langle e_1, \ldots, e_n \rangle$ and $\xi' = \langle e'_1, \ldots, e'_m \rangle$, their concatenation is $\xi.\xi' = \langle e_1, \ldots, e_n, e'_1, \ldots, e'_m \rangle$, assuming that the ordering is consistent with the events' timestamps. If ξ and ξ' indicate the same sequence of activity executions, i.e., $\langle e_1.a, \ldots, e_n.a \rangle = \langle e'_1.a, \ldots, e'_m.a \rangle$, they are of the same *trace variant*. An *event log* is a set of traces, $L = \{\xi_1, \ldots, \xi_n\}$, and we write $\mathcal{L}$ for the universe of event logs. Table 1 defines two traces, as indicated by the *'patient ID'* attribute. In the remainder, we assume the individuals of interest to be represented in at most one case. In our example, this means that only one treatment per patient is recorded in the log.

2.2 Foundations of Local Differential Privacy

Differential privacy is a definition for privacy that ensures that personal data of individuals is indistinguishable in a data analysis setting. Essentially, differential privacy aims to allow one to learn nothing about an individual, while learning useful information from a population [7]. Achieving differential privacy means that result of a query, performed on an undisclosed dataset, can be published without allowing an individual's personal data to be derived from the published result. On the contrary, methods that achieve *local* differential privacy anonymise a dataset itself in such a manner that it can be published while still guaranteeing the privacy of an individual's data [18]. This is achieved by applying noise to the data, contrary to applying it to the result of a function performed on the undisclosed data. The adoption of local differential privacy in industry is well-documented, being employed by, e.g., Apple [32], SAP [19], and Google [9].

To apply this notion in the context of event logs, we define $\alpha : \mathcal{L} \to \mathcal{L}$ as an *anonymisation function* that takes an event log as input and transforms it into an anonymised event log. This transformation is non-deterministic and is typically realised through a stochastic function. Furthermore, we define $img(\alpha) \subseteq \mathcal{L}$ as the *image* of α, i.e., the set of all event logs that may be returned by α. Finally, we define two event logs $L_1, L_2 \in \mathcal{L}$ to be *neighbouring*, if they differ by exactly the data of one individual. In our setting, this corresponds to one case and, hence, one trace, i.e., $|L_1 \backslash L_2| + |L_2 \backslash L_1| = 1$. Based on [18], we then define local differential privacy as follows:

Definition 1 (Local Differential Privacy). *Given an anonymisation function α and privacy parameter $\epsilon \in \mathbb{R}$, function α provides ϵ-local differential privacy, if for all neighbouring pairs of event logs $L_1, L_2 \in \mathcal{L}$, it holds that:*

$$Pr[\alpha(L_1) \in img(\alpha)] \leq e^\epsilon \times Pr[\alpha(L_2) \in img(\alpha)]$$

where the probability is taken over the randomness introduced by the anonymisation function α.

The intuition behind the guarantee is that it limits the information that can be disclosed by one individual, i.e., one case. The strength of the guarantee depends on ϵ, with lower values leading to stronger data protection.

2.3 Ensuring Local Differential Privacy

Mechanisms that ensure local differential privacy strive to provide privacy guarantees while keeping as much useful information as possible, i.e., they aim to maintain maximum utility of the dataset. The mechanisms typically do not delete or generalize (parts of the) data, as is done to obtain other privacy guarantees [20]. Rather, they define an anonymisation function that inserts noise into data, in order to obscure information about individuals, while retaining as many characteristics about the general population as possible. Several such mechanisms have been developed to anonymise various data types, including ones that ensure differential privacy for numerical, categorical, and boolean data:

Numerical Data – Laplace Mechanism. The Laplace mechanism [5] is an additive noise mechanism for numerical values. It draws noise from a Laplacian distribution, that is calibrated based on the privacy parameter ϵ and the sensitivity of the data distribution. The latter is defined as the maximum difference one individual can cause.

Boolean Data - Randomized Response. To ensure differential privacy of boolean data, one can use *randomized response* [37]. The algorithm is based on the following idea: A fair coin toss determines if the true value of an individual is revealed or if a randomized value is chosen instead. Here, the randomization depends on the strength ϵ of the differential privacy guarantee. In this paper, we will use a so-called *binary mechanism* [16].

Categorical Data - Exponential Mechanism. To handle categorical data, it is possible to use the *exponential mechanism* [27]. It enables the definition of a utility difference between the different potential values of the domain of the categorical value. The probability of a value being exchanged by another value depends on the introduced probability loss.

Parallel Composition of Differential Privacy. Given such mechanisms that are able to provide differential privacy for various data types, a crucial property of (local) differential privacy is that it is compositional. Intuitively, this means that when the results of multiple ϵ-differential-private mechanisms, performed on disjoint datasets, are merged, the merged result also provides ϵ-differential privacy [28]. Adapted to our notion of attributes and timestamps of events, this is formalized as follows: Let $M_i(e.d_i)$, $1 \leq i \leq p$, and $M_0(e.ts)$ be the values obtained by some mechanisms $M_0, M_1, \ldots M_p$ for the attribute values and the timestamp of an event e. Then, if all mechanisms provide ϵ-differential privacy and under the assumption of all attributes (and the timestamp) being independent, the result of their joint application to e also provides ϵ-differential privacy.

This property forms a crucial foundation for our proposed framework to privacy-aware event log publishing, as introduced next.

3 The PRIPEL Framework

The *Privacy-Preserving event log publishing* (*PRIPEL*) framework takes an event log as input and transforms it into an anonymised one that includes

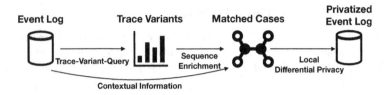

Fig. 1. Overview of PRIPEL Framework

contextual information and guarantees ϵ-differential privacy. As depicted in Fig. 1, the PRIPEL framework consists of three main steps. Given an event log L, PRIPEL first applies a *trace-variant query* Q on L. The query returns a bag of activity sequences that ensures differential privacy from a control-flow perspective. Second, the framework constructs new traces by enriching the activity sequences obtained by Q with contextual information, i.e., timestamps and attribute values, from the original log L. This is achieved in a *sequence enrichment* step, which results in a *matched* event log L_m. Finally, PRIPEL anonymises the timestamps and attribute values of L_m individually by exploiting the maxim of parallel composition of differential privacy. The resulting event log L' then guarantees ϵ-differential privacy, while largely retaining the information of the original log L.

Sections 3.1 through 3.3 outline instantiations of each of these three steps. However, we note that the framework's steps can also be instantiated in a different manner, for instance by using alternative trace-variant queries or matching techniques. It is therefore possible to tailor PRIPEL to specific use cases, such as a setting in which traces become available in batches.

3.1   Trace Variant Query

The first step of our framework targets the anonymisation of an event log from a control-flow perspective. In particular, the framework applies a trace variant query, which returns a bag of activity sequences that captures trace variants and their frequencies in a differentially private manner. Such a step is essential, given that even the publication of activity sequences from an event log, i.e., with all attribute values and timestamps removed, can be sufficient to link the identity of individuals to infrequent activity sequences [12, 25]. For example, uncommon treatment paths may suffice to resolve the identity of a specific patient.

In PRIPEL, we adopt a state-of-the-art realisation of a privacy-preserving trace variant query [25]. It employs a Laplace mechanism (see Sect. 2.3) to add noise to the result of a trace variant query. As shown for an exemplary query result in Table 2, this mechanism may alter the frequency of trace variants, remove variants entirely, and introduce new ones. Note that the size of a trace variant query typically differs from the number of traces in the original log.

The employed trace variant query is configured with two parameters, n and k, which influence the prefix-tree that the mechanism uses to generate a query result. Here, n sets the maximum depth of the prefix-tree, which determines the maximum length of an activity sequence returned by the query. Parameter k is used to bound the mechanism's state space in terms of the number of potential activity sequences that are explored. A higher k means that only more commonly occurring prefixes are considered, which reduces the runtime, but may negatively affect the resulting log's utility. The runtime complexity of the query depends on the maximal number of explored prefixes: $\mathcal{O}(|\mathcal{A}|^n)$. Yet, in practice, the exponential runtime is mitigated by the pruning parameter k.

Below, we adopt a flattened representation of the result of the trace variant query. By $Q(L) \subseteq (\mathcal{A}^*)^*$, we denote a sequence of activity sequences derived by duplicating each activity sequence returned by the trace variant query according to its frequency, in some arbitrary order. For example, if the query returns the bag $[\langle Registration, Triage\rangle^2, \langle Registration, Triage, Antibiotics\rangle]$, $Q(L)$ is defined as $\{\langle Registration, Triage\rangle, \langle Registration, Triage, Antibiotics\rangle, \langle Registration, Triage\rangle\}$.

Table 2. Illustration of a privacy-aware trace variant query

Trace variant	Count	Privatized count
$\langle Registration, Triage, Surgery\rangle$	5	6
$\langle Registration, Triage, Antibiotics\rangle$	7	5
$\langle Registration, Triage, Surgery, Antibiotics\rangle$	2	3
$\langle Registration, Triage, Antibiotics, Surgery, Antibiotics\rangle$	0	1

So far, no other designs for trace variant queries have been introduced in the literature. However, we assume that alternative query formulations suited for specific use cases will be developed in the future.

3.2 Sequence Enrichment

The second step of the framework enriches the activity sequences obtained by the trace variant query with contextual information, i.e., with timestamps and attribute values. This is achieved by establishing a trace matching between each activity sequence from $Q(L)$ and a trace of the original log L. The latter trace determines how the activity sequence is enriched with contextual information to construct a trace of the matched log L_m. Here, L_m should resemble the original log: Distributions of attribute values and timestamps, along with their correlation with trace variants in the original L shall be mirrored in the matched log L_m.

To link the activity sequences in $Q(L)$ and traces in log L, we define a matching function $f_m : Q(L) \nrightarrow L$. It is potentially partial and injective, i.e., it matches each activity sequence (again, note that activity sequences obtained from the trace variant query are duplicated according to their frequency) to a separate trace in L, such that $f_m(\sigma_1) = f_m(\sigma_2)$ implies that $\sigma_1 = \sigma_2$ for all σ_1, σ_2 that are part of $Q(L)$. However, constructing such a mapping function requires to address two challenges:

(i) Since the trace variant query introduces noise, some sequences from $Q(L)$ cannot be paired with traces in L that are of the exact same sequence of activity executions. Given a sequence $\sigma = \langle Registration, Triage, Release \rangle$ of $Q(L)$ and a trace ξ with its activity executions being $\langle Registration, Release \rangle$, for example, the trace does not provide attribute values to be assigned to a 'Triage' event. To preserve their order, the insertion of an additional event may require the timestamps of other events to be changed as well.

(ii) Since $Q(L)$ may contain more sequences than the original log L has traces, some sequences in $Q(L)$ might not be matched to any trace in L, i.e., f_m is partial. Since all sequences in $Q(L)$ must be retained in the construction of traces for the matched log to ensure differential privacy, also such *unmatched* sequences must be enriched with contextual information.

Given these challenges, PRIPEL incorporates three functions: (1) a matching function f_m; (2) a mechanism f_e to enrich a matched sequence σ with contextual information from trace $f_m(\sigma)$ to construct a trace for the matched log L_m; and (3) a mechanism f_u to enrich an unmatched sequence to construct a trace for L_m. In this paper, we propose to instantiate these functions as follows:

Matching Function. The matching function f_m shall establish a mapping from $Q(L)$ to L such that the activity sequences and traces are as *similar* as possible. This similarity can be quantified using a distance function. Here, we propose to use the Levenshtein distance [21] to quantify the edit distance of some sequence σ that is part of $Q(L)$ and the sequence of activity executions derived from a trace $\xi \in L$, denoted as $ed(\sigma, \xi)$. Using assignment optimization techniques, the matching function is instantiated, such that the total edit distance is minimized, i.e., with $Q(L) = \langle \sigma_1, \ldots, \sigma_n \rangle$, we minimize $\sum_{1 \le i \le n} ed(\sigma_i, f_m(\sigma_i))$.

Matched Sequence Enrichment. Given a matched sequence σ of $Q(L)$, the sequence σ is enriched based on the context information of trace $\xi = f_m(\sigma)$ to create a new trace ξ_σ. The proposed procedure for this is described by Algorithm 1. To create the events for the new trace ξ_σ derived from σ, we iterate over all activities in σ, create a new event, and check if there is a corresponding event e' of ξ. Using k_σ as the number of times we have observed activity a in the sequence σ (line 4), e' shall be the k_σ-th occurrence of an event in ξ with $e.a = a$ (line 7). If such an event e' exists, we assign all its attribute values to the new event e (line 9). Subsequently, we check if the timestamp of e' occurs after the timestamp of the last event of ξ_σ (line 10). If this is the case, we assign the timestamp $e'.ts$ of the original event to event e. Otherwise, we generate a new timestamp based on the following equation, assuming that the current event is the n-th event to be added to $\xi_\sigma = \langle e_1, \ldots, e_{n-1} \rangle$:

$$e_n.ts = e_{n-1}.ts + \Delta_{e_{n-1}.a, e_n.a} \tag{1}$$

Here, $\Delta_{e_{n-1}.a, e_n.a}$ denotes a timestamp difference randomly drawn from the distribution of these differences in the original log. That is, the distribution is

Algorithm 1. Matched Sequence Enrichment

INPUT: An event log L; an activity sequence σ; the matched trace $\xi = f_m(\sigma)$.
OUTPUT: A trace ξ_σ derived by enriching σ based on ξ.

1: **for** $1 \leq i \leq |\sigma|$ **do**
2:     $e \leftarrow$ create new event
3:     $e.a \leftarrow \sigma(i).a$ ▷ Assign activity to new event
4:     $k_\sigma \leftarrow |\{1 \leq j \leq |\xi_\sigma| \mid \xi_\sigma(j).a = e.a\}|$ ▷ Count a-events in new trace ξ_σ
5:     $k_\xi \leftarrow |\{1 \leq j \leq |\xi| \mid \xi(j).a = e.a\}|$ ▷ Count a-events in original trace ξ
6:     **if** $k_\sigma < k_\xi$ **then**   ▷ Get corresponding occurrence of a
7:        $e' \leftarrow \xi(j)$ with $\xi(j).a = e.a$ and $|\{1 \leq l < j \mid \xi(l).a = e.a\}| = k_\sigma$
8:        **for all** $D \in \mathcal{D}$ **do**
9:           $e.D \leftarrow e'.D$ ▷ Assign attribute values of e' to e
10:        **if** $e'.ts > \xi_\sigma(|\xi_\sigma|).ts$ **then**
11:           $e.ts \leftarrow e'.ts$
12:        **else**
13:           $e.ts \leftarrow$ derive timestamp based on Equation 1
14:     **else**   ▷ No corresponding event in ξ
15:        **for all** $D \in \mathcal{D}$ **do** $e.D \leftarrow$ draw random attribute value
16:        $e.ts \leftarrow$ draw random timestamp for activity $e.a$
17:     $\xi_\sigma \leftarrow \xi_\sigma.\langle e \rangle$
18: **return** ξ_σ ▷ Return new trace

---

obtained by considering all pairs of subsequent events in the original traces that indicate the execution of the respective activities. If no such pairs of events appeared in the original log, we resort to the distribution of all timestamp differences of all pairs of subsequent activities of the original log.

If no corresponding event e' can be found for the newly created event e, we assign randomly drawn attribute values and a timestamp to this event (lines 15–16). We draw the attributes values from the overall distribution of each attribute D in the original log L, while timestamps are calculated according to Eq. 1.

Unmatched Sequence Enrichment. For sequences in $Q(L)$ without a matching, we assign the attribute values randomly. To handle the timestamps, we randomly draw a timestamp t_{start} for the event created for the first activity in σ, from the overall distribution of all timestamps of the first events of all traces ξ in the original log L. We generate the remaining timestamps based on Eq. 1.

The runtime complexity of the whole sequence enrichment step is dominated by the assignment optimization problem, which requires $\mathcal{O}(|Q(L)|^3)$ time.

3.3 Applying Local Differential Privacy

Next, starting with the matched log derived in the previous step, we turn to the anonymisation of contextual information using local differential privacy. While the treatment of attribute values follows rather directly from existing approaches, we propose a tailored approach to handle timestamps. The runtime complexity of this step is linear in the size of the matched log L_m, i.e., we arrive at $\mathcal{O}(|L_m|)$.

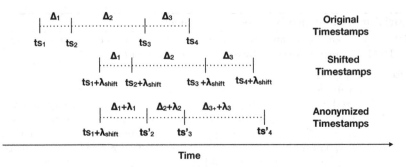

Fig. 2. Illustration of timestamp anonymisation

Anonymising Attribute Values. We differentiate between attributes of three data types: numerical, categorical, and boolean. For each type, we employ the mechanism discussed in Sect. 2.3. Under the aforementioned assumptions for parallel composition of differential privacy, the resulting values are ϵ-differentially private. Note that for each attribute, a different privacy parameter ϵ may be chosen. This way, the level of protection may be adapted to the sensitivity of the respective attribute values.

Anonymising Timestamps. To anonymise timestamps, we introduce random timestamp shifts, which is inspired by the treatment of network logs [38]. That is, we initially alter all timestamps based on some randomly drawn noise value, λ_{shift}, which is drawn, for instance, from a Laplacian distribution. The result is illustrated in the middle sequence of Fig. 2. After this initial shift, we subsequently introduce noise to the time intervals between events, depicted as Δ_1, Δ_2, and Δ_3 in the figure. To this end, we add random noise to the length of each interval, denoted by λ_1, λ_2, and λ_3. To retain the order of events, we bound the random timestamp shift to the size of the interval between two events. Since the event order was already anonymised in the first step of the framework (Sect. 3.1), introducing additional noise by re-ordering events here would just reduce the event log's utility.

After this final step, all aspects of the original log, i.e., control-flow and contextual information, have been anonymised. Based on the maxim of parallel composition, the resulting log provides ϵ-differential privacy.

4   Proof-of-Concept

This section presents a proof-of-concept of the PRIPEL framework. We first report on a prototypical implementation (Sect. 4.1), which we apply in a case study using a real-world event log (Sects. 4.2–4.3). In this manner, we aim to show the feasibility of the framework in a realistic setting and investigate its ability to preserve the utility of an event log while providing privacy guarantees.

4.1   Prototypical Implementation

We implemented PRIPEL in Python and published our implementation under the MIT licence on Github.[1] The implementation uses the PM4Py library [2] to parse and process event logs. To instantiate the framework, we implemented a Python version of the trace-variant query by Mannhardt et al. [25]. The anonymisation of contextual information is based on IBM's *diffprivlib* library [15].

4.2   Case Study Setup

We show the feasibility of PRIPEL by applying our implementation to the Sepsis event log [24]. We selected this event log given its widespread adoption as a basis for case studies, as well as due to the relevance of its characteristics in the context of our work. As shown in our earlier work [12], anonymisation techniques that perform aggregations over the whole Sepsis log have a considerable impact on the anonymised log's utility. The reason being the long tail process behaviour in terms of a relatively low number of re-occurring trace variants: 1,050 traces spread over 846 trace variants. As such, the log's challenging characteristics make it particularly suitable for a proof-of-concept with our framework.

To parametrise our implementation, we test different values of the privacy parameter ϵ, ranging from 0.1 to 2.0. Given that this parameter defines the strictness of the desired privacy guarantees (lower being stricter), varying ϵ shall show its impact on utility of the resulting anonymised log.

We select the maximal prefix length $n = 30$, to cover the length of over 95% of the traces in the Sepsis event log. To cover all potential prefixes of the original log, we would need to set $n = 185$. However, this would add a lot of noise and increase the runtime significantly. Therefore, we opt for only looking into shorter traces. For each event log, we opted for the lowest value for k that still computes the query within a reasonable time, as will be detailed in the remainder.

4.3   Case Study Results

In this section, we first focus on the runtime of the PRIPEL framework. Subsequently, we explore its ability to preserve event log utility while guaranteeing ϵ-differential privacy.

Runtime. We measured the runtime of our PRIPEL implementation for various parameter configurations, obtained on a MacBook Pro (2018) with an i5 Intel Core CPU and 8 GB memory. As shown in Table 3, we were typically able to obtain an anonymised event log in a manner of minutes, which we deem feasible in most application scenarios. However, the runtime varies considerably across the chosen configurations and the framework's three main steps.

All besides one of the anonymised logs have far more traces than the original log, due to the added noise as part of the trace variant query. However, this is not true for the log with a $\epsilon = 1.5$ differential privacy guarantee, which contains

---

[1] https://github.com/samadeusfp/PRIPEL.

only one third of the number of traces of the original log. This is due to the low
noise level and the fact that $k = 2$ cuts out all variants that appear only once.
This applies to nearly all the variants in the original log. Since only a few noisy
traces are added, the resulting log is significantly smaller than the original log.

Table 3. Runtime of *PRIPEL* for the Sepsis log

ϵ	k	$|Q(L)|$	Query	Enrichment	Anonymisation	Total
0.1	20	5,175	1 s	35 s	3 m 24 s	4 m 07 s
0.5	4	6,683	1 s	3 m 52 s	4 m 08 s	8 m 12 s
1.0	2	7,002	2 s	8 m 37 s	4 m 27 s	13 m 18 s
1.5	2	340	1 s	8 s	13 s	23 s
2.0	1	13,152	9 s	33 m 05 s	8 m 30 s	42 m 06 s

The trace variant query (Step 1 in PRIPEL), is executed in a manner of seconds, ranging from one to nine seconds, depending on the configuration. However,
this runtime could be greatly exceeded for configurations with a higher n. While
a trace variant query with $\epsilon = 1.5$ and $k = 2$ is answered in one second, a
configuration of $\epsilon = 1.5$ and $k = 1$ does not lead to any result within an hour.

Sequence enrichment (Step 2) is the step with the largest runtime variance,
from 35 s to 33 min. In most configurations, this step also represents the largest
contribution to the total runtime. This is due to the polynomial runtime complexity of the enrichment step, see Sect. 3.2. To reduce this runtime, a greedy
strategy may instead be used to match activity sequences and traces.

Anonymisation based on local differential privacy (Step 3) has a reasonable
runtime that increases linearly with the number of traces in the resulting log.

Based on these observations and the non-repetitive character of the anonymisation task, we argue that it is feasible to apply our PRIPEL framework in
real-world settings. However, if runtime plays a crucial factor in an application
scenario, it should be clear that a suitable parameter configuration must be
carefully selected.

Event Log Utility. To illustrate the efficacy of PRIPEL, we analyse the utility
of anonymised event logs. In particular, we explore measures for three scopes:
(1) the event level, in terms of *attribute value quality*, (2) the trace level, in terms
of *case durations*, and (3) the log level, in terms of overall *process workload*.

Data Attribute Values: At the event level, we compare the value distribution of
data attributes in anonymised logs to the original distribution. The Sepsis log
primarily has attributes with boolean values. The quality of their value distributions is straightforward to quantify, i.e., by comparing the fraction of true values
in an anonymised log L' to the fraction in L. To illustrate the impact of the
differential privacy parameter ϵ on attribute value quality, we assess the value
distribution for the boolean attribute *InfectionSuspected*. As depicted in Table 4,
the truth value of this attribute is true for 81% of the cases in the original log.

Table 4. Sensitivity of attribute values to parameter ϵ

Attribute	Original	$\epsilon = 2.0$	$\epsilon = 1.5$	$\epsilon = 1.0$	$\epsilon = 0.5$	$\epsilon = 0.1$
Infection suspected (fraction)	0.81	0.75	0.69	0.67	0.58	0.51
Avg. case duration (days)	28.47	36.93	7.95	37.77	37.16	34.2
Median case duration (days)	5.34	11.23	0.12	11.92	10.95	9.57

The anonymised distribution is reasonably preserved for the highest ϵ value, i.e., the least strict privacy guarantee. There, the distribution has 75% true values. However, the accuracy of the distribution drops for stronger privacy guarantees, reaching almost full randomness for $\epsilon = 0.1$. This illustrates that the quality of attribute values can be preserved for certain privacy levels, but that it may be impacted for stricter settings. Note that, given that these results are obtained by anonymising individual values, the reduced quality for stronger privacy guarantees is inherently tied to the notion of differential privacy and is, therefore, independent of the specifics of the PRIPEL framework.

Case Duration. Next, we investigate the accuracy of the case durations in the anonymised logs. Unlike the previously discussed quality of individual event attributes, the quality of case durations is influenced by all three steps of the framework. Therefore, when interpreting the results depicted in Table 4, it is important to consider that the maximal length of a trace is bound to 30 events in anonymised logs (due to the selection of parameter n), whereas the original log contains traces with up to 370 events. However, we can still observe longer case durations in the anonymised logs due to the added noise. Additionally, in all scenarios, the average case duration is far higher than the median case duration. This indicates that the log contains several outliers in terms of longer case durations. All anonymised logs reveal this insight. We conclude that *PRIPEL* preserves insights on the trace level, such as the duration of cases.

Process Workload. Finally, at the log level, we consider the total workload of a process in terms of the number of cases that are active at any particular time. Given that anonymised event logs can have a considerably higher number of traces than the original log, we consider the progress of the relative number of active cases over time, as visualized in Fig. 3. The red dots denote the original event log, while blue triangles represent the anonymised event log with $\epsilon = 1.0$.

The figure clearly shows that the general trend over time is sustained. However, the anonymised log shows a consistently higher workload than the original log. Furthermore, the variance over time is less extreme for the anonymised log. This shows that the necessary noise insertion smooths out some of the variability. Nevertheless, the results illustrate PRIPEL's ability to preserve utility for such a log-level process analysis.

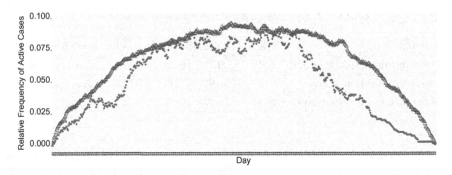

Fig. 3. Active cases over time in original log (red) vs. anonymised log (blue) (Color figure online)

5 Discussion

With *PRIPEL*, we introduced a framework that enables publishing of event logs that retain contextual information while guaranteeing differential privacy. As such, the anonymised event log can be used for rich process mining techniques that incorporate a fine-granular separation of classes of cases, without violating recent privacy regulations, such as the GDPR or CCPA.

While our general framework is generally applicable, the specific instantiations introduced earlier impose two assumptions on the event logs taken as input.

First, the employed notion for differential privacy assumes that any individual, such as a patient, is only represented in one case. To be able to guarantee differential privacy in contexts where this assumption may not hold, one can ensure that a single case exists per individual during the log extraction step, e.g., by limiting the selection of cases for which traces are derived or by constraining the time interval considered in the analysis. Alternatively, if the maximum number of cases per individual is known, the degree of noise introduced in the first step of the framework can be adjusted accordingly, by selecting the parameter ϵ. Finally, one may incorporate strategies that explicitly aim at adjusting differential privacy to handle multiple occurrences of individuals, such as [17].

Second, we assume that all attributes can be anonymised independently. Hence, the usefulness of anonymised values or the degree of privacy may be reduced for strongly correlated attributes. For instance, the independent anonymisation of the *height* and *age* of a child may result in improbable combinations.

Also, an attribute may represent a measurement that appears repeatedly in the trace, e.g., capturing the trend of a person's weight. Since the measurements are inter-related, the values to be anonymised are not independent, so that the parallel composition of differential privacy is not applicable. In that case, one can employ notions of differential privacy as developed for streaming settings [6].

Aside from these assumptions, we also acknowledge certain limitations related to our instantiation of the framework's steps. For instance, the approach chosen to determine the sensitivity of numerical attributes and timestamps is prone to outliers. Therefore, it might be necessary to reduce the number of outliers in an event log during pre-processing, in order to maintain the utility of the anonymised log. Yet, such limitations are inherent to any data anonymisation approach, since it has been shown that anonymisation reduces the utility of data [3]. Another limitation relates to the applied trace variant query. For this query mechanism, the size of the anonymised log can differ drastically from the original log. This may diminish the utility of the log for certain analysis tasks, such as the identification of performance bottlenecks.

Finally, we highlight that the PRIPEL framework, and the notion of differential privacy in general, is particularly suited for analysis techniques that aim to aggregate or generalize over the traces in an (anonymised) event log. This means that the resulting event logs are suitable for, e.g., process discovery (e.g., by a directly-follows relation over all traces), log-level conformance checking (e.g., by a frequency distribution of deviations observed in all traces), process enhancement (e.g., by aggregate performance measures for activities), and predictive monitoring (e.g., by models that generalize the correlations observed between trace features and outcomes). However, the insertion of noise can lead to the inclusion of process behaviour that never occurred in the original log, which may lead to incorrect results when performing trace-level analysis, such as the establishment of alignments for a single case. If it is important to avoid such false positives, other anonymisation approaches, such as PRETSA [12], may be more suitable.

6   Related Work

Privacy in process mining recently received a lot of attention [11, 29]. The problem was raised in [26], noticing that most individuals might agree with the usage of their data for process improvement. However, the analysis of personal data for such a goal represents so-called secondary use, which is in violation of regulations such as the GDPR and CCPA. Furthermore, in [36], it was shown that even projections of event logs can lead to serious re-identification risks.

Several approaches have been proposed to address these privacy issues. In [12], we proposed an algorithm to sanitize event logs for process discovery, which ensures k-anonymity and t-closeness. Alternative approaches [4,31] use cryptography to hide the confidential data in event logs. Other work focused on ensuring privacy for specific process mining tasks, by directly adapting analysis techniques. For instance, in [30] a technique to ensure confidentiality in role mining was proposed, while [25] introduced privacy-preserving queries to retrieve a directly-follows graph and the trace variants of a log. The work in [33] uses encryption to calculate the output of the alpha miner in a privacy-preserving manner. Other work considers process mining performed by multiple parties on an inter-organizational business process. In [22], an approach to generate a combined process model for such a business process was proposed. Similarly, [8] introduces an approach based on secure multi-party computation to answer queries relating the business process, such as the directly-follows query.

7   Conclusion

In this paper, we introduced PRIPEL, a framework to publish anonymised event logs that incorporates contextual information while guaranteeing differential privacy. In particular, PRIPEL ensures differential privacy on the basis of individual cases, rather than on an entire event log. We achieved this by exploiting the maxim of parallel composition. By applying a prototypical implementation on a real-world event log, we illustrate that the utility of anonymised event logs is preserved for various types of analysis involving contextual information.

By incorporating contextual information, for the first time, PRIPEL offers the use of rich process mining techniques in a privacy-preserving manner. In particular, anonymised event logs are now suitable for analysis techniques that incorporate a fine-granular separation of cases based on contextual information. In future work, we intend to further explore the impact that strongly correlated attributes have on the provided privacy guarantees. In addition, we aim to incorporate the handling of ongoing cases in the PRIPEL framework.

Acknowledgements. This work was partly supported by the Alexander von Humboldt Foundation.

References

1. Augusto, A., et al.: Automated discovery of process models from event logs: review and benchmark. IEEE Trans. Knowl. Data Eng. **31**(4), 686–705 (2018)
2. Berti, A., van Zelst, S.J., van der Aalst, W.: Process mining for python (PM4PY):bridging the gap between process-and data science. arXiv preprint arXiv:1905.06169 (2019)
3. Brickell, J., Shmatikov, V.: The cost of privacy: destruction of data-mining utility in anonymized data publishing. In: Proceedings of the 14th ACM SIGKDD International Conference on Knowledge Discovery and Data Mining, pp. 70–78 (2008)
4. Burattin, A., Conti, M., Turato, D.: Toward an anonymous process mining. In: 2015 3rd International Conference on Future Internet of Things and Cloud, pp. 58–63. IEEE (2015)
5. Dwork, C., McSherry, F., Nissim, K., Smith, A.: Calibrating noise to sensitivity in private data analysis. In: Halevi, S., Rabin, T. (eds.) TCC 2006. LNCS, vol. 3876, pp. 265–284. Springer, Heidelberg (2006). https://doi.org/10.1007/11681878_14
6. Dwork, C., Naor, M., Pitassi, T., Rothblum, G.N.: Differential privacy under continual observation. In: Proceedings of the Forty-Second ACM Symposium on Theory of Computing, pp. 715–724 (2010)
7. Dwork, C., Roth, A., et al.: The algorithmic foundations of differential privacy. Found. Trends® Theor. Comput. Sci. **9**(3–4), 211–407 (2014)
8. Elkoumy, G., Fahrenkrog-Petersen, S.A., Dumas, M., Laud, P., Pankova, A., Weidlich, M.: Secure multi-party computation for inter-organizational process mining. In: Nurcan, S., Reinhartz-Berger, I., Soffer, P., Zdravkovic, J. (eds.) BPMDS/EMMSAD -2020. LNBIP, vol. 387, pp. 166–181. Springer, Cham (2020). https://doi.org/10.1007/978-3-030-49418-6_11

9. Erlingsson, Ú., Pihur, V., Korolova, A.: RAPPOR: randomized aggregatable privacy-preserving ordinal response. In: Proceedings of the 2014 ACM SIGSAC Conference on Computer and Communications Security, pp. 1054–1067. ACM (2014)
10. Data Protection Working Party of the EU Commission: Opinion 05/2014 on anonymisation techniques (2014)
11. Fahrenkrog-Petersen, S.A.: Providing privacy guarantees in process mining. In: CAiSE Doctoral Consortium, pp. 23–30 (2019)
12. Fahrenkrog-Petersen, S.A., van der Aa, H., Weidlich, M.: PRETSA: event log sanitization for privacy-aware process discovery. In: International Conference on Process Mining, ICPM 2019, Aachen, Germany, 24–26 June 2019, pp. 1–8 (2019)
13. Garfinkel, S.L.: De-identification of personal information. National Institute of Standards and Technology (2015)
14. Hintze, M.: Viewing the GDPR through a de-identification lens: a tool for compliance, clarification, and consistency. Int. Data Priv. Law $8(1)$, 86–101 (2018)
15. Holohan, N., Braghin, S., Mac Aonghusa, P., Levacher, K.: Diffprivlib: The IBM differential privacy library. arXiv preprint arXiv:1907.02444 (2019)
16. Holohan, N., Leith, D.J., Mason, O.: Optimal differentially private mechanisms for randomised response. IEEE Trans. Inf. Forensics Secur. $12(11)$, 2726–2735 (2017)
17. Kartal, H.B., Liu, X., Li, X.B.: Differential privacy for the vast majority. ACM Trans. Manag. Inf. Syst. (TMIS) $10(2)$, 1–15 (2019)
18. Kasiviswanathan, S.P., Lee, H.K., Nissim, K., Raskhodnikova, S., Smith, A.: What can we learn privately? SIAM J. Comput. $40(3)$, 793–826 (2011)
19. Kessler, S., Hoff, J., Freytag, J.C.: SAP HANA goes private: from privacy research to privacy aware enterprise analytics. Proc. VLDB Endow. $12(12)$, 1998–2009 (2019)
20. LeFevre, K., DeWitt, D.J., Ramakrishnan, R.: Incognito: efficient full-domain k-anonymity. In: Proceedings of the 2005 ACM SIGMOD International Conference on Management of Data, pp. 49–60 (2005)
21. Levenshtein, V.I.: Binary codes capable of correcting deletions, insertions, and reversals. Sov. Phys. Doklady. 10, 707–710 (1966)
22. Liu, C., Duan, H., Zeng, Q., Zhou, M., Lu, F., Cheng, J.: Towards comprehensive support for privacy preservation cross-organization business process mining. IEEE Trans. Serv. Comput. $12(4)$, 639–653 (2016)
23. Maggi, F.M., Di Francescomarino, C., Dumas, M., Ghidini, C.: Predictive monitoring of business processes. In: Jarke, M., et al. (eds.) CAiSE 2014. LNCS, vol. 8484, pp. 457–472. Springer, Cham (2014). https://doi.org/10.1007/978-3-319-07881-6_31
24. Mannhardt, F.: Sepsis cases-event log, pp. 227–228. Eindhoven University of Technology. Dataset (2016)
25. Mannhardt, F., Koschmider, A., Baracaldo, N., Weidlich, M., Michael, J.: Privacy-preserving process mining. Bus. Inf. Syst. Eng. $61(5)$, 595–614 (2019). https://doi.org/10.1007/s12599-019-00613-3
26. Mannhardt, F., Petersen, S.A., Oliveira, M.F.: Privacy challenges for process mining in human-centered industrial environments. In: 14th International Conference on Intelligent Environments, IE 2018, Roma, Italy, 25–28 June 2018, pp. 64–71 (2018)
27. McSherry, F., Talwar, K.: Mechanism design via differential privacy. In: 48th Annual IEEE Symposium on Foundations of Computer Science (FOCS 2007), pp. 94–103. IEEE (2007)

28. McSherry, F.D.: Privacy integrated queries: an extensible platform for privacy-preserving data analysis. In: Proceedings of the 2009 ACM SIGMOD International Conference on Management of Data, pp. 19–30. ACM (2009)
29. Pika, A., Wynn, M.T., Budiono, S., Ter Hofstede, A.H., van der Aalst, W.M., Reijers, H.A.: Privacy-preserving process mining in healthcare. vol. 17, p. 1612. Multidisciplinary Digital Publishing Institute (2020)
30. Rafiei, M., van der Aalst, W.M.P.: Mining roles from event logs while preserving privacy. In: Di Francescomarino, C., Dijkman, R., Zdun, U. (eds.) BPM 2019. LNBIP, vol. 362, pp. 676–689. Springer, Cham (2019). https://doi.org/10.1007/978-3-030-37453-2_54
31. Rafiei, M., von Waldthausen, L., van der Aalst, W.M.: Ensuring confidentiality in process mining. In: SIMPDA, pp. 3–17 (2018)
32. Team, D., et al.: Learning with privacy at scale (2017). https://machinelearning.apple.com/2017/12/06/learning-with-privacy-at-scale.html
33. Tillem, G., Erkin, Z., Lagendijk, R.L.: Privacy-preserving alpha algorithm for software analysis. In: 37th WIC Symposium on Information Theory in the Benelux/6th WIC/IEEE SP Symposium on Information Theory and Signal Processing in the Benelux (2016)
34. van der Aalst, W., et al.: Process mining manifesto. In: Daniel, F., Barkaoui, K., Dustdar, S. (eds.) BPM 2011. LNBIP, vol. 99, pp. 169–194. Springer, Heidelberg (2012). https://doi.org/10.1007/978-3-642-28108-2_19
35. Voigt, P., Von dem Bussche, A.: The EU General Data Protection Regulation (GDPR). A Practical Guide, 1st edn. Springer, Cham (2017). https://doi.org/10.1007/978-3-319-57959-7
36. Nuñez von Voigt, S., et al.: Quantifying the re-identification risk of event logs for process mining. In: Dustdar, S., Yu, E., Salinesi, C., Rieu, D., Pant, V. (eds.) CAiSE 2020. LNCS, vol. 12127, pp. 252–267. Springer, Cham (2020). https://doi.org/10.1007/978-3-030-49435-3_16
37. Warner, S.L.: Randomized response: a survey technique for eliminating evasive answer bias. J. Am. Stat. Assoc. 60(309), 63–69 (1965)
38. Zhang, J., Borisov, N., Yurcik, W.: Outsourcing security analysis with anonymized logs. In: 2006 Securecomm and Workshops, pp. 1–9. IEEE (2006)

A Framework for Estimating Simplicity of Automatically Discovered Process Models Based on Structural and Behavioral Characteristics

Anna Kalenkova⬦, Artem Polyvyanyy⬦, and Marcello La Rosa(✉)⬦

School of Computing and Information Systems,
The University of Melbourne, Parkville, VIC 3010, Australia
{anna.kalenkova,artem.polyvyanyy,marcello.larosa}@unimelb.edu.au

Abstract. A plethora of algorithms for automatically discovering process models from event logs has emerged. The discovered models are used for analysis and come with a graphical flowchart-like representation that supports their comprehension by analysts. According to the Occam's Razor principle, a model should encode the process behavior with as few constructs as possible, that is, it should not be overcomplicated without necessity. The simpler the graphical representation, the easier the described behavior can be understood by a stakeholder. Conversely, and intuitively, a complex representation should be harder to understand. Although various conformance checking techniques that relate the behavior of discovered models to the behavior recorded in event logs have been proposed, there are no methods for evaluating whether this behavior is represented in the simplest possible way. Existing techniques for measuring the simplicity of discovered models focus on their structural characteristics such as size or density, and ignore the behavior these models encoded. In this paper, we present a conceptual framework that can be instantiated into a concrete approach for estimating the simplicity of a model, considering the behavior the model describes, thus allowing a more holistic analysis. The reported evaluation over real-life event logs for several instantiations of the framework demonstrates its feasibility in practice.

1 Introduction

Information systems keep records of the business processes they support in the form of event logs. An event log is a collection of traces encoding timestamped actions undertook to execute the corresponding process. Thus, such logs contain valuable information on how business processes are carried out in the real world. Process mining [1] aims to exploit this historical information to understand, analyze, and ultimately improve business processes. A core problem in process mining is that of automatically discovering a process model from an event log. Such a model should faithfully encode the process behavior captured

© Springer Nature Switzerland AG 2020
D. Fahland et al. (Eds.): BPM 2020, LNCS 12168, pp. 129–146, 2020.
https://doi.org/10.1007/978-3-030-58666-9_8

in the log and, hence, meet a range of criteria. Specifically, a discovered model should describe the traces recorded in the log (have good *fitness*), not encode traces not present in the log (have good *precision*), capture possible traces that may stem from the same process but are not present in the log (have good *generalization*), and be *"simple"*. These quality measures for discovered process models are studied within the conformance checking area of process mining. A good discovered model is thus supposed to achieve a good balance between these criteria [3].

In [1], Van der Aalst suggests that process discovery should be guided by the Occam's Razor principle [8,10], a problem-solving principle attributed to William of Ockham. Accordingly, "one should not increase, beyond what is necessary, the number of entities required to explain anything" [1]. Specifically to process mining, a discovered process model should only contain the necessary constructs. Various measures for assessing whether a discovered model is simple have been proposed in the literature [9,15], such as the number of nodes and arcs, density, and diameter. However, these measures address the number of constructs, i.e., the structure of the discovered models, while ignoring what these constructs describe, i.e., the process behavior.

In this paper, we present a framework that considers the model's structure and behavior to operationalize Occam's Razor principle for measuring the simplicity of a process model discovered from an event log. The framework comprises three components that can selectively be configured: (i) a notion for measuring the structural complexity of a process model, e.g., size or diameter; (ii) a notion for assessing the behavioral similarity, or equivalence, of process models, e.g., trace equivalence, bisimulation, or entropy; and (iii) the representation bias, i.e., a modeling language for describing models. A configured framework results in an approach for estimating the simplicity of process models. The obtained simplicity score establishes whether the behavior captured by the model can be encoded in a structurally simpler model. To this end, the structure of the model is related to the structures of other behaviorally similar process models.

To demonstrate these ideas, we instantiate the framework with the *number of nodes* [9] and *control flow complexity* (*cfc*) [4] measures of structural complexity, *topological entropy* [20] measure of behavioral similarity, and uniquely labeled *block-structured* [19] process models captured in the Business Process Model and Notation (BPMN) [18] as the representation bias. We then apply these framework instantiations to assess the simplicity of the process models automatically discovered from event logs by the Inductive miner algorithm [16]. This algorithm constructs *process trees*, which can then be converted into uniquely labeled *block-structured* BPMN models [14].

Once the framework is configured, the next challenge is to obtain models of various structures that specify behaviors similar to that captured by the given model, as these are then used to establish and quantify the amount of unnecessary structural information in the given model. To achieve completeness, one should aim to obtain all the similar models, including the simplest ones. As an exhaustive approach for synthesizing all such models is often unfeasible in practice, in this paper, we take an empirical approach and synthesize random models that approximate those models with similar behavior. To implement such approximations, we developed a tool that generates uniquely labeled block-structured BPMN models randomly, or exhaustively for some restricted cases, and measures their structural complexity and behavioral similarity.

The remainder of this paper is organized as follows. Section 2 discusses an example that motivates the problem of ignoring the behavior when measuring the simplicity of process models. Section 3 presents our framework for estimating the simplicity of the discovered models. In Sect. 4, we instantiate the framework with concrete components. Section 5 presents the results of an analysis of process models discovered from real-life event logs using our framework instantiations. Section 6 concludes the paper.

2   Motivating Example

In this section, we show that the existing simplicity measures do not always follow the Occam's Razor principle. Consider event log $L = \{\langle load\,page,$ $fill\,name,\ fill\,passport,\ fill\,expire\,date\rangle,\ \langle load\,page,\ fill\,name,\ fill\,expire\,date,$ $fill\,passport\rangle,\ \langle load\,page,\ fill\,passport,\ fill\,expire\,date\rangle,\ \langle load\,page,\ fill\,name,$ $fill\,expire\,date\rangle,\ \langle load\,page,\ fill\,name,\ fill\,passport\rangle,\ \langle load\,page,\ fill\,name,$ $fill\,passport,\ fill\,expire\,date,\ load\,page\rangle,\ \langle load\,page,\ fill\,name,\ fill\,expire\,date,$ $fill\,passport, load\,page\rangle, \langle load\,page, fill\,name, load\,page\rangle, \langle fill\,name, fill\,expire\,date,$ $fill\,passport\rangle,\ \langle fill\,passport,\ fill\,expire\,date\rangle\}$ generated by a passport renewal information system.[1] The log contains ten *traces*, each encoded as a sequence of *events*, or *steps*, taken by the users of the system. Usually, the user loads the Web page and fills out relevant forms with details such as name, previous passport number, and expiry date. Some steps in the traces may be skipped or repeated, as this is common for the real world event data [13], Fig. 1 and Fig. 2 present BPMN models discovered from L using, respectively, the Split miner [2] and Inductive miner (with the noise threshold set to 0.2) [16] process discovery algorithm.

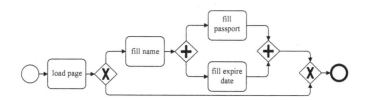

Fig. 1. A BPMN model discovered by Split miner from event log L.

It is evident from the figures that the models are different. First, they have different structures. Figure 1 shows an acyclic model with exclusive and parallel branches. In contrast, the model in Fig. 2 only contains exclusive branches enclosed in a loop and allowing to skip any of the steps. Second, the models

---

[1] This simple example is inspired by a real world event log analyzed in [13].

describe different collections of traces. While the model in Fig. 1 describes three traces (viz. ⟨load page⟩, ⟨load page, fill name, fill passport, fill expire date⟩, and ⟨load page, fill name, fill expire date, fill passport⟩), the model in Fig. 2 describes all the possible traces over the given steps, i.e., all the possible sequences of the steps, including repetitions.

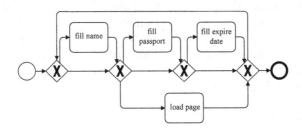

Fig. 2. A BPMN model discovered by Inductive miner from event log L.

The latter fact is also evident in the precision and recall values between the models and log. The precision and recall values of the model in Fig. 1 are 0.852 and 0.672, respectively, while the precision and recall values of the model in Fig. 2 are 0.342 and 1.0, respectively; the values were obtained using the entropy-based measures presented in [20]. The values indicate, for instance, that the model in Fig. 2 is more permissive (has lower precision), i.e., encodes more behavior not seen in the log than the model in Fig. 1, and describes all the traces in the log (has perfect fitness of 1.0); the measures take values on the interval $[0, 1]$ with larger values showing better precision and fitness.

To assess the simplicity of discovered process models, measures of their structural complexity [4, 9,15,17], such as the *number of nodes* and/or *edges*, *density, depth, coefficients of network connectivity*, and *control flow complexity*, can be employed. If one relies on the number of nodes to establish the simplicity of the two example models, then they will derive at the conclusion that they are equally simple, as both contain ten nodes. This conclusion is, however, naïve for at least two reasons: (i) the two models use ten nodes to encode different behaviors, and (ii) it may be unnecessary to use ten nodes to encode the corresponding behaviors.

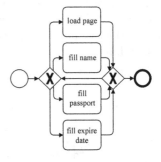

Fig. 3. A "flower" model.

The model in Fig. 3 describes the same behavior as the model in Fig. 2 using eight nodes. One can use different notions to establish similarity of the behaviors, including exact (e.g., trace equivalence) or approximate (e.g., topological entropy). The models in Figs. 2 and 3 are trace equivalent and specify the behaviors that have the (short-circuit) topological entropy of 1.0 [20]. Intuitively, the entropy measures the "variety" of traces of different lengths specified by the

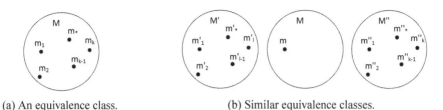

(a) An equivalence class.   (b) Similar equivalence classes.

Fig. 4. Behavioral classes of model equivalence.

model. The more distinct traces of different lengths the model describes, the closer the entropy is to 1.0. The entropy of the model in Fig. 1 is 0.185. There is no block-structured BPMN model with unique task labels that describes the behavior with the entropy of 0.185 and uses less than ten nodes. Thus, we argue that the model in Fig. 1 should be accepted as such that is simpler than the model in Fig. 2.

3   A Framework for Estimating Simplicity of Process Models

In this section, we present our framework for estimating the simplicity of process models. The framework describes standard components that can be configured to result in a concrete measure of simplicity. The *simplicity framework* is a tuple $\mathcal{F} = (\mathcal{M}, \mathcal{C}, \mathcal{B})$, where $\mathcal{M}$ is a collection of *process models*, $\mathcal{C} : \mathcal{M} \rightarrow \mathbb{R}_0^+$ is a measure of *structural complexity*, and $\mathcal{B} \subseteq (\mathcal{M} \times \mathcal{M})$ is a *behavioral equivalence* relation over $\mathcal{M}$.

The process models are captured using some process modeling language (representation bias), e.g., finite state machines [11], Petri nets [21], or BPMN [18]. The measure of structural complexity is a function that maps the models onto non-negative real numbers, with smaller assigned numbers indicating simpler models. For graph-based models, this can be the number of nodes and edges, density, diameter, or some other existing measure of simplicity used in process mining [17]. The behavioral equivalence relation $\mathcal{B}$ must define an equivalence relation over $\mathcal{M}$, i.e., be reflexive, symmetric, and transitive. For instance, $\mathcal{B}$ can be given by (weak or strong) bisimulation [12] or trace equivalence [11] relation over models. Alternatively, equivalence classes of $\mathcal{B}$ can be defined by models with the same or similar measure of behavioral complexity, e.g., (short-circuit) topological entropy [20].

Given a model $m_1 \in \mathcal{M}$, its behavioral equivalence class per relation $\mathcal{B}$ is the set $M = \{m \in \mathcal{M} \mid (m, m_1) \in \mathcal{B}\}$, cf. Fig. 4a. If one knows a model $m_* \in M$ with the lowest structural complexity in M, i.e., $\forall m \in M : \mathcal{C}(m_*) \leq \mathcal{C}(m)$, then they can put the simplicity of models in M into the perspective of the simplicity of m_*. For instance, one can use function $sim(m) = (\mathcal{C}(m_*)+1)/(\mathcal{C}(m)+1)$ to establish such a perspective.

Suppose that $\mathcal{M}$ is the set of all block-structured BPMN models with four uniquely labeled tasks, $\mathcal{B}$ is the trace equivalence relation, and $\mathcal{C}$ is the measure of the number of nodes in the models. Then, it holds that $sim(m_1) = 1.0$ and $sim(m_2) = 9/11 = 0.818$, where m_1 and m_2 are the models from Fig. 1 and Fig. 2, respectively, indicating that m_1 is simpler than m_2. To obtain these simplicity values, we used our tool and generated all the block-structured BPMN models over four uniquely labeled tasks, computed all the behavioral equivalence classes over the generated models, and collected statistics on the numbers of nodes in the models.

For some configurations of the framework, however, such exhaustive analysis may yield intractable. For instance, the collection of models of interest may be infinite, or finite but immense. Note that the number of block-structured BPMN models with four uniquely labeled tasks is 2,211,840, and is 297,271,296 if one considers models with five uniquely labeled tasks (the number of models grows exponentially with the number of allowed labels). In such cases, we suggest grounding the analysis in a representative subset $\mathcal{M}' \subset \mathcal{M}$ of the models.

Suppose that one analyzes model $m \in \mathcal{M}$ that has no other (or only a few) models in its equivalence class M, refer to Fig. 4b. Then, model m can be compared to models of lowest structural complexities m'_* and m''_* from some other equivalence classes M' and M'' which contain models that describe the behaviors "similar" to the one captured by m. To this end, one needs to establish a measure of "similarity" between the behavioral equivalence classes of models.

In the next section, we exemplify the discussed concepts by presenting example instantiations of the framework.

4   Framework Instantiations

In this section, we instantiate our framework $\mathcal{F} = (\mathcal{M}, \mathcal{C}, \mathcal{B})$ for assessing the simplicity of process models discovered from event logs and define the set of models ($\mathcal{M}$), structural complexity ($\mathcal{C}$), and the behavioral equivalence relation ($\mathcal{B}$) as follows:

- $\mathcal{M}$ is a set of block-structured BPMN models with a fixed number of uniquely labeled tasks. BPMN is one of the most popular process modeling languages. Besides, block-structured uniquely labeled process models are discovered by Inductive miner—a widely used process discovery algorithm;
- $\mathcal{C}$ is either the *number of nodes* or the *control flow complexity* measure. These measures were selected among other simplicity measures, because, as shown empirically in Sect. 5, there is a relation between these measures and the behavioral characteristics of process models; and
- $\mathcal{B}$ is the behavioral equivalence relation induced by the notion of (short-circuit) *topological entropy* [20]. The entropy measure is selected because it maps process models onto non-negative real numbers that reflect the complexity of the behaviors they describe; the greater the entropy, the more variability is present in the underlying behavior. Consequently, models from an equivalence class of $\mathcal{B}$ describe behaviors with the same (or very similar) entropy values.

For BPMN models the problem of minimization is still open and only some rules for local BPMN models simplification exist [14,22]. Although, NP-complete techniques [5] synthesizing Petri nets with minimal regions (corresponding to BPMN models [14] with minimal number of routing contracts) from the sets traces can be applied, there is no general algorithm for finding a *block-structured* BPMN model that contains a minimal possible number of nodes or has a minimal control flow complexity for a given process behavior. In this case, it may be feasible to generate the set of all possible process models for the given behavioral class (see the general description of this approach within our framework Sect. 3, Fig. 4a). However, due to the combinatorial explosion, the possible number of block-structured BPMN models grows exponentially with the number of tasks. While it is still possible to generate all block-structured BPMN models containing 4 or less tasks, for larger number of tasks this problem is computationally expensive and cannot be solved in any reasonable amount of time. In this work, we propose an approach that approximates the exact solutions by comparing analyzed models with only some randomly generated models that behave similarly. This approach implements a general approximation idea proposed within our framework (Sect. 3, Fig. 4b). Section 4.1 introduces basic notions used to describe this approach. Section 4.2 describes the proposed approach, discusses its parameters and analyzes dependencies between structural and behavioral characteristics of block-structured BPMN models.

4.1 Basic Notions

In this subsection, we define basic notions that are used later in this section.

Let X be a finite set of elements. By $\langle x_1, x_2, \ldots, x_k \rangle$, where $x_1, x_2, \ldots, x_k \in X$, $k \in \mathbb{N}_0$, we denote a finite *sequence* of elements over X of length k. X^* stands for the set of all finite sequences over X including the empty sequence of zero length.

Given two sequences $x = \langle x_1, x_2, \ldots, x_k \rangle$ and $y = \langle y_1, y_2, \ldots, y_m \rangle$, by $x \cdot y$ we denote *concatenation* of x and y, i.e., the sequence obtained by appending y to the end of x, i.e., $x \cdot y = \langle x_1, x_2, \ldots, x_k, y_1, y_2, \ldots, y_m \rangle$.

An *alphabet* is a nonempty finite set. The elements of an alphabet are its *labels*. A (formal) *language* L over an alphabet Σ is a (not necessarily finite) set of *sequences*, over Σ, i.e., $L \subseteq \Sigma^*$. Let L_1 and L_2 be two languages. Then, $L_1 \circ L_2$ is their concatenation defined by $\{l_1 \cdot l_2 \mid l_1 \in L_1 \wedge l_2 \in L_2\}$. The language L^* is defined as $L^* = \bigcup_{n=0}^{\infty} L^n$, where $L^0 = \{\langle\rangle\}$, $L^n = L^{n-1} \circ L$.

Structural Representation. The class of process models considered in this work are *block-structured* BPMN models that are often used for the representation of processes discovered from event logs, e.g., these models are discovered by the Inductive mining algorithm [16].

Block-structured BPMN models are constructed from the following basic set of elements: *start* and *end events* represented by circles with thin and thick borders respectively and denoting beginning and termination of the process;

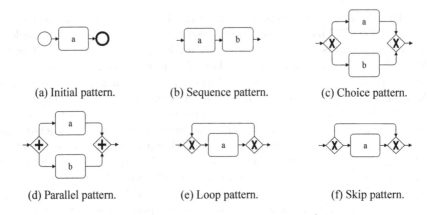

(a) Initial pattern.   (b) Sequence pattern.   (c) Choice pattern.

(d) Parallel pattern.   (e) Loop pattern.   (f) Skip pattern.

Fig. 5. Patterns of block-structured BPMN models.

tasks modeling atomic process steps and depicted by rounded rectangles with labels; routing *exclusive* and *parallel gateways* modeling exclusive and parallel executions and presented by diamonds; and *control flow* arcs that define the order in which elements are executed.

The investigated class of *block-structured* BPMN models consists of all and only BPMN models that:

1) can be constructed starting from the initial model presented in Fig. 5a and inductively replacing tasks with the patterns presented in Figs. 5b to 5f;
2) have *uniquely* labeled tasks, i.e., any two tasks have different labels;
3) when constructing a model, only patterns other than loop can be applied to the nested task of the loop pattern; only patterns other than skip and loop can be applied to the nested task of the skip pattern;

When constructing a model, the number of tasks increases if the patterns from Figs. 5b to 5d are applied, the patterns Figs. 5e to 5f can be applied no more than twice in a row, and the pattern Fig. 5a is applied only once. Hence, if we fix the number tasks (labels) in the investigated models, the the overall set of these models is finite.

After constructing the collection of models, local minimization rules are applied [14]. These rules merge gateways without changing the model semantics. An example of local reduction of gateways is presented in Fig. 6a, Fig. 6b illustrates merging of loop and skip constructs. For the detailed description of local minimization rules refer to [14].

We focus on the following complexity measures of block-structured BPMN models: (1) C_n – the *number of nodes* (including start and end events, tasks, and gateways); (2) C_{cfc} - the *control flow complexity* measure, which is defined as a sum of two numbers: the number of all splitting parallel gateways and the total number of all outgoing control flows of all splitting exclusive (choice) gateways [4].

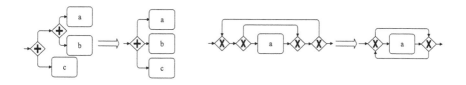

(a) Merging parallel gateways.   (b) Merging loop and skip constructs.

Fig. 6. Examples of applying local minimization rules.

Sequences of labels are used to encode executions of business processes. The ordering of tasks being executed defines the ordering of labels in a sequence. We say that a process model encodes or *accepts* a formal language if and only if this language contains all possible sequences of labels corresponding to the orderings of tasks being executed within the model and only them. Figure 7a presents an example of a block-structured model m_1 that accepts language $L_1 = \{\langle a, b, c\rangle, \langle a, c, b\rangle, \langle b, a, c\rangle, \langle b, c, a\rangle, \langle c, a, b\rangle, \langle c, b, a\rangle\}$. A block-structured BPMN model m_2 accepting an infinite language of all sequences starting with a in alphabet $\{a, b, c\}$ is presented in Fig. 7b.

Behavioral Representation. Next, we recall the notion of entropy which is used for the behavioral analysis of process models and event logs [20]. Let Σ be an alphabet and let $L \subseteq \Sigma^*$ be a language over this alphabet. We say that language L is *irreducible regular* language if and only if it is accepted by a strongly-connected automata model (for details refer to [6]). Let $C_n(L)$, $n \in \mathbb{N}_0$, be the set of all sequences in L of length n. Then, the *topological entropy* that estimates the cardinality of L by measuring the ratio of the number of distinct sequences in the language to the length of these sequences is defined as [6]:

$$ent(L) = \limsup_{n\to\infty} \frac{\log |C_n(L)|}{n}. \tag{1}$$

The languages accepted by block-structured BPMN models are *regular*, because they are also accepted by corresponding automata models [11]. But not all of them are *irreducible*, so the standard topological entropy (Eq. 1) cannot be always calculated. To that end, in [20], it was proposed to construct an irreducible language $(L \circ \{\langle \chi \rangle\})^* \circ L$, where $\chi \notin \Sigma$, for each language L, and use so-called *short-circuit* entropy $ent\bullet(L) = ent((L \circ \{\langle \chi \rangle\})^* \circ L)$. Monotonicity of the short-circuit measure follows immediately from the definition of the short-circuit topological entropy and Lemma 4.7 in [20]:

Corollary 4.1 (Topological entropy). *Let L_1 and L_2 be two regular languages.*

1. *If $L_1 = L_2$, then $ent\bullet(L_1) = ent\bullet(L_2)$;*
2. *If $L_1 \subset L_2$, then $ent\bullet(L_1) < ent\bullet(L_2)$.*

(a) Block-structured BPMN model m_1.   (b) Block-structured BPMN model m_2.

Fig. 7. Examples of block-structured BPMN models.

Note that the opposite is not always true, i.e., different languages can be represented by the same entropy value. Although the language (trace) equivalence is stricter than the entropy-based equivalence, in the next section, we show that entropy is still useful for classifying the process behavior.

In this paper, we use the notion of *normalized* entropy. Suppose that L is a language over alphabet Σ, then the normalized entropy of L is defined as: $\overline{ent}(L) = \frac{ent\bullet(L)}{ent\bullet(\Sigma^*)}$, where Σ^* is the language containing all words over alphabet Σ. The normalized entropy value is bounded, because, for any language L it holds that $L \subseteq \Sigma^*$, and hence, by Corollary 4.1 $ent\bullet(L) \leq ent\bullet(\Sigma^*)$, consequently $\overline{ent}(L) \in [0,1]$. Obviously, Corollary 4.1 can be formulated and applied to the normalized entropy measure, i.e., for two languages L_1 and L_2 over alphabet Σ, if $L_1 = L_2$, then $\overline{ent}(L_1) = \overline{ent}(L_2)$, and if $L_1 \subset L_2$, it holds that $\overline{ent}(L_1) < \overline{ent}(L_2)$.

We define the relation of behavioral equivalence $\mathcal{B}$ using the normalized entropy. Let Σ be an alphabet and let $L_1, L_2 \subseteq \Sigma^*$ be languages accepted by models m_1 and m_2 respectively, $(m_1, m_2) \in \mathcal{B}$ if and only if $\overline{ent}(L_1) = \overline{ent}(L_2)$.

Normalized entropy not only allows to define the notion of behavioral equivalence, but also to formalize the notion of behavioral similarity. For a given parameter Δ, we say that two models m_1 and m_2 are *behaviorally similar* if and only if $|\overline{ent}(L_1) - \overline{ent}(L_2)| < \Delta$, where L_1 and L_2 are the languages these models accept.

4.2   Estimating Simplicity of Block-Structured BPMN Models

In this subsection, we devise a method for assessing the simplicity of uniquely labeled block-structured BPMN models. As no analytical method for synthetizing a "minimal" block-structured BPMN model in terms of number of nodes or control flow complexity for a given behavior is known, and no computationally feasible approach for generating all possible models with a given behavior exists, we propose an approach that investigates the dependencies between the structural and behavioral model characteristics empirically, and reuse these dependencies to measure the simplicity of models.

As the set of all models $\mathcal{M}$ cannot be exhaustively constructed, we generate its subset $\mathcal{M}' \subset \mathcal{M}$ and relate analyzed models from $\mathcal{M}$ with behaviorally

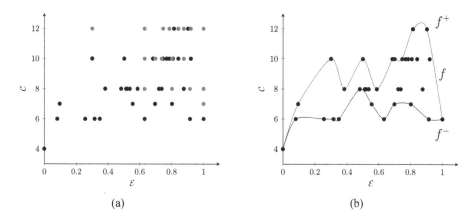

Fig. 8. Structural (C) and behavioral ($\mathcal{E}$) characteristics of process models: (a) for all models in $\mathcal{M}'$ and (b) filtered models with upper and lower envelops for $\Delta = 0.05$.

similar models from $\mathcal{M}'$, producing an approximate solution. We then estimate the simplicity of the given model by comparing its structural complexity with that of the simplest behaviorally similar models, with the complexity of these models being in a certain interval from "the best case" to "the worst case" complexity. In order to define this interval and relate it to entropy values, we construct envelope functions f^- and f^+ that approximate "the best case" and "the worst case" structural complexity of the simplest process models for a given entropy value. Below we give an approach for constructing these envelope functions and define the simplicity measure that relates the model complexity to an interval defined by these functions.

Let $\mathcal{E} : \mathcal{M}' \rightarrow [0,1]$ be a function that maps process models in $\mathcal{M}'$ onto the corresponding normalized entropy values. Figure 8a presents an example plot relating structural characteristics $C(m)$ and entropy $\mathcal{E}(m)$ values for each process model $m \in \mathcal{M}'$; the example is artificial and does not correspond to any concrete structural and behavioral measures of process models. Once such data points are obtained, we filter out all the models $m \in \mathcal{M}'$ such that $\exists m' \in \mathcal{M}' : \mathcal{E}(m) = \mathcal{E}(m')$ and $C(m) > C(m')$. In other words, we filter out a model, if its underlying behavior can be described in a structurally simpler model. This means that only the structurally "simplest" models remain. The process models that were filtered out are presented by gray dots in Fig. 8a.

Once the set $\mathcal{M}''$ of the models remaining after filtering the models in $\mathcal{M}'$ is obtained, it defines the partial function $f : [0,1] \nrightarrow \mathbb{R}_0^+$, such that $f(e) = c$ if and only if exists a model $m \in \mathcal{M}''$, where $e = \mathcal{E}(m)$ and $c = C(m)$ (Fig. 8b). This function relates the behavioral and structural characteristics of the remaining models. Then, we construct envelop functions that define intervals of the structural complexities of the remaining "simplest" models. The upper envelop $f^+ : [0,1] \rightarrow \mathbb{R}_0^+$ is a function going through the set of data points $D^+ = \{(e, f(e)) \mid \forall e' \in dom(f) : (|e - e'| < \Delta \Rightarrow f(e) \geq f(e'))\}$, where Δ is a parameter that defines classes of behaviorally similar models. Less formally, f^+ goes through all the data points that are maximum in a Δ-size window. Similarly, the lower envelop is defined as a function $f^- : [0,1] \to \mathbb{R}_0^+$ going through $D^- = \{(e, f(e)) \,|\, \forall e' \in dom(f) : (|e - e'| < \Delta \Rightarrow f(e) \leq f(e'))\}$. In general, the envelope can be any smooth polynomial interpolation or a piecewise linear function, the only restriction is that it goes through D^+ and D^- data points.

Parameter Δ defines the measure of similarity between classes of behaviorally equivalent models. In each case, Δ should be selected empirically, for instance, too small Δ will lead to local evaluations, that may not be reliable because they do not take into account global trends, while setting too large Δ results in a situation when we do not take into account entropy, relating our model with all other models from the set. In Fig. 8b, the upper and lower envelops were constructed for $\Delta = 0.05$.

Using the upper and lower envelope functions we can estimate simplicity of process models from $\mathcal{M}$. The simplicity measure is defined in Eq. (2), where $sim(m)$ is the simplicity of model $m \in \mathcal{M}$ with an entropy value $e = \mathcal{E}(m)$; α and β are parameters, such that $\alpha, \beta \in [0,1]$ and $\alpha + \beta \leq 1$.

$$
sim(m) = \begin{cases}
\alpha \cdot \dfrac{f^+(e)}{\mathcal{C}(m)} & \mathcal{C}(m) \geq f^+(e) \\[2ex]
\alpha + (1 - \alpha - \beta) \cdot \dfrac{(f^+(e) - \mathcal{C}(m))}{(f^+(e) - f^-(e))} & f^-(e) \leq \mathcal{C}(m) < f^+(e) \\[2ex]
1.0 - \beta \cdot \dfrac{\mathcal{C}(m)}{f^-(e)} & \mathcal{C}(m) < f^-(e)
\end{cases}
\tag{2}
$$

According to Eq. (2), $sim(m)$ is in the interval between zero and one. Parameters α and β are used to adjust the measure. Parameter α shows the level of confidence that some complexity values can be above the upper envelope. If the complexity $\mathcal{C}(m)$ of model m is above the upper envelope $f^+(e)$, m is more complex than "the worst case" model, then $sim(m)$ is less than or equal to α and tends to zero as $\mathcal{C}(m)$ grows. If the model complexity $\mathcal{C}(m)$ is between the envelopes $f^-(e)$ and $f^+(e)$, then $sim(m) \in (\alpha, 1 - \beta]$ and the higher $\mathcal{C}(m)$ is (the closer the model is to "the worst case"), the closer the simplicity value to α. Parameter β shows the level of confidence that some data points may be below the lower envelope. If it is guaranteed that there are no models in $\mathcal{M}$ with data points below the lower envelope it is feasible to set β to zero. Otherwise, if $\mathcal{C}(m)$ is lower than the lower envelope $f^-(e)$, then $sim(m)$ belongs to the interval $(1 - \beta, 1]$ and tends to one as $\mathcal{C}(m)$ approaches zero.

Next, we apply the proposed approach to construct upper and lower envelope functions for the number of nodes and control flow complexity measures of block-structured BPMN models with a fixed number of uniquely labeled tasks. To analyze the relations between the structural and behavioral characteristics, we generated all block-structured BPMN models with three tasks. Figure 9 contains plots with data points representing the behavioral and structural characteristics of these process models. These data points, as well as the upper and lower envelopes, are constructed using the general technique described above with window parameter $\Delta = 0.01$. Additionally, to make the envelope functions less

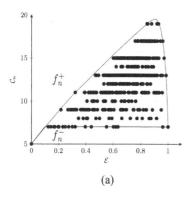 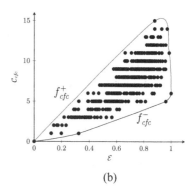

(a)   (b)

Fig. 9. Dependencies between entropy and structural complexity of block-structured BPMN models containing three tasks for the (a) number of nodes and (b) control flow complexity structural complexity measures.

detailed and reflect the main trends, we construct them only through some of the data points from D^+ and D^- sets in such a way that the second derivative of each envelope function is either non-negative or non-positive, i.e., envelope functions are either convex or concave.

In both cases, the upper envelope functions f_n^+ and f_{cfc}^+ grow monotonically, starting at the sequential model (a sequence of three tasks) with the entropy of zero, reach the maximum, and then drop to the "flower" model (see an example of a "flower" model in Fig. 3) with the entropy of one. These results show that, as the number of nodes (Fig. 9a) and complexity of the control flow (Fig. 9b) increase, the minimum possible entropy values also increase. As the model structure becomes more complex, more behavior is allowed and the lower bound of the entropy increases.

While the lower envelope for the number of nodes measure f_n^- (Fig. 9a) is flat and does not reveal any explicit dependency, the lower envelope for the control flow complexity f_{cfc}^- (Fig. 9b) grows. This can be explained by the fact that the number of nodes is reduced during the local model minimization [14], while the control flow complexity measure takes into account the number of outgoing arcs of exclusive splitting gateways and is not affected by the local minimization.

The empirical results and observations presented in this section reveal the main dependencies between the structural complexity and the behavioral complexity of block-structured BPMN models and can be generalized for an arbitrary number of tasks. They also show that this approach relies on the quality of the model generator, i.e., the set of generated models should be dense enough to reveal these dependencies. In the next section, we apply the proposed approach to assess the simplicity of process models discovered from real world event logs.

5   Evaluation

In this section, we use the approach from Sect. 4 to evaluate the simplicity of process models discovered by Inductive miner (with noise threshold 0.2) from industrial Business Process Intelligence Challenge (BPIC) event logs[2] and an event log of a booking flight system (BFS). Before the analysis, we filtered out infrequent events that appear less than in 80% of traces using the "Filter Log Using Simple Heuristics" Process Mining Framework (ProM) plug-in [7].[3] The Inductive miner algorithm discovers uniquely labeled block-structured BPMN models. As structural complexity measures, we used the number of nodes and the control flow complexity (*cfc*).

To estimate the upper and lower bounds of the structural complexity of the models, for each number of tasks (each size of the log alphabet), we generated 5,000 random uniquely labeled block-structured BPMN models. For all the models, data points representing the entropy and structural complexity of the models were constructed. We then constructed the upper and lower envelopes using the window of size 0.01, refer to Sect. 4 for the details. The envelopes were constructed as piecewise linear functions going through all the selected data points.

For both structural complexity measures, parameter α, cf. Eq. (2), was set to 0.5, i.e., models represented by the data points above the upper envelope are presumed to have simplicity characteristic lower than 0.5. In turn, parameter β was set to 0.0 and 0.1 for the *number of nodes* and *cfc* measure, respectively. In contrast to *cfc*, the lower envelope for the *number of nodes* measure is defined as the minimal possible number of nodes in any model, and this guarantees that there are no data points below it. The final equations for the *number of nodes* and *cfc* simplicity measures, where $e = \mathcal{E}(m)$ is the topological entropy of model m, $\mathcal{C}_n(m)$ is the *number of nodes* in m, $\mathcal{C}_{cfc}(m)$ is the *cfc* complexity of m, f_n^+ and f_{cfc}^+ are the upper envelopes for the *number of nodes* and *cfc* measures, and f_n^- and f_{cfc}^- are the corresponding lower envelopes, are given below.

$$sim_n(m) = \begin{cases} 0.5 \cdot \dfrac{f_n^+(e)}{\mathcal{C}_n(m)} & \mathcal{C}_n(m) \geq f_n^+(e) \\ 0.5 + 0.5 \cdot \dfrac{(f_n^+(e) - \mathcal{C}_n(m))}{(f_n^+(e) - f_n^-(e))} & f_n^-(e) \leq \mathcal{C}_n(m) < f_n^+(e) \\ 1.0 & \mathcal{C}_n(m) < f_n^-(e) \end{cases} \tag{3}$$

$$sim_{cfc}(m) = \begin{cases} 0.5 \cdot \dfrac{f_{cfc}^+(e)}{\mathcal{C}_{cfc}(m)} & \mathcal{C}_{cfc}(m) \geq f_{cfc}^+(e) \\ 0.5 + 0.4 \cdot \dfrac{(f_{cfc}^+(e) - \mathcal{C}_{cfc}(m))}{(f_{cfc}^+(e) - f_{cfc}^-(e))} & f_{cfc}^-(e) \leq \mathcal{C}_{cfc}(m) < f_{cfc}^+(e) \\ 1.0 - 0.1 \cdot \dfrac{\mathcal{C}_{cfc}(m)}{f_{cfc}^-(e)} & \mathcal{C}_{cfc}(m) < f_{cfc}^-(e) \end{cases} \tag{4}$$

Table 1 presents the original and adjusted (proposed in this paper) simplicity measures, induced by the *number of nodes* and *cfc* structural complexity measures, for the process models discovered from the evaluated event logs. Models were discovered from the filtered event logs and their sublogs that contain only traces appearing in the filtered event logs at least two or four times. Model

---

[2] BPIC logs: https://data.4tu.nl/repository/collection:event_logs_real.

[3] The filtered logs are available here: https://github.com/jbpt/codebase/tree/master/jbpt-pm/logs.

Table 1. Simplicity of uniquely labeled block-structured BPMN models discovered from industrial event logs and their sublogs; the number of unique traces (*#Traces*), number of distinct labels in the discovered models (*#Labels*) and their entropy values (*Entropy*) are specified.

Model	Event log	#Traces	#Labels	Entropy	C_n	sim_n	C_{cfc}	sim_{cfc}
m_1	BPIC'2019	3,365	6	0.484	12	0.923	5	0.767
m_2	BPIC'2019	614	6	0.333	12	0.887	5	0.697
m_3	BPIC'2019	302	6	0.377	12	0.901	6	0.714
m_4	BPIC'2018	15,536	8	0.800	25	0.684	20	0.690
m_5	BPIC'2018	1,570	7	0.432	16	0.802	10	0.680
m_6	BPIC'2018	618	7	0.638	18	0.813	15	0.676
m_7	BFS	279	6	0.378	14	0.754	5	0.723
m_8	BFS	70	6	0.847	20	0.485	13	0.723
m_9	BFS	29	6	0.258	15	0.630	7	0.516

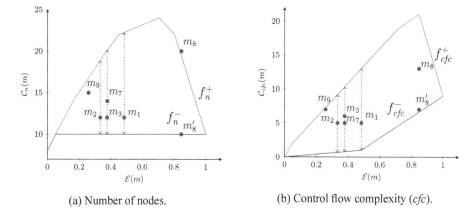

(a) Number of nodes.   (b) Control flow complexity (*cfc*).

Fig. 10. Structural complexity of block-structured BPMN models over six labels.

m_8 (refer to Fig. 11a) is an automatically discovered process model with redundant nodes. The value of $sim_n(m_8)$ is less than 0.5 because the corresponding data point is above the upper envelope (Fig. 10a). Note that the manually constructed "flower" model m_8' (Fig. 11) that accepts the same traces as m_8 has better structural complexity and, consequently, the corresponding adjusted simplicity measurements relate as follows: $sim_n(m_8') = 1.0 > sim_n(m_8) = 0.485$, and $sim_{cfc}(m_8') = 0.890 > sim_{cfc}(m_8) = 0.723$. The difference between $sim_{cfc}(m_8)$ and $sim_{cfc}(m_8')$ simplicity values is not as significant as the difference between $sim_n(m_8)$ and $sim_n(m_8')$, as despite m_8' has only two gateways the total number of outgoing sequence flows from these gateways is rather high.

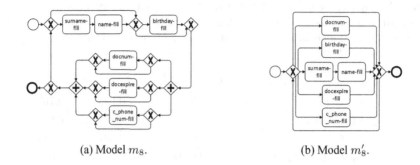

(a) Model m_8.

(b) Model m_8'.

Fig. 11. Models m_8 and m_8' discovered from the BFS event log.

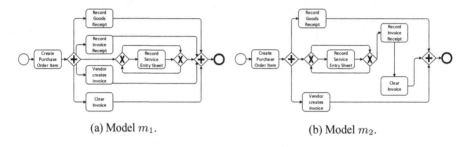

(a) Model m_1.

(b) Model m_2.

Fig. 12. Models m_1 and m_2 discovered from the BPIC'2019 event log.

Models m_1, m_2, and m_3 have the same number of nodes, but different entropy values. Model m_1 is considered the simplest in terms of the number of nodes among the three models because it is located further from the upper envelope than the other two models. Hence, its sim_n value is the highest. Models m_1 and m_2, which in addition have the same control flow complexity values, are shown in Fig. 12a and Fig. 12b, respectively. Model m_1 is considered more simple than model m_2 because it merely runs all the tasks in parallel (allowing *"Record Service Entry Sheet"* task to be skipped or executed several times). In contrast, model m_2 adds additional constraints on the order of tasks (leading to lower entropy) and, thus, should be easier to test. Note that m_1 models a more diverse behavior which in the worst case, according to the upper envelope, can be modeled with more nodes. These results demonstrate that when analyzing the simplicity of a discovered process model, it is feasible and beneficial to consider both phenomena of the structural complexity of the model's diagrammatic representation and the variability/complexity of the behavior the model describes. This way, one can adhere to the Occam's Razor problem-solving principle.

6   Conclusion

This paper presents a framework that can be configured to result in a concrete approach for measuring the simplicity of process models discovered from event logs. In contrast to the existing simplicity measures, our framework accounts for both a model's structure and behavior. In this paper, the framework was implemented for the class of uniquely-labeled block-structured BPMN models using topological entropy as a measure of process model behavior. The experimental evaluation of process models discovered from real-life event logs shows the approach's ability to evaluate the quality of discovered process models by relating their structural complexity to the structural complexity of other process models that describe similar behaviors. Such analysis can complement existing simplicity measurement techniques showing the relative aspects of the structural complexity of the model.

We identify several research directions arising from this work. First, we acknowledge that the proposed instantiation of the framework is approximate and depends on the quality of the randomly generated models. The analysis of other structural complexity measures as well as more sophisticated random model generation algorithms can lead to a more precise approach. Second, the framework described in this paper can be instantiated with other classes of process models to extend its applicability to models discovered by a broader range of process discovery algorithms. Finally, we believe that this work can give valuable insights into the improvement of existing, and the development of new process discovery algorithms.

Acknowledgments. This work was supported by the Australian Research Council Discovery Project DP180102839. We sincerely thank the anonymous reviewers whose suggestions helped us to improve this paper.

References

1. Aalst, W.: Data science in action. In: Aalst, W. (ed.) Process Mining, pp. 3–23. Springer, Heidelberg (2016). https://doi.org/10.1007/978-3-662-49851-4_1
2. Augusto, A., Conforti, R., Dumas, M., La Rosa, M., Polyvyanyy, A.: Split miner: automated discovery of accurate and simple business process models from event logs. Knowl. Inf. Syst. **59**(2), 251–284 (2018). https://doi.org/10.1007/s10115-018-1214-x
3. Buijs, J.C.A.M., van Dongen, B.F., van der Aalst, W.M.P.: On the role of fitness, precision, generalization and simplicity in process discovery. In: Meersman, R., et al. (eds.) OTM 2012. LNCS, vol. 7565, pp. 305–322. Springer, Heidelberg (2012). https://doi.org/10.1007/978-3-642-33606-5_19
4. Cardoso, J.: How to Measure the Control-flow Complexity of Web processes and Workflows, pp. 199–212 (2005)
5. Carmona, J., Cortadella, J., Kishinevsky, M.: A region-based algorithm for discovering Petri Nets from event logs. In: Dumas, M., Reichert, M., Shan, M.C. (eds.) Business Process Management, vol. 5240, pp. 358–373. Springer, Heidelberg (2008). https://doi.org/10.1007/978-3-540-85758-7_26

6. Ceccherini-Silberstein, T., Machì, A., Scarabotti, F.: On the entropy of regular languages. Theor. Comp. Sci. **307**, 93–102 (2003)
7. van Dongen, B.F., de Medeiros, A.K.A., Verbeek, H.M.W., Weijters, A.J.M.M., van der Aalst, W.M.P.: The ProM framework: a new era in process mining tool support. In: Ciardo, G., Darondeau, P. (eds.) ICATPN 2005. LNCS, vol. 3536, pp. 444–454. Springer, Heidelberg (2005). https://doi.org/10.1007/11494744_25
8. Garrett, A.J.M.: Ockham's Razor, pp. 357–364. Springer, Netherlands (1991)
9. Gruhn, V., Laue, R.: Complexity metrics for business process models. In: 9th International Conference on Business Information Systems (BIS 2006), pp. 1–12 (2006)
10. Grünwald, P.D.: The Minimum Description Length Principle (Adaptive Computation and Machine Learning). The MIT Press (2007)
11. Hopcroft, J.E., Motwani, R., Ullman, J.D.: Introduction to Automata Theory, Languages, and Computation, 3rd edn. Addison-Wesley Longman Publishing Co., Inc., USA (2006)
12. Jančar, P., Kučera, A., Mayr, R.: Deciding bisimulation-like equivalences with finite-state processes. In: Larsen, K.G., Skyum, S., Winskel, G. (eds.) ICALP 1998. LNCS, vol. 1443, pp. 200–211. Springer, Heidelberg (1998). https://doi.org/10.1007/BFb0055053
13. Kalenkova, A.A., Ageev, A.A., Lomazova, I.A., van der Aalst, W.M.P.: E-government services: comparing real and expected user behavior. In: Teniente, E., Weidlich, M. (eds.) BPM 2017. LNBIP, vol. 308, pp. 484–496. Springer, Cham (2018). https://doi.org/10.1007/978-3-319-74030-0_38
14. Kalenkova, A., Aalst, W., Lomazova, I., Rubin, V.: Process mining using BPMN: relating event logs and process models process mining using BPMN. Relating event logs and process models. Softw. Syst. Model. **16**, 1019–1048 (2017)
15. Kluza, K., Nalepa, G.J., Lisiecki, J.: Square complexity metrics for business process models. In: Mach-Król, M., Pełech-Pilichowski, T. (eds.) Advances in Business ICT. AISC, vol. 257, pp. 89–107. Springer, Cham (2014). https://doi.org/10.1007/978-3-319-03677-9_6
16. Leemans, S.J.J., Fahland, D., van der Aalst, W.M.P.: Discovering block-structured process models from event logs - a constructive approach. In: Colom, J.-M., Desel, J. (eds.) PETRI NETS 2013. LNCS, vol. 7927, pp. 311–329. Springer, Heidelberg (2013). https://doi.org/10.1007/978-3-642-38697-8_17
17. Lieben, J., Jouck, T., Depaire, B., Jans, M.: An improved way for measuring simplicity during process discovery. In: Pergl, R., Babkin, E., Lock, R., Malyzhenkov, P., Merunka, V. (eds.) EOMAS 2018. LNBIP, vol. 332, pp. 49–62. Springer, Cham (2018). https://doi.org/10.1007/978-3-030-00787-4_4
18. OMG: Business Process Model and Notation (BPMN), Version 2.0.2 (2013). http://www.omg.org/spec/BPMN/2.0.2
19. Polyvyanyy, A.: Structuring process models. Ph.D. thesis, University of Potsdam (2012). http://opus.kobv.de/ubp/volltexte/2012/5902/
20. Polyvyanyy, A., Solti, A., Weidlich, M., Ciccio, C.D., Mendling, J.: Monotone precision and recall measures for comparing executions and specifications of dynamic systems. ACM Trans. Softw. Eng. Methodol. **29**(3) (2020). https://doi.org/10.1145/3387909
21. Reisig, W.: Understanding Petri Nets: Modeling Techniques, Analysis Methods. Case Studies. Springer, Heidelberg (2013). https://doi.org/10.1007/978-3-642-33278-4
22. Wynn, M.T., Verbeek, H.M.W., van der Aalst, W.M.P., ter Hofstede, A.H.M., Edmond, D.: Reduction rules for yawl workflows with cancellation regions and or-joins. Inf. Softw. Technol. **51**(6), 1010–1020 (2009)

Online Process Monitoring Using Incremental State-Space Expansion: An Exact Algorithm

Daniel Schuster[1]([✉])[iD] and Sebastiaan J. van Zelst[1,2][iD]

[1] Fraunhofer Institute for Applied Information Technology FIT,
Sankt Augustin, Germany
{daniel.schuster,sebastiaan.van.zelst}@fit.fraunhofer.de
[2] RWTH Aachen University, Aachen, Germany
s.j.v.zelst@pads.rwth-aachen.de

Abstract. The execution of (business) processes generates valuable traces of event data in the information systems employed within companies. Recently, approaches for monitoring the correctness of the execution of running processes have been developed in the area of process mining, i.e., online conformance checking. The advantages of monitoring a process' conformity during its execution are clear, i.e., deviations are detected as soon as they occur and countermeasures can immediately be initiated to reduce the possible negative effects caused by process deviations. Existing work in online conformance checking only allows for obtaining approximations of non-conformity, e.g., overestimating the actual severity of the deviation. In this paper, we present an exact, parameter-free, online conformance checking algorithm that computes conformance checking results on the fly. Our algorithm exploits the fact that the conformance checking problem can be reduced to a shortest path problem, by incrementally expanding the search space and reusing previously computed intermediate results. Our experiments show that our algorithm is able to outperform comparable state-of-the-art approximation algorithms.

Keywords: Process mining · Conformance checking · Alignments · Event streams · Incremental heuristic search

1 Introduction

Modern information systems support the execution of different business processes within companies. Valuable traces of *event data*, describing the various steps performed during process execution, are easily extracted from such systems. The field of *process mining* [3] aims to exploit such information, i.e., the event data, to better understand the overall execution of the process. For example, in process mining, several techniques have been developed that allow us to *(i)* automatically discover process models, *(ii)* compute whether the process, as

© Springer Nature Switzerland AG 2020
D. Fahland et al. (Eds.): BPM 2020, LNCS 12168, pp. 147–164, 2020.
https://doi.org/10.1007/978-3-030-58666-9_9

148   D. Schuster and S. J. van Zelst

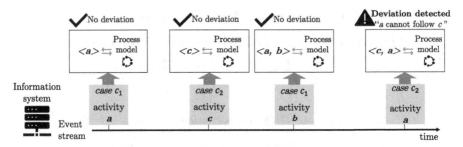

Fig. 1. Overview of online process monitoring. Activities are performed for different process instances, identified by a case-id, over time. Whenever a new activity is executed, the sequence of already executed activities within the given case/process instance is checked for conformance w.r.t. a reference process model

reflected by the data, conforms to a predefined reference model and *(iii)* detect performance deficiencies, e.g., bottleneck detection.

The majority of existing process mining approaches work in an offline setting, i.e., data is captured over time during process execution and process mining analyses are performed a posteriori. However, some of these techniques benefit from an *online application scenario*, i.e., analyzing the process at the moment it is executed. Reconsider *conformance checking*, i.e., computing whether a process' execution conforms to a reference model. Checking conformance in an online setting allows the process owner to detect and counteract non-conformity at the moment it occurs (Fig. 1). Thus, potential negative effects caused by a process deviation can be mitigated or eliminated. This observation inspired the development of novel conformance checking algorithms working in an online setting [7,8,22]. However, such algorithms provide approximations of non-conformity and/or use high-level abstractions of the reference model and the event data, i.e., not allowing us to obtain an exact quantification of non-conformance.

In this paper, we propose a novel, *exact* solution for the online conformance checking problem. We present a *parameter-free* algorithm that computes exact conformance checking results and provides an exact quantification of non-conformance. Our algorithm exploits the fact that the computation of conformance checking results can be reduced to a shortest path problem. In fact, we extend the search space in the course of a process instance execution and compute shortest paths by utilizing previous results every time new behavior is observed. Moreover, we explicitly exploit specific properties of the search space when solving the conformance checking problem. Therefore, the proposed incremental algorithm is specifically designed for online conformance checking and cannot be directly applied to general shortest path problems. The conducted experiments show that the proposed approach outperforms existing approximation algorithms and additionally guarantees exact results.

The remainder of this paper is structured as follows. In Sect. 2, we present related work regarding conformance checking and incremental search algorithms. In Sect. 3, we present preliminaries. In Sect. 4, we present the main algorithm.

In Sect. 5, we prove the correctness of the proposed algorithm. We evaluate the proposed algorithm and present the results of the experiments conducted in Sect. 6. Finally, we conclude the paper in Sect. 7.

2 Related Work

In this section, we first focus on (online) conformance checking techniques. Subsequently, we present related work regarding incremental search algorithms.

Two early techniques, designed to compute conformance statistics, are token-based replay [21] that tries to replay the observed behavior on a reference model and footprint-based comparison [3], in which the event data and the process model are translated into the same abstraction and then compared. As an alternative, *alignments* have been introduced [2,4] that map the observed behavioral sequences to a feasible execution sequence as described by the (reference) process model. Alignments indicate whether behavior is missing and/or whether inappropriate behavior is observed. The problem of finding an alignment was shown to be reducible to the shortest path problem [4].

The aforementioned techniques are designed for offline usage, i.e., they work on static (historical) data. In [22], an approach is presented to monitor ongoing process executions based on an event stream by computing partially completed alignments each time a new event is observed. The approach results in approximate results, i.e., false negatives occur w.r.t. deviation detection. In this paper, we propose an approach that extends and improves [22]. In [7], the authors propose to pre-calculate a transition system that supports replay of the ongoing process. Costs are assigned to the transition system's edges and replaying a deviating process instance leads to larger (non-zero) costs. Finally, [8] proposes to compute conformance of a process execution based on all possible behavioral patterns of the activities of a process. However, the use of such patterns leads to a loss of expressiveness in deviation explanation and localization.

In general, incremental search algorithms find shortest paths for similar search problems by utilizing results from previously executed searches [15]. In [13], the Lifelong Planning A^* algorithm is introduced that is an incremental version of the A^* algorithm. The introduced algorithm repeatedly calculates a shortest path from a fixed start state to a fixed goal state while the edge costs may change over time. In contrast, in our approach, the goal states are constantly changing in each incremental execution, whereas the edge costs remain fixed. Moreover, only new edges and vertices are incrementally added, i.e., the already existing state space is only extended. In [14], the Adaptive A^* algorithm is introduced, which is also an incremental version of the A^* algorithm. The Adaptive A^* algorithm is designed to calculate a shortest path on a given state space from an incrementally changing start state to a fixed set of goal states. In contrast to our approach, the start state is fixed in each incremental execution.

Table 1. Example *event log* fragment

Case	Activity	Resource	Time-stamp
...	...	...	...
13152	Create account (*a*)	*Wil*	*19-04-08 10:45*
13153	Create account (*a*)	*Bas*	*19-04-08 11:12*
13154	Request quote (*c*)	*Daniel*	*19-04-08 11:14*
13155	Request quote (*c*)	*Daniel*	*19-04-08 11:40*
13152	Submit order (*b*)	*Wil*	*19-04-08 11:49*
...	...	...	...

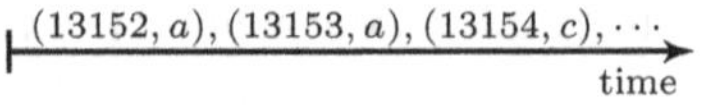

$(13152, a), (13153, a), (13154, c), \cdots$

time

Fig. 2. Schematic example of an event stream

3   Background

In this section, we present basic notations and concepts used within this paper.

Given a set X, a multiset B over X allows us to assign a multiplicity to the elements of X, i.e., $B\colon X \to \mathbb{N}_0$. Given $X = \{x, y, z\}$, the multiset $[x^5, y]$ contains 5 times x, once y and no z. The set of all possible multisets over a set X is denoted by $\mathcal{B}(X)$. We write $x \in_+ B$ if x is contained at least once in multiset B.

A sequence σ of length n, denoted by $|\sigma| = n$, over a base set X assigns an element to each index, i.e., $\sigma\colon \{1, \ldots, n\} \to X$. We write a sequence σ as $\langle \sigma(1), \sigma(2), ..., \sigma(|\sigma|) \rangle$. Concatenation of sequences is written as $\sigma \cdot \sigma'$, e.g., $\langle x, y \rangle \cdot \langle z \rangle = \langle x, y, z \rangle$. The set of all possible sequences over base set X is denoted by X^*. For element inclusion, we overload the notation for sequences, i.e., given $\sigma \in X^*$ and $x \in X$, we write $x \in \sigma$ if $\exists\, 1 \leq i \leq |\sigma|\, (\sigma(i) = x)$, e.g., $b \in \langle a, b \rangle$.

Let $\sigma \in X^*$ and let $X' \subseteq X$. We recursively define $\sigma_{\downarrow_{X'}} \in X'^*$ with: $\langle \rangle_{\downarrow_{X'}} = \langle \rangle$, $(\langle x \rangle \cdot \sigma)_{\downarrow_{X'}} = \langle x \rangle \cdot \sigma_{\downarrow_{X'}}$ if $x \in X'$ and $(\langle x \rangle \cdot \sigma)_{\downarrow_{X'}} = \sigma_{\downarrow_{X'}}$ if $x \notin X'$. For example, let $X' = \{a, b\}$, $X = \{a, b, c\}$, $\sigma = \langle a, c, b, a, c \rangle \in X^*$ then $\sigma_{\downarrow_{X'}} = \langle a, b, a \rangle$.

Let $t = (x_1, ..., x_n) \in X_1 \times \cdots \times X_n$ be an n-tuple, we let $\pi_1(t) = x_1, \ldots, \pi_n(t) = x_n$ denote the corresponding projection functions that extract a specific component from the tuple, e.g., $\pi_3((a, b, c)) = c$. Correspondingly, given a sequence $\sigma = \langle (x_1^1, \ldots, x_n^1), \ldots, (x_1^m, \ldots, x_n^m) \rangle$ with length m containing n-tuples, we define projection functions $\pi_1^*(\sigma) = \langle x_1^1, \ldots, x_1^m \rangle, \ldots, \pi_n^*(\sigma) = \langle x_n^1, \ldots, x_n^m \rangle$ that extract a specific component from each tuple and concatenate it into a sequence. For instance, $\pi_2^*(\langle (a, b), (c, d), (c, b) \rangle) = \langle b, d, b \rangle$.

Event Logs. The data used in process mining are *event logs*, e.g., consider Table 1. Each row corresponds to an *event* describing the execution of an activity in the context of an *instance* of the process. For simplicity, we use short-hand activity names, e.g., a for "create account". The events related to *Case-id* 13152 describe the activity sequence $\langle a, b \rangle$.

Event Streams. In this paper, we assume an *event stream* rather than an event log. Conceptually, an event stream is an (infinite) sequence of events. In Fig. 2, we depict an example. For instance, the first event, $(13152, a)$, indicates that for a process instance with case-id 13152 activity a was performed.

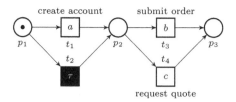

Fig. 3. Example WF-net N_1 with visualized initial marking $[p_1]$ and final marking $[p_3]$ describing a simplified ordering process. First "create account" is optionally executed. Next, either "submit order" or "request quote" is executed

Definition 1 (Event; Event Stream). *Let C denote the universe of* case identifiers *and A the universe of* activities. *An event $e \in C \times A$ describes the execution of an activity $a \in A$ in the context of a process instance identified by $c \in C$. An event stream S is a sequence of events, i.e., $S \in (C \times A)^*$.*

As indicated in Table 1, real-life events contain additional information, e.g., resource information, and are usually uniquely identifiable by an event id. However, for the purpose of this paper, we are only interested in the executed activity, the case-id of the corresponding process instance and the order of events.

Process Models. Process models allow us to describe the (intended) behavior of a process. In this paper, we focus on *sound Workflow nets* [1]. A Workflow net (WF-net) is a subclass of *Petri nets* [20]. Sound WF-nets, in turn, are a subclass of WF-nets with favorable *behavioral properties*, e.g., no deadlocks and livelocks. Consider Fig. 3, where we depict a sound WF-net. We use WF-nets since many high-level process modeling formalism used in practice, e.g. BPMN [10], are easily translated into WF-nets. Moreover, it is reasonable to assume that an experienced business process designer creates sound process models.

Petri nets consist of a set of *places P*, visualized as circles, and a set of *transitions T*, visualized as rectangular boxes. Places and transitions are connected by arcs which are defined by the set $F = (P \times T) \cup (T \times P)$. Given an element $x \in P \cup T$, we write $x\bullet = \{y \in P \cup T \mid (x, y) \in F\}$ to define all elements y that have an incoming arc from x. Symmetrically, $\bullet x = \{y \in P \cup T \mid (y, x) \in F\}$, e.g., $\bullet p_2 = \{t_1, t_2\}$ (Fig. 3).

The state of a Petri net, i.e., a *marking M*, is defined by a multiset of places, i.e., $M \in \mathcal{B}(P)$. Given a Petri net N with a set of places P and a marking $M \in \mathcal{B}(P)$, a *marked net* is written as (N, M). We denote the initial marking of a Petri net with M_i and the final marking with M_f. We denote a Petri net as $N = (P, T, F, M_i, M_f, \lambda)$. The labeling function $\lambda \colon T \to A \cup \{\tau\}$ assigns an (possibly invisible, i.e., τ) activity label to each transition, e.g., $\lambda(t_1) = a$ in Fig. 3.

The transitions of a Petri net allow to change the state. Given a marking $M \in \mathcal{B}(P)$, a transition t is *enabled* if $\forall p \in \bullet t \, (M(p) > 0)$. An enabled transition can *fire*, yielding marking $M' \in \mathcal{B}(P)$, where $M'(p) = M(p) + 1$ if $p \in t\bullet \setminus \bullet t$, $M'(p) = M(p) - 1$ if $p \in \bullet t \setminus t\bullet$, otherwise $M'(p) = M(p)$. We write $(N, M)[t\rangle$ if

Fig. 4. Three possible alignments for WF-net N_1 (Fig. 3) and trace $\langle a, b, c \rangle$

t is enabled in M and we write $(N, M) \xrightarrow{t} (N, M')$ to denote that firing transition t in marking M yields marking M'. In Fig. 3, we have $(N_1, [p_1])[t_1\rangle$ as well as $(N_1, [p_1]) \xrightarrow{t_1} (N_1, [p_2])$. If a sequence of transitions $\sigma \in T^*$ leads from marking M to M', we write $(N, M) \xrightarrow{\sigma} (N, M')$. We let $\mathcal{R}(N, M) = \{M' \in \mathcal{B}(P) \mid \exists \sigma \in T^* (N, M) \xrightarrow{\sigma} (N, M')\}$ denote the state space/all reachable markings of N given an initial marking M.

A *WF-net* $N = (P, T, F, [p_i], [p_o], \lambda)$ is a Petri net with a unique source place p_i and a unique sink place p_o, i.e., $M_i = [p_i]$ and $M_f = [p_o]$. Moreover, every element $x \in P \cup T$ is on a path from p_i to p_o.

Alignments. To explain traces in an event log w.r.t. a reference model, we use *alignments* [4], which map a trace onto an execution sequence of a model. Exemplary alignments are depicted in Fig. 4. The first row of an alignment (ignoring the skip symbol $\gg$) equals the trace and the second row (ignoring $\gg$) represents a sequence of transitions leading from the initial to the final marking.

We distinguish three types of *moves* in an alignment. A *synchronous move* (light-gray) matches an observed activity to the execution of a transition, where the transition's label must match the activity. *Log moves* (dark-gray) indicate that an activity is not re-playable in the current state of the process model. *Model moves* (white) indicate that the execution of a transition cannot be mapped onto an observed activity. They can be further differentiated into *invisible-* and *visible model moves*. An invisible model move consists of an inherently invisible transition ($\lambda(t) = \tau$). Visible model moves indicate that an activity should have taken place w.r.t the model but was not observed at that time.

In an online setting, an event stream is assumed to be infinite. A new event for a given process instance can occur at any time. Hence, we are interested in explanations of the observed behavior that still allow us to reach the final state in the reference model, i.e., *prefix-alignments*. The first row of a prefix-alignment also corresponds to the trace, but the second row corresponds to a sequence of transitions leading from the initial marking to a marking from which the final marking can still be reached. For a formal definition, we refer to [4].

Since multiple (prefix-)alignments exist, we are interested in an alignment that minimizes the mismatches between the trace and the model. Therefore, we assign costs to moves. We use the *standard cost function*, which assigns cost 0 to synchronous moves and invisible model moves, and cost 1 to log- and visible model moves. A (prefix-)alignment is optimal if it has minimal costs.

To compute an optimal (prefix-)alignment, we search for a *shortest path* in the state-space of the *synchronous product net (SPN)* [4]. An SPN is composed of a trace net and the given WF-net. In Fig. 5a, we depict an example trace net. We refer to [4] for a formal definition of the trace net. In Fig. 5b

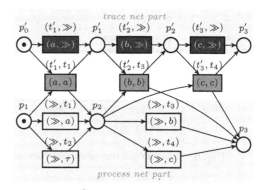

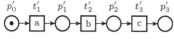

(a) Trace net of the trace $\langle a, b, c \rangle$ **(b)** SPN N_1^S of $\langle a, b, c \rangle$ and the WF-net N_1

Fig. 5. Construction of a trace net and a synchronous product net (SPN)

we depict an example SPN. Each transition in the SPN corresponds to a (prefix-)alignment move. Hence, we can assign costs to each transition. Any path in the state-space (sequence of transitions in the SPN) from $[p_0', p_1]$ to $[p_3', p_3]$ corresponds to an alignment of N_1 and $\langle a, b, c \rangle$. For the given example, a shortest path with cost 1, which corresponds to the first alignment depicted in Fig. 4, is:

$$(N_1^S, [p_0', p_1]) \xrightarrow{(t_1', t_1)} (N_1^S, [p_1', p_2]) \xrightarrow{(t_2', \gg)} (N_1^S, [p_2', p_2]) \xrightarrow{(t_3', t_4)} (N_1^S, [p_3', p_3])$$

To compute a *prefix-alignment*, we look for a shortest path from the initial marking to a marking $M \in \mathcal{R}(N_1^S, [p_0', p_1])$ such that $M(p_3') = 1$, i.e., the last place of the trace net part is marked. Next, we formally define the SPN.

Definition 2 (Synchronous Product Net (SPN)). *For a given trace σ, the corresponding trace net $N^\sigma = (P^\sigma, T^\sigma, F^\sigma, [p_i^\sigma], [p_o^\sigma], \lambda^\sigma)$ and a WF-net $N = (P, T, F, [p_i], [p_o], \lambda)$ s.t. $P^\sigma \cap P = \emptyset$ and $F^\sigma \cap F = \emptyset$, we define the SPN $N^S = (P^S, T^S, F^S, M_i^S, M_f^S, \lambda^S)$ s.t.:*

- $P^S = P^\sigma \cup P$
- $T^S = (T^\sigma \times \{\gg\}) \cup (\{\gg\} \times T) \cup \{(t', t) \in T^\sigma \times T \mid \lambda(t) = \lambda^\sigma(t') \neq \tau\}$
- $F^S = \{(p, (t', t)) \in P^S \times T^S \mid (p, t') \in F^\sigma \vee (p, t) \in F\} \cup \{((t', t), p) \in T^S \times P^S \mid (t', p) \in F^\sigma \vee (t, p) \in F\}$
- $M_i^S = [p_i^\sigma, p_i]$ and $M_f^S = [p_o^\sigma, p_o]$
- $\lambda^S : T^S \to (\mathcal{A} \cup \{\tau\} \cup \{\gg\}) \times (\mathcal{A} \cup \{\tau\} \cup \{\gg\})$ *(assuming $\gg \notin \mathcal{A} \cup \{\tau\}$) s.t.:*
  - $\lambda^S(t', \gg) = (\lambda^\sigma(t'), \gg)$ *for $t' \in T^\sigma$*
  - $\lambda^S(\gg, t) = (\gg, \lambda(t))$ *for $t \in T$*
  - $\lambda^S(t', t) = \lambda^S(\lambda^\sigma(t), \lambda(t))$ *for $t' \in T^\sigma, t \in T$*

Next, we briefly introduce the shortest path algorithm $A^\star$ since our proposed algorithm is based on it and it is widely used for alignment computation [4,9].

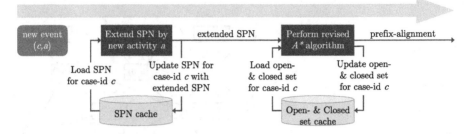

Fig. 6. Overview of the proposed incremental prefix alignment approach

$A^\star$ **algorithm.** The $A^\star$ algorithm [12] is an informed search algorithm that computes a shortest path. It efficiently traverses a search-space by exploiting, for a given state, the *estimated remaining distance*, referred to as the heuristic/h-value, to the closest goal state. The algorithm maintains a set of states of the search-space in its so-called open-set O. For each state in O, a path from the initial state to such a state is known and hence, the distance to reach that state, referred to as the g value, is known. A state from O with minimal f-value, i.e., $f = g + h$, is selected for further analysis until a goal state is reached. The selected state itself is moved into the closed set C, which contains fully investigated states for which a shortest path to those states is known. Furthermore, all successor states of the selected state are added to the open set O. Note that the used heuristic must be *admissible* [12]. If the used heuristic also satisfies *consistency* [12], states need not be reopened.

4   Incremental Prefix-Alignment Computation

In this section, we present an exact algorithm to incrementally compute optimal prefix-alignments on an event stream. First, we present an overview of the proposed approach followed by a detailed description of the main algorithm.

4.1   Overview

The core idea of the proposed algorithm is to exploit previously calculated results, i.e., explored parts of the state-space of an SPN. For each process instance, we maintain an SPN, which is extended as new events are observed. After extending the SPN, we "continue" the search for an optimal prefix-alignment.

In Fig. 6 we visualize a conceptual overview of our approach. We observe a new event (c, a) on the event stream. We check our SPN cache and if we previously built an SPN for case c, we fetch it from the cache. We then extend the SPN by means of adding activity a to the trace net part. Starting from intermediate results of the previous search, i.e., open & closed set used in the $A^\star$ algorithm, we find a new, optimal prefix-alignment for case c.

Algorithm 1: Incremental Prefix-Alignment Computation

input: $N=(P,T,F,[p_i],[p_o],\lambda), S\in(\mathcal{C}\times\mathcal{A})^*$

begin

1   **forall** $c \in \mathcal{C}$ **do**
     $\lfloor\ \mathcal{D}_\sigma(c) \leftarrow \langle\rangle, \mathcal{D}_C(c) \leftarrow \emptyset;$ // initialize cache

2    $i \leftarrow 1;$

3   **while** *true* **do**

4      $e \leftarrow S(i);$ // get i-th event of event stream

5      $c \leftarrow \pi_1(e);$ // extract case-id from current event

6      $a \leftarrow \pi_2(e);$ // extract activity label from current event

7      $\mathcal{D}_\sigma(c) \leftarrow \mathcal{D}_\sigma(c)\cdot\langle a\rangle;$ // extend trace for case c

8   let $N^S=(P^S,T^S,F^S,M_i^S,M_f^S,\lambda^S)$ from N and $\mathcal{D}_\sigma(c);$
     // construct/extend synchronous product net

9   let $h : \mathcal{R}(N^S,M_i^S)\rightarrow\mathbb{R}_{\geq0};$ // define heuristic function

10   let $d : T^S\rightarrow\mathbb{R}_{\geq0};$ // define standard cost function

11   **if** $|\mathcal{D}_\sigma(c)|=1$ **then**   // initialization for first run regarding case c

12        $\mathcal{D}_O(c) \leftarrow \{M_i^S\};$ // initialize open set

13        $\mathcal{D}_g(c) \leftarrow M_i^S\mapsto0;$ // initialize cost-so-far function

14        $\lfloor\ \mathcal{D}_p(c) \leftarrow M_i^S\mapsto(null, null);$ // initialize predecessor function

15      $\mathcal{D}_{\overline{\gamma}}(c),\mathcal{D}_O(c),\mathcal{D}_C(c),\mathcal{D}_g(c),\mathcal{D}_p(c) \leftarrow A_{\text{inc}}^*(N^S,\mathcal{D}_\sigma(c),\mathcal{D}_O(c),\mathcal{D}_C(c),$
     $\mathcal{D}_g(c),\mathcal{D}_p(c),h,d);$ // execute/continue shortest path search

16      $\lfloor\ i \leftarrow i + 1;$

In Algorithm 1 we depict the overall algorithm. As input we assume a reference process model, i.e., a WF-net N, and an event stream S. The algorithm processes every event on the stream S in the order in which they occur. First, we extract the case id and the activity label from the current event. Next we either construct the SPN if it is the first activity for the given case or we extend the previously constructed SPN. For the SPN's state space we then define a heuristic function h and the standard cost function d. If we process the first activity for a given case, we initialize the open set O with the SPN's initial marking. Afterwards, we calculate a prefix alignment by calling a modified A^* algorithm, i.e., A_{inc}^*. We obtain an optimal prefix-alignment $\overline{\gamma}$, open set O, closed set C, cost-so-far function g and the predecessor function p. The function g assigns to already discovered states the currently known cheapest costs and function p assigns the corresponding predecessor state to reach those. We cache the results to reuse them when computing the next prefix-alignment upon receiving a new event for the given case. Afterwards, we process the next event.

Note that, the approach theoretically requires infinite memory since it stores all intermediate results for all occurring cases because in general, we do not know when a case is completed in an online dimension. However, this is a general research challenge in process mining on streaming data, which is not addressed in this paper.

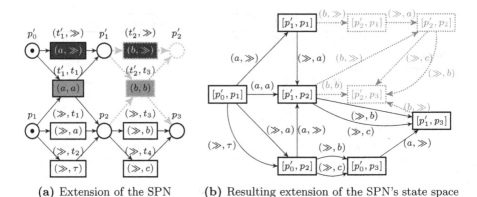

(a) Extension of the SPN   **(b)** Resulting extension of the SPN's state space

Fig. 7. Incremental extension of the SPN for the process model N_1 and a trace that was extended by a new activity b, i.e., $\langle a \rangle \cdot \langle b \rangle$

The following sections are structured according to the overview shown in Fig. 6. First, we explain the SPN extension. Subsequently, we present a revised A^* algorithm to incrementally compute optimal prefix-alignments, i.e., A^*_{inc}. Moreover, we present a heuristic function for the prefix-alignment computation.

4.2 Extending SPNs

Reconsider WF-net N_1 (Fig. 3) and assume that the first activity we observe is a. The corresponding SPN is visualized by means of the solid elements in Fig. 7a and the state space in Fig. 7b. Any state in the state-space containing a token in p'_1 is a suitable goal state of the A^* algorithm for an optimal prefix-alignment.

Next, for the same process instance, we observe an event describing activity b. The SPN for the process instance now describing trace $\langle a, b \rangle$ as well as its corresponding state-space is expanded. The expansion is visualized in Fig. 7 by means of dashed elements. In this case, any state that contains a token in p'_2 corresponds to a suitable goal state of the optimal prefix-alignment search.

4.3 Incrementally Performing Regular A^*

Here, we present the main algorithm to compute prefix-alignments on the basis of previously executed instances of the A^* algorithm.

The main idea of our approach is to continue the search on an extended search space. Upon receiving a new event (c, a), we apply the regular A^* algorithm using the cached open- and closed-set for case identifier c on the corresponding extended SPN. Hence, we incrementally solve shortest path problems on finite, fixed state-spaces by using the regular A^* algorithm with pre-filled open and closed sets from the previous search. Note that the start state remains the same and only the goal states differ in each incremental step.

Algorithm 2: $A^\star_{\text{inc}}$ (modified A^* algorithm that computes prefix-alignments from pre-filled open and closed sets)

input: $N^S = (P^S, T^S, F^S, M_i^S, M_f^S, \lambda^S), O, C \subseteq \mathcal{R}(N^S, M_i^S),$
$\qquad g\colon \mathcal{R}(N^S, M_i^S) \to \mathbb{R}_{\geq 0}, p\colon \mathcal{R}(N^S, M_i^S) \to T^S \times \mathcal{R}(N^S, M_i^S),$
$\qquad h\colon \mathcal{R}(N^S, M_i^S) \to \mathbb{R}_{\geq 0}, d\colon T^S \to \mathbb{R}_{\geq 0}$

begin

1   let $p_{|\sigma|}$ be the last place of the trace net part of N^S;

2   **forall** $m \in \mathcal{R}(N^S, M_i^S) \setminus O \cup C$ **do**   // initialize undiscovered states

3      $g(m) \leftarrow \infty$;

4      $f(m) \leftarrow \infty$;

5   **forall** $m \in O$ **do**

6      $f(m) = g(m) + h(m)$;   // recalculate heuristic and update f-values

7   **while** $O \neq \emptyset$ **do**

8      $m \leftarrow \underset{m \in O}{\arg\min} f(m)$;   // pop a state with minimal f-value from O

9   **if** $p_{|\sigma|} \in_+ m$ **then**

10        $\overline{\gamma} \leftarrow$ prefix-alignment that corresponds to the sequence of transitions $(t_1, ..., t_n)$ where $t_n = \pi_1(p(m)), t_{n-1} = \pi_1(\pi_2(p(m)))$, etc. until there is a marking that has no predecessor, i.e., M_i^S;

11   **return** $\overline{\gamma}, O, C, g, p$;

12      $C \leftarrow C \cup \{m\}$;

13      $O \leftarrow O \setminus \{m\}$;

14   **forall** $t \in T^S$ s.t. $(N^S, m)[t\rangle(N^S, m')$ **do**   // investigate successor states

15   **if** $m' \notin C$ **then**

16          $O \leftarrow O \cup \{m'\}$;

17   **if** $g(m) + d(t) < g(m')$ **then**   // a cheaper path to m' was found

18            $g(m') \leftarrow g(m) + d(t)$;   // update costs to reach m'

19            $f(m') \leftarrow g(m') + h(m')$;   // update f-value of m'

20            $p(m') \leftarrow (t, m)$;   // update predecessor of m'

In Algorithm 2, we present an algorithmic description of the A^* approach. The algorithm assumes as input an SPN, the open- and closed-set of the previously executed instance of the A^* algorithm, i.e., for the process instance at hand, a cost-so-far function g, a predecessor function p, a heuristic function h, and a cost function d (standard cost function). First, we initialize all states that have not been discovered yet (line 2). Since the SPN is extended and the goal states are different with respect to the previous run of the algorithm for the same process instance, all h-values are outdated. Hence, we recalculate the heuristic values and update the f-values for all states in the open set (line 6) because we are now looking for a shortest path to a state that has a token in the newly added place in the trace net part of the SPN. Hence, the new goal states were not present in the previous search problem. Note that the g values are not affected by the SPN extension. Thereafter, we pick a state from the open set with smallest f-value (line 7). First, we check if the state is a goal state, i.e., whether it contains a token in the last place of the trace net part (line 9). If so, we reconstruct the sequence of transitions that leads to the state, and thus, we obtain a prefix-alignment (using predecessor function p). Otherwise, we move the current state from the open- to the closed set and examine all its successor states. If a successor state is already in the closed set, we ignore it. Otherwise, we add it to the open set and update the f-value and the predecessor state stored in p if a cheaper path was found.

Heuristic for Prefix-Alignment Computation. Since the A^* algorithm uses a heuristic function to efficiently traverse the search space, we present a heuristic for prefix-alignment computation based on an existing heuristic [4] used for conventional alignment computation. Both heuristics can be formulated as an Integer Linear Program (ILP). Note that both heuristics can also be defined as a Linear Program (LP) which leads to faster calculation but less accurate heuristic values.

Let $N^S = (P^S, T^S, F^S, M_i^S, M_f^S, \lambda^S)$ be an SPN of a WF-net $N = (P, T, F, [p_i], [p_o], \lambda)$ and a trace σ with corresponding trace net $N^\sigma = (P^\sigma, T^\sigma, F^\sigma, [p_i^\sigma], [p_o^\sigma], \lambda^\sigma)$. Let $c \colon T^S \to \mathbb{R}_{\geq 0}$ be a cost function that assigns each (prefix-)alignment move, i.e., transition in the SPN, costs. We define a revised heuristic function for prefix-alignment computation as an ILP:

- *Variables*: $X = \{x_t \mid t \in T^S\}$ and $\forall x_t \in X : x_t \in \mathbb{N}_0$
- *Objective function*: $min \sum_{t \in T^S} x_t \cdot c(t)$
- *Constraints*:
  - Trace net part: $M_f^S(p) = \sum_{t \in \bullet p} x_t - \sum_{t \in p \bullet} x_t \quad \forall p \in P^S : p \in P^\sigma$
  - Process model part: $0 \leq \sum_{t \in \bullet p} x_t - \sum_{t \in p \bullet} x_t \quad \forall p \in P^S : p \in P$

The revised heuristic presented is a relaxed version of the existing heuristic used for conventional alignment computation. Admissibility and consistency can be proven in a similar way as for the existing heuristic. We refer to [4,9].

Reducing Heuristic Recalculations. In this section, we describe an approach to reduce the number of heuristic calculations. Reconsider line 6 in Algorithm 2. Before we continue the search on an extended search space, we recalculate the heuristic for all states in the open set. This is needed because the goal states differ in each incremental execution. However, these recalculations are computational expensive. Instead of recalculating the heuristic in advance (Algorithm 2, line 6), we mark all states in the open set that have an outdated heuristic value. Whenever we pop a state from the open set with an outdated heuristic value (line 8), we update its h-value, put it back in the open set and skip the remainder of the while body (from line 9). Thereby, we do not have to recalculate the heuristic value for all states in the open set. This approach is permissible because the goal states are "further away" in each iteration and hence, h-values can only grow.

5   Correctness

In this section, we prove the correctness of the approach. We show that states in the closed set do not get new successors upon extending the SPN. Furthermore, we show that newly added states never connect to "older" states. Finally, we show that the open set always contains a state which is part of an optimal prefix-alignment of the extended trace.

Lemma 1 (State-space growth is limited to frontier). *Let* $\sigma^{i-1} = \langle a_1, \ldots, a_{i-1} \rangle$, $\sigma^i = \sigma^{i-1} \cdot \langle a_i \rangle$, *and* $\sigma^{i+1} = \sigma^i \cdot \langle a_{i+1} \rangle$. *For a WF-net, N let* $N_{i-1}^S = (P_{i-1}^S, T_{i-1}^S, F_{i-1}^S, M_{i_{i-1}}^S, M_{f_{i-1}}^S, \lambda_{i-1}^S)$ *be the SPN of N and* σ^{i-1}, N_i^S *and* N_{i+1}^S *analogously.*

$$\forall M \in \mathcal{B}(P_{i-1}^S) \forall t \in T_{i+1}^S \left((N_{i+1}^S, M)[t\rangle \Rightarrow t \in T_i^S \right)$$

Proof (By construction of the SPN). Observe that $P_{i-1}^S \subset P_i^S \subset P_{i+1}^S$ and $T_{i-1}^S \subset T_i^S \subset T_{i+1}^S$. Let $p_{|\sigma^i|} \in P_{i+1}^S$ be the i-th place of the trace net part (note that $p_{|\sigma^i|} \notin P_{i-1}^S$) and let $t_{i+1} \in T_{i+1}^S \setminus T_i^S$. By construction of the SPN, we know that $p_{|\sigma^i|} \in \bullet t_{i+1}$ and $\forall j \in \{1, \ldots, i-1\} : p_{|\sigma^j|} \notin \bullet t_{i+1}$. □

Observe that, when searching for an alignment for σ^i, Algorithm 2 returns whenever place p_{σ^i} is marked. Moreover, the corresponding marking remains in O. Hence, each state in C is "older", i.e., already part of P_{i-1}^S. Thus, Lemma 1 proves that states in the closed set C do not get new successors upon extending the SPN.

Lemma 2 (New states do not connect to old states). *Let* $\sigma^i = \langle a_1, \ldots, a_i \rangle$ *and* $\sigma^{i+1} = \sigma^i \cdot \langle a_{i+1} \rangle$. *For a given WF-net N, let* $N_i^S = (P_i^S, T_i^S, F_i^S, M_{i_i}^S, M_{f_i}^S, \lambda_i^S)$ *(analogously* N_{i+1}^S*) be the SPN of N and* σ^i.

$$\forall M \in \mathcal{B}(P_{i+1}^S) \setminus \mathcal{B}(P_i^S) \forall M' \in \mathcal{B}(P_i^S) \left(\nexists t \in T_{i+1}^S \left((N_{i+1}^S, M)[t\rangle(N_{i+1}^S, M')) \right) \right)$$

Proof (By construction of the SPN). Let $t_{i+1} \in T_{i+1}^S \setminus T_i^S$. Let $p_{|\sigma^{i+1}|} \in P_{i+1}^S$ be the $(i+1)$-th place (the last place) of the trace net part. We know that $p_{|\sigma^{i+1}|} \in t_{i+1} \bullet$ and $p_{|\sigma^j|} \notin t_{i+1} \bullet \ \forall j \in \{1, \ldots, i\}$. For all other $t \in T_i^S$ we know that $\nexists M \in \mathcal{B}(P_{i+1}^S) \setminus \mathcal{B}(P_i^S)$ such that $(N^S, M)[t\rangle$. □

From Lemma 1 and 2 we know that states in the closed set are not affected by extending the SPN. Hence, it is feasible to continue the search from the open set and to not reconsider states which are in the closed set.

Lemma 3. (Exists a state in the O-set that is on the shortest path). *Let* $\sigma^i = \langle a_1, \ldots, a_i \rangle$, $\sigma^{i+1} = \sigma^i \cdot \langle a_{i+1} \rangle$, N_i^S, N_{i+1}^S *the corresponding SPN for a WF-net N, O^i and C^i be the open- and closed set after the prefix-alignment computation for σ_i. Let $\overline{\gamma}_{i+1}$ be an optimal prefix-alignment for σ_{i+1}.*

$$\exists j \in \{1, \ldots, |\overline{\gamma}_{i+1}|\}, \overline{\gamma}_{i+1}' = (\overline{\gamma}_{i+1}(1), \ldots, \overline{\gamma}_{i+1}(j)) \ s.t.$$

$$(N_{i+1}^S, M_{i+1}^S) \xrightarrow{\pi_2^*(\overline{\gamma}_{i+1}')\downarrow_T} (N_{i+1}^S, M_O) \ and \ M_O \in O^i$$

Proof. $\overline{\gamma}^{i+1}$ corresponds to a sequence of markings, i.e., $S = (M_{i+1}^S, \ldots, M', M'', \ldots, M''')$. Let $X^{i+1} = \mathcal{B}(P_{i+1}^S) \setminus C^i \cup O^i$. It holds that $X^{i+1} \cap O^i = X^{i+1} \cap C^i = O^i \cap C^i = \emptyset$. Note that $M''' \in X^{i+1}$ because $M''' \notin \mathcal{B}(P_i^S)$. Assume $\forall M \in S : M \notin O^i \Rightarrow \forall M \in S : M \in C^i \cup X^{i+1}$. Observe that $M_i^S = M_{i+1}^S \in C^i$ since initially $M_i^S \in O^0$ and in the very first iteration M_i^S is selected for expansion because it is not a goal state, Algorithm 2. We know that for any state pair M', M'' it cannot be the case that $M' \in C^i, M'' \in X^{i+1}$. Since we know that at least $M_i^S \in C^i$ and $M''' \in X_c^{i+1}$ there $\exists M', M'' \in S$ such that $M' \in C^i, M'' \in O^i$.   □

Hence, it is clear from Lemmas 1–3 that incrementally computing prefix-alignments, continuing the search from the previous open- and closed set, leads to optimal prefix-alignments.

6   Evaluation

We evaluated the algorithm on publicly available real event data from various processes. Here, we present the experimental setup and discuss the results.

6.1   Experimental Setup

The algorithm introduced in [22] serves as a comparison algorithm. We refer to it as Online Conformance Checking (OCC). Upon receiving an event, OCC partially reverts the previously computed prefix-alignments (using a given maximal window size) and uses the corresponding resulting state of the SPN as start state. Hence, the algorithm cannot guarantee optimality, i.e., it does not search for a global optimum. However, OCC can also be used without partially reverting, i.e., using window size ∞. Hence, it naively starts the computation from scratch without reusing any information, however, optimality is then guaranteed. We implemented our proposed algorithm, incremental A^* (IAS), as well as OCC in the process mining library *PM4Py* [5]. The source code is publicly available[1]. Although, the OCC algorithm was introduced without a heuristic function [22], it is important to note that both algorithms, IAS and OCC, use the previously introduced heuristic in the experiments to improve objectivity.

We use publicly available datasets capturing the execution of real-life processes [6,11,17–19]. To mimic an event stream, we iterate over the traces in the event log and emit each preformed activity as an event. For instance, given the event log $L = [\langle a, b, c \rangle, \langle b, c, d \rangle, \ldots]$, we simulate the event stream $\langle (1, a), (1, b), (1, c), (2, b), (2, c), (2, d), \ldots \rangle$. For all datasets except CCC19 [19] that contains a process model, we discovered reference process models with the Inductive Miner infrequent version (IMf) [16] using a high threshold. This results in process models that do not guarantee full replay fitness. Moreover, the discovered process models contain choices, parallelism and loops.

---

[1] https://github.com/fit-daniel-schuster/online_process_monitoring_using_incremental _state-space_expansion_an_exact_algorithm.

6.2 Results

In Table 2, we present the results. OCC-Wx represents the OCC algorithm with window size x, OCC with an infinite window size. Moreover, we present the results for the IAS algorithm that does *not* use the approach of reducing heuristic recalculations as presented in Sect. 4.3, we call it IASR. Note that only IAS(R) and OCC guarantee optimality. Furthermore, note that a queued state corresponds to a state added to the open set and a visited state corresponds to a state moved into the closed set. Both measures indicate the search efficiency.

We observe that reducing the number of heuristic re-calculations is valuable and approximately halves the number of solved LPs and hence, reduces the computation time. As expected, we find no significant difference in the other measured dimensions by comparing IAS and IASR. We observe that IAS clearly outperforms all OCC variants regarding search efficiency for all used event logs except for CCC19 where OCC variants with small window sizes have a better search efficiency. This results illustrate the relevance of IAS compared to OCC and OCC-Wx and show the effectiveness of continuing the search on an extended search space by reusing previous results. Regarding false positives, we observe that OCC-Wx variants return non-optimal prefix-alignments for all event logs. As expected, the number of false positives decreases with increasing window size. In return, the calculation effort increases with increasing window size. This highlights the advantage of the IAS' property being parameter-free. In general, it is difficult to determine a window size because the traces, which have an impact on the "right" window size, are not known in an online setting upfront.

Table 2. Results of the conducted experiments for various real-life event logs

Event log	≈ avg. queued states per trace							≈ avg. visited states per trace						
	IASR	IAS	OCC	OCC-W1	OCC-W2	OCC-W5	OCC-W10	IASR	IAS	OCC	OCC-W1	OCC-W2	OCC-W5	OCC-W10
CCC 19 [19]	774	766	14614	312	431	885	1622	756	751	12557	212	283	506	932
Receipt [6]	31	29	65	37	50	82	104	18	17	26	19	23	33	42
Sepsis [17]	73	70	532	102	146	285	450	44	43	232	47	62	103	166
Hospital [18]	21	21	42	32	41	65	71	11	11	15	14	17	23	26
BPIC 19 [11]	28	28	257	41	57	90	107	18	18	154	21	27	40	48

Event log	# traces with false positives							# variants with false positives						
	IASR	IAS	OCC	OCC-W1	OCC-W2	OCC-W5	OCC-W10	IASR	IAS	OCC	OCC-W1	OCC-W2	OCC-W5	OCC-W10
CCC 19 [19]	0	0	0	7	8	1	1	0	0	0	7	8	1	1
Receipt [6]	0	0	0	8	5	3	1	0	0	0	8	5	3	1
Sepsis [17]	0	0	0	59	60	6	1	0	0	0	58	59	6	1
Hospital [18]	0	0	0	88	88	69	32	0	0	0	49	49	39	19
BPIC 19 [11]	0	0	0	318	259	193	90	0	0	0	272	206	145	75

Event log	≈ avg. computation time (s) per trace							≈ avg. number solved LPs (heuristic functions) per trace						
	IASR	IAS	OCC	OCC-W1	OCC-W2	OCC-W5	OCC-W10	IASR	IAS	OCC	OCC-W1	OCC-W2	OCC-W5	OCC-W10
CCC 19 [19]	12.2	5.69	35.7	0.74	0.85	1.51	2.61	3345	1889	8443	338	393	658	1066
Receipt [6]	0.12	0.04	0.05	0.04	0.04	0.07	0.09	89.2	42	53	40	50	75	91
Sepsis [17]	0.59	0.28	0.6	0.09	0.11	0.23	0.35	518	226	343	104	138	247	356
Hospital [18]	0.05	0.03	0.03	0.02	0.03	0.04	0.05	63	30	35	34	42	61	66
BPIC 19 [11]	0.4	0.19	0.79	0.06	0.09	0.12	0.14	128	71	136	44	57	81	91

Regarding calculation time, we note that the number of solved LPs has a significant influence. We observe that IAS has often comparable computation time to the OCC-wx versions. Comparing optimality guaranteeing algorithms (IAS & OCC), IAS clearly outperforms OCC in all measured dimensions for all logs.

6.3   Threats to Validity

In this section, we outline the limitations of the experimental setup. First, the artificial generation of an event stream by iterating over the traces occurring in the event log is a simplistic approach. However, this allows us to ignore the general challenge of process mining on streaming data, deciding when a case is complete, since new events can occur at any time on an (infinite) event stream. Hence, we do not consider the impact of multiple cases running in parallel.

The majority of used reference process models are discovered with the IMf algorithm. It should, however, be noted that these discovered models do not contain duplicate labels. Finally, we compared the proposed approach against a single reference, the OCC approach. To the best of our knowledge, however, there are no other algorithms that compute prefix-alignments on event streams.

7   Conclusion

In this paper, we proposed a novel, parameter-free algorithm to efficiently monitor ongoing processes in an online setting by computing a prefix-alignment once a new event occurs. We have shown that the calculation of prefix-alignments on an event stream can be "continued" from previous results on an extended search space with different goal states, while guaranteeing optimality. The proposed approach is designed for prefix-alignment computation since it utilizes specific properties of the search space regarding prefix-alignment computation and therefore, generally not transferable to other shortest path problems. The results show that the proposed algorithm outperforms existing approaches in many dimensions and additionally ensures optimality.

In future work, we plan to implement the proposed approach in real application scenarios and to conduct a case study. Thereby, we want to focus on limited storage capacities, which requires to decide whether a case is considered to be completed to free storage.

References

1. van der Aalst, W.M.P.: The application of Petri Nets to workflow management. J. Circuits Syst. Comput. **8**(1), 21–66 (1998). https://doi.org/10.1142/S0218126698000043
2. van der Aalst, W.M.P., Adriansyah, A., van Dongen, B.F.: Replaying history on process models for conformance checking and performance analysis. Wiley Interdisc. Rew.: Data Min. Knowl. Discov. **2**(2), 182–192 (2012)

3. van der Aalst, W.M.P.: Process Mining - Data Science in Action, 2nd edn. Springer, Heidelberg (2016). https://doi.org/10.1007/978-3-662-49851-4
4. Adriansyah, A.: Aligning observed and modeled behavior. Ph.D. thesis, Eindhoven University of Technology, Department of Mathematics and Computer Science (2014). https://doi.org/10.6100/IR770080
5. Berti, A., van Zelst, S.J., van der Aalst, W.: Process mining for Python (PM4Py): Bridging the gap between process-and data science. In: Proceedings of the ICPM Demo Track 2019, Co-located with 1st International Conference on Process Mining (ICPM 2019), Aachen, Germany, 24–26 June 2019. pp. 13–16 (2019). http://ceur-ws.org/Vol-2374/
6. Buijs, J.: Receipt phase of an environmental permit application process ('WABO'), CoSeLoG project. Dataset (2014). https://doi.org/10.4121/uuid:a07386a5-7be3-4367-9535-70bc9e77dbe6
7. Burattin, A.: Online conformance checking for Petri Nets and event streams. In: Proceedings of the BPM Demo Track and BPM Dissertation Award co-located with 15th International Conference on Business Process Modeling (BPM 2017), Barcelona, Spain, 13 September 2017 (2017). http://ceur-ws.org/Vol-1920/BPM_2017_paper_153.pdf
8. Burattin, A., van Zelst, S.J., Armas-Cervantes, A., van Dongen, B.F., Carmona, J.: Online conformance checking using behavioural patterns. In: Weske, M., Montali, M., Weber, I., vom Brocke, J. (eds.) BPM 2018. LNCS, vol. 11080, pp. 250–267. Springer, Cham (2018). https://doi.org/10.1007/978-3-319-98648-7_15
9. Carmona, J., van Dongen, B.F., Solti, A., Weidlich, M.: Conformance Checking - Relating Processes and Models. Springer, Heidelberg (2018). https://doi.org/10.1007/978-3-319-99414-7
10. Dijkman, R.M., Dumas, M., Ouyang, C.: Semantics and analysis of business process models in BPMN. Inf. Softw. Technol. **50**(12), 1281–1294 (2008). https://doi.org/10.1016/j.infsof.2008.02.006
11. van Dongen, B.F.: BPI Challenge 2019. Dataset (2019). https://doi.org/10.4121/uuid:d06aff4b-79f0-45e6-8ec8-e19730c248f1
12. Hart, P.E., Nilsson, N.J., Raphael, B.: A formal basis for the heuristic determination of minimum cost paths. IEEE Trans. Syst. Sci. Cybern. **4**(2), 100–107 (1968). https://doi.org/10.1109/TSSC.1968.300136
13. Koenig, S., Likhachev, M.: Incremental A*. In: Dietterich, T.G., Becker, S., Ghahramani, Z. (eds.) Advances in Neural Information Processing Systems 14 (Neural Information Processing Systems: Natural and Synthetic, NIPS 2001, 3–8 December 2001, Vancouver, British Columbia, Canada), pp. 1539–1546. MIT Press (2001). http://papers.nips.cc/paper/2003-incremental-a
14. Koenig, S., Likhachev, M.: Adaptive A. In: Dignum, F., Dignum, V., Koenig, S., Kraus, S., Singh, M.P., Wooldridge, M.J. (eds.) 4th International Joint Conference on Autonomous Agents and Multiagent Systems (AAMAS 2005), 25–29 July 2005, Utrecht, The Netherlands, pp. 1311–1312. ACM (2005). https://doi.org/10.1145/1082473.1082748
15. Koenig, S., Likhachev, M., Liu, Y., Furcy, D.: Incremental heuristic search in AI. AI Mag. **25**(2), 99–112 (2004). http://www.aaai.org/ojs/index.php/aimagazine/article/view/1763
16. Leemans, S.J.J., Fahland, D., van der Aalst, W.M.P.: Discovering block-structured process models from event logs containing infrequent behaviour. In: Lohmann, N., Song, M., Wohed, P. (eds.) BPM 2013. LNBIP, vol. 171, pp. 66–78. Springer, Cham (2014). https://doi.org/10.1007/978-3-319-06257-0_6

17. Mannhardt, F.: Sepsis Cases. Dataset. 4TU.Centre for Research Data (2016). https://doi.org/10.4121/uuid:915d2bfb-7e84-49ad-a286-dc35f063a460
18. Mannhardt, F.: Hospital Billing. Dataset. 4TU.Centre for Research Data (2017). https://doi.org/10.4121/uuid:76c46b83-c930-4798-a1c9-4be94dfeb741
19. Munoz-Gama, J., de la Fuente, R., Sepúlveda, M., Fuentes, R.: Conformance checking challenge 2019. dataset. 4TU.Centre for Research Data (2019). https://doi.org/10.4121/uuid:c923af09-ce93-44c3-ace0-c5508cf103ad
20. Murata, T.: Petri Nets: properties, analysis and applications. Proc. IEEE **77**(4), 541–580 (1989). https://inst.eecs.berkeley.edu/~ee249/fa07/discussions/PetriNets-Murata.pdf
21. Rozinat, A., van der Aalst, W.M.P.: Conformance checking of processes based on monitoring real behavior. Inf. Syst. **33**(1), 64–95 (2008). https://doi.org/10.1016/j.is.2007.07.001
22. van Zelst, S.J., Bolt, A., Hassani, M., van Dongen, B.F., van der Aalst, W.M.P.: Online Conformance checking: relating event streams to process models using prefix-alignments. Int. J. Data Sci. Anal. (2017). https://doi.org/10.1007/s41060-017-0078-6

Engineering

Looking for Meaning: Discovering Action-Response-Effect Patterns in Business Processes

Jelmer J. Koorn[1]([✉]), Xixi Lu[1], Henrik Leopold[2,3], and Hajo A. Reijers[1]

[1] Utrecht University, Utrecht, The Netherlands
{j.j.koorn,x.lu,h.a.reijers}@uu.nl
[2] Kühne Logistics University, Hamburg, Germany
henrik.leopold@the-klu.org
[3] Hasso Plattner Institute, University of Potsdam, Potsdam, Germany

Abstract. Process mining enables organizations to capture and improve their processes based on fact-based process execution data. A key question in the context of process improvement is how responses to an event (action) result in desired or undesired outcomes (effects). From a process perspective, this requires understanding the action-response patterns that occur. Current discovery techniques do not allow organizations to gain such insights. In this paper we present a novel approach to tackle this problem. We propose and formalize a technique to discover action-response-effect patterns. In this technique we use well-established statistical tests to uncover potential dependency relations between each response and its effects on the cases. The goal of this technique is to provide organizations with processes that are: (1) appropriately represented, and (2) effectively filtered to show meaningful relations. The approach is evaluated on a real-world data set from a Dutch healthcare facility in the context of aggressive behavior of clients and the responses of caretakers.

Keywords: Effect measurement · Process discovery · Healthcare · Patterns

1 Introduction

The desire to improve organizational processes has led to the adoption of process mining in many industries [11,23]. One of the key advantages of process mining is that it enables organizations to understand, analyze, and improve their processes based on process execution data, so-called event logs. Such event logs capture how organizational processes are actually executed and can be extracted from various information systems that are used in organizations [1].

While the advantages of process mining have been demonstrated in many domains, the application of process mining is still associated with different challenges. One particularly important challenge is to provide the user with a process representation that a) is easy to understand and b) allows the user to obtain

© Springer Nature Switzerland AG 2020
D. Fahland et al. (Eds.): BPM 2020, LNCS 12168, pp. 167–183, 2020.
https://doi.org/10.1007/978-3-030-58666-9_10

the required insights about the process execution. To this end, various process discovery algorithms have been proposed, including the heuristic miner [27], the fuzzy miner [15], and the inductive miner [17]. What all of these algorithms have in common is that they focus on discovering the control flow of a process, i.e., the order constraints among events.

In many scenarios, however, the control flow perspective is not sufficient for understanding and improving the process. As an example, consider the care process of a residential care facility supporting clients with their daily needs. The main goal of this process is to ensure the well-being of clients. One of the main factors negatively affecting the well-being of clients are incidents of aggressive behavior, e.g. when clients verbally or physically attack other clients or staff. Staff responds to aggressive incidents with one or multiple measures ranging from verbal warnings to seclusion. A key question in the context of process improvement is which of these measures lead to desired (i.e., de-escalation of aggressive behavior) or undesired (i.e., escalation of aggressive behavior) outcomes.

From a process perspective, this requires understanding the *action-response-effect* patterns. In the healthcare process, we consider the aggressive incidents as *actions*, the countermeasures taken to the incident as *responses*, and the follow-up incidents as *effects*. Action-response-effect patterns are not accounted for in existing discovery algorithms. As a result, their application to such event logs leads to a process representation that is either hard to read (because it contains too many connections) or it does not allow the user to obtain actual insights about the process (because it does not show the effect of behavior).

Recognizing the limitation of existing algorithms with respect to showing meaningful insights into action-response-effect patterns, we use this paper to propose a novel discovery technique. We leverage well-established statistical tests to analyze event logs in order to discover simplified graphical representations of business processes. We simplify the resulting models by highlighting the statistically significant dependency relations according to statistical tests, while insignificant relations are hidden. We conduct an evaluation with an event log from a Dutch residential care facility containing a total of 21,706 aggression incidents related to 1,115 clients. We show that our technique allows to obtain important insights that existing discovery algorithms cannot reveal.

The rest of the paper is organized as follows. Section 2 describes and exemplifies the problem of discovering *action-response-effect* patterns. Section 3 introduces the formal preliminaries for our work. Section 4 describes our proposed technique for discovering *action-response-effect* patterns. Section 5 evaluates our technique by applying it to a real-world data set. Section 6 discusses related work and Sect. 7 concludes the paper.

2   Problem Statement

Many processes contain action-response-effect patterns. As examples consider healthcare processes where doctors respond to medical conditions with a number of treatments, service processes where service desk employees respond to issues with technical solutions, and marketing processes where customers may respond to certain stimuli such as ad e-mails with increased demand. Let us reconsider the example of the healthcare process in a residential care facility in order to illustrate the challenge of discovering an understandable and informing process representation from an event log containing action-response relations. The particular aspect of interest are incidents of aggressive behavior from the clients and how these are handled by staff. Table 1 shows an excerpt from a respective event log. Each entry consists of an event identifier EID (which, in this case, is equal to the incident number), a case identifier CID (which, in this case, is equal to the client identifier), a timestamp, an aggressive incident (action), and one or more responses to this event.

Table 1. Excerpt from an action-response log of a care process

EID	CID	Timestamp	Action	Response(s)
1	1	12-05 09:53	VA	Warning
2	1	13-05 13:35	PO	Distract client, seclusion
3	1	26-05 09:32	VA	Warning
4	1	26-05 11:02	PP	Distract client
5	2	21-06 14:51	VA	Distract client
6	1	23-06 21:23	VA	Distract client
7	2	24-06 17:02	VA	–
8	3	29-08 11:22	VA	Warning
9	3	31-08 08:13	PO	Warning, seclusion
10	3	31-08 10:48	PP	Distract client

Legend: EID = Event identifier, CID = Client identifier,
VA = Verbal Aggression, PP = Physical Aggression
(People), PO = Physical Aggression (Objects),

Figure 1 a) shows the directly–follows-graph that can be derived from the events of this log. It does not suggest any clear structure in the process. Although this graph is only based on twelve events belonging to three different event classes, it seems that almost any behavior is possible. In addition, this representation does not provide any insights into certain hidden patterns [2]. However, if we take a closer look, we can see that there are effects to a certain response. For instance, we can see that over time the aggressive incidents related to client 1 escalate from verbal aggression to physical aggression against objects and people. The verbal aggression event in June (EID = 6) is probably unrelated to the previous pattern since it occurs several weeks after. To gain an even deeper understanding, we need to take both the response and its effect into account. Both client 1 and 2 escalate from verbal aggression to physical aggression after the verbal aggression was only countered with a warning.

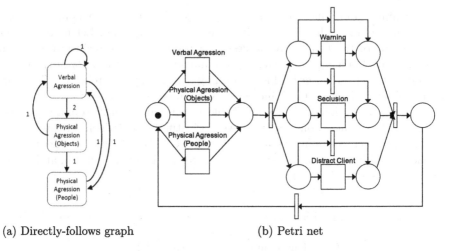

(a) Directly-follows graph   (b) Petri net

Fig. 1. Representations resulting from the action-response log from Table 1

These examples illustrates that explicitly including the responses and effects in the discovery process is important for answering the question of how to possibly respond to an action when a certain effect (e.g. de-escalating aggressive behavior) is desired. Therefore, our objective is to discover a model that: (1) shows the action-response-effect process, and (2) reveals the dependency patterns of which responses lead to a desired or undesired outcomes (effect). There are two main challenges associated with accomplishing this:

1. *Graphical representation*: From a control-flow perspective, action-response relations are a loop consisting of a choice between all actions and a subsequent and-split that allows to execute or skip each responses. Figure 1 b) illustrates this by showing the Petri net representing the behavior from the log in Table 1. Obviously, this representation does not allow to understand which responses lead to a desired or undesired effect.
2. *Effective filtering mechanism*: The possible number of responses calls for a filtering mechanisms that allows to infer meaningful insights from the model. In the example above, we only have three event classes and three event response classes (plus the "no response"). This results in eight possible responses. In case of 5 response event classes, we already face 32 ($=2^5$ possible responses. Including all these response arcs in a model will likely lead to an unreadable model that does not allow to infer the desired insights.

In the next sections, we propose a technique that creates graphical representations of dependency patterns in action-response effect logs.

3   Preliminaries

In this section, we formalize the concept of action-response-effect event logs.

Definition 1 (Action-Response-Effect Log). *Let $\mathcal{E}$ be the universe of event identifiers. Let $\mathcal{C}$ be the universe of case identifiers. Let $d_1, ..., d_n$ be the set of attribute names (e.g., timestamp, resource, location). Let A be the set of actions and R a finite set of responses. An action-response log L is defined as $L = (E, \pi_c, \pi_l, \pi_r, \pi_{d_1}, ..., \pi_{d_n}, <)$, where*

- *$E \subseteq \mathcal{E}$ is the set of events,*
- *$\pi_c : E \to \mathcal{C}$ is a surjective function linking events to cases,*
- *$\pi_l : E \to A$ is a surjective function linking events to actions,*
- *$\pi_r : E \to 2^R$ is a surjective function linking events to a set of responses,*
- *$\pi_{next} : E \to \mathcal{C}$ is a surjective function linking events to the effects,*
- *$\pi_{d_i} : E \to \mathcal{U}$ is a surjective function linking the attribute d_i of each event to its value,*
- *$< \subseteq E \times E$ is a strict total ordering over the events.*

Given an action-response log L according to Definition 1, we shall use the shorthand notation $\sigma = \langle e_1, \ldots, e_n \rangle$ in the remainder of this paper to refer to an event trace that consists of n events with an identical case identifier. Furthermore, for any pair of events e_i and e_j with $i < j$, it holds that $e_i < e_j$ according to the strict total ordering of the events in log L.

The set of response events $\{r_1^e, \ldots, r_n^e\}$ of an event e is given by the function π_r, we write $\pi_r(e) = \{r_1^e, \ldots, r_n^e\}$. For each trace $\sigma = \langle e_1, \ldots, e_n \rangle$, the sequence of responses is $\langle \pi_r(e_1), \ldots, \pi_r(e_n) \rangle$. For example, in the action-response log listed in Table 1, for event e_1: $\pi_c(e_1) = 1$ is the case of event e_1, $\pi_l(e_1) =$ "Verbal Aggression" is the action of e_1, and $\pi_r(e_1) = \{$ "Warning"$\}$ is the set of responses of e_1.

Effects of Responses. As we discussed, we aim to investigate whether a certain response to an action has an effect on the follow-up event. As such, we measure the effectiveness of a response to an action by studying the effect. For this aim, we first define the effects of events by using function π_{next} and introducing parameter ϵ for elapsed time. For each trace $\sigma = \langle e_1, ..., e_n \rangle$, we define the effect for each e_i, where $1 \leq i < n$ as follows: if the elapsed time to the next event e_{i+1} is less than ϵ, the effect $\pi_{next}(e_i)$ of e_i is the action of e_{i+1}, else we say that the effect is a silent action τ. Formally, if $\pi_{time}(e_{i+1}) - \pi_{time}(e_i) \leq \epsilon$, then $\pi_{next}(e_i) := \pi_{action}(e_{i+1})$, else $\pi_{next}(e_i) := \tau$.

To test the hypothesis whether an effect is independent of the response to an action, the number of observed events is compared to the number of expected events of different responses and effects. To calculate the number of observed events, we create a matrix (table) where each cell is filled with the number of observed events of a response and an effect. Let $a \in A$ be an action, $R = \{r_1, \cdots, r_m\}$ be a set of responses, and $C = \{c_1, \cdots, c_n\}$ a set of effects. We define a $|R| \times |C|$ matrix, where each row represents a response r_i, each column represents an effect c_j, and each cell counts the number of observed events that

Table 2. Excerpt of the event log action-response-effect

ID	Timestamp	Action	Response(s)	Effect
1	12-05 09:53	VA	Warning	PO
1	13-05 13:35	PO	Distract client, seclusion	τ
1	26-05 09:32	VA	Warning	PP
1	26-05 11:02	PP	Distract client	τ
2	21-06 14:51	VA	Distract client	VA
1	23-06 21:23	VA	Distract client	τ
2	24-06 17:02	VA	–	τ
3	29-07 11:22	VA	Warning	PO
3	31-07 08:13	PO	Warning, seclusion	PP
3	31-07 10:48	PP	Distract client	τ

Legend: VA = Verbal Aggression, PP = Physical Aggression
(People), PO = Physical Aggression (Objects)

have response r_i and effect c_j. We have

$$
freq_{a,R,C} = \begin{pmatrix} f_{1,1} & f_{1,2} & \cdots & f_{1,n} \\ f_{2,1} & f_{2,2} & \cdots & f_{2,n} \\ \vdots & \vdots & \ddots & \vdots \\ f_{m,1} & f_{m,2} & \cdots & f_{m,n} \end{pmatrix}
$$

where

$$
f_{i,j} = freq_L(a, r_i, c_j) = \quad |\{e \in L \mid \pi_l(e) = a \wedge r_i \in \pi_r(e) \wedge \pi_{next}(e) = c_j\}| \quad (1)
$$

For instance, given a log L as listed in Table 2, $freq_L($"VA", "Warning", "PO"$) = |\{e_1, e_8\}| = 2$. Considering Table 3 and omitting the column totals and row totals, it exemplifies a matrix $freq_{a,R,C}$. If the effects are independent of responses, then we should observe that the distribution of effects of a response is similar to the *total distribution*.

Each row r_i presents the distribution of effects $c_1, ..., c_k$ to the response r_i. To test whether each individual response r_i has an influence on the effects, we define $freq_{a,r,C}$ as a $2 \times |C|$ matrix:

$$
freq_{a,r,C} = \begin{pmatrix} f_{1,1} & f_{1,2} & \cdots & f_{1,n} \\ f_{2,1} & f_{2,2} & \cdots & f_{2,n} \end{pmatrix}
$$

where $f_{1,j} = freq_L(a, r, c_j)$ and

$$
f_{2,j} = \quad |\{e \in L \mid \pi_l(e) = a \wedge r \notin \pi_r(e) \wedge \pi_{next}(e) = c_j\}| \quad (2)
$$

An example of $freq_{a,r,C}$ where r is "Terminate contact" is listed in Table4. In the following section, our approach first performs a chi-squared test which

Table 3. Excerpt of the tables used to perform high-level statistical tests; horizontal categories: effect, vertical categories: response

Observed	PO	PP	VA	τ	Total
Warning	250	400	200	50	*900*
Held with force	20	50	50	10	*130*
Seclusion	30	50	20	10	*110*
Terminate contact	100	100	90	10	*300*
Distract client	100	150	40	10	*310*
Total	*500*	*750*	*400*	*100*	**1750**
Expected	PO	PP	VA	τ	Total
Warning	257.1	385.7	205.7	51.4	*900*
Held with force	37.1	55.7	29.7	7.4	*130*
Seclusion	31.4	47.1	25.1	6.3	*110*
Terminate contact	85.7	128.6	68.6	17.1	*300*
Distract client	88.6	132.9	70.9	17.7	*310*
Total	*500*	*750*	*400*	*100*	**1750**

Legend: VA = Verbal Aggression, PP = Physical Aggression (People), PO = Physical Aggression (Objects)

allows us to calculate the expected values and test the dependency between responses and effects. The chi-square test compares the observed frequencies to the expected frequencies. If they differ significantly, then the null hypothesis is rejected, which means we cannot rule out that there is a dependency relation between the response and the effect.

The complete event logs containing action-response-effect are used in the technique proposed in this paper. The next section elaborates on this.

4 Discovery Technique for Action-Response Logs

In this section, we propose an algorithm to implement a discovery technique, see Algorithm 1. This technique builds on the formalization introduced previously. The goal is to create understandable process models that provide the user with the required insights into the execution of the process. First, we describe the pre-processing that needs to take place (Input for Algorithm 1). Then, we elaborate on the technique which consists of three main stages: (1) high-level statistics (line 1–5 in Algorithm1), (2) detailed statistics (line 5–9), and (3) identifying influential points (line 9–14).

4.1 Pre-processing the Event Log

We first pre-process the log to obtain the effects of responses. As we are studying the effect of a response to an action, the duration between a response and its

Table 4. Excerpt of the tables for an individual response used to perform statistical tests; horizontal categories: effect

Observed	PO	PP	VA	τ	Total
Terminate contact = 0	300	500	210	90	1100
Terminate contact = 1	100	100	90	10	300
Total	400	600	300	100	1400
Expected	PO	PP	VA	τ	Total
Terminate contact = 0	314.3	471.4	235.7	78.6	1100
Terminate contact = 1	85.7	128.6	64.3	21.4	300
Total	400	600	300	100	1400

Legend: VA = Verbal Aggression, PP = Physical Aggression (People), PO = Physical Aggression (Objects)

effect influences the likelihood of a dependency relation between the two. Let us return to our example: if there is an aggressive incident, there is a given response to this incident. However, if the next incident takes place after a long time (e.g. a year) we doubt that this new incident is still dependent on the response to the initial action. Thus, we defined the parameter epsilon (ϵ), see Sect. 3. ϵ represents the maximum duration between two events in which the first event is still considered to have an effect on the second event. For our specific example we define ϵ equaling seven days in line with the input of an expert. Based on the ϵ, we introduce state τ. It represents the state we reach if there is no next incident within the defined duration of ϵ. In Table 2 we can see, for example, that distracting the client seems to be related to τ.

4.2   Computing High-Level Statistics

After pre-processing the event log, we investigate for each action the significant relation between the responses and the effects. In our example, the client shows a certain type of aggressive behavior (the action). Given this, we are interested in how the response of a caretaker to that incident has an effect on the follow-up incident. Hence, we will explain the technique with a fixed initial action.

In Table 3, an example of the observed and calculated expected frequencies can be found given the action is physical aggression against objects (see line 2 & 3 in Algorithm 1). This allows us to perform a Pearson Chi-square test [9] (see line 4). Based on a confidence level α (usually 95%), the calculated χ^2 is compared to the Chi-square distribution to see if there is at least one pair of response-effect significantly different. If the chi-square score is insignificant, the action is excluded from the graphical representation (see line 22). If the Chi-square is significant (see line 5), this indicates that the effects may depend on the response. We then move to the second stage, see Sect. 4.3.

We demonstrate this first stage by applying it to a designed example based on our case study presented in Table 3. Based on the observed values, we can calcu-

Algorithm 1. Compute graph

Input: Event log L
Output: Graph $G = (V, \prec)$
  1:      {*STAGE 1: High-Level Statistics*}
  2: **for** $a \in A$ **do**
  3:      Initiate matrix $O[a] \leftarrow freq_{a,R,C}$ {*see Equation 2. calculate the observed values*}
  4:      Compute matrix $E[a]$ {*calculate the expected values by following the chi-square test. see [9]*}
  5:      Compute $\chi_a^2 = \frac{(O[a]-E[a])^2}{E[a]}$ {*To test the dependence between responses R and effects $A \cup \{\tau\}$*}
  6:      **if** χ_a^2 is significant **then**
  7:          {*$O[a]$ differs from $E[a]$, thus responses R have a statistically significant influence on the effects C*}
  8:              {*STAGE 2: Detailed Statistics*}
  9:          **for** response $r \in R$ **do**
 10:              Compute matrix $O[a]_r$, $E[a]_r$, and $\chi_{a,r}^2$
 11:              **if** $\chi_{a,r}^2$ is significant **then**
 12:                  {*STAGE 3: Influential Points*}
 13:                  Compute adjusted standardized residuals ASR_c {*see Sect. 4.4*}
 14:                  **for** effect $c \in A \cup \{\tau\}$ **do**
 15:                      **if** ASR_c is significant **then**
 16:                          {*draw the arc from r to c*}
 17:                          $V \leftarrow V \cup \{a_s\} \cup \{r\}$, $\prec \leftarrow \prec \cup \{(a_s, r)\} \cup \{(r, c)\}$
 18:                      **end if**
 19:                  **end for**   {*effect*}
 20:              **else**
 21:                  {*$\chi_{a,r}^2$ is insignificant. i.e., r has no significant influence on C. We do not draw node r or any arc from r to C*}
 22:              **end if**
 23:          **end for**   {*response*}
 24:      **else**
 25:          {*Observed $O[a]$ follows the expected values $E[a]$. thus response R has no statistically significant influence on the effects C; thus. no arcs are drawn*}
 26:      **end if**
 27: **end for**   {*action*}
 28: **return** G

---

late the expected values in the table, for example, the expected value for the first cell: response *Terminate Contact* and effect $VA = \frac{N_r \times N_c}{E[a][r][c]} = \frac{300 \times 400}{1750} = 68.6$. We know from Table 3 that there are five response classes and four effect classes, so the degrees of freedom: $c = (5-1) \times (4-1) = 12$. Given all this, we can calculate the Chi-square score for the overall table: $\chi_c^2 = \sum_{i=1}^5 \frac{(O_{\text{Warning,PO}} - E_{\text{Warning,PO}})^2}{E_{\text{Warning,PO}}} +$ ....$+ \frac{(O_{\text{Distract client},\tau} - E_{\text{Distract client},\tau})^2}{E_{\text{Distract client},\tau}}$ $\chi_{12}^2 = \frac{(250-257.1)^2}{257.1} + ... + \frac{(10-17.7)^2}{17.7} = 63.47$. Now we need to determine if this score is significantly different from the mean of the Chi-distribution [14]. The formula for calculating the p-value is complex and will thus not be discussed in detail in this paper. For more details we refer to [14]. In our case the p-value (<0.001) corresponding to our Chi-square score is significant. This shows that for at least one pair of response-effect given action PO there is a significant difference from the expected frequency. Thus, we perform a Chi-square test for each individual response.

4.3   Computing Detailed Statistics

In the second stage of the algorithm, we perform the Chi-square test again on each response class to determine for which response we need to perform post-hoc statistical tests (see line 6–8 in Algorithm 1). For this purpose we create dummy variables. A dummy variable is made for each individual response, which takes the value of 0 or 1. The new table we create is a 2×4 table where the rows represent the response either taking a 0 or 1 value, see Table 4. Note that the degrees of freedom changes to three now. The same formulas are used to calculate the individual response Chi-square score and the corresponding p-value. A Bonferroni correction [16] is made to correct the critical value for the fact that on the same table multiple sets of analyses are performed. The Chi-square test identifies for which responses there is at least one effect that is significantly different from the expected frequency. If the Chi-square score is significant, we create a node for the response and perform post-hoc tests to identify the exact pairs of response-effect that are significant (see line 9).

We will demonstrate this stage on our designed example. We test five times (one for each response). Thus, we apply the Bonferroni correction [16] on confidence level of 95% (meaning $\alpha = 0.05$): $\frac{0.05}{5} = 0.01$. If we take Table 4, we can use the same formulas as presented in the previous section to calculate the expected values. Note that we assume independence of responses. Thus, if there are two responses, the action is counted twice: once for response 1 and once for response 2. Therefore, the observed frequencies in Table 3 are not necessarily equal to those in Table 4. If we perform the Chi-square test for the response *terminate contact* we get a Chi-square score of 31.96 with a p-value < 0.001. Thus, for the response *terminate contract* there is at least one effect that is significantly different from the expected frequency. A post-hoc test will identify the exact pairs for which this is true.

4.4   Identifying Influential Points

In the last stage, the post-hoc tests are performed to test which exact pairs of response-effect have a significant contribution to the Chi-square test score. For this, the adjusted standardized residuals (ASR) [3] are calculated (see line 10 in Algorithm 1). They represent a normalization of the residuals (observed - expected frequency). As the residuals can take either a positive or negative value we use two-sided testing. In order to improve the interpretability, we transform the α level into a critical value. We refer to [14] for details on this. If $|ASR| > criticalscore$ the difference between observed and expected frequency is significant. A significant score means that a specific pair of response-effect has a significant impact on the overall test score. We will refer to these as *influential points*. If the score is insignificant, no arc is drawn for that pair of response-effect

For each influential point, arcs are drawn in the graphical representation (see line 11–14). We first draw an arc from the action to the responses. On this arc, we indicate the observed frequency of the behavior. Then, we draw an arc from the response to the effect(s) for which we found a significant relation. On the arc we display the observed frequency followed by the expected frequency in brackets. If the observed frequency is larger than the expected frequency, i.e. the response leads to an increase in frequency of effect, we draw a thick arc. Correspondingly, if the observed frequency is lower than the expected frequency we draw a thin arc. The total number of graphical representations created equals the number of actions for which a significant Chi-square score is found (see line 25).

Now, we turn to the designed example. From the previous section we know that the response *Terminate contract* results in a significant Chi-square score. To calculate which points are influential points we calculate the adjusted standardized residuals for each pair. To exemplify, we show the calculation of the ASR for the pair *Terminate contact = 1* and VA: $ASR = \dfrac{90-64.3}{\sqrt{64.3*(1-\frac{64.3}{300})*(1-\frac{64.3}{300})}} = 4.08$ Given our Bonferroni correction gave us an alpha of 0.01 (see previous section), we need to test on the 99 % confidence level. The critical absolute value for this is 2.57. Thus, if our ASR value is $> |2.57|$ we mark it as influential point and draw an arc in the graphical representation. In the example of the pair Terminate contract = 1 and VA the ASR is larger than the critical score (4.08 > 2.57). Therefore, we draw a thick arc in the graphical representation of this example.

After conducting the above-described calculations for all actions, responses, and effects from the designed example, we obtain a total of three graphical representations (one for each action). In the next section, we evaluate the technique by applying it on a real-world data set.

5   Evaluation

The goal of this section is to demonstrate the capability of our technique to discover models that allow to obtain meaningful insights into action-response-effect patterns. To this end, we implemented our technique in Python and applied it to real-world data set. The scripts are publicly available for reproducibility[1].

5.1   Data Set

To evaluate our technique, we use a real-world data set related to the care process of a Dutch residential care facility. The event log contains 21,706 recordings of aggressive incidents spread over 1,115 clients. The process captured in this log concerns the aggressive behavior of clients in their facilities and the way client caretakers respond to these incidents. In the log we can find an aggressive incident of the client, which fits in one of five action classes. This is followed by some measures taken by the staff as response to this incident, which fits in one of nine response classes. In line with the description of our technique, we transformed this log into suitable triples by adding the next aggressive incident of a client as the effect, given it took place within our ϵ. Thus, the effect can be one of five classes. As there are four different classes of actions, our technique will return four different graphical representations. Below, we present and discuss the results for one class of action: physical aggression against objects.

---

[1] Source code and results: github.com/xxlu/ActionEffectDiscovery.

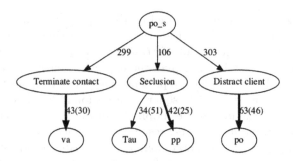

Fig. 2. Graphical representation of applying our technique on the action-response-effect event log. The initial action is physical aggression against objects.

5.2 Results

Healthcare Case Results. After applying our technique to the data set, we obtain four graphs (one for each class of action). In Fig. 2 we show the resulting graph when the initial action is physical aggression against objects ("po_s" in the figure). What we can see in the graph is the observed frequencies of the responses. For example, *terminate contact* has been observed 299 times in our data as a response to physical aggression against objects. Following this, the graph shows that in 43 events the effect to this response class is verbal aggression. From the data we know that, in total, there are four action classes, nine response classes, and five effect classes. As such, the representation for one action could potentially contain 81 ($9 * 4 + 9 * 5$) arcs. In our graphical representation, we do not draw all these arcs, we only draw seven of them.

Each arc represents a significantly higher (thick arc) or lower (thin arc) amount of observed compared to expected frequencies of interactions between the response and effect. As can be seen in the graph, this reduces the number of arcs substantially such that the impact of each individual response to a physical aggression against objects event can be studied.

Focusing on the insights we can obtain from the graphical representation in Fig. 2. The figure shows that responding to a physical aggression against objects event with *seclusion* results in a significantly higher amount of physical aggression against people ("pp" in the figure). This can be seen by the thicker arc or by comparing the observed frequency (42) with the expected frequency (25). Studying the frequencies we can conclude that we observe that the response *seclusion* is almost 1.7 times as likely to have the effect equaling physical aggression against people compared to what is expected. In similar fashion, the response *terminate contact* and *distract client* lead to a higher likelihood of one class of effect. However, the response *seclusion* leads to a significantly lower likelihood of the effect being no next aggression incident (τ).

Comparison to Control-Flow Based Discovery. Figure 3 illustrates that a control-flow based discovery approach, such as the directly-follows approach,

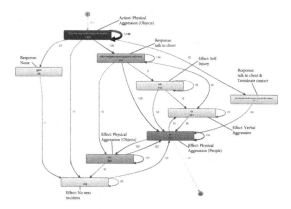

Fig. 3. Directly-follows process model of the real-world event log for the initial action physical aggression against objects. This shows the process filtered on 5% of the possible activities and paths. The model is created with Disco. Tool Website: https://fluxicon.com/disco/.

cannot provide such insights in the context of action-response-effect logs. The process model contains a large number of arcs. The number of arcs here increase exponentially with the number of responses observed. A possible solution to this could be to add information to the control-flow based representation, such as the observed frequencies of the arcs or nodes. However, filtering based on the frequencies does not always have the desired result. This can also be seen in Fig. 3. It could even be misleading since the data set is imbalanced. In this real-world scenario, a high frequency does not imply a significant pattern. This becomes obvious if we compare the approaches. From the figures we can see that none of the significant response-effect pairs from Fig. 2 are displayed in Fig. 3. In order to understand the relations in the representation, we have to account for the relative frequencies. These reveal the meaningful insights that are hidden in the representation of a discovery technique such as the control-flow. Hence, even after applying filtering mechanisms, Fig. 3 does not provide the insights that are required to answer a question such as: If a client displays aggressive behavior of class X, which response is likely to lead to an (de-)escalation or future aggression?

5.3   Discussion

Insights. The key question identified at the start of this research addressed the desire to express insights into how a response to an action can lead to a desired or undesired outcome (effect). In our problem statement we identified two main challenges associated with this that need to be overcome: (1) graphical representation, and (2) effective filtering mechanism. Studying the example of aggressive behavior highlights how the proposed technique addresses both these challenges. Figure 2 shows that our technique creates simple graphical representation that allow for insights into dependency relations that cannot be obtained using Fig. 3. In addition, comparing the same figures we can see that the use of statistics reduces the number of arcs substantially. The filtering mechanisms is effective in the sense that it filters those arcs that are meaningful, opposed to those that are merely frequent.

As a result in Fig. 2 we can see the effects of responses to aggressive incidents. Important to note is that physical aggression against people is seen as the most and verbal aggression as the least severe form of aggressive behavior. The figure shows that responding to a physical aggression against objects event with *seclusion* increases the likelihood of the next event being physical aggression against people. In other words, this response leads to an undesired outcome: escalation of the aggressive behavior of the client. In contrast, we observe that the response *terminate contact* is more likely to lead to a verbal aggressive incident. Thus, this represents a desired outcome: de-escalation of future violence. Finally, the response *distract client* has the effect that the client is more likely to repeat the same class of action ("po" in the figure), indicating a circular relation.

Implications. One interesting implication of our technique is that the generated insights can be used to support decision making processes. In our example, Fig. 2 can be used to train existing and new staff members to ensure that appropriate responses are taken. Placing this technique in a broader medical context, the technique could help make informed decisions when different treatment options are considered. In a different domain, the technique could help a marketing organization understand the effectiveness of marketing strategies in terms of response of potential customers. In short, the discovery technique provides insights into action-response-effect patterns where the objective of analyzing the process is to understand possible underlying dependency patterns.

Limitations. It is worth mentioning that, in our technique, we assume the independence of the responses. This means that each response has a unique effect on the effect and there is no interfering effect when responses are combined. For example, if response r_1 is more likely to lead to c_1 and r_2 to c_2, then performing r_1 and r_2 are more likely to lead to follow-up effects c_1 or c_2, but not a different effect c_3. Statistical pre-tests can be performed to verify this assumption. A basic approach is to create a correlation matrix for the dummies of the responses. In our example, this matrix shows that the assumption holds. In other words, no responses are strongly and significantly correlated. If the assumption is violated then the technique should consider R' as input. R' is a set of all independent classes including those groups of responses that have a potential interfering effect.

6   Related Work

Over the last two decades a plethora of process discovery algorithms were proposed [5]. The majority of these approaches generate procedural models such as Petri nets [25,26], causal nets [20,28], BPMN models [4,7] or process trees [8,17]. Some approaches also discover declarative models [6,24] or hybrid models (i.e. a combination of procedural and declarative models) [10,19]. What all these techniques have in common is that they aim to discover the control flow of a business process, that is, the execution constraints among the process' activities. Our approach clearly differs from these traditional process discovery approaches by focusing on action-response patterns instead of the general control flow.

There are, however, also alternative approaches to process discovery. Most prominently, several authors addressed the problem of artifact-centric process discovery [18,21,22]. The core idea of artifact-centric process discovery is to consider a process as a set of interacting artifacts that evolve throughout process execution. The goal of artifact-centric discovery, therefore, is to discover the lifecyles associated with these artifacts and the respective interactions among them. While artifact-centric discovery techniques move away from solely considering the control-flow of the process' activities, the main goal is still control-flow oriented. A related, yet different approach to process discovery was proposed in [12,13]. This approach focuses on the different perspectives of a process and discovers and captures how their relations using Composite State Machines.

While the technique from [12,13] is potentially useful in many scenarios we address with our technique, the insights that can be obtained with our technique differ substantially. The technique from [12,13] allows to understand how different artifact lifecycle states are related. For example, it reveals that a patient in the state *"healthy"* does no longer require a *"lab test"*. The goal of our technique is to show what actually needs to be done (or should not be done) to make sure a patient ends up in the state *"healthy"*. To the best of our knowledge, we are the first to propose a technique that discovers such action-response-effect patterns and allows the reader to develop an understanding of why certain events occur.

7   Conclusion

This paper presented a technique to discover action-response-effect patterns. We identified two main challenges that we addressed in this research: (1) graphical representation, and (2) effective filtering mechanism. In order to address these challenges, we proposed a novel discovery technique that builds on filtering influential relations using statistical tests. We evaluated our technique on a real-world data set from the healthcare domain. More specifically, we used our technique to study aggressive behavior and show that we can gain valuable and novel insights from the representations discovered by our technique. The representations also show that the technique can tackle both challenges by providing an easy-to-interpret representation that only displays meaningful relations.

In future work, we plan to further test the approach on real-world cases. In addition, we plan to extend this work in two ways: (1) by introducing more complex statistical tests to provide flexibility in the assumption of independence of the responses, and (2) by introducing statistical tests to approximate the optimal configuration of ϵ.

182   J. J. Koorn et al.

(628.011.004) and Lunet Zorg in the Netherlands. We would also like to thank the
experts from the Lunet Zorg for their valuable assistance and feedback.

References

1. Aalst, W.: Data science in action. Process Mining, pp. 3–23. Springer, Heidelberg
   (2016). https://doi.org/10.1007/978-3-662-49851-4_1
2. van der Aalst, W.M.: A practitioner's guide to process mining: limitations of the
   directly-follows graph. Proc. Comput. Sci. **164**, 321–328 (2019)
3. Agresti, A.: Categorical Data Analysis, vol. 482. John Wiley, Hoboken (2003)
4. Augusto, A., Conforti, R., Dumas, M., La Rosa, M.: Split miner: discovering accurate and simple business process models from event logs. In: 2017 IEEE International Conference on Data Mining (ICDM), pp. 1–10. IEEE (2017)
5. Augusto, A., et al.: Automated discovery of process models from event logs: review
   and benchmark. IEEE TKDE **31**(4), 686–705 (2018)
6. Bernardi, M.L., Cimitile, M., Di Francescomarino, C., Maggi, F.M.: Using discriminative rule mining to discover declarative process models with non-atomic activities. In: Bikakis, A., Fodor, P., Roman, D. (eds.) RuleML 2014. LNCS, vol. 8620, pp.
   281–295. Springer, Cham (2014). https://doi.org/10.1007/978-3-319-09870-8_21
7. vanden Broucke, S.K., De Weerdt, J.: Fodina: a robust and flexible heuristic process
   discovery technique. Decis. Support Syst. **100**, 109-118 (2017)
8. Buijs, J.C., van Dongen, B.F., van der Aalst, W.M.: A genetic algorithm for discovering process trees. In: 2012 IEEE Congress on Evolutionary Computation, pp.
   1–8. IEEE (2012)
9. Cochran, W.G.: The $\chi2$ test of goodness of fit. Ann. Math. Stat. **23**, 315–345
   (1952)
10. De Smedt, J., De Weerdt, J., Vanthienen, J.: Fusion miner: process discovery for
    mixed-paradigm models. Decis. Support Syst. **77**, 123–136 (2015)
11. De Weerdt, J., Schupp, A., Vanderloock, A., Baesens, B.: Process mining for the
    multi-faceted analysis of business processes–a case study in a financial services
    organization. Comput. Ind. **64**(1), 57–67 (2013)
12. van Eck, M.L., Sidorova, N., van der Aalst, W.M.P.: Discovering and exploring
    state-based models for multi-perspective processes. In: La Rosa, M., Loos, P., Pas-
    tor, O. (eds.) BPM 2016. LNCS, vol. 9850, pp. 142–157. Springer, Cham (2016).
    https://doi.org/10.1007/978-3-319-45348-4_9
13. van Eck, M.L., Sidorova, N., van der Aalst, W.M.: Guided interaction exploration
    in artifact-centric process models. In: 2017 IEEE 19th Conference on Business
    Informatics (CBI), vol. 1, pp. 109–118. IEEE (2017)
14. Fisher, R.A., Yates, F.: Statistical Tables: For Biological. Agricultural and Medical
    Research. Oliver and Boyd, Edinburgh (1938)
15. Günther, C.W., van der Aalst, W.M.P.: Fuzzy mining – adaptive process simplifi-
    cation based on multi-perspective metrics. In: Alonso, G., Dadam, P., Rosemann,
    M. (eds.) BPM 2007. LNCS, vol. 4714, pp. 328–343. Springer, Heidelberg (2007).
    https://doi.org/10.1007/978-3-540-75183-0_24
16. Haynes, W.: Bonferroni Correction, p. 154. Springer, New York (2013). https://
    doi.org/10.1007/978-1-4419-9863-7

17. Leemans, S.J.J., Fahland, D., van der Aalst, W.M.P.: Discovering block-structured process models from event logs - a constructive approach. In: Colom, J.-M., Desel, J. (eds.) PETRI NETS 2013. LNCS, vol. 7927, pp. 311–329. Springer, Heidelberg (2013). https://doi.org/10.1007/978-3-642-38697-8_17

18. Lu, X., Nagelkerke, M., van de Wiel, D., Fahland, D.: Discovering interacting artifacts from ERP systems. IEEE Trans. Serv. Comput. **8**(6), 861–873 (2015)

19. Maggi, F.M., Slaats, T., Reijers, H.A.: The automated discovery of hybrid processes. In: Sadiq, S., Soffer, P., Völzer, H. (eds.) BPM 2014. LNCS, vol. 8659, pp. 392–399. Springer, Cham (2014). https://doi.org/10.1007/978-3-319-10172-9_27

20. Nguyen, H., Dumas, M., ter Hofstede, A.H.M., La Rosa, M., Maggi, F.M.: Mining business process stages from event logs. In: Dubois, E., Pohl, K. (eds.) CAiSE 2017. LNCS, vol. 10253, pp. 577–594. Springer, Cham (2017). https://doi.org/10.1007/978-3-319-59536-8_36

21. Nooijen, E.H.J., van Dongen, B.F., Fahland, D.: Automatic discovery of data-centric and artifact-centric processes. In: La Rosa, M., Soffer, P. (eds.) BPM 2012. LNBIP, vol. 132, pp. 316–327. Springer, Heidelberg (2013). https://doi.org/10.1007/978-3-642-36285-9_36

22. Popova, V., Fahland, D., Dumas, M.: Artifact lifecycle discovery. Int. J. Coop. Inf. Syst. **24**(01), 1550001 (2015)

23. Rojas, E., Munoz-Gama, J., Sepúlveda, M., Capurro, D.: Process mining in healthcare: a literature review. J. Biomed. Inform. **61**, 224–236 (2016)

24. Schönig, S., Rogge-Solti, A., Cabanillas, C., Jablonski, S., Mendling, J.: Efficient and customisable declarative process mining with SQL. In: Nurcan, S., Soffer, P., Bajec, M., Eder, J. (eds.) CAiSE 2016. LNCS, vol. 9694, pp. 290–305. Springer, Cham (2016). https://doi.org/10.1007/978-3-319-39696-5_18

25. Song, W., Jacobsen, H.A., Ye, C., Ma, X.: Process discovery from dependence-complete event logs. IEEE Trans. Serv. Comput. **9**(5), 714–727 (2015)

26. Verbeek, H., van der Aalst, W.M., Munoz-Gama, J.: Divide and conquer: a tool framework for supporting decomposed discovery in process mining. Comput. J. **60**(11), 1649–1674 (2017)

27. Weijters, A.J., Van der Aalst, W.M.: Rediscovering workflow models from event-based data using little thumb. Integr. Comput.-Aided Eng. **10**(2), 151–162 (2003)

28. Yahya, B.N., Song, M., Bae, H., Sul, S.O., Wu, J.Z.: Domain-driven actionable process model discovery. Comput. Ind. Eng. **99**, 382–400 (2016)

Extracting Annotations from Textual Descriptions of Processes

Luis Quishpi, Josep Carmona$^{(\boxtimes)}$, and Lluís Padró

Computer Science Department, Universitat Politècnica de Catalunya,
Barcelona, Spain
{quishpi,jcarmona,padro}@cs.upc.edu

Abstract. Organizations often have textual descriptions as a way to document their main processes. These descriptions are primarily used by the company's personnel to understand the processes, specially for those ones that cannot interpret formal descriptions like BPMN or Petri nets. In this paper we present a technique based on Natural Language Processing and a query language for tree-based patterns, that extracts annotations describing key process elements like actions, events, agents/patients, roles and control-flow relations. Annotated textual descriptions of processes are a good compromise between understandability (since at the end, it is just text), and behavior. Moreover, as it has been recently acknowledged, obtaining annotated textual descriptions of processes opens the door to unprecedented applications, like formal reasoning or simulation on the underlying described process. Applying our technique on several publicly available texts shows promising results in terms of precision and recall with respect to the state-of-the art approach for a similar task.

1 Introduction

The consolidation of the BPM discipline in organizations is closely related to the ability of going beyond current practices, especially for the assumption that data that talks about processes is an structured source of information. In practice, this assumption is often not met, i.e., organizations document their processes in textual descriptions, as a way to bootstrap their accessibility [15].

The ubiquity of textual descriptions of processes has caused recent research in proposing mechanisms to make actionable this information source, e.g., the discovery of formal process models [7,16], the alignment between structured and non-structured process information [13,17], or the use of annotations and natural language techniques to encompass process information [10,12].

The contribution in [12] shows how formal reasoning is possible on top of *Annotated Textual Descriptions of Processes* (ATDP, see an example in Fig. 1), by equipping ATDP with a formal, trace semantics that links any ATDP specification to a linear temporal logic formula. However, in [12] (but also in similar works

© Springer Nature Switzerland AG 2020
D. Fahland et al. (Eds.): BPM 2020, LNCS 12168, pp. 184–201, 2020.
https://doi.org/10.1007/978-3-030-58666-9_11

like [10]), it is assumed that these annotations are manually crafted, thus hampering the ability to automate the application of formal analysis on annotated textual descriptions of processes.

In this paper we propose a novel technique to extract an important subset of the ATDP language. In contrast to existing approaches, we use a query language that considers the hierarchical structure of the sentences: our technique applies flexible tree-based patterns on top of the *dependency tree* corresponding to the NLP analysis of each sentence. This makes the approach very robust to variations that can arise in the discursive description of the main process elements, but also contributes to reduce considerably the number of patterns that need to be defined and maintained to perform the extraction.

The open-source tool related to this paper contributes to make ATDP specifications actionable. Currently, several functionalities are available[1]: an ATDP library, an ATDP editor, an ATDP interface to a model checker, and now an ATDP extractor.

Running Example. Figure 1 shows the results of the technique proposed in this paper. The text describes the process of examining patients in a hospital[2]. For this text, the techniques of this paper are able to automatically extract activities (highlighted in red), roles (highlighted in blue), conditions (highlighted in green), and relations between these extracted elements (e.g., control-flow relations between actions).

The paper is organized as follows: next section shortly describes the work related to this contribution. In Sect. 3 we overview the main ingredients of this paper contribution, presented in Sect. 4. Experiments and tool support are reported in Sect. 5, whilst Sect. 6 concludes the paper and provides suggestions for future work.

2 Related Work

For the sake of space, we only report here the related work that focuses on the extraction of process knowledge from textual descriptions [1,7,16] or legal documents [3,19], or the work that considers textual annotations in the scope of BPM [10,12].

For the former, the work by Friedrich et al. [7] is acknowledged as the state-of-the-art for extracting process representations from textual descriptions, so we focus our comparison on this approach. As we will see in the evaluation section, our approach is significantly more accurate with respect to the state-of-the-art in the extraction of the main process elements. Likewise, we have incorporated as well the patterns from [16], and a similar outcome is reported in the experiments. Moreover, we believe that our ideas can be easily applied in the scope of legal documents, proposed in [3,19].

---

[1] https://github.com/PADS-UPC.
[2] This example is inspired from [14].

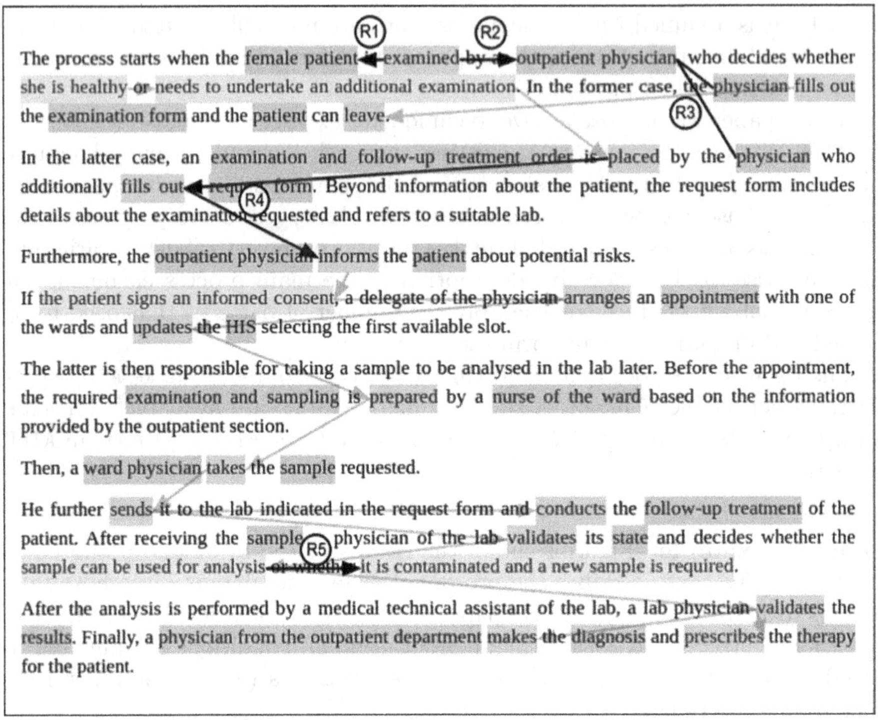

Fig. 1. Extracted annotated textual description of a patient examination process. R1: Patient of `examine` is `female patient`, R2: Agent of `examine` is `outpatient physician`, R3: Coreference between `outpatient physician` and `physician`, R4: Sequential between `fill out` and `informs`, R5: Conflict between conditions `sample can be used for analysis` and `it is contaminated and a new sample is required` (Color figure online)

For the later type of techniques [10,12], we see these frameworks as the principal application for our techniques. In particular, we have already demonstrated in the platform https://modeljudge.cs.upc.edu an application of the use of annotations in the scope of teaching and learning process modeling[3].

3   Preliminaries

3.1   Natural Language Processing and Annotation

Linguistic analysis tools can be used as a means to structure information contained in texts for its later processing in applications less related to language itself. This is our case: we use NLP analyzers to convert a textual description of

---

[3] The reader can see a tutorial for annotating process modeling exercises in the `ModelJudge` platform at https://modeljudge.cs.upc.edu/modeljudge_tutorial/.

a process model into a structured representation. The NLP processing software used in this work is FreeLing[4] [11], an open–source library of language analyzers providing a variety of analysis modules for a wide range of languages. More specifically, the natural language processing layers used in this work are:

Tokenization & sentence splitting: Given a text, split the basic lexical terms (words, punctuation signs, numbers, etc.), and group these tokens into sentences.

Morphological analysis: Find out all possible parts-of-speech (PoS) for each token.

PoS-Tagging: Determine the right PoS for each word in a sentence. (e.g. the word *dance* is a verb in *I dance all Saturdays* but a noun in *I enjoyed our dance together.*)

Named Entity Recognition: Detect named entities in the text, which may be formed by one or more tokens, and classify them as *person, location, organization, time-expression, numeric-expression, currency-expression,* etc.

Word sense disambiguation: Determine the sense of each word in a text (e.g. the word *crane* may refer to an animal or to a weight-lifting machine). We use WordNet [5] as the sense catalogue and synset codes as concept identifiers.

Dependency parsing: Given a sentence, get its syntatic structure as a dependency parse tree (DT). DT are an important element in our approach. The reader can see an example of a dependency tree in Fig. 4.

Semantic role labeling: Given a sentence, identify its predicates and the main actors (agent, patient, recipient, etc) involved in each predicate, regardless of the surface structure of the sentence (active/passive, main/subordinate, etc.). E.g. In the sentence *John gave Mary a book written by Peter*, SRL would extract two predicates: `give` (with semantic roles `Agent(John,give)`, `Patient(book,give)`, and `Recipient(Mary,give)`), and `write` (with semantic roles: `Agent(Peter,write)` and `Patient(book,write)`).

Coreference resolution: Given a document, group mentions referring to the same entity (e.g. a person can be mentioned as *Mr. Peterson, the director*, or *he*).

The three last steps are of special relevance since they allow the top-level predicate construction, and the identification of actors throughout the whole text: dependency parsing identifies syntactic subjects and objects (which may vary depending, e.g., on whether the sentence is active or passive), while semantic role labeling identifies semantic relations (the *agent* of an action is the same regardless of whether the sentence is active or passive). Coreference resolution links several mentions of an actor as referring to the same entity (e.g. in Fig. 1, *a delegate of the physician* and *the latter* refer to the same person. Also, the same object is mentioned as *the sample requested* and *it*).

---

[4] http://nlp.cs.upc.edu/freeling.

All NLP components are developed and evaluated on standard benchmarks in the area, obtaining state-of-the art results. In particular, dependency trees –which are the basic element upon which we build our proposal– are created by a Deep Learning parser [4] which obtains accuracy scores over 90%.

3.2 Annotated Textual Descriptions of Processes (ATDP)

ATDP is a formalism proposed in [12], aiming to represent process models on top of textual descriptions. This formalism naturally enables the representation of a wide range of behaviors, ranging from procedural to completely declarative, but also hybrid ones. Different from classical conceptual modeling principles, this highlight ambiguities that can arise from a textual description of a process, so that a specification can have more than one possible interpretation[5].

ATDP specifications can be translated into linear temporal logic over finite traces [2,8], opening the door to formal reasoning, automatic construction of formal models (e.g. in BPMN) from text, and other interesting applications such as simulation: to generate end-to-end executions (i.e., an *event log* [18]) that correspdond to the process described in the text, which would allow the application of *process mining* algorithms.

In Fig. 1, there are different types of fragments, distinguished by color in our visual front-end. Some fragments (shown in red) describe the atomic units of behavior in the text, that is, activities and events, while others (shown in blue) provide additional perspectives beyond control flow. For example, `outpatient physician` is labelled as a *role* at the beginning of the text, while `informs` is labelled as an *activity*. Depending on their types, fragments can be linked by means of *relations*.

ATDP models are defined over an input text, which is marked with *typed text fragments*, which may correspond to *entities*, or *activities*. Marked fragments can be related among them via a set of *fragment relations*.

Entity Fragments. The types of entity fragments defined in ATDP are:

- *Role.* The role fragment type is used to represent types of autonomous actors involved in the process, and consequently responsible for the execution of activities contained therein. An example is `outpatient physician` in Fig. 1.
- *Business Object.* This type is used to mark all the relevant elements of the process that do not take an active part in it, but that are used/manipulated by process activities. An example is the `(medical) sample` obtained and analyzed by physicians during the patient examination process.

Activity Fragments. ATDP distinguishes the following types of activity fragments:

---

[5] In this work we consider a flattened version of the ATDP language, i.e., without the notion of *scopes*.

- *Condition.* It is considered discourse markers that mark conditional statements, like: *if, whether* and *either*. Each discourse marker needs to be tailored to a specific grammatical structure.
- *Task and Event.* Those fragment types are used to represent the atomic units of work within the business process described by the text. Usually, these fragments are associated with verbs. An example task fragment is `validates` (`results`). Event fragments are used to annotate other occurrences in the process that are relevant from the point of view of the control flow, but are exogenous to the organization responsible for the execution of the process.

Fragment Relations. Text fragments can be related to each other by means of different relations, used to express properties of the process emerging from the text:

- *Agent.* Indicates the role responsible for the execution of an activity.
- *Patient.* Indicates the role or business object on which an activity is performed.
- *Coreference.* Induces a coreference graph where each connected component denotes a distinct process entity.
- *Sequential.* Indicates the sequential execution of two activity fragments A1 and A2 in a sentence. We consider two important relations from [12]: Precedence and Response. Moreover, to cover situations where ambiguities in the text prevent selecting any of the two aforementioned relations, we also incorporate a less restrictive constraint WeakOrder, that only applies in case both activities occur in a trace.
- *Conflicting.* A conflict relation between two condition activity fragments $\langle C1, C2 \rangle$ in a sentence indicates that one and only one of them can be executed, thus capturing a choice. This corresponds to the relation NonCoOccurrence from [12].

Once `ATDP` are extracted, several possibilities arise, ranging from simulation, to formal analysis. For any of the previous techniques, there are available open-source libraries (see Sect. 5).

3.3   TRegex

In this paper, we use Tregex[6] [9], a query language that allows the definition of regular-expression-like patterns over tree structures. Tregex is designed to match patterns involving the content of tree nodes and the hierarchical relations among them. In our case we will be using Tregex to find substructures within syntactic dependency trees. Applying Tregex patterns on a dependency tree allows us to search for complex labeled tree dominance relations involving different types of information in the nodes. The nodes can contain symbols or a string of characters (e.g. lemmas, word forms, PoS tags) and Tregex patterns may combine those tags with the available dominance operators to specify conditions on the tree.

---

[6] https://nlp.stanford.edu/software/tregex.html.

Additionally, as in any regular expression library, subpatterns of interest may be specified and the matching subtree can be retrieved for later use. This is achieved in Tregex using unification variables as shown in pattern (2) in Fig. 2.

Figure 2 describes the main Tregex operators used in this research to specify pattern queries.

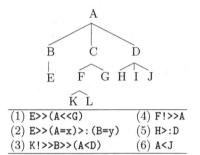

Operator	Meaning
X << Y	X dominates Y
X >> Y	X is dominated by Y
X !>> Y	X is not dominated by Y
X < Y	X immediately dominates Y
X > Y	X is immediately dominated by Y
X >, Y	X is the first child of Y
X >- Y	X is the last child of Y
X >: Y	X is the only child of Y
X $-- Y	X is a right sister of Y

(1) E>>(A<<G)   (4) F!>>A
(2) E>>(A=x)>:(B=y)   (5) H>:D
(3) K!>>B>>(A<D)   (6) A<J

Fig. 2. Some operators provided by Tregex (left). The tree on the right would match patterns (1), (2), (3), and would not match patterns (4), (5), (6). Note that unless parenthesized, all operators refer to the first element in the pattern. Pattern (2) captures nodes A and B into variables x and y.

4 Approach

Our proposed technique automatically extracts ATDP elements applying Tregex patterns on textual description of business process, commonly used in industry and business organizations [15]. The result is a set of ATDP elements that may be used to derive formal representations of process models, generate logs via simulation, or automatically reason about process behaviour (see [12] for more details on ATDP possibilities).

The technique follows the steps shown in Fig. 3. The first step consists of performing a NLP analysis to extract, among other information, a dependency tree for each sentence (see Sect. 3.1).

The obtained dependency trees (one for each sentence) are transformed to a format suitable for Tregex patterns: A node in the transformed dependency tree is a structured string, containing information about the lemma, PoS tag, and syntactic function of each word. Additionally, nodes marked as predicates by the NLP semantic role labeling step are decorated with an extra <ACTION> label, that identifies them as potential activity fragments. Figure 4 shows the transformed tree for the input sentence *"If the patient signs an informed consent, a delegate of the physician arranges an appointment with one of the wards and updates the HIS selecting the first available slot"*.

Next step consists of extracting process entities (actors and business objects) as described below in Sect. 4.1. Afterwards, we extract activity fragments relying

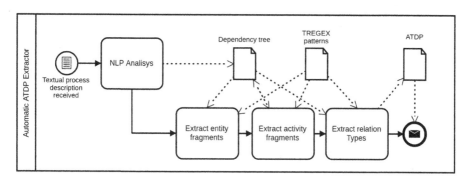

Fig. 3. General framework for automatic `ATDP` extraction

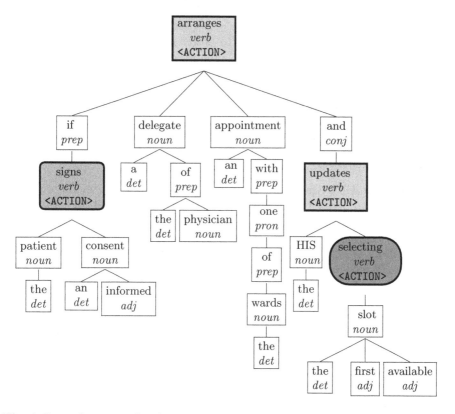

Fig. 4. Dependency tree for the sentence *"If the patient signs an informed consent, a delegate of the physician arranges an appointment with one of the wards and updates the HIS selecting the first available slot"*. Oval red node *selecting* is filtered out as a process activity since it is inside a subordinate clause. Round-corner olive *signs* is marked as a condition activity, since it is inside the conditional clause. Sharp-corner green nodes *arranges* and *updates* are kept as process activities since they are at the main clause level in the sentence (accounting for the *and* coordinating structure).

on an incremental procedure based on Tregex patters: First, a set of patterns identify which `<ACTION>` nodes are actually conditions, and change their mark to `<CONDITION>`. Next, other patterns discard non-relevant `<ACTION>` nodes, and relabel relevant ones as `<ACTIVITY>`. Finally, a last batch of patterns decide which of the remaining actions should be relabeled as `<EVENT>`. See Sect. 4.2 for details on each of these pattern sets. Finally, after relabeling the appropriate tree nodes, the last set of patterns extracts relations between the resulting activity nodes (Sect. 4.3).[7]

4.1 Extraction of Entity Fragments

Roles and Business Objects. To identify the roles – i.e. autonomous actors– of the process, we leverage the results from the NLP analysis and focus on the elements with a semantic role of *Actor*. Similarly, business object are detected extracting elements with semantic role of *Object*. For each of those elements, the extracted text should be modified to better represent the role or business object: fragments that begin with *the* or prepositions such as *by*, *of* or *from* can be modified to not contain these elements, but just the core description of the role/object.

To that end, the following Tregex pattern is recursively applied to the dependency tree to select the relevant modifiers of the main entity word (i.e. nouns and adjectives directly modifying the head noun in the phrase):

PE1 `/noun|adjective/=result > /EntityHeadWord/`

This pattern will extract only nouns and adjectives directly modifying each main entity word (note that this pattern will we instantiated for each word heading a phrase identified as *Actor* or *Object* by the NLP).

For instance, in the sentence *"The process starts when the female patient is examined by an outpatient physician, who decides whether she is healthy or needs to undertake an additional examination"* the results of the semantic role labeling step for *Agent* would return the whole subtree headed by *physician* (i.e. *an outpatient physician, who decides... examination*). The role entity fragment Tregex pattern will strip down such a long actor/object removing the determiner and the relative clause, while keeping the core actor/object and its main modifiers, thus extracting respectively `outpatient physician` as a role, and `female patient` as a business object.

4.2 Extraction of Activity Fragments

In order to extract activity fragments, we rely on the output of NLP, which marks as predicates all non-auxiliary verbs as well as some nominal predicates (e.g. *integration*, *meeting*, etc.). However, many verbs in a process description

---

[7] It is important to notice that the selection, configuration and application of rules influences the `ATDP` extraction. Exploring possible extensions and strategies to achieve a complete and minimal set of rules will be object of future research.

may be predicates from a linguistic perspective, but do not correspond to actual process activities. Thus, we use a set of patterns that discard predicates unlikely to be describing a relevant process task, or relabel them as *condition* or *event* fragment.

Condition Fragments. To detect conditional phrases, we use patterns that check for nodes having part-of-speech with a domination relation with nodes containing words such as "if", "whether" or "either". If a match is found, the tree node captured in variable `result` is marked as `<CONDITION>`. Condition patterns are:

```
PC1 /<verb>/=result >, /whether/
PC2 /<verb>|<not>/=result >, (/or/ >> /<whether>/)
PC3 /<verb>/=result >, /if/
PC4 /<verb>/=result < /either/=condition << /or/
PC5 /<verb>/=result > (/or/ >> (/<verb>/ < /either/))
```

The first pattern checks for a node `<verb>` that is the first child of a node with word "whether". In the second pattern, the matched node is either a `<verb>` or the word `<not>` that is the first child of a node with word "or" which is in turn child of node "if".

For instance, patterns PC1 and PC2 can be used to determine that `she is healthy` and `needs to undertake an additional examination` are conditions in the sentence "*... who decides whether she is healthy or needs to undertake an additional examination.*". Similarly, pattern PC3 matches the tree in Fig. 4, and extracts the condition fragment `the patient signs an informed consent`.

Finally, patterns PC4 and PC5 extract the conditional phrase in sentences containing "`either...or`" constructions.

Event Fragments. The strategy to identify events is similar to conditional fragments identification. The main difference is that, instead of conditional markers, we consider the presence of time markers such as *once, as soon, when* and *whenever*. The following Tregex expressions are used to identify event fragments:

```
PV1 /<ACTION>/=result > /once/
PV2 /<ACTION>/=result > (/be/ > /once/)
PV3 /<ACTION>/=result >> (/as/ >- /soon/)
PV4 /<ACTION>/=result <, /when/
PV5 /<ACTION>/=result < /whenever/
```

If a match is found, the tree node captured in variable `result` is marked as `<EVENT>`. For instance, in the sentence "*Once the payment is confirmed, the ZooClub department can print the card...*", after applying pattern PV2, the fragment `confirm(payment)` is identified as an event fragment.

Task Fragments. Task fragments represent the atomic activity of execution inside the process model, and their identification is done after extracting conditions and events.

PT1 /be <ACTION>/=toRemove
PT2 /start <ACTION>/=toRemove
PT3 /have <ACTION>/=toRemove
PT4 /want <ACTION>/=toRemove

These patterns simply discard verbs *be, start, have* and *want* as activities. Subjective verbs (e.g. *want, think, believe,* etc.) are unlike to describe activities and thus are filtered out. For instance in the sentence *"The process starts when the female patient is examined by an outpatient physician,..."*, *start* is removed from the activity list, while *examine* is kept.

The following patterns remove any action candidates that are in a subordinate clause under another action.

PT5 /<ACTION>/=toRemove >> /<ACTION>/=result !>> /and|or/
PT6 /<ACTION>/=toRemove >> (/<ACTION>/=result >> /and|or/)

The idea is that a subordinate clause is describing details about some element in the main clause, but it is not a relevant activity thus it must be removed. For instance, in the sentence *"..., the examination is prepared based on the information provided by the outpatient section"*, the verbs *base* and *provide* would be removed as activities, since the main action described by this sentence is just *prepare (examination)*.

The first pattern has an additional constraint, checking that the tree does not contain a coordinating conjunction (*and/or*), since in that case, both predicates are likely to be activities (e.g. in *"He sends it to the lab and conducts the follow-up treatment"*, although *conduct* is under the tree headed by *send*, the presence of *and* in between blocks the pattern application), meanwhile in the second pattern takes as reference the coordinating conjunction *and/or* to remove any action candidates that are in a subordinate clause under the main action.[8]

If a match is found by patterns PT5 or PT6, the tree node captured in variable `result` is marked as <ACTIVITY> and in the tree node captured in variable `toRemove` the tag <ACTION> is removed. For instance, in the tree in Fig. 4, the action *select (first available slot)* that is under *update (HIS)* is discarded by pattern PT5.

4.3   Relation Types

Agent, Patient and Coreference. These relations are straightforwardly extracted from the output (predicates and arguments) of the Semantic Role

---

[8] Observe that the absence of parenthesis in pattern 1 means that the "!>>/and|or/" condition is applied to the first action in the pattern, while in pattern 2, the parenthesis force that condition on the second action.

Labelling phase. However, only those involving entities or activities detected by the patterns described above are considered. For instance, in the first sentence of our running sample (Fig. 1) we have that the *agent* for activity `examine` is `outpatient physician`, while the *patient* is `female patient`,. stating that `examine` someone is under the responsibility of a `outpatient physician` and the `examine` activity operates over a `female patient` business object.

Regarding coreference, in our running example (Fig. 1), all text fragments pointing to the `patient` role corefer to the same entity, whereas there are three different physicians involved in the text: the `outpatient physician`, the `physician` and the `ward physician`, which form disconnected coreference subgraphs.

Sequential. The extraction of sequential relations is performed on the results of activity fragment extraction described in Sect. 4.2. We use patterns to capture `Precedence`, `Response` and `WeakOrder` constraints, which express the order of execution of the activities in an `ATDP` specification.

These first patterns can be used to identify a particular case of `Response` that typically occurs in conditional sentences:

PR1 /<CONDITION>/=from >, (/if/ >/<ACTIVITY>/=to)
PR2 /<CONDITION>/=from >, (/if/ >(/verb/ </<ACTIVITY>/=to))
PR3 /<CONDITION>/=from >, (/if/>(/verb/<(/be|to/</<ACTIVITY>/=to)))

These patterns capture the case where a <CONDITION> (identified by previous patterns) is inside an *if* clause (that is, below the *if* token in the dependency tree), which has an <ACTIVITY> as the condition's consequent. In those cases, it is safe to assume that the activity in the consequent *responds to* the occurrence of the condition. For instance, in the dependency tree in Fig. 4, pattern PR1 would extract that `arrange (appointment)` *responds to* `sign(consent)`.

With the following patterns we are able to extract sequential relations between <EVENT> and <ACTIVITY> nodes. These are typical cases of `Precedence`:

PP1 /<EVENT>/=from > /<ACTIVITY>/=to
PP2 /<EVENT>/=from >> (/verb/ << /<ACTIVITY>/=to)

For instance, pattern PP1 checks for an <EVENT> immediately dominated by an <ACTIVITY>, so in the sentence "*An intaker keeps this registration with him at times when visiting the patient*", it would extract the sequential relation from `visit(patient)` to `keep(registration)`.

Pattern PP2 checks for an <EVENT> that is dominated by a verb which also dominates an <ACTIVITY>. When applied to the sentence "*Once the payment is confirmed, the ZooClub department can print the card*" we are able to extract the sequence between `confirm(payment)` and `print(card)`.

We also extract sequences from one condition fragment to several activities using the following patterns:

PS1 /<CONDITION>/=to >> (/whether/ >> /<ACTIVITY>|<EVENT>/=from)
PS2 /<CONDITION>/=to >> /<ACTIVITY>|<EVENT>/=from < /either/
PS3 /<CONDITION>/=to >> (/or/ >> /<ACTIVITY>|<EVENT>/=from)

For instance in the sentence *"The process starts when the female patient is examined by an outpatient physician, who decides whether she is healthy or needs to undertake an additional examination."* pattern PS1 will extract the sequential relations examine(patient) → is healthy, and examine (patient) → needs (undertake examination).

For more general cases, the subtleties between the different order constraints cannot be easily distinguished by an automatic analyzer. In those cases, we take a conservative approach and extract the least restrictive constraint, WeakOrder, using the patterns:

PW1 /<ACTIVITY>/=from < (/and/ << (/<ACTIVITY>/=to < /then/))
PW2 /<ACTIVITY>/=from << (/and/ << (/<ACTIVITY>/=to < /then/))
PW3 /<ACTIVITY>/=from >> (/after/ > /<ACTIVITY>/=to)
PW4 /<ACTIVITY>/=from >> (/after/ > (/be/ < /<ACTIVITY>/=to))
PW5 /<ACTIVITY>/=to > (/be/>(/after/>(/<ACTIVITY>/=from>/be/)))
PW6 /<ACTIVITY>/=from < (/before/ < /<ACTIVITY>/=to)
PW7 /<ACTIVITY>|<EVENT>/=from << (/<ACTIVITY>/=to < /and/)
PW8 /<ACTIVITY>/=from < (/and/ < /<ACTIVITY>/=to)

To illustrate the WeakOrder, using pattern PW1 we can infer that generate and pay are in WeakOrder in the sentence *"The Payment Office of SSP generates a payment report and then pays the vendor"*.

Additionally, we incorporated the approach used in [16] to extract relations Response, Precedence, and Succession based on the mandatory aspect of each activity: Given a sentence stating that activity A happens before activity B, if both A and B are mandatory, the relation is marked as Succession. If B is mandatory but A is not, the result is a Response relation. If B is not mandatory, a Precedence relation is extracted. Patterns M1, M2, M3 below are used to decide whether a task is mandatory or not. Their occurrence order is determined by the patterns previously presented in this section.

M1 /<ACTIVITY>/ >/must|will|would|shall|should/
M2 /<ACTIVITY>/ >(/be/ >/must|will|would|shall|should/)
M3 /<ACTIVITY>/ >(/be/ >(/have/ >/must|will|would|shall|should/))

Conflict. Conflict relations naturally arise when conditions are introduced in a process description. In ATDP the only conflict relation is NonCoOccurrence. To that end, we consider conditional discourse markers that affect <CONDITION> nodes extracted by patterns in Sect. 4.2:

PX1 /whether/ << (/<CONDITION>/=from << (/or/<</<CONDITION>/=to))
PX2 /<CONDITION>/=from << (/or/ << /<CONDITION>/=to)

For instance, pattern PX1 would extract the constraint that the sample can not be safely used and contaminated at the same time from the sentence "... *decides whether the sample can be used for analysis or whether it is contaminated*".

Pattern PX2 extracts general conflicts, such as the conditional fragments `approve` and `deny` from the sentence "*The next step is for the IT department to analyse the request and either approve or deny it.*" are considered in conflict. In order to this pattern to work, previously the verbs `approve` and `deny` were labeled as `<CONDITION>` in Sect. 4.2, patterns PC4 and PC5.

5 Tool Support and Experiments

This section presents experiments evaluating the performance of the proposed approach[9] to automatically extract `ATDP` from text. We will report two different experiments for two types of evaluation: we will compare activity extraction with a baseline based on [6], and relation extraction with the recent approach [16].

Activity Extraction. The evaluation is performed comparing the activity fragments extracted against gold standard annotations carried out by a human, who selected just the activities deemed relevant to the process. We collected a test data set consisting of 18 of those text-model pairs, shown in Table 1. The first 13 models stem from material in the appendix of Master thesis [6], and the last 5 from our academic dataset[10] used in [13]. In both cases each example includes a textual process description paired with the corresponding BPMN models created by a human. As a gold reference for evaluation, we manually created one `ATDP` for each example following the activities in those BPMN models, i.e. marking as activity fragments only the text pieces that had a corresponding element in the BPMN model.

Since the approach in [6] is not publicly available, we wrote Tregex patterns that would mimic that reference approach. Namely, we use patterns that take the output of the NLP analysis step, we filter out weak verbs `be`, `have`, `do`, `achieve`, `start`, `exist`, and `base`, and we use conditional indicators like `if`, `whether`, and `otherwise` to detect conditions.

Table 1 shows the results obtained by our tool compared with the baseline based in [6], which relies in extracting as activities most of the verbs detected by the NLP tool. The former scenario uses all the patterns described in this paper. Precision is computed as the percentage of right fragments among predicted fragments ($P = \#ok/\#pred$). Recall is the percentage of expected fragments extracted ($R = \#ok/\#gold$). F_1 score is the harmonic mean of precision and recall ($F_1 = 2PR/(P + R)$). We only count extracted fragments as right if they match the gold annotations in words and type (`<ACTIVITY`, `<EVENT>`, `<CONDITION>`).

---

[9] https://github.com/PADS-UPC/atdp-extractor.

[10] https://github.com/setzer22/alignment_model_text/tree/master/datasets/NewData set.

Table 1. Column *#gold* contains the number of activity fragments marked by a human as relevant to the process. Columns *#pred* and #ok show the number of fragments predicted by the tool, and how many of them were in the gold annotations. Columns P, R, and F_1 show precision, recall and F-measure respectively.

Source	#gold	Patterns emulating [6]					Our patterns				
		#pred	#ok	P	R	F_1	#pred	#ok	P	R	F_1
1-1_bicycle_manufacturing	15	22	11	50	**73**	60	18	11	**61**	**73**	**67**
1-2_computer_repair	10	14	9	64	**90**	75	10	8	**80**	80	**80**
2-1_sla_violation	46	93	41	44	**89**	59	70	40	**57**	87	**69**
3-1_2009-1_mc_finalice	8	15	7	47	**88**	61	10	6	**60**	75	**67**
3-2_2009-2_conduct_directions	7	12	7	58	**100**	74	9	6	**67**	86	**75**
3-6_2010-1_claims_notification	12	19	12	63	**100**	77	15	12	**80**	100	**89**
4-1_intaker_workflow	34	55	23	42	**68**	52	49	23	**47**	68	**55**
5-1_active_vos_tutorial	8	10	8	**80**	100	**89**	10	8	**80**	100	**89**
6-1_acme	22	41	20	49	**91**	64	36	19	**53**	86	**66**
7-1_calling_leads	6	11	6	55	**100**	71	9	5	**56**	83	67
8-1_hr_process_simple	5	7	5	71	**100**	**83**	5	4	**80**	80	80
9-2_exercise_2	8	16	8	50	**100**	67	9	8	**89**	100	**94**
10-2_process_b3	15	21	14	**67**	93	**78**	21	14	**67**	93	**78**
Total	196	336	171	51	**87**	64	271	164	**61**	84	**70**
1081511532_rev3	10	14	8	57	**80**	67	10	7	**70**	70	**70**
1120589054_rev4	11	17	11	65	**100**	79	14	11	**79**	100	**88**
1364308140_rev4	12	13	9	69	**75**	72	10	8	**80**	67	**73**
20818304_rev1	12	12	8	**67**	67	**67**	11	7	64	58	61
784358570_rev2	16	27	13	48	**81**	61	22	13	**59**	81	**68**
Total	61	83	49	59	**80**	68	67	46	**69**	75	**72**
TOTAL	257	419	220	53	**86**	65	338	210	**62**	82	**71**

Obtained results show that the baseline based in [6] obtains higher recall (since it extracts more activities), but lower precision (since many of the extracted activities are not in the gold annotations, i.e. they are not relevant for the process). On the other hand, our approach is a bit more conservative and extracts less activities, thus getting slightly lower recall, but largely higher precision. Overall, the trade-off F_1 score is consistently better when using our tree-based patterns.

Relation Extraction. To evaluate the extraction of relations, we compare our approach with the one presented in [16][11]. In addition to the 18 benchmarks from Table 1, we have added the data collection used in [16]. In this later case, we exclude from the evaluation the WeakOrder constraints generated by our system, since the reference dataset does not include such relation. Table 2 reports the comparison, that shows again the tendency to improve the results both for the dataset used in [16] and our dataset.

---

[11] https://github.com/hanvanderaa/declareextraction.

Table 2. Results of performed experiments with respect to [16]. The information is the same than in Table 1, but with counts correspond to both activities and relations.

Source	#gold	Public code by [16]					Our patterns				
		#pred	#ok	P	R	F_1	#pred	#ok	P	R	F_1
1-1_bicycle_manufacturing	26	30	9	30	35	32	33	21	**64**	**81**	**71**
1-2_computer_repair	19	13	6	46	32	37	18	12	**67**	**63**	**65**
2-1_sla_violation	90	100	42	**42**	47	44	128	53	41	**59**	**49**
3-1_2009-1_mc_finalice	15	19	9	47	60	53	17	10	**59**	**67**	**63**
3-2_2009-2_conduct_directions	13	8	7	**88**	54	**67**	11	8	73	62	**67**
3-6_2010-1_claims_notification	22	23	11	48	50	49	25	13	**52**	**59**	**55**
4-1_intaker_workflow	65	101	40	40	62	48	91	43	**47**	**66**	**55**
5-1_active_vos_tutorial	13	14	6	43	46	44	16	11	**69**	**85**	**76**
6-1_acme	40	48	16	33	40	36	68	27	**40**	**68**	**50**
7-1_calling_leads	12	16	7	44	58	50	16	9	**56**	**75**	**64**
8-1_hr_process_simple	11	5	5	**100**	45	**62**	10	6	60	**55**	57
9-2_exercise_2	14	12	6	50	43	46	17	13	**76**	**93**	**84**
10-2_process_b3	27	25	14	**56**	**52**	**54**	29	14	48	52	50
Total	367	414	178	43	49	46	479	240	**50**	**65**	**57**
1081511532_rev3	18	18	8	44	**44**	44	17	8	**47**	44	**46**
1120589054_rev4	20	27	11	41	**55**	47	16	10	**63**	50	**56**
1364308140_rev4	31	16	13	**81**	42	55	22	15	68	**48**	**57**
20818304_rev1	24	12	10	**83**	42	56	24	15	63	**63**	**63**
784358570_rev2	37	31	13	42	35	38	37	18	**49**	**49**	**49**
Total	130	104	55	53	42	47	116	66	**57**	**51**	**54**
datacollection_1	132	93	69	**74**	52	61	127	94	**74**	**71**	**73**
datacollection_2	51	51	45	88	88	88	50	46	**92**	**90**	**91**
datacollection_3	201	172	123	**72**	**61**	**66**	197	120	61	60	60
Total	384	316	237	**75**	62	68	374	260	70	**68**	**69**
TOTAL	881	834	470	56	53	55	969	566	**58**	**64**	**61**

6 Conclusions and Future Work

We have proposed a novel technique to extract ATDP specifications from textual descriptions. Continuing with our effort to unleash the use of unstructured data that talks about processes, this is one of the key functionalities that was missing. When comparing our approach with the state-of-the-art technique, we witness an improvement in accuracy for the task of detecting the main process elements.

For future work, we will extend the approach to also extract other ATDP elements, specially the ones regarding *scopes* and their relations, that are a real challenge since they need to be defined at a different granularity level. Another idea to explore is the definition of patterns across sentences, that may help improving the accuracy, but needs an adaption for the use of our query language, which is defined over single sentences. Orthogonal to these two lines, we also will explore the incorporation of machine learning techniques that can use the annotations performed by an expert (e.g., in the platform Model Judge teachers annotate textual descriptions of processes), to learn automatically the patterns that define the process elements. Finally, we plan to perform a deeper evaluation of our techniques, possible including real-life data from our current projects.

Acknowledgments. This work has been supported by MINECO and FEDER funds under grant TIN2017-86727-C2-1-R, and by the Ecuadorian National Secretary of Higher Education, Science and Technology (SENESCYT).

References

1. de AR Goncalves, J.C., Santoro, F.M., Baião, F.A.: Business process mining from group stories. In: Proceedings of the 13th International Conference on Computers Supported Cooperative Work in Design, CSCWD 2009, 22–24 April 2009, Santiago, Chile, pp. 161–166. IEEE (2009)
2. De Giacomo, G., De Masellis, R., Montali, M.: Reasoning on LTL on finite traces: insensitivity to infiniteness. In: Proceedings of the 28th AAAI Conference on Artificial Intelligence, pp. 1027–1033. AAAI Press (2014)
3. Dragoni, M., Villata, S., Rizzi, W., Governatori, G.: Combining natural language processing approaches for rule extraction from legal documents. In: Pagallo, U., Palmirani, M., Casanovas, P., Sartor, G., Villata, S. (eds.) AICOL 2015-2017. LNCS (LNAI), vol. 10791, pp. 287–300. Springer, Cham (2018). https://doi.org/10.1007/978-3-030-00178-0_19
4. Dyer, C., Ballesteros, M., Ling, W., Matthews, A., Smith, N.A.: Transition-based dependency parsing with stack long short-term memory. In: Proceedings of the 53rd Annual Meeting of the Association for Computational Linguistics and the 7th International Joint Conference on Natural Language Processing, (ACL-IJCNLP 2015), Beijing, China (2015)
5. Fellbaum, C.: WordNet. An Electronic Lexical Database. Language, Speech, and Communication. The MIT Press, Cambridge (1998)
6. Friedrich, F.: Automated generation of business process models from natural language input. School of Business and Economics. Humboldt-Universität zu Berli (2010)
7. Friedrich, F., Mendling, J., Puhlmann, F.: Process model generation from natural language text. In: Mouratidis, H., Rolland, C. (eds.) CAiSE 2011. LNCS, vol. 6741, pp. 482–496. Springer, Heidelberg (2011). https://doi.org/10.1007/978-3-642-21640-4_36
8. De Giacomo, G., Vardi, M.Y.: Linear temporal logic and linear dynamic logic on finite traces. In: IJCAI (2013)
9. Levy, R., Andrew, G.: Tregex and tsurgeon: tools for querying and manipulating tree data structures. In: LREC, pp. 2231–2234 (2006)
10. López, H.A., Debois, S., Hildebrandt, T.T., Marquard, M.: The process highlighter: from texts to declarative processes and back. In: Proceedings of the Dissertation Award, Demonstration, and Industrial Track at BPM 2018 co-located with 16th International Conference on Business Process Management (BPM 2018), Sydney, Australia, 9–14 September 2018, pp. 66–70 (2018)
11. Padró, L., Stanilovsky, E.: Freeling 3.0: towards wider multilinguality. In: Proceedings of the Eighth International Conference on Language Resources and Evaluation (LREC), pp. 2473–2479 (2012)

12. Sànchez-Ferreres, J., Burattin, A., Carmona, J., Montali, M., Padró, L.: Formal reasoning on natural language descriptions of processes. In: Hildebrandt, T., van Dongen, B.F., Röglinger, M., Mendling, J. (eds.) BPM 2019. LNCS, vol. 11675, pp. 86–101. Springer, Cham (2019). https://doi.org/10.1007/978-3-030-26619-6_8
13. Sànchez-Ferreres, J., van der Aa, H., Carmona, J., Padró, L.: Aligning textual and model-based process descriptions. Data Knowl. Eng. **118**, 25–40 (2018)
14. Semmelrodt, F.: Modellierung klinischer prozesse und compliance regeln mittels BPMN 2.0 und eCRG. Master's thesis, University of Ulm (2013)
15. van der Aa, H., Carmona, J., Leopold, H., Mendling, J., Padró, L.: Challenges and opportunities of applying natural language processing in business process management. In: Proceedings of the 27th International Conference on Computational Linguistics (COLING), pp. 2791–2801 (2018)
16. van der Aa, H., Di Ciccio, C., Leopold, H., Reijers, H.A.: Extracting declarative process models from natural language. In: Giorgini, P., Weber, B. (eds.) CAiSE 2019. LNCS, vol. 11483, pp. 365–382. Springer, Cham (2019). https://doi.org/10.1007/978-3-030-21290-2_23
17. van der Aa, H., Leopold, H., Reijers, H.A.: Comparing textual descriptions to process models - the automatic detection of inconsistencies. Inf. Syst. **64**, 447–460 (2017)
18. van der Aalst, W.M.P.: Process Mining, 2nd edn. Springer, Heidelberg (2016). https://doi.org/10.1007/978-3-662-49851-4
19. Winter, K., Rinderle-Ma, S.: Detecting constraints and their relations from regulatory documents using NLP techniques. In: Panetto, H., Debruyne, C., Proper, H.A., Ardagna, C.A., Roman, D., Meersman, R. (eds.) OTM 2018. LNCS, vol. 11229, pp. 261–278. Springer, Cham (2018). https://doi.org/10.1007/978-3-030-02610-3_15

Analyzing Process Concept Drifts Based on Sensor Event Streams During Runtime

Florian Stertz$^{(\boxtimes)}$, Stefanie Rinderle-Ma, and Juergen Mangler

Faculty of Computer Science, University of Vienna, Vienna, Austria
{florian.stertz,stefanie.rinderle-ma,juergen.mangler}@univie.ac.at

Abstract. Business processes have to adapt to constantly changing requirements at a large scale due to, e.g., new regulations, and at a smaller scale due to, e.g., deviations in sensor event streams such as warehouse temperature in manufacturing or blood pressure in health care. Deviations in the process behavior during runtime can be detected from process event streams as so called concept drifts. Existing work has focused on concept drift detection so far, but has neglected why the drift occurred. To close this gap, this paper provides online algorithms to analyze the root cause for a concept drift using sensor event streams. These streams are typically gathered externally, i.e., separated from the process execution, and can be understood as time sequences. Supporting domain experts in assessing concept drifts through their root cause facilitates process optimization and evolution. The feasibility of the algorithms is shown based on a prototypical implementation. Moreover, the algorithms are evaluated based on a real-world data set from manufacturing.

Keywords: Online process mining · Concept drift · Sensor event stream · Root cause analysis · Time sequence · Dynamic Time Warping

1 Introduction

"World-class organizations leverage business process change as a means to improve performance, reduce costs, and increase profitability" [23]. Companies can react by adapting their business process to the changing requirements at a large scale, e.g., new regulations, and at a smaller scale, e.g., deviations in sensor streams in manufacturing or medicine. In any case, adaptations of the process logic result in a so called *concept drift* [25].

When adapting business processes, a concept drift might be known in case of explicitly defined and applied process changes, but also unknown and "only" recorded in so called *process event logs* that store information on business process execution in an event-based manner. If the process execution events are continuously collected during runtime, we call this a *process event stream*. Existing techniques detect concept drifts from process event logs in an offline manner (ex post) based on process execution logs [4] or in an online way based on *process event streams* [15,19,27], i.e., during runtime as the processes are executed.

© Springer Nature Switzerland AG 2020
D. Fahland et al. (Eds.): BPM 2020, LNCS 12168, pp. 202–219, 2020.
https://doi.org/10.1007/978-3-030-58666-9_12

Online concept drift detection can be crucial to react on process changes in time. However, approaches to analyze and identify the reason why a concept drift happened, i.e., its *root cause*, are missing although knowing the root cause contributes to, e.g., optimizing future occurrences of similar concept drifts.

Hence the basic question is how to identify and analyze the root cause for concept drifts at runtime. Several examples suggest that data from IoT devices, i.e., external sources such as sensors can influence the execution behavior of a process. Temperature, for example, might cause exceptions in logistics processes [3]. Variations in parameters might indicate the quality of products in manufacturing [8,12]. The data emitted by sensors is called *sensor event streams* and is captured externally, i.e., outside the process execution [16]. Sensor event streams constitute *time sequence data* [12]. Informally, a time sequence holds quantitative, time-stamped data. We opted to analyze time sequence data instead of time series data as the latter requires equidistant time intervals what is not always the case for the real world cases to be considered.

In order to facilitate root cause analysis for concept drifts, this work addresses the following research questions:

RQ1: *How can drifts in sensor event streams associated with process instances be identified?*

RQ2: *How can the analysis of these drifts help domain experts, to assess root causes and thus propose concept drifts/process evolution?*

The approach takes a *process history* [19] as input. The process history holds an ordered sequence of process models that have been mined online and are connected to per-instance sensor event streams. These sensor event streams are time sequences, and the deviations between the streams of different instances of each model are determined using *dynamic time warping (DTW)*. DTW calculates the distance between two time sequences. The challenge is to interpret the drifts in the sensor event streams to identify future concept drifts in the process model (in contrast to [19], which deals with the identification of concept drifts ex-post). The approach was implemented for a real-world IoT application from the manufacturing domain and a data set was gathered that is used to evaluate the approach. Specifically, we show how the results of the analysis support domain experts in understanding why a drift happened (root cause) and to learn what can be done to efficiently deal with it. The objective is therefore to evaluate the applicability of this approach in finding the cause for a concept drift, to evaluate the performance of this approach, i.e., how many reasons can be correctly detected in which time and to give information on how to adapt the current process model to the current situation.

This paper is outlined as follows: In Sect. 2, a running example as well as preliminaries are introduced. Section 3 features two algorithms to determine drifts in event streams from external sources. Section 4 evaluates these algorithms based on a real world IoT application. Related work is reflected in Sect. 6. Section 7 summarizes this work and gives a brief outlook of the planned future work.

2 Running Example and Fundamentals

Figure 1(a) shows the process model of a medical round for a patient of a health care facility. This model represents the current care plan for one specific patient. The general health status of a patient is checked, the blood pressure is measured, and drugs are administered. During runtime process instances are created and executed based on the process model. The execution information is stored in a process event log. Assume that a concept drift occurs, which results in the process model depicted in Fig. 1(b), i.e., an additional hydration check is added in parallel to checking the blood pressure. Another drift could be detected in the data elements of a process instance, for example, the task "Blood Pressure" is in (b) done by nurses, while it has been done in (a) by medical doctors. Existing approaches [14, 15, 19, 27] enable drift detection, but do not explain why the drift happened in the first place.

Unlike process data such as resource or patient age, typically, the temperature and humidity of the patient's room are constantly monitored by external sensors. The sensors produce event streams which consist of data points representing a single measurement. These measurements are typically not stored in a process execution log, but in a different database, since the tasks are not directly linked to any process data. We investigate whether and how such sensor event streams can be exploited in order to analyze and explain why a concept drift happened.

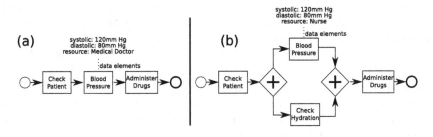

Fig. 1. Concept drift resulting in adapted process model – medical example

This work exploits *process histories* [19] to store drift information reflected by deviations in process models. A process history $HP := <M_0, M_1, .., M_n, ..>$ contains a list of viable process models $M_i, i = 0, 1, ..$ that reflect the natural evolution of a business process P. While previous work [20] focuses on data that is part of the business logic of a process (e.g., resources as in Fig. 1), this paper addresses high velocity time sequence data that is collected from external sensors, but is otherwise not utilized in the context of processes or sub-processes.

A time sequence is defined as follows in [10, p. 208]: *A sequence of time-stamped data for which the attribute values are the result of measurements of a quantitative real-valued state variable, denoted by* $y \in \mathbb{R}, y = (y(t_1), y(t_2), ..., y(t_n))$.

The challenge is to compare the time sequences in order to detect differences in the associated sensor event streams that can lead to drifts. To compare two time sequences, an alignment is calculated to determine the distances from one sequence to another. The most common distances measure are the Euclidean Distance (ED) [9] and Dynamic Time Warping (DTW) [2]. While ED has several advantages like linear computing time and being straightforward, it requires time sequences to be of the same length and is deceptive for noise. DTW is also able to globally find the best alignment and can cope with sequences of different length. The complexity is quadratic, since a $m \times n$ matrix has to be constructed, where m and n are the lengths of the time sequence.

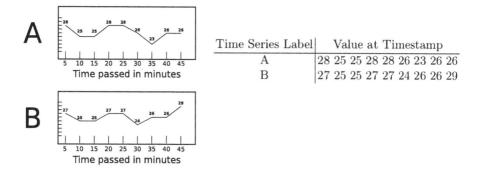

Time Series Label	Value at Timestamp
A	28 25 25 28 28 26 23 26 26
B	27 25 25 27 27 24 26 26 29

Fig. 2. Plot of two time sequences and their corresponding values

29	18	12	12	9	9	8	11	8	8
26	17	8	8	9	10	5	8	5	5
26	15	7	7	8	9	5	8	5	5
24	13	6	6	7	7	5	5	7	9
27	9	5	5	3	3	4	8	9	10
27	8	3	3	2	3	4	8	9	10
25	7	1	1	4	7	8	10	11	12
25	4	1	1	4	7	8	10	11	12
27	1	3	5	6	7	8	12	13	14

B/A   28 25 25 28 28 26 23 26 26

Fig. 3. Warp matrix constructed using DTW: orange cell = distance (Color figure online)

We use DTW as we are dealing with sequences of different lengths. Figure 2 shows time sequences A and B, together with a table containing the exact values at every timestamp. The $m \times n$ matrix D for the alignment between A and B is constructed by starting in the bottom row and filling every value from left to right, as can be seen in Fig. 3. The distance as absolute difference between the actual values is calculated, so in the bottom left corner it is $|28 - 27| = 1$. Afterwards the cheapest cost from one of the cells before is used, so $D(n, m_1)$, $D(n_1, m_1)$ and $D(n_1, m)$ is added to the distance and assigned to $D(n, m)$. The definition follows [18]: $D(i, j) = Dist(i, j) + min[D(i-1, j), D(i, j-1), D(i-1, j-1)]$.

The distance is found in the top right corner of Fig. 3. The alignment can be found using back-tracing starting in the top right corner and following the path back to the start cell in the bottom left corner, i.e., the green cells.

This work employs the DTW Barycenter Averaging (DBA) [17] algorithm. DBA uses DTW as distance measure and calculates the average time sequence for a set of time sequences. It starts by an arbitrary average sequence and adapts it iteratively by trying to minimize the sum of squared DTW distances from the average sequence to the set of sequences. The computation time of this technique is again quadratic, since a DTW matrix has to be created for each iteration.

3   Time Sequence Assignment and Root Cause Detection

This section details the main contribution of this work, i.e., how to utilize time sequence data from sensor event streams to flag process instances for closer inspection when performing a root cause analysis for concept drifts. Note that an analysis for both cases is possible, i.e., finding reasons for concept drifts that have already been detected (ex post) and – particularly during runtime – detecting and analyzing deviations in the sensor event streams that might lead to a future concept drift, i.e., a process evolution.

We start with the architecture of the solution presented in this work (cf. Fig. 4) as foundation for the subsequent considerations. Note that the components *Time Sequence Module* and *Drift Decision Detection* (both red) realize the contribution of this paper.

For detecting drifts, sensor event streams are taken as input. They can be fed into the system by any process execution engine. In the manufacturing scenario presented throughout this paper, the Cloud Process Execution Engine CPEE[1] is utilized. The sensor components provide data streams collected through tasks in ⑤ (Fig. 7). The process history is therefore extended to include all the data from the sensors. Further implementation details will be described in Sect. 4.

3.1   Time Sequence Module

This component enriches the process history by adding the average time sequence of every sensor to each new viable process model M_n. To relate a time sequence of an event stream produced by a sensor to a specific process instance, the timestamps of the first and currently last event of the stream are taken into

---

[1] http://cpee.org/.

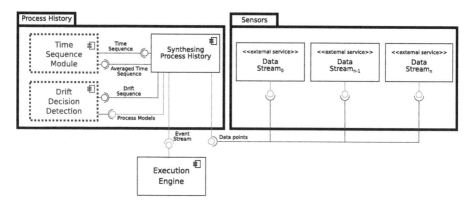

Fig. 4. Proposed architecture: red parts denote the contribution of this paper (Color figure online)

account and the corresponding time sequence is cut out for the process instance. In the example (cf. Fig. 1), time sequences between the start time of "Check patient" and end time "Administer Drugs" are mapped to a process instance for both sensors, temperature and humidity.

Algorithm 1 shows the pseudo code for the *Time Sequence Module*. The set of unfitting traces T is provided by the process history, i.e., those traces that do not conform to the current model M_n. The time sequences are provided by external sensors through the process history. In line 1, the return value is initialized as an empty dictionary. A dictionary here reflects a hash table [6] data structure with a key and a related value to it. Line 2 starts the iteration over time sequences of each sensor. At first, the time sequence for each trace out of T is collected starting in line 6. We map a time sequence from a sensor to a trace by beginning from the first time stamp of this trace to the last known time stamp of this trace, as can be seen in line 9. Since we are working in an online environment, it is possible that traces just started and contain only one event, which results in no time sequence for this specific trace.

Another important aspect of the online setting is, that each trace could have greatly varying execution times, since we do not know how long a complete trace is going to take. To diminish the impact of outliers and faulty or aborted instances, we exclude sequences with a duration shorter than the first quartile minus 1.5 times the IQR (Interquartile Range) or with a duration greater than the third quartile plus 1.5 times the IQR, similar to boxplots. The IQR is calculated here between third and first quartile. Other methods for detecting outliers can be applied here or even working with every trace.

We calculate the quartile at (lines 11 and the IQR at line 12). Afterwards the outliers of the collected time sequences are removed. Otherwise the time sequence will be taken into account (lines 14–17). In the last step (line 18), the averaged time sequence is put into the dictionary ATS with its corresponding sensor id as key. The dictionary of averaged time sequences is then sent back to the process history. The current viable process model in the process history is thereby extended by this dictionary, which is then used by the Drift Decision Detection component.

Input: ST: dictionary of a time sequence for each sensor ID
Result: ATS: dictionary of an averaged time sequence for each sensor ID

```
1  ATS = dict()
2  for w,ts in ST do
3  │   // w is id of sensor, ts its corresponding time sequence
4  │   temp_ts_list = list()
5  │   stats = list()
6  │   for t in ts do
7  │   │   if |t| < 2 then
8  │   │   │   next
9  │   │   temp_ts_list.append(time_sequence(t.first_event.timestamp,t.last_event.timestamp))
10 │   │   stats.append(temp_ts_list.last.length)
11 │   first,second,third,fourth = quartile(stats)
12 │   x = iqr(stats)
13 │   ts_list = list()
14 │   for t in temp_ts_list do
15 │   │   if |t| < first − x || |t| > third+x then
16 │   │   │   next
17 │   │   ts_list.append(t)
18 │   ATS[w] = dba(ts_list)
19 return ATS
```

Algorithm 1: Find relevant time sequences and compute avg. time sequence

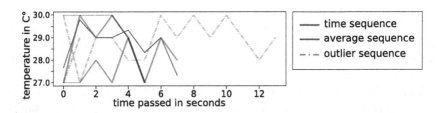

Fig. 5. Exemplary Result of Algorithm 1. The red line is the average sequence calculated using DBA. The green dashed lines represent outliers, potentially due to a faulty process instance. (Color figure online)

Figure 5 shows an example of Algorithm 1 where the following 5 sequences for the room temperature have been collected: $(27, 29)$, $(27, 27, 28, 27, 29, 27, 29, 28]$, $[30, 30, 30, 30, 29, 27)$, $(27, 30, 29, 30, 29, 27)$, $(30, 27, 29, 29, 28, 28, 30, 29, 30, 29, 30, 29, 28, 29)$. The third quartile for the lengths of these sequences would be 8, the first quartile is 6. Therefore the IQR equals 2. This excludes sequences which are shorter than 3 or longer than 11. The first sequence $(27, 29)$ and the last sequence $(30, 27, 29, 29, 28, 28, 30, 29, 30, 29, 30, 29, 28, 29)$ are not taken into account for the calculation and are printed in a green dashed line. The red time sequence shows the calculated average time sequence with DBA.

3.2 Drift Decision Detection

The second component of the solution proposed in this work is the Drift Decision Detection component.

Input: M: A list of process models with averaged time sequence dictionary
TH: Dictionary of thresholds for similarity
Result: D: Set of sensor IDs that are likely to have caused a drift
1 $D = \mathrm{set}()$
2 **for** ws_id in $M.second.ATS.keys$ **do**
3   **if** ws_id not in $M.first.ATS.key$ **then**
4 | next
5      $ts\_a = M.\mathrm{first}.ATS[ws\_id]$
6      $ts\_b = M.\mathrm{last}.ATS[ws\_id]$
7   **if** $dtw(ts\_a,ts\_b) > TH[ws\_id]$ **then**
8 | $D.\mathrm{add}(ws\_id)$
9 return D

Algorithm 2: Detecting a set of sensor data streams which caused a drift

---

Algorithm 2 shows the detection of the most likely external sensors that can have caused the drift in the process model. The process history sends two process models to this component in order to receive a set of external sensors which caused a drift from the first model to the second model. Each of these process models contains its average time sequence for each external sensor. The dictionary TH is user defined and contains for every external sensor, a related threshold for the distance between the two average time sequences. A different threshold for each external sensor is needed, because the dynamic warp distance is calculated using the differences in the data points. Assume that for the running example (cf. Fig. 1), the ideal temperature ranges between 27° and 29° C. Thus similar time sequences have a low absolute cost depending on the length of the alignment. A sensor keeping track of parts with higher tolerances can therefore have a higher warping distance for similar sequences. These thresholds can be approximated using a test set for the classification, where an expert has to define sensitivity and specificity for the sensor data. At the start, the return value D is initialized as an empty set in line 1. The loop iterates over every key that is in the dictionary of averaged time sequences (ATS) in the second model in line 2. It is to be noted that the models could have different events attached to them, but the external sensors should be the same. If a specific sensor is not present in both models, we cannot take it into account, see lines 3. The average time sequence for one sensor is retrieved for both models in line 5 and 6. If the cost of the alignment, which is reflected in the top right cell of the warping matrix, see Fig. 3, is greater than the corresponding threshold to the sensor, this sensor is added to the return value D in line 8. This set of external sensors is then returned to the process history, where it is stored.

3.3   Performance Optimizations

One problem with DTW is the computation time, since a $m \times n$ matrix has to be constructed, where m is the length of one time sequence and n the length of the other time sequence.

One approach that can be used to optimize the performance of Algorithm 1 and Algorithm 2 is FastDTW [18]. FastDTW aims at performing DTW in linear time with 3 steps. First the time sequence is shrunk into smaller time sequences that reflect the same curve approximately. Then the minimum distance warp path is computed for the smaller time sequence. Afterwards this warp path is adjusted to the original time sequence. For a length of 10000 data points the computation time can be reduced from 57.45 s to 8,42 s. The error rate for this approximation is below 1%.

Another way to speed up time warping is early abandoning [11,24]. In this strategy, if the warping distance is above a certain threshold while creating the warping matrix, the algorithm can stop the execution and label it as an outlier.

Both methods are suitable optimizations for Algorithm 2, since it uses user defined thresholds for each external sensor, but not for Algorithm 1. This is because the average time sequence is computed using the complete DTW distance score, thus not exact methods like FastDTW and early abandoning cannot be used. In Sect. 4, Algorithm 2 is evaluated using DTW and FastDTW.

4   Evaluation

The algorithms and components presented in Sect. 3 are prototypically implemented and tested based on a real-world IoT application from the manufacturing domain in order to prove the effectiveness and feasibility of the approach: The Austrian Center for Digital Production[2] produces parts called GV12 for a gas-turbine (see Fig. 6) as a prototypical solution for a customer. The requirements for the part

Fig. 6. GV12 part

include high precision manufacturing (low tolerances, i.e. some aspects allow for deviations of only 0.02 mm), and strict quality assurance for each part, including (a) detailed tracking of manufacturing data for each part and (b) measuring the adherence to tolerances for more than 12 features with automated precision measurement equipment.

The entire production is carried out automatically by implementing the interaction between the involved machines through industrial robots and transport systems. We focus on the manufacturing and quality control as shown in Fig. 7.

---
[2] https://www.acdp.at/.

Currently more than 20 processes and sub-processes are involved, and orchestrated during production of up to 40 parts per batch. Figure 7 illustrates the basic manufacturing logic:

- (1) Batches of up to 40 pieces are ordered, the manufacturing is scheduled.
- (2) The interaction between all machines and robots is orchestrated, while enforcing industrial safety principles.[3]
- (3) Individual parts are produced by using the following three steps:
  - Machining of a part from hardened steel, which takes about 4 min per part.
  - Measuring of the part by a high-speed optical micrometer,[4] while the next part is machined. This takes about 12 s per part.
  - Measuring of a part with automated precision measurement equipment,[5] which takes about 8 min per part, and is also done in parallel to the machining.
- (4) A generic machine monitoring process determines when to start data collection for both, machining and measuring.
- (5) A generic data collection process produces a continuous stream of values when the laser of the high-speed optical micrometer is scanning the surface of the part.

The "Measure with Keyence" task is done automatically by a Keyence measuring machine at no additional cost in parallel to the production of the next part. As the Keyence machine is very compact, fast, and operates without touching the part, this step is done after the robot extracted the part from the production machine, and before it puts it on the palett. On the palett it is transported to the MicroVu measuring machine, which is rather big and has to be operated in a location with low vibrations and special light and temperature conditions. The task "Measure with MicroVu", as opposed to the task "Measure with Keyence", is required by the customer, because it basically creates an objective report about the quality of a part.

After some time, deviations in the process event stream collected by (5) can be observed. These deviations can happen based on

- physical effects due to deteriorating machining tools, or temperature fluctuations.
- problems stemming from accumulating debris that affects the production quality as well as measurement quality.

Up to this point only the extreme values of the time sequence (i.e. min, max) from the Keyence machine were used, which are sufficient for detecting (a) if the part has been dropped by the robot (no part), or (b) the part appears to be too big (i.e., it is engulfed by chips). However, the extreme values proved

---

[3] https://www.iso.org/standard/51330.html.

[4] https://www.keyence.com/products/measure/micrometer/ls-9000/index.jsp.

[5] https://www.microvu.com/products/vertex.html.

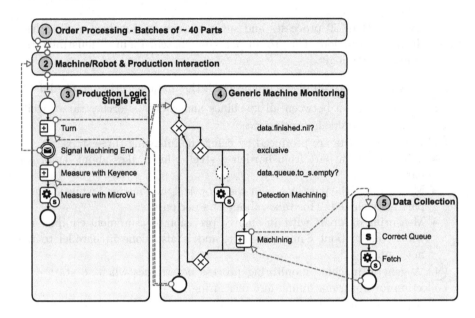

Fig. 7. Batches of GV12 parts

not to be effective for early detection of parts which do not comply to the quality requirements. If an early reliable estimation of the quality was available, it could be used to skip the 'Measure with MicroVu" altogether, which would save valuable resources.

· Hence, our approach for this evaluation is instead of taking only the extreme values of the measurement into account, to analyze the complete time sequence of the measurement. Every time the process history detects a drift in the data elements, i.e, "Measure with MicroVu" detects only faulty instances, a drift has been detected in the data model. Algorithm 1 calculates then the average sequence, e.g., Fig. 8. The threshold for Algorithm 2 is here calculated ex-post, with the results of "Measure with MicroVu".

4.1 Prototypical Implementation – RQ1

The orchestration of the BPMN 2.x based process models on the factory floor (cf. Fig. 7) is driven by the process engine CPEE[1]. The process history component subscribes to the CPEE in order to receive information about every executing event. The external sensor represented by activity "Measure with MicroVu" is a high-speed optical micrometer.[6]

The data set[7] contains 1026 traces in the XES[8] format for 37 parts and is available at the figshare repository [21]. The traces are produced by 13 different

---

[6] https://www.keyence.com/products/measure/micrometer/ls-9000/index.jsp.

[7] http://gruppe.wst.univie.ac.at/data/timesequence.zip.

[8] http://xes-standard.org/.

process models. The sensor values amount for 6.2 MiB out of 1 GiB of total data. A time sequence for this event contains on average about 776 data points. Measurements from a time sequence range from 4.09 up to 37.87 mm.

The process history creates the process models as described in [19]. The process history uses a sliding window approach to deal with infinite amount of data that is being captured by listening to streams, i.e., only a specified number of traces are used for detecting a new process model in the history.

The Time Series Module component is implemented in Python as we are using the tslearn package [22] because it provides functions for computing an alignment using DTW as well as DBA for finding the average time series. The results of this component are retrievable via a RESTful web service as well. The Drift Decision Detection component also uses these libraries. The result of Algorithm 1 on the data set is depicted in Fig. 8. Each grey sequence relates to one specific trace and shows the measurement data points of one part. As it can be seen, one time sequence only lasts for about 8 s, while the other ones last about 12 to 14 s.

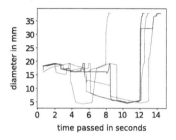

Fig. 8. Result of implementation. The red line represents the average sequence (Color figure online)

The average sequence, calculated using DBA is depicted in red. This sequence is stored as additional information in the process history for the current process model. Since this log only provides one sensor, i.e., "Keyence", only one sequence has to be calculated using DBA. To determine the feasibility of the implementation, we furthermore looked at the following questions:

- How are parameters such as the duration of a process instance or the number of traces in the process history sliding window, affecting the algorithms?
- What is the performance of these algorithms?

The performance of Algorithm 2 is only depending on the length of the average time sequence, which is hard to tweak with parameters of the process history and the number of sensors. It can be adapted by changing the amount of data points that are to be stored per time unit. The performance of Algorithm 1 on the other hand is highly dependent of the parameters set for the process history.

In order to rate the effectiveness of the approach it is possible to rely on the data provided by "Measure with MicroVu". Out of 37 parts, 18 parts were faulty. With this knowledge we first varied the threshold in order to achieve 0% false negative detection of parts. In other words: no parts that are faulty should be delivered to the customer, on the

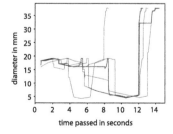

Fig. 9. Chips on GV12 - wrong measurement

other hand it is acceptable that some parts that are actually good are detected as faulty. The optimal threshold proved to be 22.

When varying the window size, i.e., the number of traces to be analyzed during the drift detection, the following results emerge:

Table 1. Results of both Algorithms

Window size	False positives	False negatives	Runtime
1	45%	0%	1.4 s
5	0%	0%	10.3 s
10	0%	0%	20.7 s

As can be seen in Table 1, a window size of 5 and a threshold of 22 is sufficient for our scenario. With these values 100% of the faulty parts can be identified, without relying on the time intensive "Measure with MicroVu" task. This means that for a rate of 18 faulty tasks, almost 50% of the production time can be saved, based on calculation of drift for sensor event streams.

4.2   Concept Drift Prediction/Process Evolution - RQ2

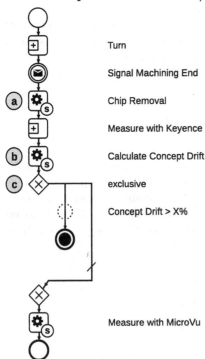

Turn

Signal Machining End

Chip Removal

Measure with Keyence

Calculate Concept Drift

exclusive

Concept Drift > X%

Measure with MicroVu

Fig. 10. GV12 prototype part

For the task "Measure with Keyence" in Fig. 7, as collected by process ⑤, the deviations for the measurements between parts have some serious repercussions that can lead to multiple possible process evolutions.

The results were discussed with three domain experts involved in the production of the GV12 parts. When discussing the results from the drift analysis, the domain experts came up with the following discussion points.

As can be seen in Fig. 9, the machining produced long chips, which entangled the part. Furthermore, the comparison of the drift for "Measure with Keyence" with the quality data from "Measure with MicroVu" (see Fig. 7) was deemed sufficient for predicting the quality of a part, thus allowing for immediate removal of faulty parts from production which decreases the overall time per batch greatly: the less "Measure with

Table 2. Runtime of Algorithm 1.

Datapoints/ Sequences	10	100	1000
5	1.17 s	1.22 s	3.53 s
10	1.18 s	1.31 s	7.01 s
50	1.29 s	4,43 s	75.83 s
100	1.22 s	4.63 s	133.00 s

Table 3. Runtime of Algorithm 2.

Datapoints	DTW	FastDTW
10	0.88 s	0.0002 s
100	0.87 s	0.0003 s
1000	0.91 s	0.001 s
10000	4.70 s	0.01 s

MicroVu" the better. This led to the proposal of the concept drifts / process evolutions shown in Fig. 10. Overall, the concept drifts can be classified as follows:

- Static Evolution (a) : an extra activity "Chip Removal" was proposed to be inserted, based on the observed drifts. A robot blows compressed air on the part, to remove debris and chips, which allows for more accurate measuring. This will allow for lower possible thresholds in future/similar scenarios.
- Dynamic Evolution (b)+(c) : The drift is to be actively calculated at runtime, based on previous process instances, and made available to the current instance. A decision (c) is proposed to be inserted, that allows for terminating single parts without "Measure with MicroVu".

Performance Evaluation: Table 2 shows the runtime of Algorithm 1 to analyze the applicability of this solution. We generated random time sequences with 10, 100, and 1000 data points on average. Algorithm 1 is then applied on a set consisting of 5, 10, 50, and 100 time sequences. The results of 10 data points on average show, that the execution time of Algorithm 1 for 100 sequences is even lower as the one for 50 sequences. This happens, because the time for the calculation is so small, that other currently running tasks of the operating system may interfere with the execution.

With 100 data points, Algorithm 1 affects the total execution time to a greater extent, especially with more sequences: 50 sequences result in a more than 3 times longer execution time than 10 sequences. With 1000 data points, the execution time with more than 50 sequences is increased by more than 10 times the execution time with 10 sequences.

Table 3 shows the comparison between DTW and FastDTW (cf. Sect. 3.3) in terms of speed. As expected, FastDTW is the faster technique as it works in linear time. Unfortunately the results differ greatly for DTW when compared to FastDTW. While, for example, the distance between 2 sequences with random values between 90 and 110 and 10000 data points was 343.2 when using DTW, the distance equals to 45299 when using FastDTW. Since both algorithms are highly depending on the global maximum of the alignment of sequences, Fast-DTW is not a suitable option.

Assessment by Domain Experts: We presented the results to a machine operator, a mechanical engineer, and a measurement engineer. All three experts were overall satisfied with the results. They highlighted that to the best of their knowledge in order to achieve similar results, additional – hard to configure – software would be necessary.

5 Discussion

Possible **limitations** in the context of the presented approach include:

- *Performance:* An important aspect for the performance of this approach is the number of data points in a time sequence. As can be seen in Table 2, even with 1000 data points and 10 time sequences the implementation took about 7 s. This of course increases linearly with number of sensors. Other techniques like FastDTW instead of DTW, reduce the runtime drastically, but the alignment using FastDTW varies greatly from the globally best alignment using DTW, which leads to worse results.
- *Sensors selection:* While in general IoT devices such as external sensors provide a valuable source for detecting the cause of a concept drift, choosing the "right" IoT device may be hard in some cases. The reason is that in many real-world scenarios there is a plethora of devices creating data streams and therefore time sequences. Taking an external sensor into account, that has no relation to the process model, for example, can produce wrong results, since the time sequences of this sensor may vary to a great extent and hence be incorrectly identified as the source of a drift. In addition, the runtime is heavily depending on the number of sensors, hence not significant sensors should be excluded. Therefore it is recommended that an expert additionally validates the results. If no sensors can be excluded by experts, a parallel optimization is advised of Algorithm 1 where each sensor can be calculated separately. This reduces the execution time of the algorithm to the execution time of the sensor with the most data points.
- *Thresholds:* Another important aspect is finding the threshold for Algorithm 2 automatically. If there is a training set, the threshold can be calculated until a specified sensitivity and specificity are met. Otherwise, an expert sets the threshold.

Also, the following **threats to validity** have to be considered: The data set of the evaluation comprises the data of one sensor. Hence, the selection of the sensors cannot be evaluated. While the increase of the runtime is predictable, the quality of the results can differ greatly, if not related sensors are taken into account. The real-world case comes from the manufacturing domain, where the selection of the sensors may be easier, since the conditions of the events are often in a controlled environment, like a factory. In other domains, like the medical domain or logistic domain where numerous external data stream sources can affect the execution of a process, the selection may be more difficult. In future work, experiments in different domains are planned.

6   Related Work

Several algorithms for offline process discovery exist [1]. Existing work shows that a selection of these algorithms can be used for online process discovery as well. This includes the heuristics miner [5], which takes the frequency of events into account and the inductive miner [13], which tries to find a certain block structure to find splits for the process model. Concept drift detection can also conducted in an offline [4] and online manner [14,15,19,27]. However, the mentioned online mining techniques neither consider external data nor analyze the root cause for concept drifts. [26] enables the visual exploration of the concept drift type. This work, by contrast, analyzes sensor event streams as time sequence data. Time series data in process mining domain have been analyzed for finding decision points by [7] in an offline manner. Other approaches exploit sensor data for outcome predictions for process instances [3] and manufacturing systems [12], but do not address concept drifts.

7   Conclusion

This paper elaborates a novel approach to predict the root cause of a concept drift in a business process based on external sensor streams. Two algorithms are introduced to compare the time sequences associated with the sensor event streams in combination with the process event stream. In the evaluation, it is shown that the algorithms are capable of detecting the drifts in the external sensor event stream with high accuracy, given a certain amount of traces for a specific setting. A big factor for this approach, is the type of available sensors. A domain expert has to distinguish which sensors are important, and is used best to verify a drift in certain aspects of a produced part. Otherwise the computation time is increased with no benefit, as some external sensors are not able to contribute to a drift in the process. Furthermore, three domain experts, based on the highlighted drifts, verified root causes, and proposed multiple concept drifts/process evolutions, thus showing the validity of the solution.

Future work aims at algorithms for predicting and explaining future drifts.

Acknowledgment. This work has been partly funded by the Austrian Research Promotion Agency (FFG) via the "Austrian Competence Center for Digital Production" (CDP) under the contract number 854187. This work has been supported by the Pilot Factory Industry 4.0, Seestadtstrasse 27, Vienna, Austria.

References

1. van der Aalst, W.M.P.: Process Mining - Data Science in Action, 2nd edn. Springer, Heidelberg (2016). https://doi.org/10.1007/978-3-662-49851-4
2. Berndt, D.J., Clifford, J.: Using dynamic time warping to find patterns in time series. In: KDD Workshop, Seattle, WA, vol. 10, pp. 359–370 (1994)
3. Borkowski, M., Fdhila, W., Nardelli, M., Rinderle-Ma, S., Schulte, S.: Event-based failure prediction in distributed business processes. Inf. Syst. **81**, 220–235 (2019)
4. Bose, R.J.C., Van Der Aalst, W.M., Zliobaite, I., Pechenizkiy, M.: Dealing with concept drifts in process mining. IEEE Trans. Neural Netw. Learn. Syst. **25**(1), 154–171 (2014)
5. Burattin, A., Sperduti, A., van der Aalst, W.M.: Control-flow discovery from event streams. In: 2014 IEEE Congress on Evolutionary Computation (CEC), pp. 2420–2427. IEEE (2014)
6. Cormen, T.H., Leiserson, C.E., Rivest, R.L., Stein, C.: Introduction to Algorithms. MIT Press, Cambridge (2009)
7. Dunkl, R., Rinderle-Ma, S., Grossmann, W., Anton Fröschl, K.: A method for analyzing time series data in process mining: application and extension of decision point analysis. In: Nurcan, S., Pimenidis, E. (eds.) CAiSE 2014. LNBIP, vol. 204, pp. 68–84. Springer, Cham (2015). https://doi.org/10.1007/978-3-319-19270-3_5
8. Ehrendorfer, M., Fassmann, J., Mangler, J., Rinderle-Ma, S.: Conformance checking and classification of manufacturing log data. In: Business Informatics, pp. 569–577 (2019)
9. Faloutsos, C., Ranganathan, M., Manolopoulos, Y.: Fast subsequence matching in time-series databases. ACM **23**, 419–429 (1994)
10. Grossmann, W., Rinderle-Ma, S.: Fundamentals of Business Intelligence. Springer, Heidelberg (2015). https://doi.org/10.1007/978-3-662-46531-8
11. Junkui, L., Yuanzhen, W.: Early abandon to accelerate exact dynamic time warping. Int. Arab J. Inf. Technol. (IAJIT) **6**(2), 144–152 (2009)
12. Kammerer, K., Hoppenstedt, B., Pryss, R., Stökler, S., Allgaier, J., Reichert, M.: Anomaly detections for manufacturing systems based on sensor data - insights into two challenging real-world production settings. Sensors **19**(24), 5370 (2019)
13. Leemans, S.J.J., Fahland, D., van der Aalst, W.M.P.: Discovering block-structured process models from event logs - a constructive approach. In: Colom, J.-M., Desel, J. (eds.) PETRI NETS 2013. LNCS, vol. 7927, pp. 311–329. Springer, Heidelberg (2013). https://doi.org/10.1007/978-3-642-38697-8_17
14. Maaradji, A., Dumas, M., Rosa, M.L., Ostovar, A.: Detecting sudden and gradual drifts in business processes from execution traces. IEEE Trans. Knowl. Data Eng. **29**(10), 2140–2154 (2017)
15. Maggi, F.M., Burattin, A., Cimitile, M., Sperduti, A.: Online process discovery to detect concept drifts in LTL-based declarative process models. In: Meersman, R., et al. (eds.) OTM 2013. LNCS, vol. 8185, pp. 94–111. Springer, Heidelberg (2013). https://doi.org/10.1007/978-3-642-41030-7_7
16. Mottola, L., et al.: makeSense: simplifying the integration of wireless sensor networks into business processes. IEEE Trans. Softw. Eng. **45**(6), 576–596 (2019)
17. Petitjean, F., Ketterlin, A., Gançarski, P.: A global averaging method for dynamic time warping, with applications to clustering. Pattern Recogn. **44**(3), 678–693 (2011)
18. Salvador, S., Chan, P.: Toward accurate dynamic time warping in linear time and space. Intell. Data Anal. **11**(5), 561–580 (2007)

19. Stertz, F., Rinderle-Ma, S.: Process histories - detecting and representing concept drifts based on event streams. In: Panetto, H., Debruyne, C., Proper, H.A., Ardagna, C.A., Roman, D., Meersman, R. (eds.) OTM 2018. LNCS, vol. 11229, pp. 318–335. Springer, Cham (2018). https://doi.org/10.1007/978-3-030-02610-3_18
20. Stertz, F., Rinderle-Ma, S.: Detecting and identifying data drifts in process event streams based on process histories. In: Cappiello, C., Ruiz, M. (eds.) CAiSE 2019. LNBIP, vol. 350, pp. 240–252. Springer, Cham (2019). https://doi.org/10.1007/978-3-030-21297-1_21
21. Stertz, F., Rinderle-Ma, S., Mangler, J.: Data set containing process execution log data with time sequence information for conference proceeding 2020 paper: analyzing process concept drifts based on sensor event streams during runtime. https://doi.org/10.6084/m9.figshare.12472634
22. Tavenard, R.: tslearn documentation (2018)
23. The Hackett Group: Enabling business process change (2019). https://www.thehackettgroup.com/business-process-change/
24. Wei, L., Keogh, E., Van Herle, H., Mafra-Neto, A.: Atomic wedgie: efficient query filtering for streaming time series. In: Fifth IEEE International Conference on Data Mining (ICDM 2005), pp. 8-pp. IEEE (2005)
25. Widmer, G., Kubat, M.: Learning in the presence of concept drift and hidden contexts. Mach. Learn. 23(1), 69–101 (1996). https://doi.org/10.1023/A:1018046501280
26. Yeshchenko, A., Di Ciccio, C., Mendling, J., Polyvyanyy, A.: Comprehensive process drift detection with visual analytics. In: Laender, A.H.F., Pernici, B., Lim, E.-P., de Oliveira, J.P.M. (eds.) ER 2019. LNCS, vol. 11788, pp. 119–135. Springer, Cham (2019). https://doi.org/10.1007/978-3-030-33223-5_11
27. van Zelst, S., van Dongen, B., van der Aalst, W.: Event stream-based process discovery using abstract representations. Knowl. Inf. Syst. 54(2), 407–435 (2018). https://doi.org/10.1007/s10115-017-1060-2

TADE: Stochastic Conformance Checking Using Temporal Activity Density Estimation

Florian Richter$^{(\boxtimes)}$, Janina Sontheim, Ludwig Zellner, and Thomas Seidl

Ludwig-Maximilians-Universität München, Munich, Germany
{richter,sontheim,zellner,seidl}@dbs.ifi.lmu.de.de

Abstract. In most processes, we have a strong demand for high conformance. We are interested in processes that work as designed, with as little deviations as possible. To assure this property, conformance checking techniques evaluate process instances by comparing their execution to work-flow models. However, this paradigm is depending on the assumption, that the work-flow perspective contains all necessary information to reveal potential non-conformance. In this work we propose the novel method TADE to check for process conformance with regards to another perspective. While traditional methods like token-based replay and alignments focus on workflow-based deviations, we developed time-sensitive stochastic estimators and prove their superiority over the competitors regarding accuracy and runtime efficiency. TADE is based on the well-known kernel density estimation. The probabilities of event occurrences at certain timestamps are modeled, so the fitness of new cases is computed considering this stochastic model. We evaluate this on a real-world building permit application process, which shows its usage capabilities in industrial scenarios.

Keywords: Process mining · Stochastic model · Conformance checking

1 Introduction

Dealing with processes of any shape, most analysts are often confronted with the question, whether all instances behave as defined or not. Deviating instances represent process entities like machines, staff or consumers. Each entity performs actions in the process, which are observed and tracked in an event log. These event logs are then used to discover a graph-like workflow net, often depicted as a Petri Net or as an equivalent structure.

However, those models usually focus on the workflow only, highlighting the order of observed events and neglecting the temporal flow of activities. Multiple works [6,11,14,19] underline that the temporal perspective is a beneficial facet for understanding a process. Divergences in the temporal perspective can often be used as an early hint on incoming changes. Also, delays in a process are

© Springer Nature Switzerland AG 2020
D. Fahland et al. (Eds.): BPM 2020, LNCS 12168, pp. 220–236, 2020.
https://doi.org/10.1007/978-3-030-58666-9_13

usually costly and have a negative impact on the process performance. While the workflow remains intact, workflow-based conformance checking will always fail to detect problems regarding the temporal flow of events. Here, we present our novel approach for conformance checking, that focuses not only on the observed order of events, but takes the actual timestamp into consideration, which is used relatively to the first event of the case. Furthermore, our approach does not work with a classical process model like the aforementioned graph-like Petri nets or similar notations. The common attempt to measure conformance is by applying token-based replay or alignments, where the former is restricted to the use with Petri nets and the latter is more generally applicable but also requires process models as a basis. Here, we are using the process log data directly to derive a probabilistic model. Since we are presenting in this paper a stochastic fitness value for conformance checking there is no form of visualization necessarily required.

An apparently fit trace is often not sufficient to fulfill specific workflow constraints. For each activity the occurrence probability for all points in time after start of a case is evaluated. Therefore, a probability density function is estimated by using the process log as a finite sample for the kernel density estimator. Furthermore, we use the Gaussian kernel as a density function. Our novel approach follows a stochastic paradigm, which means that we presume the underlying process a distribution of ordered activities but with differences in terms of occurrence times.

Besides these points, our approach is also very intuitive to understand and therefore hardly error-prone in programming. The area of application for this approach is wide e.g. it can be used to detect anomalies like security-threatening issues or trace affiliations to one another. As for the evaluation we apply our approach to a real-world dataset, BPIC 2015 [7], to solve a classification task. This task consists of assigning traces to pre-defined classes, which in our case are represented by sublogs of the same process differing by their executing resources. Those classes are covered by a trained model each. The fitness of a new case is computed based on the models and thereby it can be assigned to a class. Moreover, the fitness values for a conformance classification and the runtime performance is compared to the most common existing approaches for conformance checking, token-based replay and alignments, since there is no other approach dealing with the same problem setup as we do.

In Sect. 2 we analyze and compare approaches in relation to our contribution. The subsequent Sect. 3 provides preliminary information. In Sect. 4 we introduce Temporal Activity Density Estimation, which is subsequently used to describe our conformance checking approach in detail. We evaluate our approach experimentally in Sect. 5 and consider the results as well as propose ideas for future work in Sect. 6.

2   Related Work

Measures of the quality of a process model so far have been fitness, precision, generalization, and simplicity [4]. Traditional conformance checking relies on the measures model fitness and model precision. Fitness determines how much behavior of the log or trace is contained in the model. The more of the log can be reproduced in the process model, the greater the fitness value. On the contrary, precision accounts for the behavior of the model that is explainable by the log. The worse the precision, the more the model is underfitting. Many techniques have been developed that rely on a traditional Petri net or an equivalent workflow model. An overview over conformance checking approaches is given by Carmona et al. in [5]. Two of those approaches to determine the fitness and the precision of a model are token-based replay and alignment. Even from a theoretical perspective, conformance techniques that rely on those measures, suffer from issues as presented in [12].

Token-based replay determines the fitness of a trace by replaying the events as a firing sequence on a Petri net. This method is a prominent foundation for many other methods in process mining. However, it only utilizes the sequence of activities, without the actual temporal behavior. Alignments provide another workflow-model-based approach. Moves on both the trace of activities and on the model are performed simultaneously. In case that this is not possible, log-only or trace-only moves are performed but decrease the fitness score. Alignment-based conformance checking investigates all log-trace alignments to find the most synchronous alignment. The computation is complex and therefore requires much computation time. Also, alignments consider the workflow and neglect the actual timestamps.

Having an event log $[\langle a, b\rangle^1, \langle b, a\rangle^{99}]$ and the corresponding stochastic process model $[\langle a, b\rangle^{0.99}, \langle b, a\rangle^{0.01}]$ as in [10], the common measures fitness and precision would be perfectly fine. Even though, considering the stochastic perspective there is just an overlap of 2%. Therefore, the measures fitness and precision are not sufficient enough as a measure for conformance checking and the stochastical perspective on the data is very helpful.

Our novel method follows a stochastic approach to focus on the temporal behavior of traces instead of just the order of activities. However, instead of augmenting a Petri net and using an extension of one of both conformance checking paradigms, we follow a stochastic approach in a simple model, to improve efficiency while boosting accuracy. Stochastic process models can be derived automatically from event logs, as e.g. in [15]. A possibility to represent stochastic process models is using Hidden Markov Models, where activities are represented as transitions between states. Each transition has an execution probability to model the likeliness of different workflows. While Hidden Markov Models represent a process as a stochastic model, the temporal perspective is also neglected here. In [17], Non-Markovian models are used to predict duration times by using a stochastic Petri net. It does not solve the conformance problem directly and does not consider relations between activities. Another work by Rogge-Solti et al. [16] uses temporal density estimation to identify outliers. However, the estimators are derived using a previously discovered workflow model. Though, multiple works [6,11,14,19] underline that the temporal perspective is a beneficial facet for understanding a process. Hence, related to our extension of the plain structure with temporal behavior are timed Petri nets [13] which extend the order of the process model by timing annotations.

The first steps towards a stochastic paradigm for process models were already taken by Richter et al. in LIProMa [8] by using the Earth Movers Distance. Label-Independent Process Matching is a method to compare processes while neglecting their specific labels. Nevertheless a successful comparison is achieved by solving the temporal transportation problem based on the temporal flow of action sequences. Another stochastic approach was described by Leemans et al. [10], using stochastic language models and Earth Mover's Distance between logs and models. Their cost function measuring this distance is defined as the lowest cost for any reallocation function with given stochastic languages of the event log and the stochastic process model. Using the stochastic language, which is a set of tuples consisting of a trace and its probability, the approach is tied to the common log notation and needs to calculate the shortest distance between two languages.

In contrast to that, we follow with TADE a more direct approach by working on activity level and without a transformation between two languages. Thereby our new fitness score, TSC-fitness, regarding temporal stochastic conformance of traces are calculated in a very efficient way. To calculate the TSC-fitness for traces it is worth mentioning that we present already an algorithmic solution. Furthermore TADE yields higher accuracy than traditional conformance checking approaches.

Senderovich et al. [20] propose a stochastic versus deterministic approach to compare a schedule with a given process log. This is done by rejecting a null hypothesis claiming the F/J network of the schedule and the event log to be equal. To create a F/J network for both the schedule and the network preprocessing steps with possible information loss have to be performed, which is not necessary in our approach.

3   Preliminaries

We start with the atomic parts of a process which are events. Each event $e = (c, a, t)$ contains at least a case identifier c, an activity label a and a timestamp t. To simplify notation we define the select operator $\#$ which allows us to access a specified property of an event. For the event $e = (c, a, t)$ we define $\#_{case}(e) := c$, $\#_{act}(e) := a$ and $\#_{time}(e) := t$. An event log L is a set of events. A subset of L, that contains exactly all events with the common case identifier c is called a case. We denote a case in angle brackets as $c = \langle e_1, \dots, e_n \rangle$.

In our approach we calculate a fitness score for a case to determine conformance using the probabilities of every event in the case. The probability of an event depends on the distribution of the corresponding activity over time. This probability corresponds to the fitness of an event. To get this fitness value we need probability functions for every activity, so-called *kernels* k. Kernels are well-established algorithms in the field of machine learning. Kernels map non-linear separable problems in a higher dimensional space where those problems might be separable.

Since in most applications the temporal distribution of activities does not follow an *a priori* model but results from the event log L, we use non-parametric models. A widely spread non-parametric approach is to use the *Gaussian kernel function* $k(t)$, which is defined as follows, to obtain a non-parametric model for each previously left-aligned (cf. Sect. 4.1) event $e = (c, a, t)$:

$$k(t) = \frac{1}{\sqrt{2\pi}} \cdot exp(-\frac{t^2}{2})$$

Left-alignment indicates that the timestamps of a case are noted down relative to the first timestamp of this case.

At a specific point in time the actual probability for an event is unknown, as well. Therefore, the Kernel Density Estimator (KDE) is used to approximate the probability density of an activity. KDEs are well-established methods in machine learning, as well. For a sample $x_1, x_2, ..., x_n \in \mathbb{R}$, a kernel k and the bandwidth h, the *Kernel Density Estimator (KDE)* is defined as:

$$\hat{f}_h(t) : \mathbb{R} \to \mathbb{R}_+, \qquad \hat{f}_h(t) = \frac{1}{nh} \sum_{j=1}^{n} k\left(\frac{t - x_j}{h}\right)$$

For the quality of the approximation the choice of the bandwidth h is crucial. For deeper insights on kernels and bandwidths, we highly recommend to read the explanations in Schölkopf et al. [18].

In terms of conformance checking on processes, a sample always refers to one activity, e.g. a, and describes all occurrences of this activity a over all cases being used for training of the model, with left-aligned timestamps. We assume the bandwidth to be equally set for all activities. Thus, we note down the activity instead of the bandwidth in the index of the density estimator, $\hat{f}_a(t)$.

4   Stochastic Conformance Checking Using Temporal Activity Density Estimation

Our novel method TADE[1] utilizes a kernel density estimation to train a probability model for activity occurrences in a process, c.f. Sect. 4.1. After the model has been trained, new traces can be checked for conformance by applying the trained model to the actual trace execution. Therefore, we define a case fitness value in Sect. 4.2. Furthermore we consider a more computationally intense variation, the TADE-FC Sect. 4.3. In Sect. 4.4 we study the impact of the choice of the kernel and bandwidth and complete the approach with an analysis of the complexity in Sect. 4.5.

Usually, it is not a good idea to mingle process discovery and conformance checking. However, to apply kernel density estimation, we need proper kernel functions, which is not the usual output of discovery algorithms. Also, the majority of process owners will probably struggle to hand over a temporal kernel model

---

[1] https://github.com/Skarvir/TADE.

for analysis. Therefore, we combine discovery and conformance checking here, but we recommend to separate both parts by using a distinct training log for discovery and a different event log for the conformance testing.

4.1   Temporal Activity Density Estimation (TADE)

As input we take an event log L. All cases are handled iteratively. For each case we first *left-align* all timestamps, i.e. the starting event $e_0 = (c, a, t_0)$ of case c is transformed to $e'_0 = (c, a, 0)$ and all succeeding events of this case, $e_i = (c, *, t_i)$, consider only the relative time difference to the starting event of this case, as $e'_i = (c, *, t_i - t_0)$, instead of the original absolute timestamp t_i.

Per activity a we are interested in a probability density function $f_a(t)$ that defines the occurrence probability of this activity at a given timestamp. Since in most applications the work-flow of a process does not follow a strict and parametric statistical model there is no single distribution to cover this behavior. To obtain a probability density function anyhow, we use the process log as a finite sample to derive a non-parametric model instead. Therefore we generate singular kernels for every occurrence of an activity over all cases. Having those kernels we aggregate them to obtain an estimated probability density function $\hat{f}_a(t)$.

Having a non-parametric model we, therefore, use a non-parametric kernel function, here the *Gaussian kernel function* $K(t)$, which is defined as follows, to obtain a non-parametric model for each previously left-aligned event $e = (c, a, t)$:

$$K(t) = \frac{1}{\sqrt{2\pi}} \cdot exp(-\frac{t^2}{2})$$

For each activity a, we can now define a *probability density estimator* $\hat{f}_a(t) \approx f_a(t)$ by aggregating all corresponding Gaussian kernel functions $K(t)$:

$$\hat{f}_a(t) = \frac{1}{|a|_L \, h} \sum_{\substack{e \in L \\ \#_{act}(e) = a}} K\left(\frac{t - \#_{time}(e)}{h}\right)$$

where $|a|_L$ is the number of events that execute the activity a. The bandwidth parameter h has the property to smooth the probability density function and is examined more closely in Sect. 4.4. Each activity spans its distinct temporal activity density function.

In the left part of Fig. 1 the singular Gaussian kernel functions are depicted for every occurrence of activity a, plotted below the x-axis, over all cases in the process log and timestamps being left-aligned. The y-axis depicts the probability of the occurrence. The right part of Fig. 1 shows the aggregation of the singular kernels from the left part of this figure, the estimated kernel density.

A mixture of different activities as a common activity set is possible if activities perform simultaneous process actions. However, this requires deeper domain knowledge.

In terms of the used real-world dataset BPIC 2015, in particular for every subset separately, this means that we calculate a probability density function

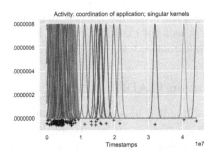
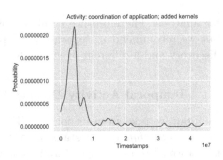

Fig. 1. Left: For each observation of one activity, a kernel function is generated, using a common bandwidth. Right: Kernel density estimation determines the mean of all singular kernels and produces a kernel mixture model.

for every activity occurring in the training phase. For the five municipality the probability density function for activity a may look very different, since every municipality works slightly different.

4.2   Temporal Stochastic Conformance (TSC) Checking

The conformance checking task is a very elementary task by having estimated the probability density functions for the activities with TADE. The value of the estimated probability density function $\hat{f}_a(t)$ covering the activity a defines the probability that the event activity is executed at this point in time relative to the time of the starting event of that specific case. To check if a case is conform we need to consider all events in this case and apply the corresponding probability density functions $\hat{f}_a(t)$ for every event, i.e. for the event activity and the event time, separately.

Having all estimated probability values for one case we use the arithmetic mean to derive the temporal stochastic conformance-fitness (TSC) value of this case regarding a temporal activity density estimation. Formally, for a given case $c = \langle e_1, \ldots, e_n \rangle$ the *temporal stochastic conformance (TSC)-fitness* is:

$$fitness_{TSC}(c) = \frac{1}{n} \cdot \sum_{e \in c} \hat{f}_{\#_{\mathrm{act}}(e)} \left(\#_{\mathrm{time}}(e) \right)$$

We use the average over all activities for the computation of the trace fitness. This is a robust approach and outperforms further methods, c.f. Sect. 5.1. From a statistics perspective, one expects the product of all probabilities to determine the probability of fitness for the whole trace. Also, the minimum of all event fitness values would be a suitable candidate. However, both approaches increase the sensitivity for outliers while emphasizing the unfit parts of the trace. The average of all event fitness values emerged as a more robust approach to expand the singular event values into a representative value for a trace fitness.

In terms of our real-world dataset, it means that we now have a new case and want to figure out to which municipality it belongs or came from. Thus, we calculate the TSC-fitness for this case for each municipality, using the probability density functions for this particular municipality.

4.3 Full Cartesian TADE (TADE-FC)

The previous baseline approach left-aligns the temporal perspective of all cases. To put it in another way, in this case we use the time difference between the first event and all subsequent events. This approach has the disadvantage of excessively weighting the impact of the first events in a case on the fitness score. Two sequential events with a short interim time are usually more correlated in time than the first and the last event of a case, which have a long time interval in-between. If we only consider the time difference between the first event and all other events, the latter events are represented by a fuzzy probability distributions. This effect is caused by the higher variance of these long intervals. Later events are often depending on the completion of previous events and temporal deviations are carried along the whole trace and accumulated in all succeeding events.

We, therefore, extend our approach to the full Cartesian activity set, considering all pairs of events in a case. This gives us a higher accuracy for the probability estimators with the disadvantage of longer calculation time.

Instead of defining a kernel function for each activity, we define *kernel functions for all relations of two temporally succeeding activities*, whereby it is not limited to directly succeeding pairs. The resulting relation set is a subset of the full Cartesian product set of all activities. It should be noted that the Cartesian product also contains pairs of the same activity and is, therefore, a reflexive relation. This covers the scenario that an activity can occur multiple times in the same case. The kernel density estimation formula from the basic TADE approach thus extends to the following form:

$$\hat{f}_{(a,b)}(t) = \frac{1}{|[a,b]|_L \, h} \sum_{\substack{e_1, e_2 \in L \\ \#_{\mathrm{act}}(e_1) = a \\ \#_{\mathrm{act}}(e_2) = b}} K\left(\frac{t - |\#_{\mathrm{time}}(e_1) - \#_{\mathrm{time}}(e_2)|}{h}\right)$$

where $|[a,b]|_L$ defines the number of temporally succeeding occurrences of a and b within the same case c as

$$|[a,b]|_L = \left| \{(e_1, e_2) \in L^2 \mid \#_{case}(e_1) = \#_{case}(e_2) \wedge \#_{act}(e_1) = a \wedge \#_{act}(e_2) = b\} \right|$$

The TSC-fitness has to be modified as well to consider all relations in a case instead of singular activities only:

$$fitness_{TSC}(c) = \frac{1}{|c^2|} \cdot \sum_{e_1, e_2 \in c} \hat{f}_{(\#_{\mathrm{act}}(e_1), \#_{\mathrm{act}}(e_2))} (|\#_{\mathrm{time}}(e_1) - \#_{\mathrm{time}}(e_2)|)$$

Since we consider relations of activities in succeeding order, the temporal difference of the corresponding timestamps is always positive. For kernel density estimation, this does not pose a problem, as the domain are the real numbers. However, if the kernel is exchanged with another estimator, this should be considered.

In Fig. 2 the estimators for a case with four activities are shown. Using the full Cartesian set of four activities, we maintain 16 density estimations. This is similar to behavioural profiles [22], which capture order relations for the Cartesian product of activities. Regarding these profiles, the set of temporal density estimation functions can be considered as a temporal behavioural profile for the log. Workflow-based behavioural profiles are used for discrete compliance checking and therefore related to our task. However, the perspectives work orthogonally and might be used as an ensemble for a generalized compliance checking technique in a future work. For the basic version of TADE, only the first row is used as sketched with a frame here. For larger activity universes, the number of estimators grows quadratic.

4.4 Kernel and Bandwidth Selection

Kernel density estimation uses a particular kernel function to approximate the densities on the singular observation level before summing up these curves. In this work, we restrict the method to Gaussian kernels only, among others because it is most widely spread. Furthermore, due to the large number of events compared to the smaller number of activities, each model contains a multitude of observations. Therefore, changing the kernel function shows only a diminished impact on the aggregated probability function after the first experiments. Still, extensive evaluations with other kernels are of interest but out of the scope of this work.

The choice of the bandwidth is of much higher importance than the choice of the kernel. We sketched this in Fig. 3. Further you can see, that using a very small bandwidth, like $bw = 0.05$, results in a very noisy probability density function, where every training event yields a mode as a density peak. The TSC-fitness is therefore subject to very sudden changes. The other extreme case is a very high bandwidth, like $bw = 2.0$. This can result in a probability density function with a single mode, neglecting all minor modes that cover important and interesting deviations of the activity. This barely reflects the original distribution. While the bandwidth has a huge impact on the estimation, the choice of the kernel is only marginally important.

A popular approach to set the bandwidth parameter is the Silverman method. However, it works best on unimodal Gaussian models, but we often observe multimodal distributions due to process loops and complex activity dependencies. Therefore, we recommend the Improved Sheather-Jones bandwidth selection [21] at this point, which minimizes the asymptotic mean integrated squared error (AMISE). It results from the mean integrated squared error (MISE) of the probability density function f and its Gaussian kernel density estimator $\hat{f}$, which is given by

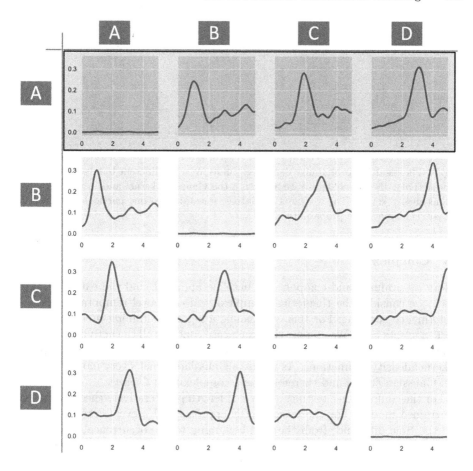

Fig. 2. All 16 density estimations for the full Cartesian set of activities a, b, c and d. Using the base version of TADE instead of TADE-FC, only the first row is used, highlighted with a frame here.

$$\mathrm{MISE}(h) = \mathbb{E}_f \int \left[\hat{f}(t; h) - f(t) \right]^2 dt$$

The AMISE is then the asymptotic approximation of the MISE. It is shown by Jones [21] that for $h\sqrt{n} \to \infty$ as $n \to \infty$, it is minimized by

$$h_0 = \left(\frac{1}{2N\sqrt{\pi}\, \|f''\|^2} \right)^{2/5}$$

h_0 minimizes the AMISE and is an approximation for the minimizer of MISE. The unknown derivation of the probability density function f'' can be estimated using the Fourier heat equation. Approaches to find a good estimator efficiently are found well-explained in the literature like in [3].

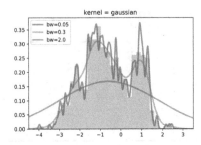 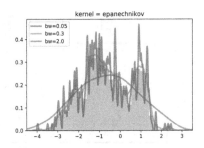

Fig. 3. The resulting probability density estimations with different bandwidths for the same activity. In the left figure we are using the Gaussian kernel and in the right the Epanechnikov kernel. The x-axis is a relative timestamp to one particular event and the y-axis displays the probability.

4.5   Complexity

Before we evaluate and compare the baseline approach and the extended approach, we consider the theoretical complexity of our novel temporal statistical conformance checking. For this, we assume a log L, containing n cases with at most m events each. We assume that each case contains all the activities. For the training phase, our baseline approach iterates over all $n \cdot m$ events and computes m kernel density estimations. As we use a Gaussian kernel, every model is a sum of n Gaussian curves and therefore has a complexity of $\mathcal{O}(nm)$.

For the conformance testing, a case c of length p is iteratively checked against the trained models. For the basic TADE approach, all p events are considered and the time difference from the case beginning to the occurrence is used. For each of those $p - 1$ time differences, the probability is yielded by the learned Gaussian kernel density estimation. This leads to the complexity of $\mathcal{O}(p)$ to compute the TSC-fitness for one case. For the full Cartesian TADE, a case of length p produces p^2 many relations. Analogously to the baseline we end up with a complexity that scales as $\mathcal{O}(p^2)$ using m^2 distinct Kernel Density Estimators.

5   Evaluation

In this section, we evaluate our novel temporal stochastic conformance checking approaches. For this we first of all have to face the fact that to the best of our knowledge there is no other temporal stochastic conformance checking approach so far against which we could compare. Furthermore, there is also no approach focusing on the temporal occurrence of an activity rather than on structural deviations. Therefore, we utilized the most common conformance checking methods token-based replay and alignment. Although they are invented to check a different kind of conformance they are the most suitable approaches to compare with.

To evaluate our approach we firstly compare different methods of how to calculate the final case-wise TSC-fitness score. Second, we show its applicability on a real-world dataset by solving a conformance classification task. Third, we expose the advantageous runtime performance by measuring the runtime on several log sizes.

5.1 Aggregation of the TSC-Fitness Score

By proposing a stochastical approach for conformance checking we calculate the probability for every event of the test case, compared to the trained model, with a kernel density estimation for the particular activity. To get the fitness value for the whole case, the TSC-fitness, we need to aggregate those probabilities suitably. Our choice for this computation is averaging all TSC-fitness values of this case even though from a statistical point of view, the product of all probabilities would be meaningful. Further valid candidates are the minimum as a lower bound or the maximum as an upper bound. Once again, we utilize the BPIC 2015 dataset, since we will compare the classification accuracy again.

Table 1. Comparison of different methods to aggregate event TSC-fitness values into a case TSC-fitness value. Choices are minimum (min), maximum (max), mean and product of the event fitness values.

	Min			Max			Mean			Product		
	prec	rec	f1	prec	rec	f1	prec	rec	f1	prec	rec	f1
BPIC15-1	0.46	0.43	0.44	0.17	0.67	0.27	**0.49**	0.45	**0.47**	0.23	**0.91**	0.37
BPIC15-2	0.43	0.48	0.45	0.07	0.02	0.03	0.45	**0.48**	**0.46**	**0.56**	0.04	0.07
BPIC15-3	0.69	0.46	0.55	0.02	0.00	0.00	0.73	**0.52**	**0.60**	**0.88**	0.18	0.30
BPIC15-4	0.59	0.44	0.50	0.06	0.03	0.04	0.63	**0.47**	**0.53**	**0.78**	0.16	0.26
BPIC15-5	0.41	0.66	0.51	0.04	0.00	0.01	**0.43**	**0.70**	**0.53**	0.42	0.12	0.19

In Table 1 we compare the quality of the classification. It can clearly be seen that the maximum is a poor choice, however, this is quite expected. The minimum of the TSC-fitness values is almost on the level of the arithmetic mean. The product has high precision values for three classes. However, this is not a great advantage as the recall is poor for those classes. It seems that a majority of cases are assigned to the first class. Therefore the product is not suitable for this task as the cases are more likely to be assigned into the first class and the models do not reflect the classes very well. As previously proposed, the arithmetic mean has proven to be the best candidate for class assignment so far.

5.2 Conformance Classification

For this experiment, we utilize the BPIC 2015 dataset [7]. This dataset consists of five sublogs, which cover building permit applications in five different municipalities. All five processes follow similar guidelines and use the same activity descriptions. We evaluate traditional token-based replay and our two approaches, TADE and TADE-FC, on the following task. The results of alignments and token-based replay have been shown to be very similar in this task, so we focus on token-based replay only due to the faster computation. On each sublog, a model is trained on one part of the traces. Then, for the remaining traces, we compute the TSC-fitness for each trace on all five models. The model that provides the best TSC-fitness determines the class of this trace. We assume that the process which produced a trace also corresponds to a model that provides the best TSC-fitness for this trace. The advantage of this dataset for this task is the known ground truth as well as the similarity of processes. Using different processes for the classification task is not appropriate as the classification would mainly rely on different activity labels than workflow and temporal behavior.

Table 2. Classification accuracy on the BPIC 2015 dataset for token-based replay, Temporal Activity Density Estimation (TADE) and TADE-Full Cartesian, separated per sublog.

	Activities	Traces	Events	Token-based replay			TADE			TADE-FC		
				prec	rec	f1	prec	rec	f1	prec	rec	f1
BPIC15-1	398	1199	52217	0.10	0.01	0.02	0.49	0.43	0.46	0.80	0.68	0.73
BPIC15-2	410	832	44354	0.00	0.00	0.00	0.42	0.45	0.44	0.59	0.70	0.64
BPIC15-3	383	1409	59681	0.02	0.01	0.02	0.72	0.51	0.60	0.86	0.67	0.75
BPIC15-4	356	1053	47293	0.33	0.85	0.33	0.63	0.45	0.52	0.88	0.72	0.79
BPIC15-5	389	1156	59083	0.16	0.16	0.16	0.41	0.70	0.52	0.60	0.88	0.72

According to best-practices, we use randomly sampled 80% of the traces as training dataset and evaluate the remaining 20% of the log as test dataset. The resulting classification quality is given as precision, recall and F1 score in Table 2. We trained five Petri nets with the Inductive Miner [9] and applied token-based replay [1], both using the implementation in pm4py [2]. For the test log traces, here 1130 cases, we determined the model that maximized the TSC-fitness of the case.

Due to the generalization purpose of process discovery, all discovered models are rather similar. Hence, the computed fitness scores for token-based replay differ only slightly and most cases are assigned to the same class. In some instances, a particular choice of training and test set partitioning causes all cases to be assigned to the fifth model, which happens if all models are equal regarding the test set. However, we chose an evaluation instance which provides different models to give workflow-model-based conformance checking a slight advantage. Even so, our new approaches TADE and TADE-FC outperform the traditional conformance checking approach token-based replay, as the results in Table 2 show.

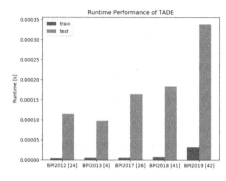 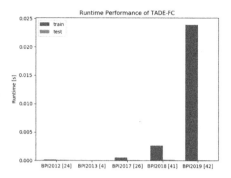

Fig. 4. The runtime for training, in blue, and conformance checking, in orange, are compared separately for several datasets of the BPI challenges. Left figure shows the results for TADE and the right one for TADE-FC. (Color figure online)

5.3   Runtime Evaluation

Previously, we evaluated the quality of the conformance checking by solving a trace classification task. The computation time of all methods for this task differs vastly. First, we consider the runtime behavior of our two novel approaches, TADE and TADE-FC, in terms of the ratio of training to testing. Secondly, we compare the runtime of TADE, TADE-FC with the common approaches for conformance checking, token-based replay and alignments. For the latter two methods, we used the pm4py implementations. For alignment, the concept for convex optimization is used as recommended, to speed up the alignment computations. It is also important to apply the traditional conformance checking methods on the whole log instead of feeding each trace separately. This causes a factor of 10 in runtime performance due to duplicate traces in the log.

In Fig. 4 the runtime for training and conformance checking, i.e. testing, are visualized separately. This is done for several datasets of the last years BPI challenges. Like before in the experiment for conformance classification, we used randomly sampled 80% of the log traces for training and evaluated on the remaining 20% of the log as test set. For TADE in the left figure, conformance checking is the distinct dominant part of the performance. While the training phase for all datasets was faster than 0.0005 s the conformance checking took almost up to 0.00035 s. For the TADE-FC version the runtime of training and testing was the other way around. This is because the large number of relations increases the model training runtime in TADE-FC. This confirms the intuition that TADE is trained very fast, whereas TADE-FC takes longer to train.

In Fig. 5 we compare the absolute computation time for the whole task for the four approaches alignment, token-based replay, TADE and TADE-FC. Considering an event-based runtime the relative runtime differences between the approaches do not change, as the used logs are the same. While alignments, even with the faster optimizer, require more than 17.5 h to complete the task, token-based replay completes the classification in under 2 h. Unfortunately, the models have low expressiveness and yield only a poor classification considering the vast time amount. TADE with the full Cartesian relation set requires almost one hour to complete the classification, yielding the most accurate results. The quality of TADE is also competitive, as it only needs one minute, which is 60 times faster then TADE-FC. This comes at the cost of reducing the accuracy by factor two, but still tremendously outperforms token-based replay regarding the fitness measures precision, recall, and f1-score, c.f. Sect. 5.2. Therefore, our two temporal-based fitness scoring methods are a suitable choice for applications that rely on a trace fitness with strong runtime performance requirements.

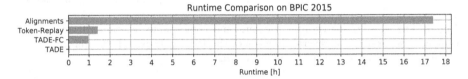

Fig. 5. Runtime comparison on the real-world dataset BPIC 2015 for the approaches alignment, token-based replay, TADE-FC and TADE.

5.4   Discussion and Limitations

The performed evaluations illustrate the capabilities of TADE to estimate conformance in a reasonable speed. However, being very fast while accurate is not the main point here. The comparison with workflow-based approaches like token-replay and alignments is fragile as they do not suit very well as direct competitors due to their limited perspective. However, we are able to determine a temporal fitness using a very simple stochastic technique without deriving complex workflow models. Adding temporal information into process models and using them for conformance checking, we are able to process many instances in a short period of time. We do not mean to outclass workflow-based conformance checking methods, but TADE provides a reasonable addition to this scope. Most non-conforming traces can be filtered out based on their temporal fitness. For the remaining test candidates, additional resources and computation time can now be utilized for a more precise analysis.

TADE's advantage lies in the simplicity of its models. The temporal density estimation does not cover parallelism and loops in its current implementation. Multiple recurrences of activities usually differ in their temporal behavior, e.g. a repair job will take some days, but if this fails, a second cycle will be more tedious to identify the initial root cause. Also, activities with certain temporal constraints e.g. a worker is not allowed to perform activity 'a' on sundays, is not represented at the moment as the kernel function assumes a continuous domain. Incorporating workflow models into the temporal model and replacing the kernel functions with more complex kernels might solve those problems, but the impact on efficiency and accuracy has to be evaluated in future works. For recurring activities within a trace, the kernel density estimation will yield several peaks in the probability function, so TADE can already cope with this issue.

6   Conclusion and Future Work

Temporal Stochastic Density Estimation is a very natural and intuitive method to define the fitness of a process trace with a high focus on the temporal perspective. Since deviations in time occur in various severities, these estimators are very sensitive and perform with much higher performance than traditional conformance checking methods. With the focus only on sequential orders, only finitely many unfit deviation types can be covered with traditional conformance checking methods, hence the stochastic approach is superior. In extensive experiments, we showed not only the quality but also the good performance of our novel and efficient conformance checking approach. Even using a full Cartesian set of activity relations outperformed token-based replay in both quality and runtime.

However, we did not cover sufficiently the occurrence of loops and parallelism in the approach. This is still a future work as the modeling of kernel functions provides much freedom in designing different representations. We introduced only a simple one by considering only timestamp differences for the estimation part. In future works, we aim at improving the quality even more by incorporating concurrency checks and workflow patterns into the approach. This could assist in modeling loop and concurrency patterns in the density estimation. Further, there is a demand for online conformance checking and our efficient approach is modifiable to check a stream of events for conformance. Last, there are many works on advanced process mining tasks, which operate on token-based replay or alignments. Those tools will also benefit from an efficiently computable and accurate alternative fitness score, out TSC-fitness.

References

1. Berti, A., van der Aalst, W.: Reviving token-based replay: increasing speed while improving diagnostics. In: Algorithms & Theories for the Analysis of Event Data (ATAED 2019), p. 87 (2019)
2. Berti, A., van Zelst, S.J., van der Aalst, W.: Process Mining for Python (PM4Py): Bridging the Gap Between Process-and Data Science, pp. 13–16 (2019)
3. Botev, Z.I., Grotowski, J.F., Kroese, D.P., et al.: Kernel density estimation via diffusion. Ann. Stat. **38**(5), 2916–2957 (2010)
4. Buijs, J.C.A.M., van Dongen, B.F., van der Aalst, W.M.P.: On the role of fitness, precision, generalization and simplicity in process discovery. In: Meersman, R., et al. (eds.) OTM 2012. LNCS, vol. 7565, pp. 305–322. Springer, Heidelberg (2012). https://doi.org/10.1007/978-3-642-33606-5_19
5. Carmona, J., van Dongen, B.F., Solti, A., Weidlich, M.: Conformance Checking - Relating Processes and Models. Springer, Heidelberg (2018). https://doi.org/10.1007/978-3-319-99414-7
6. Dixit, P.M., et al.: Detection and interactive repair of event ordering imperfection in process logs. In: Krogstie, J., Reijers, H.A. (eds.) CAiSE 2018. LNCS, vol. 10816, pp. 274–290. Springer, Cham (2018). https://doi.org/10.1007/978-3-319-91563-0_17

7. van Dongen, B.F.: BPI challenge 2015. In: 11th International Workshop on Business Process Intelligence (BPI 2015) (2015)
8. Richter, F., Zellner, L., Azaiz, I., Winkel, D., Seidl, T.: LIProMa: label-independent process matching. In: Di Francescomarino, C., Dijkman, R., Zdun, U. (eds.) BPM 2019. LNBIP, vol. 362, pp. 186–198. Springer, Cham (2019). https://doi.org/10. 1007/978-3-030-37453-2_16
9. Leemans, S.J.J., Fahland, D., van der Aalst, W.M.P.: Scalable process discovery with guarantees. In: Gaaloul, K., Schmidt, R., Nurcan, S., Guerreiro, S., Ma, Q. (eds.) CAISE 2015. LNBIP, vol. 214, pp. 85–101. Springer, Cham (2015). https:// doi.org/10.1007/978-3-319-19237-6_6
10. Leemans, S.J.J., Syring, A.F., van der Aalst, W.M.P.: Earth movers' stochastic conformance checking. In: Hildebrandt, T., van Dongen, B.F., Röglinger, M., Mendling, J. (eds.) BPM 2019. LNBIP, vol. 360, pp. 127–143. Springer, Cham (2019). https://doi.org/10.1007/978-3-030-26643-1_8
11. Polato, M., Sperduti, A., Burattin, A., Leoni, M.: Time and activity sequence prediction of business process instances. Computing **100**(9), 1005–1031 (2018). https://doi.org/10.1007/s00607-018-0593-x
12. Polyvyanyy, A., Solti, A., Weidlich, M., Ciccio, C.D., Mendling, J.: Monotone precision and recall measures for comparing executions and specifications of dynamic systems. ACM Trans. Softw. Eng. Methodol. (TOSEM) **29**(3), 1–41 (2020)
13. Ramchandani, C.: Analysis of asynchronous concurrent systems by timed Petri nets (1973)
14. Richter, F., Seidl, T.: Looking into the tesseract: time-drifts in event streams using series of evolving rolling averages of completion times. Inf. Syst. **84**, 265–282 (2019)
15. Rogge-Solti, A., van der Aalst, W.M.P., Weske, M.: Discovering stochastic Petri nets with arbitrary delay distributions from event logs. In: Lohmann, N., Song, M., Wohed, P. (eds.) BPM 2013. LNBIP, vol. 171, pp. 15–27. Springer, Cham (2014). https://doi.org/10.1007/978-3-319-06257-0_2
16. Rogge-Solti, A., Kasneci, G.: Temporal anomaly detection in business processes. In: Sadiq, S., Soffer, P., Völzer, H. (eds.) BPM 2014. LNCS, vol. 8659, pp. 234–249. Springer, Cham (2014). https://doi.org/10.1007/978-3-319-10172-9_15
17. Rogge-Solti, A., Weske, M.: Prediction of business process durations using non-Markovian stochastic Petri nets. Inf. Syst. **54**, 1–14 (2015)
18. Schölkopf, B., Smola, A.J., Bach, F., et al.: Learning with Kernels: Support Vector Machines, Regularization, Optimization, and Beyond. MIT Press, Cambridge (2002)
19. Senderovich, A., Weidlich, M., Gal, A.: Temporal network representation of event logs for improved performance modelling in business processes. In: Carmona, J., Engels, G., Kumar, A. (eds.) BPM 2017. LNCS, vol. 10445, pp. 3–21. Springer, Cham (2017). https://doi.org/10.1007/978-3-319-65000-5_1
20. Senderovich, A., et al.: Conformance checking and performance improvement in scheduled processes: a queueing-network perspective. Inf. Syst. **62**, 185–206 (2016). https://doi.org/10.1016/j.is.2016.01.002
21. Sheather, S.J., Jones, M.C.: A reliable data-based bandwidth selection method for kernel density estimation. J. Roy. Stat. Soc.: Ser. B (Methodol.) **53**(3), 683–690 (1991)
22. Weidlich, M., Polyvyanyy, A., Desai, N., Mendling, J., Weske, M.: Process compliance analysis based on behavioural profiles. Inf. Syst. **36**(7), 1009–1025 (2011)

Predictive Business Process Monitoring via Generative Adversarial Nets: The Case of Next Event Prediction

Farbod Taymouri[(✉)], Marcello La Rosa, Sarah Erfani, Zahra Dasht Bozorgi, and Ilya Verenich

The University of Melbourne, Melbourne, Australia
{farbod.taymouri,marcello.larosa,
sara.erfani,ilya.verenich}@unimelb.edu.au,
zdashtbozorg@student.unimelb.edu.au

Abstract. Predictive process monitoring aims to predict future characteristics of an ongoing process case, such as case outcome or remaining timestamp. Recently, several predictive process monitoring methods based on deep learning such as Long Short-Term Memory or Convolutional Neural Network have been proposed to address the problem of next event prediction. However, due to insufficient training data or sub-optimal network configuration and architecture, these approaches do not generalize well the problem at hand. This paper proposes a novel adversarial training framework to address this shortcoming, based on an adaptation of Generative Adversarial Networks (GANs) to the realm of sequential temporal data. The training works by putting one neural network against the other in a two-player game (hence the "adversarial" nature) which leads to predictions that are indistinguishable from the ground truth. We formally show that the worst-case accuracy of the proposed approach is at least equal to the accuracy achieved in non-adversarial settings. From the experimental evaluation it emerges that the approach systematically outperforms all baselines both in terms of accuracy and earliness of the prediction, despite using a simple network architecture and a naive feature encoding. Moreover, the approach is more robust, as its accuracy is not affected by fluctuations over the case length.

1 Introduction

Predictive business process monitoring is an area of process mining that is concerned with predicting future characteristics of an ongoing process case [19,21]. Different machine learning techniques, and more recently deep learning methods, have been employed to deal with different prediction problems, such as outcome prediction [20], remaining time prediction [18], suffix prediction (i.e. predicting the most likely continuation of an ongoing case) [1,12,18], or next event prediction [1,2,12,16,18]. In this paper, we are specifically interested in

© Springer Nature Switzerland AG 2020
D. Fahland et al. (Eds.): BPM 2020, LNCS 12168, pp. 237–256, 2020.
https://doi.org/10.1007/978-3-030-58666-9_14

the latter problem: given an ongoing process case (proxied by a prefix of a complete case), and an event log of completed cases for the same business process, we want to predict the most likely next event by determining both its label (i.e. the name of the next process activity to be performed) and its timestamp (i.e. when such activity will start or complete). This problem has been addressed in [1,2,12,18] using Recurrent Neural Networks (RNNs) with Long-Short-Term Memory (LSTM), while [16] uses Convolutional Neural Networks (CNNs) for predicting the next event label only.

Despite their popularity, deep learning methods such as LSTM or CNN, often feature thousands to millions of parameters to estimate, and for this reason require lots of labeled training data to be able to generalize well the dataset at hand, as well as to learn salient patterns [3]. In our context, this challenge is exacerbated by the limited size of real-life event logs available for training, compared to the number of parameters to be estimated. For example, an LSTM with one hidden layer containing 100 neurons has at least $4 \times (100+1)^2$ parameters to be estimated, which in turn requires at least the same number of unique training instances, i.e. the same number of unique process cases in the event log. This is hardly the case in practice, as event logs typically contain several thousand or (at best) several million complete cases, of which only a subset are unique.

Motivated by Generative Adversarial Nets (GANs) [4], this paper proposes a novel adversarial training framework to address the problem of next event prediction. The framework is based on the establishment of a *minmax game* between two players, each modeled via an RNN, such that each network's goal is to maximize its own outcome at the cost of minimizing the opponent's outcome. One network predicts the next event's label and timestamp, while the other network determines how realistic this prediction is. Training continues until the predictions are almost indistinguishable from the ground truth. During training, one player learns how to generate sequences of events close to the training sequences iteratively. Thus, it eliminates the need for a large set of ground truth sequences.

To the best of our knowledge, this is the first paper that adapts GANs to the realm of temporal sequential data, for predictive process monitoring. This approach comes with several advantages. First, we formally show that the training complexity of the proposed adversarial net is of the same order as that of a net obtained via conventional (i.e. non-adversarial) training. Second, we show that the worst-case accuracy of our approach is not lower than that obtained via conventional training, meaning that the approach never underperforms a conventional approach such as LSTM with the same architecture.

We instantiated our framework using a simple LSTM architecture for the two networks, and a naive one-hot encoding of the event labels in the log. Using this implementation, we evaluated the accuracy of our approach experimentally against three baselines targeted at the same prediction problem, using real-life event logs.

The rest of this paper is organized as follows. The background and related work are provided in Sect. 2. The presented approach is Sect. 3 while the evaluation is discussed in Sect. 4. Finally, Sect. 5 concludes the paper and discusses opportunities for future work.

2   Background and Related Work

In this section we provide background knowledge on machine learning with a focus on deep learning methods. Next, we discuss related work in predictive process monitoring, with a focus on next event prediction using deep learning.

2.1   Machine Learning and Deep Learning

The goal of *machine learning* is to develop methods that can automatically detect patterns in data, and these patterns to predict future data or other outcomes of interest under uncertainty [13]. Depending on the underlying mechanisms, the learning model can be labelled as *generative* or *discriminative*. The objective of a generative model is to generate new data instances according to the given training set. In detail, it learns a joint probability distribution over the input's features. The *naive Bayes* classifier is an example of generative models. In contrast, a discriminative model directly determines the label of an input instance by estimating a conditional probability for the labels given the input's features. *Logistic regression* is an example of discriminative models. Discriminative models can only be used in supervised learning tasks, whereas generative models are employed in both supervised and unsupervised settings [14]. Figure 1, sketches the differences between the mentioned approaches; A discriminative model learns a decision boundary that separates the classes whereas a generative model learns the distribution that governs input data in each class.

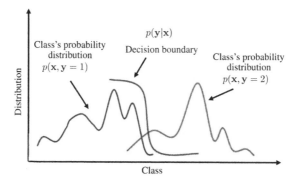

Fig. 1. Differences between a generative and discriminative approaches; $\mathbf{x}$ is the input's features, and $\mathbf{y}$ is the corresponding label

Deep Neural Networks (DNNs) are extremely powerful machine learning models that achieve excellent performance on difficult tasks such as speech recognition, machine translation, and visual object recognition [7,10,11]. DNNs aim at learning feature hierarchies at multiple levels of abstraction that allow a system to learn complex functions mapping the input to the output directly from data, without depending completely on human-crafted features. The learning process in a DNN equals to estimating its parameters, and one can do it via *Stochastic Gradient Descent (SGD)* or its modifications that are the dominant training algorithms for neural networks [3].

Recurrent Neural Networks (RNNs) are a family of DNNs with *cyclic* structures that make them suitable for processing sequential data [17]. RNNs exploit the notion of *parameter sharing* that employs a single set of parameters for different parts of a model. Therefore, the model can be applied to examples of different forms (different lengths) and generalize across them [6]. Such sharing is particularly important when a specific piece of information can occur at multiple positions within the input sequence. Two main issues in training an RNNs are *catasrophic forgetting*, i.e., the model forgets the learned patterns, and *optimization instability*, i.e., the optimization does not converge [3]. The first issue can be alleviated by invoking the *Long Short-Term Memory (LSTM)* architecture [8] which uses a few extra variables to control the information flow and thus causes the network to learn long-term patterns as well. The second issue can be mitigated by monitoring the gradient's norm of each parameter and scaling it down when it exceeds a threshold, a.k.a., *gradient clipping* [15].

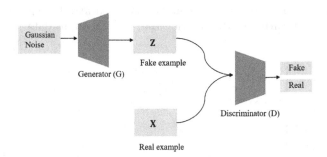

Fig. 2. Generative adversarial nets [4]; the generator produces fake examples from Gaussian noise, and the discriminator determines which of its input is real or fake.

Generative Adversarial Nets (GANs). [4] is a framework that employs two neural network models, called players, simultaneously, see Fig. 2. The two players correspond to a *generator* and a *discriminator*. The generator takes *Gaussian noise* to produce instances, i.e., *fake instances*, which are similar to input instances, i.e., *real instances*. The discriminator is a binary classifier such as logistic regression whose job is to distinguish real instances from generated instances, i.e., fake instances. The generator tries to create instances that are as realistic as possible; its job is to fool the discriminator, whereas the discriminator's job is to identify the fake instances irrespective of how well the generator tries to fool it. It is an adversarial game because each player wants to maximize its own outcome which results in minimization of the other player's outcome. The game finishes when the players reach to *Nash equilibrium* that determines the optimal solution. In the equilibrium point the discriminator is unable to distinguish between real and fake instances.

GANs provide enormous advantages compared to other strategies for training generative models. For instance, one can learn the input's joint probability even it is very sharp and degenerated, although, it needs accurate coordination of the players, i.e., neural nets, according to the problem at hand. Thus, depending on the input type, a GAN gives rise to a robust generative model that synthesizes high-quality images, texts, and sequences. Also, the GAN's discriminator can be viewed as a feature selection mechanism since it selects the most important features of its inputs to discriminate fake and real instances [5].

2.2 Predictive Process Monitoring of Next Event

This section reviews work on next event prediction using deep learning techniques. The interested reader can find an overview and comparative evaluation of different predictive process monitoring approaches in [19,21].

The work by Evermann et al. [2] uses the LSTM architecture for the next activity prediction of an ongoing trace, although the authors mention that one can predict other attributes such as the event's duration time. It uses embedding techniques to represent categorical variables by high dimensional continuous vectors; it uses a two hidden layer LSTMs with one hundred epochs, the input's dimension varies according to the embedding representation, ten-fold cross-validation, and dropout for each cell is 0.2.

Tax et al. [18] propose a similar architecture based on LSTMs. This work uses a one-hot vector encoding to represent categorical variables. Given an ongoing process execution, the approach predicts the next activity and its timestamp, and the remaining cycle time and suffix until the end of the process execution. Suffix prediction is made by next activity predictions iteratively. The proposed approach uses a variety of architectures. However, the best results are based on two hidden layers (shared and multi-task) LSTM with one hundred neurons in each layer for all the prediction tasks. Their results show that the proposed framework outperforms the technique in [2].

The work in [16] uses a Convolutional Neural Network (CNN) for the next activity prediction task in a running process execution. The authors propose a data engineering schema to represent the spatial structure in a running case like a two-dimensional image. In experiments the approach starts with a prefix of length one and increases the prefix length during the training until the best accuracy can be obtained on the validation set. They use three convolutional and max-pooling layers with 32, 64, and 128 filters, respectively. The experiments show an improvement over [2,18].

Camargo et al. [1] employ a composition of LSTMs and feedforward layers to predict the next activity and its timestamp and the remaining cycle time and suffix for a running case. The approach uses embedding techniques similar to [2] to learn continuous vectors for categorical variables and then use them for the prediction task via LSTMs. Similar to [18], different settings such as "specialized", "shared categorical", and "full shared" architectures are considered in the experiments. Also, different configurations are considered randomly from a full search space of 972 combinations. The experiments show improvements over [2,18], and for the next activity prediction task this approach sometimes outperforms that in [16].

Lin et al. [12] propose an encoder-decoder framework based on LSTMs to predict the next activity and the suffix of an ongoing case. Unlike the previous approaches, it uses all available information in input log, i.e., both control-flow and performance attributes, for the prediction tasks. Random embedding is used for each event and its attribute. The encoder maps an input sequence into a set of high dimensional vectors and the decoder returns it back into new sequence that can be used for the prediction tasks. The experimental setup of this approach is different from [1,2,16,18]. Specifically, while the previous approaches aim to fit a predictive model for each prefix length, [12] considers all possible prefix lengths at once during the training and testing phases.

3   Approach

The main aim of predictive process monitoring is to predict the corresponding attributes of ongoing process executions one or a few steps ahead of time. This paper, for an ongoing process execution (prefix), predicts an event's label and its timestamp one step ahead of time. To this end, we propose an adversarial framework inspired by GANs [4], which coordinates players, i.e., the generator, and discriminator, in a novel way for process mining context, see Fig. 3. It has two main parts, *data prepossessing*, and *adversarial predictive process monitoring net*. The first part prepares the input data in the form of prefixes for the prediction task, and adopts the required encoding to deal with categorical variables. It uses one-hot encoding to manifest the viability of the proposed adversarial net. The second part establishes a minmax game between generator and discriminator by proposing fake and real prefixes. Real prefixes are those in the training set, and fake prefixes are formed from the generator's output, i.e., predictions. The training runs as a game between two players, where the generator's goal is to maximize the accuracy of the prediction to fool the discriminator, and the discriminator's goal is to minimize its error in distinguishing real and fake prefixes, see flows (1), (2) in Fig. 3. It is an adversarial game since the generator and the discriminator compete with each other, i.e., learning from the opponent's mistake, see flows (1), (3) in Fig. 3. Thus maximizing one objective function minimizes the other one and vice versa.

The proposed adversarial net in this work has a number of major differences from the original GANs proposed by Goodfellow et al. [4], i.e., Vanilla GAN, which are the core contributions of this paper. In our work, both the discriminator and the generator are composed of RNNs (LSTM architecture) and feedforward neural networks, rather than only feedforward networks. This is due to the fact that we apply GANs for sequential temporal data that LSTMs have

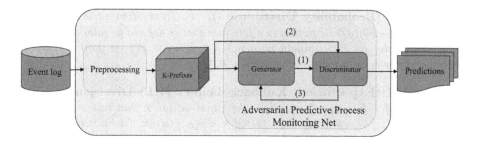

Fig. 3. Overall approach for next event prediction

been shown to perform well on [8]. Besides, the fake examples are formed by the generator's predictions and the input prefix; this is in contrast to Vanilla GAN that creates fake examples from Gaussian noise, see Fig. 2. In this way, one can adopt GAN-like frameworks to the wide range of process mining applications. Finally, the proposed framework guarantees that, in the worst case, the generator has performance as if it was trained conventionally, i.e., no adversarial game, thus, it reduces the effects of *mode collapse* in Vanilla GAN wherein the generator fails to model the distribution of the training data well enough, which in turn results in underfitting the input data and causes poor performance.

The rest of this section is organized as follows. First, the preliminary definitions are presented. Following that, we formalize the required data prepossessing. Next, RNNs training will be provided in detail, which will be used later in our framework. Finally, we give details of the adversarial predictive process monitoring net, including its training and optimization.

3.1 Preliminaries and Definitions

This section provides the required preliminaries and definitions for the formalization of the proposed approach.

Definition 1 (Vector). *A vector,* $\mathbf{x} = (x_1, x_2, \ldots, x_n)^T$, *is a column array of elements where the ith element is shown by* x_i. *If each element is in* $\mathbb{R}$ *and vector contains n elements, then the vector lies in* $\mathbb{R}^{n \times 1}$, *and the dimension of* $\mathbf{x}$, $dim(\mathbf{x})$, *is* $n \times 1$.

We represent a vector by a lowercase name in bold typeface. Beside, a set of d vectors as $\mathbf{x}^{(1)}, \mathbf{x}^{(2)}, \ldots, \mathbf{x}^{(d)}$, where $x^{(i)} \in \mathbb{R}^{n \times 1}$. Also, they can be represented by a matrix $\mathbf{M} = (\mathbf{x}^{(1)}, \mathbf{x}^{(2)}, \ldots, \mathbf{x}^{(d)})$ where $\mathbf{M} \in \mathbb{R}^{n \times d}$. We denote the *ith* row of a matrix by $\mathbf{M}_{i,:}$, and likewise the *ith* column by $\mathbf{M}_{:,i}$.

Definition 2 (Gradient). *For a function* $f(\mathbf{x})$ *with* $f : \mathbb{R}^n \to \mathbb{R}$, *the partial derivative* $\frac{\partial}{\partial x_i} f(\mathbf{x})$ *shows how f changes as only variable* x_i *increases at point* $\mathbf{x}$. *With that said, a vector containing all partial derivatives is called gradient, i.e.,* $\nabla_{\mathbf{x}} f(\mathbf{x}) = (\frac{\partial}{\partial x_1} f(\mathbf{x}), \frac{\partial}{\partial x_2} f(\mathbf{x}), \ldots, \frac{\partial}{\partial x_n} f(\mathbf{x}))^T$.

Definition 3 (Probability Distribution). *For a random variable (vector)* $\mathbf{x} \in \mathbb{R}^n$*, a probability distribution is a function that is defined as follow:* $p : \mathbb{R}^n \to [0,1]$*. Similarly, for two random variables* $\mathbf{x} \in \mathbb{R}^n, \mathbf{y} \in \mathbb{R}^m$*, a joint probability distribution is defined as:* $p : \mathbb{R}^n \times \mathbb{R}^m \to [0,1]$*.*

Definition 4 (Expectation, Kullback–Leibler (KL) Divergence). *The expectation of a function* $f(\mathbf{x})$ *where the input vector* $\mathbf{x}$ *that has a probability distribution* $p(\mathbf{x})$ *is defined as:* $\mathbb{E}_{\mathbf{x} \sim p}[f(\mathbf{x})] = \oint p(\mathbf{x})f(\mathbf{x})d\mathbf{x}$*. Given two probability distributions* $p_1()$ *and* $p_2()$*, KL divergence measures the dissimilarity between two distributions as follows:* $D_{KL}(p_1 \parallel p_2) = \mathbb{E}_{\mathbf{x} \sim p_1}[\log p_1(\mathbf{x}) - \log p_2(\mathbf{x})]$*.*

A similar concept to measure the dissimilarity between two distribution is the *cross-entropy* and defined as $H(p_1, p_2) = -\mathbb{E}_{\mathbf{x} \sim p_1}[\log p_2(\mathbf{x})]$.

Definition 5 (Event, Trace, Event Log). *An event is a tuple* $(a, c, t, (d_1, v_1),$ $\ldots, (d_m, v_m))$ *where* a *is the activity name (label),* c *is the case id,* t *is the timestamp, and* $(d_1, v_1) \ldots, (d_m, v_m)$ *(where* $m \geq 0$*) are the event attributes (properties) and their associated values. A trace is a non-empty sequence* $\sigma = \langle e_1, \ldots, e_n \rangle$ *of events such that* $\forall i, j \in \{1, \ldots, n\}$ $e_i.c = e_j.c$*. An event log* L *is a multiset* $\{\sigma_1, \ldots \sigma_n\}$ *of traces.*

A trace (process execution) also can be shown by a sequence of vectors, where a vector contains all or part of the information relating to an event, e.g., event's label and timestamp. Formally, $\sigma = \langle \mathbf{x}^{(1)}, \mathbf{x}^{(2)}, \ldots, \mathbf{x}^{(t)} \rangle$, where $\mathbf{x}^{(i)} \in \mathbb{R}^n$ is a vector, and the superscript shows the time-order upon which the events happened.

Definition 6 (k-Prefix (Shingle)). *Given a trace* $\sigma = \langle e_1, \ldots, e_n \rangle$*, a k-prefix is a non-empty sequence* $\langle e_i, e_{i+1}, \ldots, e_{i+k-1} \rangle$*, with* $i \in \{1, 2, \ldots, n - k + 1\}$*, which is obtained by sliding a window of size* k *from the left to the right of* σ*.*

The above definition, a.k.a. *k-gram*, holds when an input trace is shown by a sequence of vectors. For example, the set of 2-prefix for $\sigma = \langle \mathbf{x}^{(1)}, \mathbf{x}^{(2)}, \mathbf{x}^{(3)}, \mathbf{x}^{(4)} \rangle$, is $\{\langle \mathbf{x}^{(1)}, \mathbf{x}^{(2)} \rangle, \langle \mathbf{x}^{(2)}, \mathbf{x}^{(3)} \rangle, \langle \mathbf{x}^{(3)}, \mathbf{x}^{(4)} \rangle\}$.

3.2   Data Preprocessing

This section elaborates on preparing k-prefixes which constitute the training and test set. In detail, the approach in this paper learns a function that given a k-prefix, $\langle \mathbf{x}^{(1)}, \mathbf{x}^{(2)}, \ldots, \mathbf{x}^{(k)} \rangle$, returns a vector, $\mathbf{y}^{(k)}$, that can be viewed as the next attribute (property) prediction. For the sake of simplicity, we only predict the next *activity* and its *timestamp*, see Definition 5. For the timestamp attribute, we consider the relative time between activities, calculated as the time elapsed between the timestamp of one event and the event's timestamp that happened one step before. However, without loss of generality, one can include the prediction of other attributes.

There are several methods in literature to encode and represent categorical variables. Unlike the techniques in [1,2,12], which learn embedding representations for categorical variables, this paper, uses *one-hot encoding*. The reason to adopt this rudimentary encoding is to manifest that the viability of the presented approach owes to the adversarial architecture and not to the data engineering part. Indeed, one can integrate various embedding representations.

In a nutshell, the one-hot vector encoding of a categorical variable is a way to create a binary vector (except a single dimension which is one, the rest are zeros) for each value that it takes. Besides, we use $\langle EOS \rangle$ to denote the end of a trace. Formally:

Definition 7 (One-Hot Encoding). *Given a universal set of activity names $\mathcal{E}$, including $\langle EOS \rangle$, and trace σ, one-hot encoding is a function, $f(\sigma, \mathcal{E})$, that maps σ into a sequence of vectors $\langle \mathbf{x}^{(1)}, \mathbf{x}^{(2)}, \ldots, \mathbf{x}^{(|\sigma|)} \rangle$, where, $\mathbf{x}^{(i)} \in \{1\} \cup \{0\}^{\mathcal{E}-1}, \forall i \in \{1, 2, \ldots, |\sigma|\}$.*

For example, given $\mathcal{E} = \{a_1, a_2, a_3, a_4, a_5, \langle EOS \rangle\}$, and $\sigma = \langle a_1, a_3, a_4, \langle EOS \rangle \rangle$. The one-hot vector encoding of σ is the following sequence of vectors:

$$f(\sigma, \mathcal{E}) = \langle \underbrace{(1,0,0,0,0,0)}_{a_1}, \underbrace{(0,0,1,0,0,0)}_{a_3}, \underbrace{(0,0,0,1,0,0)}_{a_4}, \underbrace{(0,0,0,0,0,1)}_{\langle EOS \rangle} \rangle$$

Furthermore, if $\mathbf{x}^{(i)}$ shows the one-hot vector of e_i, then, one can *augment* the former with the other attributes of the latter. In this paper, as mentioned already, we augment one-hot vectors with the time elapsed between the timestamp of one event and the event's timestamp time that happened one step before.

Table 1. Preprocessing of input k-prefix

Input 3-prefix	$x^{(t)}$		$y^{(t)}$
	One-hot vector	Timestamp (s)	One-hot vector (next)
$\langle (a_1,$ 26/12/2019 00:30 AM),	$(1,0,0,0,0,0)$	0	$(0,0,1,0,0,0)$
$(a_3,$ 26/12/2019 01:02 AM),	$(0,0,1,0,0,0)$	1920	$(0,0,0,1,0,0)$
$(a_4,$ 26/12/2019 01:18 AM),	$(0,0,0,1,0,0)$	960	$(0,0,0,0,0,1)$
$(\langle EOS \rangle) \rangle$	$(0,0,0,0,0,1)$	0	*null*

For each k-prefix, $\langle \mathbf{x}^{(1)}, \mathbf{x}^{(2)}, \ldots, \mathbf{x}^{(k)} \rangle$, we couple another k-prefix $\langle \mathbf{y}^{(1)}, \mathbf{y}^{(2)}, \ldots, \mathbf{y}^{(k)} \rangle$, where $\mathbf{y}^{(t)}, \forall t \in \{1, 2, \ldots, k\}$, is the next ground truth vector after visiting $\mathbf{x}^{(t)}$. It is worth noting that, $\mathbf{x}^{(t)}$ and $\mathbf{y}^{(t)}$ might have different dimensions. For example, the former can be a one-hot vector, whereas the latter refers to the next activity's timestamp, which is scalar. A set of such paired k-prefixes is considered for training and test set. For the above example, Table 1 shows the augmented vectors, i.e., $\mathbf{x}^{(t)}$, containing one-hot vectors and non-standardized events timestamps, as well as the respective next attribute, i.e., $\mathbf{y}^{(t)}$. The last row shows the end of prefix which is discarded for the since it does not provide useful information.

3.3   Training Recurrent Neural Networks

This section provides the training of RNNs in detail, which we will use it later in our proposed framework. For the ease of exposition, we present the training for the traditional RNN [17], although, the concepts hold for any RNN architectures such as LSTM.

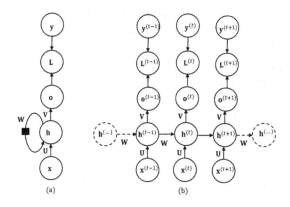

(a)   (b)

Fig. 4. (a) An RNN, (b) Time-unfolding of an RNN architecture

Given a sequence of inputs $\langle \mathbf{x}^{(1)}, \mathbf{x}^{(2)}, \ldots, \mathbf{x}^{(k)} \rangle$, an RNN computes sequence of outputs $\langle \mathbf{o}^{(1)}, \mathbf{o}^{(2)}, \ldots, \mathbf{o}^{(k)} \rangle$ via the following recurrent equations:

$$\mathbf{o}^{(t)} = \phi_o(\mathbf{V}^T \mathbf{h}^{(t)} + \mathbf{b}), \quad \mathbf{h}^{(t)} = \phi_h(\mathbf{W}^T \mathbf{h}^{(t-1)} + \mathbf{U}^T \mathbf{x}^{(t)} + \mathbf{c}), \quad \forall t \in \{1, 2, \ldots, k\} \quad (1)$$

where $\mathbf{o}^{(t)}$ is the RNN's prediction for ground truth vector $\mathbf{y}^{(t)}$; ϕ_h and ϕ_o are nonlinear element-wise functions, and the set $\theta = \{\mathbf{W}, \mathbf{U}, \mathbf{V}, \mathbf{c}, \mathbf{b}\}$, is the network's parameters. An RNN's architecture, and its time-unfolded graph are shown in Fig. 4 (a) and (b) respectively, where we hide vectors $\mathbf{c}$, $\mathbf{b}$, and functions ϕ_h, ϕ_o for the purpose of transparency.

One can estimate (learn) an RNN's parameters, i.e., θ, via the *maximum likelihood principle*, in which θ is estimated to maximize the likelihood of training instances. This way, an RNN is trained to estimate the conditional distribution of the next vector's attribute, $\mathbf{y}^{(t)}$, given the past input, $\mathbf{x}^{(1)}, \mathbf{x}^{(2)}, \ldots, \mathbf{x}^{(t)}$. In detail, to estimate θ, one minimizes the following loss function:

$$J(\theta) = \sum_{t=1}^{k} L^{(t)}, \quad \text{where} \quad L^{(t)} = -\log p_m(\mathbf{y}^{(t)} | \mathbf{x}^{(1)}, \mathbf{x}^{(2)}, \ldots, \mathbf{x}^{(t)}) \quad (2)$$

where p_m, gives the likelihood (probability) that the RNN generates the ground truth vectors. Besides, $L^{(t)}$, boils down to the cross-entropy between $softmax(\mathbf{o}^{(t)})$ and $\mathbf{y}^{(t)}$ whenever the latter is a one-hot vector, and it becomes $\| \mathbf{y}^{(t)} - \mathbf{o}^{(t)} \|_2$, a.k.a., Mean Square Error (MSE), for a continues ground truth vector. Finally, in an iterative way, the network's parameters are updated via SGD algorithm, wherein, the gradient of $J(\theta)$, i.e., $\nabla_\theta J$, is computed by *back-propagation through time (BPTT)* [17].

One can see that training an RNN or an LSTM in this way gives rise to a discriminative model, see Eq. 2 and Fig. 1. However, according to the *Bayes' theorem* the estimated conditional distribution in Eq. 2 is proportional to the joint probability distribution, i.e., $p_m(\mathbf{y}^{(k)}|\mathbf{x}^{(1)}, \mathbf{x}^{(2)}, \dots, \mathbf{x}^{(k)}) \propto p_m(\mathbf{x}^{(1)}, \mathbf{x}^{(2)}, \dots, \mathbf{x}^{(k)}, \mathbf{y}^{(k)})$. Thus, one can consider LSTMs or RNNs as generative models by using the learned distribution p_m which is an approximation to the input's ground truth joint distribution p_d. We will exploit this issue in our proposed framework.

3.4 Adversarial Predictive Process Monitoring Nets

This section presents the core contribution of this paper by proposing an adversarial process to estimate a generative model for the predictive process monitoring tasks. The proposed framework is inspired by the seminal work in [4], i.e., Vanilla GAN, which has been used for synthesizing images. However, our proposed adversarial net is devised to work with time-series data, including categorical and continuous variables; Therefore, it is fully adaptable to a wide range of process mining applications.

In the proposed adversarial architecture, shown in Fig. 5, both the generator and the discriminator are LSTMs, as explained in Sect. 3.3, and are denoted by $G(;\theta_g)$, and $D(;\theta_d)$ respectively. Precisely, the output of G is a sequence, however, the last prediction is of our concern. D is equipped with an extra dense feedforward layer which assigns a probability to its input as a real prefix. The networks' parameters are denoted by θ_g and θ_d, which are adjusted during training.

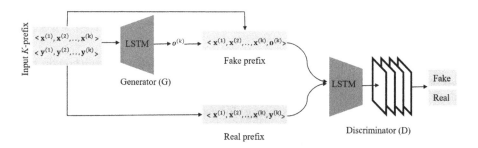

Fig. 5. Proposed GAN architecture for predicting next attributes

The generator in Fig. 5 given a k-prefix $\langle \mathbf{x}^{(1)}, \mathbf{x}^{(2)}, \dots, \mathbf{x}^{(k)} \rangle$ and its ground truth $\langle \mathbf{y}^{(1)}, \mathbf{y}^{(2)}, \dots, \mathbf{y}^{(k)} \rangle$, generates sequence $\langle \mathbf{o}^{(1)}, \mathbf{o}^{(2)}, \dots, \mathbf{o}^{(k)} \rangle$ according to Eq. 1. Thus, we want the G's last prediction, $\mathbf{o}^{(k)}$, to be as close as possible to ground truth $\mathbf{y}^{(k)}$, such that, D gets confused in discriminating $\mathbf{o}^{(k)}$ and $\mathbf{y}^{(k)}$. To make this more concrete we define the followings *fake* and *real* prefixes.

$$\mathbf{X}^{(k)} = \underbrace{\langle \mathbf{x}^{(1)}, \mathbf{x}^{(2)}, \dots, \mathbf{x}^{(k)}, \mathbf{y}^{(k)} \rangle}_{\text{Real prefix}}, \quad \mathbf{Z}^{(k)} = \underbrace{\langle \mathbf{x}^{(1)}, \mathbf{x}^{(2)}, \dots, \mathbf{x}^{(k)}, \mathbf{o}^{(k)} \rangle}_{\text{Fake prefix}} \quad (3)$$

Where $\mathbf{X}^{(k)}$ and $\mathbf{Z}^{(k)}$ are sampled from p_d and p_m distributions respectively, and differ only in their the last elements. Thus, the minmax game, as an optimization, is as follow:

$$\arg \min_G \max_D = \mathbb{E}_{\mathbf{X}^{(k)} \sim p_d} [\log \underbrace{D(\mathbf{X}^{(k)})}_{(a)}] + \mathbb{E}_{\mathbf{Z}^{(k)} \sim p_m} [\log \underbrace{(1 - D(\mathbf{Z}^{(k)}))}_{(b)}] \quad (4)$$

Equation 4 drives D to maximize the probability of assigning $\mathbf{X}^{(k)}$ to a real prefix, see (a), and assigning $\mathbf{Z}^{(k)}$ to a fake prefix, see (b). Simultaneously, it drives G in generating fake prefixes, i.e., $\mathbf{Z}^{(k)}$s, to fool D into believing its prefixes are real. In short, G minimizes the cross-entropy between the ground truths and its predictions. Hence, the training procedure is presented in Algorithm 1.

Algorithm 1. Stochastic gradient descent training of the proposed adversarial net

---

1: **for** number of epochs **do**   ▷ Number of training iterations
2:    **for** each $\langle \mathbf{x}^{(1)}, \mathbf{x}^{(2)}, \dots, \mathbf{x}^{(k)} \rangle$ **do**   ▷ A k-prefix
3:       ●Generate $\langle \mathbf{o}^{(1)}, \mathbf{o}^{(2)}, \dots, \mathbf{o}^{(k)} \rangle$ using G via Eq. 1
4:       ●Create fake and real prefixes, i.e., $\mathbf{Z}^{(k)}$ and $\mathbf{X}^{(k)}$, according to Eq. 3
5:       ●Update the discriminator, D, by *ascending* its gradient:
$$\theta_d \leftarrow \theta_d + \epsilon \left(\nabla_{\theta_d} [\log D(\mathbf{X}^{(k)}) + \log(1 - D(\mathbf{Z}^{(k)}))] \right)$$
6:       ●Update the generator, G, by *descending* its gradient:
$$\theta_g \leftarrow \theta_g - \epsilon \left(\nabla_{\theta_g} [\log(1 - D(\mathbf{Z}^{(k)})) + J(\theta_g)] \right)$$
7:    **end for**
8: **end for**

Algorithm 1 computes gradients for all prefixes in each epoch, although, one can use batches to speed up training time as well. Besides, the learning rate, i.e., ϵ, can be different for G and D. Line 5 shows that the parameters of the discriminator, i.e., θ_d, are updated (maximizing) for each pair of real and fake prefixes by ascending the gradient of mistakes. Next, in line 6, we update (minimizing) the parameters of the generator, i.e., θ_g, by descending the gradients of two terms. In the fist term, the generator exploits the discriminator's mistake in determining a fake prefix, i.e., $\mathbf{Z}^{(k)}$, to update its parameters (see flow (3) in Fig. 3). This way, the generator learns how to fool the discriminator in the next iterations by generating more realistic prefixes. The second term is the loss function as defined in Eq. 2. We incorporated this term because in some situations the D's mistake for a fake prefix, i.e., $\log(1 - D(\mathbf{Z}^{(k)}))$, does not provide sufficient gradient for G to update its weight. It happens at the beginning of training, when D easily discriminates fake and real prefixes, e.g., $\log(1 - D(\mathbf{Z}^{(k)})) = \log(1-0) = 0$, thus, adding $J(\theta_g)$ facilitates the generator's learning process.

Convergence: At equilibrium, the generator's prefixes, i.e., fake prefixes, are indistinguishable from real prefixes, and it means that the generator has learnt the input data distribution, i.e., p_d. Thereby, its predictions must be enough close to ground truths. However, learning in GANs is a difficult task, since the minmax game in Eq. 4, in general, is not a *convex* function, thus, no global optimum solution is guaranteed to obtain. In addition, in a minmax game where each player reducing their own cost at the expense of the other player, reaching *Nash equilibrium* is not guaranteed. Consequently, either of the mentioned issues causes GANs to underfit the input's data distribution which give rises to poor results [4]. Algorithm 1 alleviates the mentioned issues by invoking $J(\theta_g)$ during training. Thus, in the worst case, the generator's ability to capture p_d for the prediction task is lower bounded as if it was trained conventionally, i.e., no adversarial process.

Complexity: The complexity of Algorithm 1 boils down to computing gradients for the generator and the discriminator. In detail, for a k-prefix $\langle \mathbf{x}^{(1)}, \mathbf{x}^{(2)}, \ldots, \mathbf{x}^{(k)} \rangle$ that is paired with $\langle \mathbf{y}^{(1)}, \mathbf{y}^{(2)}, \ldots, \mathbf{y}^{(k)} \rangle$, suppose that $\mathbf{x}^{(t)}, \mathbf{y}^{(t)} \in \mathbb{R}^m$, $\forall t \in \{1, 2, \ldots, k\}$, and $\mathbf{U}, \mathbf{W}, \mathbf{V} \in \mathbb{R}^{m \times m}$. Therefore, to compute gradients of an RNN (or an LSTM architecture), one must do a forward propagation pass from left to right of the time-unfolded graph to generate $\langle \mathbf{o}^{(1)}, \mathbf{o}^{(2)}, \ldots, \mathbf{o}^{(k)} \rangle$ and to compute $J()$, see Fig. 4 (b). Following that, a backward propagation pass moving right to left through the time-unfolded graph for computing gradients. In summary, either a forward or a backward pass requires $O(km^2)$ operations [22]. Thus, for a training set containing n k-prefixes, $O(knm^2)$ operations are required in each iteration. Thereby, the proposed adversarial net's complexity is of the same order as conventional training, i.e., no minmax game. Besides, it is noteworthy that the updates of the discriminator and the generator, i.e., lines 5 and 6, can be done in parallel after creating $\mathbf{Z}^{(k)}$ and $\mathbf{X}^{(k)}$.

4   Evaluation

We implemented our approach in Python 3.6 via PyTorch 1.2.0 and used this prototype tool to evaluate the approach over four real-life event logs, against three baselines [1,16,18]. The choice of the baselines was determined by the availability of a working tool, either publicly or via the authors. For this reason, we excluded from the experiment the work by Lin et al. [12], whose tool we were not able to obtain. Moreover, the work by Evermann et al. [2] was excluded as Tax et al. [18] have already shown to outperform this approach.

The experiments were run on an Intel Core i8 CPU with 2.7 GHz, 64GB RAM, running MS Windows 10. The reason to use CPU rather than GPU is that the baselines were designed for CPU execution. However, our implantation also allows one to train discriminator and generator on separate GPUs. Running of CPU instead of GPU only affects performance, not accuracy.

4.1 Experimental Setup

Datasets: The experiments were conducted using four publicly-available real-life logs obtained from the 4TU Centre for Research Data.[1] Table 2 shows the characteristics of these logs while the description of the process covered is provided below.

- **Helpdesk:** It contains traces from a ticketing management process of the help desk of an Italian software company.
- **BPI12:** It contains traces from an application process for a personal loan or overdraft within a global financing organization. This process contains three sub-processes from which one of them is denoted as W and used already in [1,2,18]. As such, we extract two logs from this dataset: BPI12 and BPI12(W).
- **BPI17:** It contains traces for a loan application process of a Dutch financial institute. The data contains all applications filed through an online system in 2016 and their subsequent events until February 1st 2017.

Table 2. Descriptive statistics of the datasets ($|\sigma|$ is the trace length, Δt is the time difference between two consecutive event timestamps)

Log	Traces	Events	Labels	Max $|\sigma|$	Min $|\sigma|$	Avg $|\sigma|$	Avg Δt, days	St Dev(Δt), days
Helpdesk	3,804	13,710	9	14	1	3.60	3.379	6.613
BPI12	13,087	262,200	23	175	3	20.03	0.453	1.719
BPI12(W)	9,658	72,413	6	74	1	7.49	1.754	3.075
BPI17	31,509	1,202,267	26	180	10	38.15	0.588	3.211

All the above logs feature event attributes capturing process resources. This information is used by the baseline in [1] to extract extra signal for training.

Evaluation Measures: For consistency, we reuse the same evaluation measures adopted in the baselines. Specifically, to measure the accuracy of predicting the next event's label, we use the fraction of correct predictions over the total number of predictions. For the timestamp prediction, we report Mean Absolute Error (MAE), that is the average of absolute value between predictions and ground truths.

Training Setting: For both generator and discriminator we use a two layer LSTM. In addition, the discriminator is equipped with a dense layer for the binary classification task. In detail:

- We use 25 epochs and split the data into 80%–20% for training and testing respectively, by preserving the temporal order between cases. However, early stopping is used to avoid over-training. In addition, we use a batch of size five to speed up the training procedure.

---

[1] https://data.4tu.nl/repository/collection:event_logs_real.

- For each log, we consider different prefix lengths to be used for the prediction task, i.e., k-prefixes, where $k \in \{2, 4, 6, 8, 10, 15, 20, 25, 30, 35, 40, 45, 50\}$, provided such k-lengths exist in the log. In detail, we train the proposed framework for each k-length case prefix and report the value of prediction accuracy and MAE, for that k. In this way, we can also observe the *earliness* of a prediction, i.e. see how the predictions accuracy and MAE evolve over the prefix length. This experimental setup is in-line with that of [1,2,16,18]. Moreover, since the training and test set size varies for each prefix, we report the weighted average over all k-lengths for both accuracy and MAE.
- For each LSTM, we dynamically adjust the size of hidden units in each layer, and it is twice the input's size. For example if the augmented vectors dimension is 10, then each layer has 2×10 hidden units.
- *Adaptive Moment Estimation (ADAM)* is used as an optimization algorithm for both generator and discriminator. It accelerates the learning procedure by mitigating the effects of highly curvature search space [9]. The learning rate, i.e., ϵ, was set to 0.0002 for both LSTMs to avoid gradient explosion during the training. In addition, we applied gradient clipping [15] to scale down the gradient of each layer in every iteration. More specifically, let us use $\mathbf{g}$ to denote the gradient vector of a layer. Then, if $\frac{\|\mathbf{g}\|_2}{|\text{batch}|} > 10$, we scale the gradient as $\mathbf{g} = \frac{10\mathbf{g}}{\|\mathbf{g}\|_2}$. The threshold value of 10, only affects the learning speed and does not alter the learning outcome [15].

For the baselines, we used the best parameter settings, as discussed in the respective papers, or provided by the authors. These settings are provided in our tool distribution.

Table 3. Weighted average accuracy for next label prediction, and Weighted average MAE for next timestamp prediction

Approach	Weighted average accuracy				Weighted average MAE (days)			
	Helpdesk	BPI12(W)	BPI12	BPI17	Helpdesk	BPI12(W)	BPI12	BPI17
Ours	**0.9518**	**0.9158**	**0.9401**	**0.9256**	**0.8621**	**0.6528**	**0.3471**	0.4225
Tax et al. [18]	0.7419	0.7077	0.7495	**0.8941**	3.660	1.5530	0.3716	0.5026
Camargo et al. [1]	0.7384	0.7543	0.7182	0.8568	2.8996	1.8405	0.5201	**0.3646**
Pasquadibisceglie et al. [16]	0.7677	0.7734	0.7424	0.8676	–	–	–	–

4.2   Results

Next Label Prediction: The second to fifth column of Table 3 show the weighted average accuracy of our approach and of the baselines, for each of the four logs. We can see that our approach provides a considerably more accurate overall prediction compared to the baselines for each dataset. In Fig. 6 we break this result for each k-prefix length, per log. From these charts we can draw several observations. First, our approach has an accuracy that is systematically higher than that of each baseline, at any given prefix length, obtaining

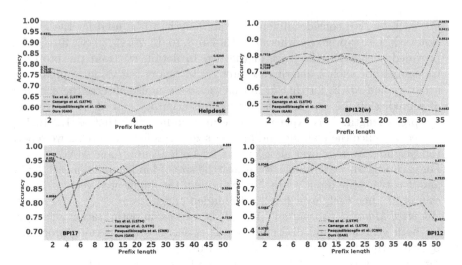

Fig. 6. Accuracy of next event label prediction on the test set for different k-prefixes, $k \in \{2, 4, \ldots, 50\}$; Our approach vs. baselines

at least 98% accuracy for all logs at the longest considered prefix length. This is achieved by using a naive feature encoding (one-hot vector) of event labels, without extracting features from further event attributes such as resources. Second, the accuracy monotonically increases (though not strictly) with the length of the prefix. In contrast, the baselines exhibit fluctuations in accuracy as the length of the prefix increases. This is mainly due to the way a neural network is trained, and secondly, to the number of training examples (sequences of events in our case) used. In detail, our approach trains a neural network via a minmax game (adversarial) in addition to the conventional training, which allows us to obtain better generalization of the datasets at hand. Above that, the proposed approach is much less sensitive to the number of training sequences since the generator learns the input's distribution, through which it can then generate training sequences close to ground truth ones, thus eliminating the need for a large training data. The lack of sufficient training data severely impacts the baselines. For example, [1] loses accuracy faster than the other baselines as the prefix length increases. This is most likely because this approach extracts features from process resource, besides event labels and timestamps, and as such it requires a much larger training data for a larger number of parameters.

Next Timestamp Prediction: The last four columns in Table 3 show the weighted average MAE in days, for each log and for each approach, except [16] as it does not support timestamp prediction. The detailed MAE for each prefix length in provided in Fig. 7. The results are consistent with those for next event label prediction, in terms of accuracy (lower error), earliness and stability. Specifically, from the charts we can see that for nearly all prefixes, our approach outperforms the baselines, except for $k = 2$ in BPI12, BPI12(W) and for $k = 2$–

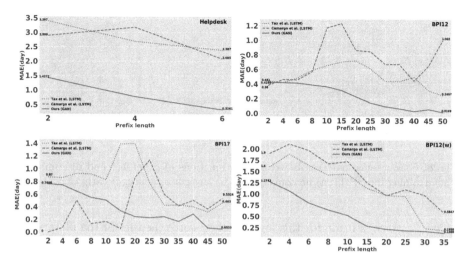

Fig. 7. MAE of next event timestamp prediction on the test set for different k-prefixes, $k \in \{2, 4, \ldots, 50\}$; Our approach vs. baselines

15 in BPI17, where [1] provides slightly better MAE. For the BPI12 log, our approach reaches an MAE of 0.0169 at the longest prefix length, while the best result, achieved by [18] is 0.2457 (14 times higher). Given that MAE is measured as number of days, this means that there is an error of 14 days in the timestamp prediction. Looking at the weighted average MAE, we can observe the most significant improvements in the Helpdesk log, where our approach achieves up to 4 times lower MAE than the baselines.

The higher MAE values of [1] for certain prefix lengths, especially in the BPI17 log, are attributable to the use of resources in the log, and are in-line with the aggregate results in Table 3, where [1] outperforms our approach for the weighted average MAE in BPI17 (0.3646 instead of 0.4225). To confirm this intuition, we re-executed the experiment without using resources (we note that [1] is the only baseline that extracts features from resources) and the accuracy obtained was lower (e.g. for BPI17, [1] obtains a weighted average MAE of 0.5537 instead of 0.3646).

In terms of stability, we can see that while we do not achieve monotonicity as in the case of next label prediction, the amplitude of the fluctuations of MAE in our approach is very small across all logs, with a clear downward trend as prefix length increases.

Behavior of the Convergence: We concluded our experiment by studying the convergence behavior of the generator and the discriminator while performing the minmax game in Algorithm 1. We provide three patterns that we observed in our experiments, as shown in Fig. 8, which plots the loss function of generator and discriminator. The patterns are the same for all datasets. As an example, we explain the pattern for the BPI17 log. Figure 8 (a) is an example where

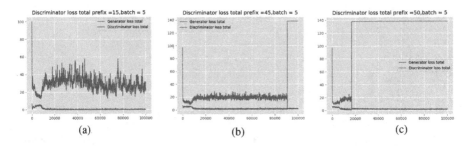

Fig. 8. Convergence patterns based on loss functions of generator and discriminator when training for BPI17: a) no convergence; b) late convergence; c) early Convergence

no convergence is made for this log. In other words, neither of the players can overcome the other. In this situation, the training continues with conventional training, as one can see from Fig. 6 where our accuracy for BPI17 and for $k = 15$ is slightly better than that in [18]. In contrast, Fig. 8 (b) and (c) are examples of late, respectively, early convergence. Here the generator exploits the adversarial game since, after many iterations, it fools the discriminator as the discriminator's loss function increases significantly, and the generator's loss function drops. In such situations, the generator has learned the input's distribution correctly. Thus, the discriminator makes mistakes in distinguishing the ground truth from the generator's predictions. The effect of this gain can be seen in Fig. 6 for BPI17 at $k = 45$ or 50, where our approach outperforms the baselines by far.

5 Conclusion

This paper put forward a novel adversarial framework for the prediction of next event label and timestamp, by adapting Generative Adversarial Nets to the realm of sequential temporal data. The training is achieved via a competition between two neural networks playing a minmax game. The generator maximizes its performance in providing accurate predictions, while the discriminator minimizes its error in determining which of the generator's outputs are ground-truth sequences. At convergence, the generator confuses the discriminator in its task. The training complexity of the proposed framework is of the same order as that of conventional training, and more importantly, we showed, both formally and empirically, that given the same network's architecture, our minmax training outperforms a network trained in conventional settings.

The results of the experimental evaluation highlight the merits of our approach, which systematically outperforms all the baselines, both in terms of accuracy and earliness. The results also show that the behavior of our approach is more robust as it does not suffer from accuracy fluctuations over the prefix length. This in turn confirms the generator's ability to learn the input distribution for generating predictions close to the ground truth, eliminating the need for a large number of training instances.

The experimental setting is limited to four (real-life) logs and three baselines. More extensive experiments should be conducted to confirm the results of this study. A further avenue for future work is to investigate alternative architectures within the proposed adversarial framework, to deal with other prediction problems such as case outcome or remaining time. More broadly, our adaptation of GANs to sequential temporal data lends itself well to various applications in process mining. For example, we foresee its use for variant analysis, automated process discovery, alignment computation in conformance checking, and process drift detection. We plan to investigate some of these opportunities in the future.

Reproducibility. The source code of our tool as well as the parameter settings used in our approach and in the baselines, in order to reproduce the experiments, can be found at https://github.com/farbodtaymouri/GanPredictiveMonitoring. This link also provides detailed experiment results.

Acknowledgments. We thank Manuel Camargo and Vincenzo Pasquadibisceglie for providing access and instructions to use their tools. This research is partly funded by the Australian Research Council (DP180102839).

References

1. Camargo, M., Dumas, M., González-Rojas, O.: Learning accurate LSTM models of business processes. In: Hildebrandt, T., van Dongen, B.F., Röglinger, M., Mendling, J. (eds.) BPM 2019. LNCS, vol. 11675, pp. 286–302. Springer, Cham (2019). https://doi.org/10.1007/978-3-030-26619-6_19
2. Evermann, J., Rehse, J.-R., Fettke, P.: Predicting process behaviour using deep learning. Decis. Supp. Syst. **100**, 129–140 (2017)
3. Goodfellow, I., Bengio, Y., Courville, A.: Deep Learning. MIT Press, Cambridge (2016)
4. Goodfellow, I., et al.: Generative adversarial nets. In: Proceedings of NIPS. ACM (2014)
5. Goodfellow, I.J.: Nips 2016 tutorial: generative adversarial networks. ArXiv (2017)
6. Goodfellow, I.J., Mirza, M., Da, X., Courville, A.C., Bengio, Y.: An empirical investigation of catastrophic forgetting in gradient-based neural networks. CoRR (2013)
7. Hinton, G.E., et al.: Deep neural networks for acoustic modeling in speech recognition. IEEE Sig. Process. Mag. **29**, 82–97 (2012)
8. Hochreiter, S., Schmidhuber, J.: Long short-term memory. Neural Comput. **9**, 1735–1780 (1997)
9. Kingma, D.P., Ba, J.: Adam: a method for stochastic optimization. CoRR (2014)
10. Krizhevsky, A., Sutskever, I., Hinton, G.E.: Imagenet classification with deep convolutional neural networks. In: Proceedings of NIPS. ACM (2012)
11. LeCun, Y., Bottou, L., Bengio, Y., Haffner, P.: Gradient-based learning applied to document recognition. In Proceedings of the IEEE. IEEE (1998)
12. Lin, L., Wen, L., Wang, J.: Mm-pred: a deep predictive model for multi-attribute event sequence. In: Proceedings of SDM. SIAM (2019)
13. Murphy, K.P.: Machine Learning - A Probabilistic Perspective. The MIT Press, Cambridge (2012)

14. Ng, A.Y., Jordan, M.I.: On discriminative vs. generative classifiers: a comparison of logistic regression and Naive Bayes. In: Proceedings of NIPS. ACM (2001)
15. Pascanu, R., Mikolov, T., Bengio, Y.: On the difficulty of training recurrent neural networks. In: Proceedings of ICML. ACM (2012)
16. Pasquadibisceglie, V., Appice, A., Castellano, G., Malerba, D.: Using convolutional neural networks for predictive process analytics. In: Proceedings of ICPM. IEEE (2019)
17. Rumelhart, D.E., Hinton, G.E., Williams, R.J.: Learning representations by back-propagating errors. Nature **323**, 533–536 (1986)
18. Tax, N., Verenich, I., La Rosa, M., Dumas, M.: Predictive business process monitoring with LSTM neural networks. In: Dubois, E., Pohl, K. (eds.) CAiSE 2017. LNCS, vol. 10253, pp. 477–492. Springer, Cham (2017). https://doi.org/10.1007/978-3-319-59536-8_30
19. Teinemaa, I., Dumas, M., La Rosa, M., Maggi, F.M.: Outcome-oriented predictive process monitoring: review and benchmark. TKDD **13**(2), 1–57 (2019)
20. Teinemaa, I., Dumas, M., Leontjeva, A., Maggi, F.M.: Temporal stability in predictive process monitoring. Data Min. Knowl. Discov. **32**(5), 1306–1338 (2018). https://doi.org/10.1007/s10618-018-0575-9
21. Verenich, I., Dumas, M., La Rosa, M., Maggi, F.M., Teinemaa, I.: Survey and cross-benchmark comparison of remaining time prediction methods in business process monitoring. ACM TIST **10**(4), 1–34 (2019)
22. Williams, R.J., Zipser, D.: Gradient-based learning algorithms for recurrent networks and their computational complexity (1995)

Exploring Interpretable Predictive Models for Business Processes

Renuka Sindhgatta[(✉)], Catarina Moreira, Chun Ouyang, and Alistair Barros

Queensland University of Technology, Brisbane, Australia
{renuka.sr,catarina.pintomoreira,c.ouyang,alistair.barros}@qut.edu.au

Abstract. There has been a growing interest in the literature on the application of deep learning models for predicting business process behaviour, such as the next event in a case, the time for completion of an event, and the remaining execution trace of a case. Although these models provide high levels of accuracy, their sophisticated internal representations provide little or no understanding about the reason for a particular prediction, resulting in them being used as black-boxes. Consequently, an interpretable model is necessary to enable transparency and empower users to evaluate when and how much they can rely on the models. This paper explores an interpretable and accurate attention-based Long Short Term Memory (LSTM) model for predicting business process behaviour. The interpretable model provides insights into the model inputs influencing a prediction, thus facilitating transparency. An experimental evaluation shows that the proposed model capable of supporting interpretability also provides accurate predictions when compared to existing LSTM models for predicting process behaviour. The evaluation further shows that attention mechanisms in LSTM provide a sound approach to generate meaningful interpretations across different tasks in predictive process analytics.

Keywords: Interpretable models · Attention-based neural networks · Predictive process models

1 Introduction

Recurrent neural networks (RNNs) have been successful in tasks that require the processing of sequential data where, predicting the next output depends on an input sequence, such as language modelling, speech recognition or time series prediction [18]. RNNs and their variants such as Long short term memory networks (LSTM) have naturally found applicability in predictive process analytics by modelling the sequential business process execution data to predict the next event in a case, remaining execution time of a running case, and remaining sequence of events [1,3,7,15,16]. Accuracy has been a dominant criterion when choosing deep learning models (such as RNNs) for predictive process analytics. The use of these sophisticated models however, comes at the cost of the models being used as 'black boxes'; i.e. they are unable to provide insights into why a

© Springer Nature Switzerland AG 2020
D. Fahland et al. (Eds.): BPM 2020, LNCS 12168, pp. 257–272, 2020.
https://doi.org/10.1007/978-3-030-58666-9_15

certain decision or prediction was drawn. Consequently, it is hard for users to understand the rationale of the black-box machinery when using predictions of the model for decision support. The opaqueness of these models often leads to lack of trust and impedes their adoption in sensitive domains such as insurance, healthcare, or law.

Recent literature has emphasised the need to understand and trust predictions from machine learning models coupled with a clear understanding of the behaviour of predictive models [13]. In parallel, there has been an increasing interest in the research community on *interpretable* or *explainable* machine learning [5]. Interpretability or explainability has not been addressed thus far in the context of predicting business process behavior when using deep learning techniques. We aim to address this gap in our work by building an attention-based LSTM model that provides insights into the important features influencing the prediction. Given an incomplete prefix representing a running case, the proposed model predicting the next activity can provide intuitive information on specific step or index in the sequence of events that influenced the prediction. For example, given a sequence of events, the model interpretation can reveal the influence of the last event or the first event on the prediction of next activity. In addition, it can reveal which attribute of an event (activity, role of a resource, or time) influenced the prediction. As a result, we present an approach to address the 'black-box' limitation using a two-level neural attention model that provides transparency of the relevant features influencing the prediction results while retaining the prediction accuracy compared to existing work on predicting business process behaviour using deep learning models. Hence, the paper makes the following contributions:

- proposes a model that facilitates interpretability in the context of predicting business process behaviour.
- presents experimental evaluation of the proposed approach and compares it to existing baselines thus addressing accuracy and interpretability.

The paper is organised as follows. A brief overview of previous studies using deep learning techniques to predict process behaviour is presented along with an introduction to the background topics such as interpretability and explainability (Sect. 2). The details of our approach to building interpretable machine learning models is presented in Sect. 3. The evaluation of the approach and the discussions on real-world event logs is presented in Sect. 4. Finally, we summarise the contributions of our work and outline future work (Sect. 5).

2 Related Work and Background

2.1 Related Work

The use of deep learning techniques in the form of RNNs and its variants for predicting process behaviour has been addressed in the literature. Layers of stacked LSTM have been used to predict next activity of an ongoing case and the time of a case until completion (or remaining time) [15,16]. The input to the model is a sequence of prior events. Each event is encoded to a feature representing the activity of the event as a one-hot vector, and additional dimensions representing the timestamp of the event. The architecture comprises a number of shared LSTM layers, and independent LSTM layers. The number of shared and independent layers are configured to achieve the best performance in terms of the accuracy of predicting the next activity and mean absolute error in predicting the time of the next event. The remaining sequence of events (suffix) of a running case is generated by iteratively predicting the next event until the end event is predicted.

Evermann et al. [3] proposed a deep learning model with two layers of stacked LSTM to predict the next event of an ongoing case. The categorical attributes of the event such as activity and resource information are transformed to n-dimensional vector or *embedding*. The effect of the dimensionality of embedding and the length of the input sequence on accuracy of the predictions are evaluated. This study acknowledges the limitation of interpreting the knowledge encoded by the model. The study further presents two mechanisms of interpreting the results of the model: i) using hallucinations to predict the suffix, and ii) using t-SNE plots to visualise the embedding matrix and the hidden states. The interpretations provide some information about the layers and cells activated for an input sequence but are limited in their ability to explain a prediction.

Lin et al. [7] propose an encoder, modulator and decoder model to predict the next event and generate the suffix of a case. The encoder comprises of an LSTM network for each event attribute. The modulator combines the hidden representations of the LSTM-based encoder to infer the weight vector. The weighted sum of the encoded vectors is used as input to a decoder layer comprising of a two layer LSTM network to predict the next activity. While the modulator computes a weight vector that could represent importance of different event attributes and provide insights into which attribute is important for the prediction, the focus of the study has been on the accuracy of the proposed architecture.

Recent work by Camargo et al. [1] presents an approach to train accurate LSTM-based models to predict process behaviour. The approach consists of a pre-processing phase that extracts n-grams or fixed length sequences of events, an LSTM training phase, and a post-processing phase to select the predicted next event. The majority of state-of-the-art research focus uniquely on the accuracy of the models. The focus of this work is to infuse some form of interpretability directly into an LSTM-based predictive model predicting business process behaviour without impacting accuracy.

2.2   Interpretable Models for Predicting Process Behaviour

Existing state-of-the-art techniques for constructing predictive models for business processes usually adopt a "black-box" approach. Black-box models commonly refer to the use of machine learning models where the internal mechanisms of the models are either unknown or known but not understandable to users. The challenge is to endow complex models with capabilities to explain the underlying predictive mechanisms in a way that helps users understand and scrutinize the behaviour. To achieve interpretability, the body of literature is divided into two major paradigms of approaches towards interpretability of black-boxes: (1) interpretable models; and (2) post-hoc models.

- **Interpretable models** are interpretable by design, promoting a more transparent, white-box approach for prediction. An interpretable model is capable of explaining a decision it takes or explaining how it works [5]. Examples include decision trees, Bayesian networks, linear regression. These systems enable an understanding of how features correlate with each other and how they contribute to the predictions.
- **Post-hoc models**, which are model-agnostic, aim to provide local explanations for a specific decision and make it reproducible on demand (instead of explaining the whole model's behaviour). The two most representative post-hoc models in the literature are LIME [12] and SHAP [8], and they are based on two completely different mechanisms. While LIME makes use of feature perturbations to build a linear surrogate model out of it (such as a decision-tree), SHAP is based on game theory, where predictions are explained by assuming that each feature value of the instance is a "player" in a game where the prediction is the payout. SHAP makes use of Shapley values, which is a method to fairly distribute the "payout" among different features [9].

When it comes to extracting interpretations out of deep learning models such as RNNs and LSTM, concerns have been raised on post-hoc explanation models as these explanation methods can be an inaccurate representation of the original model [13]. Although several approaches exist in the literature to probe and interpret deep neural networks [2,4,6,10], when it comes to interpretable models within predictive process analytics, the literature proposals are limited and their efficiency has not been thoroughly analysed. Recent research has acknowledged the need for extracting interpretations by illustrating the potential of explainable models for a manufacturing business process [11].

2.3 Attention-Based Models for Interpretations

Attention-based models can be seen as neural network architectures that enable the learning of sequential input-output relations when the input and output sequences have different lengths. This type of structure is of particular interest to predictive process behavior, because traces have different lengths. While existing predictive process analytics methods in the literature compress the sequential input into a fixed sized vector in order to feed it to a neural network architecture, attention-based models can use variable-length inputs without the constraint of fixed-sized vector by using a variable-length memory. In general, the attention mechanism allows a predictive model to focus on (or attend to) specific elements in a given input sequence for a prediction task.

Attention-based models also provide an underlying mechanism for interpretability [14]. Since these models require the computation of a distribution of weights over inputs, the attention weights can provide some insights to a decision-maker of *why* a certain prediction was computed by means of not manipulating directly the input features (as it happens in LIME), but rather by manipulating the distribution of weights, which are associated to the input [14].

Current studies in the literature have used attention-based models mainly in Natural Language Processing tasks [4,6,17]. For a model to be interpretable, it must not only suggest explanations that make sense to the user, but also ensure that those explanations accurately represent the true reasons for the model's decision [14]. This is, however, nearly impossible to verify in traditional post-hoc models, such as LIME and SHAP, since these algorithms build models around local interpretations, providing approximations to the predictive black box, instead of reflecting the true underlying mechanisms of the black box (as pointed out by [13]). With attention-based models, since the interpretability is extracted directly from the weights that are used to train the black box, one can get interpretations that better reflect the underlying mechanisms of the black box. In the next section, we present how attention models can be used as an interpretable mechanism in the context of predictive process analytics.

3   Approach

This section details our approach to predict process behaviour. We first describe the input features used for our model. Next, we describe the neural network architectures, which extend from models based on reverse and dual attention mechanisms [2,10].

Input Features: The objective of the model is to predict the next activity given the trace of an incomplete case. A *trace* is a sequence of events of a case. The input to the model are multiple prefix traces of different lengths. A *prefix trace* of length k contains the first k events of a trace. For simplicity, we describe the model input for a single prefix trace.

An event e_i in a prefix trace is represented as (a_i, rl_i, t_i), where $a_i \in A$ is the activity of the event, $rl_i \in RL$ is the role of the resource performing the activity, and $t_i \in \mathbb{R}$ is the timestamp associated with the event. We assume that each event has a timestamp associated with the completion of the activity. For each event, we represent the activity vector as a binary vector $v_{a_i} \in \{0,1\}^{|A|}$ where $v_{a_{i,p}}$ is set to 1, if p is the activity of the event and the rest are set to 0. Similarly the role vector is a binary vector $v_{rl_i} \in \{0,1\}^{|RL|}$ with the role of resource associated to the event set to 1 and 0 otherwise. The time feature is computed as the time elapsed between the completion time of the event and that of its previous event. The time feature for event e_i is computed as $\Delta t_i = t_i - t_{i-1}$. Fixed length sequences are extracted from each trace as detailed in the Sect. 4, in line with the previous work [1]. Each fixed length sequence of events $(e_1, e_2, \ldots, e_i)$ has an event represented by an activity vector, a role vector, and a continuous time interval value $(v_{a_i}, v_{rl_i}, \Delta t_i)$.

Attention-Based LSTM Models: The section presents an overview of the three models used in this work: i) prefix-index attention model that provides insights into the events influencing the prediction, ii) prefix-index and event attribute attention model that enables interpreting the events as well as the input features (representing event attributes) influencing the prediction, and iii) an attention-based interpretable model to predict next activity and its completion time. The model architectures are based on an interpretable model used in the health-care domain to predict patients at risk [2].

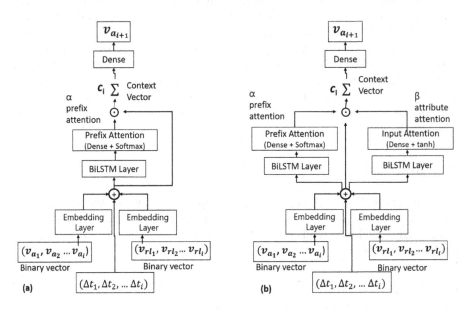

Fig. 1. Model architectures (a) Prefix-index attention (b) Prefix-index and event attribute attention

Prefix-Index Attention Model: Figure 1(a) presents the model that predicts the next activity of a running case, given an input prefix of events. The model takes as input, a fixed length sequence of activity vectors, role vectors along with sequences of time intervals. An embedding layer is used to convert the categorical values of the activity and the role represented as binary vectors to continuous vectors. The activity embedding, role embedding, and the time interval value are concatenated as v_{emb_i}. The concatenated input representing the sequence of events $(v_{emb_1}, v_{emb_2}, \ldots, v_{emb_i})$ is passed to a bidirectional LSTM. Compared to a traditional LSTM which processes sequence information in one direction or from the first input in the sequence to the last input, a bidirectional LSTM computes additional set of hidden state vectors by considering reverse order of the input. The reverse order is useful to consider in our scenario, as in a case execution, the next activity relies on the information about what has happened previously (reverse order of activities). The output of the BiLSTM is a hidden state vector $(h_1, h_2, \ldots, h_i)$ for each index in the sequence. The attention layer takes as input the hidden state vectors and generates the index attention $(\alpha_1, \alpha_2, \ldots, \alpha_i)$, a distribution of values that sum to 1. The attention values are element-wise multiplied with the concatenated input vector and added to obtain a context vector $c_i = \sum_{j=1}^{i} \alpha_j \odot v_{emb_j}$, where $\odot$ indicates element wise multiplication. The context vector is used as the input to a neural network dense layer to predict the next activity. The attention mechanism allows the model to focus on specific indices in the prefix when predicting the next activity. Finding the indices in a prefix that contributes to a prediction can be derived based on α values - the higher the value, the more influential the event at that index was in predicting the next activity. Hence, the model architecture enables interpreting the indices and thus the events influencing a prediction.

Prefix-Index and Event Attribute Attention Model: In addition to identifying the events in a prefix influencing the prediction, it would also be useful to reason which of the event attributes influenced the prediction (activities, resource roles, or the previous execution time). To support event attribute-level attention, another BiLSTM layer is used and hidden vectors are computed (Fig. 1(b)). The variable-level attention weights β are derived from the hidden vectors of the BiLSTM layer. The details on how to achieve variable-level attention can be found in [2].

In brief, the context vector c_i is computed using the α weights, the β weights, and the input vector embeddings. The context vector, $c_i = \sum_{j=1}^{i} \alpha_j \beta_j \odot v_{emb_j}$. If there are m activities and r roles, the input to the BiLSTM layer representing an event is an $(m+r+1)$ dimension vector (including the time interval dimension). The β-weight for each event is an $(m+r+1)$ vector. As the input features are binary vectors, the context vector indicates the influence of each input dimension on the prediction. For activities and roles, the $\alpha\beta \odot v_{emb}$ weight itself represents its influence on the prediction. For non-binary time interval input, the weight $\alpha_j \beta_j \times \Delta t_j$ is able to provide insight of the contribution of the time interval for predicting the next activity.

Prefix-Index and Event Attribute Attention Model for Remaining Time Prediction: The prefix-index and event attribute attention-based model is used to predict next activity, role and remaining time (Fig. 2). The model is used to compare the accuracy of attention-based model with existing approaches. In this model, the input features remain the same. The output context vector is used as input to three dense layers. The model shares the context vector. The next activity, the resource role and the time interval are predicted by the three dense layers. This model is further used to generate the complete trace. This is achieved by injecting continuous feedback to the model for each new predicted event, until the end of the trace (stop event) is reached. The time interval for each event is predicted and the remaining time for case execution can be computed as a sum of the time intervals.

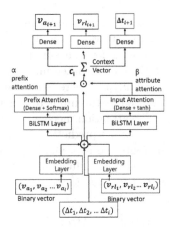

Fig. 2. Model predicting next activity, role and remaining time

4 Evaluation and Results

This section describes the datasets used, the pre-processing of the input event attributes, and three experimental evaluations. The first experiment evaluates the prefix-index attention model for accuracy and uses the α attention weights to interpret the influential events. The second experiment evaluates prefix-index and event attribute attention model to interpret the influence of the event attributes on the prediction. We finally compare the performance of the attention-based model with existing baseline approaches.

4.1 Datasets and Processing

The experiment uses five real-world business process event logs available at the 4TU center for research data[1]. The distinct characteristics of the event logs is presented in Table 1. The logs represent traces of short lengths (Helpdesk and BPIC 2013) with an average of 5 events per trace, to long running cases with with 20–30 events per trace (BPIC 2012 and BPIC 2015-5).

Input Sequence Extraction: The activity, resource, and completion time of the event are used as input features. Resources are grouped into roles based on the work by Camargo et al. [1] and the role of the resource associated to the event is used as the input feature. The categorical attributes of the event, i.e. activity and role are one-hot encoded (i.e. represented as a binary vector). The use of one-hot encoding improves interpretability as described in Sect. 3. Fixed length sequences are generated for each trace by extracting n-grams. An example of n-grams of length 5 extracted for a trace containing the following sequence of activities [A, B, C, F, K, R] is shown in Table 2. For each trace, a start and end activity is added before the extraction of n-grams. A similar approach is used

---

[1] https://data.4tu.nl/repository/collection:event_logs_real.

Table 1. Event logs and the summary statistics

Event log	# Traces	# Activities	Mean events/trace	Median events/trace	Mean duration	Median duration
Helpdesk	4580	14	4.6	4	40.9 days	39.9 days
BPIC 2013	13087	7	4.4	3	179.2 days	82 days
BPIC 2012-W	9685	6	7.5	6	11.4 days	8.5 days
BPIC 2012	13087	36	20	11	8.6 days	19.5 h
BPIC 2015-5	1156	41	31.3	31	98.3 days	77.1 days

to generate the n-grams of roles associated to the events in the trace and the time intervals of the events. An n-gram of size k effectively constitutes to k prior events of the case used to predict the next activity.

The **time interval** input is a continuous value. We scale continuous values to its z-score (i.e. zero mean and unit variance) resulting in values in the $[-1, 1]$ range. This is a standard normalisation approach used by the deep learning implementations.

Sequence	Next activity
[0, 0, 0, 0, 0]	A
[0, 0, 0, 0, A]	B
[0, 0, 0, A, B]	C
[0, 0, A, B, C]	F
[0, A, B, C, F]	K
[A, B, C, F, K]	R
[B, C, F, K, R]	END

Table 2. Generation of n-grams

Training Details: For each event log, we temporally split into train set and test dataset in a 0.7:0.3 ratio. The training set consists of the first 70% of the cases. The n-grams are extracted for the cases in the train set. The train set is further split into training and validation sets in a 0.85:0.15 ratio. The validation set is used to determine the values of the hyperparameters including the number of LSTM cells, and the regularisation parameters.

4.2 Prefix-Index Attention Model

Table 3 summarises the accuracy of the prefix-index attention model for different logs and different n-gram lengths. The length of the n-gram is chosen based on the average and median number of activities per trace. For the `Helpdesk, BPIC 2013` log, n-gram length is chosen to be 5 as the average number of events per trace is low (<5). For longer traces, the n-gram with different lengths are evaluated. Table 3 indicates that the accuracy of the models does not significantly change with the increase in length of the n-gram. We use the attention weights to gain insights into the prediction accuracy of the models. Figure 3 plots the α-attention weights for the 8 models presented in Table 3. The x-axis is the index of the n-gram or the input sequence of events (ranging from 0 to n-gram length). The α-weight is computed for each prediction in the test dataset (30% of unseen data). The y-axis is the average α-weight at each index. Figure 3 shows that the

Table 3. Accuracy predicting next event with different n-gram size

No.	Event log	n-gram length	Accuracy
1	Helpdesk	5	0.7922
2	BPIC 2013	5	0.4609
3	BPIC 2012-W	5	0.7682
4	BPIC 2012-W	10	0.7789
5	BPIC 2012	5	0.7900
6	BPIC 2012	10	0.7900
7	BPIC 2012	15	0.7904
8	BPIC 2015-5	15	0.3682

α-weight for the last event is 0.80 for the models trained using the Helpdesk, and BPIC 2013 event logs indicating that these models predominantly use the last event to predict the next event. The influence of the last event is lower in other models as indicated by α-weights of the last index ($\leq$0.5 for BPIC 2012, BPIC 2012W, and BPIC 2015-5). We observe that with BPIC 2015-5, the average α-weights of the last state is low with all prior indices having similar weights. The model accuracy is also low (0.35). Here, we hypothesis that with less training data (550 traces), the model is unable to learn and the attention layer has not yet converged to a stable set of weights.

To validate the influence of α-weights, we train models on all event logs by considering only the last two events; i.e. an input n-gram length of 2 only. For models that indicated high α-weights for the last two events (>0.8), we expect that the accuracy of predictions should continue to remain high if we reduce the n-gram size to 2. Table 4 shows the accuracy of the models trained using lower input sequence lengths. Models trained on Helpdesk, BPIC 2013 have the same accuracy as shown in Table 3. The model trained on BPIC 2012-W reduces moderately. The accuracy lowers considerably for models trained on BPIC 2012 and BPIC 2015-5, as considering only last two events results in loss of input information; i.e. the sum of α-weights of the last two events is lower than 0.7 with prior events influencing the prediction of next event. The results validate the interpretation provided by α-weights thus providing information about the events influencing the prediction.

Table 4. Accuracy predicting next event

No.	Event log	n-gram length	Accuracy
1	Helpdesk	2	0.7930
2	BPIC 2013	2	0.4633
3	BPIC 2012-W	2	0.7604
4	BPIC 2012	2	0.7261
5	BPIC 2015-5	2	0.3295

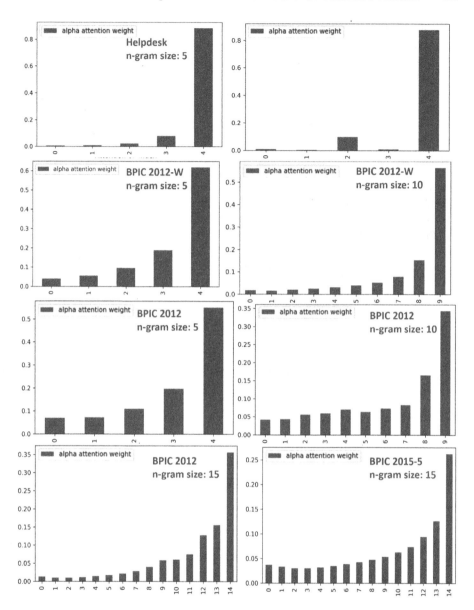

Fig. 3. The mean distribution of α-weights for the index values of the test dataset predictions with n-gram index (x-axis) in the range of [5, 15] when predicting next activity.

4.3 Prefix-Index and Event Attribute Attention Model

The prefix-index and event attribute attention model is trained to support interpretations on the most influential events (α-weights) in a running case and the event attributes attention-weights ($\alpha\beta \odot \boldsymbol{v_{emb}}$) that contribute to the prediction. The models are trained on all five event logs. For each prediction in the test dataset, the most influential index in the sequence of inputs is identified, i.e. the input index with the highest α-weights. The β-weights of the input attributes are also computed. The mean attention weights are presented for all five event logs in Fig. 4. The attention weights are in the range $[-1.0, 1.0]$. The absolute value of the weight is important as both positive and negative values indicate the influence of an attribute on the prediction. To understand the attributes influencing the prediction using attention weights, we further perform an ablation study of the time and resource features. The basic idea of an ablation is to remove features systematically and investigate how a feature impacts the prediction task. The attention weights in Fig. 4 indicate that time interval feature does not influence the prediction of next activity for models trained on the event logs BPIC 2012, BPIC 2015-5, Helpdesk. Hence, in these cases, not including time as an attribute would not reduce the accuracy. As expected, we observe minimal impact on accuracy when the time feature is excluded (AR (-T)) on

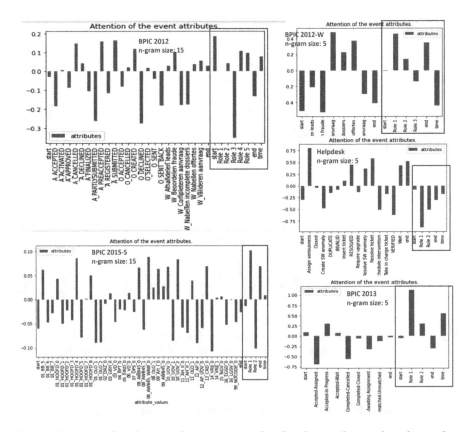

Fig. 4. The mean distribution of attention-weights for the attribute values for prefix-index and event attribute attention model when predicting next activity.

models trained using these logs in Table 5. The resource role feature influences the prediction as indicated by attention weights. Removal of resource role as a feature (A (-R -T)) reduces accuracy of all models. The influence is higher on models where there are more number of roles with higher attention weights (e.g. BPIC 2012) as compared to models with lower number of role values (e.g. Helpdesk).

Table 5. Activity (A), Role of the Resource (R), Time (T) feature ablation on the prefix-index and event attribute attention model

No.	Event log	ART	AR (-T)	A (-R -T)
1	Helpdesk	0.7961	0.7855	0.7829
2	BPIC 2013	0.4648	0.4638	0.4598
3	BPIC 2012-W	0.7741	0.7697	0.7684
4	BPIC 2012	0.7874	0.7841	0.7625
5	BPIC 2015-5	0.3624	0.3581	0.3551

Generally, the prefix-index and event attribute attention model provides richer insights for the same n-gram length vis-a-vis the prefix-index attention model. The attention weights offer information about the influential events and the event attributes while maintaining the same or better accuracy when compared to the prefix-index attention model.

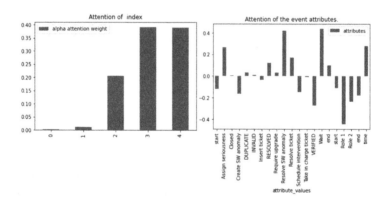

Fig. 5. The attention weights: prefix index attention-weight, and event attribute attention-weights for a single prediction.

Local Interpretations: The attention weights presented so far are global interpretations or interpretations that have been aggregated (we use arithmetic mean for aggregation). However, the model provides local interpretations or is able to provide the reasoning for a particular prediction. Figure 5 presents the attention weight for a single input prefix for model trained using `Helpdesk` event log. For this specific instance of an input, the model considers the last three events and further uses time interval as an important feature when predicting the next event.

4.4 Accuracy and Interpretability of Models

The aim of training the attention-based activity and remaining time prediction model is to assess the performance of the model when predicting the next event, the remaining sequence of events (i.e. suffixes), and the remaining time given the input prefixes of varying lengths. For each prefix, the next activity is predicted and the accuracy is measured. For suffix and remaining time prediction, the *hallucination* approach outlined by earlier studies [1,3] is used till the end of the case is reached. The model predicts the remaining time Δt_{i+1}, which is the difference between the timestamp of the last event in the prefix from the timestamp of the last hallucinated event. The Damerau–Levenshtein (DL) measure (which applies to pairs of strings), is used to measure the similarity for suffix prediction [1]. The Mean Absolute Error (MAE) metric is used to measure the error in predicting remaining time. MAE is computed by taking the absolute value of the difference between the true value of remaining time and the predicted value, and then calculating the average value of these magnitudes.

Table 6. Next event, suffix, and remaining time prediction performance

Implementation	Next event			Suffix prediction distance			Remaining cycle time MAE (days)	
	Help desk	BPIC 2012	BPIC 2012-W	Help desk	BPIC 2012	BPIC 2012-W	Help desk	BPIC 2012-W
Our approach	0.796	0.787	0.774	0.910	0.319	0.467	8.12	9.3
Camargo et al.	0.789	0.786	0.778	0.917	0.632	0.525	6	9.1
Evermann et al.	0.798	0.780	0.623	0.742	0.110	0.297	–	
Tax et al.	0.712		0.760	0.767		0.353	6	9.1 -
Lin et al.	0.912	0.974		0.874	0.281		–	–

We use the `Helpdesk`, `BPI2012W and BPI2012` event logs evaluated in previous studies. Table 6 summarizes the average accuracy for the next-event prediction task, the average similarity between the predicted suffixes and the actual suffixes, and the MAE of the remaining time. For the task of next-event prediction, our approach performs similar to all existing state-of-the-art approaches [1,3,15] except for the baseline of Lin et al. [7]. For the task of suffix prediction, our approach has the performance similar to Camargo et al. [1] for suffix prediction on Helpdesk log, but underperforms with the other logs. Our approach has higher MAE for the remaining time prediction as compared to Camargo et al. While the focus of our work has been to improve interpretability of the models, these results suggest that the model is able to achieve good performance when predicting categorical variables. The model requires further optimisation and tuning with respect to predicting the continuous value of remaining time. However, we observe that the approach presented in this work leads to deriving interpretations from the models without a significant trade-off on accuracy when predicting process behaviour.

5   Conclusion and Future Work

This paper presents an attention-based LSTM model that provides interpretations to predict the next event and its attributes: event activity, the role of the resource, and the timestamp associated with the event. The attention mechanisms provide insights into the events in a case and the event attributes that influence prediction of the next event. We use the model to generate the suffix and estimate remaining time by iteratively predicting the next event until the end of the case is reached. To process the input, we continue to use the one-hot encoding for categorical data but convert the binary vectors to continuous vectors. The paper presents three network architectures. Firstly, the prefix-index attention model supports interpretations regarding which events influenced a prediction. Secondly, prefix-index and event attribute attention model identifies which events and event attributes influenced the prediction. Finally, we extend the model to support the prediction of three event attributes: the activity, role of the resource and its timestamp.

In this work, we have limited the input features to three event attributes by considering the activity, resource and time perspective. The data perspective and inclusion of other generic features has not been considered. Additional process attributes can have a significant impact when predicting the next event for certain business processes. We would extend the current model to include the data perspective as a part of the future work. Our work provides a starting point for building and evaluating models that explain their predictions. Providing insights to business users on the predictions can be a very challenging task and remains as an open research question in the scientific community [13].

Acknowledgement. We particularly thank Manuel Camargo, Marlon Dumas, and Oscar González Rojas for the high quality code they released which allowed fast reproduction of the experimental setting and the processing of event logs. This paper was partly supported by ARC Discovery Grant DP190100314.

Reproducibility: The source code and the event logs can be downloaded from https://git.io/JvSWl.

References

1. Camargo, M., Dumas, M., González-Rojas, O.: Learning accurate LSTM models of business processes. In: Hildebrandt, T., van Dongen, B.F., Röglinger, M., Mendling, J. (eds.) BPM 2019. LNCS, vol. 11675, pp. 286–302. Springer, Cham (2019). https://doi.org/10.1007/978-3-030-26619-6_19

2. Choi, E., Bahadori, M.T., Sun, J., Kulas, J., Schuetz, A., Stewart, W.F.: RETAIN: an interpretable predictive model for healthcare using reverse time attention mechanism. In: Annual Conference on NeurIPS, pp. 3504–3512 (2016)

3. Evermann, J., Rehse, J., Fettke, P.: Predicting process behaviour using deep learning. Decis. Support Syst. **100**, 129–140 (2017)

4. Ghaeini, R., Fern, X.Z., Tadepalli, P.: Interpreting recurrent and attention-based neural models: a case study on natural language inference. In: Proceedings of the 2018 Conference on Empirical Methods in Natural Language Processing (2018)

5. Guidotti, R., Monreale, A., Ruggieri, S., Turini, F., Giannotti, F., Pedreschi, D.: A survey of methods for explaining black box models. ACM Comput. Surv. **51**(5), 93:1–93:42 (2018)

6. Lee, J., Shin, J.H., Kim, J.S.: Interactive visualization and manipulation of attention-based neural machine translation. In: Proceedings of the 2017 Conference on Empirical Methods in Natural Language Processing: System Demonstrations (2017)

7. Lin, L., Wen, L., Wang, J.: MM-Pred: a deep predictive model for multi-attribute event sequence. In: Berger-Wolf, T.Y., Chawla, N.V. (eds.) Proceedings of the 2019 SIAM International Conference on Data Mining, SDM, pp. 118–126. SIAM (2019)

8. Lundberg, S.M., Lee, S.I.: A unified approach to interpreting model predictions. In: Proceedings of the 31st Conference on Advances in Neural Information Processing Systems (NIPS) (2017)

9. Molnar, C.: Interpretable Machine Learning: A Guide for Making Black Box Models Explainable. Leanpub (2018)

10. Qin, Y., Song, D., Chen, H., Cheng, W., Jiang, G., Cottrell, G.W.: A dual-stage attention-based recurrent neural network for time series prediction. In: IJCAI, pp. 2627–2633 (2017)

11. Rehse, J., Mehdiyev, N., Fettke, P.: Towards explainable process predictions for industry 4.0 in the DFKI-smart-lego-factory. KI **33**(2), 181–187 (2019). https://doi.org/10.1007/s13218-019-00586-1

12. Ribeiro, M.T., Singh, S., Guestrin, C.: "Why should I trust you?": explaining the predictions of any classifier. In: Proceedings of the 22nd ACM SIGKDD, pp. 1135–1144 (2016)

13. Rudin, C.: Stop explaining black box machine learning models for high stakes decisions and use interpretable models instead. Nat. Mach. Intell. **1**(5), 206–215 (2019)

14. Serrano, S., Smith, N.A.: Is attention interpretable? In: Proceedings of the 57th Conference of the Association for Computational Linguistics, ACL, pp. 2931–2951. Association for Computational Linguistics (2019)

15. Tax, N., Verenich, I., La Rosa, M., Dumas, M.: Predictive business process monitoring with LSTM neural networks. In: Dubois, E., Pohl, K. (eds.) CAiSE 2017. LNCS, vol. 10253, pp. 477–492. Springer, Cham (2017). https://doi.org/10.1007/978-3-319-59536-8_30

16. Verenich, I., Dumas, M., Rosa, M.L., Maggi, F.M., Teinemaa, I.: Survey and cross-benchmark comparison of remaining time prediction methods in business process monitoring. ACM TIST **10**(4), 34:1–34:34 (2019)

17. Wang, Y., Huang, M., Zhu, X., Zhao, L.: Attention-based LSTM for aspect-level sentiment classification. In: Proceedings of the 2016 Conference on Empirical Methods in Natural Language Processing (2016)

18. Williams, R., Zipser, D.: A learning algorithm for continually running fully recurrent neural networks. Neural Comput. **1**, 270–280 (1989)

Triggering Proactive Business Process Adaptations via Online Reinforcement Learning

Andreas Metzger$^{(\boxtimes)}$ ⓘ, Tristan Kley ⓘ, and Alexander Palm ⓘ

paluno – The Ruhr Institute for Software Technology,
University of Duisburg-Essen, Essen, Germany
{andreas.metzger,tristan.kley,alexander.palm}@paluno.uni-due.de

Abstract. Proactive process adaptation can prevent and mitigate upcoming problems during process execution by using predictions about how an ongoing case will unfold. There is an important trade-off with respect to these predictions: Earlier predictions leave more time for adaptations than later predictions, but earlier predictions typically exhibit a lower accuracy than later predictions, because not much information about the ongoing case is available. An emerging solution to address this trade-off is to continuously generate predictions and only trigger proactive adaptations when prediction reliability is greater than a predefined threshold. However, a good threshold is not known a priori. One solution is to empirically determine the threshold using a subset of the training data. While an empirical threshold may be optimal for the training data used and the given cost structure, such a threshold may not be optimal over time due to non-stationarity of process environments, data, and cost structures. Here, we use online reinforcement learning as an alternative solution to learn when to trigger proactive process adaptations based on the predictions and their reliability at run time. Experimental results for three public data sets indicate that our approach may on average lead to 12.2% lower process execution costs compared to empirical thresholding.

Keywords: Machine learning · Business process monitoring · Prediction · Adaptation · Accuracy · Earliness

1 Introduction

Predictive business process monitoring predicts how an ongoing case will unfold [2,16,35]. To this end, predictive business process monitoring uses the sequence of events produced by the execution of a case to make predictions about the future state of the case. If the predicted future state of the case indicates a problem, the ongoing case may be proactively adapted; e.g., by re-scheduling process activities or by changing the assignment of resources [19,24,37]. Proactive business process adaptation can prevent the occurrence of problems and it

© Springer Nature Switzerland AG 2020
D. Fahland et al. (Eds.): BPM 2020, LNCS 12168, pp. 273–290, 2020.
https://doi.org/10.1007/978-3-030-58666-9_16

can mitigate the impact of upcoming problems during business process execution [26,28,36]. As an example, a delay in the expected delivery time for a freight transport process may incur contractual penalties. If a delay is predicted, faster, alternative transport activities (such as air delivery instead of road delivery) can be scheduled to prevent the delay and thus the penalty.

Problem Statement. There are two key requirements for predictive business process monitoring when used for proactive process adaptation [20,22,35]. First, predictions should be *accurate*. When adaptation decisions are based on inaccurate predictions, this may imply unnecessary adaptations (e.g., if a delay is falsely predicted) or missed adaptations (e.g., if an actual delay is not predicted). Second, predictions should be produced *early* during process execution. Earlier predictions leave more time for adaptations, which typically have non-negligible latencies. However, there is an important trade-off between generating accurate predictions and generating them early. Earlier predictions typically have a lower accuracy than later predictions, because not much information about the ongoing case is available [20,35].

An emerging solution to address this trade-off is to continuously generate predictions and dynamically determine when a prediction is sufficiently reliable [9,22,34–36]. Only a reliable prediction is used to trigger a proactive process adaptation. Typically, this entails generating, for each prediction, an estimate of the prediction's reliability. A simple example for a reliability estimate is the class probability generated by a random forest classifier. A prediction is considered reliable if the reliability estimate is greater than a given threshold. As an example, all predictions with a class probability higher than 95% may be considered reliable predictions.

By setting different thresholds, one can trade earliness against accuracy [22,36]. If earlier predictions are preferred, a lower threshold may be chosen, at the risk that predictions are not very accurate. On the other hand, if accurate predictions are required, a higher threshold may be chosen, at the risk that adaptations will be triggered too late as to be effective. Experimental results indicate that a higher threshold (and thus more conservative stance in taking adaptation decisions) may help achieve cost savings even if the individual adaptations are expensive [19,22]. Yet, this more conservative stance comes at the expedient of achieving smaller cost saving on average. Based on these observations, a process manager with a lower risk affinity may set a higher threshold than a process manager with a higher risk affinity. However, how to set a concrete threshold that is optimal in the given situation remains open.

Another approach, which eliminates the need to manually set a threshold, is to empirically determine a threshold. This so called *empirical thresholding* is performed via a dedicated training process involving a separate training data set and knowledge about the concrete cost structure of process execution [8,36]. This ensures that the threshold is optimal for the training data used and the given cost structure. However, the threshold may not remain optimal over time due to non-stationarity of process environments, data, and cost structures.

Contributions. Here, we introduce an alternative approach that does not require manually determining a threshold nor does it require a-priori information to empirically determine such threshold. In fact, our approach does not aim to determine an optimal threshold at all. Instead, we combine two emerging machine learning paradigms to decide when to trigger proactive business process adaptations. On the one hand, we use ensembles of deep learning models to generate predictions and their reliability estimates. On the other hand, we use online reinforcement learning (RL) to learn at run time when to trigger an adaptation based on the predictions and their reliability estimates.

We use the predictions and reliability estimates generated by a predictive monitoring system developed in our previous work [20,22]. To provide a more fine-grained signal to online RL, we extended this system from classification to regression in order to generate numeric instead of binary predictions.

We build on our online RL approach presented in earlier work [25], and extend it with respect to three main aspects:

- *Stronger reward function:* The reward function is a key element in RL, because rewards quantify the feedback for executing an action (i.e., an adaptation in our case). RL aims to find an action-selection policy that maximizes long-term rewards. Here, we present a reward function that provides a strong signal to the RL algorithm. For the BPIC2017 data set used in [25], this led to 36.9% lower costs on average than the initial reward function proposed in [25]. In addition, we decouple rewards from the concrete cost structure of process execution, which eliminates the need to re-tune the reward function when the cost structure changes.
- *Additional data sets:* In addition to the BPIC 2017 data set used in [25], we experimentally evaluate our approach on two additional BPM data sets: BPIC 2012 and Traffic. In particular, the Traffic data set visibly exhibits non-stationarity and thus serves to demonstrate how our approach can capture non-stationary process environments.
- *Comparative analysis:* We perform a comparative analysis of our approach with empirical thresholding, as a state-of-the-art approach [8,36]. When compared with empirical thresholding, our approach leads to 12.2% lower process execution costs on average across all three data sets.

In the remainder, Sect. 2 describes our overall approach and its realization. Section 3 reports on the experimental evaluation of our approach. Section 4 discusses validity risks and limitations. Section 5 analyzes related work. Section 6 concludes with an outlook on future work.

2   Overall Approach

Our approach combines two emerging machine learning paradigms as shown in Fig. 1. We leverage *online reinforcement learning (RL)* to learn at run time when to trigger proactive business process adaptations. As input to online RL, we use predictions and their reliability estimates generated via *ensemble deep supervised learning*. We explain these two elements of our approach below.

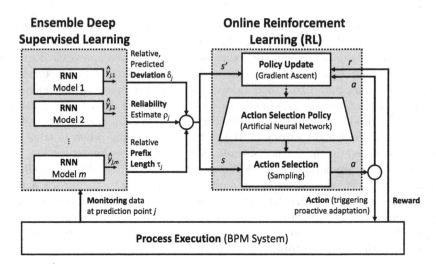

Fig. 1. Combination of machine learning for proactive adaptation

2.1 Ensemble Deep Supervised Learning

As we presented the details of ensemble deep learning for predictive process monitoring in our previous work [20,22], here we only provide a brief summary and the extensions from classification to regression. Regression facilitates computing numeric predictions, which provide a more fine-grained signal to online RL than binary predictions computed via classification.

As shown on the left hand side of Fig. 1, we compute predictions and reliability estimates from ensembles of deep learning models, specifically Recurrent Neural Networks (*RNNs*). RNNs can naturally handle arbitrary length sequences of input data [10] and provide generally high prediction accuracy [7,33]. To implement our approach, we use RNNs with Long Short-Term Memory (LSTM) cells as they better capture long-term dependencies in the data [17,33] and build on the architecture and realization presented by Tax et al. [33].

Ensemble prediction is a meta-prediction technique where the predictions of m prediction models, so called *base learners*, are combined into a single prediction [27,38]. Ensemble prediction is primarily used to increase aggregate prediction accuracy, while it also allows computing reliability estimates [1]. Computing reliability estimates is the main reason why we use ensembles of RNN models in our approach. We use bagging (bootstrap aggregating [6]) as a concrete ensemble technique to build the individual prediction models of our RNN ensemble. Bagging generates m new training data sets from the whole training set by sampling from the whole training data set uniformly and with replacement. For each of the m new training data sets a separate RNN model is trained.

The ensemble of RNN models creates a *prediction* $\hat{y}_j$ at each potential prediction point j. In our case, a prediction is generated after each event of the running case. These prediction points are thus characterized by their prefix length j, which gives the number of events that were produced up to the prediction point [13,35].

At each prediction point j, each of the m base learners of the ensemble delivers a prediction result $\hat{y}_{i,j}$, with $i = 1, \ldots, m$. Following the typical approach for combining regression models of an ensemble [38], we compute the ensemble prediction as the mean of all predictions:

$$\hat{y}_j = \frac{1}{m} \cdot \sum\nolimits_{i=1}^{m} \hat{y}_{j,i}.$$

To determine whether this numeric prediction indicates a violation (and thus may require a proactive adaptation), we compute the *relative predicted deviation* δ_j of the prediction from the planned process outcome A:

$$\delta_j = \frac{\hat{y}_j - A}{A}.$$

Without loss of generality, we assume $\delta_j > 0$ means violation. As an example, if the predicted duration of a transport process is longer than its planned duration, this means a violation, as the planned delivery time will not be met.

The *reliability* estimate ρ_j for the ensemble prediction $\hat{y}_j$ is computed as the fraction of the base learners that predicted a violation or a non-violation. We compute the relative deviation $\delta_{i,j}$ for each ensemble prediction and use this to determine the reliability estimate as follows:

$$\rho_j = max_{i=1,\ldots,m}\left(\frac{|i : \delta_{i,j} > 0|}{m}, \frac{|i : \delta_{i,j} \leq 0|}{m}\right).$$

2.2 Online Reinforcement Learning (RL)

RL learns the effectiveness of an agent's actions through the agent's interactions with its environment [31]. As shown on the right hand side of Fig. 1, the agent selects and executes an action a in response to environment state s. As a result, the environment transitions to s' and the agent receives a reward r for executing the action. The goal of RL is to maximize cumulative rewards.

The reward function $r(s)$ specifies the numeric reward the system receives when reaching the new environment state s' after executing action a. Thereby, the reward function quantifies the learning goal to achieve. As an example, a simple reward function provides a positive reward $r = 100$ if action a had the desired effect (i.e., led to the desired new environment state), and a negative reward $r = -100$ if it did not.

The successful application of RL depends on how well the learning problem, and in particular the reward function, is defined [5]. Below, we first explain how we define a suitable learning problem for triggering proactive process adaptations, and then provide details on our concrete RL realization.

Learning Problem. We formalize the learning problem of when to trigger a proactive process adaptation by defining actions a, states s and rewards r.

We define an action a as either triggering ($a =$ true) or not triggering ($a =$ false) a proactive process adaptation.

We build the state s from the output of the predictive monitoring system, which includes the predicted deviation δ_j, the reliability estimate ρ_j as well as information about the current prediction point j given as the relative prefix length τ_j, i.e., each state s is represented by $s = (\delta_j, \rho_j, \tau_j)$. In addition to the relative deviation δ_j and the prediction reliability ρ_j introduced in Sect. 2.1, we also use the relative prediction point τ_j of the current case as input. Using τ_j provides an important signal to the RL algorithm about the earliness of the prediction. This relative prediction point can be computed by dividing the prediction point j by the case length. In situations, where the case length is not known a-priori, the case length may be estimated by the upper bound of process lengths observed in the training data for the RNN ensemble.

Finally, the most important part of formalizing the learning problem is to define suitable rewards r. By giving a reward function, one expresses the learning goal in a declarative fashion. As mentioned above, the aim of the learning process is to maximize cumulative rewards. Therefore, finding a suitable reward function is key to successful learning. One obvious approach is to model the reward function as close as possible to the actual problem domain, which is what we did in our previous work [25]. Here, this would mean to define rewards to be the concrete costs of process execution as encoded in the underlying cost model of the process (see Sect. 3.2). Defining the reward function in such a way has the appeal of a direct mapping between rewards and the behavior of a system in its respective application domain [4]. Yet, it exhibits the following two shortcomings.

First, using the cost model as a reward function means that learning strongly depends on the concrete costs. Whenever the cost model changes, this would require an update of the reward function. We thus decouple the rewards from the actual process costs. In particular, this decoupling should facilitate our RL approach to become more robust against changing cost structures at run time.

Table 1. Reward function r based on prediction contingencies

	Predicted Violation	Predicted Non-violation
Actual Violation	$+1 \cdot (1 - \tau_j)$ (*necessary adaptation*)	-1 (*missed adaptation*)
Actual Non-violation	$-.5 - .5 \cdot (1 - \tau_j)$ (*unnecessary adaptation*)	$+1$ (*no adaptation*)

Second, using the cost model as reward function may not provide a strong enough reward signal to steer the learning process in the right direction and facilitate convergence. In particular, a successful process execution (true negative prediction) would entail zero costs (see Sect. 3.2). However, zero provides only a weak signal to the learner. We thus formulate strong rewards for each of the prediction contingencies as shown in Table 1.

We provide a strong positive reward signal $(+1)$ if no adaptation was needed and none was triggered (*no adaptation*). Similarly, we provide a strong positive reward signal in the case of a *necessary adaptation*. However, we take into account that not all adaptations triggered may be effective. As explained in Sect. 1, the chances for effective adaptations are the highest at the beginning of the case. We thus discount the reward by a factor of $(1 - \tau_j)$.

We provide a strong negative reward (-1) for a *missed adaptation*. Similarly, we provide a negative reward signal in the case of *unnecessary adaptations* by penalizing the adaptation itself $(-.5)$, as well as the potential compensations that may be required if the adaptation was effective $(-.5 \cdot (1 - \tau_j))$.

We break down the RL problem into suitable episodes, each episode matching the execution of a single case. For each prediction point (process activity), our approach decides whether to adapt or not. Whenever the approach decides to adapt or when the end of the case is reached, we provide a reward r as described above; otherwise, we provide a reward of zero as illustrated in Fig. 2. In order not to discount the reward received at the end of the case, we consequently set the discount factor of the RL algorithm to $\gamma = 1$. The discount factor is a standard hyper-parameter[1] in RL and defines the relevance of future rewards.

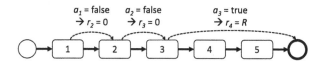

Fig. 2. Episodic learning problem

Realization. We realize our approach using the *policy-based* RL framework for self-adaptive information systems we introduced in [25]. We use policy-based RL, because it offers two main benefits over classical, value-based RL algorithms, such as SARSA and Q-Learning [31]. Value-based RL algorithms often use a lookup table to represent the learned knowledge, which requires manually quantizing environment states to facilitate scalability if the environment has a high number of states or if the environment state is represented by continuous variables. In our case, reliability estimates and predictions are represented by continuous variables. In addition, to facilitate convergence of learning, value-based RL algorithms require manually fine-tuning exploitation versus exploration, i.e., using current knowledge versus gathering new knowledge. When applying RL in an online setting, as we do, value-based RL therefore poses the challenge of when and how to modify the exploration rate to capture non-stationary environments [31].

---

[1] Hyper-parameters are used to configure the machine learning algorithms and thereby control the learning process.

The fundamental idea behind policy-based RL is to directly use and maximize a parametrized stochastic action selection policy [23,32]. This *action selection policy* (see Fig. 1) maps states to a probability distribution over the action space (i.e., set of possible actions). Actions are selected by sampling from this probability distribution. In our approach, we represent the policy as an artificial neural network (concretely a multi-layer perceptron), because this facilitates generalizing over unseen states.

At run time, *action selection* (see Fig. 1) samples an action a from the probability distribution given by the policy for the current state s. Action selection determines whether there is a need for triggering a proactive adaptation. The generated actions constitute proactive adaptation triggers.

The actual online learning happens via *policy updates* (see Fig. 1). During a policy update, the policy parameters are perturbed based on the rewards received, such that the resulting probability distribution is shifted towards a direction which increases the likelihood of selecting actions leading to a higher cumulative reward. As we represent the policy as an artificial neural network, the policy parameters (the weights of the neural network) are updated via so-called policy gradient methods. These methods update the policy according to the gradient of a given objective function, such as average rewards over the last q actions. Because of this sampling and the probabilistic nature of the policy, policy-based RL does not require manually fine-tuning the balance between exploitation and exploration. Exploration is automatically performed, because sampling over the probability distribution given by the policy leads to some degree of random action selection.

As a concrete policy-based RL algorithm, we use proximal policy optimization (PPO [29]) in the form of OpenAI's baseline implementation[2]. PPO is rather robust for what concerns hyper-parameter settings. Thereby, we avoid the need for extensive hyper-parameter tuning compared to other policy-based RL algorithms. In addition, PPO avoids too large policy updates by using a so called clipping function. A too large policy update may destroy the learned knowledge in a single policy update. To represent the policy, we used multi-layer perceptrons with two hidden layers of 64 neurons each. The input layer consists of three neurons representing the three state variables; the output layer consists of one neuron representing the action variable.

3   Experimental Evaluation

To demonstrate the feasibility and applicability of our approach, we experimentally analyze whether we can learn good proactive adaptation policies at run time. To this end, we analyze how learning evolves over time. We also compare the process execution costs of our approach with the costs when using thresholds determined by empirical thresholding as state-of-the-art baseline.

---

[2] https://openai.com/blog/openai-baselines-ppo/.

3.1   Experimental Setup

The experimental setup includes the prototypical implementation of our approach, which consists of code to train and evaluate the RNN-LSTM ensembles, as well as code to perform RL at run time. We use three real-world data sets that are among the ones frequently used to evaluate predictive process monitoring approaches [35]. Table 2 provides key characteristics of these data sets. We chose data sets, which had a large enough size – in terms of number of cases and predictions – to observe the effects of learning (also see the discussion in Sect. 4). Similar to [35], we only considered prefix lengths up to a certain length (99% quantile in our case) in order not to bias the results towards very long cases. All artifacts, including code, data sets, prediction results, as well as experimental outcomes, are publicly available to facilitate replicability[3].

Table 2. Data sets used in experiments

Name	Domain	# Cases	# Predictions	Max. Prefix Len.
BPIC2012	Credit application	4,361	57,665	49
BPIC2017	Credit application	10,500	232,397	73
Traffic	Traffic fines	50,117	140,536	6

3.2   Cost Model

To quantify and compare process execution costs, we use a cost model based on [22,36]. Table 3 shows the cost model in the structure of a contingency table.

Table 3. Cost model

	Prediction $\hat{y}_j$ = positive		$\hat{y}_j$ = negative
	Effective adaptation	Non-effective adaptation	
Actual y_j = positive	Adaptation costs	Adaptation costs + Penalty	Penalty
y_j = negative	Adaptation costs + Compensation costs	Adaptation costs	0

A proactive adaptation decision entails different costs depending on whether the decision is based on a false positive or a false negative prediction. In addition, the costs depend on whether a proactive adaptation was *effective* or not. We consider an adaptation non-effective if the problem persists after the adaptation.

---

[3] https://git.uni-due.de/predictive-process-monitoring/bpm-2020-artefacts/.

The cost model considers three main cost factors of proactive process adaptation. *Adaptation costs* incur, because the adaptation of a running case typically requires effort and resources. As an example, adding more staff to speed up the execution of a case incurs additional personnel costs for the execution of this case. *Penalty costs* incur if the process outcome does not match the planned or expected outcome. As an example, a penalty may have to be paid for late deliveries in a transport process. Penalties may be faced in two situations. First, a necessary proactive adaptation may be missed. Second, a proactive adaptation may not be effective and thus the problem remains after adaptation. *Compensation costs* incur if the adaptation turns out to be an adaptation based on false positive predictions, and thus such wrong adaptation may require roll-back or compensation activities. As an example, if a credit card is falsely blocked, this may entail additional costs for issuing a new credit card to the customer to compensate for this false blocking.

To keep the number of experimental variables manageable, we express adaptation costs c_a and compensation costs c_c as a fraction κ of penalty costs c_p, i.e., $c_a = c_c = \kappa \cdot c_p$. By varying κ, we can reflect different situations that may be faced in practice concerning how costly a process adaptation or compensation in relation to a penalty may be.

We use α to represent the probability that an adaptation is effective. To model the fact that earlier prediction points provide more options and time for proactive adaptations than later prediction points, earlier proactive adaptations are given a higher α than later adaptations. Specifically, we vary α in our experiments such that it linearly decreases from $\alpha_{\max} = 1$ for the first prediction point to $\alpha_{\min}$ for the last prediction point. We consider two different settings for $\alpha_{\min}$ to cover different possible circumstances: (1) $\alpha_{\min} = 0.5$ to model that late adaptations may still be feasible, (2) $\alpha_{\min} = 0$ to model that late adaptations are not feasible.

3.3   Experimental Results

We first analyze how the learning process evolves over time in order to demonstrate that RL is able to learn when to trigger proactive process adaptations. Figure 3 show the respective results for the three data sets.

The charts show how the rate of adaptations, earliness, the rate of correct adaptation decisions, and overall rewards evolve (costs are discussed further below). We measure earliness in terms of relative prefix-length when an adaptation was made, i.e., 0 means an adaptation was made at the beginning of the process, while 1 means it was made at the end. Charts start at case # 100, because the points in the charts are averaged over the last 100 cases (for stability reasons).

Part (a) of the charts shows the learning process until convergence can be observed, while part (b) shows the learning process for the whole test data set. We consider convergence to happen as soon as cumulative rewards averaged over the last 100 cases reaches the cumulative rewards averaged across the whole data set, which is indicated as the dashed red line.

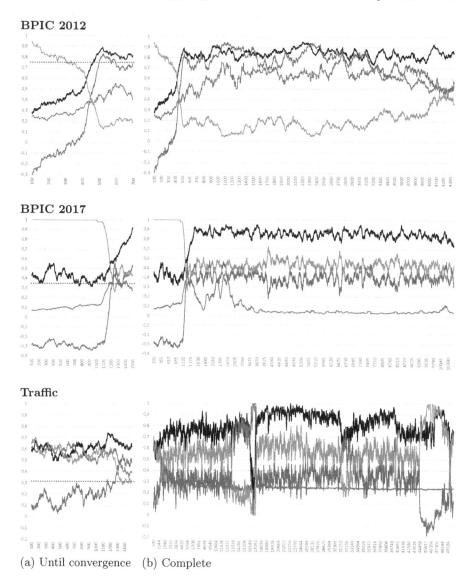

Fig. 3. Learning behavior; green: rate of adaptations; **blue:** earliness (0 = beginning, 1 = end of process); **black:** rate of correct adaptation decisions; red: overall reward/100 (Color figure online)

Across all four data sets, the convergence of the learning process is evident when observing the development of the reward curve. Convergence happens after around 500 cases for BPIC 2012, 1200 for BPIC 2017, and 1300 for Traffic. It can also be seen that the approach indeed is able to learn when to adapt in order to maximize rewards. For all three data sets, the approach starts with a very high rate of adaptations that are triggered very early in the process. However, this has negative impact on rewards, as the approach has not yet learned that (1) adaptations should only be triggered for positive predictions, (2) not all predictions may be accurate, (3) there is a trade-off between accuracy and earliness. This is also evident in the rate of correct adaptation decisions (which is very low before convergence). After the point of convergence is reached, it can be observed that the approach has learned to be more conservative with triggering adaptations (the rate of adaptations goes down), and also that later predictions may be more accurate (earliness goes up). This results in a higher rate of correct adaptation decisions and thus a higher reward.

Having observed convergence of learning, we now compare the process execution costs of our approach with the process execution costs when using empirical thresholding [36]. Results are given in Tables 4 and 5 for the different settings of α_{min}. We used different concrete process execution costs (expressed as different settings for κ; see Sect. 3.1). For each κ, we computed the optimal threshold based on a 1/3 subset of the test data set and compared the costs of both approaches for the remaining 2/3 of the test data set. For the RL approach, this implies that we compare the results once learning has converged. Note that for Traffic, we consider an excerpt of the data set (including only the first 14,000 cases), because the data set visibly exhibits non-stationarity after that point, which we further analyze below.

Table 4. Average process execution costs of *RL* and empirical *thr*esholding for different relative costs κ and $\alpha_{min} = 0.5$ (all differences are significant with a p-value < 0.001)

$\alpha_{min} = 0.5$	$\kappa = .1$			$\kappa = .2$			$\kappa = .3$			$\kappa = .4$			$\kappa = .5$			Avg
	RL	Thr	Diff	RL	Thr	Diff	RL	Thr	Diff	RL	Thr	Diff	RL	Thr	Diff	
Traffic (excerpt)	27,7	25,2	9,1%	37,5	41,4	-10,5%	47,2	57,6	-22,0%	56,9	73,8	-29,6%	66,7	89,9	-34,9%	-14,6%
BPIC 2012	17,8	17,8	0,0%	20,3	21,1	-3,6%	22,8	23,6	-3,3%	25,3	25,9	-2,1%	27,8	28,1	-1,1%	-2,0%
BPIC 2017	8,2	8,8	-7,8%	14,8	15,2	-2,5%	21,5	21,5	0,2%	28,2	27,6	1,9%	34,8	33,7	3,3%	-1,7%
Average			0,4%			-5,5%			-8,4%			-9,9%			-10,9%	-6,1%
Traffic (full)	17,6	17,4	1,2%	23,8	28,0	-17,6%	30,1	38,6	-28,5%	36,3	49,3	-35,7%	42,6	59,9	-40,8%	-20,3%
Average			-2,2%			-7,9%			-10,6%			-12,0%			-12,9%	-8,0%

Table 5. Average process execution costs for $\alpha_{min} = 0$

$\alpha_{min} = 0.0$	$\kappa = .1$			$\kappa = .2$			$\kappa = .3$			$\kappa = .4$			$\kappa = .5$			Avg
	RL	Thr	Diff	RL	Thr	Diff	RL	Thr	Diff	RL	Thr	Diff	RL	Thr	Diff	
Traffic (excerpt)	28,4	27,8	1,9%	38,1	43,9	-15,3%	47,8	60,0	-25,5%	57,5	76,1	-32,3%	67,2	92,2	-37,1%	-19,0%
BPIC 2012	22,3	22,6	-1,3%	24,6	25,3	-2,7%	27,0	28,0	-3,7%	29,4	30,6	-4,2%	31,7	32,7	-3,1%	-2,7%
BPIC 2017	8,3	11,0	-32,5%	15,0	17,7	-18,1%	21,6	23,4	-8,4%	28,2	29,1	-3,1%	34,9	33,1	5,1%	-13,5%
Average			-1,8%			-6,0%			-8,1%			-9,2%			-9,5%	-6,4%
Traffic (full)	17,7	19,8	-11,7%	23,9	30,3	-26,7%	30,2	40,9	-35,4%	36,4	51,5	-41,2%	42,7	62,0	-45,3%	-20,3%
Average			-15,2%			-15,8%			-15,9%			-16,2%			-14,4%	-12,2%

Results indicate that the proactive process adaptations triggered by our approach result on average in 6.1% ($\alpha_{min} = 0.5$) resp. 6.4% ($\alpha_{min} = 0$) less process execution costs when compared to empirical thresholding.

As we mentioned above, one of the principle advantages of the RL approach is to capture non-stationarity in the data. The Traffic data set shows such non-stationarity between around case # 14,000 and # 16,000, and again after around case # 45,000. Deeper analysis shows that this is due to the fact that the average prediction accuracy for cases # 14,000 to # 16,000 is 65% higher than the average accuracy for the whole data set, while for all cases after case # 45,000 the average accuracy is 51% lower than the average accuracy for the whole data set. We thus now use the complete Traffic data set to analyze how our approach captures non-stationarity. Results are shown in the last row of Tables 4 and 5 respectively. In the presence of non-stationary, our RL approach shows high improvements over empirical thresholding, leading to 20.3% lower costs on average for both settings of $\alpha_{\min}$. We consider the capability of capturing such non-stationary situation one of the key benefits of our approach. Overall, this leads to average savings of 8% resp. 12.2% when we compare our approach for all three complete data sets against empirical thresholding.

The above results also show the robustness of RL in the presence of different concrete costs (expressed as different values of κ). In 24 out of the 30 situations, RL delivers the same or less costs than empirical thresholding. Note that while the optimal empirical threshold is computed for each value of κ, the RL approach is independent of κ.

Finally, Table 6 compares the costs of the strong reward function with the costs of the weak reward function we used in our previous work and which we applied to the BPIC 2017 data set [25]. As can be seen, the stronger reward function leads to a clear increase in the performance of the RL approach, leading to 36.9% less costs on average. This is an important improvement contributing to our RL approach being able to outperform empirical thresholding.

Table 6. Average process execution costs of strong and weak reward function

| | $\kappa=.1$ | | | $\kappa=.2$ | | | $\kappa=.3$ | | | $\kappa=.4$ | | | $\kappa=.5$ | | | |
	r_{strong}	r_{weak}	Diff	r_{strong}	r_{weak}	Diff	r_{strong}	r_{weak}	Diff	r_{strong}	r_{weak}	Diff	r_{strong}	r_{weak}	Diff	Avg
BPIC 2017	8,2	17,4	-52,9%	14,8	25,0	-40,6%	21,5	32,6	-34,0%	28,2	40,2	-30,0%	34,8	47,8	-27,2%	-36,9%

4 Discussion

4.1 Threats to Validity

Internal Validity. We repeated each of the experiments multiple times in order to assess potential random effects due to the stochastic nature of the neural networks. Even though there were differences in the speed of convergence, the principle learning behavior was consistent across these repetitions. We also purposefully used a multi-layer perceptron as a simple neural network to represent the policy for the RL approach. Using deep learning models, such as RNN-LSTM, to represent the policy may lead to different results.

External Validity. We used three large, real-world data sets from two different application domains, which differ in key characteristics. To consider the effect of cost factors on the overall process execution costs, we varied the relative adaptation and compensation costs (variable κ). However, we used a rather abstract cost model. For instance, we assumed that the concrete costs for each of the cost factors do not depend on the type of adaptation or severity of a problem, i.e., we only used constant cost functions for adaptation costs and penalties. As such, the effects observed may differ when considering different shapes of cost functions faced in practice. Further experiments, e.g., following the setup described in [18], thus would strengthen external validity.

4.2 Limitations

Speed of Convergence. RL may require quite many learning cycles until the learning process converges. In our experiments, learning required feedback from up to 1,300 cases to converge. This was also one of the reasons why our approach was not applicable to the Cargo 2000 data set, which we used previously in [18,22]. This data set only contains 1,313 cases and we could not reasonably observe convergence. Until RL has converged, the system may execute inefficient adaptations, because not enough observations have yet been made. Inefficient adaptations may lead to negative effects, because they are executed in the live system. Solutions to speed up convergence include finding good initial estimates for the learned knowledge and offline learning via simulations of the system.

Non-stationarity. While our RL approach can capture non-stationarity at run time, we still rely on predictions generated by a supervised deep learning model that is trained once on training data. As non-stationarity of the process data may have an impact on the prediction model (e.g., see the differences in accuracy for the Traffic data set discussed above), one enhancement may be to exploit process drift detection [14,15] and re-train the prediction model if needed.

Multiple Adaptions. We currently formulate the RL problem in such a way as to consider only one possible adaptation. In practice, different adaptation alternatives may exist. In principle, the RL problem can be extended to accommodate more than one action. The RL agent can learn when it is better to execute which of these adaptation alternatives; e.g., by considering different costs for different adaptation actions [8].

Parallel Process Instances. Our RL approach does not consider the influence adaptation actions may have on concurrently running cases. One potential enhancement thus may be to build on existing work such as [3], which facilitates predictions across multiple cases.

5 Related Work

We discuss related work along two complementary streams: (1) addressing the trade-off between earliness and accuracy in predictive process monitoring, and (2) using RL in the context of business process management.

Balancing Earliness and Accuracy. In the literature, the trade-off between prediction accuracy and earliness was approached from different angles.

Several authors use prediction earliness as a dependent variable in their experiments. This means they evaluate their predictive process monitoring techniques by considering prediction earliness in addition to prediction accuracy. As an example, Kang et al. [12], Teinemaa et al. [35], and we in our earlier work [21] measured the accuracy of different prediction techniques for the different prediction points along process execution. Results presented in the aforementioned works clearly show the trade-off between prediction earliness and accuracy. However, it was left open how to resolve the trade-off between accuracy and earliness.

In our previous work, we use reliability estimates computed from ensembles of RNN-LSTM models to decide on proactive adaptation [22]. We dynamically determine the earliest prediction with sufficiently high reliability and in turn use this prediction as basis for proactive adaptation. However, our previous approach required the manual definition of a reliability threshold.

Teinemaa et al. introduce the concept of alarm-based prescriptive process monitoring [8,36]. They use class probabilities generated by random forests (ensembles of decision trees) as reliability estimates to determine whether to raise an alarm to trigger a proactive adaptation. The reliability thresholds above which alarms are raised are determined empirically using a dedicated training data set, taking into account a concrete cost model. This ensures that the threshold is optimal for the specific training data used and the given cost model. Yet, the threshold may not be optimal over time due to non-stationarity of process environments and data, and concrete cost structures.

Reinforcement Learning in BPM. In the literature, a few different RL approaches in the context of BPM were proposed. Huang et al. employ RL for the dynamic optimization of resource allocation in operational business processes [11]. However, they do not consider the proactive adaptation of processes with respect to resources at run time. Also, they use Q-Learning as a classical RL algorithm, and thus assume the environment can be represented by a finite, discrete set of states. As mentioned above, our approach does not have this limitation, but it can directly handle large and continuous environments.

Silvander proposes using Q-Learning with function approximation via a deep neural network (DQN) for the optimization of business processes [30]. They suggest defining a so called ϵ decay rate, to reduce the amount of exploration over time. However, they do not consider using RL at run time, and thus do not take into account how to increase the rate of exploration in the presence of non-stationarity. As mentioned above, our approach does not require tuning the exploration rate and thus does not face this problem.

In our previous work, we proposed a generic framework and implementation for using policy-based RL for self-adaptive information systems [25]. Here, we customized this framework specifically for the problem of triggering proactive process adaptations. In particular, we integrated this framework with our work on predictive process monitoring [22]. In addition, we formulated the reward function in a much stronger and more robust way by decoupling it from actual process costs. Finally, we performed a much broader range of experiments, including two additional data sets and the comparison with a state-of-the-art baseline.

6   Conclusions and Perspectives

We combined two emerging machine learning paradigms – ensemble deep supervised learning and policy-based reinforcement learning – to learn when to trigger proactive process adaptations at run time. Experimental results indicate lower process execution costs when compared to the state of the art, in particular in the presence of non-stationarity.

We plan enhancing our approach in order to speed up the convergence of the reinforcement learning process; e.g., by using simulations to perform offline pre-training. In addition, we plan further experiments to analyze potential benefits of using deep learning models to represent the reinforcement learning policy. Finally, we plan collecting empirical insights from applying the approach in actual business operations.

Acknowledgments. We cordially thank the anonymous reviewers for their constructive comments. Our research received funding from the EU's Horizon 2020 R&I programme under grants 871493 (DataPorts) and 780351 (ENACT).

References

1. Bosnic, Z., Kononenko, I.: Comparison of approaches for estimating reliability of individual regression predictions. Data Knowl. Eng. **67**(3), 504–516 (2008)
2. Cabanillas, C., Di Ciccio, C., Mendling, J., Baumgrass, A.: Predictive task monitoring for business processes. In: Sadiq, S., Soffer, P., Völzer, H. (eds.) BPM 2014. LNCS, vol. 8659, pp. 424–432. Springer, Cham (2014). https://doi.org/10.1007/978-3-319-10172-9_31
3. Conforti, R., de Leoni, M., Rosa, M.L., van der Aalst, W.M.P., ter Hofstede, A.H.M.: A recommendation system for predicting risks across multiple business process instances. Decis. Support Syst. **69**, 1–19 (2015)
4. D'Angelo, M., et al.: On learning in collective self-adaptive systems: state of practice and a 3D framework. In: Litoiu, M., Clarke, S., Tei, K. (eds.) 14th International Symposium on Software Engineering for Adaptive and Self-Managing Systems, SEAMS@ICSE 2019, Montreal, QC, Canada, pp. 13–24. ACM (2019)
5. Dewey, D.: Reinforcement learning and the reward engineering principle. In: 2014 AAAI Spring Symposia, Stanford University, Palo Alto, California, USA, 24–26 March 2014. AAAI Press (2014)

6. Dietterich, T.G.: Ensemble methods in machine learning. In: Kittler, J., Roli, F. (eds.) MCS 2000. LNCS, vol. 1857, pp. 1–15. Springer, Heidelberg (2000). https://doi.org/10.1007/3-540-45014-9_1
7. Evermann, J., Rehse, J., Fettke, P.: Predicting process behaviour using deep learning. Decis. Support Syst. **100**, 129–140 (2017)
8. Fahrenkrog-Petersen, S.A., et al.: Fire now, fire later: alarm-based systems for prescriptive process monitoring. CoRR abs/1905.09568 (2019)
9. Di Francescomarino, C., Ghidini, C., Maggi, F.M., Petrucci, G., Yeshchenko, A.: An eye into the future: leveraging a-priori knowledge in predictive business process monitoring. In: Carmona, J., Engels, G., Kumar, A. (eds.) BPM 2017. LNCS, vol. 10445, pp. 252–268. Springer, Cham (2017). https://doi.org/10.1007/978-3-319-65000-5_15
10. Goodfellow, I., Bengio, Y., Courville, A.: Deep Learning. MIT Press, Cambridge (2016)
11. Huang, Z., van der Aalst, W.M.P., Lu, X., Duan, H.: Reinforcement learning based resource allocation in business process management. Data Knowl. Eng. **70**(1), 127–145 (2011)
12. Kang, B., Kim, D., Kang, S.: Real-time business process monitoring method for prediction of abnormal termination using KNNI-based LOF prediction. Expert Syst. Appl. **39**(5), 6061–6068 (2012)
13. Leontjeva, A., Conforti, R., Di Francescomarino, C., Dumas, M., Maggi, F.M.: Complex symbolic sequence encodings for predictive monitoring of business processes. In: Motahari-Nezhad, H.R., Recker, J., Weidlich, M. (eds.) BPM 2015. LNCS, vol. 9253, pp. 297–313. Springer, Cham (2015). https://doi.org/10.1007/978-3-319-23063-4_21
14. Liu, N., Huang, J., Cui, L.: A framework for online process concept drift detection from event streams. In: 2018 International Conference on Services Computing, SCC 2018, San Francisco, CA, USA, pp. 105–112. IEEE (2018)
15. Maaradji, A., Dumas, M., La Rosa, M., Ostovar, A.: Fast and accurate business process drift detection. In: Motahari-Nezhad, H.R., Recker, J., Weidlich, M. (eds.) BPM 2015. LNCS, vol. 9253, pp. 406–422. Springer, Cham (2015). https://doi.org/10.1007/978-3-319-23063-4_27
16. Márquez-Chamorro, A.E., Resinas, M., Ruiz-Cortés, A.: Predictive monitoring of business processes: a survey. IEEE Trans. Serv. Comput. **11**(6), 962–977 (2018)
17. Mehdiyev, N., Evermann, J., Fettke, P.: A multi-stage deep learning approach for business process event prediction. In: Loucopoulos, P., Manolopoulos, Y., Pastor, O., Theodoulidis, B., Zdravkovic, J. (eds.) 19th Conference on Business Informatics, CBI 2017, Thessaloniki, Greece, pp. 119–128. IEEE Computer Society (2017)
18. Metzger, A., Bohn, P.: Risk-based proactive process adaptation. In: Maximilien, M., Vallecillo, A., Wang, J., Oriol, M. (eds.) ICSOC 2017. LNCS, vol. 10601, pp. 351–366. Springer, Cham (2017). https://doi.org/10.1007/978-3-319-69035-3_25
19. Metzger, A., Föcker, F.: Predictive business process monitoring considering reliability estimates. In: Dubois, E., Pohl, K. (eds.) CAiSE 2017. LNCS, vol. 10253, pp. 445–460. Springer, Cham (2017). https://doi.org/10.1007/978-3-319-59536-8_28
20. Metzger, A., Franke, J., Jansen, T.: Ensemble deep learning for proactive terminal process management at duisport. In: vom Brocke, J., Mendling, J., Rosemann, M. (eds.) Business Process Management Cases, vol. 2. Springer, Heidelberg (2020)
21. Metzger, A., Neubauer, A.: Considering non-sequential control flows for process prediction with recurrent neural networks. In: 44th Euromicro Conference on Software Engineering and Advanced Applications, SEAA, Prague, Czech Republic, pp. 268–272. IEEE Computer Society (2018)

22. Metzger, A., Neubauer, A., Bohn, P., Pohl, K.: Proactive process adaptation using deep learning ensembles. In: Giorgini, P., Weber, B. (eds.) CAiSE 2019. LNCS, vol. 11483, pp. 547–562. Springer, Cham (2019). https://doi.org/10.1007/978-3-030-21290-2_34

23. Nachum, O., Norouzi, M., Xu, K., Schuurmans, D.: Bridging the gap between value and policy based reinforcement learning. In: Advances in Neural Information Processing Systems 12 (NIPS 2017), pp. 2772–2782 (2017)

24. Nunes, V.T., Santoro, F.M., Werner, C.M.L., Ralha, C.G.: Real-time process adaptation: a context-aware replanning approach. IEEE Trans. Syst. Man Cybern. Syst. **48**(1), 99–118 (2018)

25. Palm, A., Metzger, A., Pohl, K.: Online reinforcement learning for self-adaptive information systems. In: Dustdar, S., Yu, E., Salinesi, C., Rieu, D., Pant, V. (eds.) CAiSE 2020. LNCS, vol. 12127, pp. 169–184. Springer, Cham (2020). https://doi.org/10.1007/978-3-030-49435-3_11

26. Park, G., Song, M.: Prediction-based resource allocation using LSTM and minimum cost and maximum flow algorithm. In: International Conference on Process Mining (ICPM 2019), Aachen, Germany, pp. 121–128 (2019)

27. Polikar, R.: Ensemble based systems in decision making. IEEE Circuits Syst. Mag. **6**(3), 21–45 (2006)

28. Poll, R., Polyvyanyy, A., Rosemann, M., Röglinger, M., Rupprecht, L.: Process forecasting: towards proactive business process management. In: Weske, M., Montali, M., Weber, I., vom Brocke, J. (eds.) BPM 2018. LNCS, vol. 11080, pp. 496–512. Springer, Cham (2018). https://doi.org/10.1007/978-3-319-98648-7_29

29. Schulman, J., Wolski, F., Dhariwal, P., Radford, A., Klimov, O.: Proximal policy optimization algorithms. CoRR abs/1707.06347 (2017)

30. Silvander, J.: Business process optimization with reinforcement learning. In: Shishkov, B. (ed.) BMSD 2019. LNBIP, vol. 356, pp. 203–212. Springer, Cham (2019). https://doi.org/10.1007/978-3-030-24854-3_13

31. Sutton, R.S., Barto, A.G.: Reinforcement Learning: An Introduction. MIT Press, Cambridge (2018)

32. Sutton, R.S., McAllester, D.A., Singh, S.P., Mansour, Y.: Policy gradient methods for reinforcement learning with function approximation. In: Advances in Neural Information Processing Systems 12 (NIPS 1999), pp. 1057–1063 (2000)

33. Tax, N., Verenich, I., La Rosa, M., Dumas, M.: Predictive business process monitoring with LSTM neural networks. In: Dubois, E., Pohl, K. (eds.) CAiSE 2017. LNCS, vol. 10253, pp. 477–492. Springer, Cham (2017). https://doi.org/10.1007/978-3-319-59536-8_30

34. Teinemaa, I., Dumas, M., Maggi, F.M., Di Francescomarino, C.: Predictive business process monitoring with structured and unstructured data. In: La Rosa, M., Loos, P., Pastor, O. (eds.) BPM 2016. LNCS, vol. 9850, pp. 401–417. Springer, Cham (2016). https://doi.org/10.1007/978-3-319-45348-4_23

35. Teinemaa, I., Dumas, M., Rosa, M.L., Maggi, F.M.: Outcome-oriented predictive process monitoring: review and benchmark. TKDD **13**(2), 17:1–17:57 (2019)

36. Teinemaa, I., Tax, N., de Leoni, M., Dumas, M., Maggi, F.M.: Alarm-based prescriptive process monitoring. In: Weske, M., Montali, M., Weber, I., vom Brocke, J. (eds.) BPM 2018. LNBIP, vol. 329, pp. 91–107. Springer, Cham (2018). https://doi.org/10.1007/978-3-319-98651-7_6

37. Weber, B., Sadiq, S.W., Reichert, M.: Beyond rigidity - dynamic process lifecycle support. Comput. Sci. - R&D **23**(2), 47–65 (2009)

38. Zhou, Z.H.: Ensemble Methods: Foundations and Algorithms. Chapman and Hall/CRC, Boca Raton (2012)

Video-to-Model: Unsupervised Trace Extraction from Videos for Process Discovery and Conformance Checking in Manual Assembly

Sönke Knoch[(✉)], Shreeraman Ponpathirkoottam, and Tim Schwartz

German Research Center for Artificial Intelligence (DFKI), Saarland Informatics Campus, Saarland University, Stuhlsatzenhausweg 3, 66123 Saarbrücken, Germany
soenke.knoch@dfki.de

Abstract. Manual activities are often hidden deep down in discrete manufacturing processes. To analyze and optimize such processes, process discovery techniques allow the mining of the actual process behavior. Those techniques require the availability of complete event logs representing the execution of manual activities. Related works about collecting such information from sensor data unobtrusively for the worker are rare. Papers either address the sensor-based recognition of activities or focus on the process discovery part using process mining-compatible data sets. This paper builds on previous works to provide a solution on how execution-level information can be extracted from videos in manual assembly. The test bed consists of an assembly workstation equipped with a single RGB camera. A neural network-based real-time object detector delivers the input for an algorithm, which generates trajectories reflecting the movement paths of the worker's hands. Those trajectories are automatically assigned to work steps using hierarchical clustering of similar behavior with dynamic time warping. The system has been evaluated in a task-based study with ten participants in a laboratory under realistic conditions. The generated logs have been loaded into the process mining toolkit ProM to discover the underlying process model and to measure the system's performance using conformance checking.

Keywords: Process mining · Computer vision · Unsupervised learning · Industry 4.0

1 Introduction

Manual assembly workflows usually involve numerous work steps to be performed involving multiple material parts and tools. The creation of models to control, analyze, and optimize such workflows is oftentimes costly, necessitating

---

S. Knoch and S. Ponpathirkoottam—These authors contributed equally.

D. Fahland et al. (Eds.): BPM 2020, LNCS 12168, pp. 291–308, 2020.
https://doi.org/10.1007/978-3-030-58666-9_17

interviews, workshops, and observations to generate models of existing workflows. Process discovery offers a data-driven alternative with the prerequisite of detailed logs containing event traces about the workflow with information such as case identifiers, activity names, and time stamps. Gathering such logs and subsequent process discovery in manual assembly requires sensors which can provide fine-grained and accurate data about the steps and a technique that extracts the relevant information from raw sensor data.

According to van der Aalst 2012 [2], event log generation for process mining from raw data remains a challenge. The analysis of related works in Diba et al. 2019 [7] shows that most works focus on the event data extraction and abstraction from information available in databases and not from sensors. The modeling of manual workflows as business processes directly from videos is an emerging field. The literature review by Mannhardt et al. [13] analyzes work about sensor-based activity recognition in industrial environments and shows that work based on raw videos of manual assembly procedures is sparse, dominated by supervised recognition techniques, and that the connection to process discovery is a promising direction for future research.

A seamless method to generate process mining logs and to discover workflows in manual assembly processes using cameras is suggested. Video data from cameras is used and processed with the help of a hand detection framework to generate data elements representing the hand positions. To abstract these data elements to events in the process trace, the data elements are combined into hand movement trajectories and assigned to work-step events using unsupervised clustering techniques and dynamic time warping. The developed pipeline, from hand detection, to trajectory building and clustering, to the identification of work steps, has been evaluated in a task-based user study in the laboratory.

The remainder of this paper is organized as follows: In Sect. 2, related work about video-based workflow discovery is presented. Section 3 describes the preliminary context and the selected use case. In Sect. 4, the concept and implementation of all steps towards the log generation from videos is explained. The evaluation containing the study design and the process mining analysis is presented in Sect. 5. The paper concludes with Sect. 6.

2   Related Work

One of the earliest proofs of concept of workflow discovery in manual assembly was by Kaczmareka et al. [9], describing an assembly station equipped with an additional RGB depth camera (RGB+D). They analyzed the depth picture information and build a dictionary of images of assembly states and hand gestures. This dictionary is used to identify different work steps and build a workflow. Müller et al. [14] proposed a more versatile approach called the smart assembly workplace, an environment designed to impart knowledge on assembly to unskilled users. It is an *supervised* approach, which uses an RGB+D camera to observe predefined activity zones to extract work steps performed by workers. The depth data is used to filter interest regions, and the skin color is used for hand localization. Though the method is inspiring as a concept, without good quality depth data and highly controlled worker movements, the work step identification would be inaccurate.

Roitberg et al. [17], in a more recent work, observed assembly activities using a multi-modal setup involving two infrared cameras specialized for hand and finger detection and an RGB+D camera for body tracking. They devise a *supervised* technique to identify different work steps by fusing many features from the different sensors. With a huge data set, they are able to demonstrate a powerful technique, but as with any other supervised method, the dependency on a large data set makes their idea less scalable.

Nater et al. [15], proposed one of the earliest ideas to observe a car-assembly scene from a ceiling-mounted camera and identify workflows in an *unsupervised* way. Entire camera frames were used as feature vectors after dimensionality reduction and clustered into group frames corresponding to the same task. The crucial assumption of a cyclic workflow in their work enabled them to filter the noise. Although suitable for tracking frame-level changes in an assembly environment, their method is not suitable for fine-grained understanding of events.

Bauters et al. [4] aim to identify (1) optimal movement paths for fast work step completion and (2) abnormal paths of workers, in a large room where assembly is performed. They use five cameras to segment the location of the workers in an assembly room consisting of an assembly station, where assembly is performed, and racks, where parts are stored. The trajectories traced by the worker while picking up parts and bringing them to the station are grouped using unsupervised techniques to identify normal and abnormal work steps, and to derive performance indicators for each step (like speed of movement, cycle time etc.). The focus of the authors was not to derive workflows. Inspired by this work, we adapted the use of hierarchical clustering and dynamic time warping for clustering hand motion patterns in manual assembly at a single workstation. Table 1 provides a feature comparison between the related works and the suggested Video-to-Model approach.

Table 1. Feature comparison between related works and this work.

Feature/Work	[9]	[14]	[17]	[15]	[4]	Video-to-Model
Activity Recognition	✗	✗	✓	✗	✗	✗
Designed for Single Workstation	✗	✓	✓	✗	✗	✓
Camera-based Hand Detection	✗	✗	✓	✗	✗	✓
Motion Pattern Analysis	✗	✗	✗	✗	✓	✓
Unsupervised Learning	✗	✗	✗	✓	✓	✓
Workflow Discovery	✓	✓	✗	✓	✓	✓
Flexibility/Scalability	✗	✗	✗	✓	✓	✓
Video-based	✓	✓	✓	✓	✓	✓

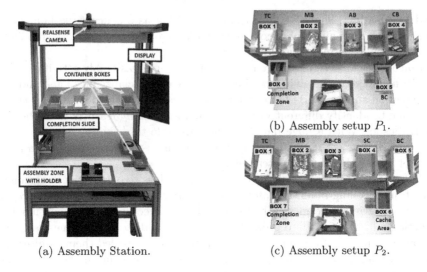

(b) Assembly setup P_1.

(c) Assembly setup P_2.

(a) Assembly Station.

Fig. 1. Manual assembly workstation equipped with RGB camera. (Color figure online)

3   Preliminaries

A *process model* triggers a set of *task execution sequences* which are called the execution sequences of a model; cf. Carmona et al. [6, p. 30 et seq.]. According to the authors, the recording of a single activity is called an *event* and is an atomic representation of such an activity. Events are summarized in one *case*. A time series of events is called a *trace*. The challenge of the Video-to-Model approach lies in the extraction of event data from videos and the abstraction of this data to process mining-compatible events. Based on the concepts provided in Carmona et al. 2018, Diba et al. 2019 distinguish between event data extraction, event correlation, and event abstraction. Event data *extraction* is concerned with the derivation of data elements, event *correlation* with the association of data elements to traces of a case, and event *abstraction* with the transition for those elements to events in the log representing activity executions. Mapping this terminology to our work, for extraction a *hand detector* from computer vision is used to extract hand locations which form the data elements. For abstraction, those data elements are connected to *trajectories* which are defined as a sequence of detected hands in the video. Finally, those hand motion trajectories are *clustered* and mapped to events that correspond to *activity executions*. The events are *work steps* forming the *trace*, which corresponds to an assembly process describing the construction of one specific *product* executed by a *worker*. The terminology and proposed pipeline is illustrated in Fig. 2.

In the presented Video-to-Model approach we aim at the discovery of manual work behavior in the form of work steps in video recordings. To illustrate the approach, an assembly workstation was chosen as an example objective to explore the potential of the developed software artefact. A camera perspective showing

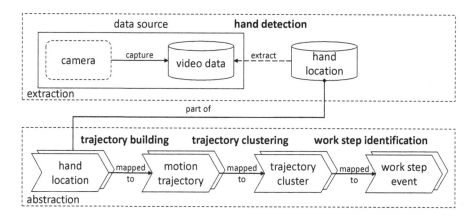

Fig. 2. Trajectory clustering and work step identification based on [7].

the worker's hands from above, as shown on the right of Fig. 1, minimizes possible
interference caused by the worker's assembly activities and protects their privacy,
since the worker can remain anonymous. Such a view provides consistent information about the worker's hand movements, which are in the focus of attention
when analyzing a manual assembly process. This low degree of instrumentation
makes the suggested approach highly flexible and scalable when several workstations have to be instrumented. The only requirement that must be fulfilled is the
visibility of the hands during assembly and the availability of stable light conditions. This requirement is usually satisfied in a manufacturing context, since
assembly workstations usually include their own light sources at the top of the
installation.

Figure 1 shows the manual assembly workstation which has been designed
and constructed according to industry standards. The station has two levels:
one top level serving materials and one lower level acting as the desk for assembly tasks, containing tools and further materials. Material parts are stored in
standard container boxes, referred to as small load carriers (SLC), which are
common instruments for organizing material storage at an assembly station in
manufacturing. In addition, the workstation is equipped with a display showing
worker guidance instructions and a work piece holder fixing the product during assembly in front of the worker. A completion slide on the left side carries
finalized products to the back of the workstation for follow-up tasks, such as
inspection or packaging.

For the assembly, we used a mock-up product with no real function that was
taken from the SmartF-IT research project [20] funded by BMBF. It includes two
variants consisting of the material parts connecting board (CB), an application
board (AB), a main board (MB), top casing (TC), bottom casing (BC), and
several screws (SC) stored in Euro SLCs and fixed together using a common
screwdriver as the only tool.

4   Concept and Implementation

Figure 2 provides an overview of the implemented pipeline consisting of four steps. It is divided into event data *extraction* at the top and *abstraction* at the bottom of the figure. The extraction starts with the video capture of manual assembly activities. This video data is stored and processed by the *hand detection* and delivers information about the hand location. Those hand locations form the input for the abstraction, which starts with the *trajectory building*, connecting the hand location coordinates to hand motion trajectories representing the grasp paths of the worker's hands. The trajectories are the input for the *trajectory clustering* which groups similar grasp paths. Finally, during *work step identification* the clusters are mapped to work steps using the vicinity of a cluster to the position of a material box. A material box is labeled by the material name, which uniquely identifies the work step activity. It must be noted that the trajectory clustering is an unsupervised form of the work step identification. The positions of material boxes are used, due to their availability, to verify the identification and to automatize the work step labeling, making the final step semi-supervised. The details about each step are explained in the following.

4.1   Hand Detection

In order to discover the workflow in manual assembly, it is necessary to gather information about the worker's hand positions. Object detection and localization delivers information about the object's presence and position within an image in the form of a bounding box surrounding the detected object. Current state-of-the-art object detection approaches use deep neural networks (DNN). The major advantage of DNNs is the re-usability of the feature representations learned for new object detection tasks, making them highly scalable. A popular object detector maintained and used by a large community is the YOLOv3 object detector [16] which was originally trained for multi-class object detection. The feature representations learned by this detector are reused for detecting hands by retraining it with a suitable hand detection data set. Except for one recent work [18] there are no explicit hand data sets for the industrial context. In this work we used data sets where the appearance and usage of hands are comparable to those in industrial context.

Inspired by the work of [19] where the camera view is similar to ours, we started with the Ego-Hand data set [3], re-training the YOLOv3 detector for hand detection. It consists of a two-person interaction recorded from an egocentric camera, including 48 Google Glass videos of interaction between two persons at a table, 4, 800 video frames with 15, 053 hand labels, and annotations about the left and right hand. The code for re-training of the YOLOv3 detector is provided by its authors; see [16]. With a data set available in the format as expected by the code, the model can be retrained.

Since the accuracy observed during tests in the evaluation setup indicated scope for improvement, we improved the performance by selecting the VIVA hand detection challenge data set. It includes videos from YouTube and videos of hands of car drivers and their front seat passengers. It contains 7 views including the first person view, left and right hand annotations, 5, 500 frames of annotated training data and 5, 500 frames of test data. A pre-study with five participants assembling 20 products of variant one from the evaluation, see Sect. 5, was conducted. It was found that the combination of the VIVA and Ego-Hands data sets, augmented with vertically flipped versions of the images in both sets, sufficiently covered the variations in hand pose and appearance required for the assembly use case.

4.2   Trajectory Building

A trajectory is constructed representing the movement of one of the worker's hands in order to perform a work step. Since all the assembling activity is performed in the assembly zone marked with a blue tape as shown in Fig. 1, trajectories are constructed whenever the hands move outside the assembly zone. Ideally, a trajectory represents a work step. A representative point of the bounding box delivered by the hand detector is sufficient for building such hand motion trajectories. The midpoint of the top horizontal edge of the bounding box is chosen for this purpose and is called the *pivot point*. Since the hand motion paths corresponding to different work steps can cross each other, a simple spatial clustering of the pivot point coordinates in the image will not be sufficient to distinguish different work steps. Hence, the pivot points occurring with consecutive time stamps are connected to build a *valid hand motion trajectory* which can be mapped to a single work step event.

The hand detection is performed on each frame of the given video of the assembly process. Hands detected in subsequent time instances, not necessarily in subsequent frames, are assembled to form trajectories. Hence a trajectory is defined as a set of hands arranged in ascending order of time stamps. A trajectory t of length l can be represented as $t = \{h_1, h_2, \ldots, h_l\}$ and $h_1 < h_2 < h_l$. Trajectories are built whenever the hands move outside the assembly zone. This explains the white box with no trajectories shown in Fig. 3b and 3c. As each frame is processed, the set of detected hands is used to build two lists of trajectories—a list of active trajectories is represented as T_A, and a list of inactive trajectories as T_I. A trajectory in T_A is moved to T_I when no new hand is added to it over a period of 1 s or 60 frames since our video is recorded at 60 FPS. In order to filter trajectories caused by random, uninteresting hand movements as well as noisy trajectories caused by false positives in the hand detection, a trajectory is removed if it contains less than 5 hand positions. Prior to moving trajectories from T_A to T_I, all the hands in a given frame are to be suitably handled.

Each detected hand can belong to exactly one trajectory. Let $H_D = \{h_i, i = 1, 2 \ldots n\}$ correspond to the set of all hands detected in the current frame. Further, $box(h_i)$ refers to the detected hands' bounding box and $point(h_i)$ to the pivot point of this box. Now, let $T_A = \{t_k, k = 1 \ldots K\}$ be the set of all active trajectories where $t_k = \{h_1^{(k)}, h_2^{(k)}, \ldots, h_l^{(k)}\}$, and $h_1^{(k)} < h_2^{(k)} < h_l^{(k)}$, ascending by time, is the kth active trajectory. The last detected hand in the kth active

Algorithm 1. Trajectory building

```
 1: {T_A = {t_k, k = 1 ... K}}
 2: {The for loop is run for each frame of the video.}
 3: for all h_i in H_D do
 4:    foundTrajectory := False
 5:    minDistance := 10,000
 6:    minTrajIndex := -1
 7:    {Phase 1:}
 8:    for all h_l^(k) in T_A do
 9:       if overlap(box(h_i), box(h_l^(k))) > 0.3 then
10:          add h_i to t_k
11:          foundTrajectory := True
12:          break
13:       else
14:          if distance(point(h_i), point(h_l^(k))) < minDistance then
15:             minDistance = distance(point(h_i), point(h_l^(k)))
16:             minTrajIndex = k
17:          end if
18:       end if
19:    end for
20:    {Phase 2:}
21:    if not foundTrajectory then
22:       if minDistance < 50px then
23:          add h_i to t_{minTrajIndex}
24:       else
25:          add h_i to t_{k=K+1} in T_A as new trajectory
26:          {T_A = {t_k, k = 1 ... K + 1}}
27:       end if
28:    end if
29: end for
30: {Moving trajectories from active list to inactive list}
31: for all t_k in T_A do
32:    if time.of(h_i) - time.of(h_l^(k)) > 1sec then
33:       if |t_k| >= 5 then
34:          add t_k to T_I
35:       end if
36:       remove t_k from T_A
37:    end if
38: end for
```

trajectory is $h_l^{(k)}$. All the hands in H_D are compared with the last hand in each active trajectory, $\{h_l^{(k)}, k = 1, 2 \ldots K\}$, based on two different criteria (referred to as phases) and added to the respective active trajectory. If a particular hand h_i does not satisfy either of the two criteria to be added to an active trajectory, a new active trajectory is started with h_i as the first hand in it.

Algorithm 1 shows the procedure of building trajectories. Each detected hand in H_D is handled in two phases as stated earlier. For each hand h_i in H_D, two variables, $foundTrajectory$ and $minDistance$, are initialized. Then, in *phase 1*, the overlap between the bounding box of the detected object h_i and the bounding box of the last hand $h_l^{(k)}$ in each trajectory in the set of active trajectories T_A is checked. If an overlap by more then 30% is identified, then the object h_i is added to the respective trajectory t_k. If multiple objects provide an overlap of more than 30%, the one with the maximum overlap is chosen. When the overlap criteria is satisfied, phase 1 is finished. If the overlap criteria is not satisfied, the distance between the pivot point of h_i and $h_l^{(k)} \forall k$ in $[1, 2 \ldots K]$ is checked.

The minimum distance is stored in $minDistance$ and the minimum index is stored in $minTrajIndex$ used in *phase 2*.

Phase 2 is invoked if the hand h_i could not be assigned to any of the active trajectories based on the overlap criteria. It is needed in cases when the hand moved too fast even to be detected by the camera capture at 60 FPS. Such fast hand movements were caused by the freedom given to users to perform actions in a natural way. One way of handling this would have been to reduce the overlap criteria even further, which in turn would have led to a high number of false positives in the trajectories. Phase 2 is also necessary when the hand detector has failed to recognize hands in a certain frame. Then, the value of $minDistance$ is checked. If it is lower then 50px, then h_i is added to the trajectory t_k, where the last object's pivot point was close to h_i's pivot point. Otherwise, h_i is used to create a new trajectory, which is added to the list of active trajectories T_A.

The constants chosen to define the overlap of two bounding boxes, the distance between two pivot points and the validation of a constructed trajectory regarding time and the number of points have been identified during tests in the evaluation setup in order to minimize the number of broken trajectories. If the workstation setup, the frame rate of the camera and its position changes or the observed user behavior differs widely, they may require adjustment.

4.3   Trajectory Clustering

Hierarchical clustering, an unsupervised, standard procedure in multivariate data analysis, was chosen to cluster trajectories of the same work step. It was selected because it does not require the number of clusters to be known in advance and provides, with the dendrogram, a nice visualization of the relation between different clusters. To achieve a clustering that is not too general (clusters contain a large share of objects) and not too specific (clusters contain a small share of objects), a depth of k at which the hierarchy is cut needs to be defined carefully by the user. The type of clustering may be divisive (top-down) or agglomerative (bottom-up). Since divisive clustering is computationally more expensive due to its consideration of all possible divisions into subsets, we chose *bottom-up agglomerative clustering*, starting with the maximum number of clusters.

During clustering, each trajectory is first treated as a separate cluster. Then the following two steps are continually repeated: (1) identify two clusters that are similar to each other based on a distance measure, and (2) merge the two most similar clusters. To measure the distance, a metric computing the distance between two points, such as the Euclidean, Manhattan, or Mahalanobis Distance, can be chosen. The criteria for merging of two clusters can be estimated by using the distance between the farthest, closest or centroid elements of two clusters.

The points within trajectories occur with different frequencies and with different time distances, due to the different speed of the hand movements and also due to mis-detections. Thus, a simple distance measure will not provide an accurate comparison between clustered trajectories. Dynamic time warping (DTW) [5], which is often used in automatic speech recognition where temporal sequences of speech units are compared, provides a more advanced similarity measure. To match two sequences optimally, time is stretched (warped), repeating some points in the sequence, which gave this method its name. DTW ensures that a different speed of observation occurrence in time sequences with different length does not affect the similarity measure between them.

The implemented clustering handles each trajectory as an individual data point. Using DTW, the trajectories are compared with 1 norm as a distance measure. The DTW approach was combined with Ward's variance, as suggested by [12], in order to be more accurate and consistent, especially for small data sets. The depth of k was chosen heuristically based on tests with the data collected during evaluation. The clusters refer to the work steps in the assembly process.

4.4   Work Step Identification

Ideally, if there are no mis-detections, a trajectory starts when the hand leaves the assembly zone and ends when it enters the assembly zone again as mentioned in Sect. 4.2. The starting and ending time stamps of a trajectory, which are the first and the last frame with a detected hand in the hand motion path, represent the start and end time stamps of the work step. In the absence of predefined zones for the boxes, each trajectory represents a work step, and clustering groups all the trajectories of the same workstep into one group. Hence, under ideal conditions, the work step identification described in this paper is an unsupervised offline technique developed to work on recorded video data.

In the current approach, due to hand mis-detections, the trajectories constructed need to be filtered and broken trajectories grouped. Also, for the discussed target scenario, the work steps within a work plan (referred to as the assembly process) differ regarding the materials which are involved; the material picking is defined as a reference point. Since the locations of the material boxes are available to us, we are able to map each cluster to a work step ID as the activity name. Therefore, we use the concept of activity zones surrounding the material box. Such a labeling is shown, e.g., in Fig. 1 (c): seven activity zones indicate the position of materials, the assembly zone, and the slide for finalized products. Such activity zones have to be defined in advance to allow the automatic identification of work steps and the process discovery. This generates a log of valid traces consisting of PersonID (resource), ProductID (case), WorkStepID (activity), StartTime and EndTime. This can be considered a semi-supervised approach, since human input is given in the form of activity zones.

The work step identification was realized by implementing a voting procedure, allowing each trajectory within a cluster to vote for its work step name. The voting procedure was required since the trajectories of left and right hands from the same user can be very different and can sometimes be assigned to the wrong activity zone. The voting procedure eliminates this error. For each trajectory, the point most distant from the assembly zone is chosen to be the *voting point* of the respective trajectory. Then, for all voting points, the distance to the left or right edge (whichever is closer) of the activity zone is measured. If the distance is below a defined threshold, the vote is counted. Otherwise the

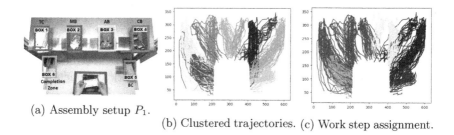

(a) Assembly setup P_1.

(b) Clustered trajectories. (c) Work step assignment.

Fig. 3. Trajectory clustering and work step identification.

Table 2. Excerpt from the event log for P_1, T_1 generated during evaluation with reference (REF), discovered (DISC), and ground truth (GT) work steps IDs.

Index	PersonID	ProductID	WorkStepID			StartTime	EndTime
log_{DISC}	(resource)	(case)	$model_{REF}$	log_{DISC}	log_{GT}		
295	P12	Prod42	Box 1	Box 1	Box 1	14:13:45.18	14:13:46.37
296	P12	Prod42	Box 2	Box 2	Box 2	14:13:49.64	14:13:50.81
297	P12	Prod42	Box 3	Box 3	Box 3	14:13:53.86	14:13:54.81
298	P12	Prod42	$\gg$	Box 5	junk	14:13:59.40	14:13:59.95
299	P12	Prod42	Box 4	Box 4	Box 4	14:13:59.03	14:14:00.26
300	P12	Prod42	Box 5	Box 5	Box 5	14:14:09.46	14:14:10.67
301	P12	Prod42	Box 6	Box 6	Box 6	14:14:15.90	14:14:18.52
302	P12	Prod42	$\gg$	Box 6	Box 6	14:14:21.70	14:14:21.89

trajectory is marked as a *junk path*. Since left hand trajectories tend to be closer to the left edge and right hand trajectories to the right edge of the activity zone, this information about the direction from which a box was approached is used to classify the path as left or right handed. After voting, all trajectories in a cluster are labeled with the ID of the activity zone that received the maximum number of votes in the cluster.

Figure 3 shows the trajectory clustering and work step identification graphically. Figure 3b shows the clustered trajectories where each cluster is identified by an arbitrary color. Figure 3c shows the clusters assigned to work steps using the color of the relevant material box from the setup in Fig. 3a. In Table 2 an excerpt for one case from the event log generated during the evaluation can be seen. Two examples of abnormal behavior can be seen highlighted in grey: *junk* indicates a falsely classified work step due to hand movements not related to the assembly, and there is a false repetition of step 6 due to a split of the grasp path caused by missing hand detections resulting in two separate trajectory clusters. Both leads to a move ($\gg$) in the log which can not be executed according to the model during conformance checking. A model move would occur, for example, when a work step was not identified and is absent in the log.

5   Evaluation

The study was conducted at the assembly workstation described in Sect. 3. The task-based study design is described in Sect. 5.1. Section 5.2 describes the conducted process mining analysis evaluating the presented work step identification pipeline. The results are discussed in Sect. 5.3.

5.1   Study Design

In order to simulate workflow variations, the assembly instructions are varied to control the human behavior through three different *assembly tasks* (T_1, T_2 and T_3) for two different *product variants* (P_1 and P_2). Aside from the different material parts, the number of boxes changes between product variant one and two (P_1 and P_2), as shown in the Figs. 1b and 1c.

The *first task* T_1 in each product scenario reflects high standardization with no variation, where the user has a minimal degree of freedom and the assembly is performed one part at a time in sequential order. It was designed to provide ideal conditions for the hand detection. In the *second task* T_2, an optimized behavior is directed: grasping two parts at a time with both hands. T_2 represents a process variation and was designed to evaluate whether or not the system can discover the variation in the workflow. The *third task* T_3 reflects the highest degree of freedom for the worker, since he or she was asked to assemble the product without further restrictions. It was designed to test how well the system can discover the dominant workflow under these varying conditions. Within each task, the participants assembled five products to allow the system to extract recurring patterns over a period of observations.

Before starting the assembly, every participant was instructed to keep their hands in the assembly region when not in use. In addition, one material part was to grasped at a time unless the grasping of two parts was specifically requested in the instructions. Parts which were not in use were not to be held in the hands. Within P_2, screws that were not used had to be placed back in their box unless the use of a defined storing region on the table was permitted. Between each task, there was a pause lasting a minimum of one and a maximum of three minutes. During assembly, a supervisor dismantled assembled products and refilled the material boxes from the back side of the station, due to the limited amount of available parts during the experiment.

To guide participants through the assembly process, instructions for each task (out of six) were shown on a display screen adjacent to the assembly desk as shown in Fig. 1. On the screen, all material parts and assembly steps were described. Before the start of each task, the supervisor demonstrated the assembly one time and the participant repeated the assembly a maximum of two times to clarify any doubts.

Ten persons ($5f$, $5m$) participated in the study. The participants were divided into two groups of five persons each. One group started with product one, the other group with product two, to avoid a learning effect in support of one of the product variants. Four participants were left-handed. There was no discernible

Table 3. (1) conformance between $model_{REF}$ and log_{GT}; (2) conformance between $model_{DISC}$ and log_{GT}.

Metric	P_1, T_1	P_1, T_2	P_1, T_3	P_2, T_1	P_2, T_2	P_2, T_3
(1) Trace fitness	0.9420	0.9472	–	0.9127	0.8023	–
(1) Move-model fitness	0.9867	0.9933	–	0.9871	0.9778	–
(1) Move-log fitness	0.9071	0.9101	–	0.8742	0.6943	–
(2) Trace fitness	0.9630	0.9760	0.9581	0.9343	0.7297	0.9536
(2) Move-model fitness	0.9867	0.9933	0.9932	0.9905	1.0000	0.9810
(2) Move-log fitness	0.9454	0.9632	0.9325	0.9160	0.7297	0.9480
Classification accuracy	0.9260	0.9528	0.9729	0.9952	0.9414	0.8847

pattern noticed in the usage of specific hands for specific parts, except that in order to access a particular box, participants preferred using the hand closest to the box. With more participants and a longer observation period, more conclusive remarks could be made.

5.2 Result

Two kinds of logs have been generated from the evaluation study for each task and product variant (in total twelve): the *discovered workflow* log_{DISC} from the trajectory building and clustering, and the *annotated workflow* log_{GT} from the human annotations. For each task and product variant, each log is based on five products assembled by ten participants, and thus contains 50 execution sequences which are mined for a process. The logs were loaded into the process mining tool ProM [8] and converted into the eXtensible Event Stream (XES) format. The logs have been made available in [10].

Performance Indication for Hand Detection and Trajectory Building. In the following, $model_{ref}$ and log_{GT} are compared. $model_{ref}$ includes four Petri nets which were modeled based on the instructions given to the participants within tasks 1 and 2 in both product variants. These reference workflows are used to evaluate the performance of the hand detection and trajectory building. For this, two assumptions were made: (1) the participants follow the instructions thoroughly and (2) the ground truth log represents 100% accurate hand detection and trajectory building. The nets were created in the Yasper Petri net editor (see www.yasper.org) and imported into ProM, and are available under [10]. To prepare the conformance checking, an initial marking was set to the first place and a final marking to the last place in each net to achieve a simplified Petri net for replay. For this, we used the ProM plugins by Adriansyah and Verbeek. This procedure allows the computation of the fitness metric for all four reference models. The conformance checking was conducted using the replay technique by [1]. In the configuration, we chose a replay technique based on

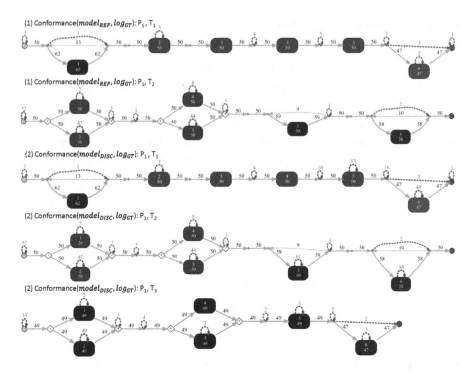

Fig. 4. (1) Reference (*model_REF*) and (2) discovered models (*model_DISC*) for P_1 with work step IDs and number of occurences from ProM's inductive miner; Tau transitions have been faded out for better legibility.

integer linear programming. For the classification, the start events were chosen, and thus complete and dummy events were assigned with zero costs. The results from conformance checking for P_1 are shown in Fig. 4 and in Table 3 indexed with (1). In the figure, the number of occurrences is indicated per work step ID. Red-dashed edges indicate inserted events additional to the model and activities which have been skipped in the model.

Performance Test Trajectory Clustering and Work Step Identification.
To evaluate the performance of trajectory clustering and work step identification, a workflow model *model_DISC* was generated in the form of a Petri net from the discovered log *log_DISC* using the inductive miner by [11] (variant=infrequent, noise threshold = 0.2) for all six tasks across both products. The model was then used to check the conformance between the net and the annotated ground truth log *log_GT* again using the replay technique by [1]. Since *log_DISC* reflects the result from the clustering and work step identification and *model_DISC* represents an aggregated form of this information, the conformance between *model_DISC* and *log_GT* provides insights about the performance of the suggested approach of the trajectory clustering and work step identification. It states how well a discovered

model fits the reality captured in the ground truth. The three models for P_1 from the inductive mining are presented in Fig. 4 below the two reference models. The rows in Table 3 indexed with (2) show the results from the second conformance checking in terms of numbers.

Confusion Matrix. Figure 5 shows the confusion matrices accumulating the number of trajectories during all tasks per product variant. This is a common metric to analyze multi-class classification. For example, it is stated in the matrix for P_1 in Fig. 5a that box 2 was discovered one time, but during annotation it was labeled as box 1. We refer to such a confusion with $C(i,j)$, where $i \neq j$. Summing up all such mis-classifications and dividing them by the sum of correct classifications in the diagonal line, an accuracy of 0.9479 was achieved for P_1 and 0.8923 for the more complex product P_2. The accuracy values for each task per product are listed in the last row of Table 3.

Ann/Disc	Junk	Box 1	Box 2	Box 3	Box 4	Box 5	Box 6
Junk	15					8	6
Box 1	5	152	1				17
Box 2			153				
Box 3				150			1
Box 4					152	12	
Box 5						167	
Box 6							170

(a) Confusion matrix P_1.

Ann/Disc	Junk	Box 1	Box 2	Box 3	Box 4	Box 5	Box 6	Box 7
Junk	92				2	1	41	2
Box 1	25	155	1	1				3
Box 2	1		149	2				
Box 3			2	153	1		1	
Box 4				11	285		2	
Box 5	7				6	154	31	
Box 6	2					2	244	1
Box 7	3	1						151

(b) Confusion matrix P_2.

Fig. 5. Confusion matrices showing the accumulated number of trajectories.

5.3 Discussion

During *task 1* for the first product, the confusions $C(1,6)$ and $C(4,5)$ led to the insertion of loops in the discovered Petri net available in [10] and indicated by the backward facing edges in Fig. 4. In addition, multiple trajectories were generated for one work step, which led to more activities for box 5 and 6 in the log than process traces, indicating repetitions; see Table 2. During *task 2*, the same errors influenced the process discovery. Temporal filtering can be used to combine such activities, but the estimation of a suitable threshold is difficult because the system might become robust against the detection of real repetitions.

For *task 3*, no restrictions were posed for the assembly. In the discovered workflow, it was clearly visible that most people decided to follow the parallel grasping of parts in boxes $1 + 2$ and $3 + 4$; see the model on the bottom of Fig. 4. The trace fitness of 0.9581 when replaying the annotated ground truth log on the discovered Petri net shows that the clustering and work step identification led to a model which reflects the dominant behavior captured in the ground truth, and the hand detection was, at 97.29% accuracy, sufficiently accurate, which is supported by the confusion matrix for this task.

Similar to the results during the assembly of P_1 in *task 1*, during P_2, the confusions $C(1,7)$ and $C(4,5)$, such as the high number of trajectories for the work step related to box 4 containing bulk material (screws), led to a workflow behavior which was different from what was expected. One difficulty was that it was accessed using the left hand by only one user, which led to the set of generated trajectories being grouped into the wrong cluster. This is a known behavior of hierarchical clustering and with more samples where the left hand was used for accessing box 4, the error would not occur. Nevertheless, the discovered Petri net is able to replay most cases indicated by the fitness values in Table 3.

In *task 2*, during P_2, the confusion $C(5,6)$ was high and the caching of screws caused a lot of events related to work step 6. This was the reason for the inductive miner to exclude steps 5 and 7. Increasing the sensitivity of the mining algorithm and including both start and stop classes uncovers such behavior in a more complex Petri net. Since the parameters were kept equal among all tasks and products, the Petri net presents only the most dominant process behavior. Again, the conformance checking of the reference model helps to identify the critical steps during work step identification, also indicated by the corresponding fitness value of 0.8023 in Table 3.

During *task 3* a few participants picked parts sequentially, while others picked them in parallel. As in task 2, the confusion $C(5,6)$ influenced the discovery. Nevertheless, in the discovered model [10] it is clearly visible that most users decided not to cache the screws in box 6, but picked them directly from box 4.

6   Conclusion

The suggested procedure for work step identification based on trajectory building and clustering showed how process traces can be extracted from videos that show assembly processes from a top-down perspective. The approach was evaluated in a study with ten participants and delivered good test results even with a small number of samples. Due to its simplicity, the setup removes barriers that may hinder companies deploying such a system. The system itself is not limited to manufacturing, but could also be used in other domains, such as healthcare.

In future work, it might be interesting to deploy such a system in a real factory to analyze the system's performance on a larger test set and show the benefit for companies running such a system. A further application would be the observation of concept drift in assembly workflows and the use of online detection in combination with online conformance checking.

Acknowledgments. We thank Peter Fettke and Jana Koehler for discussions related to this work. This research was funded in part by the German Federal Ministry of Education and Research under grant number 01IS19022E (project BaSys4.2). The responsibility for this publication lies with the authors.

References

1. Adriansyah, A., van Dongen, B.F., van der Aalst, W.M.P.: Conformance checking using cost-based fitness analysis. In: 2011 IEEE 15th International Enterprise Distributed Object Computing Conference, pp. 55–64, August 2011

2. van der Aalst, W., et al.: Process mining manifesto. In: Daniel, F., Barkaoui, K., Dustdar, S. (eds.) BPM 2011. LNBIP, vol. 99, pp. 169–194. Springer, Heidelberg (2012). https://doi.org/10.1007/978-3-642-28108-2_19

3. Bambach, S., Lee, S., Crandall, D.J., Yu, C.: Lending a hand: detecting hands and recognizing activities in complex egocentric interactions. In: Proceedings of the IEEE International Conference on Computer Vision, pp. 1949–1957 (2015)

4. Bauters, K., Cottyn, J., Claeys, D., Slembrouck, M., Veelaert, P., Van Landeghem, H.: Automated work cycle classification and performance measurement for manual work stations. Robot. Comput.-Integr. Manufact. **51**, 139–157 (2018)

5. Berndt, D.J., Clifford, J.: Using dynamic time warping to find patterns in time series. In: KDD Workshop, Seattle, WA, vol. 10, pp. 359–370 (1994)

6. Carmona, J., van Dongen, B., Solti, A., Weidlich, M.: Conformance Checking: Relating Processes and Models. Springer, Heidelberg (2018). https://doi.org/10.1007/978-3-319-99414-7

7. Diba, K., Batoulis, K., Weidlich, M., Weske, M.: Extraction, correlation, and abstraction of event data for process mining. WIREs Data Min. Knowl. Discov. **10**(3), e1346 (2020)

8. Eindhoven Technical University: Prom6.8 - revision 38904 (2010). http://www.promtools.org/doku.php?id=prom68

9. Kaczmarek, S., Hogreve, S., Tracht, K.: Progress monitoring and gesture control in manual assembly systems using 3D-image sensors. Procedia CIRP **37**, 1–6 (2015)

10. Knoch, S., Ponpathirkoottam, S., Schwartz, T.: Video-to-model data set, March 2020. https://doi.org/10.6084/m9.figshare.12026850.v1. https://figshare.com/articles/Video-to-Model_Data_Set/12026850

11. Leemans, S.J.J., Fahland, D., van der Aalst, W.M.P.: Discovering block-structured process models from event logs - a constructive approach. In: Colom, J.-M., Desel, J. (eds.) PETRI NETS 2013. LNCS, vol. 7927, pp. 311–329. Springer, Heidelberg (2013). https://doi.org/10.1007/978-3-642-38697-8_17

12. Lerato, L., Niesler, T.: Investigating parameters for unsupervised clustering of speech segments using TIMIT. In: Twenty-Third Annual Symposium of the Pattern Recognition Association of South Africa, p. 83 (2012)

13. Mannhardt, F., Bovo, R., Oliveira, M.F., Julier, S.: A taxonomy for combining activity recognition and process discovery in industrial environments. In: Yin, H., Camacho, D., Novais, P., Tallón-Ballesteros, A.J. (eds.) IDEAL 2018. LNCS, vol. 11315, pp. 84–93. Springer, Cham (2018). https://doi.org/10.1007/978-3-030-03496-2_10

14. Müller, B.C., et al.: Motion tracking applied in assembly for worker training in different locations. Procedia CIRP **48**, 460–465 (2016)

15. Nater, F., Grabner, H., Van Gool, L.: Unsupervised workflow discovery in industrial environments. In: 2011 IEEE International Conference on Computer Vision Workshops (ICCV Workshops), pp. 1912–1919. IEEE (2011)

16. Redmon, J., Farhadi, A.: YOLOv3: an incremental improvement (2018). https://arxiv.org/abs/1804.02767

17. Roitberg, A., Somani, N., Perzylo, A., Rickert, M., Knoll, A.: Multimodal human activity recognition for industrial manufacturing processes in robotic workcells. In: Proceedings of the 2015 ACM on International Conference on Multimodal Interaction, pp. 259–266. ACM (2015)

18. Shilkrot, R., Narasimhaswamy, S., Vazir, S., Hoai, M.: WorkingHands: a hand-tool assembly dataset for image segmentation and activity mining (2019)
19. Victor, D.: Real-time hand tracking using SSD on tensorflow (2017). https://github.com/victordibia/handtracking
20. Wahlster, W.: SmartF-IT - cyber-physical IT systems to master complexness of a new generation of multi-adaptive factories (2016). http://www.smartf-it-proj ekt.de

Enhancing Event Log Quality: Detecting and Quantifying Timestamp Imperfections

Dominik Andreas Fischer[1]([✉]), Kanika Goel[2], Robert Andrews[2],
Christopher Gerhard Johannes van Dun[1], Moe Thandar Wynn[2],
and Maximilian Röglinger[1]

[1] FIM Research Center, Project Group Business and Information Systems
Engineering of the Fraunhofer FIT, University of Bayreuth, Bayreuth, Germany
{dominik.fischer,christopher.vandun,maximilian.roeglinger}@fim-rc.de
[2] Queensland University of Technology, Brisbane, Australia
{k.goel,r.andrews,m.wynn}@qut.edu.au

Abstract. Timestamp information recorded in event logs plays a crucial role in uncovering meaningful insights into business process performance and behaviour via Process Mining techniques. Inaccurate or incomplete timestamps may cause activities in a business process to be ordered incorrectly, leading to unrepresentative process models and incorrect process performance analysis results. Thus, the quality of timestamps in an event log should be evaluated thoroughly before the log is used as input for any Process Mining activity. To the best of our knowledge, research on the (automated) quality assessment of event logs remains scarce. Our work presents an automated approach for detecting and quantifying timestamp-related issues (timestamp imperfections) in an event log. We define 15 metrics related to timestamp quality across two axes: four levels of abstraction (event, activity, trace, log) and four quality dimensions (accuracy, completeness, consistency, uniqueness). We adopted the design science research paradigm and drew from knowledge related to data quality as well as event log quality. The approach has been implemented as a prototype within the open-source Process Mining framework ProM and evaluated using three real-life event logs and involving experts from practice. This approach paves the way for a systematic and interactive enhancement of timestamp imperfections during the data preprocessing phase of Process Mining projects.

Keywords: Process Mining · Event log · Data quality · Timestamps · Data quality assessment

1 Introduction

Process Mining, a sub-discipline of data science and business process management (BPM), is a powerful technique that allows deriving insights into business

© Springer Nature Switzerland AG 2020
D. Fahland et al. (Eds.): BPM 2020, LNCS 12168, pp. 309–326, 2020.
https://doi.org/10.1007/978-3-030-58666-9_18

process performance and behaviour using historical records from event logs [1]. Previous research shows that Process Mining is widely applied in practice [7,10]. Thereby, using an event log as the fundamental data source for Process Mining, organizations gain insights into process performance, conformance of processes to existing process models, and process improvement opportunities [26]. Reliable Process Mining results are, however, contingent on starting with high-quality event log(s) [1,4,13]. In practice, event logs are often far from the desired quality [7,26]. Therefore, an event log should not be naively used for Process Mining without ensuring that it is of adequate quality [1]. Data scientists spend up to eighty percent of their work with identifying, assessing, and remedying data quality issues [32]. Therefore, in the BPM community the interest in exploring the roots of data quality problems and the related assurance of accurate data is rising [2,32]. Following the words of Edward Deming ("you can't manage what you can't measure"), it is essential to have a set of metrics for detecting and quantifying event log quality [32].

However, to the best of our knowledge, research that focuses on the (automated) quality assessment of event logs remains scarce. We intend to bridge this gap in research specifically for timestamp-related data quality issues since timestamps are the principal means for ordering events and the foundation for many use cases [9,12,13]. Precise timestamps are essential to reproduce the correct ordering of activities and, thus, to obtain accurate process models (*discovery*), to measure the alignment between the process model and the actual process flow (*conformance*), and to determine effectiveness and efficiency in the execution of activities (*performance*) [9,12]. In contrast, inaccurate and coarse timestamps often lead to convoluted process models that may result in erroneous analyses [9]. This paper, therefore, focuses on the following research question: *How can we detect and quantify timestamp-related data quality issues in event logs?*

To address the research question, we adopt the design science research (DSR) paradigm [11] and develop an automated approach for detecting and quantifying timestamp imperfections in an event log. We evaluate the quality of timestamps in an event log across two axes: four levels of abstraction (event, activity, trace, log) and four quality dimensions (accuracy, completeness, consistency, uniqueness). We define 15 timestamp quality-related metrics and demonstrate how they can be computed. Following the DSR process by Peffers et al. [21] and the evaluation framework by Sonnenberg and vom Brocke [24], the remainder of this paper is structured as follows: In Sect. 2, we derive essential design objectives for a timestamp quality quantification approach from mature knowledge on data and event log quality. Section 3 introduces the required preliminaries and explains the approach employed. Section 4 demonstrates the prototype implemented in the Process Mining framework ProM. In Section 5, we describe the evaluation of our approach by using three real-life event logs and involving experts from research and practice. The paper concludes with Sect. 6.

2   Background

In this section, we present a brief overview of the background on data quality and event log quality research in Process Mining and propose two design objectives that underpin our approach.

It is well-recognised that the quality of input data is of high importance to Process Mining techniques [1,13]. Previous research, therefore, established data quality dimensions for evaluating data quality as they verify the "fitness for use" of data by data consumers [32]. A variety of studies on data quality dimensions exist that are renowned and widely adopted (see [18,22,29,30]). However, they often do not provide metrics for measuring data quality in databases or event logs. Hence, we conducted a scan of recent literature on data and event log quality while focusing on extracting metrics for quantifying event log quality.

We analysed 48 papers synthesized from a larger set of results (n = 412) by abstract screening and subsequently by text screening [31]. We created a concept matrix in which we attributed data quality dimensions to each article and whether the studies provide metrics for quality quantification [31]. We identified six studies that provide metrics for data quality quantification [3,5,15,17,23,25]. Furthermore, we clustered 118 different data quality dimensions that were named by the literature based on syntactic and semantic similarities which finally led us to 25 different data quality dimensions.

Since we aim to optimize the automation of our technique, we excluded dimensions that are not quantifiable without user input according to the literature (e.g., objectivity, usability, valued-added). This reduced our set to eight different data quality dimensions. From these dimensions, we excluded dimensions, that do not align with our intention to quantify timestamp quality (e.g., conciseness, understandability) and decided on the four data quality dimensions: *accuracy*, *completeness*, *consistency*, and *uniqueness*. We specify the following design objective (DO):

> **DO 1.** An approach for detecting and quantifying timestamp imperfections should consider multiple data quality dimensions, such as *accuracy*, *completeness*, *consistency*, and *uniqueness*.

Regarding event log quality, which refers to the data quality of event logs, the IEEE Task Force on Process Mining provides maturity levels for the suitability of different data sources for Process Mining [13]. For instance, they categorize semantically annotated logs of BPM systems as the pinnacle of high-quality event logs (★★★★★) while they rank paper-based medical records to the lowest level (★). They consider logs that at least fulfil the conditions of 3-stars (★★★) as suitable for Process Mining techniques. However, most real-life logs do not comply with these conditions as they tend to be incomplete, noisy, and imprecise [7,10].

To understand which quality issues affect event logs, Suriadi et al. [26] proposed eleven event log imperfection patterns often found in real-life logs. Three of these patterns highlight timestamp-related issues, namely *form-based event capture*, *inadvertent time travel*, and *unanchored event* [26]. The *form-based event capture* pattern describes the existence of sets of events that mostly occur at the same time. Electronic-based forms creating multiple events with equal timestamps commonly cause the presence of this pattern. The *Inadvertent time travel* pattern outlines the existence of inaccurate timestamp values that lead to incorrect ordering of events. The *unanchored event* pattern characterizes timestamps that are recorded in a different format than expected from the Process Mining tool. The confusion between the month-day and day-month format is a frequent manifestation of the named pattern.

Beyond the mentioned timestamp-related issues, we identified other factors that may impact Process Mining analysis. *Mixed granularity of traces* may cause incorrect event ordering [9]. For instance, in a hospital log, 'admission' may be recorded at second-level granularity, e.g., '03 Feb 2019 10:23:12', while within the same trace 'examination by the doctor' may be recorded at hour-level, e.g., '03 Feb 2019 10:00:00'. In the discovered process model, this will lead to incorrect orderings: the 'admission' activity follows the 'examination by the doctor' activity. In the majority of cases, the 'admission' activity may happen before the 'examination by the doctor', but, as the example has shown, in some instances, mixed granularity may cause *incorrect and infrequent event ordering* [9].

There exists an approach which tests for an *inconsistent format* to detect the *unanchored event* pattern. This aims, for instance, to identify date specifications in the format common in the United States ('MM-DD-YYYY'). Studies also discover timestamp issues through *stacked or parallel events* [8,19]. For instance, let the doctor submit a form at the end of each examination in which he declares having 'measured blood pressure', 'measured temperature', and 'intercepted airways'. Submitting a form may lead to three events in the log containing the same timestamp, i.e. the time the form was submitted (see *form-based event capture* in [26]) rather than the time these three events happened. We also identified research that addresses the issue of *overlapping events*, which aims to detect resource overlap between events. For instance, according to the log, a nurse may begin a new patient transfer before completing the previous patient transfer [6]. As a result, for our approach, we specified the following objective:

> **DO 2.** An approach for detecting and quantifying timestamp imperfections should consider existing imperfection detection approaches, such as *inconsistent format* (satisfies the *unanchored event* pattern), *mixed granularity of traces*, *infrequent event ordering* (satisfies the *inadvertent time travel* pattern), *overlapping events*, and *stacked events* (satisfies the *form-based event capture* pattern).

3   Approach

3.1   Preliminaries

Before we present our approach, we introduce required definitions and preliminaries. An event log is the necessary input to gain insights into a recorded process via Process Mining techniques. Central to Process Mining are the notions of *case* and *trace* in such event logs. A case is the set of events carried out in a single process instance with a *trace* being the execution sequence of the events in a case. Consequently, to conduct Process Mining analysis, an event log needs to contain, at a minimum, enough information such that each event record can be attributed to a case, and can be placed in sequence within the case. For ordering events, timing information (e.g., date and time) of when an event occurred is frequently used, although some discovery algorithms rely on implicit ordering of events in an event log instead of explicit timestamps. Optionally, an event record may contain attributes such as a resource and costs [7,9,13].

Definition 1 (event, attribute, event log). *Let $\mathcal{E}$ be the set of all possible event identifiers and $AN = \{a_1, a_2, .., a_n\}$ be the set of all possible attribute labels. For each attribute $a_i \in AN$ ($1 \leq i \leq n$), $\mathcal{D}_{a_i}$ is the set of all possible values for the attribute a_i. For any event $e \in \mathcal{E}$ and an attribute name $a \in AN$, we denote $\#_a(e) \in \mathcal{D}_a$ as the value of attribute named a for event e.*

For any event $e \in \mathcal{E}$ we define the following standard attributes: $\#_{id}(e) \in \mathcal{D}_{id}$ is the event identifier of e; $\#_{case}(e) \in \mathcal{D}_{case}$ is the case identifier of e; $\#_{act}(e) \in \mathcal{D}_{act}$ is the activity label of e; $\#_{time}(e) \in \mathcal{D}_{time}$ is the timestamp of e; $\#_{ts}(e) \in \mathcal{D}_{ts}$ is the lifecycle transition of e. We also define $\#_{res}(e) \in \mathcal{D}_{res}$ as the resource who triggered the occurrence of e as an optional attribute. An event log $\mathcal{L} \subseteq \mathcal{E}$ is a set of events.

Definition 2 (case, trace). *Let $\mathcal{C}$ be the set of all possible case identifiers. For any $c \in \mathcal{C}$ and an attribute name $a \in AN$, we denote $\#_a(c) \in \mathcal{D}_a$ as the value of the attribute named a for case c. We denote $\mathcal{E}^*$ as the set of all finite sequences of events over $\mathcal{E}$ where a finite sequence of length n over $\mathcal{E}$ is a mapping $\sigma \in \{1, \cdots, n\} \to \mathcal{E}$ and is represented as $\sigma = \langle e_1, e_2, \cdots, e_n \rangle$ where $e_i = \sigma(i)$ for $1 \leq i \leq n$. We define the special attribute $\#_{trace}(c) \in \mathcal{E}^*$ as representing the trace of case c, which consists of all events associated with c. We denote $\hat{c} = \#_{trace}(c)$ as shorthand for referring to the trace of a case and further note that the ordering in a trace should respect timestamps, i.e. for any $c \in \mathcal{L}, i, j$ such that $1 \leq i \leq j \leq |\hat{c}| : \#_{time}(\hat{c}(i)) \leq \#_{time}(\hat{c}(j))$.*

Next, we define quality metrics and position each metric along two axes: four quality dimensions (accuracy, completeness, consistency, uniqueness) and four levels of abstraction (event, activity, trace, log).

Definition 3 (quality dimensions, quality metrics, abstraction levels). *Let $DQ = \{dq_1, dq_2, \cdots, dq_n\}$ be the set of quality dimensions labels, $M = \{m_1, m_2, \cdots, m_n\}$ be the set of quality metrics labels and $V = \{v_1, v_2, \cdots, v_n\}$ be the set of quality attributes labels. Let $LL \subseteq AN^*$ be the set of all possible log abstraction levels. For any $ll \in LL$ we denote $\mathcal{E}_{ll}$ as the set of all event identifiers such that for any event $e \in \mathcal{E}_{ll}$ only attributes $a \in ll$ are accessible. We define some special log abstraction levels as: $ll_{event} = \{eventid, timestamp\}$; $ll_{activity} = \{eventid, activity\ label, transition, timestamp\}$; $ll_{trace} = \{eventid, traceid, transition, timestamp\}$; $ll_{log} = AN$.*

For any metric $m \in M$ and quality attribute $v \in V$ we denote $\#_v(m) \in \mathcal{D}_v$ as the value of quality attribute v for metric m where $\mathcal{D}_v$ is the set of all possible

Table 1. Timestamp quality assessment framework

	OVERALL TIMESTAMP QUALITY			
	Accuracy	Completeness	Consistency	Uniqueness
Log Level		Missing Trace[c]	Mixed Granularity of the Log[c] Format[a]	Duplicates within Log[c]
Trace Level	Infrequent Event Ordering[a] Overlapping Events per Resource[a]	Missing Activity[c]	Mixed Granularity of Traces[a]	Duplicates within Trace[b]
Activity Level		Missing Event[c]	Mixed Granularity of Activities[c]	Duplicates within Activity[c]
Event Level	Future Entry[c] Precision[c]	Missing Timestamp[c]		

values for the quality attribute v. We define the following attributes for each metric $m \in M$: $\#_{score}(m) \in [0,1]$; $\#_{weight}(m) \in \mathbb{R}^+$; $\#_{ll}(m) \in \mathcal{D}_{ll}$ and $ll \in LL$; $\#_{dq}(m) \in \mathcal{D}_{ll}$ and $dq \in DQ$. In a similar way we denote: $\#_{score}(dq) \in [0,1]$ and $dq \in DQ$; $\#_{weight}(dq) \in \mathbb{R}^+$ and $d \in DQ$; $\#_{score}(ll) \in [0,1]$ and $ll \in LL$.

3.2   Detection and Quantification of Timestamp Imperfections

Table 1 depicts our proposed framework to detect and quantify timestamp imperfections in an event log. We measure the quality of timestamps at various log abstraction levels (event, activity, trace, log) [1], using the four data quality dimensions *accuracy, completeness, consistency,* and *uniqueness* (DO 1). In total, we defined a set of 15 novel quality metrics, consisting of metrics based on existing detection approaches[a] (DO 2), modifications of existing detection approaches[b] and ten new detection approaches that we designed ourselves[c] based on insights from literature. However, we found no metrics that apply to accuracy at log or activity level. Nonetheless, the framework should be seen as an extensible foundation in event log quality quantification and, thus, further metrics or dimensions can be integrated.

We now describe all four quality dimensions and one exemplary metric for each dimension and show how we detect timestamp-related quality issues and quantify each metric to receive a score between 0 and 1. Due to lack of space, we provide details on all 15 metrics here: http://bit.ly/33hz4SM.

QD$_1$: Accuracy describes the deviation of the recorded value from the real value represented by the data [29]. Following the stated definition, we allocated every metric that investigates imprecise timestamps to accuracy. At the event level, we inspect the (*precision* (M$_4$) of timestamps. We examine to what granularity the timestamp of an individual event is recorded in the log. For instance, we consider the quality of a timestamp that contains information down to millisecond as optimal while hour-level granularity is not. We also developed the metric *future entry* at the event level, which indicates whether there are future-dated timestamps in an event log. At the trace level, we quantify accuracy through the metric *infrequent event ordering* as this phenomenon often occurs as a result of inaccurate timestamps [9]. Infrequent event ordering also covers the *inadvertent time travel* pattern since this pattern typically manifests itself in the existence of some traces in which event ordering deviates significantly [26]. We also detect *overlapping events* per resource provided that the start and end times of an activity that is executed by a resource are recorded in an event log. This can indicate imprecise recordings of start or end timestamps of activities if we assume that a resource does not multitask since the metric identifies activities that are started by a specific resource before they finished their prior activity [6].

M$_4$: Precision (Quality dimension: accuracyabstraction level: event)aims to detect events containing coarse timestamps. Particularly events that are mostly recorded manually show coarse granularity as it is difficult for the user to provide information, for instance, about milliseconds granularity.
Detection. For each event $e \in \mathcal{L}$, we determine (i) the granularity $g(e)$ by investigating up to which time unit $tu \in \mathcal{TU} = \{year, month, ..., millisecond\}$ an event is recorded, and (ii) the number $\#_{tu<g(e)}(e)$ of time units tu that are more granular than $g(e)$.
Quantification. By default, the scores of all metrics should indicate a similar influence on Process Mining techniques. Hence, we assign a power value to each metric. Using this and $\#_{tu<g(e)}(e)$ of each event e, we calculate the score of *precision* with the following equation:

$$\#_{score}(precision) = (1 - \frac{\sum_{e \in \mathcal{L}} \#_{tu<g(e)}(e)}{6 * |\mathcal{L}|})^2 \tag{1}$$

QD$_2$: Completeness manifests as the recording of all values for a specific variable [29]. We quantify completeness at the event level through the metric *missing timestamp* of events. For this purpose, we examine whether a timestamp is recorded for each event. Furthermore, if an event contains a timestamp before the year 1971, this timestamp is also considered as missing, since many systems convert time-related null values into the year 1970 (so-called Unix time). At the activity level, we check for *missing events* (M$_7$). Since an activity requires at least an event with a start transition and an event with a complete transition, we consider an activity that either has no start event or end event as an indicator of a missing event. At the trace level, we aim to detect *missing activities*. To identify this issue, we first scan the event log for infrequent predecessor-follower relations. If a trace contains an infrequent relation, the trace is investigated to see whether it contains an activity that frequently follows the predecessor under investigation. Unless we are unable to find a frequent follower, we assume that an activity is missing in this trace. Lastly, we detect possible *missing traces* at the log level by examining differences between timestamps of the first events of two consecutive traces. We consider a gap between two traces that is significantly larger than the expected mean value as an indicator of a missing trace in between.

M$_7$: Missing event (completeness, activity) describes cases in which an activity is either missing a start or an end event. Potential reasons are failures or omissions in recording the start or end event, or the expected event has been mapped to the wrong trace.

Detection. In each trace, we count all events e with $\#_{act}(e) = a$ and $\#_{ts}(e) = start$. We then count all events e in the trace with $\#_{act}(e) = a$ and $\#_{ts}(e) = complete$. If the two counts are not the same, the trace contains missing events for activity a.

Quantification. To calculate a score, we use the ratio of affected activities to total activities and the ratio of affected traces to total traces in the log. Let $\mathcal{L}_{act} = \{\#_{act}(e) | e \in \mathcal{L}\}$ be the set of all activity labels and $\mathcal{L}_{case} = \{\#_{case}(e) | e \in \mathcal{L}\}$ be the set of all case identifiers in log $\mathcal{L}$. We define *affected* : $\mathcal{L} \times \mathcal{L}_{case} \times \mathcal{L}_{act} \to \mathbb{N}$ such that $affected(\mathcal{L}, c, a)$ returns the difference between the number of events $e \in \mathcal{L}$ with $\#_{case}(e) = c$, $\#_{act}(e) = a$ and $\#_{ts}(e) = start$ and those with $\#_{ts}(e) = complete$. $\#affected\ activities = \sum_{c \in \mathcal{L}_{case}, a \in \mathcal{L}_{act}} affected(\mathcal{L}, c, a)$. Let $T = \{\#_{case}(e) | e \in \mathcal{L}, affected(\mathcal{L}, \#_{case}(e), \#_{act}(e)) > 0\}$ be the set of traces which contain at least one affected activity and $\#affected\ traces = |T|$. Then Thus, we calculate the score for using the following equation:

$$\#_{score}(missing\ events) = (1 - \frac{\#affected\ activities}{2 * |\mathcal{L}_{act}|} - \frac{\#affected\ traces}{2 * |\mathcal{L}_{case}|})^4 \quad (2)$$

QD$_3$: Consistency means the equal representation of data values in all events [29]. As multiple units are necessary to evaluate equality, it is not possible to measure consistency for a single event at the event level. At the activity level, we group all events according to their activity label. After that, we examine whether all timestamps of a specific activity show the same granularity because mixed granularity potentially leads to the wrong order of activities [9]. We also inspect individual traces for *mixed granularity of traces* at the trace level. For this metric, we group the events according to their trace IDs. Furthermore, at the log level, we compare the granularity of all events applying the metric *mixed granularity of the log* (M$_9$) regardless of trace and activity labels. We also assess whether all event timestamps have been recorded in the same day-month *format*. As addressed by the imperfection pattern *unanchored event* [26], a log may contain timestamps that have been stored in a day-month format and timestamps that have been stored in a month-day format when logs from multiple systems are combined in a single event log.

M_9: **Mixed granularity of the log** (consistency, log) measures the extent of mixed granularity of the events in the log. We check whether certain events are recorded in coarser or finer granularity. This may occur, among others, if parts of the log are recorded automatically through electronic systems while other parts are recorded manually by the user.

Detection. $g(e)$ of each event $e \in \mathcal{E}$ by investigating up to which time unit $tu \in TU = \{year, month, ..., millisecond\}$ an event is recorded. Then, we count how often each time unit tu was found as the most precise granularity and determine the dominating time unit $max(TU)$. Thereupon, we calculate the observed granularity distribution and the expected granularity distribution. We calculate the observed distribution as follows:

$$d_{\text{obs}}(tu) = \frac{tu}{|TU|} \tag{3}$$

We use $max(TU)$ for the calculation of the expected distribution. For instance, let $max(TU) = second$, we assume that $d_{\text{exp}}(second) = 59/60$. The remaining $1/60$ is distributed accordingly over the coarser time units. From there, we calculate the deviation of the two distributions:

$$dev = \sum_{tu \in TU} \frac{|d_{\text{exp}}(tu) - d_{\text{obs}}(tu)|}{2} \tag{4}$$

Quantification. To determine a score for the metric *mixed granularity of the log* we use the following equation:

$$\#_{\text{score}}(mixed\ gran.\ (log)) = (1 - dev)^2 \tag{5}$$

QD_4: **Uniqueness** is defined as the existence of unwanted duplicates within or across systems for a particular data set [29]. At the activity level, we measure uniqueness using the metric *duplicates within activity*. Therefore, we detect all activities that contain more than one event with the same timestamp. Frequently detected issues include identically timestamped start and end events for the same activity. We identify *duplicates within trace* (M_{14}) at trace level. This metric detects events of a trace that show the same timestamp. As the imperfection pattern *form-based event capture* shows, several events of a trace are often recorded using the same timestamp through e-forms, even though they happened in a sequence [26]. Finally, applying the metric *duplicates within log*, we reveal events that do not belong to the same trace but use the same timestamp. This issue may also be caused by electronic form-based event storage, for instance, if the user can record multiple trace start events through an e-form.

M_{14}: **Duplicates within trace** (uniqueness, trace) aims to detect events with an exact same timestamp in the same trace. As the imperfection pattern *form-based event capture* shows, recording of events after the fact (e.g., via e-forms) often causes multiple events stored with equal timestamps, although these events did not happen concurrently in real life [26].

Detection. As duplicates within a trace we describe a set of n events $\mathcal{E}_{dt} \subseteq \mathcal{E}$ where for every event $e_i \in \mathcal{E}_{dt}$: $\#_{trace}(e_i)$ is equal, $\#_{time}(e_i)$ is equal, and $\#_{act}(e_i)$ is unequal.

Quantification. To calculate a score,To calculate a score, we use the ratio of detected events to total events, and the ratio of affected traces to traces. Let $\mathcal{L}_{time} = \{\#_{time}(e)|e \in \mathcal{L}\}$ be the set of all timestamps, and $\mathcal{L}_{case} = \{\#_{case}(e)|e \in \mathcal{L}\}$ be the set of all case identifiers in log $\mathcal{L}$. We define $duplicates : \mathcal{L} \times \mathcal{L}_{case} \times \mathcal{L}_{times} \rightarrow \mathbb{N}$ such that $duplicates(\mathcal{L}, c, t)$ returns the number of events $e \in \mathcal{L}$ with $\#_{case}(e) = c$ and $\#_{time}(e) = t$ having distinct values of $\#_{act}(e)$.

Let $\#detected\ events = \sum_{c \in \mathcal{L}_{case}, a \in \mathcal{L}_{ts}} duplicates(\mathcal{L}, c, t)$.

Let $T = \{\#_{case}(e)|e \in \mathcal{L}, duplicates(\mathcal{L}, \#_{case}(e), \#_{time}(e)) > 1\}$ be the set of traces which contain at least one timestamp with multiple events and $\#affected\ traces = |T|$. Thus, we calculate the score for the metric *duplicates within trace* with the following equation:

$$\#_{score}(duplicates\ (trace)) = (1 - \frac{\#detected\ events}{2 * |\mathcal{L}|} - \frac{\#affected\ traces}{2 * |\mathcal{L}_{case}|}) \quad (6)$$

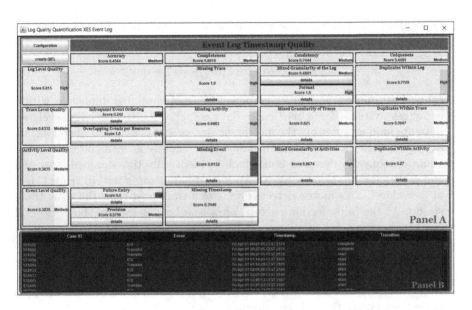

Fig. 1. Main window: the quality quantification of the MIMIC-III log (panel A) and the error list (panel B) of the metric *duplicates within trace* (Color figure online)

4   Implementation

4.1   Software Prototype

Figure 1 shows the main window of the prototype that displays the results of metrics and calculated scores in Panel A after importing an event log in XES format. The top row and the left column indicate the aggregated scores for each quality dimension and event log level. The scores are also visualized with colours: red, yellow, green for low (under 0.25), medium (0.25–0.75), and high (above 0.75), respectively. These thresholds are configurable in the prototype.

By using the "details" button for a metric, the prototype provides the user with a list of detected issues for a particular metric (Panel B). For instance, using the metric *duplicates within trace*, the list shows the case id, event label, timestamp, and lifecycle transition for all events detected by the corresponding metric as duplicate events. Thus, the user is able to discover which events are affected. This list can also be sorted by all columns.

A separate "User Configuration" window (not shown here) can be accessed through the button "Configuration". It allows the user to suppress metrics or dimensions which are not of concern and to adjust the weight of metrics. The default weight per metric is one. Any positive real number can be assigned. The accumulated dimension and event log scores are then recalculated for the new configuration. The option of suppressing irrelevant measures or dimensions and adjusting the weight of metrics turns our approach into a domain-agnostic solution, as it allows the user to customize the timestamp quality quantification for the specific use case and to address the issue of potential dependencies between metrics. For instance, the results of the metric *precision* may have an impact on the results of the consistency and uniqueness metrics. Thus, the user can hide the metric *overlapping events per resource* if multitasking is possible in the examined use case or lower the weight of *precision* if millisecond granularity is not necessary in the case under consideration. Using the "create QIEL" (QIEL = "quality-informed event log") button, the configuration information set by the user as well as the assessment results are stored in the metadata of the imported XES log file. Thus, the quality information can be used in later Process Mining phases.

4.2   Sources

The implementation of the automated approach for detecting and quantifying timestamp imperfections is available in the ProM nightly build which can be downloaded here: http://bit.ly/38KVKvJ [28]. The source code is available in the package "LogQualityQuantification" : http://bit.ly/39OAgj0. In addition, we provide detailed instructions for the use of the prototype in the appendix (http://bit.ly/33hz4SM) and describe the implemented features.

Among the three event logs used for the evaluation, log A and log B are logs from Australian partners and, therefore, cannot be made available publicly in accordance with relevant Australian legislation. Log C, however, is openly available and can be accessed after completing the CITI "Data or Specimens Only Research" course here: http://bit.ly/3aNRnkW [14].

5   Evaluation

5.1   Evaluation Strategy

Aligning with DSR purposes, our overall goal is to evaluate the usefulness and applicability of the proposed approach and give an indication towards its real-world fidelity [24]. The evaluation, therefore, involves analyzing three diverse real-life event logs and comparing the outcomes created by the application of our approach to the manual assessment of log experts. We define log experts as persons with Process Mining experience who are capable of making informed data quality statements about a particular event log. In showing that our approach returns similar quality assessments as log experts in three varying circumstances and in a fraction of the time needed for manual analysis, we provide evidence that the approach adequately supports users in detecting and quantifying timestamp-related data quality issues in event logs and, therefore, addresses our research question. The three used logs are:

- **Log A**: represents the activities related to processing of 2090 annual progress reports for PhD students at an Australian University
- **Log B**: represents the waypoints (dispatched, on scene, at patient, ...) in over 40,000 ambulance attendances to, and transport to hospital of, patients injured in road traffic crashes in Queensland, Australia
- **Log C**: represents an openly available data set comprising desensitized health data associated with 40,000 critical care patients. It includes demographics, vital signs, laboratory tests, medications, and more [14]

We decided on these logs, as many of the addressed issues are present (i.e. insufficient precision and duplicates in log A, ordering and granularity issues in log B, and future timestamps and completeness issues in log C).

We defined an iterative evaluation process (Fig. 2). One evaluation round contains the following steps: First, the timestamp quality of log A was assessed using the prototype and its results compared to a quality report manually created by a corresponding log expert A. If the quality report created by expert A matched the outcomes of the prototype closely enough (see definition below), we proceeded with expert B and log B and, subsequently, with expert C and log C.

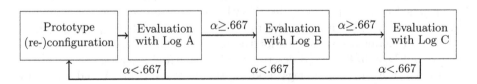

Fig. 2. Evaluation process (performed both with internal and with external experts)

When, at one point in this process, the outcomes of the prototype differed from the results reported by the expert, we reconfigured and improved the prototype based on the insights from the respective evaluation round and subsequently started a new round, again starting with log A. The process terminates when the prototype results match the experts' quality reports in all three cases.

The manual reports are based on ordinal quality levels (low $\hat{=}$ 1, medium $\hat{=}$ 2, and high $\hat{=}$ 3), the prototype output has been scaled down accordingly. To determine whether the assessment of an event log by the prototype matches the report created by the respective expert, we calculated the agreement ratio and reliability value α using Krippendorff's alpha [16]. Following the recommendations of Krippendorff, we consider the outcomes as reliable if $\alpha \geq 0.667$ [16].

We decided first to run the evaluation within the author team to preconfigure the prototype. Thus, three co-authors (who have worked with the respective logs before) represented the log experts for log A, B, and C until the approach passed each evaluation step. After the internal evaluation was completed, we also went through the evaluation process with three external log experts from academia and practice. The detailed results are presented in the following.

Table 2. Evaluation of the applied metrics

	1.A			2.A			2.B			2.C			3.A			3.B			3.C		
	P_s	P_{ql}	A	P_s	P_{ql}	A	P_s	P_{ql}	B	P_s	P_{ql}	C	P_s	P_{ql}	A	P_s	P_{ql}	B	P_s	P_{ql}	C
M_1	.616	2	3	.616	2	3	.674	2	1	.242	1	2	.616	2	3	.674	2	2	.242	1	2
M_2	1	3	3	1	3	3	1	3	2	1	3	3	1	3	3	1	3	3	1	3	3
M_3	1	3	3	1	3	3	1	3	3	0	1	1	1	3	3	1	3	3	0	1	1
M_4	.683	2	2	.683	2	2	.586	2	2	.576	2	2	.586	2	3	.586	2	2	.576	2	2
M_5	.977	3	-	.977	3	-	.983	3	3	1	3	3	.977	3	3	.983	3	3	1	3	-
M_6	.936	3	3	.936	3	3	.947	3	3	.998	3	3	.936	3	3	.947	3	3	.998	3	2
M_7	.951	3	2	.741	2	2	0	1	1	.013	1	1	.741	2	2	0	1	1	.013	1	1
M_8	1	3	3	1	3	3	1	3	3	.395	2	2	1	3	3	1	3	3	.395	2	1
M_9	.956	3	3	.956	3	3	.393	2	2	.489	2	2	.956	3	3	.393	2	2	.489	2	2
M_{10}	1	3	3	1	3	3	1	3	3	1	3	3	1	3	3	1	3	2	1	3	3
M_{11}	.918	3	3	.918	3	3	.533	2	2	.621	2	2	.918	3	3	.533	2	2	.621	2	3
M_{12}	.956	3	3	.956	3	3	.972	3	3	.867	3	3	.956	3	3	.972	3	3	.867	3	3
M_{13}	.695	2	3	.869	3	3	.601	2	2	.771	3	2	.869	3	3	.601	2	2	.771	3	3
M_{14}	.488	2	3	.397	2	2	.820	3	2	.305	2	2	.397	2	2	.820	3	3	.305	2	2
M_{15}				.509	2	2	.999	3	3	.270	2	3	.509	2	2	.999	3	3	.270	2	3
M_{16}[a]	.522	2	3																		
AG	**64.29%**			**92.86%**			**80.00%**			**80.00%**			**86.67%**			**93.33%**			**64.29%**		
α	**0.082**			**0.842**			**0.777**			**0.801**			**0.670**			**0.890**			**0.692**		

P_s = indicated scores of the prototype; P_{ql} = indicated quality levels of the proto-type; A, B, C = quality levels assigned by experts; AG = agreement; α = reliability
[a]The initial version of the prototype (for the first evaluation) contains the metric M_{16}: form-based event capture instead of the metric M_{15}: duplicates within activity.

5.2   Findings

Overall, one evaluation within the author team and one evaluation with external experts were completed and one prototype reconfiguration was performed. Below, we describe these evaluation rounds and the implemented changes.

For the **first internal evaluation round** (see Table 2, 1.A), the assigned quality levels of expert A regarding log A and the results of the prototype did not match closely enough. A number of changes were made in the prototype as a result. One main difference is the score for the metric *form-based event capture*. Expert A is certain that no events of log A were recorded through electronic forms and, therefore, the score should not be less than 3. After further analysis, we noticed that this metric detects sets of events which have the same timestamps in the same trace but for different activities. Such a pattern does not only occur due to the *form-based event capture* pattern but can also be caused by other reasons. Thus, we removed the metric *form-based event capture* and proposed a new metric *duplicates within activity* that detects sets of events with the same timestamp, the same event name and in the same trace. Originally, the metric *duplicates within log* detected sets of events with the same timestamp and same event name. However, using this detection method, we identified issues that are already covered by *duplicates within activity* or *duplicates within trace*. Thus, we modified the metric *duplicates within log* so that it detects sets of events with the same timestamp but in different traces. For the metric *missing event*, we adjusted the score quantification. Initially, we considered only the ratio of affected events to total events. For event log A, just 1.26% of total events were affected and, thus, the prototype assigns a high score to the metric *missing event*. However, expert A observed that 12.85% of the total traces were affected by *missing events* and, therefore, expected the score to be medium. Hence, we concluded that, in terms of score quantification, it is necessary to consider the ratio of affected traces to total traces.

In the **second internal evaluation round** (see Table 2, 2.A–2.C), the outcomes of the reconfigured prototype met the expectations of each expert for at least 12 of 15 metrics. As we obtained sufficient reliability, we assumed the internal evaluation to be successful.

We continued with an **evaluation round involving external experts** from academia and practice who were not engaged in the design of the approach. A data expert from an Australian university acted as the expert for log A, a data scientist working in the healthcare domain as the expert for log B, and a research associate from Germany with Process Mining focus as the expert for log C. Each of these external experts has gathered expertise with the corresponding log during previous research or industry projects and is therefore capable of providing information on all relevant quality characteristics of these logs. In all steps of the evaluation with external experts (see Table 2, 3.A–3.C), we obtained sufficient reliability and, therefore, assumed the external evaluation to be successful.

Our evaluation allowed us to improve our approach iteratively. Morever, by using real-life logs and automatically delivering outcomes matching the quality levels manually assigned by log experts from academia and practice in a fraction of the time needed for manual analysis, we demonstrate the approach's applicability in practice. Real-world fidelity is indicated by successfully using the prototype with three logs with different characteristics. We received feedback from the experts regarding the usefulness of both our approach and the prototype: The experts confirmed that timestamps are the cornerstones of event logs and should be analyzed in detail. Therefore, the approach as a way of detecting and quantifying timestamp quality issues in event logs was deemed useful to practitioners and researchers alike. This applies to both the proposed framework (Table 1) as well as the underlying set of metrics. At the same time, the experts frequently proposed two extensions to further increase the approach's usefulness and completeness: (i) including domain-specific metrics to increase the approach's usefulness in highly specific fields and (ii) including more intelligent metrics to increase the explanatory power and guidance of the approach. The implementation as part of the ProM framework allows for interoperability with other tools and was therefore welcomed by all experts. In summary, we are confident that the approach and its implementation adequately support users in detecting and quantifying timestamp quality issues in event logs and address our research question.

6 Conclusion

Following DSR principles, we designed and implemented an approach for detecting and quantifying timestamp imperfections in event logs based on 15 novel data quality metrics structured along four data quality dimensions and log levels each. The applied metrics and dimensions were subsequently evaluated using real-life event logs and involving experts from academia and practice. Our framework focuses on timestamp quality issues and provides a first step in quantifying event log quality. The approach can detect common timestamp-related issues and measure the quality of timestamp information in event logs. Furthermore, our approach is domain-agnostic (e.g. by suppressing irrelevant metrics or adjusting the weight of metrics). Thus, we support process stakeholders in determining the suitability of an event log for Process Mining analysis. We also assist data scientists in automatically identifying and assessing data quality issues in event logs. Finally, our approach paves the way for future research on detecting and quantifying quality issues of further event log components (e.g., activity labels).

These insights come with limitations: First, we intend to minimize the risk that existing issues remain undetected (false negatives). This sensitivity, however, can cause the approach to identify issues that may be false alarms (false positives) such as uniqueness issues caused by batched events [20]. However, we mitigate potential over-detection by allowing users to review detected issues and plan to implement a white-list functionality as part of future work. Second, the evaluation was only performed on three different logs and under the assumption that expert assessments are correct. Thus, we are running the risk of the prototype being configured improperly if experts are biased or the logs only capture very special situations. We consider this risk to be low, given that the logs cover a broad range of characteristics and the assessments of the internal and external experts for each log were very similar. Although we followed established principles and systematically identified potential timestamp-related quality issues from the literature and our evaluation showed promising results for the approach and the prototype, a more thorough evaluation involving further logs and experts should be conducted in the future (see [24]). Thereby, evaluations (with case studies or controlled experiments) need to focus on generality and completeness of the metrics and further examine the real-world fidelity of the approach's results.

We also identified areas where the approach can be extended. First, we want to provide a more interactive detection approach whereby fine-grained user configuration can be taken into account (e.g., for minimum and maximum values or rules for certain metrics to detect violations). Second, the framework should be seen as a foundation for future extensions. Therefore, we want to encourage researchers to introduce further metrics to underpin the quality dimensions. Third, our approach can also be extended with other log attributes such as event labels. Moreover, research so far lacks a systematic approach on how to define quality measures. Our work, therefore, constitutes a starting point to design a set of axioms for the definition of measures [27]. Finally, a natural extension to this work is to provide the user with an opportunity to repair the detected timestamp issues in a similar manner to those presented in [8,9]. Our vision is to provide an integrated approach to detecting, quantifying, repairing and tracking (timestamp) quality issues in event logs.

Acknowledgements. We would like to thank Queensland's Motor Accident Insurance Commission and the Queensland University of Technology for allowing us access to their datasets.

References

1. van der Aalst, W.M.P.: Process Mining: Data Science in Action, vol. 2. Springer, Heidelberg (2016). https://doi.org/10.1007/978-3-662-49851-4
2. van der Aalst, W.M.P., Bichler, M., Heinzl, A.: Responsible data science. Bus. Inf. Syst. Eng. **59**(5), 311–313 (2017). https://doi.org/10.1007/s12599-017-0487-z
3. Alkhattabi, M., Neagu, D., Cullen, A.: Assessing information quality of e-learning systems. Comput. Hum. Behav. **27**(2), 862–873 (2011). https://doi.org/10.1016/j.chb.2010.11.011
4. Andrews, R., van Dun, C.G.J., Wynn, M.T., Kratsch, W., Röglinger, M.K.E., ter Hofstede, A.H.M.: Quality-informed semi-automated event log generation for process mining. Decis. Support Syst. **132**(3) (2020). https://doi.org/10.1016/j.dss.2020.113265
5. Askham, N., et al.: The six primary dimensions for data quality assessment (2013)
6. Awad, A., Zaki, N.M., Di Francescomarino, C.: Analyzing and repairing overlapping work items. Inf. Softw. Technol. **80**, 110–123 (2016). https://doi.org/10.1016/j.infsof.2016.08.010
7. Bose, R.P.J.C., Mans, R.S., van der Aalst, W.M.P.: Wanna improve process mining results? In: CIDM 2013, pp. 127–134. IEEE (2013). https://doi.org/10.1109/CIDM.2013.6597227

8. Conforti, R., la Rosa, M., ter Hofstede, A.H.M.: Timestamp repair for business process event logs. Technical report, University of Melbourne (2018)
9. Dixit, P.M., et al.: Detection and interactive repair of event ordering imperfection in process logs. In: Krogstie, J., Reijers, H.A. (eds.) CAiSE 2018. LNCS, vol. 10816, pp. 274–290. Springer, Cham (2018). https://doi.org/10.1007/978-3-319-91563-0_17
10. Emamjome, F., Andrews, R., ter Hofstede, A.H.M.: A case study lens on process mining in practice. In: Panetto, H., Debruyne, C., Hepp, M., Lewis, D., Ardagna, C.A., Meersman, R. (eds.) OTM 2019. LNCS, vol. 11877, pp. 127–145. Springer, Cham (2019). https://doi.org/10.1007/978-3-030-33246-4_8
11. Gregor, S., Hevner, A.R.: Positioning and presenting design science research for maximum impact. MIS Q. 337–355 (2013). https://doi.org/10.25300/MISQ/2013/37.2.01
12. Gschwandtner, T., Gärtner, J., Aigner, W., Miksch, S.: A taxonomy of dirty time-oriented data. In: Quirchmayr, G., Basl, J., You, I., Xu, L., Weippl, E. (eds.) CD-ARES 2012. LNCS, vol. 7465, pp. 58–72. Springer, Heidelberg (2012). https://doi.org/10.1007/978-3-642-32498-7_5
13. van der Aalst, W., et al.: Process mining manifesto. In: Daniel, F., Barkaoui, K., Dustdar, S. (eds.) BPM 2011. LNBIP, vol. 99, pp. 169–194. Springer, Heidelberg (2012). https://doi.org/10.1007/978-3-642-28108-2_19
14. Johnson, A.E.W., et al.: MIMIC-III, a freely accessible database. Sci. Data 3, 160035 (2016). https://doi.org/10.1038/sdata.2016.35
15. Kherbouche, M.O., Laga, N., Masse, P.A.: Towards a better assessment of event logs quality. In: IEEE SSCI 2016, pp. 1–8. IEEE (2016). https://doi.org/10.1109/SSCI.2016.7849946
16. Krippendorff, K.: Reliability in content analysis. Hum. Commun. Res. 30(3), 411–433 (2004). https://doi.org/10.1111/j.1468-2958.2004.tb00738.x
17. Lee, Y.W., Pipino, L.L., Funk, J.D., Wang, R.Y.: Journey to Data Quality. The MIT Press, Cambridge (2009). https://doi.org/10.7551/mitpress/4037.001.0001
18. Lee, Y.W., Strong, D.M., Kahn, B.K., Wang, R.Y.: AIMQ: a methodology for information quality assessment. Inf. Manag. 40(2), 133–146 (2002). https://doi.org/10.1016/S0378-7206(02)00043-5
19. Lu, X., et al.: Semi-supervised log pattern detection and exploration using event concurrence and contextual information. In: Panetto, H., et al. (eds.) OTM 2017. LNCS, vol. 10573, pp. 154–174. Springer, Cham (2017). https://doi.org/10.1007/978-3-319-69462-7_11
20. Martin, N., Swennen, M., Depaire, B., Jans, M., Caris, A., Vanhoof, K.: Retrieving batch organisation of work insights from event logs. Decis. Support Syst. 100, 119–128 (2017). https://doi.org/10.1016/j.dss.2017.02.012
21. Peffers, K., Tuunanen, T., Rothenberger, M.A., Chatterjee, S.: A design science research methodology for information systems research. J. Manag. Inf. Syst. 24(3), 45–77 (2007). https://doi.org/10.2753/MIS0742-1222240302
22. Pipino, L.L., Lee, Y.W., Wang, R.Y.: Data quality assessment. Commun. ACM 45(4), 211–218 (2002). https://doi.org/10.1145/505248.506010
23. Sattler, K.U.: Data quality dimensions. In: Liu, L., Özsu, T.M. (eds.) Encyclopedia of Database Systems, pp. 612–615. Springer, Heidelberg (2009). https://doi.org/10.1007/978-0-387-39940-9_108

24. Sonnenberg, C., vom Brocke, J.: Evaluations in the science of the artificial – reconsidering the build-evaluate pattern in design science research. In: Peffers, K., Rothenberger, M., Kuechler, B. (eds.) DESRIST 2012. LNCS, vol. 7286, pp. 381–397. Springer, Heidelberg (2012). https://doi.org/10.1007/978-3-642-29863-9_28

25. Stvilia, B., Gasser, L., Twidale, M.B., Smith, L.C.: A framework for information quality assessment. J. Am. Soc. Inf. Sci. Technol. **58**, 1720–1733 (2007). https://doi.org/10.1002/asi.20652

26. Suriadi, S., Andrews, R., ter Hofstede, A.H.M., Wynn, M.T.: Event log imperfection patterns for process mining. Inf. Syst. **64**, 132–150 (2017). https://doi.org/10.1016/j.is.2016.07.011

27. Tax, N., Lu, X., Sidorova, N., Fahland, D., van der Aalst, W.M.P.: The imprecisions of precision measures in process mining. Inf. Process. Lett. **135**, 1–8 (2018). https://doi.org/10.1016/j.ipl.2018.01.013

28. Verbeek, H.M.W., Buijs, J.C.A.M., van Dongen, B.F., van der Aalst, W.M.P.: XES, XESame, and ProM 6. In: Soffer, P., Proper, E. (eds.) CAiSE Forum 2010. LNBIP, vol. 72, pp. 60–75. Springer, Heidelberg (2011). https://doi.org/10.1007/978-3-642-17722-4_5

29. Wand, Y., Wang, R.Y.: Anchoring data quality dimensions in ontological foundations. Commun. ACM **39**(11), 86–95 (1996). https://doi.org/10.1145/240455.240479

30. Wang, R.Y., Strong, D.M.: Beyond accuracy: what data quality means to data consumers. J. Manag. Inf. Syst. **12**(4), 5–33 (1996). https://doi.org/10.1080/07421222.1996.11518099

31. Webster, J., Watson, R.T.: Analyzing the past to prepare for the future: writing a literature review. MIS Q. **26**(2), 13–23 (2002). https://doi.org/10.5555/2017160.2017162

32. Wynn, M.T., Sadiq, S.: Responsible process mining - a data quality perspective. In: Hildebrandt, T., van Dongen, B.F., Röglinger, M., Mendling, J. (eds.) BPM 2019. LNCS, vol. 11675, pp. 10–15. Springer, Cham (2019). https://doi.org/10.1007/978-3-030-26619-6_2

Automatic Repair of Same-Timestamp Errors in Business Process Event Logs

Raffaele Conforti[1], Marcello La Rosa[2], Arthur H.M. ter Hofstede[3], and Adriano Augusto[2(✉)]

[1] Process Diamond, Melbourne, Australia
rconforti@processdiamond.com
[2] The University of Melbourne, Melbourne, Australia
{marcello.larosa,a.augusto}@unimelb.edu.au
[3] Queensland University of Technology, Brisbane, Australia
a.terhofstede@qut.edu.au

Abstract. This paper contributes an approach for automatically correcting "same-timestamp" errors in business process event logs. These errors consist in multiple events exhibiting the same timestamp within a given process instance. Such errors are common in practice and can be due to the logging granularity or the performance load of the logging system. Analyzing logs that have not been properly screened for such problems is likely to lead to wrong or misleading process insights. The proposed approach revolves around two techniques: one to reorder events with same-timestamp errors, the other to assign an estimated timestamp to each such event. The approach has been implemented in a software prototype and extensively evaluated in different settings, using both artificial and real-life logs. The experiments show that the approach significantly reduces the number of inaccurate timestamps, while the reordering of events scales well to large and complex datasets. The evaluation is complemented by a case study in the meat & livestock domain showing the usefulness of the approach in practice.

1 Introduction

In real-life scenarios, one regularly finds inaccurate or unreliable data in the records of business process executions (known as *event logs*) [1,2]. A common case of inaccurate data in event logs regards the recording of timestamps. Each event in an event log captures the start or completion of a process activity and as such has a timestamp, e.g. activity "Reject purchase order" was completed at 12:30:00 pm of 23/02/2020. A common type of timestamp error is when a set of events related to the same process instance have the same timestamp. This error can be due to delays during the logging process, e.g. when the logging system becomes overloaded; or to the granularity of the logging, e.g. the events do not

---

R. Conforti—Work done while the author was at The University of Melbourne and Queensland University of Technology.

D. Fahland et al. (Eds.): BPM 2020, LNCS 12168, pp. 327–345, 2020.
https://doi.org/10.1007/978-3-030-58666-9_19

capture the time but only the date. This is a frequent issue when the logging is done manually [3] or when the logging system is a legacy system.

Analyzing event logs that have not been screened for timestamp errors is likely to lead to wrong or misleading insights. For example, in the context of automated process discovery, where the objective is to automatically discover a process model from an event log, the presence of such errors may lead to mixing up order dependencies between process activities, especially if the logging system does not guarantee that events are recorded in the order of completion of the respective activities, or if the logging system may collect data from different sources. For example, given two activities A and B with same timestamp, these may erroneously be assumed to be concurrent, i.e. they can be executed in any order in the resulting process model, while in reality A is causal to B, i.e. A must always precede B in any instance of the process model. Any insights derived from a process model whose activities have wrong order dependencies, will be misleading. Timestamp errors can also affect performance statistics derived from the event log such as activity durations and waiting times. These statistics are used in the context of performance mining, variant analysis and conformance checking techniques, for example when checking the conformance of the as-is process to business rules that involve temporal aspects of the process. Thus, timestamp errors may also lead to wrong insights on the performance or conformance of the process at hand.

While many approaches have been proposed to filter out or repair events in order to improve the overall quality of an event log [4–12], only two of them [6,8] address the problem of repairing timestamp errors and they do so under a strict requirement: the presence of a (reference) process model with execution time annotations as input.

In this paper, we propose an automated approach to repairing timestamp errors in event logs. Specifically, we address the case where multiple events belonging to the same process instance (called *trace*) have the same timestamp. Our approach to tackle the "same-timestamp" error relies on two techniques. The first technique estimates, for each trace, the most-likely order between the events affected by the same-timestamp error, using information from correctly-ordered events in the log, and repairs the log accordingly. The second technique assigns a timestamp to each event that has been reordered, based on an estimation of the duration of each process activity in the log.

We implemented our approach in a software prototype and conducted a series of experiments with artificial and real-life logs, aimed at measuring the accuracy and time performance of our approach in correcting same-timestamp errors, under different settings. In addition, we carried out a case study with an Australian organization in the meat & livestock domain as an initial assessment of the usefulness of our approach in practice.

This paper is organized as follows. Section 2 introduces the required background and discusses approaches for event log filtering and repair. Section 3 presents our approach. Section 4 reports the experimental evaluation, including our case study. Section 5 concludes the paper and discusses future work.

2 Background and Related Work

Organizations often keep records of the execution of their business processes, e.g. order-to-cash or procure-to-pay processes, in the form of event logs. An *event log* is a set of *traces* where each trace captures the execution of a particular process instance (a.k.a. *case*). Traces are recorded as sequences of events and are identified by a unique case identifier (case id). Each *event* refers to the execution of a specific activity within a process case at a specific time. For example, the event with an activity labeled "Invoice released", a case id "134", and timestamp "23-02-2020T12:30:00", indicates that an invoice has been released for case 134 at 12:30 of 23 February 2020.

Process mining aims at automatically extracting actionable process knowledge from event logs [13,14]. This knowledge may take the form of a process model, a process performance report, and other artifacts. Data pre-processing is that phase of a process mining project where raw data is transformed into an understandable format, so that it can be used as input for knowledge discovery techniques. A key step of data pre-processing is *data cleaning*, which includes: (i) the removal of outlier data, and (ii) the correction of erroneous data. When the data under consideration is an event log, the two activities are known as log filtering and log repair.

Log filtering is a de-facto practice performed before starting any type of process mining analysis. Filtering a log generally follows an unstructured approach as different logs may be affected by different issues. Previous studies [1,2] have identified a collection of recurrent quality issues that commonly affect event logs, among these issues also incorrect timestamps. However, in the literature, log filtering is usually addressed from a noise-oriented perspective, focusing on removing infrequent traces and/or events from an event log [4,5,9] or event stream [11,12].

The goal of *log repair* is to detect erroneous or missing data (e.g. an event or its attributes) and repair it by relying on a reference model or observed correct data. Rogge-Solti et al. [6] propose to identify and restore missing events using a reference stochastic Petri net annotated with execution times. The method aligns each trace in the log to the model and, if the alignment is not perfect, the trace is repaired using the minimum cost alignment. Then, each event added as a result of the repair is assigned a timestamp computed via Bayesian networks. Similarly, Wang et al. [7] design an approach that, given a causal net, detects the events having an incorrect activity label and uses the net to restore the correct activity label. The main difference with [6] is that Wang et al. do not add new events to the log, but only repair the erroneous ones. Complementing the work of Wang et al., Shaoxu et al. [8] propose an approach to repair missing and incorrect timestamps, e.g. timestamps capturing only the hours. This approach determines the most likely correct timestamps with the aid of input time constraints between the observation of two consecutive activities. The new timestamps are assigned with the goal of minimizing the distance from input time constraints. Finally, Sani et al. [10] propose a general repair approach for infrequent behavior. Their main idea is to identify pairs of subtraces that are observed frequently (in different traces) having a third (variable) subtrace in between. Once the pairs are identified, the occurrences of the inner subtraces are analyzed to detect the least frequent ones, which are then replaced by frequent ones.

3   Approach

In this section, we present our approach for repairing event logs that contain traces where multiple events have the same timestamp and may, as such, be incorrectly ordered. We start by formally introducing the required preliminary concepts. Then, we describe our approach to reorder timestamp-equivalent events; we analyse its complexity and show its ILP formulation. Finally, we discuss a complementary technique to assign a timestamp to each reordered event.

3.1   Preliminaries

We define the notion of event log and the strictly-before and directly-follows relations between events. Using these, we provide the notion of log automaton.

Definition 1 *[Event Log]. Let Γ be a finite set of activities. A log $\mathcal{L}$ over Γ is defined as $\mathcal{L} \triangleq (\mathcal{E}, \mathcal{C}, \mathcal{A}, \mathcal{T}, <)$ where $\mathcal{E}$ is the set of events, $\mathcal{C} : \mathcal{E} \to \mathbb{N}$ is a surjective function linking events to cases, $\mathcal{A} : \mathcal{E} \to \Gamma$ is a function linking events to activities, $\mathcal{T} : \mathcal{E} \to \mathbb{N}$ is a function linking events to timestamps, and $< \subseteq \mathcal{E} \times \mathcal{E}$ is a strict total ordering over the events based on the sequential position of the events (as recorded in the event log and not according to their timestamp).*

Definition 2 *[Strictly-Before Relation]. Given a log $\mathcal{L}$ and two events $e_1, e_2 \in \mathcal{E}$, e_1 comes strictly-before e_2, i.e. $e_1 \sqsubset e_2$, iff $e_1 < e_2 \wedge \mathcal{C}(e_1) = \mathcal{C}(e_2) \wedge \nexists e_3 \in \mathcal{E} \mid \mathcal{C}(e_3) = \mathcal{C}(e_1) \wedge e_1 < e_3 \wedge e_3 < e_2$.*

Definition 3 *[Directly-Follows Relation]. Given a log $\mathcal{L}$ and two activities $x, y \in \Gamma$, y directly follows x, i.e. $x \rightsquigarrow y$, iff $\exists e_1, e_2 \in \mathcal{E} \mid \mathcal{A}(e_1) = x \wedge \mathcal{A}(e_2) = y \wedge e_1 \sqsubset e_2$. Additionally, we introduce the function $\# : \Gamma \times \Gamma \to \mathbb{N}$ which retrieves the number of times a directly-follows relation occurs in the underlying log.*

The directly-follows relations recorded in a log can be summarised with a directed graph, where each node represents an activity, and each arc connecting two nodes represents a directly-follows relation between the corresponding activities. From here on, we refer to this graph as the *log automaton* (L-automaton).

Table 1. Example log.

Example log
$\langle a, b, d, f \rangle$
$\langle a, b, c, d, f \rangle$
$\langle a, b, d, f \rangle$
$\langle a, b, c, b, d, f \rangle$
$\langle a, d, b, c, f \rangle$
$\langle a, c, d, b, f \rangle$
$\langle a, d, c, f \rangle$

Depending on the log quality, the L-automaton may contain several infrequent directly-follows relations. In fact, filtering the log or its L-automaton is common in many process discovery techniques [15,16]. To improve the quality of the L-automaton, and the effectiveness of our technique, we recommend to apply one of the many techniques to remove infrequent behavior from the log [4,5,9]. In this paper, we rely on the method in [5]. We refer to the filtered L-automaton as the *filtered log automaton* (F-automaton). By construction, the F-automaton's arc set is a subset of the L-automaton's arc set. Figures 1a and 1b show the L-automaton and the F-automaton of the log in Table 1.

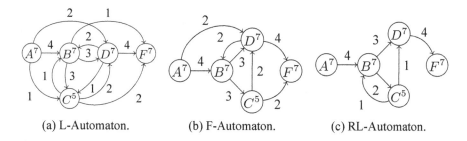

Fig. 1. Automata examples.

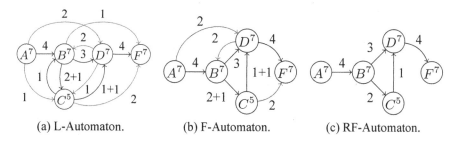

Fig. 2. Automata examples – UDFRs highlighted in red. (Color figure online)

3.2   Repairing Events Order

Starting from the F-automaton, we designed a technique to reassign the total order among the events having the same timestamp, namely *timestamp-equivalent events*.

Definition 4 *[Timestamp-Equivalent Events]. Given a log $\mathcal{L}$ and two events $e_1, e_2 \in \mathcal{E}$, e_1 is timestamp-equivalent to e_2, i.e. $e_1 \dot{\sim} e_2$, if and only if (iff) they belong to the same trace and they have the same timestamp. Formally, $e_1 \dot{\sim} e_2 \Leftrightarrow \mathcal{C}(e_1) = \mathcal{C}(e_2) \wedge \mathcal{T}(e_1) = \mathcal{T}(e_2)$. It is possible to identify the set of the timestamp-equivalent events as the quotient set of $\mathcal{E}$ by $\dot{\sim}$, formally, $\Omega \triangleq \mathcal{E}/\dot{\sim}$.*

The presence of timestamp-equivalent events may lead to *unreliable directly-follows relations* (UDFRs). In the context of this paper, we say that a directly-follows relation, e.g. $d \rightsquigarrow b$, is unreliable iff it is derived from two timestamp-equivalent events, i.e. $d \dot{\sim} b$.

Definition 5 *[Unreliable Directly-Follows Relation (UDFR)]. Given two activities $x, y \in \Gamma$, there exists an unreliable directly-follows relation between x and y, i.e. $x \rightsquigarrow_u y$, iff $x \rightsquigarrow y \wedge \exists e_1, e_2 \in \mathcal{E} \mid \mathcal{A}(e_1) = x \wedge \mathcal{A}(e_2) = y \wedge e_1 \dot{\sim} e_2$.*

By construction, an L-automaton and even an F-automaton may include UDFRs. The log in Table 1 displays in red the timestamp-equivalent events. Projecting this information on the L-automaton and the F-automaton we can highlight the UDFRs, captured in red in Figs. 2a and 2b.

It is possible to remove the UDFRs from both the L-automaton and the F-automaton. If we remove the UDFRs from the L-automaton, we refer to the resulting automaton as the *refined L-automaton* (RL-automaton, Fig. 1c), while, if we remove the UDFRs from the F-automaton, we refer to the resulting automaton as the *refined F-automaton* (RF-automaton, Fig. 2c). Given that techniques that remove infrequent directly-follows relations are based on frequencies, in general, filtering the RL-automaton may not result into the RF-automaton. We rely on the RF-automata to repair timestamp-equivalent events.

Exploiting the frequency of a directly-follows relation, we introduce the function $\Phi : \Gamma \times \Gamma \to [0, 1]$, which provides an estimate of the confidence level of a directly-follows relation in an RF-automaton. This function is defined as:

$$\Phi(x, y) \triangleq \frac{\#(x, y)}{\sum_{z \in \Gamma} \#(x, z)} \tag{1}$$

Then, we identify the optimal order of timestamp-equivalent events by selecting the most likely sequence of timestamp-equivalent events among all their possible sequences. Given a set of timestamp-equivalent events $\omega \in \mathcal{P}(\mathcal{E})^1$, first, we define the set of all possible sequences of timestamp-equivalent events in ω as:

$$\mathcal{S}(\omega) \triangleq \{\overline{\omega} \in \mathcal{E}^* \mid |\overline{\omega}| = |\omega| \wedge \forall e \in \omega \ \exists 1 \leq i \leq |\omega| \ [e = \overline{\omega}_i]\} \tag{2}$$

Then, using the confidence level of the directly-follows relations, we measure the confidence level of a sequence through the function $\% : \mathcal{E}^* \to [0, 1]$. The latter function is ultimately used to discover the most likely sequence of a set of timestamp-equivalent events. Formally, given a set of timestamp-equivalent events $\omega \in \mathcal{P}(\mathcal{E})$, we refer to the sequence with the highest confidence level (i.e. the most likely sequence of a set of timestamp-equivalent events) as $\overline{\omega}^o \in \mathcal{S}(\omega)$, such that $\%(\overline{\omega}^o) \geq \%(\overline{\omega}) \ [\forall \overline{\omega} \in \mathcal{S}(\omega)]$.

Following a pure probabilistic approach, the first implementation to come to mind for the function $\% : \mathcal{E}^* \to [0, 1]$ is the following:

$$\%(\overline{\omega}) \triangleq \prod_{i=1}^{|\overline{\omega}|-1} \Phi(\mathcal{A}(\overline{\omega}_i), \mathcal{A}(\overline{\omega}_{i+1})) \tag{3}$$

where the confidence level of the entire sequence is based on the likelihood of pairs of events following each other. While in theory this implementation works, in practice it may lead to a fault. Let us assume that we have three timestamp-equivalent events e_1, e_2, and $e_3 \in \mathcal{E}$, with $\mathcal{A}(e_1) = a, \mathcal{A}(e_2) = b$, and $\mathcal{A}(e_3) = c$. Also, let us assume that only the following directly-follows relations hold: $a \rightsquigarrow b$ and $a \rightsquigarrow c$ (with a confidence level of 0.5 and 0.1, respectively). Then, all the possible sequences that can be generated out of the three events will have a confidence level of 0 (since $b \rightsquigarrow c$ is missing), while, a sequence with $a \rightsquigarrow b$ should be preferred over other possible sequences (since $\Phi(a, b)$ is the highest). For example, we may consider the sequence $\langle a, b, c \rangle$ or $\langle c, a, b \rangle$ as the most likely.

---

[1] The powerset of $\mathcal{E}$.

Algorithm 1: Repair Log

input: Event log $\mathcal{L} = (\mathcal{E}, \mathcal{C}, \mathcal{A}, \mathcal{T}, <)$

1 **Set** $T \leftarrow$ getTraces($\mathcal{L}$);
2 **for** $t \in T$ **do**
3   **for** $\omega \in t/\tilde{\sim}$ **do**
4   **for** $e_1 \in \omega$ **do**
5   **for** $e_2 \in \omega$ **do** remove (e_1, e_2) from $<$;
6   Sequence $\overline{\omega}^b \leftarrow$ getHighestConfidenceSequence($\mathcal{S}(\omega)$);
7   **for** $i \leftarrow 1$ **to** $|\overline{\omega}^b| - 1$ **do** add $(\overline{\omega}_i^b, \overline{\omega}_{i+1}^b)$ to $<$;

8 **return** $(\mathcal{E}, \mathcal{C}, \mathcal{A}, \mathcal{T}, <)$

Following this reasoning, an improved version of the function $\% : \mathcal{E}^* \to \mathbb{R}$ is:

$$\%(\overline{\omega}) \triangleq \sum_{i=1}^{|\overline{\omega}|-1} \frac{\Phi(\mathcal{A}(\overline{\omega}_i), \mathcal{A}(\overline{\omega}_{i+1}))}{|\overline{\omega}| - 1} \tag{4}$$

We note, however, that in the case of a set of events that are only observed as timestamp-equivalent, also this revised version of the function $\%$ would always return 0. We acknowledge this as a potential limitation of our approach, since it is designed to repair the timestamp-equivalent events on the grounds of other observations of the same events with different timestamps.

Returning to our working example, the log in Table 1 contains three traces affected by timestamp-equivalent events (highlighted in red), specifically, $\overline{\omega}_1 = \langle d, b, c \rangle$, $\overline{\omega}_2 = \langle c, d, b \rangle$, and $\overline{\omega}_3 = \langle c, d \rangle$. Our technique fixes each of the three sequences separately. Working on the RF-automaton (Fig. 2c), we measure the confidence level of each possible sequence of the timestamp-equivalent events by analysing the confidence level of each arc of the RF-automaton. We recall that the confidence level of an arc, e.g. $\Phi(b, d)$, is equal to the number of times (b, d) is traversed divided by the sum of the number of times each arc with source b is traversed, i.e. $\Phi(b, d) = 0.60$ as there are $2 + 3 = 5$ ways to leave node b, 3 of which are through the arc (b, d).

Let us consider, $\overline{\omega}_1 = \langle d, b, c \rangle$, Table 2 shows all the possible sequences and the respective confidence levels. We can see that the most likely sequence of events is $\overline{\omega}_1^o = \langle b, c, d \rangle$. Considering $\overline{\omega}_2 = \langle c, d, b \rangle$, we would reach the same result, since the set of timestamp-equivalent events is the same as $\overline{\omega}_1$. While for the sequence $\overline{\omega}_3$, which contains only two events, we can trivially determine that $\overline{\omega}_3^o = \langle d, c \rangle$, since $\Phi(c, d) = 0$.

Table 2. Selecting the sequence with the highest confidence level.

Sequence (ϖ)	%(ϖ)
$\langle d, b, c \rangle$	$\left(\varPhi(d,b) + \varPhi(b,c)\right)/2 = 0.2$
$\langle d, c, b \rangle$	$\left(\varPhi(d,c) + \varPhi(c,b)\right)/2 = 0.0$
$\langle b, c, d \rangle$	$\left(\varPhi(b,c) + \varPhi(c,d)\right)/2 = 0.7$
$\langle b, d, c \rangle$	$\left(\varPhi(b,d) + \varPhi(d,c)\right)/2 = 0.3$
$\langle c, b, d \rangle$	$\left(\varPhi(c,b) + \varPhi(b,d)\right)/2 = 0.3$
$\langle c, d, b \rangle$	$\left(\varPhi(c,d) + \varPhi(d,b)\right)/2 = 0.5$

Algorithm 1 synthesises how our approach operates to repair a log affected by timestamp-equivalent events. For each trace t in the log, we retrieve all the sets containing the timestamp-equivalent events belonging to that trace (ω, see line 2 and 3). Then, we perform two major operations over each set ω. First, we remove the original strict total order defined for each pair of events $(e_1, e_2) \in \omega$ (lines 5). Second, we introduce the repaired total order based on the sequence of events with the highest confidence level (lines 6 and 7). After iterating this procedure for each trace in the log, we return the repaired log.

3.3   Time Complexity and ILP Formulation

Time Complexity. The identification of the most likely sequence of events is an NP-hard problem. We provide a sketch of its complexity by providing a polynomial time transformation from the Maximum Travelling Salesman Problem (Max TSP) (a well known NP-complete problem [17]) to the most likely sequence of events problem. The Max TSP is the problem of identifying a Hamiltonian cycle (a tour that passes through all the vertices) with maximum cost in a complete asymmetric graph with non-negative weights. It is straightforward to show that a Max TSP problem can be reduced to an instance of the most likely sequence of events problem. This can be achieved through the application of the following six polynomial steps: (1) select a random vertex v of the Max TSP problem; (2) introduce two new vertices v_i and v_o; (3) for each incoming arc of v, i.e. $a = (s, v)$, create a new arc $a_i = (s, v_i)$; (4) for each outgoing arc of v, i.e. $a = (v, t)$, create a new arc $a_o = (v_o, t)$; (5) remove all arcs connected to v; (6) remove vertex v. Now the Max TSP problem corresponds to determining the most likely sequence

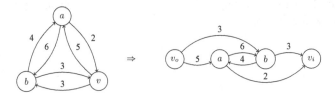

Fig. 3. Example, Max TSP reduction to most likely sequence of events problem.

of events leading from v_o to v_i. Figure 3 shows how to reduce a Max TSP problem to a most likely sequence of events problem. In the example, the asymmetric graph contains three vertices, $V = \{a, b, v\}$. These three vertices are connected via six weighted arcs $A = \{(a, b, 6), (a, v, 2), (b, a, 4), (b, v, 3), (v, a, 5), (v, b, 3)\}$. As part of the reduction two new vertices v_i and v_o are introduced, as well as arcs connecting these vertices to vertices which were originally connected to v.

ILP Formulation. In Sect. 3.2, we defined $\overline{w}^o$ as the most likely sequence over the set $\mathcal{S}(w)$ of possible sequences. To determine the most likely sequence over the set $\mathcal{S}(w)$ we propose the application of Integer Linear Programming (ILP), where the confidence level of a sequence is measured using the function proposed in Eq. 4.

Given a log $\mathcal{L}$, the inputs for our problem are the set of events $w \in \mathcal{E}/\dot{\sim}$, the event $s \in \mathcal{E}$ (not affected by timestamp error) which should precede the sequence $\overline{w}^o$, and the event $f \in \mathcal{E}$ (not affected by timestamp error) which should follow the sequence $\overline{w}^o$. Finally, for convenience we define the set $w^f \triangleq w \cup \{f\}$, and $w^{fs} \triangleq w \cup \{s, f\}$. Using w^{fs} instead of w allows us to take into account the context of the sequence w when repairing the order of the events.

Before presenting the ILP formulation, we also need to introduce the following variables: i) for each event $e \in w^{fs}$ there exists an auxiliary variable $u_e \in \mathbb{Z}$;[2] ii) for each couple of events $(e_1, e_2) \in w^{fs} \times w^{fs}$ if $e_1 \neq e_2$ there exists a variable $x_{e_1,e_2} \in \{0, 1\}$. If the solution of the ILP problem is such that $x_{e_1,e_2} = 1$, event e_2 directly follow event e_1 in the most likely sequence.

The ILP problem aims at maximizing the confidence level of the sequence as proposed in Eq. 4. We model the ILP problem of determining the best sequence as a traveling salesman problem (TSP) [18]. Our formulation presents two main differences from the original formulation. First, we try to maximize the distance instead of minimizing it (see Eq. 5).

$$\max \sum_{e_1 \in w^{fs}} \sum_{e_2 \in w^{fs}} \Phi(\mathcal{A}(e_1), \mathcal{A}(e_2)) \cdot x_{e_1,e_2}. \tag{5}$$

Second, we impose that f must close the cycle on s (see Eq. 6). The constraints of our ILP problem (Eq. 5) are captured by Eq. 6, 7, 8, and 9.[3]

$$x_{f,s} = 1 \tag{6}$$

$$\sum_{e_2 \in w^{fs} \setminus \{e_1\}} x_{e_1,e_2} = 1 \tag{7}$$

$$\sum_{e_2 \in w^{fs} \setminus \{e_1\}} x_{e_2,e_1} = 1 \tag{8}$$

$$u_{e_1} - u_{e_2} + |w^{fs}| \cdot x_{e_1,e_2} \leq |w^{fs}| - 1 \tag{9}$$

---

[2] u_e is a mathematical escamotage to ensure that the combination of equations will all have a strict order, which is defined by the ILP solver when it finds the solution.

[3] Equation 7, 8, and 9 come from Miller et al. [18].

In plain English they are the following. Equation 6; we connect the final event to the start event to prevent them from being in the middle of the sequence. Equation 7; we force each event $e_1 \in \omega^f$ to precede one and only one event (Eq. 7). Equation 8; we force each event $e_1 \in \omega^f$ to follow one and only one event (Eq. 8). Equation 9; for each couple of events $(e_1, e_2) \in \omega^f \times \omega^f$ where $e_1 \neq e_2$, we prevent the presence of sub-tours in the TSP problem, i.e. we enforce the tour to visit all cities in one go (Eq. 9). The latter, in our context, means that we enforce the presence of a single sequence covering all events.

3.4 Event Timestamp Estimation

Reordering timestamp-equivalent events does not fix their timestamps. Consequently, we complement our events-reordering approach with a technique to assign a timestamp to each reordered event.

To estimate an event timestamp, we rely on the distribution of the time elapsed between the event and the preceding event within the same trace. For simplicity, we refer to such time as *duration* of the event, whose distribution corresponds to its *probability density function* (PDF). Given an event $e \in \mathcal{E}$, we formally define its duration with the function $\mathcal{D} : \mathcal{E} \to \mathbb{N}$.

$$\mathcal{D}(e) \triangleq \begin{cases} \mathcal{T}(e) - \mathcal{T}(e_p) & \text{if } \exists e_p \mid e_p \sqsubset e_2 \wedge \mathcal{T}(e) \neq \mathcal{T}(e_p), \\ \epsilon & \text{otherwise} \end{cases} \tag{10}$$

Where ϵ is an arbitrary small value to avoid that when assigning a timestamp we will cause two events to be timestamp-equivalent.

Given activity $a \in \Gamma$, we can define the multiset of its events' durations as $\mathcal{D}_a \triangleq \{(d, n) \in \mathbb{N} \times \mathbb{N} \mid \exists e \in \mathcal{E}_{a,d} \wedge n = |\mathcal{E}_{a,d}|\}$ where $\mathcal{E}_{a,d}$ is the subset of $\mathcal{E}$ containing only events of activity a that have a given duration d, i.e. $\mathcal{E}_{a,d} \triangleq \{e \in \mathcal{E} \mid \mathcal{A}(e) = a \wedge \mathcal{D}(e) = d\}$. We use the multiset to estimate the PDF of the duration of events of activity a. For this purpose we define the function estimating the duration of an event of activity a as $f_a^{est} : \mathbb{N} \times \mathbb{N} \to (\mathbb{N} \to \mathbb{R})$, where the range is the PDF (f_a) we want to estimate. This can be achieved using approaches as the one proposed by Silverman [19] for the estimation of multimodal distributions using kernel density.

Once the PDF of each activity is known, we can assign a new timestamp to each ordered event following the durations dictated by the PDF. The new timestamp is:

$$\mathcal{T}^+(e) \triangleq \begin{cases} \mathcal{T}(e_p) + \overline{f_{\mathcal{A}(e)}} & \text{if } \exists e_p \mid e_p \sqsubset e_2 \wedge \mathcal{T}(e) \neq \mathcal{T}(e_p) \\ \epsilon + \overline{f_{\mathcal{A}(e)}} & \text{otherwise} \end{cases} \tag{11}$$

where $\overline{f_{\mathcal{A}(e)}}$ extracts a likely duration from the PDF $f_{\mathcal{A}(e)}$. Finally, the new timestamp for event e substitutes the old one in the log, i.e. $\mathcal{T} \Leftarrow \mathcal{T} \oplus \{(e, \mathcal{T}^+(e))\}$.

4   Evaluation

We implemented our approach as a standalone Java application,[4] and used this prototype tool to evaluate the accuracy and time performance of our approach using artificial and real-life datasets. (See footnote 4) Finally, we conducted a case study to gain initial evidence on the usefulness of our approach in practice.

All the experiments reported in this section were performed on a 6-core Xeon E5-1650 3.5 Ghz with 128 GB of RAM running JVM 8 with 48 GB of heap space.

4.1   Datasets and Setup

We generated the artificial dataset from the BPMN model shown in Fig. 4. We used this model since it exhibits properties often found in models discovered from real-life logs, such as high degree of concurrency, unstructuredness, skips and loop structures. Starting from a reference log obtained by simulating this model, we injected different amounts of timestamp-equivalent events at three levels of granularity by changing the percentage of affected events, traces, or unique traces in increments of 5%, ranging from 5% to 40%. This produced three sets of eight logs, for a total of 24 logs. Each of the 24 logs (as well as the reference log) contains 3,000 traces, 45,330 events, and 24 activity labels. The logs' unique traces range from 1,391 to 2,361, while the reference log counts only 1,277. Even though all the artificial logs were generated from a single artificial model as opposed to generating each log from different artificial models, we note that the validity of the assessment of our approach is grounded on the variety and amount of timestamp-equivalent events in each artificial log rather than on the variety of the behavior captured by the underlying model.

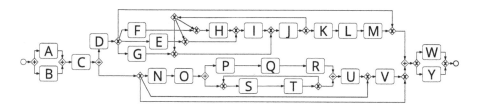

Fig. 4. Process model used to generate the artificial log

Alongside the artificial logs, we used the real-life log from the BPI Challenge 2014 [20]. We chose only this log out of the collection available at the 4TU Data Center[5] because it was the only one affected by timestamp-equivalent events for which we had access to the correct version (i.e. the original log without events' ordering errors), which we used as ground-truth in our experiments. The BPI2014 log counts 46,616 traces, 466,737 events, 39 activity labels, 22,632

---

[4] Available at https://doi.org/10.6084/m9.figshare.11868969.

[5] https://data.4tu.nl/repository/collection:event_logs_real.

unique traces. The 39% of its events are timestamp-equivalent, for a total of 182,027, of which 113,334 are incorrectly ordered.

Using our approach we repaired the logs and measured the accuracy of the repair by applying the *Levenshtein edit distance* [21] between the proposed repair and the reference log. We adapted the Levenshtein distance to the concept of traces, where instead of inserting, removing, or replacing characters we insert, remove, or replace events. We decided to use this metric since it provides a fine-grained measurement that allow us to assess the quality of a technique even in cases where the optimal solution is not identified. For the artificial logs, we also measured the fitness [22] of the repaired logs w.r.t. the BPMN model used as input, and the root-square mean error (RSME) between the assigned timestamp and the correct one.

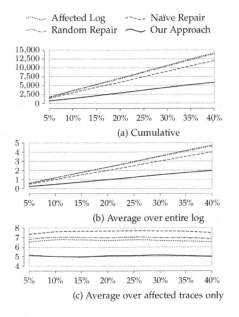

(a) Cumulative

(b) Average over entire log

(c) Average over affected traces only

Fig. 5. Edit distance for the logs $N5_e - N40_e$.

We compared our approach against three baselines: *no-repair*, *random repair*, and *naïve repair*. *No-repair* simply does not apply any change to the affected log, this baseline serves as bottom-line for improvement. *Random repair* randomly reorders the timestamp-equivalent events. *Naïve repair*, for each set of timestamp-equivalent events, it collects all the traces containing such a set of events and it selects the most frequent trace out of them, then it reorders the specific set of timestamp-equivalent events according to the events' order in the most frequent trace. We could not use any of the timestamp repair methods available in the literature [6,8] because they address different types of timestamp errors, and both require as input a reference model annotated with execution times information.

4.2   Results

Tables 3 and 4 show the results of our evaluation. They report: the number of traces affected by timestamp-equivalent events, cumulative edit distance (cum.), maximum edit distance, average edit distance computed over the entire log and its standard deviation, average edit distance computed using only traces affected by timestamp-equivalent events and its standard deviation, RMSE and fitness (for artificial logs only).

Overall, the results show that our approach outperforms the three baselines in all the measurements, performing consistently better across the whole dataset, as captured by the values in bold in the tables. Figure 5 shows the plots of the cumulative edit distance, the average edit distance over the entire log, and the average edit distance over the affected traces only. Two things can be evinced from the graphs. First, the number of remaining timestamp-equivalent events is proportional to the number inserted, regardless of the approach we use. Second, our approach is the only one to always achieve an average edit distance on the affected traces that is below the one of the affected log (see Fig. 5c). This implies that the *random* and *naïve* baselines are only repairing traces that are easy to repair, i.e. with an edit distance below the average. On the other hand, *our approach can repair complex traces*, in fact it reduced the average edit distance by 60% (on average across the dataset), and lowered the maximum edit distance by 12.5% (on average across the dataset).

Further, the results obtained when timestamp-equivalent events are injected at unique trace level are remarkable (see Table 4, logs $N5_{ut}$ – $N40_{ut}$). In fact, the *random* and *naïve* baselines are not able to repair the log, i.e. they reduce the cumulative edit distance on average by 0% and 5% compared to the *no-repair* baseline, while our approach maintains an average improvement of 60%. Figures 6a and 6b provide a graphical snapshot of the benefits of our technique, as we can see, the curve representing our technique (black in colour) sits well below the baselines. While, the *random* and *naïve* baselines almost overlap with the *no-repair* baseline.

In terms of accuracy when assigning a timestamp to an event,

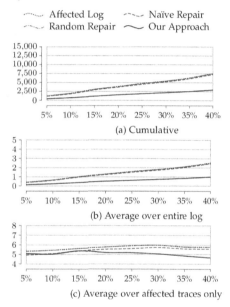

Fig. 6. Edit distance for the logs $N5_{ut}$ – $N40_{ut}$.

we improve the RMSE on average by 54%, with a minimum of 48% (achieved over the most complex log: $N40_{ut}$) and a maximum of 59%. Additionally, it should be noted that the *random* and *naïve* baselines only achieve on average an improvement of 0% and 4% (respectively). Moreover, the fitness of the logs repaired by our approach is the highest across all tests.

Finally, the results on the real-life log support the fact that our approach noticeably outperforms the three baselines. Indeed, while the *random repair* and the *naïve repair* improve the cumulative edit distance of 3% and 2% (resp.) compared to the *no-repair* baseline, our approach brings an improvement of 47%. These results, alongside those obtained on the artificial logs, confirm the efficacy of our approach.

Table 3. Results of the experimental evaluation - Part 1.

Log	Approach	#Affected Traces	Distance		Entire Log		Affected Traces		RMSE in Days	Fitness
			Cum.	Max	Average Distance	Stand. Dev.	Average Distance	Stand. Dev.		
$N5_e$	No-repair	273	1785	26	0.595	2.397	6.538	4.927	121.62	0.972
	Our	**143**	**729**	**23**	**0.243**	**1.438**	**5.098**	**4.318**	**42.65**	**0.999**
	Naïve	202	1481	26	0.494	2.306	7.332	5.372	114.27	0.981
	Random	249	1735	26	0.578	2.394	6.968	4.950	121.53	0.973
$N10_e$	No-repair	531	3590	26	1.197	3.289	6.761	4.849	123.99	0.945
	Our	**286**	**1412**	**23**	**0.471**	**1.919**	**4.937**	**4.071**	**42.82**	**0.998**
	Naïve	394	2996	26	0.999	3.192	7.604	5.230	117.45	0.962
	Random	504	3533	26	1.178	3.290	7.010	4.852	123.94	0.946
$N15_e$	No-repair	792	5349	26	1.783	3.868	6.754	4.808	122.78	0.920
	Our	**444**	**2185**	**23**	**0.728**	**2.342**	**4.921**	**4.052**	**43.16**	**0.997**
	Naïve	594	4546	26	1.515	3.801	7.653	5.100	117.15	0.941
	Random	747	5252	26	1.751	3.874	7.031	4.810	122.75	0.922
$N20_e$	No-repair	1062	7102	26	2.367	4.326	6.687	4.897	123.58	0.894
	Our	**586**	**2971**	**24**	**0.990**	**2.744**	**5.070**	**4.228**	**44.28**	**0.996**
	Naïve	777	5960	26	1.987	4.290	7.671	5.240	117.77	0.924
	Random	997	6962	26	2.321	4.339	6.983	4.909	123.52	0.897
$N25_e$	No-repair	1314	8885	26	2.962	4.668	6.762	4.904	123.98	0.867
	Our	**734**	**3742**	**24**	**1.247**	**3.027**	**5.098**	**4.221**	**44.83**	**0.995**
	Naïve	974	7504	26	2.501	4.680	7.704	5.233	118.29	0.905
	Random	1237	8723	26	2.908	4.689	7.052	4.909	123.94	0.871
$N30_e$	No-repair	1600	10673	26	3.558	4.898	6.671	4.921	123.47	0.840
	Our	**876**	**4496**	**24**	**1.499**	**3.249**	**5.132**	**4.182**	**44.46**	**0.994**
	Naïve	1175	9004	26	3.001	4.981	7.663	5.256	117.87	0.886
	Random	1511	10490	26	3.497	4.929	6.942	4.931	123.45	0.843
$N35_e$	No-repair	1881	12440	26	4.147	5.042	6.614	4.922	123.57	0.813
	Our	**1030**	**5226**	**24**	**1.742**	**3.416**	**5.074**	**4.134**	**43.87**	**0.993**
	Naïve	1374	10496	26	3.499	5.211	7.639	5.260	118.09	0.866
	Random	1756	12185	26	4.062	5.093	6.939	4.935	123.54	0.818
$N40_e$	No-repair	2168	14177	30	4.726	5.073	6.539	4.874	123.34	0.785
	Our	**1174**	**5884**	**23**	**1.961**	**3.542**	**5.012**	**4.096**	**43.86**	**0.992**
	Naïve	1598	11969	30	3.990	5.339	7.490	5.224	117.94	0.847
	Random	2046	13926	30	4.642	5.132	6.806	4.888	123.29	0.791
$N5_t$	No-repair	150	995	26	0.332	1.826	6.633	4.989	120.68	0.984
	Our	**75**	**398**	**22**	**0.133**	**1.092**	**5.307**	**4.496**	**51.92**	**0.999**
	Naïve	106	811	26	0.270	1.748	7.651	5.481	112.58	0.989
	Random	139	971	26	0.324	1.822	6.986	5.014	120.62	0.985
$N10_t$	No-repair	300	1985	26	0.662	2.511	6.617	4.862	121.55	0.970
	Our	**158**	**800**	**22**	**0.267**	**1.485**	**5.063**	**4.193**	**50.86**	**0.999**
	Naïve	223	1647	26	0.549	2.415	7.386	5.286	114.29	0.979
	Random	284	1951	26	0.650	2.509	6.870	4.875	121.50	0.970
$N15_t$	No-repair	450	2947	26	0.982	2.974	6.549	4.746	122.08	0.955
	Our	**235**	**1167**	**22**	**0.389**	**1.764**	**4.966**	**4.125**	**50.31**	**0.998**
	Naïve	331	2430	26	0.810	2.867	7.341	5.152	114.87	0.969
	Random	427	2901	26	0.967	2.974	6.794	4.750	122.05	0.956
$N20_t$	No-repair	600	4043	26	1.348	3.444	6.738	4.793	123.63	0.938
	Our	**318**	**1584**	**23**	**0.528**	**2.022**	**4.981**	**4.047**	**51.00**	**0.998**
	Naïve	445	3382	26	1.127	3.351	7.600	5.150	117.09	0.956
	Random	560	3960	26	1.320	3.446	7.071	4.790	123.60	0.939
$N25_t$	No-repair	750	5082	26	1.694	3.799	6.776	4.826	123.44	0.924
	Our	**417**	**2066**	**22**	**0.689**	**2.295**	**4.954**	**4.095**	**50.88**	**0.997**
	Naïve	564	4318	26	1.439	3.726	7.656	5.125	117.79	0.944
	Random	705	4990	26	1.663	3.804	7.078	4.821	123.41	0.926
$N30_t$	No-repair	900	6065	26	2.022	4.087	6.739	4.887	123.65	0.909
	Our	**489**	**2475**	**24**	**0.825**	**2.526**	**5.061**	**4.208**	**51.65**	**0.996**
	Naïve	664	5105	26	1.702	4.027	7.688	5.221	117.74	0.934
	Random	842	5949	26	1.983	4.096	7.065	4.886	123.62	0.911
$N35_t$	No-repair	1050	7038	26	2.346	4.316	6.703	4.901	123.81	0.895
	Our	**578**	**2928**	**24**	**0.976**	**2.727**	**5.066**	**4.229**	**52.07**	**0.996**
	Naïve	770	5906	26	1.969	4.277	7.670	5.248	117.97	0.925
	Random	985	6903	26	2.301	4.329	7.008	4.908	123.79	0.897
$N40_t$	No-repair	1200	8031	26	2.677	4.504	6.692	4.883	123.90	0.880
	Our	**657**	**3317**	**24**	**1.106**	**2.868**	**5.049**	**4.202**	**51.08**	**0.995**
	Naïve	881	6741	26	2.247	4.492	7.652	5.230	118.06	0.914
	Random	1132	7891	26	2.630	4.521	6.971	4.889	123.87	0.882

Table 4. Results of the experimental evaluation - Part 2.

Log	Approach	#Affected traces	Distance		Entire log		Affected traces		RMSE in days	Fitness
			Cum.	Max	Average distance	Stand. dev.	Average distance	Stand. dev.		
N5$_{ut}$	No-repair	235	1253	22	0.418	1.878	5.332	4.340	109.84	0.978
	Our	**87**	**444**	**16**	**0.148**	**1.077**	5.103	**3.833**	**55.71**	**0.999**
	Naïve	235	1160	22	0.387	1.821	**4.936**	4.457	104.74	0.984
	Random	235	1252	22	0.417	1.878	5.328	4.343	109.82	0.978
N10$_{ut}$	No-repair	363	1978	25	0.659	2.377	5.449	4.539	114.36	0.967
	Our	**151**	**761**	**19**	**0.254**	**1.402**	5.040	**3.865**	**58.06**	**0.999**
	Naïve	363	1849	25	0.616	2.319	5.094	4.652	110.99	0.974
	Random	363	1975	25	0.658	2.376	5.441	4.544	114.34	0.968
N15$_{ut}$	No-repair	549	3092	25	1.031	2.956	5.632	4.672	114.92	0.949
	Our	**219**	**1181**	**19**	**0.394**	**1.777**	5.393	**4.039**	**57.98**	**0.999**
	Naïve	549	2946	25	0.982	2.911	5.366	4.773	112.68	0.958
	Random	549	3089	25	1.030	2.955	5.627	4.676	114.90	0.950
N20$_{ut}$	No-repair	674	3895	25	1.298	3.288	5.779	4.715	116.26	0.950
	Our	**305**	**1587**	**21**	**0.529**	**2.028**	5.203	**4.016**	**59.31**	**0.998**
	Naïve	674	3736	25	1.245	3.250	5.543	4.816	114.44	0.949
	Random	674	3895	25	1.298	3.288	5.779	4.715	116.23	0.939
N25$_{ut}$	No-repair	802	4745	25	1.582	3.565	5.916	4.680	116.36	0.925
	Our	**362**	**1879**	**19**	**0.626**	**2.160**	5.191	**3.871**	**60.14**	**0.998**
	Naïve	802	4507	25	1.502	3.511	5.620	4.792	113.70	0.938
	Random	802	4739	25	1.580	3.564	5.909	4.684	116.34	0.926
N30$_{ut}$	No-repair	911	5449	25	1.816	3.764	5.981	4.663	116.51	0.915
	Our	**440**	**2225**	**19**	**0.742**	**2.330**	5.057	**3.897**	**59.83**	**0.997**
	Naïve	911	5228	25	1.743	3.722	5.739	4.763	114.48	0.928
	Random	911	5446	25	1.815	3.764	5.978	4.665	116.49	0.916
N35$_{ut}$	No-repair	1093	6341	25	2.114	3.949	5.801	4.626	115.02	0.902
	Our	**530**	**2567**	**20**	**0.856**	**2.450**	4.843	**3.829**	**59.63**	**0.997**
	Naïve	1093	6117	25	2.039	3.914	5.597	4.704	113.24	0.916
	Random	1093	6335	25	2.112	3.948	5.796	4.629	115.00	0.903
N40$_{ut}$	No-repair	1313	7584	25	2.528	4.134	5.776	4.505	114.83	0.882
	Our	**649**	**3023**	**19**	**1.008**	**2.575**	**4.658**	**3.695**	**60.13**	**0.996**
	Naïve	1313	7330	25	2.443	4.100	5.583	4.569	112.86	0.895
	Random	1313	7582	25	2.527	4.134	5.775	4.506	114.82	0.882
BPI2014	No-repair	36442	144957	63	3.110	3.445	3.978	**3.425**	-	-
	Our	**19838**	**77312**	**63**	**1.658**	**2.968**	**3.897**	3.461	-	-
	Naïve	35000	142072	63	3.048	3.482	4.059	3.471	-	-
	Random	34070	140199	63	3.008	3.505	4.115	3.501	-	-

Time Performance. On the artificial logs, our event-reordering technique achieved an average execution time of 4.9 s (min: 0.9 s, max: 20.2 s), linearly increasing with the number of timestamp-equivalent events. The time required to repair the BPI2014 log was over 45 m, due to the high number of affected events (over 180, 000), with an average time to fix a single event of 15 ms. Overall, the bulk of the time is taken by our timestamp estimation technique, with an average of 4.7 m on the artificial logs (min: 1.8 m, max: 24.4 m), and 5.4 m for the BPI2014 log. Such performance is expected, due to the inherent complexity of estimating the probability density function (via kernel estimation) associated with the duration of each event.

4.3   Case Study

In collaboration with an Australian consultancy company we applied our app-roach to an event log from the meat & livestock domain. The process recorded in the log covers all stages livestock goes through from when cows are bred or pur-chased at the market, to when they are slaughtered and the meat is processed. The event log contains data originating from four different cattle farms (for a total of 18,192 events), and records the processing of 3,032 cows over a timeframe of about two years. In this context, thus, each animal identifies a process case. Each cow is RFID-tagged, to record the activity each cow is involved in (e.g. breading, backgrounding, feeding) throughout the various stages of this process.

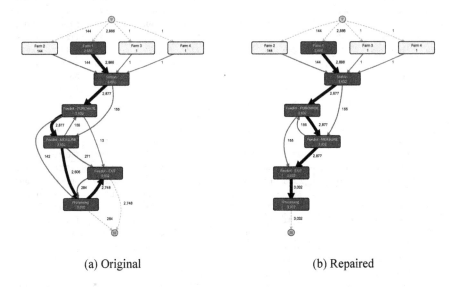

(a) Original   (b) Repaired

Fig. 7. Directly-follows graph of the log before and after repairing (shown in Disco).

When analysing the event log, we observed it contained 5,496 timestamp-equivalent events out of 18,192. Specifically, the timestamp of these events did not capture the time when the event occurred (i.e. hours and minutes) but only the date. As already mentioned, this type of problem is frequent in real-life event logs, and depends on the granularity of the logging system. In our case study, this resulted in 2,748 cases where cows were slaughtered (activity "Processing") before leaving the feeding lot (activity "Feedlot - EXIT"), as can be observed in Fig. 7a. This transition is not possible in reality, as confirmed by domain experts.

The application of our approach required no domain knowledge or additional processing of the log. Figure 7b shows the directly-follows graph of the log after repair, where the order of activities "Feedlot - EXIT" and "Processing" has been swapped. Our approach was able to repair all inaccurate cases, requiring on average 66.5 ± 3.08^6 sec to repair the log. The resulting graph is less cluttered and

---

[6] Over a set of five executions.

thus more readable. For example, the process cases that inaccurately transitioned from "Feedlot - PURCHASE" to "Processing" have now converged into the edge going from "Feedlot - PURCHASE" to "Feedlot - EXIT". This graph was validated by the business analyst involved in the case study, who confirmed the correct sequencing of activities.

5 Conclusion

We proposed an automated approach for correcting same-timestamp errors in event logs. These errors are quite common in real-life event logs [1–3], and may lead to quality issues in process mining analysis. The approach first detects the correct order of the events having the same timestamp, and then assigns a timestamp to each reordered event relying on a multimodal distribution of the duration of process activities.

We implemented our approach and assessed its effectiveness and efficiency via an experimental evaluation with artificial and real-life logs, and a case study. The experiments show that our approach reduces the amount of incorrect timestamps by at least 50%, both on artificial and real-life logs, while, the case study conducted in the meat & livestock domain provides initial results on the usefulness of our approach in practice. However, more experiments in real-life settings need to be conducted to obtain confirmatory evidence.

A possible avenue for future work is to fix events erroneously recorded with incorrect (different) timestamps by humans. This scenario occurs when the corresponding activities are performed one shortly after the other. For example, this has been observed for activities performed just after midnight in healthcare logs, where the date is incorrectly recorded as that of the previous day, while the time is recorded correctly. This issue of data quality is known as the "inadvertent time travel" pattern [1]. Another human error leading to this pattern is when the user inadvertently presses keys adjacent to the intended ones when entering an event timestamp into a log [1]. An idea would be to adapt our approach by introducing a preliminary step that, using our probabilistic model, identifies such cases and assigns them an equal timestamp. This would allow us to treat them by applying the approach proposed in this paper.

Lastly, another interesting avenue for future work is to extend the current approach to repair event logs with same-timestamp errors in the presence of multiple life-cycle events for each activity. Specifically, if there are only start and complete events for each activity, we can process all the start events and all the complete events separately, fixing the two types of event in two stages. On the other hand, the presence of multiple life-cycle events per activity would warrant a more elaborated approach.

Acknowledgments. This research is partly funded by the Australian Research Council (DP180102839).

References

1. Suriadi, S., Andrews, R., ter Hofstede, A., Wynn, M.: Event log imperfection patterns for process mining: towards a systematic approach to cleaning event logs. Inf. Syst. **64**, 132–150 (2017)
2. Bose, R., Mans, R., van der Aalst, W.: Wanna improve process mining results? In: 2013 IEEE (CIDM), pp. 127–134. IEEE (2013)
3. Mans, R.S., van der Aalst, W.M.P., Vanwersch, R.J.B., Moleman, A.J.: Process mining in healthcare: data challenges when answering frequently posed questions. In: Lenz, R., Miksch, S., Peleg, M., Reichert, M., Riaño, D., ten Teije, A. (eds.) KR4HC/ProHealth -2012. LNCS (LNAI), vol. 7738, pp. 140–153. Springer, Heidelberg (2013). https://doi.org/10.1007/978-3-642-36438-9_10
4. Ghionna, L., Greco, G., Guzzo, A., Pontieri, L.: Outlier detection techniques for process mining applications. In: An, A., Matwin, S., Raś, Z.W., Ślęzak, D. (eds.) ISMIS 2008. LNCS (LNAI), vol. 4994, pp. 150–159. Springer, Heidelberg (2008). https://doi.org/10.1007/978-3-540-68123-6_17
5. Conforti, R., La Rosa, M., ter Hofstede, A.: Filtering out infrequent behavior from business process event logs. IEEE TKDE **29**(2), 300–314 (2016)
6. Rogge-Solti, A., Mans, R.S., van der Aalst, W.M.P., Weske, M.: Improving documentation by repairing event logs. In: Grabis, J., Kirikova, M., Zdravkovic, J., Stirna, J. (eds.) PoEM 2013. LNBIP, vol. 165, pp. 129–144. Springer, Heidelberg (2013). https://doi.org/10.1007/978-3-642-41641-5_10
7. Wang, J., Song, S., Lin, X., Zhu, X., Pei, J.: Cleaning structured event logs: a graph repair approach. In: Proceedings of IEEE ICDE, pp. 30–41. IEEE (2015)
8. Song, S., Cao, Y., Wang, J.: Cleaning timestamps with temporal constraints. VLDB Endow. **9**(10), 708–719 (2016)
9. Sani, M.F., van Zelst, S.J., van der Aalst, W.M.P.: Improving process discovery results by filtering outliers using conditional behavioural probabilities. In: Teniente, E., Weidlich, M. (eds.) BPM 2017. LNBIP, vol. 308, pp. 216–229. Springer, Cham (2018). https://doi.org/10.1007/978-3-319-74030-0_16
10. Sani, M., van Zelst, S., van der Aalst, W.: Repairing outlier behaviour in event logs using contextual behaviour. EMISAJ **14**, 1–24 (2019)
11. van Zelst, S.J., Fani Sani, M., Ostovar, A., Conforti, R., La Rosa, M.: Filtering spurious events from event streams of business processes. In: Krogstie, J., Reijers, H.A. (eds.) CAiSE 2018. LNCS, vol. 10816, pp. 35–52. Springer, Cham (2018). https://doi.org/10.1007/978-3-319-91563-0_3
12. van Zelst, S., Fani Sani, M., Ostovar, A., Conforti, R., La Rosa, M.: Detection and removal of infrequent behaviour from event streams of business processes. Inf. Syst. **90**, 101451 (2019)
13. Aalst, W.: Data science in action. Process Mining, pp. 3–23. Springer, Heidelberg (2016). https://doi.org/10.1007/978-3-662-49851-4_1
14. Dumas, M., La Rosa, M., Mendling, J., Reijers, H.: Fundamentals of Business Process Management, 2nd edn. Springer, Heidelberg (2018)
15. Leemans, S.J.J., Fahland, D., van der Aalst, W.M.P.: Discovering block-structured process models from event logs containing infrequent behaviour. In: Lohmann, N., Song, M., Wohed, P. (eds.) BPM 2013. LNBIP, vol. 171, pp. 66–78. Springer, Cham (2014). https://doi.org/10.1007/978-3-319-06257-0_6
16. Augusto, A., Conforti, R., Dumas, M., La Rosa, M., Polyvyanyy, A.: Split miner: automated discovery of accurate and simple business process models from event logs. Knowl. Inf. Syst. **59**(2), 251–284 (2019)

17. Lewenstein, M., Sviridenko, M.: Approximating asymmetric maximum TSP. In: SODA, Society for Industrial and Applied Mathematics (2003)
18. Miller, C., Tucker, A., Zemlin, R.: Integer programming formulation of traveling salesman problems. J. ACM **7**(4), 326–329 (1960)
19. Silverman, B.: Using kernel density estimates to investigate multimodality. J. R. Stat. Soc. Ser. B (Methodol.) **43**, 97–99 (1981)
20. van Dongen, B.: BPI challenge 2014: activity log for incidents (2014)
21. Levenshtein, V.I.: Binary codes capable of correcting deletions, insertions and reversals. In: Soviet Physics doklady, vol. 10, p. 707 (1966)
22. Adriansyah, A., van Dongen, B., van der Aalst, W.: Conformance checking using cost-based fitness analysis. In: EDOC, pp. 55–64. IEEE (2011)

Management

Explorative Process Design Patterns

Michael Rosemann[(✉)]

Centre for Future Enterprise, Queensland University of Technology, Brisbane, Australia
m.rosemann@qut.edu.au

Abstract. The dominating process lifecycle models are characterized by deductive reasoning; that is, during the process analysis stage, problem-centered approaches such as Lean's seven types of waste are used to identify pain points (e.g., bottlenecks), and defined response patterns are deployed to overcome these. As a result, exploitative business process management (BPM) has reached a high level of maturity. However, explorative BPM, with its focus on adding new value to business processes, lacks an equally mature, deductive set of design patterns. This paper proposes to close this gap by offering seven explorative process design patterns that support the identification of options to create new value from existing business processes. Derived from secondary data analysis, the patterns are presented and comprehensively exemplified. Contributing these seven types of process exploration has the potential to help complement the focus on operationally excellent processes with a view on revenue-resilient business processes.

Keywords: Explorative BPM · Process design · Value generation · Revenue resilience

1 Introduction

Until today, business process improvement, in practice and academia, has largely been built on the hypotheses that (1) a process exists, (2) weaknesses of this process can be identified, and (3) methods are available or need to be developed to overcome these weaknesses. A typical example is Lean Management [1]. At the core of this approach is a set of seven defined types of waste (e.g., re-work, over-engineering), which define the pain points motivating process improvement. In a similar way, Six Sigma addresses process shortcomings grounded in variation, and robotic process automation deals with consistency and performance issues resulting from the deployment of human resources. In addition to such broader methodologies, a number of papers have proposed more fine-granular *process improvement patterns*; that is, heuristics for enhancing particular aspects of business processes (typically time, cost, quality) that may or may not be useful in a specific context [2].

These approaches to process improvement have in common that they are reactive (responding to a pain point), deductive (a model correlates an issue with a response), and reductionist (they lead to a streamlined version of an existing process). Examples are the knockout principle to streamline decision-making processes [2] or the elimination

© Springer Nature Switzerland AG 2020
D. Fahland et al. (Eds.): BPM 2020, LNCS 12168, pp. 349–367, 2020.
https://doi.org/10.1007/978-3-030-58666-9_20

pattern to accelerate a process [3]. It has been argued that such an approach to rationalizing a process is a legacy of Taylorism and Industrial Engineering [4]. As a result, improved processes tend to be more cost-effective, faster, and compliant (e.g., with quality expectations) [2–4]. This improvement paradigm has been labeled *exploitative business process management (BPM)* [5].

However, in the opportunity-rich environment of emerging digital technologies, innovative business models, and new co-engagement models with external stakeholders, exploitative BPM is no longer sufficient. The main reason is that exploitative BPM's focus on operational efficiency does not include a response strategy for disruptive threats to the revenue model of a customer-facing business process. Thus, organizations need to deploy ambidextrous BPM and explore previously untapped revenue opportunities as they relate to their existing business processes. This structured investigation of new sources of process value is called *explorative BPM* [5].

Exploitative and explorative BPM differ in the body of related knowledge and the set of tools, methods, and techniques available. BPM professionals have been very much sensitized to and matured the practice of responding to pain points *("What is broken?")* within a business process. For example, a bottleneck within a process is a well-defined construct, and possible response patterns (e.g., reduce demand, increase capacity) are well documented and understood. The exploration of opportunity points *("What is possible?")*, however, is absent in the practice and academic study of BPM.

This paper is driven by the aim to identify a set of patterns that provides deductive guidance on how to expand a business process in the search for new value propositions. This could materialize as new revenue in a for-profit company or new forms of relevance within the public sector. Therefore, the research question of this paper is, *"What are the explorative process design patterns that help to create new process value?"* The focus on value creation [6] is a clear difference to the aim of identifying non-value-adding activities, which dominates exploitative BPM and techniques such as value-stream mapping. Value capture [6], however, is out of scope as part of this paper.

In order to address this research question, first, the existing body of knowledge on process improvement was comprehensively studied, and patterns relevant in the context of this paper were identified. Then, secondary data in the form of documented cases of growth-minded organizations were studied, and a conceptualization of the identified practices in the form of process design patterns took place. Both approaches together led to seven explorative process design patterns that will be presented here.

There are, of course, a variety of ways for how an organization can create new value by offering entirely new processes. For example, a product company might start to also offer complementary service processes. Such entirely new forms of value are out of scope in this paper due to the very comprehensive space from which such ideas could come from. Furthermore, specific technology-induced process improvements will not be considered due to the plethora of possibilities, the speed of emergence, and the fragility of these. For example, a blockchain-empowered process might facilitate provenance along a supply chain and as a result might allow a surcharge for products.

This paper is structured as follows. Section 2 contextualizes the research by summarizing the body of knowledge on exploitative process improvement before introducing the notions of revenue resilience and explorative BPM. Section 3 is the core of the paper as it presents the research method and the seven explorative process design patterns, which are discussed and compared in Sect. 4. The final section, Sect. 5, summarizes the paper, discusses its limitations, and outlines future research directions.

2   Research Context

2.1   Exploitative Process Improvement

Exploitative process improvement is dedicated to process efficiency and effectiveness within a given value proposition. Related approaches are either comprehensive methodologies (e.g., Lean Management, Six Sigma, Theory of Constraints, Business Process Reengineering) or sets of fine-granular, operational improvement heuristics. The former tend to concentrate on the issue identification and are either light and unstructured (e.g., brainstorming) or very narrow (e.g., how to overcome variation) in terms of suggesting actual improvements. The latter are grounded in the tradition of TRIZ—that is, the theory of the resolution of invention-related tasks—which proposes a set of generalizable solution patterns [7]. Examples for such process improvement patterns are elimination (delete an activity), integration (merge two activities), automation (automate an activity), or optionality (make an activity optional for some stakeholders).

Reijers and Mansar [3] have written influential papers describing process redesign heuristics derived from literature and personal experience, and later [8] assessed these via surveys with experts. These improvement patterns have been evaluated along the exploitative dimensions of time, cost, quality, and flexibility. One of the seven components in their framework captures customer-oriented patterns. However, the related patterns are about a more efficient interaction with the customer (e.g., reduce the number of customer contacts) and less about creating new value for customers.

Hanafizadeh, Moosakhani, and Bakhshi [9] further built on this research and proposed a method to correlate redesign practices with organizational strategy. Kim et al. [10] present 16 process patterns concentrated on changes in the control flow. A consolidating framework for exploitative process improvement patterns has been proposed by Zellner [11, 12]. A comparison of process improvement patterns with patterns from domains such as software development, enterprise application integration, or workflow management is presented by Falk et al. [13]. The focus here has been on process problems; that is, "the issue that needs to be solved by means of the [...] pattern" (e.g., dissolve bottleneck) [13]. The concentration on pain points is also exemplified by proposals to highlight process weaknesses [14]. A comprehensive literature review on business process improvement patterns can be found in Missaoui and Ghannouchi [15].

Lohrmann and Reichert [2] have assessed exploitative process improvement patterns considering real-world constraints, such as the role of senior stakeholders or the cost of adapting available information technology systems. A quantitative, value-based, and mainly exploitative approach for process improvement has been proposed by Bolsinger et al. [16]. This value-based approach has been used, among others, to decide about those instances of a process that help to maximize its value contribution [17].

Process anti-patterns (aka weakness patterns [18, 19]) describe insufficient solutions and are recognized by the appearance of failures [20] (see the seven types of waste as part of the Lean Management approach as a high-level example). Thus, process anti-patterns could trigger the deployment of process improvement patterns [21].

A holistic framework that puts process improvement patterns in the context of other factors, such as aims, actors, or tools, can be found in Vanwersch et al. [22]. A consolidating Process Orbit has been suggested by Dumas et al. [23]. The rapid process improvement approach NESTT is characterized by the co-existence of exploitative and explorative improvement techniques [24].

Alternative views on process improvement can be found in papers that either focus on a specific digital technology (e.g., blockchain, [25]) or specific types of process modifications (e.g., process individualization, [26]).

2.2 Revenue Resilience

Since the days of Scientific Management and Taylorism, the primary process design ambition has been on operational efficiency. This has been supported by exploitative process improvement tools, methods, and techniques that continue to reach new levels of sophistication (see e.g., robotic process automation). However, since the emergence of disruptive innovation [27], organizations are aware that operational efficiency is a necessary but no longer sufficient condition for success. An operationally efficient process can become obsolete when the value proposition of the business process is threatened, and the process itself could ultimately become non-relevant. This becomes tangible when the (process) revenue curve is below the (process) cost curve (Fig. 1).

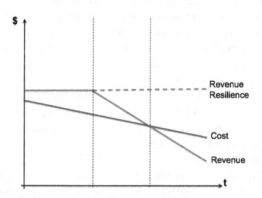

Fig. 1. Revenue resilience

Revenue resilience describes the capability to sufficiently defend and grow the revenue base in light of disruptive forces. Thus, revenue resilience as a design paradigm matters for customer-facing processes that are revenue-sensitive. However, so far, there is only an *implicit* relationship between process goals and revenue in the assumption that a time- and cost-efficient and quality-conform process will attract customers.

The search for new revenue (i.e., monetized value) models for a business process is the focus of explorative BPM. Unlike the reductionist approach of exploitative BPM, explorative BPM is a constructionist approach as it creates new, additional process features in an attempt to open new revenue channels.

A revenue-specific lens on business process is non-existent, and this needs to be the focus of explorative BPM. *Inductive* approaches (e.g., process mining) are not an option as explorative BPM is dedicated to creating new value, and this cannot be inductively derived from historical data, which are largely used as part of process mining. There are a number of approaches proposing *abductive* ways for the design of new processes (e.g., design thinking) [28, 29]. Here, customer behavior is studied and process designs are iteratively built. The shortcomings of abductive exploration, however, are the lack of predictability in the outcomes and the dependence on (non-reliable) customer input [30]. *Deductive* approaches have proven to be of value for exploitative BPM, and it is proposed to develop similar patterns for explorative BPM; that is, heuristics that prompt specific design actions.

The aim of explorative BPM—the search for new value—is comparable to the intentions of a *business model*; that is, a description of how an organization creates, captures, and monetizes value. Common approaches, such as the Business Model Canvas [31], propose nine elements that provide structure to this investigation. A dedicated business process lens, however, is missing in business models. Implicitly, a process perspective can be found in the elements of key activities and channels. In terms of the value to be generated from a business process, the elements of value proposition, cost structure, and revenue streams are most relevant. As such, this paper and its proposed set of explorative process design patterns complement a business model by (1) providing an explicit view on processes as a source of new value, and (2) shifting the dominating focus of exploitative BPM, which concentrates on cost structures, to the study of how business process explorations can lead to new revenue streams.

The business model literature has also proposed *business model patterns*; that is, architectural components that could trigger new business models (e.g., Robin Hood, add-on, two-sided market) [32, 33]. Though most of these business model patterns are not process-specific, some of them can be tailored to business process design. Therefore, the related literature has also inspired the explorative business model patterns to be presented in the next section.

3 Process Exploration via Design Patterns

3.1 Research Method

First, a comprehensive analysis of existing, deductive process improvement patterns was conducted (see Sect. 2.1) to derive an understanding of the level of granularity of those exploitative heuristics that have been successful in academia and practice. This provided important guidance for the subsequent conceptualization. Second, organizations with expanding revenue models were studied. These were either global, growth-minded organizations, such as Amazon and Uber, or Australian cases, such as Qantas or Domino's. Their growth model was then re-interpreted with a view of the underlying process design implications. Prerequisites were that the organization's actions:

– had to have an impact on the revenue resilience of the organization;
– could be conceptualized from a process viewpoint;

- were not grounded in the design of a new process, as the possibilities of entirely new process designs were regarded too difficult to conceptualize and would follow an abductive and not a deductive approach; and
- could be articulated in the form of an explorative design pattern similar in granularity to established process improvement patterns.

As patterns are proven solutions to recurring situations [34], further examples needed to be identified based on secondary data once the pattern was identified to ensure a wider applicability. In the following, we present the seven explorative *process design patterns* derived from this process. Unlike reductionist process improvement patterns (e.g., elimination), the following patterns all extend the process model; that is, lead to a more comprehensive process. Each pattern will be described as follows: (1) the *context* describes comparable, dominating exploitative views and the contextual factors leading to the emergence of this design pattern; (2) a *definition* provides clarity on the nature of the design pattern; (3) the type of *value*[1] (e.g., product revenue, commission model) catalyzed by this pattern will be described; (4) a simple conceptual model of the *pattern* provides a semi-formal visualization in terms of the pattern's schematic impact on an existing process model; (5) the *example* describes the organizations which inspired this pattern and, with this, provides clarity on the pattern's deployment in practice; and (6) finally, a *guideline* provides design support for the application of the pattern, including a description of relevant process characteristics.

The purpose of explorative design patterns is to increase the awareness of a process designer for the existence of growth opportunities leading to a larger process design space. The assessment of the actual (technical, ethical, legal) feasibility, desirability, and viability of the opportunities arising from the deployment of these patterns is context-specific and, therefore, beyond the scope of this paper.

3.2 Process Generalization

Context – The essence of a business process is the interplay of the control flow logic of the process model and the item (e.g., a product, a person) that is processed along the defined process. Exploitative process improvement takes the item for granted and centers on a reductionist approach to streamline the flow of the item.

Definition – Process generalization is the exploration of an existing process capability that can be used for additional items; that is, the provision of new products or services with only minor changes to the process. Therefore, process generalization re-purposes (re-uses) a process and facilitates the generation of new value by providing new products or services cost-effectively to the market.

Value – Process generalization allows new revenue to be generated from new products or services via the re-use of an existing process capability leading to economies of scope (multiple products/services sharing a process) and a higher return on the process.

---

[1] In this paper, revenue is used as a proxy for value monetization.

Pattern – Unlike in data modeling, the generalization of process models is far less studied. The dominating view is on specialization as the decomposition of a process activity into a sub-process. In order to deploy process generalization, the process designer needs to determine the essential process capability and then identify further items that could capitalize on this capability. As a process pattern (Fig. 2), one could think of process generalization as a way to *add new tokens* to an existing process model. While most organizations first create a new service or product and then build the required processes related to procurement, production, and distribution ('process follows product'), process generalization represents a 'product follows process' paradigm.

Fig. 2. Process generalization

Example – The ride-sharing company Uber is a story of process generalization. In 2011, Uber launched a platform model offering ride-sharing services in San Francisco. As is well known, Uber's ride-sharing service is now available in many countries around the world. Uber's process capability comprises the facilitation of crowdsourced mobility as a service. The process consists of (1) booking via an app, (2) pick-up, (3) transportation, (4) arrival, (5) integrated payment, and (6) an optional mutual rating.

Process generalization in the context of Uber prompts the question, *'What other items beyond people could be transported between two points?'* In 2014, UberEats provided the answer: food. Since then, UberEats has delivered millions of pizzas, burritos, and hamburgers, largely re-using the process capability that has been built as part of the ride-sharing solution. The addition of the token food to Uber's process capability required modifications to the process, as the drivers now had to find parking when picking up the food and when delivering it to the customer. Going up into buildings to deliver food added a further, sometimes time-consuming, activity for the driver.

Uber's process generalization has further continued. Since November 2017, Uber has partnered with the Australian airline Qantas, and it is now possible to book an Uber to or from selected Australian airports using the Qantas app. In this case, Uber's process capability is seamlessly embedded within a flight booking process, with the trigger of the booking now coming from a Qantas system as opposed to the Uber app. This example shows how the token 'airline passenger' has been added to Uber's process.

A further process generalization took place in March 2018, when Uber Health was launched in the United States, and the token 'patient' was added to Uber's process. Uber Health allows healthcare professionals to order an Uber ride for patients going to and from the care they need. An Uber Health API (application programming interface) facilitates the integration into healthcare products. The patient does not require the Uber app and can receive notifications via calls or texts.

In October 2019, Uber Pets added the token, 'pet,' to the Uber process. For an additional fee, passengers can take their pet with them on their ride. Finally, in April

2020, Uber Direct added the token 'delivery from grocery stores,' and Uber Connect allowed sending the token 'parcel' via Uber's established process capability.

This sequence of adding tokens shows how a core process capability, initially designed for the transport of people, has been generalized toward pizza, passengers, patients, pets, and parcels. Once this pattern of exploration has been established, it is not only a descriptive but also a potential predictive method. For example, one can easily imagine how Uber might add express medication (pills) to its process capability.

A further example for process generalization is Amazon's extension from being an e-commerce company selling books to scaling up its process capability to purchase, store and distribute a vast diversity of products ranging from toys to tomatoes.

Companies mastering process generalization can create value going beyond revenue generation when they make significant societal contributions due to their ability to re-deploy their processes. For example, the French luxury goods producer LVMH was able to switch from producing Christian Dior perfumes to the production of much-needed hand sanitizers to fight COVID−19 in a mere 72 h. In a similar way, textile factories produced masks quickly, and the German car manufacturer Volkswagen re-deployed 3D printing capabilities for medical equipment.

Guideline – In order to explore process generalization, a process designer needs to identify items that would benefit from the process capability. This requires specifying the essence of the process capability and then identifying items with similar characteristics (e.g., books and toys) and demands (e.g., the need to move people and food).

An organization could consider process generalization if it provides a mainstream process (e.g., e-commerce, mobility) for a subset of the possible items that could benefit from this process. Following this argument, one could envisage that an organization that has the process infrastructure to broker video content might enter the music brokerage market, and vice versa.

3.3 Process Expansion

Context – Scoping a process is one of the most fundamental process design decisions. The more comprehensive the scope, the higher the potential to generate, and charge for, additional value for customers. As such, process expansion is in sharp contrast to established, reductionist value-stream mapping approaches, which focus on identifying those activities that do *not* add value and are then targets for elimination.

Definition – Process expansion is an assessment to test if an existing process could create additional value by adding further activities to the process. Such an expansion needs to be grounded in a competitive advantage (e.g., the availability of data that facilitates the process expansion).

Value – The organization creates new billable value in addition to the value proposition of the existing process.

Pattern – When an organization deploys process expansion, it *adds new activities* to the process. These activities can be visible to the customer or not and could be at the start (see Fig. 3) or at the end of the process.

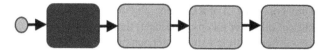

Fig. 3. Process expansion

Example – Food delivery companies such as Deliveroo, DoorDash, UberEats, or Swiggy offer an order-to-delivery process. Their process capability consists of the ability to take a food order, to source the food from a provider, transport and deliver the food to the customer, process the payment, and facilitate a customer rating. While conventional, exploitative process improvement techniques would seek to streamline (e.g., tour optimization) or modernize (e.g., voice-enabled ordering) this process capability, process expansion encourages us to look beyond the existing process boundaries by capitalizing on available data. In the case of food delivery companies, these are the location-sensitive purchase orders of customers. This dataset provides insights into what types of food are popular in what areas and into the average distance between the restaurant and the customer. An analysis of this geo-information points to popular types of food with high delivery times. It is exactly this kind of analysis that has motivated many of these food delivery companies to open dark (or ghost) kitchens; that is, setting up new places where food is produced for the exclusive purpose of food delivery. A similar example of process expansion is Netflix entering the market for the production of content based on customer preferences and so-called micro-genres.

As indicated, process expansion might also occur at the end of a process. In particular, this will be the case if continuous connectivity can be established [35]; that is, via a sensor, the product-providing company stays in touch with the customer (e.g., Tesla continues to sell upgrades to its customers after the purchase of the car).

Guidelines – Process designers interested in process expansion need to assess the datasets which are emerging within the process and evaluate the contents of the triggering event (e.g., purchase orders). These data then need to be studied in terms of competitive insights; that is, does producing rather than sourcing provide a path to new value?

Processes that could trigger a consideration of process expansion are high volume processes with start events that have a high number of attributes. These attributes need to inform a possible process expansion (e.g., point to products or services in demand).

3.4 Process Differentiation

Context – The reductionist lens of process exploitation has made the elimination of process variants and the standardization of processes a core design principle. An explorative view on a process, however, is about the assessment of how a new process differentiation can satisfy the demands of distinct groups of process customers.

Definition – Process differentiation is the creation of one or more additional process variants with the aim of offering a new value proposition for a subset of the existing process customers or attracting entirely new customers to the process. Process differentiation is not the conceptual opposite of process generalization. While process generalization is about identifying entirely new tokens (products) that benefit from the existing process capability, process differentiation focuses on nuancing what is largely the same offering in terms of process qualities such as response time.

Value – An additional process variant creates new value when it provides a new form of convenience for a subset of process customers for which they are (1) willing to pay or (2) appreciate the opportunity to pay less. Process differentiation is grounded in differential pricing for process variants, each with a distinct performance promise. The willingness to pay a surcharge in return for an improved process performance (e.g., faster processing time, personalized service) creates a new process revenue model. It can, however, also create new revenue if a downscaled process variant (i.e., lower process performance for a lower fee) attracts customers who would have otherwise regarded the previous service as unattractive. Thus, process differentiation provides an organization with the opportunity to up-sell or to down-sell.

Pattern – When an organization deploys process differentiation, it introduces a triaging point with new, distinct process variants into a business process (Fig. 4). The new process variant still provides the same product or service (e.g., resolving a call enquiry), but with either improved process features (e.g., talking to an expert) or with reduced process features (e.g., interacting with a chatbot or self-service).

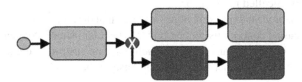

Fig. 4. Process differentiation

Example – A typical example of process specialization is a new money-for-time process variant. In this case, an additional fee is charged to the process customer in return for an accelerated processing time. Such examples can be witnessed in theme parks, airport security checks, or repair processes for electronics. Call centers of some airlines charge a fee for a staff-supported booking as opposed to a self-managed online booking. Payment does not require a process-specific payment but could be a cumulated payment, like in airline loyalty programs, and subsequently leads to a reduced waiting time. An elaboration on these and further examples can be found in Sandel [36].

Guideline – A process designer who explores process differentiation needs to assess if there is a market (i.e., a willingness to pay) for a variant of the existing process that outperforms the existing variant (e.g., in terms of time or quality of service) or if an additional process variant that is a downgraded version would attract new customers.

This process design pattern needs to be carefully studied in light of its ethical value. For example, retailers, unlike airlines, are reluctant to deploy this pattern in their super-markets; that is, high-spending customers do not get a fast check-out, as retail shopping is seen as an egalitarian space. Process differentiation requires a time-sensitive process to make waiting time (or the lack of it) a purchasable item. Thus, these tend to be processes with a high process volume and a rather simple value proposition.

3.5   Process Initiation

Context – A dominating focus of exploitative process improvement is the acceleration of a business process; that is, minimizing the time between the start and the final event. This metric is commonly known as the time-to-customer or processing time. The digital economy, with its richness of sensors and data, however, provides an opportunity to explore if a process could be initiated earlier by identifying new triggering events.

Definition – Process initiation is the exploration of how new data sources can be used to reduce process latency; that is, the time between the occurrence of a demand and the initiation of the related process. This metric is also called time-to-process.

Value – Process initiation leads to new value if a reduced process latency constitutes a source of competitive advantage; that is, organizations that respond faster to an event than others will secure a higher share of the market.

Pattern – Process initiation is about the exploration of the ideal starting event for the process with an ambition to create or access this event as soon as possible (Fig. 5).

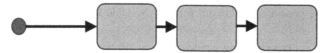

Fig. 5. Process initiation

Example – Examples for how to reduce time-to-process can be found in the domain of the Internet of Things. For example, a manufacturer using sensors to monitor the status of a machine will be able to trigger a predictive maintenance process faster and, in turn, create new value for its customers (who no longer have to monitor the machine). In a similar way, a retailer providing the opportunity to order its products via voice-enabled assistants will have a competitive advantage over those that require a customer to enter such orders on an e-commerce site. Amazon Dash Replenishment, the successor of the simple dash button, is an example of a sensor that leads to the generation of events trigging a re-fill process (e.g., for printer cartridge). These are all examples of where the process-owning organization has invested in the creation of new data (e.g., via a sensor). Advanced analytics can be used to create leading as opposed to lagging signals and early fulfillment (e.g., Amazon's predictive shopping process).

Guidelines – In order to explore process initiation, a process designer needs to identify those signals that could act as (earlier) triggering events for a business process. This requires two alternative assessments of the process: (1) Can new (technical or social) sensors be created? (2) Could the ability to conveniently create a new event be embedded in existing channels (e.g., by developing an Alexa skill)?

3.6 Process Commercialization

Context – Exploitative business process improvement is very much characterized by making the business process the unit of analysis and then working with the variables as defined within this unit of analysis. This leads to a careful analysis of the various process elements (e.g., control flow, data, resources) and how these could be arranged in more efficient and effective ways. Explorative process improvement, however, goes beyond the business process and explores further environmental opportunities in its search for process-enabled, new revenue models. The next three design patterns have such a lens and explore new value opportunities as they relate to third parties.

Definition – Process commercialization is an assessment of whether there is a market external to the organization that would be interested in deploying the entire process, or relevant parts of it, as a service.

Value – Selling a process capability to a third party creates an entirely new revenue channel and leads to new markets, new customers, and pricing and process provision models in addition to the existing value proposition of the process for its current customer base.

Pattern – The entire process or, more typically, a subset of the process is provided as a service to a third party (Fig. 6). In a much broader definition of this design pattern, one might also consider making (idle) resources (e.g., machines or staff) of the process or data as they are generated within this process available to third parties or platforms.

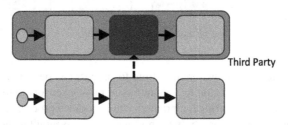

Fig. 6. Process commercialization

Example – Airlines have, over the years, matured the process capability to calculate prices dynamically; that is, based on a number of relevant context factors, such as calendar time, time of the day, weather, events, etc., the ticket price is re-adjusted frequently. The capability of the dynamic pricing process is a feature unique to this industry and has only recently been adopted, for example, in the domain of e-commerce. However, there are a number of industries that would benefit from having access to a process capability helping them to calculate the price of a product or service dynamically (e.g., cinemas). Other examples of process commercialization can be found in the domain of open banking. Here, a bank makes specific capabilities (e.g., budget calculation, savings management) available as a plug-in solution to third-party customers. Amazon Web Services was at least at the start of commercializing a 'storage-as-a-service' process.

Guideline – A process designer exploring process commercialization needs (1) to conduct an environmental scan in order to assess the market demand for the capabilities of the process and (2) assess the feasibility to make this capability available as a process-as-a-service offering. Relevant processes will need to have an isolatable capability.

3.7 Process Integration

Context – Common BPM approaches focus on the activities of a process and assess these in terms of their value, degree of automation, variation, weaknesses, and so on. Events—the other constitutional element of a business process—have attracted far less attention and are often only seen in their immediate role within the process. While the design pattern process initiation has a temporal focus (process latency) and is dedicated to exploring earlier access to the starting event, process integration is about exploring the value of events for third parties and integrating their process-centered value proposition within a larger ecosystem of business processes.

Definition – Within process integration, an event is assessed beyond its value for the process, and it is evaluated if the event could meaningfully trigger complementary third-party processes (trigger-as-a-service).

Value – Process integration creates a new revenue channel if third parties are willing to pay a commission for accessing and benefiting from the event. The process-owning organization acts in this case as an event broker.

Pattern – As part of the deployment of the process integration pattern, an event will fire more than the existing process and also trigger additional third-party processes (Fig. 7). These could be events in all stages of a process, from start to end events.

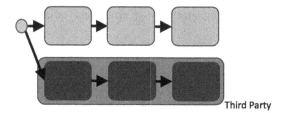

Fig. 7. Process integration

Example – A customer booking a flight creates a digital signal that he/she will not be at home. As there is a high probability that a pet might require attention during the absence of the traveler—the Australian airline Qantas, for example, estimates that two-thirds of its customer base are pet owners—the related event has potential high economic value for relevant service provides. Thus, Qantas has started a partnership with a company called

Mad Paws that provides insured pet sitting as a service. As part of the flight booking process, the related event ('customer expressed an interest in pet sitting') is brokered to Mad Paws, and Qantas monetizes this event brokerage accordingly. In a similar way, Qantas embeds Uber services in its process (see Sect. 3.2).

Guideline – Similar to process commercialization, process integration requires a strong environmental sensing capability, as complementary third parties need to be identified who might be interested in, and benefit from, access to events within the control of the business process. This will be of particular relevance when the process provider only satisfies a subset of the customer's needs.

3.8 Process Attention

Context – The uptake of process monitoring and tracking in the form of smart things and geo-information systems has placed increased emphasis on process observation. Customers can now follow the item they have ordered (e.g., food, a parcel) via convenient interfaces. Such process observations lead to an increased (digital) attention that is devoted to processes and can be the source of new value for the organization.

Definition – Process attention is the exploration of whether the time a user spends observing a process could be utilized to generate new value.

Value – Value via process attention is generated if the attention of the process user can be channeled in a two-sided business model toward promotional intentions of third parties. If so, an organization acts as a broker of attention time.

Pattern – Process attention adds an additional layer to an existing and otherwise unchanged business process. This layer is the sphere of the process that is observed by the process customer, and the time invested in this observation might be the source of commercial value as it is valuable for a third party (Fig. 8). Process attention might be in addition to the process (complementary advertisement) or embedded in the process.

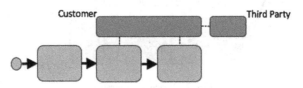

Fig. 8. Process attention

Example – The pizza chain Domino's developed a so-called pizza tracker that allows customers to track each stage of their order in real time, covering the main stages of pizza making, baking, and delivery. The Domino's GPS driver tracker even allows customers to geo-track the progress within the delivery. According to Domino's, an analysis of customer behavior has shown that customers are spending up to 8 min observing the progress of their order through the various stages. This 'share of digital attention' has now the potential to stream additional advertisements. An example of an advertisement that is embedded in the process is the New York-based start-up FreeATM that provides free-of-charge ATM services with integrated, context-sensitive (e.g., time of the day, socioeconomic status) 10-s videos before cash is provided to the customer.

Guideline – Applying process attention to one's business processes will require either a public process monitoring capability that is widely used (e.g., tracking of deliveries) or the ability to integrate advertisements within the process, without that the customer opts out or switches immediately to another provider. Like process differentiation, process attention demands a careful assessment of its ethical concerns.

4   Discussion

Identifying revenue opportunities related to existing business processes is a task of increasing relevance, but which, so far, has been out of scope for the BPM community. The seven explorative process design patterns presented here are a first attempt to provide a simple set of deductive prompts so that a revenue-sensitive lens on the management of business processes becomes more reliable.

The seven patterns have been presented in isolation, but, of course, can be deployed in combination as they complement each other in various ways; that is, they are a system of patterns. For example, process differentiation and process attention go hand-in-hand if an organization offers a process in which one variant includes an advertisement and the other a payment for not being exposed to the advertisement. This is common in music-streaming processes, for example. In a similar way, the same third party might be interested in accessing an event of the business process (process integration) and promote its services (process attention). Uber providing embedded services for Qantas is a combination of process generalization (people > passenger) and process integration.

Table 1 provides a consolidating overview of the seven explorative process design patterns. Unlike (reductionist) exploitation, process exploration is additive, and the specific additions to the existing business process are listed below. The first four patterns create new value within the organization, while the last three create a new revenue model involving a third party. Finally, the type of new revenue generated varies greatly across these seven patterns. Process generalization is the most straight forward as it adds new products to the business process. Process expansion and differentiation facilitate the opportunity to charge for new activities, either as an additional element for the entire process or in the form of a differentiated process variant. Process initiation creates a more indirect revenue impact in cases where process latency (time-to-process) is a competitive advantage.

The last three patterns create new market models (the last two are two-sided market models) as they facilitate revenue streams in addition to the existing business process. This could come in the form of a licensing model (charging for the use of a capability as part of process commercialization) or as a commission model when charging occurs for access to a process event (process integration) or customers' time (process

Table 1. Comparison of the seven design patterns.

Pattern	Addition	Third party?	Revenue model
Process generalization	New product	No	New product offering
Process expansion	New activity	No	New margin grounded in new value-adding activity
Process differentiation	New variant	No	New margin grounded in the tailored provision of alternative process performances
Process initiation	New (start) event	No	New customers because of earlier process provision
Process commercialization	New customer for activity	Yes	License for use (e.g., per-per-use)
Process integration	New customer for the event	Yes	Commission model (e.g., pay-per-event or conversion)
Process attention	New customer for attention	Yes	Commission model (e.g., pay-per-click or time)

attention). In these three patterns, third party involvement is needed, while it may be part of the design in some of the other patterns (e.g., process generalization: UberEats involves restaurants). The involvement of third parties also shows that an idea that started with deploying an explorative business design pattern can quickly become a more comprehensive undertaking, relying on further factors far beyond business processes—for example, establishing a mutually beneficial partnership model. This demonstrates how tightly coupled some of the proposed patterns are with the domain of business model innovation and business model patterns.

5   Conclusions, Limitations, and Future Work

Explorative BPM is dedicated to creating new value from existing business processes. Thus, it goes beyond the established, reactive time–cost–quality-bound approach of exploitative BPM. However, while the latter is nowadays a mature discipline, the body of knowledge, including the tools, methods, and techniques for explorative BPM, is still in its infancy. This is concerning, as disruptive innovation tends to threaten an organization's revenue model and its business processes as opposed to its model of operational excellence. As a result, exploitative BPM can be seen as a necessary—and explorative BPM as the sufficient—condition for revenue-sensitive processes.

This paper contributes to the understanding of explorative BPM by proposing seven design patterns that help as heuristics in identifying new sources of revenue models for existing business processes—process generalization, process expansion, process differentiation, process initiation, process commercialization, process integration, and process attention. However, unlike exploitative process improvement patterns (e.g., elimination), which tend to lead to predictable outcomes as most variables are under the organization's control (e.g., bottleneck disappeared), explorative design patterns are far less predictable in their results. Rather, endogenous variables are important too for their success (e.g., customers or third parties need to desire and adopt a new process value on offer). This also explains why explorative process improvement patterns are close to business models and broader than exploitative process improvement patterns.

This paper is largely conceptual in nature and, as a result, comes with a set of limitations. First, the paper is not grounded in a comprehensive secondary or primary data set, and it can be assumed that this absence of empirical insights has led to compromises in terms of the detailed understanding of each of the seven patterns or the completeness of this list of patterns. Second, at this stage, there is only a schematic and not a formal articulation of each pattern provided. Third, a structured analysis of revenue models as they are discussed within the business model literature [31, 32] has not been conducted. Fourth, the guidelines are limited; that is, we must ask under what circumstances is a pattern applicable, what capabilities are required, and what are its implications?

As one of the first contributions toward explorative process design patterns, this paper has the potential to trigger a number of future investigations. One obvious pathway would be the detailed study of the contextual factors that constitute the relevance and ultimate success of these patterns. For example, what are the process characteristics and contextual factors (e.g., customer and markets) that lead to the successful deployment of a proposed design pattern (i.e., the generation of new value)? Future research could also study comparative benefits between the design patterns, such as articulate these as a design selection problem and help prioritization among them. Finally, case-based research could lead to a deeper understanding of the deployment of these patterns and related assessments, including their feasibility, viability, and desirability.

References

1. Womack, J.P., Jones, D.T.: The machine that changed the world. Productivity Press (2007)
2. Lohrmann, M., Reichert, M.: Effective application of process improvement patterns to business processes. Softw. Syst. Model. 15(2), 353–375 (2014). https://doi.org/10.1007/s10270-014-0443-z
3. Reijers, H.A., Mansar, S.L.: Best practices in business process redesign: an overview and qualitative evaluation of successful redesign heuristics. Omega 33(4), 283–306 (2005)
4. Davenport, T.J., Short, J.E.: The new industrial engineering: information technology and business process redesign. Sloan Manag. Rev. 4, 11–27 (1990)
5. Rosemann, M.: Proposals for future BPM research directions. In: Ouyang, C., Jung, J.-Y. (eds.) AP-BPM 2014. LNBIP, vol. 181, pp. 1–15. Springer, Cham (2014). https://doi.org/10.1007/978-3-319-08222-6_1
6. Bowman, C., Ambrosini, V.: Value creation versus value capture: towards a coherent definition of value in strategy. Br. J. Manag. 11(1), 1–15 (2000)
7. Hua, Z., Yang, J., Coulibaly, S., Zhang, B.: Integrating TRIZ with problem-solving tools: a literature review from 1995 to 2006. Int. J. Bus. Innov. Res. 1(1–2), 111–128 (2006)
8. Reijers, H.A., Mansar, S.L.: Best practices in business process redesign: use and impact. Bus. Process Manag. J. 13(2), 193–213 (2007)

9. Hanafizadeh, P., Moosakhani, M., Bakhshi, J.: Selecting the best strategic practices for business process redesign. Bus. Process Manag. J. **15**(4), 609–627 (2009)
10. Kim, D., Kim, M., Kim, H.: Dynamic business process management based on process change patterns. In: Proceedings of International Conference on Computer and Network Technology (ICCNT), pp. 1154–1161, Gyeongju (2007)
11. Zellner, G.: A structured evaluation of business process improvement approaches. Bus. Process Manag. J. **17**(2), 203–237 (2011)
12. Zellner, G.: Towards a framework for identifying business process redesign patterns. Bus. Process Manag. J. **19**(4), 600–623 (2013)
13. Falk, T., Griesberger, P., Johannsen, F., Leist, S.: Patterns for business process improvement – a first approach. In: Proceedings of the 21st European Conference on Information Systems (ECIS), Utrecht, The Netherlands, 5–8 June 2013
14. zur Mühlen, M., Ho, D.T.: Service process innovation: a case study of BPMN in practice. In: Proceedings of the 41st Hawaii International Conference on System Sciences (HICSS), Walkolao, 7–10 January 2008
15. Missaoui, N., Ayachi Ghannouchi, S.: Pattern-based approaches for business process improvement: a literature review. In: Park, J.H., Shen, H., Sung, Y., Tian, H. (eds.) PDCAT 2018. CCIS, vol. 931, pp. 390–400. Springer, Singapore (2019). https://doi.org/10.1007/978-981-13-5907-1_42
16. Bolsinger, M., Bewernik, M.A., Buhl, H.U.: Value-based process improvement. In: Proceedings of the 19th European Conference on Information Systems (ECIS), Helsinki, Finland, 9–11 June 2011
17. Bolsinger, M., Elsässer, A., Helm, C., Röglinger, M.: Process improvement through economically driven routing of instances. Bus. Process Manag. J. **21**(2), 353–378 (2015)
18. Becker, J., Bergener, P., Breuker, D., Räckers, M.: An empirical assessment of the usefulness of weakness patterns in the business process redesign. In: Proceedings of the 20th European Conference on Information Systems (ECIS), Barcelona, 11–13 June 2012
19. Bergener, F., Delfmann, P., Weiss, B., Winkelmann, A.: Detecting potential weaknesses in business processes: an exploration of semantic pattern matching in process models. Bus. Process Manag. J. **21**(1), 25–54 (2015)
20. Koschmider, A., Laue, R., Fellmann, M.: Business process model anti-patterns: a bibliography and taxonomy of published work. In: Proceedings of the 27th European Conference on Information Systems (ECIS), Stockholm & Uppsala, Sweden, 8–14 June 2019
21. Höhenberger, S., Delfmann, P.: Supporting business process improvement through business process weakness pattern collections. In: Proceedings of the 12th Wirtschaftsinformatik Conference, pp. 378–392, Osnabrück, 4–6 March 2015
22. Vanwersch, R.J.B., et al.: A critical evaluation and framework of business process improvement methods. Bus. Inform. Syst. Eng. **58**(1), 43–53 (2016)
23. Dumas, M., La Rosa, M., Mendling, J., Reijers, H.: Fundamentals of Business Process Management. Springer, Berlin (2018). https://doi.org/10.1007/978-3-642-28409-0
24. Rosemann, M.: The NESTT. In: Mendling, J., vom Brocke, J. (eds.) Business Process Management Cases, pp. 169–185. Springer, Switzerland (2018). https://doi.org/10.1007/978-3-319-58307-5_10
25. Mendling, J., et al.: Blockchains for business process management – challenges and opportunities. ACM Trans. Manag. Inf. Syst. **9**(1), 1–16 (2018)
26. Wurm, B., Goel, K., Bandara, W., Rosemann, M.: Design patterns for business process individualization. In: Hildebrandt, T., van Dongen, Boudewijn F., Röglinger, M., Mendling, J. (eds.) BPM 2019. LNCS, vol. 11675, pp. 370–385. Springer, Cham (2019). https://doi.org/10.1007/978-3-030-26619-6_24
27. Christensen, C.M., Raynor, M.E., McDonald, R.: What is disruptive innovation. Harvard Bus. Rev. **95**(6), 44–53 (2015)

28. Brown, T.: Design thinking. Harvard Bus. Rev. **88**(6), 84–92 (2008)
29. Lübbe, A., Weske, M.: Bringing design thinking to business process modelling. In: Plattner, H., et al. (eds.) design Thinking, pp. 181–195. Springer, Berlin (2011). https://doi.org/10. 1007/978-3-642-13757-0_11
30. Flach, P.A., Kakas, A.C.: Abductive and inductive reasoning: background and issues. In: Flach, P.A., Kakas, A.C. (eds.) Abduction and Induction. Essays on their Relation and Integration, pp. 1–27. Springer, Dordrecht (2000). https://doi.org/10.1007/978-94-017-060 6-3_1
31. Osterwalde, A., Pigeur, Y.: Business Model Generation. Wiley, New York (2010)
32. Amshoff, B., Dülme, C., Echterfeld, J., Gausemeier, J.: Business model patterns for disruptive technologies. Int. J. Innov. Manag. **19**(3), 1–22 (2015)
33. Gassmann, O., Frankenberger, K., Csik, M.: The Business Model Navigator: 55 Models That Will Revolutionise Your Business. Pearson, Harlow (2014)
34. Alexander, C., Ishikawa, S., Silverstein, M.: A Pattern Language. Oxford University Press, England (1977)
35. Siggelkow, N., Terwiesch, C.: The age of continuous connection. Harvard Bus. Rev. **99**(3), 64–73 (2019)
36. Sandel, M.J.: What Money Can't Buy. The Moral Limits of Markets. Farrar, Straus and Giroux, New York (2012)

Quo Vadis, Business Process Maturity Model? Learning from the Past to Envision the Future

Vanessa Felch[✉] and Björn Asdecker

University of Bamberg, Feldkirchenstr. 21, 96050 Bamberg, Germany
{vanessa.felch,bjoern.asdecker}@uni-bamberg.de

Abstract. To support companies in systematically improving their business processes, academia has developed and published various business process maturity models in recent decades. Tarhan et al. (2016) expressed initial doubts about the quality of many of the models in their literature review. This paper extends their review by five years (2015–2019) and additionally analyzes the publication outlets as an indicator of model quality. The results strongly provide that business process maturity models are mainly released in less-recognized journals. A reason for this might be problems with replicability and relevance, which are the main criteria for acceptance in higher-quality journals. This finding motivated the derivation of literature-based criteria to increase the transparency, the replicability, and the content relevance of these models. These criteria are a first step to support researchers in publishing more transparent and replicable business process maturity models and to guide reviewers when evaluating papers that are considered for publication. In addition, practitioners benefit from more useful and accessible models.

Keywords: Business process · Business process management · Maturity model · Systematic literature review · Publication outlets · Transparency · Replicability

1 Introduction

To be able to compete in today's environment with permanent competitive pressure, more complex value chains, and economic uncertainty, a continuous improvement of the underlying business processes is necessary. Business process maturity models (BPMMs) are regarded as an essential instrument [26] when determining the organization's status, deriving improvement measures, and conducting cross-company comparisons [15]. Thus, these models offer a structured approach to initiate and support short-term operational projects as well as facilitate long-term strategic changes [15]. As a response to practical interest, a steady increase in publications can be observed over recent decades [46, 48]. Pöppelbuß and Röglinger were the first to reflect critically on this and therefore questioned "[…] whether high quantity goes along with high quality" [46, p. 1]. Tarhan et al. [56] conducted a systematic review of the literature published between 1990 and

Electronic supplementary material The online version of this chapter (https://doi.org/10.1007/978-3-030-58666-9_21) contains supplementary material, which is available to authorized users.

D. Fahland et al. (Eds.): BPM 2020, LNCS 12168, pp. 368–383, 2020.
https://doi.org/10.1007/978-3-030-58666-9_21

2014. In line with Pöppelbuß and Röglinger [46] observation, one of their findings was initial doubt about the quality and usefulness of some reviewed BPMMs. Since then, five years have passed. Therefore, this paper complements the previous review with a detailed search for and analysis of recent BPMM developments. Accordingly, the first research question is:

(1) Considering the most recent BPMM publications, how has the state of research regarding BPMMs changed in the last five years?
The results indicate only minor changes in the research area. To further investigate whether a critical perspective on the quality of some BPMMs may be justified, we additionally address the following research question:
(2) How well recognized are the publication outlets of BPMM articles?
The findings indicate that the papers are mainly published in less-recognized journals. This can be attributed to a low reproducibility of the design/concept and method as well as little relevance to theory and practice, which are fundamental requirements for publication in highly ranked journals [7]. To improve on these issues, we posit a third research question:
(3) Which criteria should authors consider when publishing BPMMs?
The study at hand contributes to existing knowledge (1) by guiding researchers in implementing greater transparency and thus creating a solid and substantiated BPMM and (2) by providing reviewers with a detailed checklist to rely on when evaluating submitted models in the future, which will also lead to more applicable models in practice.

The remainder of the article is structured as follows: The next chapter describes the approach and the results of the extended literature review. In addition, the publication outlets of all journal publications are analyzed. Subsequently, criteria for publishing transparent and replicable BPMMs are first derived and then applied to five recently released models. This research concludes with a summary of the key results, theoretical and managerial implications, and the description of further research opportunities.

2 The Status Quo in BPMM Research

In the past, several literature reviews of BPMMs have been conducted, e.g., [58, 61]. The most comprehensive review was published by Tarhan et al. [56]; their review focuses on challenges in the field of BPMM and tries to stimulate further research. The review is conducted in a general "all-inclusive manner" with no specific focus on a certain domain or aspect of business process management (BPM). They examined studies that were published between 1990 and 2014 in academic journals, conference proceedings, and books. Overall, 61 studies out of 2,899 references were selected for further analysis. In line with Wendler [61], they state that the majority of publications involved the development of a BPMM, the application of a model, or a comparison between models. A key finding is the lack of empirical research on model development. In addition, Tarhan et al. [56] call for more prescriptive rather than descriptive models to provide more guidance for organizations to progress to the next maturity level. They stress that a major prerequisite for a model to fulfill its prescriptive purpose is comprehensive documentation. Most notably, the authors report that only a few studies examine the relationship between BPMMs and improved business performance. Therefore, they conclude: "[...] 4 out of 9 leading maturity models have not been subjected to an empirical validation reported in the existing literature at all [...]. These numbers indicate that there is very limited empirical evidence on [...] the usefulness of the maturity models." [56, p. 128].

2.1 Review of Recently Published BPMM Research

Because Tarhan et al. [56] review process ended in 2014, this paper extends the previous search with a detailed analysis of the latest BPMM developments (2015–2019). The original search (OS) adopted search terms and databases from Tarhan et al. [56] and is complemented by a forward (FS) and backward search (BS). Initially, 5,221 references (OS: 2,744; FS: 489; BS: 1,988) were retrieved, with 69 of those (OS: 49; FS: 16; BS: 4) considered relevant for further analysis. Combined with the 61 articles that have been identified by Tarhan et al. [56], these findings indicate that in almost 30 years, 130 articles have been published in the field of BPMM. Moreover, the publication rate has increased considerably in recent years (see Fig. 1), and the publication type has changed. While the majority of studies used to be published in conference proceedings (journals: 25; conferences: 29; books: 7), in the last five years, articles are more frequently published in journals (journals: 39; conferences: 30; books: 0).

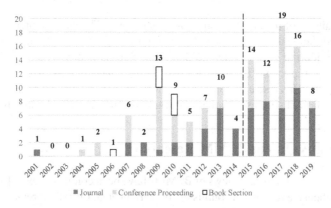

Fig. 1. Distribution of articles by year.

A more detailed analysis shows that McCormack and Johnson's maturity model (BPO-MM) [37] (27 studies), Rosemann and de Bruin's model (BPM-CF) [49] (24), and OMG's BPMM (BPMM-OMG) [45] (23) are the ones most frequently referred to in the literature. These three models, along with the Capability Maturity Model Integration (CMMI) [54], reveal the strongest increase in publications between 2015 and 2019. Moreover, the BPO-MM, BPM-CF, and BPMM-OMG are the most commonly used models to examine the relationship between BPMMs and improved business performance (1990–2014: 7; 2015–2019: 7). Nevertheless, the total number of those articles remains low. Tarhan et al. [56] reported a set of nine 'leading' maturity models based on the recognition that the models received in academia. Based on the findings of this complementary review, we suggest adding another three to the list of 'leading' models – the CMMI, the Process Performance Index (PPI) [50], and the Business Process Maturity (BPM-MC) [35]. To analyze the most recent research streams, all articles were classified in terms of content and focus in accordance with the procedure used by Tarhan et al. [56] (see Appendix A). The subcategories 'description' (20), 'empirical study on application/validation' (24/22), and 'theoretical analysis' (21) show the strongest increase (see Fig. 2).

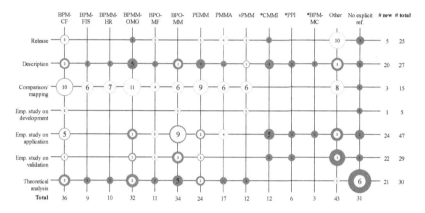

Fig. 2. Number of articles per BPMM by research content (Note: An article may have multiple research contents and may address multiple BPMMs).

The number of studies presenting a developed model ('release') clearly decreased (5). The call for more empirical research on the development of maturity models has not yet been accounted for. The subcategory 'meta-analysis' replaces 'development' as the one with the most published studies (see Fig. 3). The other three subcategories, in particular 'meta-analysis' (23), have experienced strong growth.

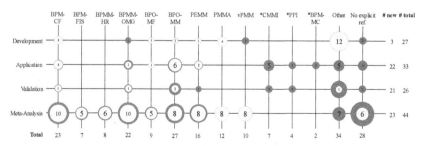

Fig. 3. Numeric distribution of articles per BPMM by main research focus (Note: An article may address multiple BPMMs).

Returning to Tarhan et al. [56] hypotheses, it can be stated that hardly anything has changed in the area of BPMMs (see Table 1). H2 and H3 remain valid, whereas minor progress has been made concerning H1 and H4. It appears that most of Tarhan et al. [56] recommendations, e.g., refining the prescriptive features of existing BPMMs, have been neglected to date, which leads us to the conclusion that the initial doubts about the quality of BPMMs remain valid. To substantiate this hypothesis, we extend the literature analysis by examining the publication outlets of the individual articles in the following paragraph. Highly ranked journals are known to pay particular attention to scientific standards, so it should be difficult to publish articles with qualitative weaknesses in such outlets. Thus, if the assumption of lower quality is substantiated, this should be reflected in the publication outlets.

Table 1. Summary of the findings regarding the hypotheses proposed by Tarhan et al. [56].

Hypothesis by Tarhan et al. [56]	Results (2016) (p. 129)	Results (2020)
H1: The BPM academic community has put more effort and emphasis on developing maturity models than empirically evaluating them.	Around one-third of the studies introduce a BPMM (20 models in 61 studies). Only 2 out of 9 leading models are referred to by studies that involve empirical works on their development, application, and validation.	Around 7 % of the studies introduce a BPMM (5 models in 69 studies). None of the three leading models have been used in empirical works on the development, application, and validation of BPMMs.
H2: There is a lack of studies validating that an increased process maturity level of an organization with respect to a BPMM leads to an improved business performance.	Only 7 out of 61 studies confirm that an increased process maturity level leads to an improved business performance.	Only 7 out of 69 studies confirm that an increased process maturity level leads to an improved business performance.
H3: Most BPMMs display descriptive rather than prescriptive characteristics.	The majority of the proposed models possess descriptive properties and show limited prescriptive features.	The three leading models possess mainly descriptive properties and have limited prescriptive features.
H4: The distinction between a maturity model and an assessment model is not well defined in the BPMM research.	Only 2 out of 9 leading models make a distinction between the maturity model and the assessment model.	2 out of 3 leading models make a distinction between the maturity model and the assessment model.

2.2 Publication Outlets of BPMM Research

From a BPMM author's perspective, the journal's level of recognition plays a decisive role, as it impacts the highest possible model application and dissemination rate. Consequently, authors will try to publish their models in the most highly recognized journals.

Over the years, there has been a growing interest in creating systematic and objective evaluation methods to determine the quality of a journal. Several researchers, including Garfield [19] and Hirsch [24], have proposed so-called impact factors. In general, the higher the impact factor is, the higher the ranking of the journal and thus the reputation of the published paper. Accordingly, we analyze the publication outlets of the 64 articles that have been published in academic journals (1990–2019). This accounts for 49% of all 130 reviewed publications. To determine the value of the publications, three impact factors are used: (1) the index by Thomson Reuters (Reuters Index) [60], (2) the H Index by Hirsch [24], and (3) the SCImago Journal Rank (SJR) indicator [51]. The impact factors are based on data from SJR – SCImago Journal & Country Rank (www.scimagojr.com, as of January 2020). Unlisted journals, such as "Computer and Information Science", are rated with an impact factor of 0. Beyond that, the mean values of each impact factor are calculated (see Table 2). Considering all publications (1990–2019), the average Reuters Index is 2.4, the average H Index is 43.6, and the average SJR index is 0.5. Furthermore, the analysis is extended to several subcategories that are related to model development and application in general. When comparing the means, the values from the 2015–2019 publications are mostly below those of the 1990–2014 publications. Herein, the subcategories 'release', 'empirical study on application', and 'application' show the greatest differences between the periods.

To assess the influence and relevance of the journals, the mean values (1990–2019) are compared with the average impact factor of selected overarching subject categories of the journals. For that purpose, the top 50 journals were identified using the SJR website to calculate their average impact factor (see Table 3). It is striking that for the period from 1990–2019, the highest values of the considered article categories (see Table 2; Reuters Index: 3.2 for 'release' publications, H Index: 47.7 for 'development' publications, SJR: 0.6 for multiple categories) only reach the lowest mean values of the selected subject categories (see Table 3; Reuters Index: 2.8, H Index: 47.4, SJR: 1.0 in each case for 'Management Information Systems') and are well below their average values (Ø subject categories, as shown in Table 3). To better understand the significance of the individual values, Table 3 also lists the lowest and highest values of each index across all subject categories and across the selected overarching subject categories. Although it must be acknowledged that impact factors change over time, the comparison provides a strong indication that articles about BPMMs are published in less-recognized journals, which are of minor relevance in the scientific community. This finding is supported by van Looy, who notes that "[…] the many existing BPMMs are assumed to differ in quality" [57, p. 18]. Reasons for this might be an insufficient theoretical foundation and methodology as well as unsatisfactory model documentation; these reasons can lead to a lack of replicability, which seems to be a general problem with maturity models [2, 5, 13, 38]. Since the replicability of a design/concept and the methodology are key criteria that are regularly used in peer-review processes and by editors when evaluating submissions [7], these results are hardly surprising. To improve on this issue, researchers need to pay particular attention to transparency, which serves as a strong indicator of the ability to replicate research results [1, 10]. Furthermore, to increase the chances of publication, research has to be considered relevant to theory and practice. Research is considered relevant if it is significant or useful [9]. To ensure this for BPMMs, authors

Table 2. Impact factors of BPMM research.

Article classification	Period	# Articles	Reuters Index	H Index	SJR
Release	1990–2014	6	3.9	59.8	0.4
	2015–2019	4	2.1	27.5	0.5
	1990–2019	10	3.2	46.9	0.5
Description	1990–2014	4	1.2	33.3	0.3
	2015–2019	11	2.5	43.3	0.8
	1990–2019	15	2.2	40.6	0.6
Empirical study on application	1990–2014	10	3.8	60.3	0.9
	2015–2019	11	1.3	20.6	0.3
	1990–2019	21	2.5	39.5	0.6
Development	1990–2014	9	2.9	51.3	0.4
	2015–2019	3	2.8	36.7	0.7
	1990–2019	12	2.9	47.7	0.4
Application	1990–2014	6	5.2	83.0	1.2
	2015–2019	10	1.4	20.8	0.3
	1990–2019	16	2.8	44.1	0.6
Total	1990–2014	25	3.4	61.8	0.7
	2015–2019	39	1.8	31.9	0.4
	1990–2019	64	2.4	43.6	0.5

Note: The mean values include the impact factors of publications from FS and BS. Since Tarhan et al. did not perform any FS or BS, we also analyzed the mean values without articles found in the FS and BS, which revealed only minor differences and did not affect the conclusions

should refer to empirically studied cause-effect relationships when defining the model content, especially with respect to the BPM application fields. This addresses our third research question. In an endeavor to provide better guidance for authors, reviewers, and editors, we again review existing literature to identify transparency and content criteria and thus seek to increase not only the quantity but also the quality of publications in the years ahead.

3   Transparency and Content Criteria for BPMM Development

To date, only a few publications have contributed to the development and communication of maturity models in general: on the one hand, procedure models, such as those by Becker et al. [5] or de Bruin et al. [12], have been published; on the other hand, general design principles by Pöppelbuß and Röglinger [46] have been released. None of the related work has aimed at deriving transparency and content criteria. Our study represents a first step to address this issue. Against this background, we conducted a literature search in the EBSCO, Google Scholar, ScienceDirect, and Web of Science databases with the search terms 'maturity model', 'capability model', 'design science', 'transparency', 'business process management', 'business process', 'business performance',

Table 3. Impact factors of the top 50 journals in selected subject categories.

Subject category according to SJR	Reuters Index	H Index	SJR
Range incl. all subject categories	{0;206.9}	{0;1096}	{0.1;72.6}
Range incl. 12 selected subject categories	{0;19.4}	{0;335}	{0.1;30.5}
Business and International Management	5.3	103.1	3.1
Business, Management and Accounting (misc.)	3.7	84.5	1.9
Computer Science Applications	7.4	144.6	2.6
Economics and Econometrics	5.6	137.2	7.4
Industrial and Manufacturing Engineering	5.2	101.8	1.8
Information Systems	6.0	93.3	1.8
Information Systems and Management	3.5	57.9	1.1
Management Information Systems	2.8	47.4	1.0
Management of Technology and Innovation	4.7	98.4	2.5
Management Science and Operations Research	3.7	85.2	1.8
Software	6.8	124.3	2.2
Strategy and Management	5.6	123.7	3.5
Ø Subject categories	5.0	100.1	2.6

'empiric*', and 'valid*'. It should be noted that our search included only academic literature and excluded publications, such as white papers, expressions of opinions, student papers, PowerPoint presentations, and papers published in nonacademic journals and magazines. After reviewing the titles, abstracts, keywords, content, and removing duplicate studies, a total of 33 relevant articles were identified [4, 5, 8, 12, 14, 16, 17, 20–23, 25, 27–29, 31–34, 36–42, 44, 46, 47, 52, 55, 59, 61]. The criteria proposed in the publications were highlighted, were then structured according to their intended use, and duplicates were eliminated. Finally, they were grouped according to the three dimensions: (1) methodology, (2) model documentation, and (3) model content scope (see Tables 4 to 6). Although we do not claim that the derived set of criteria is exhaustive, we are confident that it will provide a good starting point for further research and discussion.

3.1 Literature-Based Criteria

Methodology: To ensure scientific rigor and to create a theoretically sound model, an appropriate methodology must be adopted in the design and evaluation process. Drawing on existing knowledge, several procedure models, such as de Bruin et al. [12] and Becker et al. [5], have been proposed to provide standardized and methodological steps (see Table 4). For model development, explorative research methods – especially focus groups, case studies, or Delphi studies – are suggested in addition to literature reviews [5, 12, 32, 59]. Simulations, experiments or qualitative research methods, e.g., expert interviews, can be considered for improving models [5, 21, 55]. For model validation, the studies suggest the use of field experiments, surveys, expert interviews, focus groups, and case studies [38, 55, 61].

Table 4. BPMM criteria for the dimension 'methodology'.

Element	Criteria for BPMM publication
Procedure model	e.g., Becker et al. [5], de Bruin et al. [12]
Development method	Literature review, case study, Delphi study, focus group
Evaluation method	Demonstration with prototype, experiment with prototype or system, benchmarking, survey, expert interview, focus group
Application method	Case study, field experiment, survey, expert interview, focus group

Model Documentation: Due to model application and dissemination depending on documentation quality, the provision of a high degree of transparency is important for the respective user groups. Therefore, describing the model's purpose (descriptive, prescriptive, or comparative) is essential [46] (see Table 5). In addition, model components, such as the title and a description for each maturity level, the number of dimensions and elements, and a description for each activity, should be provided [17, 34, 46]. Depending on the model purpose, additional elements should be published. For descriptive models, the evaluation criteria and methodology should be described, whereas for prescriptive models, improvement measures, decision criteria, and methodology should be highlighted [46].

Table 5. BPMM criteria for the dimension 'model documentation'.

Element	Criteria for BPMM publication
Purpose of use	Descriptive, prescriptive, comparative
Basic components	Number of levels, descriptor for each level, generic description of the characteristics of each level, number of dimensions, number of elements for each process area, description of each activity as it might be performed at each maturity level
Components of descriptive maturity models	Intersubjectively verifiable criteria for each maturity level and level of granularity, target group-oriented assessment methodology
Components of prescriptive maturity models	Improvement measures for each maturity level and level of granularity, decision calculus for selecting improvement measures, target group-oriented decision methodology

Model Content Scope: To assess the content of the model, we rely on BPM factors, whose influence on business performance has been empirically confirmed by at least two independent studies. This resulted in five relevant constructs: (1) organization, (2) supply chain integration, (3) process, (4) IT, and (5) employees (see Table 6). 'Organization' addresses the company structure, which is adapted to the process view

Table 6. BPMM criteria for the dimension 'content scope'.

Element	Criteria for BPMM publication
Organization	Organizational structure, strategic alignment, culture
Supply chain integration	Supplier orientation, customer orientation
Process	Process focus, process owner, definition and documentation of processes and process measurement, design of processes, measurement of processes, improvement of processes
IT	Support of IT tools
Employees	Design of jobs and workplace, employee development, employee involvement and motivation, employee information exchange

[e.g., 8, 29]. Furthermore, the strategic focus determines the alignment of the business processes, whereas the corporate culture is based on teamwork, willingness to change, and a cooperative management style [e.g., 39, 47]. 'Supply chain integration' addresses the relationships among companies, their suppliers and customers. It is mainly about joint planning, forecasting, and process improvement between suppliers and companies as well as understanding customer needs and increasing their satisfaction [e.g., 8, 39]. The third construct 'process' relates to the coordination and improvement of business processes. In addition to the process view, this includes the determination of process owners [e.g., 25, 28]. The definition and documentation of the essential processes are the starting point for the design, evaluation, and continuous improvement of the processes [e.g., 36, 40, 44, 52]. The construct 'IT' involves the redesign and application of suitable IT systems both within and across companies [e.g., 14, 47]. The construct 'employees' addresses the recruitment, commitment, and development of staff [e.g., 8, 25, 47]. Moreover, it places emphasis on the interaction and communication between employees and management [e.g., 23, 31]. These dimensions represent capabilities that have a proven effect on the organization's performance. Therefore, at least one construct should be thematically addressed by BPMMs.

3.2 Evaluation of Recently Published BPMMs

To further emphasize the observation that many BPMM publications show qualitative weaknesses, we assessed the five models that, according to the literature review in Sect. 2.1, were released between 2015–2019: (1) the MM-AND [3], (2) the MM-BER [6], (3) the MM-CHA [11], (4) the MM-FRO [18], and (5) the MM-SLI [53]. Using a structured content analysis [30], the coding process was performed using MAXQDA Plus 2018. Each article represents a unit of analysis. Initially, coder A, who developed the criteria, coded the articles based on the codebook. To confirm that the criteria application is not limited to one researcher, a second coder (coder B, who has studied maturity models for years) independently worked on the same five models. Criteria that are not included in the codebook but mentioned in the articles were assigned to the category 'others' and analyzed separately. This category was used for the evaluation method of the MM-AND, as informal interviews, secondary documents, and observations were applied in addition to expert interviews. After the coding process, both files were merged, and the coded sections were compared against each other. An "agreement rate" (representing the number of matching recordings divided by the number of all recordings) of 84.03% was achieved. This value falls within the range that is considered reliable [43, p. 143]. Before the data were interpreted, all disagreements were discussed until a consensus decision was reached. The detailed results of the analysis can be found in Appendix B.

Although procedure models for the creation of maturity models have been publicly available for approximately ten years, only two articles (articles about the MM-BER and the MM-SLI) refer to such procedure models. When developing models, the authors draw solely on existing literature; other methods are not applied. One article reports an extensive evaluation process using different methods, such as case studies and interviews (MM-AND), whereas the other articles do not even address the evaluation of their models. It remains unclear whether an evaluation took place or whether the evaluation is simply not described. In contrast, validation in practice is reported more frequently (MM-BER, MM-CHA, MM-FRO), mainly using case studies (MM-CHA, MM-FRO). Furthermore, it can be concluded that basic components are usually documented, including the number of maturity levels, the descriptors for each level, and the number of elements for each process area. However, the important criterion 'description of each activity as it might be performed at each maturity level' is not addressed, although this criterion is crucial for both model applicability and dissemination in practice. No article adequately addressed criteria for descriptive models, and criteria for prescriptive purposes are not considered at all. We therefore conclude that the previously described lack of quality [46, 57] has not improved in recent years – at least not with regard to the five models under investigation. Two models consider almost all content criteria (the MM-BER and the MM-CHA), whereas the others have room for improvement. The criteria 'strategic alignment' and 'definition and documentation of processes and process measurement', which are incorporated by all five models, are considered to be particularly important. It is striking, however, that 'process focus' and 'design of jobs and workplace' are addressed by only one model each. 'Management of financial resources' and 'management contract' are, for example, elements that are not included in the codebook but mentioned in the maturity models. Our literature search did not identify at least two independent studies that verified the influence of these factors on business performance. Thus, no statement about the relevance of these elements can be made. Furthermore, it can be concluded that in almost all cases, comprehensive documentation that would allow for replicability and self-assessment by companies is not accessible. This reinforces the approach of improving transparency and relevance to achieve greater replicability and to publish BPMMs in higher quality journals.

4   Conclusion

This paper provides several theoretical contributions. First, it updates the exhaustive literature review that was conducted by Tarhan et al. [56]. We find that in the past five years, more BPMM articles have been published, but the research gaps originally identified by Tarhan et al. [56] remain valid. Special focus should be given to contributions that address the impact of BPMMs on business performance. However, empirical studies on the development of maturity models should also be further emphasized. Second, we extended Tarhan et al. [56] work by analyzing the outlets in which BPMMs were published. We find that BPMM articles of the past three decades have been mainly published in less-recognized journals. We argue that an important reason for this is a lack of methodological rigor and a low level of model documentation, which both limit the model's replicability, a key factor by reviewers in high-quality journals. Third, the study introduces criteria in three dimensions (methodology, model documentation, and content scope) to improve the transparency and relevance of BPMMs. The criteria were assessed using five previously published BPMMs. In particular, the dimension 'methodology' has been strongly neglected. The 'model documentation' and 'model content scope' dimension were addressed better; however, decisive criteria that would allow the application of the model in practice are still missing. The results underpin the need to increase transparency to achieve greater replicability and consequently to publish these models in higher-quality journals that have more relevance and influence on both the scientific community and practice.

Our proposed criteria constitute a first step towards overcoming this challenge but do not represent an exhaustive list of criteria that must be followed. Instead, these criteria are a starting point towards better BPMMs that can provide some orientation. The criteria can be valuable for (1) supporting academia in the publication of scientifically sound and transparent work on BPMMs and (2) providing reviewers with a detailed checklist to rely on when evaluating submitted models in the future. In addition, decision makers in companies can also benefit from well-founded and more transparent BPMMs. Thus, more efficient model selection and application can be ensured. Moreover, this study is a good starting point for decision makers who are thinking about applying a maturity model to improve business processes. By extending the literature review (2015–2019), practitioners obtain an overview of which current and 'leading' BPMMs are suitable for each area and where limitations exist. Finally, the extended overview enables researchers to build on the identified research gaps. A limitation of the paper is that the criteria are based solely on the literature. To confirm the criteria's usefulness, a long-term study would have to be conducted. Furthermore, the criteria have only been tested on a small number of models. An application to other maturity models should be considered. In addition to the lack of quality, there may be other reasons for not publishing BPMMs in higher quality journals. Further investigations are needed, such as examining the reviews of BPMM papers that are submitted to highly-ranked journals. Despite the limitations mentioned herein, we believe that such research helps to improve BPMMs, which is warranted to further support the continuous improvement of business processes in times of increasing competitive and economic pressure.

Appendix A. Categorization of the Studies

Due to page restrictions, the complete list of the 69 references for the supplementary systematic literature analysis (2015–2019) (see Digital Appendix A) and their categorization of the studies (see Digital Appendix B) can be found in the supplementary material.

Appendix B. Overview of the Five Analyzed BPMMs

Criteria for transparency	MM-AND	MM-BER	MM-CHA	MM-FRO	MM-SLI
Literature review	x	x		x	x
Case study					
Delphi study					
Focus group					
Procedure model		x			x
Demonstration with prototype					
Experiment with prototype or system					
Benchmarking					
Survey					
Expert interview	x				
Focus group					
Others	x				
Case study			x	x	
Field experiment					
Survey		x			
Expert interview					
Focus group					
Descriptive	x	x	x	x	x
Prescriptive	x				x
Comparative					x
Number of levels	x	x	x		x
Descriptor for each level	x	x	x		x
Generic description of each level	x	x	x		x
Number of dimensions	x	x	x	x	x
Number of elements for each process area	x	x	x	x	x
Description of each activity					
Intersubjectively verifiable criteria	x	x			x
Assessment methodology			x		x
Improvement measures					
Decision calculus to select measures					
Decision methodology					
Organizational structure		x		x	x
Strategic alignment	x	x	x	x	x
Culture		x	x		
Supplier orientation		x	x		
Customer orientation	x	x	x		
Process focus			x		
Process owner		x	x		
Definition and documentation	x	x	x	x	x
Design of processes	x	x	x	x	
Measurement of processes	x	x	x	x	
Improvement of processes		x	x		x
Support by IT-tools	x	x	x	x	
Design of jobs and workplace				x	
Employee development		x	x	x	x
Employee involvement and motivation		x			x
Employee information exchange		x	x		

References

1. Aguinis, H., Ramani, R.S., Alabduljader, N.: What you see is what you get? Enhancing methodological transparency in management research. Acad. Manag. Ann. **12**(1), 83–110 (2018)
2. Albliwi, S.A., Antony, J., Arshed, N.: Critical literature review on maturity models for business process excellence. In: International Conference on Industrial Engineering and Engineering Management, Selangor, pp. 79–83 (2014)
3. Andriani, M., Ari Samadhi, T.M.A., Siswanto, J., Suryadi, K.: Aligning business process maturity level with SMEs growth in indonesian fashion industry. Int. J. Organ. Anal. **26**(4), 709–727 (2018)
4. Babić-Hodović, V., Mehić, E., Arslanagić, M.: The influence of quality practices on BH companies' business performance. Int. J. Manag. Cases **14**(1), 305–316 (2012)
5. Becker, J., Knackstedt, R., Pöppelbuß, J.: Developing maturity models for IT management – a procedure model and its application. Bus. Inf. Syst. Eng. **51**(3), 213–222 (2009)
6. Berger, R., Wellbrock, W., Aksoy, O., Mulzer, D.: Process orientation. An approach to optimize cross-company supply chains – insights from a descriptive study. In: Annual NOFOMA Conference, Kolding, pp. 289–304 (2018)
7. Bornmann, L., Nast, I., Daniel, H.D.: Do editors and referees look for signs of scientific misconduct when reviewing manuscripts? A quantitative content analysis of studies that examined review criteria and reasons for accepting and rejecting manuscripts for publication. Scientometrics **77**(3), 415–432 (2008)
8. Bronzo, M., de Resende, P.T.V., de Oliveira, M.P.V., McCormack, K.P., de Sousa, P.R., Ferreira, R.L.: Improving performance aligning business analytics with process orientation. Int. J. Inf. Manag. **33**(2), 300–307 (2013)
9. Cachon, G.P., Girotra, K., Netessine, S.: Interesting, important, and impactful operations management. Manufact. Serv. Oper. Manag. **22**(1), 214–222 (2020)
10. Campbell, L., Loving, T.J., LeBel, E.: Enhancing transparency of the research process to increase accuracy of findings: a guide for relationship researchers. Pers. Relat. **21**(4), 531–545 (2014)
11. Chaghooshi, A.J., Moghadam, M.M., Etezadi, S.: Ranking business processes maturity by modified rembrandt technique with considering CMMI dimensions. Iran. J. Manag. Stud. **9**(3), 559–578 (2016)
12. De Bruin, T., Freeze, R., Kaulkarni, U., Rosemann, M.: Understanding the main phases of developing a maturity assessment model. In: Australasian Conference on Information Systems, pp. 8–19, Sydney (2005)
13. De Carolis, A., Macchi, M., Negri, E., Terzi, S.: A maturity model for assessing the digital readiness of manufacturing companies. In: Lödding, H., Riedel, R., Thoben, K.D., von Cieminski, G., Kiritsis, D. (eds.) APMS 2017. IAICT, vol. 513, pp. 13–20. Springer, Cham (2017). https://doi.org/10.1007/978-3-319-66923-6_2
14. Diller, H., Ivens, B.: Process oriented marketing. Mark. J. Res. Manag. **2**(1), 14–29 (2006)
15. Felch, V., Asdecker, B., Sucky, E.: Maturity models in the age of Industry 4.0 – do the available models correspond to the needs of business practice? In: Proceedings of the 52nd Hawaii International Conference on System Sciences, pp. 5165–5174, Wailea (2019)
16. Forsberg, T., Nilsson, L., Antoni, M.: Process orientation: the Swedish experience. Total Qual. Manag. **10**(4–5), 540–547 (1999)
17. Fraser, P., Moultrie, J., Gregory, M.: The use of maturity models/grids as a tool in assessing product development capability: a review. In: IEEE International Engineering Management Conference, pp. 244–249, Cambridge (2002)

18. Froger, M., Bénaben, F., Truptil, S., Boissel-Dallier, N.: A non-linear business process management maturity framework to apprehend future challenges. Int. J. Inf. Manag. **49**, 290–300 (2019)
19. Garfield, E.: Citations analysis as a tool in journal evaluation. Science **178**(4060), 471–479 (1972)
20. Gustafsson, A., Nilsson, L., Johnson, M.D.: The role of quality practices in service organizations. Int. J. Serv. Ind. Manag. **14**(2), 232–244 (2003)
21. Helgesson, Y.Y.L., Höst, M., Weyns, K.: A review of methods for evaluation of maturity models for process improvement. J. Softw. Evol. Process **24**(4), 436–454 (2012)
22. Hellström, A., Eriksson, H.: Among fumblers, talkers, mappers and organisers: four applications of process orientation. Total Qual. Manag. **24**(6), 733–751 (2013)
23. Hernaus, T., Pejic Bach, M., Bosilj Vukšić, V.: Influence of strategic approach to BPM on financial and non-financial performance. Baltic J. Manag. **7**(4), 376–396 (2012)
24. Hirsch, J.E.: An index to quantify an individual's scientific research output. Proc. Natl. Acad. Sci. **102**(46), 16569–16572 (2005)
25. Ittner, C.D., Larcker, D.F.: The performance effects of process management techniques. Manag. Sci. **43**(4), 522–534 (1997)
26. Kalinowski, B.T.: Business process maturity models research – a systematic literature review. In: International Scientific Conference on Economic and Social Development, pp. 476–483, Warsaw (2018)
27. Kohlbacher, M., Gruenwald, S.: Process ownership, process performance measurement and firm performance. Int. J. Prod. Perform. Manag. **60**(7), 709–720 (2011)
28. Kohlbacher, M., Gruenwald, S.: Process orientation: conceptualization and measurement. Bus. Process Manag. J. **17**(2), 267–283 (2011)
29. Kohlbacher, M., Reijers, H.A.: The effects of process-oriented organizational design on firm performance. Bus. Process Manag. J. **19**(2), 245–262 (2013)
30. Krippendorff, K.: Content Analysis. An Introduction to its Methodology, 4th edn. SAGE, Los Angeles (2019)
31. Kumar, V., Movahedi, B., Lavassani, K.M., Kumar, U.: Unleashing process orientation. Bus. Process Manag. J. **16**(2), 315–332 (2010)
32. Lahrmann, G., Marx, F., Winter, R., Wortmann, F.: Business intelligence maturity models: an overview. In: Conference of the Italian Chapter of AIS, Naples (2010)
33. Leyer, M., Stumpf-Wollersheim, J., Pisani, F.: The influence of process-oriented organisational design on operational performance and innovation: a quantitative analysis in the financial services industry. Int. J. Prod. Res. **55**(18), 5259–5270 (2017)
34. Maier, A.M., Moultrie, J., Clarkson, P.J.: Developing maturity grids for assessing organizational capabilities: practitioner guide. IEEE Trans. Eng. Manag. **59**(1), 138–159 (2009)
35. McCormack, K.: Business Process Maturity. Theory and Application. Booksurge, South Carolina (2007)
36. McCormack, K.: Business process orientation: do you have it? Qual. Prog. **34**(1), 51–58 (2001)
37. McCormack, K., Johnson, W.: Business Process Orientation. Gaining the E-Business Competitive Advantage. St. Lucie press, Boca Raton (2001)
38. Mettler, T.: Thinking in terms of design decisions when developing maturity models. Int. J. Strateg. Decis. Sci. **1**(4), 76–87 (2010)
39. Milanović Glavan, L., Bosilj Vukšić, V.: Examining the impact of business process orientation on organizational performance: the case of croatia. Croat. Oper. Res. Rev. **8**(1), 137–165 (2017)
40. Movahedi, B., Miri-Lavassani, K., Kumar, U.: Operational excellence through business process orientation: an intra- and inter-organizational analysis. TQM J. **28**(3), 467–495 (2016)

41. Münstermann, B., Eckhardt, A., Weitzel, T.: The performance impact of business process standardization. An empirical evaluation of the recruitment process. Bus. Process Manag. J. **16**(1), 29–56 (2010)
42. Münstermann, B., Joachim, N., Beimborn, D.: An empirical evaluation of the impact of process standardization on process performance and flexibility. In: Americas Conference on Information Systems, San Francisco (2009)
43. Neuendorf, K.: The Content Analysis Guidebook. SAGE, Thousand Oaks (2002)
44. Nilsson, L., Johnson, M.D., Gustafsson, A.: The impact of quality practices on customer satisfaction and business results: product versus service organizations. J. Qual. Manag. **6**(1), 5–27 (2001)
45. Object Management Group, https://www.omg.org/spec/BPMN/2.0/PDF/. Accessed 26 Feb 2020
46. Pöppelbuß, J., Röglinger, M.: What makes a useful maturity model? A framework for general design principles for maturity models and its demonstration in business process management. In: European Conference on Information Systems, Helsinki (2011)
47. Pradabwong, J., Braziotis, C., Tannock, J., Pawar, K.S.: Business process management and supply chain collaboration: effects on performance and competitiveness. Supply Chain Manag. Int. J. **22**(2), 107–121 (2017)
48. Rosemann, M.: The service portfolio of a BPM center of excellence. In: vom Brocke, J., Rosemann, M. (eds.) Handbook on Business Process Management 2. IHIS, pp. 381–398. Springer, Heidelberg (2015). https://doi.org/10.1007/978-3-642-45103-4_16
49. Rosemann, M., de Bruin, T.: Towards a business process management maturity model. In: European Conference on Information Systems, Regensburg, pp. 521–532 (2005)
50. Rummler-Brache Group. https://www.rummlerbrache.com/sites/default/files/Process-Performance-Index.pdf. Accessed 26 Feb 2020
51. SJR – SCImago Journal & Country Rank, https://www.scimagojr.com/journalrank.php. Accessed 17 Jan 2020
52. Skrinijar, R., Bosilj Vukšić, V., Indihar-Stemberger, M.: The impact of business process orientation on financial and non-financial performance. Bus. Process Manag. J. **14**(5), 738–754 (2008)
53. Sliz, P.: Concept of the organization process maturity assessment. J. Econ. Manag. **33**(3), 80–95 (2018)
54. Software Engineering Institute. https://cmmiinstitute.com/. Accessed 26 Feb 2020
55. Sonnenberg, C., vom Brocke, J.: Evaluation patterns for design science research artefacts. In: Helfert, M., Donnellan, B. (eds.) EDSS 2011. CCIS, vol. 286, pp. 71–83. Springer, Heidelberg (2012). https://doi.org/10.1007/978-3-642-33681-2_7
56. Tarhan, A., Turetken, O., Reijers, H.A.: Business process maturity models: a systematic literature review. Inf. Softw. Technol. **75**, 122–134 (2016)
57. Van Looy, A.: Business Process Maturity: A Comparative Study on a Sample of Business Process Maturity Models. Springer, Cham (2014). https://doi.org/10.1007/978-3-319-04202-2
58. Van Looy, A., de Backer, M., Poels, G.: Which maturity is being measured? A classification of business process maturity models. In: Proceedings of the SIKS/BENAIS Conference on Enterprise Information System, pp. 7–16 (2010)
59. Van Steenbergen, M., Bos, R., Brinkkemper, S., van de Weerd, I., Bekkers, W.: The design of focus area maturity models. In: Winter, R., Zhao, J.L., Aier, S. (eds.) DESRIST 2010. LNCS, vol. 6105, pp. 317–332. Springer, Heidelberg (2010). https://doi.org/10.1007/978-3-642-13335-0_22
60. Web of Science Group. https://clarivate.com/webofsciencegroup/solutions/journal-citation-reports/. Accessed 28 Nov 2019
61. Wendler, R.: The maturity of maturity model research: a systematic mapping study. Inf. Softw. Technol. **54**(12), 1317–1339 (2012)

A Typological Framework of Process Improvement Project Stakeholders

Charon Abbott[1] ⓘ, Wasana Bandara[1(✉)] ⓘ, Paul Mathiesen[2], Erica French[3] ⓘ, and Mary Tate[4] ⓘ

[1] School of Information Systems, Queensland University of Technology, 2 George Street, Brisbane, Australia
charon.abbott@hdr.qut.edu.au, w.bandara@qut.edu.au
[2] Independent BPM and Business Innovation Practitioner, Brisbane, Australia
p.mathiesen@connect.qut.edu.au
[3] Queensland University of Technology, Business School, 2 George Street, Brisbane, Australia
e.french@qut.edu.au
[4] School of Information Management, Victoria University of Wellington, Wellington, New Zealand
mary.tate@vuw.ac.nz

Abstract. Stakeholder engagement is well established as a critical success factor in Business Process Management (BPM) projects. Yet, guidelines to identify the relevant stakeholder groups and their specific activity is lacking. This study addresses this gap through a typological framework of stakeholder groups in process improvement (PI) projects. The framework is developed inductively from an in-depth case study and contextualized through a synthesis of literature from two different areas; process management and stakeholder research. The resulting framework offers a comprehensive matrix of six diverse stakeholder groups based on their affiliation to a BPM project and their role in the process. The framework differentiates between internal and external stakeholders and identifies three categories of each, namely; those *impacted by*; a *catalyst for*; and/or a *facilitator of*; the process improvement efforts. The framework recognizes the fundamental differences between BPM stakeholders with insight into the origin of those differences and provides a basis for planning and executing engagement activities with different stakeholder groups.

Keywords: Business Process Management · Process improvement · Stakeholders · Stakeholder-Groups · Stakeholder engagement · Stakeholder identification · Framework

1 Introduction

Organizations invest in continuous improvement of their business processes to achieve efficiency and innovation objectives, making the study of Business Process Management (BPM) a rapidly growing field. While BPM should be a continuous practice that facilitates efficiency and effectiveness, in reality it is often practiced in organizations through

© Springer Nature Switzerland AG 2020
D. Fahland et al. (Eds.): BPM 2020, LNCS 12168, pp. 384–399, 2020.
https://doi.org/10.1007/978-3-030-58666-9_22

short-term process improvement (PI) projects aiming to solve specific inefficiencies or create specific gains. Process improvement (PI) projects are often diverse in nature [1] but commonly go through lifecycle stages of process identification; discovery; analysis; redesign; implementation; and monitoring and controlling [2]. The current body of BPM research has been effective in sharing technical developments that have proven to show high impact outcomes [3]. However, managerial and organisational challenges have not been so well addressed by the existing technically oriented research [4]. The literature does recognise the critical role that people play in BPM initiatives [e.g. 4, 5] but the management of the non-technical (human) aspects of BPM initiatives requires more attention and is noted as an under-researched area in BPM [4, 6].

There are many success stories involving BPM projects, but also substantial failures reported [7–9]. It is suggested that 60–80% of BPM projects fail, [9, 10] representing a significant waste of organisational resources. Such failure rates also challenge the relative value of BPM generally. Fundamental to the success of any BPM project is the identification, engagement and management of stakeholders [9, 11, 12]. Although this can be said of any project, given the continuity and wide-spread nature of BPM practices, it demands a fresh look at understanding stakeholder engagement. Given that BPM is meant to be an organisational-wide, ongoing, practice, the relationship between parties involved in diverse improvement projects differs from discrete, non-BPM projects. This difference can be expected to amplify the importance of stakeholder engagement, as the legacy of one BPM activity builds upon the next.

The importance of stakeholder engagement is being increasingly acknowledged. Furthermore, appropriate stakeholder engagement has specifically been listed as a critical success factor for process improvement (PI) initiatives [e.g. 9, 13–15]. Yet to date, there is very little guidance on stakeholder enagement in BPM projects, with no consistency in the definition; the various terms used to describe different stakeholders, and confusing discussions on who are the stakeholder groups influencing BPM projects. For example, the literature refers to various groups such as 'users' [13], 'front-line staff' [9] and 'process participants' [2], among others. The lack of a clear understanding of key BPM stakeholders inhibits the ability to identify, plan, and interact with them which is essential in enabling appropriate stakeholder engagement. The lack of a guiding framework leads to practitioners grouping stakeholders in different ways, potentially missing some groups entirely in engagement plans for PI initiatives. Excluding stakeholders could contribute to project failure.

This research aims to answer "what are the key stakeholder groups involved in and affected by Process Improvement Projects?" to gain insights into the roles they play and their influence within projects.

While there are many definitions of the term stakeholder we adopt Freeman's [16] widely used definition "any group or individual who can affect or is affected by the achievement of the organization's objectives". Freeman's definition covers both individuals and groups however, in this research, we focus on 'stakeholder groups' as organizations manage most of their stakeholders as 'groups' (or clusters) rather than individually. In the paper we present a review of related work (Sect. 2), the study method (Sect. 3), and the findings (Sect. 4) presenting the typological framework and the supporting evidence base (Table 2). Each of the six identified stakeholder groups of the framework is detailed. The paper concludes with a discussion and outlook for future work.

2 Literature Review

This section summarizes two key areas of related research, both intended to further delineate the research gap. In Sect. 2.1 we summarize different stakeholder theories popular in general organizational contexts, critiquing their applicability in the context of process improvement projects. The second Sect. 2.2 presents a brief overview of how existing BPM studies cluster and discuss stakeholders, highlighting the lack of any formal approach to systematically and holistically identifying BPM stakeholder groups. Insights from here[1] are used to triangulate and support empirical insights that emerged from the case study (see Sects. 3 and 4).

2.1 Stakeholder Theories

The question of 'who is a stakeholder?' is a complex one [e.g. 17, 18]. Many theories have been put forward, however the topic is still debated [19]. In this section we outline two popular theories which have been used in BPM literature, Freeman's [16, 20] stakeholder theory and Mitchell et al.'s [21] theory of stakeholder identification and salience. Finally, we also consider a more recent theory by Miles [22] which has attempts to provide different categories of stakeholders. Each theory offers a different perspective on stakeholders; Freeman focuses on taking a stakeholder perspective in managing organizations; Mitchell [21] emphasizes which stakeholders should be focused upon during a project, and Miles [22] attempts to define a meta-theory.

Freeman's Stakeholder theory [16, 20] covers many complex issues including the identification and management of stakeholders. He concentrates on managing organizations from a stakeholder perspective, instead of a shareholder one and argues this has an influence on activities and performance, including value creation, ethics and managerial mindset [18]. Freeman [16] delineates between 'primary' stakeholders as those who are of critical importance to the ongoing viability of the company, and 'secondary' stakeholders who influence the primary stakeholders. Freeman acknowledges the groups he identifies as high level [16] and while this appears to be a comprehensive view of stakeholder groups, it does not take into account (i) the different situations under which activities are conducted; nor (ii) which stakeholders are key to the organization in different contexts. Yet, these limitations are important, for example, where customers may be identified as a key stakeholder group in a situation where a Customer Relationship Management (CRM) system is implemented, but they may not be a key group in a different context.

The Theory of Stakeholder Identification and Salience by Mitchell et al. [21] attempts to address the issue of context and importance when identifying stakeholders. This theory posits that there are three important attributes held by stakeholders in differing degrees; 'power' - the level of influence held by the stakeholder; 'legitimacy' - the characteristic of the relationship between the stakeholder and the company; and, 'urgency' - the

---

[1] Together with a systematic literature review that was conducted as explained in Sect. 3.

nature of the claim of the stakeholder and how soon those claims require attention [21]. Mitchell et al.'s [21] theory considers 8 groups of stakeholders split into 4 key sub-groups accessing varying degrees of the three attributes (power, legitimacy and urgency). While their classification is very useful for understanding the shifting priorities during a (PI) project, the concept of 'power' in a project is a subjective assessment which may differ between evaluators. Detailed guidelines on how to identify those stakeholders that fall into the different groups are not provided. This is a considerable gap especially when considering the transitory nature of the stakeholder groups.

In recent times, further attempts have been made to define stakeholders. For example, Miles [22] built a stakeholder model which incorporates 855 classifications of stakeholders from previous research to define a meta-theory. The author classified stakeholders into four groups, influencer, claimant, collaborator, and recipient. Influencers have the ability to influence an organization; a claimant lacks power but has a claim on the company which they actively pursue; the collaborator also lacks power but does not have a strategy; unlike the claimant. Finally, the recipient also lacks power and passively is impacted by the organization. Like Mitchell et al. [21] Miles [22] does not address the subjective nature of the concept of 'power'.

Despite the influence of both Freeman et al. [16] and Mitchell et al. [21] the categorizations they provided have not been widely used in practice, hence the continuing attempts to afford definitive solutions. One reason is the problematic concept of stakeholder power. Power is not something that is easy to identify or demarcate, hence we argue against its practical applicability when trying to identify different stakeholders. Furthermore, in the context of PI projects stakeholder groups are likely to fall into the different categories at different points within the project, for example an end user may be a different stakeholder during the initiation phase of a project than they are during its implementation phase. Davison et al. [23] recognizes the need for different stakeholder categories at different times in their framework, utilizing four stakeholder groups based on 'group needs'. However, their framework does not go far enough to distinguish between internal and external stakeholder groups, nor do they acknowledge different contexts for stakeholder groups.

2.2 Stakeholders Within Process Management Literature

While 'stakeholders' are often acknowledged within the process management literature, much of the literature either does not define the term or does so with very general expressions, such as 'employee', 'users' or 'management'. An example of this is Stary [24] who focuses on stakeholder involvement in Business Process Management (S-BPM) activities but, rarely refer to any specific group, beyond giving occasional examples, such as 'employee'. A similar approach is taken by Fleitchmann & Stary [25]. This general approach may be appropriate when focusing on the transactional nature of the interaction with stakeholders, however, it is not useful when seeking to influence stakeholder buy-in. General categorizations, such as 'employees', are too broad and fail to acknowledge the extensive range of different factors influencing such a group. Bandara et al. [13] addresses this generalization by referring to three primary stakeholder groups relevant to their research. However, other groups of stakeholders were referenced by the interviewees specifically; 'process owner', 'middle management' 'leadership', 'employee' [13] indicating a breadth previously ignored.

Stakeholder type and role are also used to distinguish stakeholders. Trkman (10) defines the type of stakeholder as 'specialist' or 'generalist'. This is relevant in PI projects as the specialists' narrower, but deeper skillset can produce higher productivity and quality, whereas the generalists' broader, but shallower skillset may make them more flexible and adaptable to change [9]. While offering a viable segregation of stakeholders, as it is possible that the level of engagement for each of these groups may differ. The reasons for this may vary according to the level of personal investment committed to the activity or the depth of their knowledge. Dumas [3] and Lederer & Groeke [25] offer a focus on roles in BPM but their inclusion is not extensive. Roles, while valid as specific job roles, may not be able to be utilized to build a comprehensive stakeholder management plan, as those impacted by the BPM change and those required to implement it may not be included.

In sum, there is little evidence in the process management field which attempts to comprehensively define all stakeholders relating to a project. One exception is Hailemariam and vom Brocke [26], where all stakeholders of an Ethiopian government service were defined. They supported all the stakeholders in the organization contributing to a coalition. However ultimately the groups were so wide-ranging including 'suppliers' and 'society', as to exclude them from any meaningful engagement due to their all-encompassing nature.

3   Methodology

We aimed to explore the characteristics of different stakeholder groups and selected a typological analysis following [27] to develop a set of *"related but distinct"* BPM stakeholder groups that are *"easily recognizable"*. The study deployed an inductive approach where the supporting evidence was primarily from a single case study, contextualized and triangulated through literature synthesis from two areas; process management and stakeholder research.

Single case studies are known to provide rich insights and to be well suited for exploring under-researched phenomena [28, 29]. The case selection criteria determined that; the (i) PI project studied be an end-to-end improvement process (ii) with multiple teams *impacted* (their day–to-day processes were changed) or *were involved with* (were part of the project team who implemented the change) the improvement initiative (iii) the PI project had been completed within the past six months. The case study was undertaken in Bank ABC[2], an ASX listed regional Australian bank, with its Head Office in Brisbane, Queensland. The PI project selected as the unit of analysis applied robotic process automation (RPA) to enhance the process of receiving credit applications for asset purchases for businesses, received from bank branches and a broker network. The data collection occurred from April 2019 to Sept 2019. The investigation was exploratory, aiming to develop a deeper understanding of stakeholder groups within a PI initiative.

---

[2] Bank ABC is a pseudonym to protect the anonymity of the organization and participants as per agreed data collection agreements and research ethics adhered to.

Case data were collected through nine (9) in-depth interviews (as summarized in Table 1). The respondents were selected to represent the different organizational and project roles pertaining to the selected PI project.

Table 1. Overview of case study interviewees

#	Organizational-role level	Project-role
1	Team Leader	Project Manager
2	Senior Management	Project team member (business representative)
3	Team Leader	End user
4	Individual Contributor	Project team member
5	Middle Manager	End user
6	Individual Contributor	Project team member
7	Individual Contributor	End user
8	Individual Contributor	End user (external)
9	Senior Management	Project sponsor

[*Note:* The organisational level represents the reporting hierarchy within the case study. *Senior Management*, reports to an executive (a category not included in the sample respondents); a *Middle Manager,* has team leaders report to them; a *Team Leader* has individual contributors report to them and; an *Individual Contributor* have no direct reports].

The interviews were complemented with related project documents. These included project updates, annual reports, post-implementation review and an RPA strategy document. Interviews were the primary evidence base and were augmented through document analysis for further detail and triangulation. Several respondents were initially identified via a key informant who was intimate with the project and identified others who played a significant role within the project. The initial list grew through snowball sampling [30] as the interviews unfolded allowing us to track important participants. The interviews were semi structured in nature, where the respondents were asked to describe their own role(s) and the roles of others within the selected project's whole lifecycle. Details such as the perceived nature of engagement, related challenges, organizational and process contexts etc. were discussed in the interviews to create opportunities to obtain deeper insights. Each interview was approximately 60 min, and were audio recorded and transcribed. A structured literature review (following guidelines outlined by [31]) was also undertaken[3] as another source of input for this exploratory investigation, where a total of 123 papers were collected and analyzed. The emerging case study findings were constantly compared with and supported by the literature.

The overall case analysis approach was inductive, drawing on supportive insights from the literature. It included multiple coding phases, following the four-step process to typology building suggested by [27] slightly adapted for our research context.

---

[3] The paper extraction strategies applied are detailed as ancillary material at (https://drive.google.com/file/d/1YjuEceQt_WLJ_-p6SLGKZp8yN574YxFx/view?usp=sharing).

The steps include: 1) Identify existing organizing frameworks. This was done based on our analysis of stakeholder literature and was used to suggest areas that might serve as points of difference that can be used to distinguish between categories. These major themes were used to guide the development of questions for a semi-structured interview process. 2) Analyse the data. Major themes were developed inductively from the data based on 243 initial open codes, and the research team used constant comparison with literature to contextualize the codes. 3) Derive dimensions of commonality and difference. As the data was analyzed, the research team analyzed and discussed important sources of commonality and variation between the various stakeholder groups included in the case data. 4) Develop typological categories. The team looked within those sources of commonality and variation for patterns of similarity and difference. The identified patterns of similarity and difference were then developed into "ideal types" which form the categories in the typology.

The overall analysis was governed by coding guidelines and rules and supported by NVivo 12 (a qualitative data analysis tool). Coding quality was validated by a second coder throughout the analysis and the coded content was reviewed through regular coder corroboration sessions where the coding was discussed, challenged and improved.

4 Study Findings

The first distinction in our findings was the classification of the stakeholders as '**internal**' or '**external**' (see Table 2). This categorization typically refers to whether a stakeholder group is from inside the organization or external to it, which aligns with Freeman's [20] concept of 'primary' and 'secondary' stakeholders. This distinction is important as there are some fundamental differences between such stakeholders, specifically job security; information flow; and numerous vested interests. The organizational boundary between internal and external stakeholders can differ based on the scope of the PI. For example, in an improvement to the payroll process for an organizational group, 'internal' would be anyone within that company group. However, if the PI impacted a subsidiary of the organization, then the scope of the subsidiary would be where the internal boundary would be drawn. Groups external to the company should be considered separately to stakeholders within the organization as the relationships are fundamentally different. Such groups often share different information than internal stakeholders and will either be in a client/consultant relationship or similar which will moderate behaviors [32] and require different treatments with alternate engagement opportunities.

Our analysis resulted in a further categorization of initial stakeholder groups. Namely, those who can be either **impacted by** the PI project, a **catalyst for** it, or a **facilitator of** the PI efforts (see Table 2). The stakeholders who are impacted by the change are likely to be those whose role is most disrupted by the PI project and who could be perceived as having the most 'to lose'. A catalyst is a stakeholder personally invested in it and advocating for its success. A facilitator of the change includes those who seek to ensure the project is a success, however, is unlikely to be as invested in the change to the same degree as a catalyst.

Table 2. Summary Case study findings

1	2	3								
Stakeholder Group	Roles and responsibilities	Case evidence found through interviewee responses								
		1	2	3	4	5	6	7	8	9
Internal-Catalyst: Stakeholders who instigate the PI project and are employees of the company. They set overall objectives and provide resources to effect the change *e.g.: Executives, top level management, senior management, top leadership, middle management[a], decision makers, process owner, management team* [2, 9, 13, 14, 23, 33, 34]	- Instigate PI project - Provide resources - Provide direction during PI - Confirm scope - Set measures for success - Clears roadblocks during PI - Accountable for PI outcomes	√	√	√		√		√	√	√
Internal-Facilitator: Employees who undertake the project This group has been tasked with implementing the process change *e.g. Facilitator, system engineer, BPM group, Process analysts, Business Process consultant, Business Process architect, change agents, project team* [2, 23, 24, 35–37]	- Clearly define scope - Manage project implementation - Manage stakeholders - Determine/provide/build solution - Supply specialist solution knowledge/skills - Responsible for PI outcomes Monitor results	√	√	√	√	√	√	√	√	√
Internal-Impacted: Employees of the company and whose day-to-day work will change as a result of the PI project *e.g. Users, front line staff, process participants, system engagers, employee, staff, middle management, internal participants* [2, 13, 23, 35–40]	- Provide information to project team - Follow new process directions	√	√	√	√	√	√	√	√	√
External-Catalyst: External stakeholder-group who have the power to force change upon the company or to directly influence the instigation of a PI project within the organisation *e.g. Government, other regulatory bodies, customer, investor, society* [23, 26]	- Direct change requirements, or - Directly influence instigation of PI				√	√				√
External-Facilitator: External stakeholders who have been engaged to implement the PI. These stakeholders may work inside the company offices or remotely *e.g. External consultant, IT vendor, system engineers, supply chain partners* [2, 13, 33, 41–44]	- Manage project implementation - Manage stakeholders - Provide/build solution - Supply specialist solution knowledge/skills - Work to contractual obligations and/or statement of work.	√	√	√	√	√	√	√	√	√

(continued)

Table 2. (*continued*)

1	2	3								
Stakeholder Group	Roles and responsibilities	Case evidence found through interviewee responses								
		1	2	3	4	5	6	7	8	9
External-Impacted: This stakeholder-group will notice a change in their interactions with the company as a result of the PI project being implemented *e.g. Customer, Front-end/Back end partners, suppliers, investor, external participants* [26, 39, 40, 44]	- Adopt/choose to adopt solution		√	√		√		√	√	

[a]Refer to internal-catalyst stakeholder-group section for an explanation of how middle managers can potentially belong to multiple stakeholder-groups, based on different contextual factors.

In summary, our analysis identified six stakeholder groups, namely; internal-catalyst, internal-facilitator, internal-impacted, external-catalyst, external-facilitator and external-impacted. Table 2 summarizes the supporting evidence. Column 1 lists and defines each stakeholder group, providing examples of designations extracted and mapped from the literature. Column 2 further elaborates on the stakeholder group by listing typical roles and responsibilities (observed from the case data and supported by literature) pertaining to each group. Column 3 presents an overview of the case data depicting which interviewees supported the suggested stakeholder grouping. The next sub-sections further describe each stakeholder group.

The categories of internal and external stakeholders are mutually exclusive, as they refer to being employed by the organization. Although internal stakeholders are likely to fall into one group, due to technical or organizational context, it is possible that individual stakeholders may fall into more than one group e.g. be both a catalyst and a facilitator. This insight can be valuable when considering engagement. For example, if stakeholders are in both Internal-Facilitator and Internal-Impacted groups, they are likely to be highly motivated to ensure the change is successful and would require different treatment to stakeholders who were solely impacted by the change.

4.1 The Internal–Catalyst Role

Seven of the nine interviewees (with 73 coding references) contributed to identifying and confirming the Internal-Catalyst as an important stakeholder group for PI projects, describing them as; *"Group executives and senior management who are the ones who decide on what processes should be automated"* (Interviewee 1), and mentioning that *"at a senior level, [they] would have a very strong interest in the fact that they had spent a considerable amount of money on external resources"* (Interviewee 1).

Although prior research does not classify PI stakeholders as we do in this study, they do mention the eminent role of those who 'support' the initiative; often inferring corporate executive support. Despite the lack of clarity over what 'support' is in practice, it is considered critical to the success of PI projects [9, 13, 14, 38]. Some mention 'decision-makers' [23], 'executives' [34] and 'senior managers' [45]. The role of the 'process owner' loosely defined yet considered a critical success factors for PI implementations is also referred to as a 'driving force' for continuous improvement and being responsible for "initiating…. improvement projects" [2].

Whilst the name of this stakeholder group may vary, the described role is to instigate process change, provide resources and be seen to support the change throughout the PI project lifecycle. The role is often perceived as being particularly critical at the start of a PI project as it holds the ultimate authority over whether an initiative is able to commence [23]. It should be noted that different characteristics of different processes and organizations and PI projects would result in different levels of management being the catalyst. For example, a project to improve an operational level process may be instigated by middle management as it may have a more concentrated scope and lower organizational visibility, whereas a strategic process may have a much higher profile and broader impact resulting in senior management being the catalyst.

4.2 The Internal-Facilitator Role

All nine interviewees (100%) identified the Internal-Facilitator as an important stakeholder group with 206 coding references. Interviewee 2 described them as those; "*making sure as a consultant/overseer that the optimisation was headed in the right direction and focused on the right things, in particular, the outcomes, and they also made sure that it minimised the impact to the business*".

Stary [24] describes 'facilitators' as those who transfer knowledge to staff about the changes being undertaken. Davison et al. [23] use the same term but defines the role differently, as being involved in system builds and having a key role in the management of other stakeholders. Other authors divide this group further into subgroups based upon their technical skills. For example, Dumas et al. [2] use the terms 'process analysts' (those who undertake modelling and improvement activities), 'BPM Group' (the team overseeing the BPM efforts) and 'system engineers' (those responsible for building and implementation of systems). Lederer Antonucci and Gocke [35] describe; 'Business Process Consultants' as those who are responsible for the 'change and project management' and 'Business Process Architects' as those who support senior management in the design of process changes and defining the standard terminology to be used within the organization. 'Process Analysts' are also mentioned as one group heavily involved with 'the business' and the implementation of changes [35].

Whilst some authors provide very detailed definitions of this group, other authors give vague definitions. De Waal & Batenberg [36] identified stakeholders who implement the PI project as 'change agents. This group is responsible for how the change gets implemented, including managing other stakeholders and the methods used to implement the change [36]. A similar approach to defining the group implementing change is also used by Finney [37], who call them the 'project team'. These descriptions are problematic, first, because it is too vague and, the second, because the people facilitating the change may not actually form part of the formal 'project team' causing further confusion.

4.3 Internal-Impacted

All nine interviewees (100%) referred to the Internal-Impacted stakeholder group with 370 coding references, where the respondents' statements typically exclaimed *"it very much has directly impacted everything I do"* (Interviewee 7).

This group is rarely defined in the PI project literature and existing category descriptions vary. Dumas [2] describe this group of stakeholders specifically as 'process participants' and similarly to Davison et al. [23], 'process participants' are described as those who carry out the process daily. Trkman [9] deconstructs this stakeholder group into specialists and generalists where reasoning for this distinction is based on the notion of a 'trade off' between the role types. Since generalists have a broader set of skills, they are more adaptable as processes change, whereas specialists have a deep yet narrower set of skills and are thus less able to develop new skills, but their specialization allows them to produce higher quality work and they are also more productive [9]. Common terms used for those impacted by a PI project are frequently abstract. As much of the literature relates to system implementation, it is unsurprising that the term 'users' is commonly found [e.g. 13, 39, 46, 47]. Another abstract term is that of 'employee' [e.g. 13, 26, 39, 46, 47]. This group of stakeholders most impacted through the PI project activity have been defined in many different ways including role type or extent of expertise.

4.4 External-Catalyst

Evidence of the External-Catalyst stakeholder group surfaced in three interviews (33%), with 3 coding references with respondent statements defining this group as *"executives are sold a very good story from people like [external consultancy] externally because it does work"* (Interviewee 5). The case evidence shows that the external catalyst did not force change upon the company, however it did directly persuade the company to instigate change. This stakeholder group are those who have a direct role in the PI project, therefore customers would not fit into this category of stakeholders unless organized such as a lobby group, or a particularly influential customer.

Davison et al. [23] defines external stakeholder groups as 'outside agencies', who initialize PI projects and conflates many different types of groups under the same definition. Hailemariam and vom Brocke [26] refers to the 'government' as an external instigator of projects but also includes 'society' which is somewhat vague and could be seen to incorporate numerous other groups such as, customers, and investor stakeholder-groups.

4.5 External-Facilitator

Presence of an External-Facilitator stakeholder group emerged in all nine interviews (100%) (with 83 coding references) and the respondents identified the potential impact on the organization as *"the [external facilitator] guys were really nice and cool to work with, but they're very time constrained to what they need to do, and they've only got a certain amount of time to do it,"* (Interviewee 8) balanced by the statement that *"for the more difficult things we used the consultants to help us where we got stuck"* (Interviewee 2).

Davison et al. [23] refer to those who are involved in the implementation of the project as 'suppliers' or 'contractors'. Bandara et al. [13] names 'vendors' as one of the three major groups of stakeholders in PI projects because this group have a different 'agenda', that is, to successfully sell their systems to users and PI experts. Dezdar and Ainin [33] also refer to external stakeholders as 'vendors', or 'consultants'. However, other researchers consider external stakeholders somewhat differently supporting the proposition that they a distinct 'facilitator' group. Ravensteyn et al. [41] refer to 'process consultants' and 'developers' as external parties involved in the change. Dumas et al. [2] have a similar view identifying the group as responsible for system development and roll out, 'system engineers'. They suggest this stakeholder group could be internal however they recognize their responsibilities are often 'outsourced to external providers' [2]. The key difference between facilitator groups in this typology is that the External Facilitators have different motivations to the Internal-Facilitators but have a skill set necessary to implement the changes.

4.6   External-Impacted

Five of the nine interviewees (55%) discussed the presence of an External-Impacted stakeholder group, with 51 coding references, which displayed similarities with the internal-impacted group. The key difference between the internal and external impacted stakeholder groups is that the external stakeholder group may elect to use the product or not. This is demonstrated in comments made by the interviewees such as "*It's a lot easier to tell branches, 'let's roll it out, bang, everyone use this, we're getting rid of the checklists.' It's completely different with brokers when they can deal with five to six different financiers, and they'll have a different form for everyone, when previously they can just send in their own version*" (Interviewee 8). This quote demonstrates the choice these external stakeholders have in using the service provided.

A clear understanding of this group is not presented in the existing literature. The idea of suppliers and customers as stakeholders is however acknowledged by Ohlsson et al. [44]. They address them as 'back-end' and 'front-end' network partners. Other literature conflates customers and employees into one group, called 'end-users' [39].

5   Discussion and Conclusion

This study aimed to provide a comprehensive typological framework of stakeholder groups in PI projects. A case study analysis was used to identify patterns and groupings that consistently identify all stakeholders and to compare activities within and across a PI project. The internal/external dichotomy and the catalyst/facilitator/impacted trichotomy creates a simple yet comprehensive 2×3 matrix of six stakeholder groups based on their position in relation to the PI improvement initiatives and their role in the PI project. In conclusion the answer to the research question "What are the key stakeholder groups involved in and affected by Process Improvement Projects" involves a framework of six (6) stakeholder types. Furthermore, the categorization presented here is holistic and complete, where all stakeholders of a given PI project can fit and be represented by one or more of the six categories outlined. The framework recognizes the fundamental differences between the internal and external stakeholders. This is a valuable distinction when considering factors that influence stakeholder engagement.

Additionally, the inclusion of the project facilitators both internal and external to the company ensures the recognition of all influencing stakeholder groups who can impact the outcome of the project.

As the stakeholder groups are not based on an organizational structure, or the level of the stakeholder within the organization we argue that this gives the framework a high degree of flexibility. This means the framework can be adopted in a multitude of situations. For example, diverse improvement projects such as one instigated by a government directive, a Group Executive or a Team Leader can all be accommodated by this framework. Another factor that contributes to the value of the model is that, unlike the stakeholder groups proposed in other models our framework does not make assumptions about the subjective attributes of stakeholders, such as their commitment or level of power, and thus can be applied consistently. This objectivity will allow direct comparisons to be made across different PI projects. It will also aid clearer analysis into how stakeholders and their treatment influence project success, which can be used to understand or develop strategies to improve success rates.

The study contributes to the current research in understanding stakeholders involved in and impacted by process improvement initiatives, thus contributing to a better understanding of the 'people' aspect of BPM. It contributes to current stakeholder research by providing a clear categorization of stakeholders for PI projects. This contribution will provide a basis for comparing the results of research across different studies, through the use of a common language. Providing the basis for such common language is as a valuable theoretical contribution as outlined by Gregor [48]. In addition, as the definitions provided are clear and comprehensive this assists with efforts taken to compare study results. The framework can also be used in future BPM research, as a tool to identify and study participants.

The typological framework has multiple practical contributions and implications. For example, using the stakeholder categorization as a checklist can help practitioners to avoid overlooking any key stakeholder group in the design and execution of critical engagement and communication plans. Study findings can provide an alternative way of viewing targeted strategies for engagement, through focused engagement initiatives for the different stakeholder groups. Due to the fact that the categories presented here are not job/role specific (i.e. does not refer to specific organizational roles such as 'executives', or 'users') it is applicable to all types and sizes of PI projects regardless of project-based specificities. In addition, the consistent categorization of stakeholders provides a mechanism to capture and compare stakeholder learnings across different projects. Future researchers can use this typological framework to assist with their study designs; specifically, sample framing.

As with most research there are limitations to this study. The current results are based on the analysis of data from a single case study. A larger sample of cases could be used to explore multiple PI project contexts, including collating further data on all stakeholder groups. The model can be further enhanced by identifying key sub-groups, which could include stakeholders who fit into more than one of the six groups or other aspects such as stakeholder power, suggested in some stakeholder theories [e.g. 21, 22]. Future research could be undertaken to derive an understanding of the potential influences that each stakeholder group offers and how such influence changes across the different stages of a PI project's lifecycle. Researchers can also expand this framework by identifying stakeholder engagement factors pertaining to the different stakeholder groups to gain a deeper understanding of how each of these different stakeholder groups may engage in PI projects. As stated in Sect. 4, it is possible that stakeholders can be members of more than one stakeholder group. Future research could investigate how being members of more than one group impacts engagement and how that impacts PI outcomes. Another worthy area of study would be undertaking research to understand how the different stakeholder groups influence each other.

References

1. vom Brocke, J., Zelt, S., Schmiedel, T.: On the role of context in business process management. Int. J. Inf. Manag. **36**(3), 486–495 (2016)
2. Dumas, M., La Rosa, M., Mendling, J., Reijers, H.A.: Fundamentals of Business Process Management. Springer, New York (2013). https://doi.org/10.1007/978-3-642-33143-5
3. van der Aalst, W.M.P.: Business process management: a comprehensive survey. ISRN Softw. Eng. **2013**, 37 (2013)
4. Alter, S., Recker, J.: Using a work system perspective to expand BPM research use cases. J. Inf. Technol. Theory Appl. **18**(1), 47–70 (2017)
5. Van Looy, A.: On the synergies between business process management and digital innovation. In: Weske, M., Montali, M., Weber, I., vom Brocke, J. (eds.) BPM 2018. LNCS, vol. 11080, pp. 359–375. Springer, Cham (2018). https://doi.org/10.1007/978-3-319-98648-7_21
6. Looy, A.: On the importance of non-technical process capabilities to support digital innovations. In: vom Brocke, J., Schmiedel, T. (eds.) BPM - Driving Innovation in a Digital World. MP, pp. 259–274. Springer, Cham (2015). https://doi.org/10.1007/978-3-319-14430-6_17
7. Abdolvand, N., Albadvi, A., Ferdowsi, Z.: Assessing readiness for business process reengineering. Bus. Process Manag. J. **14**(4), 497–511 (2008)
8. Beckett, C., Myers, M.D.: Organizational culture in business process management: the challenge of balancing disciplinary and pastoral power. Pac. Asia J. Assoc. Inf. Syst. **10**(1), 37–62 (2018)
9. Trkman, P.: The critical success factors of business process management. Int. J. Inf. Manag. **30**(2), 125–134 (2010)
10. Chen, C.-K., Reyes, L.: A quality management approach to guide the executive management team through the product/service innovation process. Total Qual. Manag. Bus. Excell. **28**(9–10), 1003–1022 (2017)
11. Thennakoon, D., Bandara, W., French, E., Mathiesen, P.: What do we know about business process management training? Current status of related research and a way forward. Bus. Process Manag. J. **24**(2), 478–500 (2018)
12. vom Brocke, J., Schmiedel, T., Recker, J., Trkman, P., Mertens, W., Viaene, S.: Ten principles of good business process management. Bus. Process Manag. J. **20**(4), 530–548 (2014)
13. Bandara, W., Indulska, M., Chong, S., Sadiq, S. (eds.) Major issues in business process management: an expert perspective. In: The 15th European Conference on Information Systems. University of St. Gallen, St Gallen, Switzerland (2007)
14. Hernaus, T., Vuksic, V.B., Štemberger, M.I.: How to go from strategy to results? Institutionalising BPM governance within organisations. Bus. Process Manag. J. **22**(1), 173–195 (2016)
15. Kohlbacher, M., Gruenwald, S.: Process orientation: conceptualization and measurement. Bus. Process Manag. J. **17**(2), 267–283 (2011)

16. Freeman, R.E.: Strategic Management: A Stakeholder Approach. Pitman, Boston (1984)
17. McGrath, S.K., Whitty, S.J.: Stakeholder defined. Int. J. Manag. Proj. Bus. **10**(4), 721–748 (2017)
18. Freeman, R.E., Harrison, J.S., Wicks, A.C., Parmar, B.L., De Colle, S.: Stakeholder Theory: The State of the Art. Cambridge University Press, Cambridge (2010)
19. Griffin, J.J.: Tracing stakeholder terminology then and now: convergence and new pathways. Bus. Ethics: Eur. Rev. **26**(4), 326–346 (2017)
20. Freeman, R.E., Harrison, J.S., Wicks, A.C.: Managing for Stakeholders: Survival, Reputation, and Success. Yale University Press, New Haven (2007)
21. Mitchell, R.K., Agle, B.R., Wood, D.J.: Toward a theory of stakeholder identification and salience: defining the principle of who and what really counts. Acad. Manag. Rev. **22**(4), 853–886 (1997)
22. Miles, S.: Stakeholder theory classification: a theoretical and empirical evaluation of definitions. J. Bus. Ethics **142**(3), 437–459 (2017). https://doi.org/10.1007/s10551-015-2741-y
23. Davison, J., Thompson, J.B., Deeks, D.A., Lejk, M.: PisoSIA® a stakeholder approach to assist change in information systems development projects and aid process improvement. Softw. Qual. J. **14**(1), 25–36 (2006). https://doi.org/10.1007/s11219-006-5999-6
24. Stary, C.: Transfer of learnings between disciplines: what S-BPM facilitators could ask progressive educators (and might not dare to do). In: Stephanidis, C., Antona, M. (eds.) UAHCI 2014. LNCS, vol. 8514, pp. 431–442. Springer, Cham (2014). https://doi.org/10.1007/978-3-319-07440-5_40
25. Fleischmann, A., Stary, C.: Whom to talk to? A stakeholder perspective on business process development. Univ. Access Inf. Soc. **11**(2), 125–150 (2012). https://doi.org/10.1007/s10209-011-0236-x
26. Hailemariam, G., vom Brocke, J.: What is sustainability in business process management? A theoretical framework and its application in the public sector of Ethiopia. In: zur Muehlen, M., Su, J. (eds.) BPM 2010. LNBIP, vol. 66, pp. 489–500. Springer, Heidelberg (2011). https://doi.org/10.1007/978-3-642-20511-8_45
27. Ayres, L., Knafl, K.: Typological analysis. In: Given, L.M. (ed.) The SAGE Encyclopedia of Qualitative Research Methods, vol. 1, p. 900-1. SAGE Publications, Inc., Thousand Oaks (2008)
28. Yin, R.K.: Case Study Research: Design and Methods, 4th edn. Sage Publications, Thousand Oaks (2009). xvi, 181 p.
29. Lee, A.S.: A scientific methodology for MIS case studies. MIS Q. **13**, 33–50 (1989)
30. Tracy, S.J.: Qualitative Research Methods: Collecting Evidence, Crafting Analysis, Communicating Impact, 2nd edn. Wiley, Newark (2019)
31. Bandara, W., Furtmuller, E., Gorbacheva, E., Miskon, S., Beekhuyzen, J.: Achieving rigour in literature reviews: insights from qualitative data analysis and tool-support. Commun. Assoc. Inf. Syst. **37**(1), 8 (2015)
32. Lehtinen, J., Aaltonen, K., Rajala, R.: Stakeholder management in complex product systems: practices and rationales for engagement and disengagement. Ind. Mark. Manag. **79**, 58–70 (2019)
33. Dezdar, S., Ainin, S.: Examining ERP implementation success from a project environment perspective. Bus. Process Manag. J. **17**(6), 919–939 (2011)
34. Huq, Z., Martin, T.N.: The recovery of BPR implementation through an ERP approach: a hospital case study. Bus. Process Manag. J. **12**(5), 576–587 (2006)
35. Lederer Antonucci, Y., Goeke, R.J.: Identification of appropriate responsibilities and positions for business process management success. Bus. Process Manag. J. **17**(1), 127–146 (2011)
36. de Waal, B.M.E., Batenburg, R.: The process and structure of user participation: a BPM system implementation case study. Bus. Process Manag. J. **20**(1), 107–128 (2014)

37. Finney, S.: Stakeholder perspective on internal marketing communication: an ERP implementation case study. Bus. Process Manag. J. **17**(2), 311–331 (2011)
38. Hung, R.Y.-Y.: Business process management as competitive advantage: a review and empirical study. Total Qual. Manag. Bus. Excell. **17**(1), 21–40 (2006)
39. Sousa, K., Mendonça, H., Lievyns, A., Vanderdonckt, J.: Getting users involved in aligning their needs with business processes models and systems. Bus. Process Manag. J. **17**(5), 748–786 (2011)
40. Trkman, P., Klun, M.: Leveraging social media for process innovation. a conceptual framework. In: vom Brocke, J., Schmiedel, T. (eds.) BPM - Driving Innovation in a Digital World. MP, pp. 59–73. Springer, Cham (2015). https://doi.org/10.1007/978-3-319-14430-6_5
41. Ravesteyn, P., Batenburg, R.: Surveying the critical success factors of BPM-systems implementation. Bus. Process Manag. J. **16**(3), 492–507 (2010)
42. Taylor, H.: Outsourced IT projects from the vendor perspective: different goals, different risks. J. Glob. Inf. Manag. **15**(2), 1–27 (2007)
43. Pradabwong, J., Braziotis, C., Tannock, J.D.T., Pawar, K.S.: Business process management and supply chain collaboration: effects on performance and competitiveness. Supply Chain Manag: Int. J. **22**(2), 107–121 (2017)
44. Ohlsson, J., Han, S., Johannesson, P., Carpenhall, F., Rusu, L.: Prioritizing business processes improvement initiatives: the seco tools case. In: Jarke, M., et al. (eds.) CAiSE 2014. LNCS, vol. 8484, pp. 256–270. Springer, Cham (2014). https://doi.org/10.1007/978-3-319-07881-6_18
45. Herzig, S.E., Jimmieson, N.L.: Middle managers' uncertainty management during organizational change. Leadersh. Organ. Dev. J. **27**(8), 628–645 (2006)
46. Aladwani, A.M.: Change management strategies for successful ERP implementation. Bus. Process Manag. J. **7**(3), 266–275 (2001)
47. Orlikowski, W.J., Baroudi, J.J.: Studying information technology in organizations: research approaches and assumptions. Inf. Syst. Res. **2**(1), 1–28 (1991)
48. Gregor, S.: The nature of theory in information systems. MIS Q. **30**(611–642), 2006 (2006)

BP-IT Alignment in SMEs: A Game-Based Learning Approach to Increase Stakeholders' Maturity

Mahi Samir Ismail[✉] and Ralf Klischewski

German University in Cairo, New Cairo City, Egypt
{mahi.samir,ralf.klischewski}@guc.edu.eg

Abstract. This research addresses the lack of sufficient guidance to SMEs with regards to how BP-IT alignment can be achieved in an affordable and scalable manner. The design science approach focused on SME managers and consultants as potential users of the *Aligner* that incorporates game-based training for raising awareness and maturity building. The deliverables are the *Aligner* design manual, a game design document as well as a prototype of the user interface, all of which can be considered a blueprint for game production. All parts of the blueprint are based on theoretical grounding and/or support from the literature and were demonstrated to and evaluated with the relevant stakeholders. Evaluation by representatives of both user groups indicate that the concept and UI prototype of the *Aligner* are indeed suitable for addressing SME-specific circumstances of BP-IT alignment. Given also the affordance and scalability of a gamified solution in principle, the validated blueprints promise to be useful for the development and application of practical games and incorporate transferable know-how for BPM-related game design regarding BP-IT alignment in SMEs.

Keywords: Business process management · Strategic alignment · BP-IT alignment · SMEs · Design science · Gamification · Game-based learning

1 Introduction

The alignment between IT and business has been in top three of the most important IT management issues for many years (Kappelman et al. 2019), and also business process management (BPM) requires the successful integration of change management, IT management, and project management. As companies are proceeding with digital transformation, a holistic process-oriented view seems to be even more important, and the conceptualization and measurement of maturity in business process orientation has been on the research agenda for more than a decade (e.g. Willaert et al. 2007).

However, the organizational challenges faced during the process of aligning IT with the business processes vary depending on factors like industry, size and business strategy. In particular, small and medium enterprises (SMEs) tend to struggle with BPM from concept to implementation and often lack the capability of appropriately integrating processes, people and technology. While SMEs are essential for both developed and

© Springer Nature Switzerland AG 2020
D. Fahland et al. (Eds.): BPM 2020, LNCS 12168, pp. 400–416, 2020.
https://doi.org/10.1007/978-3-030-58666-9_23

developing economies, only few research attempts address the need for an IT-business alignment solution that fits the specific SMEs circumstances.

In search for a solution which guides the IT-business alignment practice and which is easily scalable and affordable for SMEs, we focus on a game-based learning approach for providing the know-how of BP-IT alignment specifically to stakeholders in SMEs and their environment, aiming to increase the maturity of their alignment activities. Accordingly, the question of this research is "How can a game-based learning approach support SMEs in their alignment of IT with their business processes?" A design science approach was chosen, and contextualization, demonstration and evaluation of the artifact were carried out in Egypt, where SMEs are also considered a main pillar of economic growth and employment.

This paper is structured as follows. After analyzing the BP-IT alignment challenges in SMEs, the research methodology and its corresponding findings are presented in terms of design science phases. Then, the research contribution is related to other game-based learning attempts in the BPM area, and the conclusion reflects on the research limitations and points to future research.

2   BP-IT Alignment Challenges in SMEs

The support of information technology (IT) for business processes is one of the key success factors of BPM. IT can provide a variety of functions within business processes, and it may have various roles in business process re-engineering (Eardley et al. 2008). The BP-IT alignment is part of the overall effort of strategically aligning business and IT (e.g. Avison et al. 1996). This not just a single-time activity but rather a constant balancing action (Burn 1997). IT alignment could be nurtured as a cultural phenomenon where all associates within the firm and business partners not only care about it but also attempt to integrate it in how they do their job (Chan and Reich 2007). Meanwhile large organizations have mostly understood that they can ensure the effective use of IT in business improvement only through a clearly focused integration between corporate strategy and IT strategy, both of which now being increasingly merged as a digital strategy (Schallmo et al. 2018; Yeow et al. 2018). However, SMEs cannot simply follow the same path.

The term 'SME' covers multiple definitions and measures that vary from one country to another. The criteria, based on which SMEs are defined, mostly include the number of employees, total net assets, sales and investment level. Notably, the most common foundation for definition is employment, and along that line SMEs are defined to have up to 250 employees (Ayyagari et al. 2007). SMEs dominate the economic structure also in Egypt just as in most other Mediterranean countries (El-Saady 2011) and are perceived as an enabler to sustainable growth and a dynamic employment force in developing countries (El-Said et al. 2014).

There are many factors that characterize SMEs and differentiate them from large firms in terms of both internal and external business operations. For instance, with less internal differentiation in SMEs, many capabilities like strategic planning, purchasing and information technology infrastructure tend to be more centralized (Hong and Jeong 2006). While for some decades of the last millennium ICT usage as well as internet penetration was clearly lacking behind in SMEs, the gap between larger firms and SMEs is still significant but narrowing (Barba-Sánchez et al. 2007). Hicks et al. (2006) have shown that IT in general may still be considered a problem area for SMEs, as the main issues recognized by SMEs were related to a failure in the information exchange both internally between applications and with external entities.

SMEs like all operating enterprises entail a number of business processes. However, SMEs have always faced considerable challenges in integrating IT into their business processes, often leading to a failure (Brown and Lockett 2004). Bazhenova et al. (2012) argue that SMEs make limited use of BPM concepts due to the lack of entrepreneurs' confidence in attaining the benefits of BPM as well as to the management's adherence to obsolete principles. For example, SMEs make only little use of IT systems to measure business performance (Placide et al. 2008). Often this is due to operating inadequate information systems. Inadequacy here means the lack of several performance characteristics such as capability of handling integrated data from numerous sources, ability to present data and/or information in real time to users, reducing the probability of data overload via supplying the right users with performance information, proving reliability through delivering accurate performance information to its users, and facilitating access of information (Garengo and Bititci 2007; Aranda and Arellano 2010; Taylor and Taylor 2014).

The literature does provide guidelines for strategic IT alignment (e.g. Avison et al. 2004; Chan et al. 2006) as well as for applying BPM and BPR with a focus on alignment of IT with business processes (e.g. Miao 2010; Santos et al. 2008). Yet, all of these approaches have no clear distinctiveness for SMEs, i.e. it lacks alignment approaches that take into account the specific challenges of SMEs in BPM. It is certainly true also for SMEs that "a better organization of business processes and a strong culture can be beneficial towards any company, regardless of the number of employees" (Şerban 2015). Therefore SMEs should not be discouraged to reap the potential benefits of BPM, and the classic BPM lifecycle for optimizing business process and aligning the necessary human, technological and other resources with strategic goals (Lederer et al. 2017) should be the basis also for SMEs. However, SMEs often face a lack of capabilities needed to accomplish successful BP-IT alignment, thus bearing a higher risk of failure to their BPM activities.

Extant research not having addressed the still noticeable lack of BPM competencies in SMEs is considered as the research gap and as the starting point for the design science journey. The artifacts aims to increase the maturity of the stakeholders involved in alignment, i.e. mainly management, BP owners, IT decision makers, and consultants. Here 'maturity' firstly relates to the individual capabilities of understanding the challenges and accomplishing the BP-IT alignment. However, the individual gains will only have a sustainable effect when increasing the BP-IT alignment capabilities of the SME as an organization – e.g. moving from *ad hoc* approaches to more systematic and controlled activities – just as maturity is used as a measure to evaluate organizational capabilities in software development or BPM (Rosemann and De Bruin 2005). This is in line with the shifting focus of alignment research to focus on the continuous process of interrelating IT and business resources (Yeow et al. 2018).

Building up and strengthening BPM competencies in SMEs in support of BP-IT alignment must take into account that (a) SMEs have, in comparison, less resources for training and consultancy and (b) the number of SMEs is huge and therefore personal interaction might not be a viable option on a large scale. Considering affordance and scalability as the main requirements, we focus on game-based learning. The idea of game-based learning is to teach knowledge and/or skills using a game, which is a contained unit with a definitive start, game play and ending (Kapp 2012). In the same line, Gartner (Burke 2014) defined gamification as "the use of game mechanics and experience design to digitally engage and motivate people to achieve their goals." A serious game typically comprises a primary purpose, target audience, technology strategy, core gameplay, and key mechanics, while each element varies from a single organizational scenario to the other (Raftopoulos and Greuter 2015).

The application of game-based learning in the enterprise has shown to be an effective catalyst to many business processes, and a valid solution to multiple organizational problems including technological illiteracy, employee compliance issues, employee lack of motivation and many more (Baxter et al. 2017; Friedrich et al. 2020; Larson 2020). Specifically, Kapp (2012) stated that gamification is helpful for scenarios where the leaders must constantly update their employees' knowledge, which is the case in almost every automation process or IT-related scenario. However, exploitation, manipulation, harms, as well as social negative impacts are some of the ethical issues that were found as drawbacks of the gamification practice in enterprises (Kim and Werbach 2016). These pros and cons of game-based learning apply also to SMEs.

3 Methodology: Designing and Evaluating the *Aligner*

The research adopted a design science approach as outlined by Peffers et al. (2007). Accordingly, the following sections present methodology and results of the phases through which the artefact (named *Aligner*) has been created and evaluated with the aim of supporting SMEs in their alignment of IT with their business processes.

The research model shown in Fig. 1 illustrates the two types of stakeholders that are intended to use the artifact. The key figure is the SME manager (CEO, CIO, BP owner, head of IT, or whoever is responsible for the alignment; could be more than one per company) who is challenged with addressing the problem "how to align" between the business processes of the SME and its IT (including external IT capabilities). The alignment is conceptualized as three stages: clarifying expectations before IT implementation and/or BPR, activities during implementation (e.g. change management, system customization), and evaluation of alignment results after implementation and utilization. The model also proposes the IT and/or BP consultant as a possible use case. The main role of the consultant is to advise the SME manager, i.e. to contribute to competency building and raising maturity (and not to replace the internal role).

3.1 Problem Identification and Objectives of the Artifact

The artifact outcomes and the design objectives were developed on the basis of data collected from interviews along with re-visiting the literature. The literature review indicated

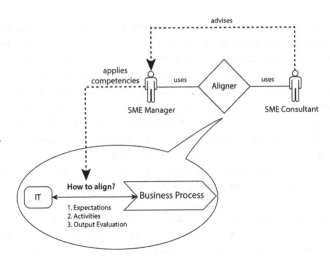

Fig. 1. Research model for designing and evaluating the *Aligner* artifact

that the lack of specific BP-IT alignment guidance constitutes a problem for SMEs. To confirm this problem identification in practice and to develop a better understanding of the problem dimensions, an interview guide was designed as the data collection instrument. The aim was to address the three stages of IT alignment to the SMEs business processes (see Fig. 1) through inquiring details about acquiring the IT solution, the management expectations prior to implementation, the method of following up on the role of IT in their company, the activities done during implementation from both internal and external stakeholders, whether the expectations were met, and finally the method of measuring the return on IT investment. The semi-structured interviews were conducted with three SME managers as well as two experienced IT consultants in Egypt in order to obtain in-depth multi-dimensional knowledge about the alignment challenges in SMEs. After documenting the interview recordings[1], main issues faced by SMEs were analyzed according to the three stages of alignment in the research model. One company was identified as an outlier because the main IT used was only an online tool without relation to core business processes, and accordingly the aforementioned alignment phases were non-existent in that case.

In order to ensure the practicality and appropriateness of the artifact design, another survey[2] was developed and administered for the purpose of clarifying the typical SME managers' needs with regards to game utilization. This instrument allowed for efficiently reaching a wider scope of SME managers as the *Aligner's* main target user. The questionnaire was based on the experience design process and method proposed by Kim et al. (2011). 16 SME managers were surveyed in order to identify the main game design

---

[1] The full interviews are available at https://drive.google.com/file/d/1JW8nZ7sMaHTPXDu9W RMypXvidBfCqaLZ/view?usp=sharing.

[2] The survey details are available at https://drive.google.com/file/d/1vgo9fm6XDKs8qzyY0OKV hd86duVyUuPL/view?usp=sharing.

needs for ensuring the highest possible user likeability, understandability and eventually learning impact.

3.2 Design and Development of the Artifact

Implementing a full game was out of the scope of this research. Hence, the artifact includes only the blueprints for a gamified learning tool which aim to provide the recipe required for the game-based learning that can be implemented in multiple forms: mobile game, video game or through an online web application.

The design and development phase started with developing the game concept and ideology. The game-based learning literature was analyzed to ensure the inclusion of important gamification features. The most common game mechanics were identified to be: achievements, exercises and synchronizing with the community, time and luck cf. (Dale 2014). Based on the artifact design objectives as well as the game needs survey results, achievements, exercises, synchronizing with the community and time were chosen to be incorporated in the solution design. The solution was planned with the intention to fulfill each one of the design objectives (see Sect. 4.1) in order to maximize the potential of achieving the desired outcomes. Case-based learning was applied to address the first and sixth objectives 'Include and communicate the BP-IT alignment lessons learned' and 'Provide case-based learning'. 'Entail step-by-step (sequential) learning' was met through providing a phased approach to the *Aligner*, in which each phase has levels and each level builds up knowledge based on the previous levels. Integrating the alignment phases (as per research model) with theoretical material aimed to satisfy the third and eighth objectives 'Provide the know-how of integrating IT into their business processes' and 'the artifact should cover the three alignment phases'. In order to accomplish the objective 'Easy to use by managers', it was planned to conduct feedback interviews in the evaluation phase.

Furthermore, there are two gamification learning practices: retrieval practice and spaced retrieval combined, they form a strong basis for increased learning and retention of knowledge. Retrieval practice involves the learner recalling information previously communicated in the game, whereas the idea behind spaced retrieval is to space the content provided to the learners over time rather than all at once (Kapp 2012). Both learning practices were used to reach the objective 'It should have an interactive app-roach'. Finally, certain elements of games were used to guarantee effective game-based learning challenge, immediate feedback (score and providing correct answer after the user submission), problem-solving, a sense of accomplishment, autonomy and mastery (trophies, leader board and user profiles).

3.3 Demonstration and Evaluation

The demonstration of the solution was used to test the understandability and logic of the *Aligner* for both target groups, i.e. SME managers and consultants. The demonstration process conducted included first introducing and briefly explaining the purpose of the *Aligner* to the SME managers, then presenting the design manual and going through its different levels. They would then evaluate the *Aligner's* usability through answering the evaluation criteria questions prepared for the next phase. Finally, the interviewees were asked a pre-established list of questions before and after playing the *Aligner* using the UI developed in order to test their understanding of BP-IT alignment and whether the game increases their level of maturity. The UI prototype was tested in the evaluation phase with two managers in one of the SMEs interviewed in the data collection phase. The demonstration process with the consultants/experts took on similar steps except for not asking to play the game but allowing the experts to read the content of the UI design through which the design features are highlighted. This was followed by noting down their impressions and comments with regards to the concept and game design. The GDD was not included in the evaluation phase as the focus here was on understandability and user experience and the developer was accordingly not seen as a relevant stakeholder to the game outcomes.

To evaluate the artifact, the IT consultants were subjected to two rounds of feedback interviews. The criteria for artifact evaluation were selected from the set of criteria provided by Prat et al. (2014) classified into goal, environment, structure, activity and evolution. The first round of evaluation took place after developing both the game design manual as well as part of the UI which had not yet been finalized. In the first round of interviews, the *Aligner* design manual was fully showcased to two consultants who have dealt with several SME clients and only a few screenshots of the *Aligner* UI were presented. They were asked to evaluate the solution according to the criteria selected. After the game design manual and UI were developed, a feedback interview was conducted with a different third consultant in the second iteration who was also asked to evaluate after carrying out a full demonstration on all artifact components. The list of criteria addressed to the consultants in the feedback interviews to evaluate the artifact included validity, generalizability, understandability, ease of use, fitness with target organizations (SMEs), simplicity to the target users (SME managers), clarity, level of detail sufficiency, and utility to people and organizations.

The second iteration also involved an evaluation with a sample SME, including answering a set of questions[3] before and after the manager playing the *Aligner* as well as directly asking about the selected criteria, i.e. performance, efficacy, and utility. The intention was to test the user's understanding before and after playing the *Aligner* to view if there would be any difference in the user's maturity with regards to the three alignment phases.

Finally, communication of the research findings included direct communication with the practice stakeholders involved in the research. Academically, the work has been submitted as M.Sc. thesis as a basis for this submission. Dissemination of the artifact for further development and application in practice is still under consideration.

4 The *Aligner* as a Maturity Accelerator

4.1 Problem Identification and Objectives of the Artifact

The interviews largely confirmed the research problem identified upfront, yet they provided further depth to the research problem with regards to the problems faced by SMEs that specifically impact their BPM-IT alignment:

---

[3] Full testing questionnaire with the SME manager's before & after results is available at: https://drive.google.com/file/d/1WdkNdSBQ7PvDbIVm2UFeHCcWOfI0Sca0/view?usp=sharing.

- SME managers generally understand the necessity of process automation and their *expectations* extend to a variety of benefits of IT usage in their companies. However, they lack the awareness of the need to follow up on the role of IT in their company, they have unclear ROI expectations and do not envision a change management initiative as a BPR/BPM success factor.
- SMEs are usually unready for the solution implementation in the *activities* phase as they provide data of low quality to the consultants and/or vendors. Not only do the SME clients almost never have an internal team dedicated for the implementation, but it was also stated that there is no valid form of following up neither on the system's alignment with strategy nor on the system's functionality with regards to their business needs. Additionally, neither proper testing nor analysis takes place to understand their business problem and their need for BPM. It has also been mentioned that SME clients typically do not understand the IT consultants' plans or any of their approaches to provide BPM services or to achieve the IT alignment. The issues leading to failed alignment include the non-existent awareness when it comes to the selection of the solution as well as insufficient analysis carried out by internal management. The SME managers select the solution based on trustworthiness and price, with little consideration for technical integration or business process alignment.
- Results of analyzing the answers to the questions tackling the *evaluation* phase include the insufficient business needs analysis from the SME's side which is due to not being aware of the importance of such activity, leading to improper understanding of this alignment between technical and business dimensions in their company. There is neither a standardized nor a consistent way of continuously evaluating the solution in relation to their ongoing business processes. None of the SME managers interviewed expressed a need for evaluation; however, methods to obtain the return on their investment included speed of operations, higher productivity and efficiency.

The following desired outcomes of the artifact were the result of the analysis: increase SME managers' overall understanding of the role of IT in their company business processes, increase SMEs' ability to align BPR with IT, increase SME managers' confidence in attaining the benefits of BPM-making (Bazhenova et a. 2012), and finally to teach the critical role interdependence plays between technology, practice, and strategy (Akhavan et al. 2006). These outcomes are what the research artifact aims to achieve in order to solve the research problem.

The results of the game needs survey showed that the autonomy need was dominant, which is why the game should entail a unique private user profile that displays their status and where they stand in the game. The factor competence also represented major importance to the survey respondents, accordingly, a trophies system was created in order to encourage a sense of achievement and boost the users' self-confidence regarding their performance. The online gaming approach was found to be the most suitable so as to connect the different managers across the enterprise, allowing the generation of the relatedness factor since it averagely scores third in priority. Accordingly, managers get to view the other users' current game status and the trophies collected as well as to engage together to a certain extent in a few of the game sections.

The main artifact design objectives can be summarized as follows: include and communicate the BPR-IT alignment lessons learned; entail step-by-step (sequential) learning; provide the know-how of integrating IT into their business processes; it should be easy to use by SME managers and have an interactive approach; provide case-based learning; it should have a scoring model that forms the feedback to the user based on questions and answers; the artifact should cover the BPR-IT expectations; activities during implementation, and IT alignment evaluation.

4.2   Design and Development of the *Aligner*

The artifact deliverables include a game design manual, a game design document (GDD) and a prototype of the User Interface (UI). According to practitioner's recommendation, each deliverable was developed for a different target group: the game design manual is for the game designer who is responsible for the designs and layouts of the game; the game design document is for the game developer who turns those designs into a functioning game; and the UI prototype is for demonstration and evaluation purposes.

The *Aligner* design manual[4] comprises two sections, one that discusses the theoretical background of the *Aligner*, followed by the storyline section containing the script of all *Aligner* phases shown in Fig. 2. Each phase consists of separate levels that the user must pass in order to move on to the next phase. Essentially, the *Aligner* consists of three main phases according to the three identified alignment stages, i.e. expectations, activities and evaluation. The levels were created in order to tackle different sub-concepts that are crucial to ensure the user understanding of the phase through the use of cases. The cases upon which the potential game users are tested were selected based on the BPM lifecycle (Dumas et al. 2013) considering the close relation between the lifecycle phases and the BP-IT alignment stages identified in the research model. Eventually, the BP-IT alignment itself accounts only for a smaller fraction of the *Aligner* content because user must acquire important pre-requisite knowledge in order to fully understand the BPM-IT alignment material that is introduced towards the end of the game.

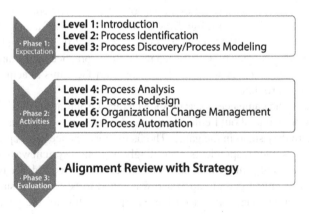

Fig. 2.   The *Aligner's* hierarchy of levels.

---

[4] The full *Aligner* Design Manual is available at https://drive.google.com/file/d/1qmuteISwek1 jXeBZzyArTGwTM0IiMA0H/view?usp=sharing.

Stage 1 "Expectations" comprises three levels. The first one is an introductory level that provides the user with the minimum of understanding required to proceed with the game (Dumas et al. 2013), and Levels 2 and 3 were mapped to the first two stages in the BPM lifecycle,

Stage 2 "Activities" consists of four different levels. Levels 4 and 5 were mapped to the third and fourth stages in the BPM lifecycle, respectively. Levels 6 and 7 follow the main concepts of the fifth stage in the lifecycle as explained by Dumas et al. (2013, p. 2). However, the content of Level 6 was taken from Scheer et al. (2003), solely focusing on BP change management activities. And the content of Level 7 was obtained from the process automation chapter of Dumas et al. (2013; 297–347).

Stage 3 "Evaluation" is designed to develop the users' awareness of the need to assess their IT alignment as well as their ability to do so. Accordingly, it clarifies the role of IT alignment in a case company followed by an application exercise through which users may relate to their own SME scenario. The case used is based on real life case (as described by a local advertising agency director) to specify KPIs, strategy and business needs as realistic as possible. The second question, inspired by the strategic alignment model by Avison et al. (2004), focuses on the strategic alignment between IT and the business strategy (obtained as an input from the user in Level 2). The last question provides the user with the knowhow needed to assess the IT alignment with the business performance based on the KPIs obtained from the user in the opening page of the *Aligner* (see Fig. 3).

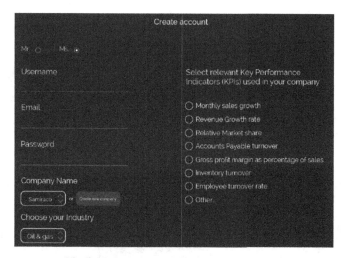

Fig. 3. Opening page (clipping) of the *Aligner*

The scoring, more specifically the trophy system, in the *Aligner* is based on the progressive percentage concept as in the BPR maturity model proposed by Ramzi et al. (2016). There are a total of five trophies in the game: 1-'*Kick-Start*' is obtained by the end of the introduction level regardless of the score or amount of correct answers obtained by the user as it is based on the initial maturity level, which does not yet demonstrate any development in the user's expectations. This trophy is granted to the user regardless of his/her performance, only as a form of boosting their self-confidence and sense of achievement. As soon as the user has correctly solved 15% of the game after level 2, the 2-'*all-set*' trophy is received along with the user's initial 150 points. After correctly solving 50% and 70% of the game after Level 2, the third and fourth trophy are received, respectively. Finally, the *Aligner* trophy is only granted when the user is able to solve 100% of the game correctly. Apart from the trophy system, each question is given 50 points, and each trophy grants 100 extra bonus points. This is how the score is calculated for each user.

The prototype of the UI[5] was designed by a professional graphic designer to whom the results of the game needs survey and the design objectives were communicated. The UI development entailed regular meetings to ensure that the UI reflects the core game concepts and functionality for higher validity of demonstration and evaluation results. It mainly shows samples of the different question types, the various features that fulfill the several game needs including the user profile and the company scoreboard (see Fig. 4). The user profile shows the user status in the *Aligner* along with a leader-board on the right hand side that displays the status of the user in comparison to those of the other managers in the same company. This feature would only exist in the multi-player mode. The color palette was meant to have a darker nature as explained in the GDD to give the user a sense of elegance and seniority to fit with the company managers as target users for the game. The GDD[6] is a document through which the core concepts necessary for the game development are shown along with the game play and the game mechanism.

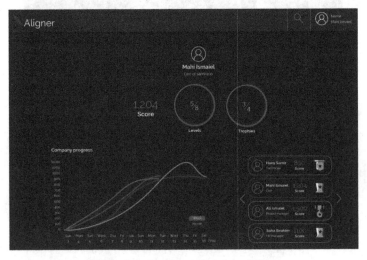

Fig. 4. Sample user profile of the *Aligner*

---

[5] The UI design is available at https://drive.google.com/file/d/1UuIJ1tbX45AMRTt8WMbnZDQ 64nEDDWAa/view?usp=sharing.

[6] The full GDD is available at https://drive.google.com/file/d/1-BR6teKO-3ZbWzv3aOakknTD UMKZPfV6/view?usp=sharing.

4.3   Demonstration and Evaluation: Increasing Stakeholders' Maturity?

The first round of demonstration and feedback interviews revealed some significant comments and suggestions. The artifact suggestions were all based on the consultants' conduct with their clients and the awareness level they believed was needed from the clients' end. For example, one consultant proposed the idea of allowing the user to specify certain benefits/expectations during the expectations phase to be used later on in the evaluation phase in order to assess the extent of fulfillment to these benefits. Other suggestions included: adding more options in different MCQs; "process automation" (level 7) as a focus to allow the user to propose how automation can be executed in certain scenarios; translating the *Aligner* into Arabic for reaching the local user base (however, this remained controversial among the consultants). In general, efficacy and validity were rated "high" (out of low, moderate or high), the ease of use was rated "high" and also the simplicity and clarity of message. Generalizability was rated "high" for industrial sectors with strong SME participation (assuming that the game will not be relevant in industries with complicated processes like oil & gas or car manufacturing).

The second round of demonstration and evaluation included a feedback interview with another consultancy. The interviewee believed the word 'IT' can be slightly misleading for SMEs based on his experience with clients. However, his feedback was generally positive as he described the *Aligner* as a solution particularly to those SMEs that have clear objectives, which could even benefit third parties (like themselves) through facilitating the consultation and knowledge transfer needed to deliver successful projects. The only threat from his perspective was that *Aligner's* success is largely dependent on the user who is playing, implying that the target segment should only be the ones who are willing to learn and change their company to the better. The validity of solution was ranked high but generalizability was ranked low since it would work only with a specific type of SME managers. Understandability was rated as high, yet emphasizing the need for Arabic translation.

The SME manager described the *Aligner* as easy to use, simple, clear with sufficient level of detail, and that the nature of the game fits with the target organizations (SMEs). A dynamic method of user interaction like audios or videos was suggested. The quality of the solution in practical use to people was rated as 4, whereas, for organizations as 3–4 (out of 1 = lowest to 5 = highest). Finally, the manager solved the questions before and after playing the *Aligner* manually on paper during the feedback session. The results indicated that the user's understanding increased after playing the game as his answers to many of the questions changed. The interviewee's evaluation results to the *Aligner* were similar to that of the consultant in this round of evaluation.

5   Contribution to Game-Based Learning of BPM

The deliverables of this research are the *Aligner* design manual, the game design document as well as a prototype of the user interface, all of which can be considered as blueprints for game production. All parts of the blueprint are created based on theoretical grounding and/or support from the literature. Some of the game levels are even in line with approaches of the big players in the field; e.g. the communication management and the introduction of different training phases and types at Level 6 (Organizational

Change Management) in the *Aligner* design manual has shown great resemblance with the change management plan utilized by SAP (as participating consultant at an SAP partner has confirmed during evaluation).

A few attempts towards gamification in the area of BPM exist, but not in the same directions as this research. For example, Elise Olding (research director at Gartner) argues that the appropriate gamification could tackle BPM challenges such as creating a culture of continuous improvement, sharing best practices and having process visibility (Mak 2012). To that end, she provides rather general recommendations (which have been taken into account also in our design process) including defining process objectives, metrics and desired outcomes; understanding what works in a particular culture; assign value to each activity or task; planning for iterations and increasing the challenges; finding the needed skills to help with user interface design, game design or implementation. However, the Gartner report discusses the gamification of business processes as such (with the aim to foster continuous improvement), but does not address the issue of IT alignment.

From the research perspective, a well-elaborated approach (also based on a design science) is the gamification of collaborative business process modeling as presented by Pflanzl (2016): the prototype provides an experimental set of quality metrics addressing aspects of the readability, understandability and completeness of process models and has been tested and evaluated through a controlled student experiment. Typical game elements such as points, badges and a leaderboard were implemented so that users would learn more about the quality of business process modeling. However, the deliverables of this research do not include a game manual or a game design document that could serve as a transferrable blueprints.

Mancebo et al. (2017) presented a tool that supports the definition of games on BPMS platforms and enables their evaluation from execution logs. The authors aim to improve the sustainability of business processes through encouraging users to be more environmentally friendly, and to that end they proposed different process measures. The transferable deliverables include a UML diagram of the domain model as well as list of derived measures proposed to assess sustainability. The research elaborates more on the (required) game functionalities, however, it does not report about any test or evaluation of the game.

Pflanzl and Vossen (2018) concluded that the current state of the art offers numerous possibilities for research at the intersection between process modelling and games, among which finding new application scenarios in other phases of the BPM life cycle. The unique contribution of this research is that it has created blueprints for the gamification of disseminating knowledge and raising awareness regarding the BP-IT alignment, taking into account the specific circumstances of SMEs – both of which had not been addressed by research before.

The *Aligner* as the artifact in focus received a somewhat positive evaluation. However, this research could not test the actual effect of utilizing the *Aligner*'s in context with respect to increasing motivational affordances, raising maturity and invoking expected behavioral outcomes. Hence, the question "Does gamification work?" (Hamari et al. 2014), i.e. whether the *Aligner* actually supports SMEs in their alignment of IT with their business processes, remains to be answered in future research.

6 Conclusion

This research aimed to address the problem of insufficient BP-IT alignment in SMEs, and the research gap was found to be the lack of sufficient guidance to SMEs with regards to how BP-IT alignment can be achieved in an affordable and scalable manner. The design science approach focused on SME managers and IT consultants as the stakeholders and potential users of the artifact that incorporates gamified training for raising awareness and maturity building. The deliverables are the *Aligner* design manual, a game design document as well as a prototype of the user interface, all of which can be considered a blueprint for game production. All parts of the blueprint are created based on theoretical grounding and/or support from the literature. The blueprints were demonstrated through various ways to both relevant stakeholders, and feedback of the first iteration was incorporated into the design. Evaluation by representatives of both user groups indicate that the concept and UI prototype of the *Aligner* are indeed suitable for addressing SME-specific circumstances of BP-IT alignment, particularly to build up maturity from a basic level of understanding.

The research contribution could be allocated to the field of business process orientation and/or of process-aware organizations. The validated blueprints are useful for practical game development and application and provide transferable know-how for BPM-related game design regarding BP-IT alignment in SMEs. Given also the affordance and scalability of a gamified solution in principle, the developed artifact has the potential of contributing to raising alignment maturity in SMEs.

Limitations of the research include:

- Aging of basic BPM literature and limited sources with the needed level of depth; in result some cases in the game (e.g. a university case) lack relevance to SMEs.
- Some game aspects were "tweaked" to suit the audience targeted and to increased likeability and decrease complexity; this may have reduced the reliability of the knowledge dissemination
- The *Aligner* does not touch on all aspects regarding the BPM lifecycle and how to properly carry out its activities; only qualitative process analysis is introduced in level 4 to users (since the consultants emphasized on the need to provide lowest level of complexity possible with the highest level of knowledge provision).
- A low number of interviews conducted in both the data collection and the evaluation phases as well as possible bias of interviewees challenge the generalizability of the results.
- Time and other resource limitation resulted in limiting the game to only a blueprint rather than a fully functioning game, i.e. not being able to carry out a full demonstration and evaluation. In particular, the effect of utilizing the *Aligner* on BP-IT alignment in an SME context was not tested.

Future research should involve a higher number of the stakeholders to increase the findings' generalizability, develop a full game for demonstration and evaluation, and perform longitudinal case studies to test the impact on alignment capabilities and maturity in context. Furthermore, the game design would highly benefit from the competition aspect (as indicated in game needs survey), and this needs further understanding in order to successfully improve game features as well as game outcomes.

References

Akhavan, P., Jafari, M., Ali-Ahmadi, A.R.: Exploring the interdependency between reengineering and information technology by developing a conceptual model. Bus. Process Manag. J. **12**(4), 517–534 (2006)

Aranda, C., Arellano, J.: Strategic performance measurement systems and managers' understanding of the strategy: a field research in a financial institution. J. Account. Organ. Change **6**(3), 330–358 (2010)

Avison, D., Jones, J., Powell, P., Wilson, D.: Using and validating the strategic alignment model. J. Strateg. Inf. Syst. **13**(3), 223–246 (2004)

Avison, D.E., Eardley, W.A., Powell, P.: How strategic are strategic information systems? Aust. J. Inf. Syst. **4**(1), 11–20 (1996)

Ayyagari, M., Beck, T., Demirgüç-Kunt, A.: Small and medium enterprises across the globe. Small Bus. Econ. **29**(4), 415–434 (2007). https://doi.org/10.1007/s11187-006-9002-5

Barba-Sánchez, V., Martínez-Ruiz, M.D.P., Jiménez-Zarco, A.I.: Drivers, benefits and challenges of ICT adoption by small and medium sized enterprises (SMEs): a literature review. Probl. Perspect. Manag. **5**(1), 103–114 (2007)

Bazhenova, E., Taratukhin, V., Becker, J.: Impact of information and communication technologies on business process management on small and medium enterprises in the emerging countries. In: Proceedings 11th International Conference of Perspectives in Business Informatics Research, Nizhny Novgorod, Russia, pp. 65–74 (2012)

Baxter, R.J., Holderness Jr., D.K., Wood, D.A.: The effects of gamification on corporate compliance training: a partial replication and field study of true office anti-corruption training programs. J. Forensic Acc. Res. **2**(1), A20–A30 (2017)

Brown, D.H., Lockett, N.: Potential of critical e-applications for engaging SMEs in e-business: a provider perspective. Eur. J. Inf. Syst. **13**(1), 21–34 (2004)

Burke, B.: Gartner Redefines Gamification. Gartner Blog Network, 4 April 2014 (2014). https://blogs.gartner.com/brian_burke/2014/04/04/gartner-redefines-gamification/

Burn, J.M.: A professional balancing act – walking the tightrope of strategic alignment. In: Sauer, C., Yetton, P.W. (eds.) Steps to the Future – Fresh Thinking on the Management of IT-Based Organizational Transformation, pp. 55–88. Jossey-Bass Publishers, San Francisco (1997)

Chan, Y.E., Reich, B.H.: IT alignment: an annotated bibliography. J. Inf. Technol. **22**(4), 316–396 (2007)

Chan, Y.E., Sabherwal, R., Thatcher, J.B.: Antecedents and outcomes of strategic IS alignment: an empirical investigation. IEEE Trans. Eng. Manag. **53**(1), 27–47 (2006)

Dale, S.: Gamification: making work fun, or making fun of work? Bus. Inf. Rev. **31**(2), 82–90 (2014)

Dumas, M., La Rosa, M., Mendling, J., Reijers, H.A.: Fundamentals of Business Process Management. Springer, Heidelberg (2013). https://doi.org/10.1007/978-3-642-33143-5

Eardley, A., Shah, H., Radman, A.: A model for improving the role of IT in BPR. Bus. Process Manag. J. **14**(5), 629–653 (2008)

El-Saady, R.: The role of SMEs in Mediterranean economies: The Egyptian experience SME unit. General Authority for Investment, Cairo (2011)

El-Said, H., Al-Said, M., Zaki, C.: Small and medium enterprises landscape in Egypt: new facts from a new dataset. Int. J. Entrepreneurship Small Bus. **20**(3), 286–309 (2014)

Friedrich, J., Becker, M., Kramer, F., Wirth, M., Schneider, M.: Incentive design and gamification for knowledge management. J. Bus. Res. **106**, 341–352 (2020)

Garengo, P., Bititci, U.: Towards a contingency approach to performance measurement: an empirical study in Scottish SMEs. Int. J. Oper. Prod. Manag. **27**(8), 802–825 (2007)

Hamari, J., Koivisto, J., Sarsa, H.: Does gamification work? A literature review of empirical studies on gamification. In: Proceedings 47th Hawaii International Conference on System Sciences, pp. 3025–3034. IEEE (2014)

Hicks, B.J., Culley, S.J., McMahon, C.A.: A study of issues relating to information management across engineering SMEs. Int. J. Inf. Manag. **26**(4), 267–289 (2006)

Hong, P., Jeong, J.: Supply chain management practices of SMEs: from a business growth perspective. J. Enterp. Inf. Manag. **19**(3), 292–302 (2006)

Kapp, K.M.: The Gamification of Learning and Instruction: Game-Based Methods and Strategies for Training and Education. Pfeiffer, San Francisco (2012)

Kappelman, L., Torres, R., McLean, E., Maurer, C., Johnson, V., Kim, K.: The 2018 SIM IT issues and trends study. MIS Q. Executive **18**(1) (2019). Article no. 7

Kim, J., Park, S., Hassenzahl, M., Eckoldt, K.: The essence of enjoyable experiences: the human needs. In: Marcus, A. (ed.) DUXU 2011. LNCS, vol. 6769, pp. 77–83. Springer, Heidelberg (2011). https://doi.org/10.1007/978-3-642-21675-6_9

Kim, T.W., Werbach, K.: More than just a game: ethical issues in gamification. Ethics Inf. Technol. **18**(2), 157–173 (2016). https://doi.org/10.1007/s10676-016-9401-5

Larson, K.: Serious games and gamification in the corporate training environment: a literature review. TechTrends **64**(2), 319–328 (2019). https://doi.org/10.1007/s11528-019-00446-7

Lederer, M., Knapp, J., Schott, P.: The digital future has many names—how business process management drives the digital transformation. In: Proceedings 6th International Conference on Industrial Technology and Management (ICITM), pp. 22–26. IEEE (2017)

Mak, H.W.: Gamification Potential for Business Process Management. Gartner Report, 24 September 2012. https://www.gamification.co/2012/09/24/gartner-bpm-gamification/

Mancebo, J., Garcia, F., Pedreira, O., Moraga, M.A.: BPMS-Game: tool for business process gamification. In: Carmona, J., Engels, G., Kumar, A. (eds.) BPM 2017. LNBIP, vol. 297, pp. 127–140. Springer, Cham (2017). https://doi.org/10.1007/978-3-319-65015-9_8

Miao, Y.-J.: How does the enterprise implement business process reengineering management. In: Proceedings International Conference on E-Business and E-Government, pp. 4100–4102 (2010)

Peffers, K., Tuunanen, T., Rothenberger, M.A., Chatterjee, S.: A design science research methodology for information systems research. J. Manag. Inf. Syst. **24**(3), 45–77 (2007)

Pflanzl, N.: Gameful business process modeling. In: Proceedings 7th International Workshop on Enterprise Modeling and Information Systems Architectures (EMISA). Vienna, Austria, pp. 17–20 (2016)

Pflanzl, N., Vossen, G.: What do business process modelling and super mario bros. have in common? A games-perspective on business process modelling. Int. J. Concept. Model. Spec. Issue Concept. Model. Honour of Heinrich C. Mayr, 69–76 (2018). https://doi.org/10.18417/emisa.si.hcm.7

Placide, P.-N., Raymond, L., Fabi, B.: Adoption and risk of ERP systems in manufacturing SMEs: a positivist case study. Bus. Process Manag. **14**(4), 530–545 (2008)

Prat, N., Comyn-Wattiau, I., Akoka, J.: Artifact evaluation in information systems design-science research-a holistic view. In: Proceeding of the 19th Pacific Asia Conference on Information Systems (PACIS 2014), p. 23 (2014)

Raftopoulos, M., Walz, S., Greuter, S.: How enterprises play: towards a taxonomy for enterprise gamification. In: Proceedings of the Annual Conference of the Digital Games Research Association (2015)

Rosemann, M., De Bruin, T.: Towards a business process management maturity model. In: Proceedings 13th European Conference on Information Systems. Regensburg, Germany, pp. 26–28 May 2005

Santos, J., Sarriegi, J.M., Serrano, N.: A support methodology for EAI and BPM projects in SMEs. Enterp. Inf. Syst. **2**(3), 275–286 (2008)

Schallmo, D., Williams, C.A., Lohse, J.: Clarifying digital strategy – detailed literature review of existing approaches. In: Proceedings 29th ISPIM Innovation Conference, Stockholm, Sweden, pp. 17–20 June 2018

Scheer, A.W., Abolhassan, F., Jost, W., Kirchmer, M.F. (eds.): Business Process Change Management: ARIS in Practice. Springer, Berlin (2003). https://doi.org/10.1007/978-3-540-247 03-6

Şerban, A.I.: Business process reengineering on SME's: evidence from Romanian SME's. In: Proceedings 9th International Management Conference, pp. 175–182 (2015)

Taylor, A., Taylor, M.: Factors influencing effective implementation of performance measurement systems in small and medium-sized enterprises and large firms: a perspective from Contingency Theory. Int. J. Prod. Res. **52**(3), 847–866 (2014)

Willaert, P., Van den Bergh, J., Willems, J., Deschoolmeester, D.: The process-oriented organisation: a holistic view developing a framework for business process orientation maturity. In: Alonso, G., Dadam, P., Rosemann, M. (eds.) BPM 2007. LNCS, vol. 4714, pp. 1–15. Springer, Heidelberg (2007). https://doi.org/10.1007/978-3-540-75183-0_1

Yeow, A., Soh, C., Hansen, R.: Aligning with new digital strategy: a dynamic capabilities approach. J. Strateg. Inf. Syst. **27**, 43–58 (2018)

Understanding Quality in Declarative Process Modeling Through the Mental Models of Experts

Amine Abbad Andaloussi[1]([✉]), Christopher J. Davis[2], Andrea Burattin[1], Hugo A. López[3,5], Tijs Slaats[3], and Barbara Weber[4]

[1] Software and Process Engineering, Technical University of Denmark,
2800 Kgs., Lyngby, Denmark
amab@dtu.dk
[2] University of South Florida, Saint Petersburg, FL, USA
[3] Department of Computer Science, University of Copenhagen, Kbenhavn, Denmark
[4] Institute of Computer Science, University of St. Gallen, St. Gallen, Switzerland
[5] DCR Solutions A/S, Copenhagen, Denmark

Abstract. Imperative process models have become immensely popular. However, their use is usually limited to rigid and repetitive processes. Considering the inherent flexibility in most processes in the real-world and the increased need for managing knowledge-intensive processes, the adoption of declarative languages becomes more pertinent than ever. While the quality of imperative models has been extensively investigated in the literature, little is known about the dimensions affecting the quality of declarative models. This work takes an advanced stride to investigate the quality of declarative models. Following the theory of Personal Construct Psychology (PCT), our research introduces a novel method within the Business Process Management (BPM) field to explore quality in the eyes of expert modelers. The findings of this work summarize the dimensions defining the quality of declarative models. The outcome shows the potential of PCT as a basis to discover quality dimensions and advances our understanding of quality in declarative process models.

Keywords: Process model understandability · Declarative process models · Model quality · Personal construct psychology · Repertory Grid

1 Introduction

In the development of process-aware information systems (PAIS), process models are used for enactment and management purposes [4]. Besides their ability to

A. Abbad Andaloussi, A. Burattin, H.A. López, T. Slaats, B. Weber: Work supported by the Innovation Fund Denmark project *EcoKnow* (7050-00034A). T. Slaats: Work supported by the Danish Council for Independent Research project *Hybrid Business Process Management Technologies* (DFF-6111-00337). H.A. López: Work supported by the European Union's Horizon 2020 research and innovation programme under the Marie Sklodowska-Curie grant agreement BehAPI No. 778233.

D. Fahland et al. (Eds.): BPM 2020, LNCS 12168, pp. 417–434, 2020.
https://doi.org/10.1007/978-3-030-58666-9_24

provide a blueprint for process execution, process models are used for requirement elicitation, communication and process improvement. Process models are expressed using languages from either the *imperative* or *declarative* paradigm. While imperative models describe all the process executions explicitly, declarative models rather specify the constraints guiding the overall process and allow any execution not violating the given constraints to occur. When dealing with rigid and repetitive processes, imperative languages are the best candidates. However, when it comes to knowledge-intensive processes where flexibly is an inherent requirement, imperative languages become unable to represent processes concisely. Alternatively, the constraint-based approach of declarative languages allows abstracting the details of specific process executions and modeling the general interplay of events. The flexibility of declarative languages comes at the cost of their understandability [16]. Considering the rich semantics of declarative languages and the different ways in which constraints can interact, it becomes hard for the reader to infer the process executions allowed by the model [34].

To support the understandability of declarative models, several hybrid representations extending models with textual annotations and simulations have emerged (review in [3]). Nevertheless, understandability challenges remained apparent [1]. Refining models to improve their quality is an alternative to overcome these limitations. While there is a rich body of literature investigating the quality of imperative models (e.g., [10,17,29,30]), only a few contributions exploring the comprehension of declarative models exist (e.g., [20,37]). A review by Corradini et al. [10] identified 50 guidelines addressing the quality of process models. However, many are limited to imperative languages and several of their focal constructs (e.g., gateways, pools and lanes, message events) are not relevant to declarative models. Similarly, the use of a single start event and the necessity to minimize concurrency in the model [10] are guidelines common to imperative modeling that counteract the constraint-based approach of declarative languages. Indeed, declarative models can have several entry-points [37]. Likewise, imposing a sequential-flow would need to over constrain the declarative model, increasing its complexity - and reducing its understandability. In addition, modeling with constraints introduces conceptual challenges (e.g., hidden dependencies [37]), which are absent when modeling imperatively. Nonetheless, guidelines addressing the visual clarity of models (e.g., avoiding overlapping elements and line crossings) can be applied to both language paradigms. As a step towards the development of a more comprehensive framework for assessing the quality of declarative models, we use Personal Construct Theory (PCT) [24] to elicit quality dimensions used by experts when evaluating declarative models. Afterwards, we turn to the literature to discuss the similarities with existing guidelines and mark the key disparities requiring further investigation.

PCT directly fulfills our aim to elicit the criteria used by experts to judge model quality. It postulates that individuals develop a set of personal constructs (i.e., scales) to frame their experiences based on their similarities and differences [24]. In our context, the constructs offer scalar dimensions used by experts to differentiate the qualities of process models. Tapping into these constructs provide a means to articulate each expert's mental model, making the criteria by which model components are judged more tractable. Moreover, grounding our study in PCT overcomes many of the limitations of interpretive studies exploring the quality of process models, in particular those reliant on techniques such as interviews and think-aloud (e.g., [6,37]). Insights obtained from interviews are usually bound by the interviewer's questions, leaving no chance to discover other relevant aspects beyond the repertoire of questions. As for think-aloud, it helps people to voice their thoughts out-loud and thus reveal their inner thoughts. However, as individuals tend to know more than they can readily articulate [12], part of their thought remains tacit and not readily evident in verbal utterances. PCT overcomes this limitation by removing the bounds of predetermination - the interview structure - offering in its place a framework for a series of comparisons. The similarities and differences between elements (e.g., those of process models) provide the basis for - and scope of - the technique. Through this comparison process, each individual's constructs can be articulated without constraint. Collectively, these benefits motivate our choice of PCT to articulate the constructs under girding judgments of quality. Following analysis based on grounded theory [8], the constructs articulated are aggregated to propose a multi-dimensional framework for the assessment of declarative model quality.

Our contribution is twofold. Firstly, we develop a multi-dimensional framework that has the capacity to more comprehensively assess the quality of declarative models. Secondly we demonstrate the potential of PCT in conducting interpretive analysis of process modeling. Our findings enhance the understanding of the dimensions of quality in declarative modeling and promote their use in industry. Moreover, these emergent dimensions of quality have the clear potential to support teaching of declarative modeling, helping students identify pertinent aspects requiring more attention when modeling processes declaratively. Finally, further adoption of PCT in the process modeling field would add to the stream of research exploring the mental models of practitioners. Sect. 2 presents the background, Sect. 3 introduces the related work, Sect. 4 explains the research method, Sect. 5 presents the findings, Sect. 6 discusses the findings and Sect. 7 wraps-up the key contributions and delineates the future work.

2   Background

DCR Graphs. DCR Graphs consist of nodes and edges: the nodes indicate *events*, the edges indicate *relations* between the events. Events can be assigned to *roles*. To maximize flexibility, events that are unconstrained can be executed at any time and any number of times. Events have a state marking, which is a tuple of three Boolean values: *executed, included* and *pending. Executed* indicates that the event has executed at least once in the past. *Included* indicates whether the event is currently relevant for the process: irrelevant (*excluded*) events cannot be executed, but also cannot constrain the execution of other events. *Pending* indicates that the event must be executed some time in the future, i.e. the event is a requirement that must be fulfilled before we can end the process. Pending events are generally referred as *required events*.

There are five basic relations. A *condition* restricts an event by stating that it cannot be executed before another event has fired at least once. *Milestones* constrain an event by stating that as long as a particular other event is pending, it cannot be executed. The *exclusion* and *inclusion* relations can be used to remove or add back an event from or to the process, effectively toggling event's included state. Finally, the *response* relation indicates that the execution of one event makes another event pending (i.e., required). The last three relations imply a dynamic behavior in the model as they are not constraints in the traditional sense, but rather capture *effects* that some events have on others. Relations and events can be combined together to model specific *behavioral patterns*.

Several extensions complement the core notation above. Hierarchy can be achieved through *nesting* [21], which allows one to group several events together (into a *nest event*), and then add a single relation to or from all of them. It simply acts as a shorthand for having a relation for each individual event and therefore does not add additional semantic meaning. The notion of *multi-instance sub-processes* [13] on the other hand, significantly extends the language by allowing one to model sub-process templates which can be instantiated many times. For example, a funding application round may consist of many individual applications, each application instance having their own unique internal state. Finally one can model the influence of contextual *data* on the process by adding *data expressions* to relations, indicating under what circumstances they should be activated [36]. For example, a response relation between "check expenses report" and "flag report" can be activated only if the amount exceeds a thousand euros.

Mental Models and Personal Construct Psychology. A mental model is an abstract representation of a situation or a system in the individual's mind [18]. Research on mental models addresses two aspects: their structure and change over time. Studies of the structure of mental models contribute to the theory of human reasoning and are used to evaluate individuals' decision making [23]. Change-oriented studies focus on dynamics where the system state changes over time. These studies investigate how individuals' mental models evolve and adapt [19]. In this work, we lean to the former, striving to articulate mental models whose structure reveals experts' judgement of declarative process models. The structure of the mental model - comprised of scalar constructs - provides direct insight into the criteria on which their assessment of quality is based.

To tap into individuals' mental models, we refer to the PCT theory of George Kelly [24]. Kelly assumed that individuals develop unique systems of interrelated personal constructs (i.e., scales), allowing them to understand and predict their surrounding world [24]. These personal constructs emerge from the individuals' past and ongoing experiences. Individuals organize and differentiate their experiences through judgement of similarities and differences, evolving a system of constructs, which they use to frame and predict the consequences of their own

actions and interpret those of others [12]. The commonality of a system of constructs enables them to be used as a basis to explain interpersonal relations. This
is particularly pertinent to personal experiences that share a cognitive medium
or framework. PCT posits that individuals sharing common experiences can
develop similar personal constructs [12].

In the view of Kelly, a personal construct is bipolar. It is composed of two
ends (e.g., good versus bad). Eliciting constructs is challenging because individuals are generally unable to access the structure of their own cognitive system
and verbalize their implicit knowledge [12]. *Repertory Grid* is a knowledge elicitation technique developed to help people identify and articulate their personal
constructs [12,24]. In a nutshell, the approach comprises a series of trials where
a participant is asked to identify similarities and differences between different
elements – such as process models in DCR Graphs. The result of each comparison is then used to articulate the participant's personal constructs and their
meaning. A step-by-step explanation of the Repertory Grid process is provided
in Sect. 4.2. Repertory Grid has been used in a wide range of domains (e.g.,
technology acceptance [12]). However, its potential has not yet been exploited in
the field of process modeling. This work builds upon the PCT theory and adapts
the Repertory Grid technique to derive a comprehensive framework delineating
the dimensions used by experts to evaluate the quality of declarative process
models.

Grounded Theory. Grounded Theory adopts a qualitative inductive approach
to analyzing and conceptualizing data [8]. A multi-phase process of coding is a
central to grounded theory, enabling the phenomena emerging from data to be
identified and classified. Three coding techniques – *initial-coding, focused-coding*
and *axial-coding* – are common [8]. Initial-coding highlights salient aspects in
the data; focused coding allows these aspects to be grouped based on similarity
of their traits, while axial-coding establishes relationships between the identified codes. Typically, a qualitative analysis starts with initial-coding, followed
by focused-coding and finally axial-coding. In model comprehension studies,
grounded theory has been used to analyze the verbal utterances of participants
when interacting with different representations of process models (e.g., [1,37]).
Building on these works, our analysis uses the coding techniques of grounded
theory to analyze the personal constructs verbalized by the experts throughout
the different steps of the Repertory Grid.

3   Related Work

Model quality frameworks have emerged in different contexts. In conceptual
modeling, guidelines addressing the use of graphical notations and the overall
quality of conceptual models have emerged (e.g., [26,28,31]). In process modeling, a large body of literature focusing on the quality of imperative models
exists (for an overview see the literature reviews in [10,17]). In addition, a set of
guidelines have been proposed on how to create process models of good quality

(e.g., [27,29,30,35]). However, when it comes to declarative languages, only a very limited number of studies exploring specific aspects of declarative models have emerged. Namely, the authors in [20] suggested that the comprehension of declarative models could be affected by the layout and the complexity of the used constraints. As for [37], the author suggested that modularization could support the comprehension of declarative models when solving a particular type of tasks.

Our study differs from the earlier works in several aspects. As opposed to [26,28,31] where guidelines are generic to any model-based representation, our work emphasizes declarative models, in particular those in DCR graphs, providing a closer examination of the quality dimensions relevant for that matter. With regards to [10,17,27,29,30,35], many of the proposed guidelines either do not apply to declarative models or need further investigation to ensure their applicability (cf. Sect. 1). Alternatively, our research bases its analysis on declarative models and compares to related work to highlight the similarities and disparities between imperative and declarative guidelines (cf. Sect. 6). When it comes to studies looking into declarative process models, we argue that model quality was not well emphasized. Instead, the focus was on exploring the use of declarative models [20] or assessing the impact of modularization [37] on the performance of users. Conversely, our work emphasizes the quality of declarative process models and aims at providing a multi-dimensional quality framework to further promote their use in practice. Besides, our study design (based on PCT, cf. Sect. 4) differs from the existing qualitative designs as explained in Sect. 1.

4   Research Method

This section introduces our research method including the research question (cf. Sect. 4.1), data collection (cf. Sect. 4.2) and analysis procedures (cf. Sect. 4.3).

4.1   Research Question

This work addresses the need for a comprehensive framework allowing to evaluate the quality of declarative process models, particularly DCR Graphs. Our research question is formulated as follows: **Which quality dimensions are used by experts when comparing DCR Graphs?**

4.2   Data Collection

Data was collected using a step-wise approach underpinned by PCT. The following sections explain our data collection process in detail, introduce the research setting, and describe the materials used in the study.

Approach. Following the theoretic position set out in Sect. 2, we use the Repertory Grid to identify the constructs used by experts to evaluate the quality of DCR Graphs. The elicitation process is initiated by the *selection of a set of elements* referring to different instances of a universe of discourse [24]. Repertory

Grid studies use different types of elements. In clinical contexts, elements are usually represented as roles (i.e., people); however, in other studies, elements are represented as working tasks [12]. In our study, we consider the elements as models provided by modelers with different levels of expertise. *Collecting the models* representing the elements of the grid is, then, the first phase of our data collection. To this end, we have shared a process description with a set of participants and asked them to design the corresponding model in DCR Graphs. The resulting models are available in our online repository [2].

Once the models defining the elements of the grid have been collected, we move to the second phase of our data collection, where participants recruited for their expertise evaluate the quality of the collected models. This phase begins by *eliciting of personal constructs*. Through a series of trials, the participant is given a triad (i.e., set of three) of models and asked, following the minimum context form described by Kelly [12,24]), to *(1)* identify the "*odd model out*" (i.e., the model that differs from the other two models of the triad) *(2)* and explain "*why*", that is to say, what –in her terms – makes it odd. This articulates one dimension of the scale used to differentiate the models (elements). The participant is then asked what –if anything– makes the remaining (non-odd) elements similar. Often, this is a simple negation: for instance, a triad composed of 3 process models might be differentiated because one model *has color coded events*, while in the other two *all events have the same color*. In this sense, the construct defined with the poles *has color coded events* versus *all events have the same color* is an example of a participant's personal construct. A construct is thus articulated as two distinct poles drawn from the difference between the odd model and the similarity of the other two models.

The identification of personal constructs is usually complemented by a discussion of the meaning of the constructs to the participant. The discussion is moderated using *laddering up* and *laddering down* techniques used respectively to elaborate or abstract the insights offered by the participant, further articulating their relevance [12]. The same triad approach is repeated until a theoretical saturation of constructs is reached. Rather than data saturation, where all possible triads should be visited, we follow a theoretical saturation approach, striving to provide the participant with new triads until no more new constructs emerge. On average, most constructs were articulated after 7 triads, which falls within the same range of triads generally used to identify the most salient constructs [11]. Figure 1a summarizes the process of eliciting personal constructs.

Following the identification of constructs, the participant is given a grid where columns represent the collected models and rows show the identified constructs. During this process, the participant is allowed to review and edit her constructs before being asked to *rate each of the models based on the identified constructs*. The literature discusses different rating methods [12], in our study, we use a five-point scale following the insights in [12]. As the constructs usually emerge from comparisons within triads of models, some constructs might not apply to all models. In such a case the participant is told to skip these particular grid cells. Analysis of the numeric ratings enables the grid to illustrate underlying

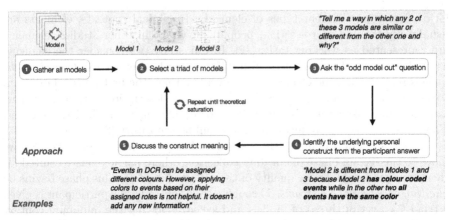

(a) The process of eliciting the participants' personal constructs

Personal Construct Poles	Elements						Personal Construct Poles
	Model 1	Model 2	Model 3	Model 4	Model 5	Model 6	
Has color coded events	5	4	2	5	3	1	All Events have the same color
...	3		2		5	1	....

(b) Fragment of a Repertory Grid

Fig. 1. Illustrations of the different steps of the Repertory Grid approach

but unseen associations between elements and constructs and thus their meaning using concrete terminology drawn from the participants 'world', which in turn supports the analysis of these personal constructs. A fragment of a Grid is illustrated in Fig. 1b. The collected grids are available in our online repository [2].

The *talkback interview* is the last step. It aims at reflecting the overall process and scrutinize the personal constructs based on the obtained qualitative insights and the grid ratings. While some studies conduct further statistical analysis to investigate the correlations between constructs and elements, our work rather focuses on the insights obtained throughout the different steps of the Repertory Grid and analyzes them following grounded theory. To keep track of these insights, the conversations with the participants were fully recorded.

Participants. To collect the models representing the elements of the grid, we have recruited 13 participants with different levels of expertise in DCR Graphs. Novice participants (3 students) have taken a BPM course where they have been introduced to process modeling in general. Intermediate participants (4 students) have been familiarized with DCR Graphs for at least one semester. Whereas expert participants (2 professors, 2 postdocs and 2 industry practitioners) are more deeply immersed through their use of and research into DCR Graphs. The heterogeneity of participants enabled us to explore the range of model complexities and reflect different modeling practices employed by users with different levels of expertise. This heterogeneity also provides the basis to allow differences between novices and experts - and novice models and expert models - to emerge.

To evaluate the models, we used 4 experts among the pool of participants in the first phase. Each expert was exposed to the 12 models collected from the other participants and her model as well. Including experts' own models in the comparison gave them the opportunity to reflect on their models (compared to others) which in turn enriched the analysis. Overall, 94 bi-polar personal constructs were elicited from the models [2].

Material. The process description used to collect the models representing the elements of the grid is inspired by a real-world use-case study presented in [15]. The process description (cf. online repository [2]) was shared with 13 participants, who were asked to design the corresponding process model in DCR Graphs.

4.3 Data Analysis

The analysis started by listening to the audio recordings of the repertory grid procedure, time stamping the periods where each of the constructs was discussed, and then taking notes of the collected insights. Here, the verbal utterances provided by each participant were related directly to the ratings of the relevant model in the repertory grid providing concrete, context-specific articulations of the participant's insights. Afterwards, we turned to grounded theory to investigate the participants' constructs and their meanings. To reduce subjectivity during the coding process, we recruited two coders. We followed the code-confirming strategy [25] to distribute the tasks between the primary and the secondary coders. The primary coder was responsible for conducting the first round of coding, while the secondary coder was recruited to critically scrutinize the codes and trigger discussions to improve the coding. Both coders are researchers within the BPM field. For each grid, the primary coder conducted the first round of initial-coding to the participant's constructs [7] based on the constructs' poles. In case the poles were not clear, the primary coder referred to the collected notes. Afterwards, the secondary coder reviewed the initial-coding and performed the second round of coding, which was, in turn, discussed by both coders to reach an agreement. Next, the constructs obtained from all the participants were combined and subjected to focused-coding [7] grouping repeating and overlapping initial codes to identify the commonality or focus among the concepts articulated. The resulting codes reveal the different *dimensions* used by the participants to evaluate the quality of declarative process models. The relationships between the revealed dimensions were elaborated using axial coding [7]. Here, the revealed dimensions were organized according to recurrent themes and then categorized. This phase was conducted in 2 rounds by both coders, followed by a discussion where the final codes were agreed. An excel sheet illustrating this process is available as part of our online repository [2]. The resulting categories, themes and dimensions are presented in Sect. 5.

5 Findings

The analysis of the constructs allowed the identification of seven themes organized into 2 categories. Sections 5.1 and 5.2 present the themes associated with the semantic qualities and pragmatic qualities of process models respectively.

5.1 Semantic Qualities

Semantics denotes the ability of the model to make true statements about the way the business process operates in the real-world [35]. The semantics of a model is a relative indicator of quality as the model behavior is subjective to the process specifications. The analysis of experts' personal constructs, drawn from their interpretation of the models, gave rise to 4 themes overarching a number of dimensions capable of assessing the semantic quality of DCR Graphs: these are *modeling behavior, modeling patterns, modeling events* and *modeling data*.

Modeling Behavior. Within this theme, several dimensions have emerged. *Comprehensiveness of behavior* is identified throughout our analysis of personal constructs. Here, experts used this dimension to evaluate the completeness of the model. When it comes to the alignment between the process specifications and the model behavior, the experts elicited the *presence of behavioral errors* dimension to assess the validity of the behavior supported by the model.

Flow-based versus *declarative modeling* is a relevant dimension used by the experts to evaluate flexibility. They identified a spectrum of modeling behaviors ranging from very flexible to over-restricted ones. Overall, the experts asserted that declarative models should support parallel behavior and avoid being restrictive. Nevertheless, they also advised avoiding both extremes (being too flexible or too restrictive) and advised to rather comply to the *process specifications*.

Modeling of required events is another relevant dimension identified by the experts. This dimension evaluates the modeling of events that must eventually be executed in the process. These events are regarded as goals which must be fulfilled in any execution [22]. Identifying these events in the specifications and modeling them correctly are important criteria to model behavior consistently. In DCR Graphs, required events can be modelled by assigning a specific marking to events at design time or by using the response relation (cf. Sect. 2).

The experts identified the dimension *Modeling of end-events* to assess whether the model allows termination. In DCR Graphs, end-events refer to events whose execution disable the rest of events in the model from executing. While some experts recommended to model termination, other experts asserted that one cannot generalize that all processes should incorporate termination. In some cases, process specifications require processes to be *suspended* rather than terminated, leaving the possibility to resume them at any point in time. For such processes, only the no-longer relevant events should be removed from the process before suspension. Similarly, the experts identified the dimension *Modeling of start-events* (i.e., events initiating the process) to assess whether the models identify the process start-events appropriately. In this respect, some experts advised using a unique start-event, while other experts affirmed that this depends on the process specifications. Nonetheless, experts advised checking whether the non-constrained events in the model are good candidates for being start-events to the process, if not, then these events must be constrained by others to prevent their occurrence when the process is first initiated.

Additionally, the *Multi-instance processing* dimension emerged to compare the extent to which multi-instance sub-processes are supported (cf. Sect. 2). From this perspective, the experts noticed that most of the models do not comply with the given process specifications as they do not offer the possibility to indicate the parts which can be executed multiple times concurrently.

The *Modeling against IT silliness* dimension addresses the experts' felt need to assess the flexibility of the models in tackling failures that prevent occurred events from being registered by the PAIS. In this context, the distinction between *unlawful behavior* (i.e., the behavior violating the constraints of the process) and *impossible behavior* (i.e., a behavior which would never occur in the real-world) has emerged. While the former is crucial to avoid, the latter can be tolerated assuming that the PAIS might fail to register some non-value adding events at their occurrence (e.g., granting a loan without signing the contract must never be allowed, whereas, signing the contract without receiving it, could be tolerated by the model assuming that the PAIS failed to register that event).

The *purpose of the model* is a dimension used by the experts to evaluate the granularity of the models. Accordingly, the level of detail exposed by the scope or bounds of the business process can be adjusted to fit the intended purpose (e.g., enactment, management). The identification of the model purpose is a crucial aspect because it goes beyond the semantic qualities of the model also to affect the pragmatics of the model. In that sense, a model intended for enactment can be hard to interpret if used for management purposes.

Modeling Patterns. Modeling patterns denote the set of mechanisms used to represent specific behaviors when modeling processes. The elicited insights focused on the *use of standard patterns*, which encompass the conventional modeling patterns advised for modeling different behaviors. For experts, standard patterns provide a clear representation of the intended model behavior. The use of standard patterns also reoccurred while inspecting the way modelers represented common behavior, exceptional behavior, and termination.

The dimension *Condition-response* versus *Include-exclude patterns* emerged when comparing the common behavior represented in the models. The *condition* and *response* relations can be used together to model a wide range of specifications. However, a similar behavior can be achieved using *exclude* and *include* relations, which was recurrent in many models. During the discussion, the experts advised adhering to the *condition-response* pattern when modeling common behavior for the following reasons: *(1)* The dynamic behavior of the *include* and *exclude* relations (cf. Sect. 2) is more likely to create hidden dependencies between events, adding unnecessary complexity to the model. *(2)*

The *include* and *exclude* relations are rather used for modeling exceptions and termination.

The dimension *Treatment of exception pattern* assesses whether the modeler uses the appropriate pattern to treat exceptions clearly. For the experts, exceptional events are not part of the main process and thus they should initially be excluded in the model and included (using the include relation) only when exceptions occur. Likewise, the dimension *Use of termination pattern* addresses whether termination is modeled using the appropriate pattern. Here, the experts recommended grouping events into a nest event (cf. Sect. 2) and add one exclude relation from the end-event to the nest event.

Modeling Events. The experts used the *Role assignment* dimension to check the assignment of roles to events and asserted that it is crucial for clarifying "who is doing what?", which in turn supports better traceability and access control.

Use of intermediate events is a pertinent dimension. In DCR, intermediate events denote the events used to enforce specific behaviors, without being explicitly mentioned in the process specifications. Intermediate events can be used to automate some actions or to model decisions. For the experts, although their use might be necessary (e.g., for implementation), intermediate events can hinder the understandability of the model and should be avoided whenever possible.

Besides, the *implicitness of events* dimension was introduced to evaluate whether all the events mentioned in the process specifications are explicitly represented in the model. Indeed, some modelers merged several events into one. For the experts, modelers should ensure a one-to-one correspondence between the events of the process specifications and those represented in the model.

Modeling Data. The dimension *Encoding decisions explicitly or using data expressions* was used by the experts to evaluate whether decisions are encoded using intermediate events or using data expressions. As mentioned in Sect. 2, data events allow assigning values to variables, which in turn are used in the evaluation of data expressions. Following the experts, the activation of the DCR relations in a model can be controlled by assigning them data expressions. At run-time, if the expression evaluates to *true*, then the semantics of the relation applies in the model, otherwise, it does not. Data expressions can be difficult to interpret. However if used purposefully for modeling decisions, they can reduce the complexity of the model (e.g., by removing intermediate decision events).

Besides, the experts identified the dimension *Appropriate choice of data types for data variables* to indicate cases where the data types of variables were not correctly chosen. Here, the experts highlighted the necessity of choosing a data type which infers meaning about the use of the variable it represents.

The *Local/global effect of data variables* dimension emerged to describe whether a data variable is evaluated immediately after being assigned a value (using a data event), or postponed to a later stage of processing. On that matter, the experts recommended evaluating data variables immediately after assigning them values, making the correspondence between the data event and its subsequent evaluation clearer. However, depending on the process specifications, an immediate evaluation of data variables is not always feasible. In this case, the experts advised a consistent naming of data events and data variables, making the correspondence between both easily perceived (cf. Sect. 5.2).

5.2 Pragmatic Qualities

Pragmatics denotes the correspondence between the model and the reader's understanding of it [35]. The pragmatic qualities of a model do not formally affect its behavior. However, they might have direct consequences on the use of the model as a communication artifact. The experts' meanings revealed 3 themes related to pragmatic qualities: *Model Layout, Event Layout, Data Layout.*

Model Layout. The experts used the dimension *Alignment and positioning of elements* to appraise the way models are laid out. They highlighted the extraneous visual complexity raising from models where elements (i.e., events, relations) overlap, and advised a careful alignment and spacing of events. Here, two strategies were used: the former evaluates whether the events assigned to the same role are aligned along the same vertical axis, while the second strategy assesses whether the events are aligned following their likely order of occurrence during execution. For the experts, these strategies could improve the pragmatic quality of the model. In addition, the experts looked into the way models were oriented and suggested a left-to-right or top-to-bottom orientation, indicating that start-events should be positioned at the left-most top-most part of the model.

The *grouping of events* dimension evaluates the way events are grouped in the model. Nest events (cf. Sect. 2) allow gathering events belonging to the same phase or assigned to the same role. With a preference for phase-based nesting, the experts associated the use of nesting with an enhanced understandability of the model. In the same vein, multi-level hierarchy was raised by experts to emphasize the benefits of going beyond a single level of nesting.

Visual conciseness focuses on the overall clarity of the model. This dimension was defined by the previously mentioned aspects e.g., alignment and grouping of events, but also in relation to the optimized use of constraints and the absence of intermediate events. These characteristics embrace both pragmatic and semantic qualities, showing that the themes and dimensions emerging within both categories influence the experts' perception of visual conciseness.

Event Layout. The experts emphasized particularly the internal pragmatics of events. The dimension *Meaningful naming of events* was used to assess the meaningfulness of events' names. For experts, events should be assigned comprehensible names which can be easily traced back to the process specifications.

Furthermore, the experts used the dimension *Verb-object* versus *noun-based naming of events* to evaluate the phrasing of the events' names. Here, they recommended a verb-object phrasing, except for the intermediate events used for modeling decisions, where a noun-based format could be acceptable.

Color coding was another identified dimension. Although, DCR allows assigning colors to events, some experts were confused by the meaning of these colors, and asserted that they are hard to interpret when no explicit legend is provided. Hence, several experts suggested avoiding to color events.

Data Layout. The dimension *Correspondence between variable names and data events' names* was used by the experts to evaluate whether the data event altering the value of a data variable can be easily recognized in the model. For experts, data events and data variables should be assigned the same name because data variables might not be evaluated immediately after being assigned a value. Hence, with the lack of a clear matching between a variable name and its corresponding data event's name, it becomes hard for the reader to infer the variable's value when being evaluated in a data expression as all the previously executed data events could presumably change the value of that data variable.

6   Discussion

The dimensions identified by the experts share many similarities with the existing imperative process modeling guidelines. For instance, comprehensiveness of behavior and presence of behavioral errors (two of the identified semantic qualities) relate to the notions of completeness (i.e., the coverage of the relevant statements of a particular domain) and validity (i.e., the correctness of the statements in the model) discussed in [28]. Moreover, the importance of designing models fitting their intended purpose (i.e., enactment, management) both in terms of granularity and target audience was not only recognized by our experts, but also emphasized in [28]. In terms of pragmatic qualities, the insights about the alignment and positioning of elements intersect with the findings in [10,30], while the recommendations about assigning meaningful names to events and phrasing them following a verb-object format have been discussed in [10,30]. Regarding the use of colors to mark events, there was no agreement between experts. This concurs with literature on the usage of color in the context of imperative processes which is also inconclusive [5,10].

The use of standard patterns is among the pertinent dimensions, which experts argued it enhances the understandability of the model. While catalogues of patterns showing how to model certain re-occurring problems exist for imperative models [14], we cannot currently rely on such resources when modeling declaratively. Additional research is needed to elicit a catalogue for DCR Graphs and to empirically evaluate its impact on model quality. Our findings show that the general idea of using decomposition to reduce process model complexity is shared with imperative models [37]. However, additional guidelines – on when and how to decompose declarative models – are missing. Decomposition in imperative models involves identifying particular points in the flow where a complex behaviour can be abstracted into an individual step with a single entry and exit point. This is not as easy in declarative modeling, where different parts of the model may interact in different ways, making it challenging to find clear distinctions between the entangling constraints of the model. There is also a need for empirical research on the impact of modularization on the quality of declarative models. Existing research [37] suggests that modularization enables abstraction and information hiding, which in turn supports the comprehension of the model. Contrarily, modularization also risks fragmentation, giving rise to split-attention effects and a need for integration between different parts of the model.

Existing guidelines on the usage of gateways for modeling decisions are not applicable to declarative models, including DCR graphs. Experts mentioned the modeling of decisions using either intermediate events or data expressions. The use of events to model decisions would lead to construct overload as a single notational element is being used to represent multiple concepts (i.e., actions and decisions). Existing research states that construct overload impacts the understandability of the model negatively [31]. Alternatively, experts suggested modeling decisions using data expressions. However, the implications of using data expressions on the understandability of declarative models are questionable and require additional research. Regarding the modeling of start-events, existing guidelines [30] advise use of a single start-event. While some experts agreed, others questioned the general applicability of this guideline and suggested that it depends on the process. Due to the constraint-based approach of declarative languages, any non-constrained event is a possible entry-point to the process. This makes modeling of start-events in declarative languages more complex than imperative languages since in declarative modelers one must check all non-constrained events to ensure that they are good candidate start-events for the process or constrain them to prevent their occurrence when the process is first initiated.

While several insights agree with the literature on imperative process models, our study identified some contradictions. For instance, our findings promote the concurrency of behavior in declarative models, whereas existing guidelines [10] advise minimizing concurrency when modeling imperatively. Moreover, existing guidelines [32] assume that processes should eventually terminate. Conversely, our insights relax this assumption by evoking the possibility of suspension instead of termination. However, little is known about when to use what, which necessitates detailed guidelines. Moreover, while the use of single end-events is recommended to ensure understandable models [30], the impact of modeling processes without explicit end-events is yet to be explored.

The results of this study have impacts on research, education and practice. The insights obtained advance our understanding of quality in declarative models. While several of the findings concur with prior research on imperative modeling, our study also revealed several dimensions where further investigation is required. The positive effects of standard patterns on both quality and comprehension of declarative models suggest a potential hypothesis worthy of test in the light of the existing theory. A further hypothesis might address effects of applying modularization on the understandability of declarative models. Moreover, the applicability of PCT in process modeling paves the path for new studies exploring the mental models of practitioners when dealing with different aspects of process models. With regards to education, our findings support the teaching of declarative process modeling (particularly in DCR Graphs) by providing a set of dimensions allowing students to focus their attention on the pertinent quality aspects to improve their design of declarative models. Our findings also have implications for practice. Several of the identified semantic qualities (relating to modeling of events and data) and pragmatic qualities (related to model, event and data layouts) can be automatically inferred from the model and thus could be implemented by tool vendors to assess the quality of process models at design time offering the potential of customized tool-support for modelers.

Limitations. Our research has some limitations. Our sample is relatively small: however, in common with other Repertory Grid studies (e.g., [9,33]) the scale and richness of the elicitation process gave rise to over 400 numeric data points, highlighting both the cognitive focus and demand of the approach, which required some 4–5 h per session. Another limitation might arise through bias during the coding procedure. To minimize this risk, we recruited a secondary coder who was purposefully critical of the coding of the primary coder. Finally, our results do not address syntactical qualities since the models were all designed using a tool (i.e., dcrgraphs.net) which automatically resolves syntax-dependent errors.

7   Conclusion and Future Work

This work investigates the quality of declarative process models. The results present a set of quality dimensions identified by experts in DCR Graphs. Similarities with existing guidelines highlight qualities shared with imperative models – while clear differences identify candidate aspects worthy of further investigation. Future work could subject the different qualities to further theoretical and empirical investigation. Several hypotheses have already emerged, as noted above. Moreover, our data could be used to investigate how different quality dimensions affect each other. The models provided by the different groups of participants could be further analyzed to discern patterns characterizing the modeling of novices, intermediates and experts, which in turn could guide the profiling of modelers at run-time and optimizing tool support. Our approach also offers sound potential to contribute to studies that explore the mental models of practitioners and their interaction with process models.

References

1. Abbad Andaloussi, A., Burattin, A., Slaats, T., Petersen, A.C.M., Hildebrandt, T.T., Weber, B.: Exploring the understandability of a hybrid process design artifact based on DCR graphs. In: Reinhartz-Berger, I., Zdravkovic, J., Gulden, J., Schmidt, R. (eds.) BPMDS/EMMSAD -2019. LNBIP, vol. 352, pp. 69–84. Springer, Cham (2019). https://doi.org/10.1007/978-3-030-20618-5_5

2. Abbad Andaloussi, A., Davis, C.J., Burattin, A., López, H.A., Slaats, T., Weber, B.: Online repository: used material, collected data and full analysis (2020). https://doi.org/10.5281/zenodo.3724609
3. Andaloussi, A.A., Burattin, A., Slaats, T., Kindler, E., Weber, B.: On the declarative paradigm in hybrid business process representations: a conceptual framework and a systematic literature study. Inf. Syst. **91**, 101505 (2020)
4. Becker, J., Rosemann, M., von Uthmann, C.: Guidelines of business process modeling. In: van der Aalst, W., Desel, J., Oberweis, A. (eds.) Business Process Management. LNCS, vol. 1806, pp. 30–49. Springer, Heidelberg (2000). https://doi.org/10.1007/3-540-45594-9_3
5. Bera, P., Soffer, P., Parsons, J.: Using eye tracking to expose cognitive processes in understanding conceptual models. MIS Q. **43**(4), 1105–1126 (2019)
6. Bernstein, V., Soffer, P.: How does it look? exploring meaningful layout features of process models. In: Persson, A., Stirna, J. (eds.) CAiSE 2015. LNBIP, vol. 215, pp. 81–86. Springer, Cham (2015). https://doi.org/10.1007/978-3-319-19243-7_7
7. Bryant, A., Charmaz, K.: The SAGE Handbook of Current Developments in Grounded Theory. SAGE Publications, Thousand Oaks (2019)
8. Charmaz, K.: Constructing Grounded Theory, Introducing Qualitative Methods series. SAGE Publications (2014)
9. Christie, D.F., Menmuir, J.G.: The repertory grid as a tool for reflection in the professional development of practitioners in early education. Teach. Devel. **1**(2), 205–218 (1997)
10. Corradini, F., et al.: A guidelines framework for understandable BPMN models. Data Know. Eng. **113**, 129–154 (2018)
11. Curtis, A.M., Wells, T.M., Higbee, T., Lowry, P.B.: An overview and tutorial of the repertory grid technique in information systems research. Commun. Assoc. Inf. Syst. **23**(3), 37–62 (2008)
12. Davis, C.J., Hufnagel, E.M.: Through the eyes of experts: a socio-cognitive perspective on the automation of fingerprint work. MIS Q. **31**(4), 681–703 (2007)
13. Debois, S., Hildebrandt, T.T., Slaats, T.: Replication, refinement & reachability: complexity in dynamic condition-response graphs. Acta Informatica **55**(6), 489–520 (2017). https://doi.org/10.1007/s00236-017-0303-8
14. van Der Aalst, W.M., Ter Hofstede, A.H., Kiepuszewski, B., Barros, A.P.: Workflow patterns. Distrib. Parallel Database **14**(1), 5–51 (2003)
15. Elgammal, A., Turetken, O., van den Heuvel, W.J., Papazoglou, M.: Formalizing and appling compliance patterns for business process compliance. Softw. Syst. Model. **15**(1), 119–146 (2014). https://doi.org/10.1007/s10270-014-0395-3
16. Fahland, D., et al.: Declarative versus imperative process modeling languages: the issue of understandability. In: Halpin, T., Krogstie, J., Nurcan, S., Proper, E., Schmidt, R., Soffer, P., Ukor, R. (eds.) BPMDS/EMMSAD -2009. LNBIP, vol. 29, pp. 353–366. Springer, Heidelberg (2009). https://doi.org/10.1007/978-3-642-01862-6_29
17. Figl, K.: Comprehension of procedural visual business process models. Bus. Inf. Syst. Eng. **59**(1), 41–67 (2016). https://doi.org/10.1007/s12599-016-0460-2
18. Forrester, J.W.: Industrial dynamics. Pegasus Communications (1961)
19. Groesser, S.N., Schaffernicht, M.: Mental models of dynamic systems: taking stock and looking ahead. Syst. Dyn. Rev. **28**(1), 46–68 (2012)
20. Haisjackl, C., et al.: Understanding declare models: strategies, pitfalls, empirical results. Softw. Syst. Model. **15**(2), 325–352 (2016)

21. Hildebrandt, T., Mukkamala, R.R., Slaats, T.: Nested dynamic condition response graphs. In: Arbab, F., Sirjani, M. (eds.) FSEN 2011. LNCS, vol. 7141, pp. 343–350. Springer, Heidelberg (2012). https://doi.org/10.1007/978-3-642-29320-7_23

22. Hildebrandt, T.T., Mukkamala, R.R.: Declarative event-based workflow as distributed dynamic condition response graphs. EPTCS **69**, 59–73 (2011)

23. Johnson-Laird, P.N.: Mental models and deduction. Trends Cogn. Sci. **5**(10), 434–442 (2001)

24. Kelly, G.A.: The psychology of personal constructs Norton. New York (1955)

25. King, N., Horrocks, C., Brooks, J.: Interviews in Qualitative Research. SAGE Publications, Thousand Oaks (2018)

26. Krogstie, J.: Model-Based Development and Evolution of Information Systems: A Quality Approach. Springer Science & Business Media, Heidelberg (2012). https://doi.org/10.1007/978-1-4471-2936-3

27. Krogstie, J.: Some future directions for business process modeling. Quality in Business Process Modeling, pp. 227–239. Springer, Cham (2016). https://doi.org/10.1007/978-3-319-42512-2_6

28. Lindland, O.I., Sindre, G., Solvberg, A.: Understanding quality in conceptual modeling. IEEE Softw. **11**(2), 42–49 (1994)

29. Mendling, J.: Metrics for Process Models. LNBIP, vol. 6. Springer, Heidelberg (2008). https://doi.org/10.1007/978-3-540-89224-3

30. Mendling, J., Reijers, H.A., van der Aalst, W.M.: Seven process modeling guidelines (7PMG). Inf. Softw. Technol. **52**(2), 127–136 (2010)

31. Moody, D.: The "physics" of notations: toward a scientific basis for constructing visual notations in software engineering. IEEE Trans. Softw. Eng. **35**(6), 756–779 (2009)

32. Moreno-Montes de Oca, I., Snoeck, M.: Pragmatic guidelines for business process modeling (2014). Available at SSRN 2592983

33. Phythian, G.J., King, M.: Developing an expert support system for tender enquiry evaluation: a case study. Eur. J. Oper. Res. **56**(1), 15–29 (1992)

34. Pesic, M.: Constraint-based workflow management systems: shifting control to users. Ph.D. thesis, TU Eindhoven (2008)

35. Reijers, H.A., Mendling, J., Recker, J.: Business process quality management. In: vom Brocke, J., Rosemann, M. (eds.) Handbook on Business Process Management 1. IHIS, pp. 167–185. Springer, Heidelberg (2015). https://doi.org/10.1007/978-3-642-45100-3_8

36. Slaats, T., Mukkamala, R.R., Hildebrandt, T., Marquard, M.: Exformatics declarative case management workflows as DCR graphs. In: BPM Proceedings (2013)

37. Zugal, S.: Applying cognitive psychology for improving the creation, understanding and maintenance of business process models. Ph.D. thesis, University of Innsbruck (2013)

Adding Intelligent Robots to Business Processes: A Dilemma Analysis of Employees' Attitudes

Amy Van Looy(⊠) 🆔

Faculty of Economics and Business Administration, Department of Business Informatics and Operations Management, Ghent University, Tweekerkenstraat 2, 9000 Ghent, Belgium
Amy.VanLooy@UGent.be

Abstract. Given the advancements in artificial intelligence, organizations are increasingly interested in applying robotics to their business processes. Unlike the many technological implications, we focus on the human side of robotics which remains under-investigated for higher-skilled employees. We particularly consider employee acceptance of intelligent robots with cognitive skills. During 48 interviews, hypothetical dilemmas regarding manual work, full- and semi-automation are discussed by office workers, managers and IT consultants. The results show that employees are positive about intelligent robots. The majority are willing to transfer repetitive tasks as long as humans can control outputs for accountability. However, employees prefer keeping tasks with creativity and human interaction. Many tasks can thus already be replaced by robotics, but more attention is needed for the facilitating role of organizations (e.g., training). The findings affect innovation strategies for implementing intelligent robots with reduced social implications. The idea of a step-by-step plan encourages a gradual adoption.

Keywords: Digital process innovation · Intelligent robots · Acceptance · Dilemma analysis

1 Introduction

Process innovation is of all times. The term was mainly used as from the 1990s with the reengineering wave [1]. However, during all industrial revolutions, organizations have paid attention to rethinking their way of working to obtain performance gains (e.g., higher quality, efficiency, effectiveness), and this by also reconsidering the ratio of human-machine cooperation [2, 3]. Nowadays, disruptive technologies are triggering a fourth industrial revolution, called Industry 4.0 [2]. Likewise, Industry 4.0 provides opportunities for process innovation and drastic changes in the job market, among others by artificial intelligence (AI) and robotics [3]. Nonetheless, employees have always been able to adapt their skills and entrepreneurs have created new jobs based on the technological advancements [2]. For instance, in the novel of "Charlie and the Chocolate Factory" from the mid-1960s, [4] already described a visionary leader who replaced employees by robots while Charlie's father was rehired for a new job related to machine maintenance.

© Springer Nature Switzerland AG 2020
D. Fahland et al. (Eds.): BPM 2020, LNCS 12168, pp. 435–452, 2020.
https://doi.org/10.1007/978-3-030-58666-9_25

This study focuses on intelligent robots, which are one of the pillars in Industry 4.0 [3]. With the recent AI advancements, robots have become able to conduct cognitive tasks [5], and so affecting the business processes of all employee types. Questions, however, remain which jobs and which business processes (or process tasks) are desired to be replaced by robots while respecting employees' potential. In this regard, our study tackles three gaps in the business process management (BPM) literature.

- First, contemporary studies have mainly focused on job replacements by machine-based robots for manual workers in industrial sectors (i.e., often performed by lower-skilled employees) [6], rather than intelligent robots affecting the jobs of other employee types and in service sectors. For instance, [7] and [8] state that robotics are negatively correlated to the employment rate of low-skilled employees but positively correlated to high-skilled employees (i.e., after being reskilled for new job contents like data analysts). Other authors agree that digital process innovation demands for new job contents focusing on education, support, development and production of such technologies [9, 10].
- Secondly, the BPM discipline recognizes the advantages of robotic process automation (RPA), which aims to innovate repetitive tasks rather than cognitive tasks [11]. More research is needed for process automation by different types of intelligence (i.e., mechanical, analytical, intuitive and empathic), and the extent to which employees should adapt their skills accordingly [5]. Moreover, although robotics are typically associated with performance gains [12], [13] states that automating tasks is still frequently done according to Taylorism (i.e., by dividing business processes into smaller tasks and optimizing them). Nonetheless, this does not necessarily lead to full performance benefits (e.g., because of reducing employees' implicit knowledge).
- Thirdly, the ratio of human-machine collaboration raises ethical discussions and new training needs [14], which have received little attention in the BPM discipline. Some authors are concerned that digitalization will affect prosperity when many jobs disappear [12], and thus impacting on the social security systems [10]. Since employee skills need to be reconsidered, governments should promote lifelong learning and introduce educational programs to better prepare people for human-machine collaboration [7, 15].

Consequently, more knowledge is needed about the adoption of robotics and the psychological reactions of employees [16]. When robots are increasingly seen as colleagues instead of resources, the issue is raised over how people will react. A complementary human-robot cooperation requires new leadership styles, but also a new organizational culture for accepting such major changes [6]. More research is needed about the balance between technology and society for better implementing process innovations by intelligent robots [8]. Hence, our research question is:

- **RQ. Which factors explain why employees would (partly) leave their work practices (i.e., business processes) to intelligent robots?**

Our purpose is to gain insight into the employees' attitudes (e.g., points of view, concerns, needs) for using intelligent robots in daily work, and we verify for which kind of business processes this digitalization will be more or less accepted. An interview-based research will be presented using on a dilemma analysis about hypothesized situations regarding future job contents. This article focuses on higher-skilled employees (i.e., office workers, managers and IT consultants), as a novel target group. We start from a well-established but generic IT acceptance theory [17] to thematically group a rich set of uncovered sub-factors specific to robotics and digital process innovation. Instead of theory testing, our qualitative research approach aims at distilling refinements or precautions that help organizations. This paper investigates which social problems should be addressed for organizations to adapt their policies. More specifically, by working towards a training curriculum and discussing ethical issues, we intend to derive a step-by-step plan that facilitates the gradual adoption of intelligent robots in organizations during digital process innovations.

The remainder is structured as follows. Section 2 describes related works. The research method is explained in Sect. 3, while results are presented in Sect. 4. A discussion is followed in Sect. 5. The paper concludes with Sect. 6.

2 Research Background

2.1 Digital Process Innovation and Intelligent Robots

Digital process innovation refers to the innovation of business processes by means of emerging technologies like STARA (i.e., smart technology, AI, robotics and algorithms) [18]. This paper targets intelligent robots because their applications will become more extensive given the fast developments in robotics [19]. Intelligent robots are defined as "*a machinery system that has comprehensive improvements in perception, decision-making and performance compared with a traditional robot, and can simulate human behaviors, emotions and thinking*" [40] (p. 525). A regular robot can execute the different tasks for which it is programmed. What makes a robot intelligent is that it can observe and think independently [19]. Based on their application domains, intelligent robots can be industrial robots, service robots and specialized robots [40]. Alternative classifications exist, such as based on the degree of intelligence (e.g., sensor type, interactive, and autonomous robots) [19].

An example of regular robots is RPA. The RPA-compatible tasks were initially time-consuming and with little added value [11]. While RPA remains one the most recent technological developments within BPM to reduce the costs of collecting data [11], future employees will be given more tasks of providing information to intelligent robots [20]. Most studies about the implementation of robotics, however, have been conducted in sectors like manufacturing and healthcare [21]. Among others, more research is needed for the new generation of service robots [22].

2.2 Digital Process Innovation and IT Acceptance Theory

During digital process innovation, organizations are frequently confronted with employees who are not willing to change their working methods [23]. Studies showed that the business value of new technologies can be completely erased by the rejection of employees [24]. Nonetheless, organizations may still underestimate the importance of employees' attitudes because of the expected performance gains. For instance, [25] showed that organizations are generally positive towards smart robots, and particularly IT organizations are highly positive.

Recent studies have been conducted related to accepting process changes, STARA and robotics. For instance, [26] argued that employees' attitudes towards BPM implementation changes strongly depend on their trust in the organization's management, rather than the hierarchical position or sector. Research related to robotics showed that employees who feel less secure about their job are more likely to deal with intelligent robots in a conservative way [27]. In another study, [18] explained that a higher STARA awareness by employees is linked to a lower job satisfaction and involvement, leading to cynicism, indifference, depression and fear for dismissal. Similarly, [23] argued that employees' attitudes towards innovation primarily depend on internal factors, such as intrinsic motivation and self-confidence. Additionally, [16] showed that employees prefer to see colleagues being replaced by other people. But when it comes to their own job, employees rather choose to be replaced by robots.

Hence, a proper preparation is essential because it gives employees more confidence in robotics and therefore more intention to collaborate with intelligent robots [28]. Also human resource managers play a role for recruiting and training employees who are employable in changing circumstances [29]. However, more research is required to uncover dedicated factors that help the acceptance of intelligent robots.

[30] describe IT acceptance as the degree of users' willingness to use IT for defined tasks (i.e., tasks for which it is designed to support). A large number of models and frameworks have been developed to explain the adoption and acceptance of technologies. These models introduce factors that affect end users [31]. The unified theory of acceptance and use of technology (UTAUT) [17] is still extensively used by researchers to explain the acceptance of new IT in Industry 4.0 [32], and will therefore be used as the common basis for our study. UTAUT identifies four key factors and four moderators [17]. The key factors are: (1) expected performance, (2) expected effort, (3) social influence, and (4) facilitating conditions. The four moderators are: (1) age, (2) gender, (3) experience, and (4) voluntariness. Based on these general parameters, UTAUT can predict the behavioral intention and actual use of a technology. For our RQ, we distill dedicated sub-factors to refine the UTAUT factors and gain insight into those elements facilitating employees' acceptance of intelligent robots.

3 Dilemma Analysis as Research Method

The future-oriented research question calls for a qualitative research approach. More specifically, a dilemma analysis presents hypothetical scenarios to practitioners [33]; in our case office worker, managers and IT consultants. Since a dilemma is seen as a conflicting choice between various alternatives, there are no correct answers so that the focus is placed on the respondents' reasoning [34]. Asking about the willingness of employees to leave certain duties to intelligent robots is situational, and thus an appropriate subject for in-depth interviews. Each respondent was asked about their opinion about a situation different from the current one, and this individually in order to give each interviewee the opportunity to clarify personal answers and to go to the heart of the hypothetical situation [35].

3.1 Selection of Respondents

Data was collected in 2019. We conducted 49 face-to-face, semi-structured interviews [36] with practitioners belonging to our university network (i.e., working at internship companies for our Master students in IT Management), of which 48 were considered complete. The pre-existing relationships with internship mentors ensured a commitment for making sufficient time available for the in-depth interviews, while simultaneously targeting the intended audience of office workers, managers and IT consultants. The average time per interview was 38 min, with a standard deviation of 13 min. The response rate was 59%, namely a total of 83 practitioners were invited, of which sixteen did not respond and eighteen refused. The main reasons for non-participation were related to a busy period at work or a holiday.

The final sample consisted of five practitioners working on the operational level, 19 working on the supportive level, 14 managers and 10 C-levels. Table 1 shows an equal division among small and medium enterprises (SMEs) and large organizations, as well as among consultancy and non-consultancy firms (i.e., across diverse sectors).

Table 1. Cross tabulation for organization sector by size.

Sector/size	Small and medium-sized enterprises (SMEs)	Large organizations	Total
Manufacturing	6	5	11
Services	3	7	10
Public & social profit	1	2	3
IT consultancy	14	10	24
Total	24	24	48

3.2 Variables

We asked whether intelligent robots can replace the respondents' job in three dilemmas (i.e., about full manual work, full automation and semi-automation). Namely:

"The following questions are purely hypothetical. They question your personal opinion or perception, regardless of whether your organization is currently more or less innovative. Suppose that in the future (so within an indefinite period of time) a robot would exist that is so intelligent that it can handle any activity and every process (or every series of activities). With robots, therefore, do not necessarily think of physical machines that can only take over manual labor, but also software that can take over complex thinking processes. This would mean

that within the dilemmas everything can be achieved with technology, and that you do not have to doubt the technical feasibility. We will deal with three dilemma situations regarding your duties, and start with the first dilemma. Please consider tasks rather as a process or series of individual activities."

- *[Dilemma 1] Are there core tasks in your current duties (or work package) that you think an intelligent robot could support you with, namely through some form of semi-automation or partial automated support?*
- *[Dilemma 2] Which core tasks from your current duties (or work package) would you never want to give to an intelligent robot? In other words: you would rather continue to perform these tasks yourself.*
- *[Dilemma 3] Which core tasks from your current duties (or work package) would you like to leave completely to an intelligent robot? In other words: you can see these tasks perfectly transferable without your input.*
- *[General attitude] What is your general view of the arrival of intelligent robots that will increasingly perform work-related tasks? Why? With what score on five would you describe your opinion? (1 = negative; 2 = rather negative; 3 = neither negative/nor positive; 4 = rather positive; 5 = positive).*

For each dilemma, we asked five sub questions related to the five UTAUT independent variables (i.e., why do you think robots can be useful, easy to use, affect performance and social influence, and which facilities do you expect?) (Table 2).

Table 2. An overview of the main variables in the dilemma analysis, based on UTAUT [17].

Independent variables	Individual determinants	Organizational determinants	Dependent variable
Expected efforts: usefulness	Gender	Size	General attitude towards intelligent robots
Expected efforts: ease-of-use	Age	Sector	
Expected performance	Experience: education level	Perceived market competition	
Expected social influence	Experience: seniority in current position		
Expected facilitating conditions	Voluntariness: adoption of private IT use [37]		

3.3 Coding

A unique code was assigned per interview question. Based on the interview transcripts, the codes facilitated assigning more specific themes or labels to text excerpts [38]. By grouping the most important labels from the first coding phases into comparative tables (i.e., analyzing by frequency and coherence with other labels), clear differences and similarities became visible. The identified concepts were thus related to each other and linked to the literature in order to extract patterns for better understanding the explanatory factors about the acceptance of intelligent robots.

We assigned 558 codes, from which 83 themes specific to intelligent robots were uncovered as sub-factors of UTAUT (Table 3). Supplementary documentation: https://drive.google.com/file/d/1Ul6VKPXiG5Ioblkwq41LGqJf8sqa2eVb/view.

Table 3. The number of factors or themes, and the underlying codes.

Main UTAUT-related factors	No. of sub-factors or themes	No. of initial codes
Task names and characteristics	30	203
Expected efforts: usefulness	15	63
Expected efforts: ease-of-use	2	59
Expected performance	15	42
Expected social influence	2	64
Expected facilitating conditions	9	90
General attitude	10	37
Total:	83	558

3.4 Evaluation Criteria

Diversity in organizational and individual characteristics stimulated data triangulation [38]. Credibility was addressed by including the UTAUT factors. Since the interviews were conducted by teams of four to six interviewers and via a semi-structured questionnaire allowing additional sub questions, personal bias was minimized. However, since all respondents were located in Western Europe and about half of them were working in IT consultancy, generalization to all sectors worldwide remained limited [35]. For instance, the public and social profit sector was underrepresented.

4 Results

We present the task names and characteristics per dilemma, before looking at the observed sub-factors underlying UTAUT and the respondents' general attitude.

4.1 Task Names and Characteristics

The work mentioned per dilemma is presented in Table 4. We observed two overlaps. Respondents had mixed opinions about doing accountancy work, namely whether it should be fully automated or semi-automated. The second overlap related to work planning and matching employees' availability to tasks or projects, with a discussion about semi-automation or no automation.

The work described per dilemma was characterized differently (Table 5). In the "no automation" dilemma, work was seen as social, creative and dealing with sensitive material. While the fully automated work was described as time-consuming and non-value adding, the semi-automated was rather dependent on various factors.

Interestingly, the three dilemmas were characterized by knowledge-intensive tasks but for different purposes, namely data-intensive for "semi-automation", contextual decision-making for "no automation", and processing a large amount of mails or testing for "full automation". Also the non-knowledge-intensive tasks were differently described, namely for computing complex data in "semi-automation" and no-brainer tasks in "full automation" situations. Likewise, the non-creative tasks had a different interpretation, namely for conformance checking with manual interventions in "semi-automation" and merely following well-defined rules in "full automation" situations.

Table 4. Top-5 of frequently mentioned task names per dilemma (N = 48).

	Semi-automation (no. of respondents)	No automation (no. of respondents)	Full automation (no. of respondents)
1	Doing accountancy work (8 respondents)	Managing customer relationships (16 respondents)	Doing accountancy work (9 respondents)
2	Collecting, analyzing and reporting on data (8 respondents)	Coaching and talent reviews (9 respondents)	Doing administrative work (7 respondents)
3	Gathering requirements, modelling and analyzing processes (7 respondents)	Directing employees, delegating tasks (5 respondents)	Programming software and software testing (7 respondents)
4	Managing contracts (2 respondents)	Planning work and matching employee availability to tasks (5 respondents)	Managing timesheets (6 respondents)
5	Planning work and matching employee availability to tasks (2 respondents)	Determining a business strategy (2 respondents)	Managing meetings (5 respondents)

Table 5. Top-5 of task characteristics per dilemma (N = 48).

	Semi-automation (no. of respondents)	No automation (no. of respondents)	Full automation (no. of respondents)
1	Can be knowledge-intensive (e.g., data-intensive) or not knowledge-intensive (e.g., computing complex data) (37 respondents)	Social (e.g., importance of human interaction), also for motivating/convincing (43 respondents)	No-brainer tasks (e.g., repetitive or not-knowledge-intensive tasks) (36 respondents)
2	Repetitive (e.g., generic and/or frequently done) (30 respondents)	Knowledge-intensive (e.g., contextual decisions) (25 respondents)	Non-creative, following well-defined rules (15 respondents)
3	Non-creative (e.g., conformance checking) (14 respondents)	Creative thinking, solution-oriented thinking (23 respondents)	Knowledge-intensive (e.g., processing data such as mails or testing) (15 respondents)
4	Variable input and/or output (11 respondents)	Human language and empathy (15 respondents)	Time-consuming (3 respondents)
5	Dependent on many different factors (9 respondents)	Sensitive or confidential material (14 respondents)	Non-value adding (2 respondents)

4.2 Expected Efforts: Usefulness and Ease-of-Use

The perceived usefulness arguments are given in Table 6. For the "no automation" dilemma, manual work was esteemed useful for human contact (i.e., to support or convince people) as well as for non-factual decision-making. It was raised that people do not like talking to robots and that the elimination of human contact is unethical.

Table 6. Top-5 of usefulness arguments per dilemma (N = 48).

	Semi-automation (no. of respondents)	No automation (no. of respondents)	Full automation (no. of respondents)
1	More time for specialization or value-adding tasks (12 respondents)	Importance of human contact (30 respondents)	Boring tasks do not motivate and are often neglected (15 respondents)
2	Robots have a high computational capacity (7 respondents)	Robots lack empathy and cannot think creatively (30 respondents)	More time for customer interaction and specialization (4 respondents)
3	Robots can provide an overview of suitable alternatives (4 respondents)	For non-factual decision-making (10 respondents)	Robots have a high computational capacity (2 respondents)
4	Decreasing random decisions (2 respondents)	People do not like talking to robots (10 respondents)	Robots are self-learning (2 respondents)
5	Effort savings (2 respondents)	Unethical to stop human contact (5 respondents)	Streamlining business processes (1 respondent)

In the "full automation" dilemma, robots were considered useful for so-called boring tasks to give employees more time for specialization and customer interaction. Robots were also appreciated for their computational and self-learning capacity.

While similar arguments applied to the "semi-automation" dilemma, the focus was also on the specialization opportunities for employees (e.g., regarding creative or managerial tasks, for coaching, for decision-making, for interpretation and customer-related issues), and so making better use of people's full potential.

Regarding ease-of-use, all respondents agreed that the "no automation" dilemma remained difficult to digitalize. This was mainly because: (1) communication and emotions are complex (e.g., underlying meanings, body language, cultural differences) (35 respondents), (2) seeking consensus requires discussion (13 respondents), (3) trustful and respectful human relationships are of high value (10 respondents), (4) external or non-defined factors (e.g., strategy, planning) are to be considered (9 respondents), and (5) tailoring or customization is complex (5 respondents).

Differentiated views were presented in the other dilemmas, albeit with similar arguments. Twenty-nine respondents considered the use of intelligent robots difficult for "semi-automation", while 19 respondents found it simple. For the "full automation" dilemma, 28 respondents agreed with simple while 15 said it would be difficult.

4.3   Expected Performance and Expected Social Influence

The expected performance gains were similar for "semi-automation" and "full automation", namely highly related to time and cost savings, and quality gains (Table 7). The reasons why intelligent robots would not trigger such performance incentives in the "no automation" dilemma involved the personal touch, complex interactions, individual decision-making and accountability for risks.

Interestingly, the performance gains were critically addressed by five respondents in the "semi-automation" dilemma (i.e., because robot set-ups take time and robots cannot prevent errors) and three respondents in the "no automation" dilemma (i.e., because quality and shared ideas outweigh performance) (Table 7).

The expected performance seemed linked to the expected social pressure. Most respondents were expecting positive stimuli for the "no automation" dilemma (44 respondents), followed by 34 respondents for "full automation", and 28 respondents for "semi-automation". Positive stimuli were seen from the Board, shareholders, market and competitors (i.e., for performance gains), but also from employees (i.e., for facilitating jobs), and customers and stakeholders (i.e., for quality). Negative pressures were expected from employees and trade unions because of a fear for job losses, privacy, IT security and ethical concerns (e.g., being accepted as humans).

Table 7. Top-5 of performance arguments per dilemma (N = 48).

	Semi-automation (no. of respondents)	No automation (no. of respondents)	Full automation (no. of respondents)
1	Time savings (40 respondents)	Allowing for a personal touch (18 respondents)	Time savings (34 respondents)
2	Higher quality (13 respondents)	Interpreting complex conversations and body language (18 respondents)	Higher quality (12 respondents)
3	Performance advantages should not be overestimated (5 respondents)	Allowing refinements, not just rational thinking (17 respondents)	More time for core business and value-adding tasks (8 respondents)
4	Less delays (3 respondents)	Taking accountability (8 respondents)	Higher employee satisfaction (5 respondents)
5	Cost savings (3 respondents)	Shared ideas are more important (3 respondents)	Cost savings (5 respondents)

4.4 Expected Facilitating Conditions

Major findings were observed across nine groups of facilitation needs (Table 8).

Table 8. Main needs for facilitation across the dilemmas (N = 48).

Facilitation needs	Number of respondents
Training, coaching, reskilling	48 respondents
Mindset for change	16 respondents
Top management actions	16 respondents
Budget investments	15 respondents
Employee involvement	14 respondents
IT aspects	11 respondents
Reconsideration of work (i.e., business processes and rules)	11 respondents
Ethics and guarantees to employees	13 respondents
Time investments	10 respondents

4.4.1 Training, Coaching and Reskilling

Organizations should consider internal and/or external courses for reskilling employees. Besides training in business knowledge, a new curriculum should include:

- Training in how a robot works (e.g., explaining which data is accessed and why, and which capacity robots have)

- Training in how to interact with, control and correct robots
- Training in new job contents (e.g., estimating which input is needed, monitoring and analyzing master data, interpreting output, and conceptual thinking).
- Training in people interaction and empathy (e.g., coaching).

Such courses should supplement on-the-job learning. Extra facilities should be given during work by means of: (1) instruction manuals on how to use intelligent robots, (2) 24/7 support teams or service desks (e.g., for questions, problems, and to set-up robots), and (3) basic IT support (e.g., for tools like MS Excel, a mailbox). It is important to create a learning organization, not only by providing training but also by stimulating informal contacts (e.g., for networking and asking for advice), and by allowing experts to transfer knowledge to other employees (e.g., to inspire as coaches)

4.4.2 Mindset for Change

Organizations should let their employees think more about innovation by applying change management to facilitate adoption. Most importantly, managers should preach values like efficiency, empowerment, entrepreneurship and team spirit, while employees should also be formally appraised for considering those corporate values. Such values can become tangible by stimulating collaboration between teams or departments. Corporate communication should focus on creating trust in intelligent robots, among others by offering success stories to prove evidence, informing how robots and employees can add value without job losses (i.e., intelligent robots should not be seen as a threat nor intimidation), as well as emphasizing the advantages for employees and customers. Innovation can also be stimulated by alternative work variants like homeworking for a better work-life balance and incentives by self-driving company cars.

4.4.3 Top Management Actions

Top managers should have a clear vision and strategic objectives derived from a business case with related automation projects. By conducting return-on-investment (ROI) calculations, robot performance can be assessed (e.g., possibly switching back to manual work). Also benchmarking is needed, both internal and with competitors.

4.4.4 Budget Investments

Budget investments are not only needed to finance robotics, but also to invest in sufficient resources (i.e., including staff) and more commercial data as input for robots. Budget is needed for an expert to experiment with robotics via trial-and-error.

4.4.5 Employee Involvement

Organizations should consult employees when deciding on the robots' tasks, inputs and outputs. It is essential to ask advice or feedback from all employee types, each with their own competencies. Employees should not only be involved during the preparation and transition period, but also after the robot implementation to stimulate knowledge sharing among colleagues (e.g., sharing customer experiences).

An alternative view on employee involvement is out-of-the-box job counselling to help employees orient themselves to new job positions, including brainstorming about personal wishes and employee participation.

4.4.6 IT Aspects

Organizations should invest in IT infrastructure and excellent Internet connection, as well as continue to support basic IT tools (e.g., MS Excel). They should stay up-to-date about IT trends (e.g., via conferences or training by IT consultants). Before robot implementations can be made, organizations should have workshops with technical people. Both internal developments and IT outsourcing should be considered, and consultants should be hired when extra knowledge is required on a certain topic.

4.4.7 Reconsideration of Work (I.E., Business Processes and Business Rules)

Before considering robotics, business processes and business rules should be rethought first. Well-described business processes and procedures help employees know what is expected from them.

4.4.8 Ethics and Guarantees to Employees

Organizations should create an ethical framework that states what robots are allowed to do, while also analyzing and justifying the human-related side effects (e.g., reskilling needs, downsizing, and burn-outs). Also privacy seems a struggle, which requires organizations to explain which personal data is monitored for what purpose. Employees wish strong employer commitments by means of some guarantees, like:

1. Guarantee that intelligent robots are able to perform the tasks to be automated (i.e., to build up confidence in robotics)
2. Guarantee that employees can control a robot's output for accountability
3. Guarantee that internal expertise of automated processes remains (i.e., having employees who know which process changes can occur)
4. Guarantee that robots are not used for talent management (e.g., not for personal promotions or dismissals)

4.4.9 Time Investments

Organizations should take time for a transition period (i.e., combining the old and new ways of working), and start with a trial or pilot. Experts should get time to make robots smarter, and employees need timeslots to participate in innovation projects.

4.5 General Attitude Towards Intelligent Robots

The vast majority felt positive about intelligent robots. Although multiple respondents added critical reflections, Fig. 1 shows that only 7 out of 48 respondents translated their concerns into a neutral or rather negative attitude (i.e., score 2 and score 3 on a 5-point Likert scale).

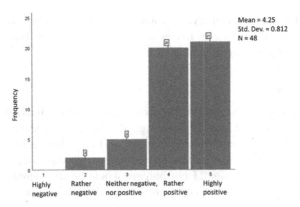

Fig. 1. Histogram of the general attitude towards intelligent robots (N = 48).

The comments are summarized in Table 9. Since the critical comments require extra efforts from organizations or governments, we now elaborate on them.

Table 9. Main comments typifying the respondents' general attitude towards robotics (N = 48).

Tone	Reasoning	Number of respondents
Neutral comments	Natural evolution in society	11 respondents
	Uncertainty (wait-and-see)	7 respondents
	Evolution in IT	3 respondents
Optimistic comments	Changes in and creation of job contents	20 respondents
	Increased job satisfaction	14 respondents
	Solutions to society	2 respondents
Critical comments	Fears of employees	17 respondents
	Inclusion/exclusion in society	11 respondents
	Ethical concerns	9 respondents
	Lack of education and reskilling needs	7 respondents

The fear for job losses should not be underestimated. Besides the need of a mindset that fosters change, businesses should recognize that job variety is important (e.g., repetitive tasks help employees to relax). Repetitive tasks should also exist for employees who are not capable of doing creative work to avoid a social gap. Ethical concerns were repeated regarding the use of medical or privacy data (e.g., robots should not decide about euthanasia) and accountability (e.g., who is responsible when robots cause defects). Governments should control that robots are properly used. Because finding IT-skilled employees remains difficult, governments should also change educational programs for teaching more on creative thinking and logical reasoning.

5 Discussion

Although our next research step is to consider the individual and organizational determinants as well (Table 2), our work has launched a call for not only looking at robotics for acquiring economic sustainability (i.e., performance gains), but also for considering the social sustainability of work (i.e., in organizations and in society).

Our findings attempt to stimulate the integration of intelligent robots in the business world. The overview of tasks that office workers, managers and IT consultants usually want to leave to robots require relatively little persuasiveness when implementing robotics. On the other hand, we clarified which tasks those higher-skilled employees prefer to perform themselves. For the latter, organizations can set a proper innovation strategy to involve their staff. New job contents are likely to focus on robot maintenance and controlling, while training curricula are needed which focus on creativity, exception handling and value-adding tasks (e.g., conceptual thinking and the interpretation of data instead of operational data input).

5.1 Research Agenda

Besides social sustainability, green sustainability deserves attention as well (e.g., the energy consumption or recycling of intelligent robots) [39].

Furthermore, research is needed to investigate how employees deal with the fact that robots are able to show empathy because Sect. 4.1 until Sect. 4.3 focused on empathy-related aspects in the "no automation" dilemma. Scholars can also investigate a more differentiated transition to intelligent robots among different types of higher-skilled employees. This transition might affect the state of mind about team work as well (Sect. 4.4.2).

Since the ethical aspects were only considered to a minor extent in Sect. 4.4.8, additional work can reflect on how far society can go in robotics. For instance, if robots become able to replace business executives and CEOs, to which extent will they take over our human-based economy, and how would robots be taxed in the future? The latter is especially crucial for countries with a budget deficit, and to address societal issues related to inequalities between rich and poor.

Finally, Sect. 4.5 emphasized that the labor market determines the direction of education (i.e., starting in primary and secondary schools). For instance, should governments cancel certain specialization areas while defining more future-proof areas? Perhaps automation can offer training solutions by using more digital platforms.

5.2 Step-by-Step Plan for a Gradual Adoption of Intelligent Robots

Based on the UTAUT facilitation factor and the nine uncovered sub-factors (Sect. 4.4), we have derived a step-by-step plan for organizations to better guide their employees through the implementation of intelligent robots. This roadmap allows organizations to reduce the implementation costs by facilitating employees to follow process innovations with intelligent robots faster and more efficiently (Table 10). Business executives and managers are advised to timely respond to employees' opinions. Alternatively, technology developers can respond to these needs and particularly employee aversion to intelligent robots.

While Table 10 is derived from our interviews, additional evaluations are required to examine how far this roadmap can lead to the desired goal of digital process innovation by intelligent robots.

Table 10. Roadmap for gradually adopting intelligent robots in process innovation projects.

Facilitation needs	Before implementation	During implementation	After implementation
Training (Subsect. 4.4.1)	• Start reskilling • Also focus on business knowledge	• How robots work • How to interact with robots (input/output)	• Offer a support desk • Learn on-the-job • Share knowledge
Mindset (Subsect. 4.4.2)	• Rethink values • Collaborate	• Apply change management to build trust	• Apply human resource management
Top management (Subsect. 4.4.3)	• Create a vision and business case for innovation projects • Start with quick wins • Calculate pre-ROI	• Check ROI • Possibly readjust the project (with more or fewer robots)	• Calculate post-ROI • Share as success story • Continue benchmarking
Budget (Subsect. 4.4.4)	• Collect data • Buy and experiment with robots (experts)	• Provide sufficient resources (also staff)	• Invest in more data (especially customer-related)
Employee involvement (Subsect. 4.4.5)	• Allow trial-and-error • Stimulate coaching • Job counselling	• Consult for the robots' input and output	• Allow for controlling robots • Talk about customers
IT aspects (Subsect. 4.4.6)	• Start from an IT architecture • Provide 24/7 Internet (Wi-Fi, backups)	• Consider outsourcing and/or internal developments	• Observe IT trends • Invest in IT licenses
Work (Subsect. 4.4.7)	• Rethink work alternatives	• Document innovated work	• Follow business processes
Ethics (Subsect. 4.4.8)	• Be GDPR compliant • Give guarantees	• Explain privacy and security issues	• Conduct periodical conformance audits
Time (Subsect. 4.4.9)	• Free timeslots to innovate (employees)	• Start with a pilot • Use transition periods	• Free timeslots for self-learning (experts)

6 Conclusion

The UTAUT factors have helped us uncover sub-factors for explaining the attitudes of office workers, managers and IT consultants towards adding intelligent robots to business processes. The study concludes that those employee types generally see robots and employees as complementary. While the majority of respondents do not bother leaving administrative and repetitive tasks to intelligent robots, some tasks are preferably not to be replaced because of customer interactions and creativity. In follow-up research, we dig deeper into the individual and organizational determinants.

References

1. Hammer, M.: Reengineering work. Harv. Bus. Rev. **68**(4), 104–112 (1990)
2. Cascio, W.F., Montealegre, R.: How technology is changing work and organizations. Ann. Rev. Org. Psych. Org. Behav. **3**(1), 349–375 (2016)
3. Karabegović, I., Karabegović, E., Mahmić, M., Husak, E.: Implementation of industry 4.0 and industrial robots in the manufacturing processes. In: Karabegović, I. (ed.) NT 2019. LNNS, vol. 76, pp. 3–14. Springer, Cham (2020). https://doi.org/10.1007/978-3-030-18072-0_1
4. Dahl, R.: Charlie and the Chocolate Factory. Alfred A. Knopf, New York (1964)
5. Huang, M.-H., Rust, R.T.: Artificial intelligence in service. J. Serv. Res. **21**(2), 155–172 (2018)
6. Kaivo-oja, J., Roth, S., Westerlund, L.: Futures of robotics. Int. J. Technol. Manag. **73**(4), 176–205 (2017)
7. Balsmeier, B., Woerter, M.: Is this time different? How digitalization influences job creation and destruction. Res. Policy **48**(8), 1–10 (2019)
8. Frey, C.B., Osborne, M.A.: The future of employment. Tech. Forecast. Soc. Change **114**, 254–280 (2017)
9. Neves, F., Campos, P., Silva, S.: Innovation and employment: an agent-based approach. J. Artif. Soc. Soc. Simul. **22**(1), 1–32 (2019)
10. Vermeulen, B., Kesselhut, J., Pyka, A., Saviotti, P.P.: The impact of automation on employment. Sustainability **10**(5), 1–27 (2018)
11. Flechsig, C., Lohmer, J., Lasch, R.: Realizing the full potential of robotic process automation through a combination with BPM. In: Bierwirth, C., Kirschstein, T., Sackmann, D. (eds.) Logistics Management. LNL, pp. 104–119. Springer, Cham (2019). https://doi.org/10.1007/978-3-030-29821-0_8
12. Gomes, O.: Growth in the age of automation: foundations of a theoretical framework. Metroeconomica **70**(1), 77–97 (2018)
13. Holford, W.D.: The future of human creative knowledge work within the digital economy. Futures **105**, 143–154 (2019)
14. Green, B.P.: Ethical reflections on artificial intelligence. Sci. et Fides **6**(2), 9–31 (2018)
15. Frank, M.R., Sun, L., Cebrian, M., Youn, H., Rahwan, I.: Small cities face greater impact from automation. J. Royal Soc. Interf. **15**(139), 1–11 (2018)
16. Granulo, A., Fuchs, C., Puntoni, S.: Psychological reactions to human versus robotic job replacement. Nat. Hum. Behav. **3**(10), 1062–1069 (2019)
17. Venkatesh, V., Morris, M.G., Davis, G.B., Davis, F.D.: User acceptance of information technology. MIS Q. **27**(3), 425–478 (2003)
18. Brougham, D., Haar, J.: Smart technology, artificial intelligence, robotics, and algorithms (STARA). J. Manag. Organ. **24**(2), 239–257 (2017)

19. Lai, R., Lin, W., Wu, Y.: Review of research on the key technologies, application fields and development trends of intelligent robots. In: Chen, Z., Mendes, A., Yan, Y., Chen, S. (eds.) ICIRA 2018. LNCS (LNAI), vol. 10985, pp. 449–458. Springer, Cham (2018). https://doi.org/10.1007/978-3-319-97589-4_38

20. Fletcher, S.R., Webb, P.: Industrial robot ethics: the challenges of closer human collaboration in future manufacturing systems. In: Ferreira, M.I.A., Silva Sequeira, J., Tokhi, M.O., Kadar, Endre E., Virk, G.S. (eds.) A World with Robots. ISCASE, vol. 84, pp. 159–169. Springer, Cham (2017). https://doi.org/10.1007/978-3-319-46667-5_12

21. Qureshi, M.O., Syed, R.S.: The impact of robotics on employment and motivation of employees in the service sector, with special reference to health care. Saf. Health Work 5(4), 198–202 (2014)

22. Savela, N., Turja, T., Oksanen, A.: Social acceptance of robots in different occupational fields. Int. J. Soc. Robot. 10(4), 493–502 (2018)

23. Hausberg, P., Hülsdau, M., Moysidou, K., Teuteberg, F.: Employees' adoption of workplace innovations. Informatik P-275, 1399–1411 (2017). https://doi.org/10.18420/in2017_140

24. Talukder, M.: Causal paths to acceptance of technological innovations by individual employees. BPM J. 25(4), 582–606 (2019)

25. Morikawa, M.: Firm's expectations about the impact of AI and robotics: evidence from a survey. Econ. Inquiry 55(2), 1054–1063 (2017)

26. Pereira, V.R., Maximiano, A., de Souza Bido, D.: Resistance to change in BPM implementation. BPM J. 25(7), 1564–1586 (2019)

27. Nam, T.: Citizen attitudes about job replacement by robotic automation. Futures 109, 39–49 (2019)

28. You, S., Robert Jr, L.P.: Human-robot similarity and willingness to work with a robotic co-worker. In: International Conference on Human-Robot Interaction, pp. 251–260. ACM/IEEE, Chicago (2018)

29. Maity, S.: Identifying opportunities for artificial intelligence in the evolution of training and development practices. J. Manag. Dev. 38(8), 651–663 (2019)

30. Dillon, A., Morris, M.G.: User acceptance of information technology. Ann. Rev. Inf. Sci. Technol. 31, 3–32 (1996)

31. Taherdoost, H.: A review of technology acceptance and adoption models and theories. Procedia Manuf. 22, 960–967 (2018)

32. Dwivedi, Y.K., Rana, N.P., Jeyaraj, A., Clement, M., Williams, M.D.: Re-examining the unified theory of acceptance and use of technology (UTAUT). Inf. Syst. Front. 21, 719–734 (2019)

33. Marshall, C., Rossman, G.B.: Designing Qualitative Research. Sage, California (2011)

34. Scager, K., Akkerman, S.F., Pilot, A., Wubbels, T.: Teacher dilemmas in challenging students in higher education. Teach. High. Educ. 22(3), 318–335 (2016)

35. Malterud, K.: Qualitative research. Lancet 358(9280), 483–488 (2001)

36. Castillo-Montoya, M.: Preparing for interview research. Qual. Rep. 21(5), 811–830 (2016)

37. Rogers, E.M.: Diffusion of innovations. Free Press, New York (2003)

38. Belotto, M.: Data analysis methods for qualitative research. Qual. Rep. 23(11), 2622–2633 (2018)

39. Couckuyt, D., Van Looy, A.: Green BPM as a business-oriented discipline: a systematic mapping study and research agenda. Sustainability 11(15), 1–22 (2019)

40. Wang, T.-M., Tao, Y., Liu, H.: Current researches and future development trend of intelligent robot: a review. Int. J. Autom. Comp. 15(5), 525–546 (2018)

How to Keep RPA Maintainable?

Philip Noppen[1], Iris Beerepoot[1(✉)], Inge van de Weerd[1], Mathieu Jonker[2], and Hajo A. Reijers[1]

[1] Utrecht University, Utrecht, The Netherlands
[2] Artilience, Utrecht, The Netherlands
i.m.beerepoot@uu.nl

Abstract. Robotic Process Automation (RPA) is a term for software tools that operate on the user interface while trying to mimic a real user. Organizations are eager to adopt RPA, since the technology promises significant benefits such as cost savings. However, it is unclear how organizations should govern RPA. The burden of maintenance, in particular, can become high once an organization scales up its RPA efforts. To prevent or diminish high maintenance efforts, we propose in this paper 11 guidelines to establish low-maintenance RPA implementations. The guidelines are particularly applicable in those contexts where business units themselves oversee these implementations with a Center of Excellence in the background. The guidelines are derived from a literature study and four case studies; they are validated with experts using the Delphi method.

Keywords: Robotic Process Automation · Governance · RPA maintenance · Federated organizational model · RPA Center of Excellence

1 Introduction

Robotic Process Automation (RPA) is a tool among a diverse set of other tools that enable higher productivity as part of an automation and digitization strategy. It refers to software tools operating on the user interface that try to mimic a real user [1]. RPA is non-invasive to the underlying IT infrastructure, as opposed to traditional BPM solutions [16]. It is used to automate processes that are structured, rule-based, and repetitive [13,34,41]. A typical use case is creating invoices. To create an invoice a bot can be tasked to retrieve data from an Excel sheet and enter the invoice data from that sheet into the correct fields of an SAP form. Once all the data is pasted into SAP, the bot creates the invoice by running all the transactions. This example emphasizes a notable strength of RPA, which is to connect different applications without human intervention.

Organizations that aim to establish quick wins to save costs are eager to implement RPA [20]. Bots are relatively quick and easy to build compared to traditional automation solutions. When the application of RPA within an organization starts spreading beyond initial experiences, the issue of governance comes

D. Fahland et al. (Eds.): BPM 2020, LNCS 12168, pp. 453–470, 2020.
https://doi.org/10.1007/978-3-030-58666-9_26

up. Some organizations choose for a *decentralized* model by letting business units develop bots autonomously, completely bypassing the IT department [39]. In other settings, as for example described in [30], a *centralized* unit takes overall responsibility and accountability of RPA within an organization. This could be a newly created Center of Excellence (CoE) or the traditional IT department. Finally, it is possible to mix these approaches into a *federated* model, where self-sufficient business units take care of RPA implementations but receive support from a CoE. Regardless of the model, however, each organization must face the problem of an increased burden of maintenance; such efforts are often much higher than expected [27]. Illustrative is the following remark of an RPA project manager, cited in [34]:

> You always underestimate the complexity of things, even if it is simple. There is more need for monitoring and maintenance than we thought one year ago. [....] We just wanted to get started, and our focus was on delivering solutions.

Because widespread organizational RPA use is still in its early stages, there is a gap of knowledge on how to deal with the maintenance challenge, which brings us to the following research question: *How can organizations minimize maintenance problems related to RPA implementations?*

The contribution of this paper is that it presents a set of 11 guidelines for the creation and sustenance of low-maintenance RPA implementations. The guidelines are considered to be particularly useful in the setting of a federated model for RPA, i.e. when RPA is driven by business units that receive support through a CoE. Organizations that have adopted a centralized model can use these guidelines to investigate or structure a business case to transition to a federated model. Those organizations that are completely new to RPA can use the guidelines to improve or critically review their business case.

To develop the guidelines that are presented in this paper, a mix of methodologies was adopted. A survey of the literature was used to develop an initial list of guidelines. Case studies within four different Dutch organizations were carried out to supplement this list. Finally, a survey-based Delphi method was used to validate the guidelines.

The remainder of the paper is structured as follows. Section 2 elaborates on the related research focusing on RPA governance structures and enabling business units. It is followed by the research methods used to create and validate the guidelines. Sect. 4 presents the guidelines. We conclude the paper in Sect. 5 with a reflection on the implications and limitations of this study.

2   Background

For governing RPA, three distinct organizational models can be identified: the decentralized, federated and centralized organizational model [27]. In a centralized organizational model, a Center of Excellence (CoE) is created containing the entire RPA capability. In practice, as observed by Schmitz, Dietze and Czarnecki [30] this can mean that a centralized team of project leaders are responsible for multiple smaller automation teams. The project leaders have a role in the identification, design and implementation of RPA use cases that contribute to the overall objective of increased process automation. Employees tasked with the processes to be automated are closely involved as they can share their expertise with the people that are tasked to automate a process. Their detailed operational understanding can also help to identify and prioritize ideas for future RPA use cases. A decentralized approach places the RPA capability in different business units without a governing body in place. Osmundsen, Iden and Bygstad [27] identify advantages of a decentralized approach. It creates enthusiasm for digitization due to the deep involvement of local employees within the RPA initiative. Employees realized how they could employ RPA software and make improvements themselves without the help of the IT department. By establishing local ownership, the employees knowing the processes were better involved. A decentralized approach can however have significant downsides [3,27]. For instance, it lacks control mechanisms to coordinate and prioritize the different RPA initiatives. Another downside is the lack of an end-to-end process view. Process automation is done within departments without a perspective of how processes are part of and affect other parts of the organization.

A federated approach combines the decentralized and centralized approach [27,39]. This organizational model retains the benefits of local ownership and business involvement of the decentralized approach. The disadvantages of the decentralized approach are avoided by retaining a CoE. Adopting a federated organizational model can spread out the maintenance effort more evenly across the organization. By organizing RPA within business units, local employees possessing the knowledge of the processes are more involved. Many organizations have claimed success by organizing RPA within business units [16,27,34,40].

However, also with a federated approach, pitfalls may emerge. First, the IT department has to be part of the RPA initiative as they can ensure that RPA solutions work securely, consistently and are scalable [32]. Furthermore, business people will run into issues that are initially invisible to them, but not to IT, such as capacity planning, fail-over for servers and storage, licensing of virtual machines and network latency [32]. This kind of collaboration between business units and the IT department can lead to ambiguity in terms of ownership and responsibilities. Indeed, establishing RPA development teams consisting mainly of business people without a background in IT can create tensions with the IT department as such a development task is often associated with software development [6,27,34]. These stakeholders can have different views on RPA and how to approach it. For example, in one case study the IT department reacted negatively to RPA as they viewed it as a temporary IT solution that was improperly integrated [34]. The IT department was concerned that RPA developers did not apply the methods and best practices that software developers use.

Second, the maintenance of bots can be more burdensome than initially expected [27,34]. RPA can scale rapidly in a relatively short time and exacerbate problems if insufficient preparation has taken place. It is recommended to continuously monitor bots, and as such RPA software often comes with a performance dashboard [7]. Such a dashboard can show average processing time per case, but also provide more insight into the exceptions. Cooper, Holderness, Sorensen and Wood [7] describe a case in which an organization operates over a thousand bots. This organization has created a manned control room where all bots are monitored 24/7, highlighting the need for continuous monitoring. An increasing need for low maintenance can lead to discussions related to ownership and responsibilities and alternative solutions [27,34].

To summarize, three governance structures for RPA can be identified, of which the federated model is the most promising. Nevertheless, when adopting a federated model, certain potentially negative consequences must be considered. The aim of this study is to prevent these negative consequences with the help of the identification of guidelines. These guidelines are specifically targeted at organizations that have adopted the federated model and that aim for low maintainability of their RPA solutions.

3   Methods

This section discusses the different research methods used to set up this research and to create and validate the guidelines. First, in Sect. 3.1, we outline the literature review. We then explain our multi-case study in Sect. 3.2. We successively (1) provide a summary of the case organizations and (2) discuss the data collection and analysis approach. We end the section with an explanation of the validation of the guidelines (Sect. 3.3). Figure 1 illustrates the steps we have taken to arrive at the guidelines, using this mix of research methods.

3.1   Literature Review

A list of both scientific literature and grey literature was created using a search on Google Scholar and Google. As search terms, we used 26 different combinations of the term "Robotic Process Automation" combined with a term such as "lessons learned", "core problems", or "implementation". Both the results from Google Scholar and Google were analyzed on their contents by scanning through titles, abstracts, and, if necessary, the article contents. We used the following inclusion criteria for evaluating entries:

– Describes an RPA implementation process
– Describes lessons learned from an RPA implementation process
– Mentions strategies to minimize the negative aspects or reinforce positive aspects

The highest ranked entries on both Google Scholar and Google yielded several useful results. Further down the search results, fewer and fewer useful articles could be identified. When stopped finding useful entries (based on the inclusion criteria), we stopped our search. This resulted in 14 scientific papers that we

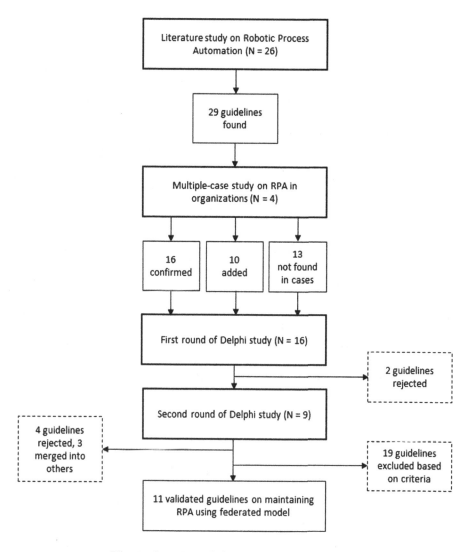

Fig. 1. Overview of the derivation of guidelines

found on Google Scholar and 12 items of grey literature found on Google. The list of grey literature consists of website entries and reports from RPA vendors and consultancy firms. The total of 26 papers and documents were summarized and reflected upon by focusing on the lessons learned by the organizations. From this, we derived a set of 29 preliminary guidelines that could potentially help organizations develop low-maintenance RPA solutions.

3.2   Multi-case Study

As we are interested in a contemporary phenomenon in its context, a multi-case study was conducted, which was the next step in our overall approach. The case study methodology is suitable when the phenomenon is difficult to study in isolation [29,42]. For this study, it was difficult to isolate RPA, since it is part of an organizational process and involves different stakeholders. Furthermore, the case study methodology is suitable for an exploratory research purpose that seeks to find out what is happening and to gain more insight [29].

Another advantage of the case study approach is triangulation, as studying the phenomenon from different angles provides a broader picture and strengthens the evidence [28,29,42]. Furthermore, fulfilling *multiple* case studies increases the generalizability and provides more insight [25].

Case Organizations. Four organizations participated in the case studies. One organization requested to be anonymized and will be referred to as BankX. The other participating organizations are the Rabobank, PostNL, and the municipality of Rotterdam. All four organizations either adopted a federated model or were moving towards a federated model. An overview of the participating organizations can be found in Table 1.

The Rabobank is a large Dutch bank and is among the 30 largest financial institutions in the world[1]. The Rabobank is an early adopter of RPA, starting with a first prototype, or Proof of Concept (PoC), in the summer of 2016, and moving beyond a PoC in 2017. In terms of RPA adoption and, more specifically, automation of processes, it is ahead of the other case organizations.

BankX is a bank as well, but is significantly smaller and only services institutional customers. BankX started with a PoC in October 2016 and moved beyond their PoC in January 2017.

PostNL is a mail, parcel, and e-commerce corporation.[2] It has its operations mainly in the Netherlands, but also in Germany, Italy, Belgium, and the United Kingdom. PostNL came into contact with RPA at the end of 2017 and subsequently started their PoC.

The municipality of Rotterdam is the second largest city of the Netherlands with more than 600,000 inhabitants. The city council of the municipality started exploringy RPA at the end of 2018 and plans to have 4–10 operational bots before the end of 2020.[3]

Data Collection and Analysis. An overview of the data collection is shown in Table 2. Semi-structured interviews form the main source of data collected from the case studies. The interviews were held with different participants from the selected organizations. The questions that were asked related to the arrangement of RPA within the organization and the choices that were made, such as: "To

---

[1] https://www.rabobank.com/en/home/index.html.

[2] https://www.postnl.nl/en/.

[3] https://www.rotterdam.nl/english/.

Table 1. Overview of the organizations participating in the case studies

Case organization	Industry	Total employees	Operational bots
Rabobank	Financial services	59,000	150
BankX	Financial services	450	50
PostNL	Distribution	38,000	17
Municipality of Rotterdam	Municipality	11,000	4–10

what extent has RPA been scaled up and are there specific factors that could hinder this? Have certain choices been made to facilitate upscaling?" And: "To what extent and how are employees being involved in the development of bots?"

The collected data were coded in NVivo, based on the guidelines as derived from literature in the previous step. As a result, 16 of the guidelines from literature were confirmed in the case studies. 10 guidelines that were not found in the literature, but did emerge in the case studies, were added to the provisional list of guidelines. 13 guidelines that had been found in literature, were not found during the case studies. We transferred the full set of 39 guidelines to the next step, the validation.

Table 2. Overview of data collection

Case organization	Type	Roles
Rabobank	2 semi-structured interviews	IT Delivery and Solution Architect; Lead Product Owner RPA
BankX	2 semi-structured interviews	Head of Process Improvement; Change Manager
PostNL	1 semi-structured interview	Platform Manager RPA
Municipality of Rotterdam	1 semi-structured interview; 3 unstructured interviews	Team Manager; Employee; RPA Developer

3.3 Validation

To validate the created guidelines the Delphi method was used. The Delphi method is defined as *"a method for structuring a group communication process so that the process is effective in allowing a group of individuals, as a whole, to deal with a complex problem"* [21]. The method is based on the premise of collective intelligence that enhances individual judgment by capturing the collective opinions of experts. In this study, we used two rounds of surveys to collect the expert opinions, allowing for participants that are both geographically close and far away to contribute anonymously [36]. This allowed for higher expert selection criteria that have academic publications related to RPA.

The 39 guidelines derived from literature and the case studies were separated into 52 statements, which allowed for a more detailed analysis. Each statement was presented in a survey to the participants, in most cases followed by a 9-point Likert scale to determine the corresponding agreement (ranging from 1 point for complete disagreement to 9 points for complete agreement). With Delphi research, there are no set criteria available to determine at which percentage consensus has been reached [38]. McKenna [24] and Loughlin and Moore [22] suggest consensus is reached if there is 51% agreement amongst respondents. In other research, percentages of 70% or 80% have been recommended. Two studies with a similar Delphi setup using a 9-point Likert scale adopted a consensus of 70% and 75% respectively [2,36]. Based on consensus percentages used in other studies, we determined the level of consensus by establishing for each statement whether a range of three consecutive points on the scale was selected by over 70% of the experts.

The Delphi study required two rounds of surveys sent to selected experts after which sufficient consensus was reached. These experts were selected based on publications related to RPA. They were working mostly in academia, but also in industry. In the first round we received 16 responses, while we received 9 responses in the second round. In both rounds we used statements to determine consensus, in this way testing support for the guidelines. As mentioned, the first survey round consisted of 52 statements, excluding demographic questions. For each statement there was an opportunity for the experts to leave a comment. The collected comments were used to refine a number of statements that did not lead to sufficient consensus. After the first round, two guidelines were eliminated because consensus was not achieved. This meant that the second round the survey covered statements related to 37 guidelines only. After this second round, 4 guidelines were rejected; 3 guidelines were merged into other guidelines, since they were determined to be similar.

After the validation, 30 guidelines derived from literature and/or the case studies were validated successfully by the experts. We then brought further focus by including only those guidelines that are relevant to organizations that have adopted a federated model and contribute towards achieving maintainability in terms of their RPA solutions. For example, the guideline *choose the organizational model with the best organizational fit* is crucial for all organizations, but as we focus on organizations that have already adopted the federated model, this is out of scope for our study.

Based on the criteria of relevancy to organizations adopting a federated model and focusing on maintainable RPA, we excluded a further 19 guidelines; 11 guidelines remained.

4   Guidelines

This section presents the 11 guidelines that went through the entire research process, such as described in the previous section. Figure 2 presents an overview of the guidelines, in relation to the different phases of RPA adoption, which we will further explain below.

4.1   Phases of RPA Adoption

In order to bring structure to the guidelines, we grouped them into three phases: *Establish Capability*, *Develop Capability*, and *Mature Capability*. The phase *Develop Capability* is subdivided into the phases *assess*, *configure*, and *test*. The phases are not intended as a proposed approach for integrating RPA in an organization, but purely function as clarification of the distinctive character of the guidelines.

The first phase, *Establish Capability*, generally consists of vendor selection, creating a business case, and developing a Proof of Concept. In this phase, organizations build the foundation of their RPA capability. The *Develop Capability* phase concerns the development phase in which the initial RPA capability is built. Bot development is divided into three parts, namely: assess, configure, and test. The *Mature Capability* phase marks the middle and ending point of scaling up the number of bots. It is also a phase that is characterized by continuous improvement and maintenance.

4.2   Guidelines to Maintainable RPA Using a Federated Model

In what comes next, we will explain the guidelines one by one. A number of guidelines are accompanied by literature references that are part of the basis of those respective guidelines. The guidelines without a reference originate exclusively from the case studies. Furthermore, each guideline is followed by one or more statements as used in the Delphi survey. The statements are accompanied by a percentage conveying the level of agreement. In addition to this percentage, a range is displayed, which denotes the degree of acceptance between that specific interval on a 9-point Likert scale. For example, for Guideline 2, 89% of the experts scored the statement with a 7, 8, or 9 on the 9-point Likert scale. Guideline 10 is the exception, which will be in the respective section.

Guideline 1: Consider Enabling Business Units to Develop and Maintain Bots. [16,27,34,40]

- Temporarily extending a business unit that is lacking the expertise to successfully develop bots with an expert from the CoE enables that business unit to successfully develop bots - 100%, 6–8
- Training and mentoring-on-the-job facilitated by the CoE should be sufficient for business units with a moderate amount of IT affinity that want to start building bots - 88%, 6–8

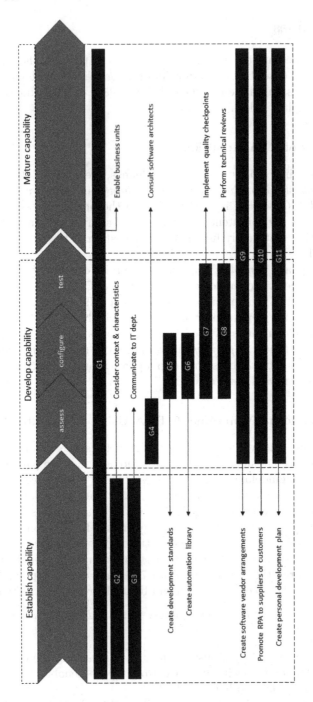

Fig. 2. Overview of the presented guidelines

One of the key characteristics of RPA as opposed to traditional BPM solutions is that it is relatively easy to configure, meaning users without a specific technical background are able to develop bots [14]. This allows organizations to use RPA in order to adopt a bottom-up approach, contrasted to a top-down standardising approach [37]. In line with this, the results from the case studies show that organizations can enable their business units to develop and maintain bots if they are deemed sufficiently capable. The statement of temporarily extending a business unit that is lacking the expertise to successfully develop bots was accepted (100%, 6–8). A transition can be facilitated by the CoE, which can help set up a robotics team within a business unit. This includes recruiting qualified people from within the business unit who are able to work with the tools provided.

Guideline 2: When Selecting RPA Vendors, Take the Context and Characteristics of the Organization into Account as Much as the Financial Aspects [8,15,20].

– Organizations aiming for medium to long-term RPA implementations should take the context and characteristics of the organization into account as much as the financial aspects when selecting RPA vendors - 89%, 7–9

Vendors can compete with each other on various aspects such as the total cost of ownership, ease of use, control, analytics and vendor support. Choosing the right vendor depends on variables such as the scope and size of the to be realized RPA capability, expertise within the organization and financial resources. For example, ease of automation can be a more important aspect for an organization lacking IT affinity and know-how among its business units. Easier to use solutions require less training and accelerate the development of bots. Vendors can differentiate the amount of support offered. In conclusion, organizations should be aware of their needs and aspirations. Choosing the right vendor can save costs and reduce the chance of failure.

Guideline 3: Demonstrate and Structure Communication to the IT Department Regarding RPA [9,26].

– Organizations should have an internal communication plan when introducing RPA to the IT department that describes the capabilities of RPA, its benefits and limitations, the role of IT and the envisioned roadmap - 87%, 7–9
– Transparent communication to the IT department about the capabilities of RPA, its benefits and limitations, the role of IT and the envisioned roadmap is effective for minimizing the resistance to RPA - 80%, 7–9

As mentioned earlier, there are specific advantages of adopting a federated model as opposed to a centralized or decentralized model. On the one hand it exploits the benefits of local ownership and on the other hand there are the benefits of a central governance body and knowledgebase of a CoE. In order to achieve these benefits, however, good communication between the parties involved is vital, not only between the CoE and the business. What became clear in the case studies is that organizations should also communicate the capabilities, benefits, limitations, role of IT and the envisioned roadmap to the IT department.

Preconceived opinions regarding RPA that can reside within the IT department should be addressed and discussed among IT personnel. Discussing the envisioned roadmap should inform IT personnel about what RPA means for their own internal roadmap. Additionally, the role of IT should be discussed as they are in a supporting role. Friction between the business and IT side can develop if the roles and responsibilities are unknown.

Guideline 4: Consult Software Architects During a Process Assessment.

– Software architects should be consulted when assessing a process - 71%, 7–9

In line with the previous guideline, the importance of communication with software architects is especially evident during process assessment. Although RPA is characterized by the fact that its development can be led by business units, this does not mean that there is no knowledge to be gained from specialists. On the contrary, our results show that business units wanting to automate a process should consult software architects. Software architects can also be part of the CoE. A board of architects can determine how the process should be automated. In some instances, a permanent solution using traditional automation is more appropriate than using RPA. Alternatively, RPA can be used as a temporary solution until a permanent solution becomes available.

Guideline 5: Create RPA Development Standards to Create Uniformity Across the Organization [12,16,18,23,26,31,39].

– Organizations should create RPA development standards to create uniformity across the organization - 89%, 7–9
– A CoE should recommend development standards to create uniformity across the organization - 78%, 7–9

The main goal of implementing RPA solutions is to achieve improved operational efficiency, for example by reducing transaction processing cost [15,18]. As operations often transcend business units, RPA development needs to be streamlined both between business units and within them in order to achieve and maintain operational efficiency. Organizations should therefore create development standards to ensure uniformity across the organization. The case organizations that have implemented a federated model have their CoE provide development guidelines and standards to ensure a certain quality standard throughout the organization. These standards can be related to for instance coding conventions, documentation and testing. Implementing such development standards should lead to improved bots. The role of the CoE should be to recommend standards and moderately enforce these standards.

Guideline 6: Create an Automation Library for Reusing Modules [5,16–18,33].

– Organizations should create an automation library for reusing modules - 73%, 7–9

As automation is not seldomly completely new to organizations implementing RPA, the mantra is often to 'think big, but start small' [10]. One way to do so is starting with smaller simpler bots and reusing parts to build more complex ones. Accordingly, our results show that re-usability and modularity principles should be applied to bot development. Reusable components can be created for steps such as logging into SAP systems. Another benefit of modularity is its support for granular development and testing. Aside from increasing development efficiency, reusable components can bolster maintenance procedures. Updates to reused components can be applied to multiple processes across the organization.

Guideline 7: Implement Quality Checkpoints During Bot Development to Audit the Usage of RPA Development Standards.

- Organizations should implement quality checkpoints during bot development to audit the usage of RPA development standards - 78%, 7–9

During development, organizations should implement quality checkpoints to audit the usage of RPA development standards. This is done to prevent an accumulation of issues that is discovered during a technical review by the CoE at what is supposed to be the final phase in development. At the Rabobank, a coordinator from the CoE is assigned to a business unit to observe the development process. This coordinator can examine the progress made and provide guidance.

Guideline 8: Have the Center of Excellence Perform a Technical Review of a Bot that a Business Unit Considers Finished.

- It is good practice to have the CoE perform a technical review of a bot that a business unit considers finished to determine if that bot is ready for a live environment - 78%, 7–9

The technical review done by the CoE takes place once a bot is considered finished by a business unit. This is done to ensure that a bot is up to a certain standard defined by the CoE and is ready for a live environment. The municipality plans to impose quality checkpoints during development and during the final sprint. The goal of the quality checkpoints is to ensure that development guidelines are utilized to prevent the need for rework in the future. More specifically, the bots are reviewed in terms of re-usability of components, robustness, testability and resilience to future changes to reduce the risk of vendor lock-in.

Guideline 9: Create arrangements with software vendors delivering software used by RPA.

- Organizations should create arrangements with software vendors, who deliver software that is used by RPA - 75%, 7–9

Organizations cannot control the updating schedule of external sources that are accessed by their bots. They should try to obtain information regarding the updating schedule and change-logs to anticipate to updates in advance. This reduces the chance of sudden exceptions created by changes within applications. Agreements with software vendors should be made, if possible, to be prepared for future changes. BankX has made arrangements with software suppliers to be informed two months in advance on any changes made in the software. However, it was not always possible to make such arrangements, which was often the case with external websites.

Guideline 10: Promote RPA and share RPA-related knowledge with suppliers or customers.

- An organization should promote RPA and share RPA related knowledge with their suppliers or customers, when an organization is *halfway* at scaling up and can be considered experienced in RPA - 57%
- ... when an organization has *finished* scaling up and can be considered an expert in RPA - 29%

This guideline does not include a range, as the participants were asked to choose whether an organization should promote RPA/share related knowledge (a) halfway the scaling up, (b) after the scaling up, or (c) never.

The rationale behind the guideline is that a bot may rely on external information sent by a customer or supplier. Such information needs to be highly standardized and uniform in all cases. Automatically generating documents such as Excel sheets using RPA can ensure that every sent Excel sheet adheres to a certain set of standards, barring failures. As a result, promoting and sharing knowledge related to RPA could have a positive effect on RPA adoption at customers or suppliers. This can contribute to further standardization requiring less maintenance and leading to fewer exceptions. 57% of the experts agreed organizations should start promoting and sharing knowledge when it is halfway at scaling up and can be considered experienced in RPA. 29% of the experts agreed that organizations should undertake this once it has finished scaling up and can be considered an expert in RPA. BankX stated that it was investigating whether processes at customers could be automated using RPA, to further automate and standardize the entire chain of linked processes.

Guideline 11: Create or Adapt a Personal Development Plan Based on an Impact Assessment [4].

- Organizations should create or adapt a personal development plan based on the impact assessment - 80%, 7–9

One last but major theme that is often associated with RPA is fear: either with bots in general or with potential job loss as a result of automation [35]. Attention to the human aspects RPA implementation should therefore not be evaded. Communication to involved employees is key. It is advised to create or adapt an existing personal development plan for employees affected within a business unit by RPA. Studies done within an organization on the overall impact of RPA on employees performing work to be automated can be used to further structure a personal development plan. RPA can have effects on employees ranging from changes to job contents to transferring to different business units or being involved in the development of RPA. A personal plan is the process of establishing the aims and objectives in the short, medium and long term in one's career.

It addresses the current situation and identifies the needs for skills, knowledge or competences to achieve the desired objectives. Subsequently, it addresses the appropriate development activities to meet the needed expertise. The personal development plan can then be used to obtain an overview of desired future plans [4]. This information can be valuable for matching employees with new opportunities that may or may not arise from RPA. Additionally, it can be used to match employees with different business units if necessary.

5   Discussion and Conclusion

Organizations were eager to adopt RPA in the last five years, but they must look into stemming the maintenance burden if they do not want to succumb under this enthusiasm. How they will be able to deal with this depends among others on the type of governance structure they choose. One of the most important choices they need to make is which one of three organizational models they adopt: decentralized, centralized, or federated [16, 17, 19, 27, 39]. Implementing the federated model provides advantages over the other models, but does not guarantee success.

This study speaks specifically to organizations that adopt a federated model, which assumes a high autonomy of business units and a CoE on RPA for centralized support. Based on a literature study and four case studies, 11 guidelines were formulated that attempt to mitigate the potential burden of maintenance and mismanagement of the technology. Specifically, they relate to the observed burden of maintenance cf. [27, 34], the mismanagement of the technology cf. [11], and the ambiguity of the roles and responsibilities. All guidelines were validated using a Delphi methodology.

The practical implications of this work are as follows. Organizations planning to adopt RPA are encouraged to consider to review their plans and account for the issues described. For instance, they may want to investigate the capabilities of their business units and the organizational model that fits them best. For many organizations, it may be attractive to balance a relatively high autonomy of decentralized units to develop their own bots with a CoE to provide guidance and support to such units. Organizations that have progressed beyond the choice for such a model and have already engaged with RPA may currently be struggling with maintenance issues. For those organizations, the list of guidelines we provided are particularly useful. We believe that business professionals that carry out, oversee, or advise RPA projects will find it beneficial to review our recommendations, for example on engaging software architects in their endeavors or on investing in the development of standards for documentation and testing. In fact, we would be pleased if our guidelines themselves will become parts of the standards that circulate within organizations applying RPA. While the guidelines themselves may not be so surprising for people who are familiar with software development, they are aimed at business professionals with no or limited experience in this area.

A limitation of this research concerns the surveys used during the Delphi study. The survey had to be brief and concise to reduce the drop-out rate.

Due to this limitation, the survey contents were less elaborate than we aspired for. Another threat concerns the selection of experts used for the Delphi study. The experts were selected based on RPA-related publications, resulting in a minority of participants that work in the industry. The threat herein is a possible discrepancy between theory and practice and certainly shapes venues for follow-up work and further validation.

References

1. van der Aalst, W.M., Bichler, M., Heinzl, A.: Robotic process automation (2018)
2. Agha, R.A., et al.: The scare 2018 statement: updating consensus surgical CAse REport (SCARE) guidelines. Int. J. Surg. **60**, 132–136 (2018)
3. Asatiani, A., Kämäräinen, T., Penttinen, E., et al.: Unexpected problems associated with the federated IT governance structure in Robotic Process Automation (RPA) deployment (2019)
4. Beausaert, S., Segers, M., Fouarge, D., Gijselaers, W.: Effect of using a personal development plan on learning and development. J. Workplace Learn. **25**(3), 145–158 (2013)
5. Chandler, S., Power, C., Fulton, M., Van Nueten, N.: Who Minds the Bots? Why Organisations Need to Consider Risks Related to Robotic Process Automation. PricewaterhouseCoopers, London (2017)
6. Chappell, D.: Introducing Blue Prism (2010)
7. Cooper, L.A., Holderness Jr., D.K., Sorensen, T.L., Wood, D.A.: Robotic Process Automation in public accounting. Accounting Horizons (2018)
8. Dilmegani, C.: RPA tools & vendors: In-depth vendor selection guide (2019). https://blog.aimultiple.com/robotic-process-automation-rpa-vendors-comparison/#rpa-tool-list
9. Fernandez, D., Aman, A.: Impacts of robotic process automation on global accounting services. Asian J. Account. Gov. **9**, 123–132 (2018)
10. Fung, H.P.: Criteria, use cases and effects of information technology process automation (ITPA). Adv. Robot. Autom. **3**, 1–10 (2014)
11. Gadre, A., Jessel, B., Karan, G.: Rethinking Robotics? Take a Step Back. Henley Business School - Capco Institute (2017)
12. Horton, R., Gordeeva, M., Green, J.: The robots are waiting Are you ready to reap the benefits? (2018)
13. Kroll, C., Bujak, D.A., Darius, V., Enders, W., Esser, M.: Robotic Process Automation - Robots conquer business processes in back offices (2016)
14. Lacity, M., Willcocks, L., Yan, A.: Are the robots really coming? Service automation survey findings. Pulse Mag. **17**, 14–21 (2015)
15. Lacity, M., Willcocks, L.: Robotic process automation: the next transformation lever for shared services. London School of Economics Outsourcing Unit Working Papers 7 (2015)
16. Lacity, M., Willcocks, L.P.: Dynamic Innovation in Outsourcing. Springer, Heidelberg (2018). https://doi.org/10.1007/978-3-319-75352-2
17. Lacity, M., Willcocks, L.P., Craig, A.: Robotic process automation: mature capabilities in the energy sector (2015)
18. Lacity, M.C., Willcocks, L.P.: A new approach to automating services. MIT Sloan Manag. Rev. **58**(1), 41–49 (2017)

19. Le Clair, C.: RPA Operating Models Should be Light and Federated: A 10-Point Control Framework Helps Manage the Digital Workforce of the Future. Forrester Research, Cambridge (2017)
20. Le Clair, C., Cullen, A., King, M.: The Forrester Wave: Robotic Process Automation, Q1 2017. Forrester Research, Cambridge (2017)
21. Linstone, H.A., Turoff, M., et al.: The delphi method. Addison-Wesley, Reading (1975)
22. Loughlin, K.G., Moore, L.F.: Using Delphi to achieve congruent objectives and activities in a pediatrics department. J. Med. Educ. **54**(2), 101–106 (1979)
23. Madakam, S., Holmukhe, R.M., Jaiswal, D.K.: The future digital work force: robotic process automation (RPA). JISTEM **16**, 1–17 (2019)
24. McKenna, H.P.: The Delphi technique: a worthwhile research approach for nursing? J. Adv. Nurs. **19**(6), 1221–1225 (1994)
25. Miles, M.B., Huberman, A.M., Saldana, J.: Qualitative Data Analysis: A Methods Sourcebook. Sage Publications, Thousand Oaks (2018)
26. Muraleedharan, V., Abel, M., Griffiths, J., Ives, R.: Getting robots right - how to avoid the 6 most damaging mistakes in scaling-up RPA (2016)
27. Osmundsen, K., Iden, J., Bygstad, B.: Organizing robotic process automation: balancing loose and tight coupling. In: HICSS (2019)
28. Pervan, G., Maimbo, M.: Designing a case study protocol for application in IS research. In: PACIS, pp. 1281–1292 (2005)
29. Runeson, P., Höst, M.: Guidelines for conducting and reporting case study research in software engineering. Empir. Softw. Eng. **14**(2), 131 (2009). https://doi.org/10.1007/s10664-008-9102-8
30. Schmitz, M., Dietze, C., Czarnecki, C.: Enabling digital transformation through robotic process automation at Deutsche telekom. In: Urbach, N., Röglinger, M. (eds.) Digitalization Cases. MP, pp. 15–33. Springer, Cham (2019). https://doi.org/10.1007/978-3-319-95273-4_2
31. Schuler, J., Gehring, F.: Implementing robust and low-maintenance Robotic Process Automation (RPA) solutions in large organisations. Available at SSRN 3298036 (2018)
32. Slaby, J.R.: Cheap, easy-to-develop software robots will eventually supplant many offshore FTEs, p. 18 (2012)
33. Slaby, J.R.: Robotic Automation Emerges as a Threat to Traditional Low-Cost Outsourcing. HfS Research Ltd. (2012)
34. Stople, A., Steinsund, H., Iden, J., Bygstad, B.: Lightweight IT and the IT function: experiences from robotic process automation in a Norwegian bank. Bibsys Open J. Syst. **25**(1) (2017)
35. Suri, V.K., Elia, M., van Hillegersberg, J.: Software bots - the next frontier for shared services and functional excellence. In: Oshri, I., Kotlarsky, J., Willcocks, L.P. (eds.) Global Sourcing 2017. LNBIP, vol. 306, pp. 81–94. Springer, Cham (2017). https://doi.org/10.1007/978-3-319-70305-3_5
36. Syed, A.M., Hjarnø, L., Krumkamp, R., Reintjes, R., Aro, A.R.: Developing policy options for SARS and SARS-like diseases-a Delphi study. Glob. Public Health **5**(6), 663–675 (2010)
37. Syed, R., et al.: Robotic process automation: contemporary themes and challenges. Comput. Ind. **115**, 103162 (2020)
38. Van Zolingen, S.J., Klaassen, C.A.: Selection processes in a Delphi study about key qualifications in senior secondary vocational education. Technol. Forecast. Soc. Chang. **70**(4), 317–340 (2003)

39. Willcocks, L.P., Lacity, M., Craig, A.: The IT function and Robotic Process Automation (2015)
40. Willcocks, L.P., Lacity, M., Craig, A.: Robotic Process Automation at Xchanging (2015)
41. Willcocks, L.P., Lacity, M., Craig, A.: Robotizing global financial shared services at Royal DSM. J. Finan. Transf. (Automation# 46) **46**, 1–26 (2017)
42. Wohlin, C., Runeson, P., Höst, M., Ohlsson, M.C., Regnell, B., Wesslén, A.: Experimentation in Software Engineering. Springer, Heidelberg (2012). https://doi.org/10.1007/978-3-642-29044-2

A Consolidated Framework for Implementing Robotic Process Automation Projects

Lukas-Valentin Herm$^{(\boxtimes)}$ⓘ, Christian Janiesch$^{(\boxtimes)}$, Alexander Helm,
Florian Imgrund, Kevin Fuchs, Adrian Hofmann, and Axel Winkelmann

Julius -Maximilians -Universität, Würzburg, Germany
{lukas-valentin.herm,christian.janiesch,alexander.helm,
florian.imgrund,kevin.fuchs,adrian.hofmann,
axel.winkelmann}@uni-wuerzburg.de

Abstract. Robotic process automation (RPA) is a disruptive technology to automate already digital yet manual tasks and subprocesses as well as whole business processes. In contrast to other process automation technologies, RPA only accesses the presentation layer of IT systems and imitates human behavior. Due to the novelty of this approach and the varying approaches when implementing the technology, up to 50% of RPA projects fail. To tackle this issue, we use a design science research approach to develop a framework for the initiation of RPA projects. We analyzed a total of 23 case studies of RPA implementation projects to derive a preliminary sequential model. We then used expert interviews to validate and refine the model. The result is a consolidated framework with variable stages, that offers guidelines with enough flexibility to be applicable in complex and heterogeneous corporate environments. We conclude the paper with a discussion and an outlook on research opportunities on adapting and scaling RPA technology in projects.

Keywords: Robotic process automation · Implementation framework · Interview study

1 Introduction

Companies compete in an international market [31] that can be highly volatile. Therefore, it is getting increasingly important for companies to be more efficient and agile to remain competitive [42]. As many processes are already performed using computers, digitalization offers a variety of potentials for optimization [12] such as the analysis and improvement of processes using event data.

Business Process Management (BPM) is the management discipline enables business processes to be identified, documented, and digitalized [9,17]. Traditionally processes are managed and optimized in mid-size or large cross-organizational projects focusing on high-value processes [9]. Due to resource constraints, these projects can only focus on a handful of processes at a time

© Springer Nature Switzerland AG 2020
D. Fahland et al. (Eds.): BPM 2020, LNCS 12168, pp. 471–488, 2020.
https://doi.org/10.1007/978-3-030-58666-9_27

[9,19]. Imgrund et al. [19,20] and van der Aalst et al. [2] have pointed out that there are more processes that should be actively managed. However, traditional off-the-shelf (legacy) software (such as enterprise software) as well as BPM software itself have turned out to be too inflexible for quick and light-weighed automation projects due to the lack of application programming interfaces (API) and the necessity to provide custom (micro) services that can be called from a process model [42].

Robotic process automation (RPA) is a recent addition to techniques to automate previously already digital yet manual tasks or subprocesses within business processes [1,28]. The technology can be valuable for companies, as manual tasks, typically performed repetitively on a daily, weekly, or monthly schedule, are associated with high administrative efforts [32]. In contrast to the use of traditional BPM systems, RPA is a software-based approach that interacts with the already existing graphical user interfaces rather than requiring an additional API [28,35]. Further, since many tasks can be implemented through scripting or intelligent recording techniques rather than authoring services, RPA projects typically involve comparably little cost. Consequently, RPA is economically relevant alternative, since a return on investment can be achieved in a short time due to the light-weight automation approach [1].

Despite the interest and growth as well as the associated high expectations, RPA technology faces several challenges. On the one hand, RPA is, according to Gartner Inc., at the peak of the hype cycle of exaggerated expectations [24]. This indicates a lack of transparency within the RPA market, which results in a mistaken understanding of RPA and its potential. On the other hand, from a research perspective RPA is poorly understood and only in the early stage of scientific research. Hence, several areas have not yet been sufficiently investigated and pose challenges [6,42].

Although RPA is generally considered to be an easy to implement technology, in-depth knowledge is necessary to create reliable and scalable RPA processes. As a result, between 30% and 50% of initial RPA implementations are estimated to fail [36]. Although academic literature already provides several case studies, most of them refer to specific companies and therefore do not enable a generalization of the findings to support RPA projects. Gotthardt et al. [15] identify broader challenges, but they are not broken down to a project level. Similarly, literature reviews such as [22,42] only highlight overarching challenges. Consequently, a more in-depth study of RPA and its implementations is necessary. This leads to the following research questions:

RQ1: Which stages in RPA projects phases are typically mentioned in reported case studies?

RQ2: How should a consolidated framework for the implementation of RPA projects look like?

In answering these questions, we attempt to contribute to several challenges that Syed et al. [42] have put forward, namely contributing to better methodological support for the adoption and implementation, socio-technical implementation, and in particular the systematic design, development, and evolution of RPA projects. We present our contribution in six sections: Sect. 2 describes our research methodology. Section 3 comprises the literature analysis and the preliminary model of reported phases to answer RQ1. Section 4 reports on the expert interviews. To answer RQ2, we analyze the results of the data collection in Sect. 5, where we introduce the consolidated framework as well as its phases and stages. In the final section, we provide a discussion and reflect on limitations of our contribution.

2 Research Methodology

Our research is design science research. Our research methodology follows the approach described by Peffers et al. [34]. We extend their procedure through theory-building elements from the interpretative research method grounded theory as well as with a structured literature review [41, 44]. Our approach is applied in four distinct phases: problem formulation and objectives, data collection and analysis, design and development, and demonstration and evaluation. See Fig. 1 for an overview. All phases are sequential but have been iterated until the consolidated framework emerged.

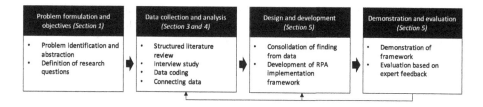

Fig. 1. Research methodology based on Peffers et al. [34]

Problem Formulation and Objectives. In line with the challenges put forward by Syed et al. [42], the artifact of this research is a consolidated framework to facilitate and guide the introduction of RPA in companies to aid the systematic design, development, and evolution of RPA implementations.

Data Collection and Analysis. To examine the current state-of-the-art, we conducted a systematic literature review following the recommendations of Webster and Watson [44] to answer RQ1. From the analysis of the articles, we designed a first iteration of the framework. In the second iteration, we conducted semi-structured interviews to verify the first iteration of the framework and adapt it according to the input we received from the interviewees [10, 33]. These were recorded, anonymized, and transcribed [25]. To extract the relevant information from the interviews, we coded the transcripts iteratively (using open and axial coding) and analyzed them with the grounded theory approach of Strauss and Corbin [41].

Design and Development. Based on the evaluation of the structured literature analysis through the interview study, we combined the identified stages or phases from both analyses. Our consolidated framework emerged from the results of the literature analysis, which were adapted and supplemented by the expert interviews. If stages from the literature were not considered applicable and not considered relevant in practice by the experts, we have removed them. On the other hand, when new stages were identified by the experts, we added them to the framework.

Demonstration and Evaluation. Ultimately, we presented the consolidated framework to the interviewed experts again and collected their feedback. We evaluated and if necessary adapted the framework. Lastly, we present the framework and describe its stages to answer RQ2.

3   Literature Review

For our systematic literature review, we searched in the databases AIS Electronic Library (AISel), ACM Digital Library, Business Source Complete, EconBiz, Emerald Insight, ESCBOhost, IEEE Xplore Digital Library, Research Papers in Economics (RePEc), and ScienceDirect for the search term 'robotic process automation | RPA' in title, abstract, and keywords where available in the database. We then screened the resulting 72 hits for articles that contain stages of RPA projects and conducted a forward/backward search to identify case studies that were not listed in the databases. This was important as due to the novelty of the technology as several well-cited publications have not been published in peer-reviewed journals or conferences. We examined these non-peer reviewed contributions critically for their relevance and rigor. The final set of articles comprises 23 examples of RPA implementation projects. See Fig. 2 for a quantitative overview of the literature review process.

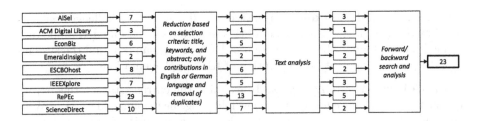

Fig. 2. Overview of literature review

Most of the articles are case study reports and their analyses. Other articles focus on RPA software, RPA and artificial intelligence, methodological support for RPA, and RPA and society. During the literature review, we have analyzed the 23 contributions in terms of their content for action patterns within the introduction of RPA projects. Similar patterns were grouped together into unified stages. Subsequently, we checked all contributions again for the occurrence of these patterns. Table 1 summarizes the stages we identified in each case study. Table 2 provides a short description each.

Table 1. Results of analyzed literature

Stage	Asatiani Penttinen (2016) [6]	Aguirre Rodriguez (2017) [3]	Slaby (2012) [39]	Willcocks et al. (2015a) [46]	Geyer-Klingeberg et al. (2018) [13]	Schneider (2019) [38]	Bitkom e.V. (2019) Case 1 [11]	Bitkom e.V. (2019) Case 2 [11]	Bitkom e.V. (2019) Case 3 [11]	Ravn et al. (2016) [5]	Lacity et al. (2015) [27]	Lacity et al. (2016) [28]	Langmann und Turi (2020) [30]	Hallikainen et al. (2018) [16]	Lacity Willcocks (2016) [26]	Willcocks et al. (2015b) [47]	Bitkom e.V. (2019) [11]	Camin (2018) [7]	Willcocks et al. (2017) [45]	Jimenez-Ramirez et al. (2019) [23]	IT-economics GmbH (2019) [21]	Schmitz et al. (2019) [37]	Smeets et al. (2019) [40]
												Use cases											
RPA demand	•		•							•		•		•					•	•	•		•
Screening of technologies		•							•	•		•		•							•		•
Process selection		•					•	•		•	•			•	•	•	•	•	•	•		•	•
RPA software selection												•			•	•	•					•	•
Proof of concept	•	•		•	•	•	•	•	•	•			•	•	•	•	•	•	•	•		•	•
Business case creation		•	•		•	•				•		•					•	•	•	•	•	•	•
Scaling of RPA services		•			•					•	•	•		•	•	•			•			•	•
Center of Excellence		•	•			•				•		•				•	•		•	•	•	•	•
Long-term service of RPA					•														•		•		•
RPA rollout						•										•	•		•	•	•		•
Transfer																						•	•
Stage count	1		3					4						5					6			8	11

Table 1 illustrates the distribution of the phases or stages we found across the different case studies. In addition, we segmented the contributions by the count of stages they used. It is apparent that most contributions only consider between three and five stages for an RPA implementation project. While this may be due to the limited space in scholarly publications, not all case studies had page limits. Hence, we assume that this lack of comprehensiveness may also be due to the lack of methodological guidance on the systematic design, development, and evolution of RPA projects.

Furthermore, while some stages such as *proof of concept* (PoC) are ubiquitous and most cases use some sort of *process selection* and *business case*. Very few cases approach RPA projects in a structured fashion early on or consider the long-term benefits and challenges: that is not many cases report on a structured *RPA demand* analysis or *RPA software selection* let alone provide thoughts on *long-term service* or the *transfer* of results.

In summary, our literature review summarizes the current state of academic literature on the different phases or stages within RPA implementation projects and, thus, serves as our answer to RQ1.

Table 2. Description of stages from the literature review

Stage	Description
RPA demand	– Identification of need for process automation
Screening of technologies	– Screening of potential automation techniques
Process selection	– Identification of processes that are suitable for RPA – Definition of relevant process attributes
RPA software selection	– Evaluation of RPA platforms
Proof of concept	– Examination of the technical and financial feasibility
Business case creation	– Derivation of the business case from PoC – Closing the gap between PoC and scaling of RPA
Scaling of RPA services	– Development of a RPA library – Extension of RPA team, software licenses, etc.
Center of Excellence	– Determination of basic structural decisions – Definition of roles, skills, KPI, etc.
Long-term service of RPA	– Ensure long-term operation of RPA robot
RPA rollout	– Implementation in the production process flow
Transfer	– Application of RPA knowledge to further processes

4   Expert Interviews

Using RPA software ourselves, we identified and contacted experts from the XING group 'Robotic Process Automation (RPA) - Practitioner Network'. Overall, eight practitioners with different backgrounds in terms of roles, industries, and company sizes agreed to an interview to share their experiences. Since these experts are from the German-speaking countries, the interview study was conducted in German and the concepts were later translated into English language. We understand the term 'expert' as someone who possesses special knowledge that can only be attained under special circumstances, that is in our case someone who has participated in at least one real-world RPA project. The interviewees and their backgrounds are summarized anonymously in Table 3.

Due to the novelty of the topic and the low number of potential interviewees locally, we opted for telephone interviews to enable synchronous communication and enable inquiries across a distance. We followed a semi-structured interview guideline with three parts: background information and skills, alignment between theory and practice as well as discussion of the identified stages. The questions could be answered openly to include emerging ideas. The interviews have been recorded, transcribed, and the data has been coded and analyzed based on the grounded theory approach by Strauss and Corbin [41].

Table 3. Interviewees

Interview	Date	Role	Company size
I1	2019-06-21	Internal consultant	1,000 employees
I2	2019-06-28	Internal consultant	300,000 employees
I3	2019-06-28	External consultant	Small and medium-sized enterprises to large enterprise customers
I4	2019-07-02	Internal consultant	250 employees
I5	2019-07-03	Internal consultant	100 employees
I6	2019-07-04	External consultant	1,000 - 10,000 employees
I7	2019-07-10	RPA provider	75 employees, large enterprise customers
I8	2019-07-15	Internal consultant	4,500 employees

In total, our audio recordings have a length of 583 min. This is equivalent to 150 pages of transcriptions.[1] When analyzing the stages from the case studies with the RPA experts, the experts generally confirmed, compressed but also expanded the findings derived from the literature review.

RPA Demand. Interviewees gave various arguments for this stage. I1 considers the potential to automate manual tasks to be particularly important. I7 identifies the potential especially for frequently repeating and more formalized processes. I5 sees potential for increasing the size of the company while keeping the number of employees constant.

Screening of Technologies. I1 points out that this step is often skipped in RPA projects. On the other hand, I8 remarks that software selection decisions are made individually for each case study. I3 also explains that other simpler technologies are often sufficient: *"We often find that this can be done with a simple Excel macro, so we can quickly add an interface with batch files or other*

---

[1] The interview guideline, the interview transcriptions (where permitted), and the coding used in this research are available in the B2SHARE repository as CC-BY-NC-SA [18].

things." Therefore, this step may have to be adapted individually for each company.

Process Selection. Almost all experts (except I7) named execution frequency as a key indicator for process selection. Standardized processes are also particularly relevant (I1–2, I5–7). Many experts (I1–2, I5–6, I8) considered further technologies such as process mining to be particularly relevant to shorten and improve the selection process. In addition, simple processes (I3, I5, I8), which are financially lucrative to automate (I5), should be used for initial RPA projects. I3 notes though that simple processes may only be appropriate candidates *"if you want quick wins and collect low-hanging fruits"*.

RPA Software Selection. The most important point when selecting RPA software is cost (I1–3, I6, I8). In addition, factors such as reputation (I5, I8), consulting support (I4, I8), transparency in the creation of robots (I3, I7), or stability (I2) should be considered. Despite the availability of some criteria, I6 illustrates that some selection processes rather proceed like *"someone in the company [...] is convinced by a tool and that's it"* or that *"RPA is so new for many that they cannot objectify the decision as there are so many factors involved that they do not know about."*

Proof of Concept. According to the experts, the RPA PoC should focus on simple pilot processes (I3, I6–7). It is important *"so that everybody sees - aha - how does it work, what is it about?"* Important tasks are the evaluation of the technical and financial feasibility (I1, I5, I6) and a comparison with the previous process flow (I7). A PoC is also used for a test alignment with corporate governance (I3, I6). I6 states that *"technical feasibility is more or less irrelevant"* in an RPA PoC.

Business Case Creation. The surveyed experts agree on the creation of a business case as an important stage. On the one hand, the business case is supposed to compare the automated processing times to manual processing times. On the other hand, the aim of the case is a proof that the change will reduce cost (I1, I4–I8). This also depends on the number of processes, which can be automated, as a high number of processes can result in a faster return on investment (I4–5, I7). I4 and I7 recommend using consulting services to benefit from their know-how from prior projects due to the novelty of the technology.

Scaling of RPA Services. Within this stage, the experts emphasize the need to set up a competence center (I1, I3–4, I7). After all, *"there is, of course, no point in always sourcing this from an external consultancy. One must also build up one's own competencies."* (I4). The competence center can also create templates and training for RPA robots (I1–2) and thus increase the complexity of the processes being implemented (I2, I8). I3 and I5 highlight that there is practically no end in automating processes with RPA since you always discover new processes while automating.

Center of Excellence. Centers of Excellence (CoE) should be introduced especially in larger companies (I3–4). This results from the problem of hiring RPA experts. I6 points out that *"in Germany, you currently have to look for experts for RPA like a needle in a haystack."*. If introduced, CoE should be positioned on the business side (I3, I5, I8) and represent a central department (I2–I5, I8). An executive department as an organizational form would also be feasible (I1, I5). At the same time the CoE can be used to take over BPM functions (I5).

Long-term Service of RPA. The long-term support and maintenance of the robots is not considered as a separate stage by the experts, but rather included in the CoE and in further RPA support processes (I1, I3, I5–6).

RPA Rollout. The RPA rollout identified in the literature is not considered by the experts explicitly as an individual stage, but as a necessary procedure within the implementation (I1, I6). It cannot be left out.

Transfer. The transfer implies the transfer of knowledge from previous RPA projects to new projects. In literature, this aspect is often addressed separately. In contrast, the analysis of the interviews survey suggests that the experts consider this aspect to be part of the *CoE* as well as *scaling of RPA services* stage (I1–2, I6–7).

Further, the interviewees stressed that the company should address questions regarding the usefulness, benefits, and added value of introducing RPA at an early stage. Therefore, an *alignment with business strategy* must be performed at an early stage to determine whether and how RPA can positively influence corporate targets. Already, the need to acquire adequate project support from management justifies an additional stage to reflect this (I5, I7). I5 describes this as follows: *"I actually have to integrate the corporate strategy into this. That is quite decisive. Because there has to be a corporate goal. It is not a departmental goal or anything else."*

Lastly, our survey indicates that stages such as *long-term service of RPA* and *transfer* have not been mentioned by our experts. Simultaneously, it is their opinion that these stages can be integrated into other stages listed above. For example, *long-term service* and *transfer* can be integrated in the *scaling of RPA services* stage as well as in a *CoE*.

All in all, the experts agreed to the stages we proposed. Some argued about their ordering. In the end, most experts agreed that the stages are never purely sequential but overlap. For example, I1 stated that building a CoE has to be established from the beginning of the project, even if it just consists of one person.

Order of Stages. Simultaneously, we also asked the experts to identify the stages described above in the chronological order they would consider them. Table 4 provides an overview of their suggestions which influenced the ordering of stages in of the consolidated framework.

Our interviews revealed that the final framework should have a high degree of flexibility, as there is no generally valid procedure, especially with regard to the concrete sequence of the individual stages, which always depends on company-specific circumstances. Nevertheless, it is still possible to make explicit specifications, since certain steps are necessary for the execution of the subsequent steps

Table 4. Preferred ordering of stages by experts

	Identification	Alignment	Screening	Process selection	RPA software selection	Proof of concept	Evaluation of business case	RPA rollout	Adaption and scaling
I1	1.	2.		3.	4.		5.		6.
I2	1.	2.	3.	4.	5.	6.	7.	8.	9.
I3	1.	2.	3.	4.	5.		6.	7.	8.
I4	1.	2.	3.	4.	5.	6.	7.	8.	9.
I5	1.	2.			3.	5.	4.		6.
I6	6.	1.	2.	3.	4.	5.			
I7	6.	1.	2.	3.	4.	5.	8.	7.	9.
I8	1.	2.	3.	4.	5.	6.	8.	7.	9.

and therefore cannot be moved around arbitrarily. Therefore, using the majority of the choices seems to be a good fit.

5   Consolidated Framework for Implementing RPA Projects

In the following, we present our RPA implementation framework first compiled in Sect. 3 and validated and consolidated in Sect. 4. See Fig. 3 for an overview and the temporal relation of the phases and stages. With the presentation of our consolidated framework we address RQ2.

The framework is divided into three phases for implementing RPA projects: initialization, implementation, and scaling. Some of its stages are performed once per project, while others are repeated continuously. These continuous steps represent project-external influences that support RPA implementation: in particular, this is the establishment and enhancement of a CoE. As the framework has been developed through 23 literature use cases as well as 8 expert interviews from different companies, the framework represents a comprehensive model to support the systematic design, development, and evolution of RPA projects. Further, it is flexible and can consequently be adapted to the different local conditions within distinct companies and industries. It allows for the integration of external consultants for a more sophisticated RPA implementation as well as the possibility of assisting in developing a company-internal CoE for knowledge transfer and continuous improvement.

Initialization, Implementation, and Scaling. Each RPA project runs through three project phases. In the *initialization phase*, *identification*, *alignment*, and *technology screening* are completed and the *implementation phase* stages of *process selection*, *software selection*, *PoC*, and the *business case* start. All of the latter may involve external consultants (if the project is not run by an

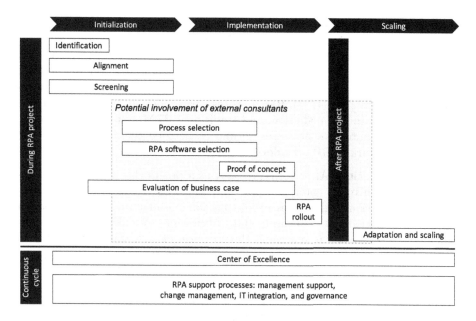

Fig. 3. Consolidated framework for RPA implementation projects

external consultancy in its entirety). The *implementation phase* completes all of these stages and ends with the *RPA rollout*. The *scaling phase* only starts after the RPA project has been completed and focuses on the *adaptation and scaling* of results for further RPA implementations. All stages are complemented by a continuous cycle of *RPA support processes* and through a *CoE*.

Identification of Automation Need. The first stage focuses on the identification of process automation needs and opportunities. Evaluating and determining current processes in enterprises for automation can be realized amongst other techniques with workshops, surveys, or reviews [6] as well as document analysis. Additionally, the need of automation for processes can be verified in normal conversation within departments or daily business discussions [27]. Depending on the level of digitalization, enterprises can discover whether manually executed processes should be automated using the existing information technology [37] (I5, I7) and process mining [13].

Alignment with Business Strategy. Companies need to consider importance, usefulness, and added value of introducing RPA early on (I3), that is they need to identify RPA success factors for their organization (I7). Hence, early alignment with business strategy is important to understand where RPA can positively influence strategic goals (I5, I7). Otherwise, the application of RPA should not be considered further. In addition, organizational issues should be addressed already at the start of a project, for example questions of principle about involved roles and functions need to be asked and answered (I3).

Screening of Different (RPA) Technologies. This stage helps to determine whether an organization can apply RPA usefully and which kind of technology is most suitable to solve the problem. This may entail that RPA turns out not to be the first candidate for automation. The implementation of the methods for screening potential depends on the individual case and can be executed proactive or exploratory [16], (I1–4). Rapid process reengineering, aspects of machine learning, custom-tool remediation, and traditional BPM systems can be alternate options to automate processes [8] and need to be considered besides the offerings of the various RPA vendors.

Processes Selection. After verifying RPA as a practicable and efficient technological solution to an enterprise problem, this stage focuses on the prioritization and selection of processes candidates for automation. Process selection requires information from end users and stakeholders to make better decisions (I4–5). Moreover, taking into account the processes of involved departments can significantly improve business understanding [37]. Most of the case studies predominantly consider processes with a low complexity for initial implementation and testing [16,27,37,39], (I8). In addition, the degree of standardization and the process maturity should be considered for the selection because mature processes are typically better documented [27], (I1–2, I5–7). Furthermore, the execution frequency and volume of processes indicate high automation potential promise an increase in efficiency [16,37], (I1–8, I8). Wanner et al. [43] have proposed a candidate for a quantifiable method of process selection for RPA projects. Their approach also entails that the relevant processes are already digitized and therefore have a digital input and output, which is a mandatory requirement for RPA. Non-digitized processes must be digitized first.

RPA Software Selection. This stage focuses the selection of the suitable software for automation. Among other things, the cost of the software (I1–3, I6, I8), skill requirements as well prior (successful) implementations represent important factors in the decision-making (I1) although the market seems to mature quickly (I2) resulting in rather organizational than technical factors to consider for software selection. Further mentioned criteria included availability of skills with external consultants, vendor support, vendor reputation and software maturity as well as security and data protection of RPA cloud solutions.

Proof of Concept Implementation. The PoC serves as a verification of the functionality as well as the technical and financial feasibility of RPA technology for the given case [5,26], (I1, I5–6). Thus, a company can verify whether it is reasonable to introduce RPA into its operations. Verification factors may include process quality or return on investment calculation [26], (I1, I5, I7). For these analyses, it is recommended that a PoC should be executed for several months to provide a detailed data-driven analysis [28]. For the PoC, simple processes should be chosen initially, as stakeholders often only become aware of the inherent challenges by dealing directly with the issue at hand [16], (I7).

Evaluation of Business Case. The business case is essential to bridge the gap between the small-scale PoC and the subsequent scaling of RPA technology within the company [5]. Defining a business case is also highly recommended to ensure long-term management support [46]. In order to gather such support, typical indicators such as processing times, (human) error rates, infrastructure, and IT cost should be considered [39], (I1, I4–8). A technology-based support in process discovery can be pursued through process mining [2, 13, 43], (I4).

RPA Rollout. The RPA rollout comprises all activities concerned with making available and activating the implemented software robot(s) in the enterprise's daily operations. Although this stage has been mentioned in the literature in various case studies such as [7, 11, 23], it has not been explicitly highlighted by the expert interviewees. Hence, while RPA rollout strategies may not be RPA-specific but apply for many software projects, rollout is a necessary stage (I1, I6) and should be subject to further research including socio-technical aspects of human and machine cooperation [42].

Adaptation and Scaling of RPA Services. After a successful PoC and a precisely defined business case have resulted in a successful RPA rollout, an extension of the RPA portfolio can subsequently take place, facilitated by the creation of RPA libraries and related templates [37], (I1–2). The complexity of the processes should continuously increase so that the RPA team can understand RPA and the automation feasibility of the corporate processes gradually (I2, I8). The integration of external service providers can provide support for more complex processes as well (I1, I4, I7). The automation of further processes also requires a step-wise increase in software licenses [26, 46], (I7). At the same time, the employees affected by the introduction of software robot must be involved at an early stage to ensure a continuing positive working attitude [29].

Center of Excellence. The implementation of software robots using RPA within the company should be accompanied by setting up a CoE [26] to support the definition of necessary roles, skills, key performance indicators, etc. The tasks of the CoE vary from the monitoring and maintenance of the software robots to the identification of appropriate further processes for automation [4], (I1, I3, I5, I7). The CoE is also responsible for process innovation, the development of new services, and efficiency improvements [3], (I6). Organizationally, the CoE is usually not anchored in the IT department, but on the business side [28], (I3). Furthermore, it is important to note that implementing a CoE requires a high amount of resources, so this step is usually only feasible for large companies [4, 47], (I3–4). Small and medium-sized enterprises should consider making available at least one full-time equivalent to manage RPA knowledge and chaperon projects.

RPA Support Processes. The expert survey revealed that continuous support from the top management is necessary as with any project to enable a consistent financial support as well as a strategic orientation and awareness within the company for the capabilities and limitations of software robots. Further, the adaptation of governance guidelines is a practical requirement. Likewise, the integration of change management and IT integration is essential to support continuous changes within the processes towards adjustments in the RPA implementations. They ensure long-term service of RPA integrated in the production processes and cooperation between humans and machines.

6   Discussion and Conclusion

In this paper, we investigated the status quo of RPA research focusing on the challenge of the systematic design, development, and evolution of RPA projects [42]. Following a structured literature review that revealed eleven stages in RPA projects and an interview study to uncover differences and similarities between practice and scholarly literature, we developed a consolidated framework of three phases and nine project-based stages and two continuous stages of project support. Our discrepancy analysis showed that there is a substantial overlap between theory and practice. Nevertheless, while promising concepts have already been developed in theory, companies have generally not yet addressed these issues in practice. In response, our consolidated framework can narrow the gap between theory and practice as all expert interviewees saw value in the framework. It provides a clear methodological contribution on how to approach RPA implementation projects comprehensively and it is of practical value for companies as confirmed by the RPA experts.

While eight interviewees only suggest limited authority and external validity in quantitative research, our study was largely qualitative and throughout the interviews, we noticed a state of theoretical saturation, where the marginal return of additional data became neglectable [14]. We observed this saturation in all relevant dimensions. All experts considered the framework as meaningful, relevant, instantiable and found it to be sufficiently flexible as well as complete with the addition of strategic and organizational alignment.

We noticed that interviewees from large enterprises tended to agree more than interviewees from small and mid-sized enterprises, which can be expected due to their narrower scope of work. Due to the diversity of interviewees in terms of their roles, industries, and BPM maturity, we do not expect the framework to have any significant biases. Nevertheless, smaller companies may need to trim the framework to their needs more comprehensively than others. Recently, we have applied the framework successfully at SYSTHEMIS AG, a German software development and IT consulting company, and have not encountered tasks that were incompatible with or missing in the framework.

Throughout the interviews we noted several reoccurring topics, which should also be taken into consideration when embarking on RPA projects. First, the understanding of 'what RPA does' and 'what RPA does not' varies widely. This is in line with Gartner's placement of RPA at the peak of the hype cycle of exaggerated expectations. Second, RPA does not entail the loss of jobs for human workers. None of the case studies or interviewees reported on terminations of work contracts but rather on freeing up capacity. Furthermore in the long term, using (software) robots seems to be beneficial for the competitiveness of the company and thus for job security [43]. Third, although the interaction of business and IT in RPA projects was clarified by the interviewees, the understanding of RPA in practice can be further increased by a detailed investigation of the interaction of these two areas. In the end, IT departments often only provide the RPA platform, while the functional business areas define the business logic of the software robots. This results in new organizational challenges.

Furthermore, our research showed that an analysis of the interdependencies between RPA and traditional BPM are necessary in the near future, since the two approaches have many similarities and the RPA momentum is typically originating from a BPM-friendly department or a BPM CoE. We observed that established BPM approaches, such as the hybrid BPM approach for the holistic management of business processes [20] can be transferred to RPA in a similar form [27], (I2). Consequently, on the one hand it is possible to explore the transfer of hybrid BPM approaches to the implementation of process improvements using RPA. On the other hand, approaches that integrate traditional approaches of BPM with agile improvements using software robots based on RPA technology should be developed, where RPA software is one option of automating processes and process integration using BPM software another.

Since RPA research is still in an early phase, there are many other issues that need to be addressed [42]. In particular, during our study we observed the need for an in-depth analysis of the economic viability of RPA systems, which also includes the determination of the technological debt introduced by RPA that is caused, among other things, by superficial implementation and the resulting low level of application integration. Ultimately, we can conclude that RPA has already established itself in many companies and contributes to the achievement of individual corporate goals. However, the technology is still in its infancy so that further innovations and improvements must follow to make the 'automation revolution' described by Lacity and Willcocks [46] a reality.

References

1. van der Aalst, W.M.P., et al.: Views on the past, present, and future of business and information systems engineering. Bus. Inf. Syst. Eng. **60**(6), 443–477 (2018). https://doi.org/10.1007/s12599-018-0561-1
2. van der Aalst, W.M.P., Bichler, M., Heinzl, A.: Robotic process automation. Bus. Inf. Syst. Eng. **60**(4), 269–272 (2018). https://doi.org/10.1007/s12599-018-0542-4
3. Aguirre, S., Rodriguez, A.: Automation of a business process using robotic process automation (RPA): a case study. In: Figueroa-García, J.C., López-Santana, E.R., Villa-Ramírez, J.L., Ferro-Escobar, R. (eds.) WEA 2017. CCIS, vol. 742, pp. 65–71. Springer, Cham (2017). https://doi.org/10.1007/978-3-319-66963-2_7
4. Anagnoste, S.: Setting up a robotic process automation center of excellence. Manag. Dyn. Knowl. Econ. **6**(2), 307–332 (2018)
5. Asatiani, A., Penttinen, E.: Get ready for robots: why planning makes the difference between success and disappointment. J. Inf. Technol. Teach. Cases **6**(2), 67–74 (2016)
6. Asatiani, A., Penttinen, E.: Turning robotic process automation into commercial success-Case OpusCapita. J. Inf. Technol. Teach. Cases **6**(2), 67–74 (2016)

7. Camin, T.: Roboter im shared service center. Controll. Manage. Rev. **62**(8), 30–37 (2018). https://doi.org/10.1007/s12176-018-0068-0
8. DeBrusk, C.: Five robotic process automation risks to avoid. MIT Sloan Manag. Rev. **October**(1) (2017)
9. Dumas, M., Rosa, M.L., Mendling, J., Reijers, H.A.: Fundamentals of Business Process Management. Springer, Heidelberg (2018). https://doi.org/10.1007/978-3-662-56509-4
10. Edwards, R., Holland, J.: What is Qualitative Interviewing? Bloomsbury Academic, London (2013)
11. Fick, A., et al.: Robotic Process Automation (RPA) im digitalen Büro (2019). https://www.bitkom.org/Bitkom/Publikationen/Robotic-Process-Automation-RPA-im-digitalen-Buero. Accessed 20 May 2020
12. Fischer, M., Imgrund, F., Janiesch, C., Winkelmann, A.: Strategy archetypes for digital transformation: Defining meta objectives using business process management. Inf. Manag. Online First (2020)
13. Geyer-Klingeberg, J., Nakladal, J., Baldauf, F., Veit, F.: Process mining and robotic process automation: a perfect match. In: Proceedings of the 16th International Conference on Business Process Management (BPM), CEUR Workshop Proceedings, Sydney, vol. 2196, pp. 124–131 (2018)
14. Glaser, B., Strauss, A.: Grounded theory: the discovery of grounded theory. Sociol. J. Br. Sociol. Assoc. **12**, 27–49 (1967)
15. Gotthardt, M., Koivulaakso, D., Paksoy, O., Saramo, C.: Current state and challenges in the implementation of robotic process automation and artificial intelligence in accounting and auditing. ACRN Oxford J. Finan. Risk Perspect. **8**(2), 31–46 (2019)
16. Hallikainen, P., Bekkhus, R., Pan, S.L.: How Opuscapita used internal RPA capabilities to offer services to clients. MIS Q. Exec. **17**(1), 41–52 (2018)
17. Hammer, M.: What is business process management? In: vom Brocke, J., Rosemann, M. (eds.) Handbook on Business Process Management 1. IHIS, vol. 1, pp. 3–16. Springer, Heidelberg (2015). https://doi.org/10.1007/978-3-642-45100-3_1
18. Helm, A., Herm, L.V., Imgrund, F., Janiesch, C.: Interview guideline, transcriptions, and coding for "a consolidated framework for implementing robotic process automation projects". EUDAT B2SHARE. http://doi.org/10.23728/b2share.402d2d1544124d24902182652d1bc77a. Accessed 15 June 2020
19. Imgrund, F., Fischer, M., Janiesch, C., Winkelmann, A.: Managing the long tail of business processes. In: Proceedings of the 25th European Conference on Information Systems (ECIS), Guimarães, pp. 595–610 (2017)
20. Imgrund, F., Fischer, M., Janiesch, C., Winkelmann, A.: Conceptualizing a framework to manage the short head and long tail of business processes. In: Weske, M., Montali, M., Weber, I., vom Brocke, J. (eds.) BPM 2018. LNCS, vol. 11080, pp. 392–408. Springer, Cham (2018). https://doi.org/10.1007/978-3-319-98648-7_23
21. IT-economics: Robotic Process Automation: eine Erfolgsgeschichte im Rahmen der Digitalisierung für Syneco (2019). https://www.it-economics.de/digitalisierung/2019-10/robotic-process-automation-eine-erfolgsgeschichte. Accessed 20 May 2020
22. Ivančić, L., Suša Vugec, D., Bosilj Vukšić, V.: Robotic process automation: systematic literature review. In: Di Ciccio, C., et al. (eds.) BPM 2019. LNBIP, vol. 361, pp. 280–295. Springer, Cham (2019). https://doi.org/10.1007/978-3-030-30429-4_19
23. Jimenez-Ramirez, A., Reijers, H.A., Barba, I., Del Valle, C.: A method to improve the early stages of the robotic process automation lifecycle. In: Giorgini, P., Weber, B. (eds.) CAiSE 2019. LNCS, vol. 11483, pp. 446–461. Springer, Cham (2019). https://doi.org/10.1007/978-3-030-21290-2_28

24. Kenneth, B., Svetlana, S.: Hype cycle for artificial intelligence. https://www. gartner.com/en/documents/3883863/hype-cycle-for-artificial-intelligence-2018. Accessed 20 May 2020
25. Kuckartz, U.: Qualitative Inhaltsanalyse. Methoden, Praxis, Computerunterstützung. Beltz Juventa, Weinheim, 2nd edn. (2014)
26. Lacity, m., Willcocks, L., Craig, A.: Robotic process automation at telefónica o2. In: The Outsourcing Unit Working Research Paper Series, vol. 15, no. 2 (2015)
27. Lacity, M., Willcocks, L.P., Craig, A.: Robotic process automation: mature capabilities in the energy sector. In: The Outsourcing Unit Working Research Paper Series, vol. 15, no. 6 (2016)
28. Lacity, M., Willcocks, L., Craig, A.: Robotizing global financial shared services at royal DSM. Paper Ser. Finan. Serv. **46**(1), 62–76 (2016)
29. Lacity, M.C., Willcocks, L.P.: A new approach to automating services. MIT Sloan Manag. Rev. **58**(1), 41–49 (2017)
30. Langmann, C., Turi, D.: Robotic Process Automation (RPA) - Digitalisierung und Automatisierung von Prozessen. Springer, Wiesbaden (2020). https://doi.org/10. 1007/978-3-658-28299-8
31. Levitt, T.: The globalization of markets. Harv. Bus. Rev. **61**(3), 92–102 (1993)
32. Mendling, J., Decker, G., Hull, R., Reijers, H.A., Weber, I.: How do machine learning, robotic process automation, and blockchains affect the human factor in business process management? Commun. Assoc. Inf. Syst. **43**(1), 297–320 (2018)
33. Paré, G.: Investigating information systems with positivist case study research. Commun. Assoc. Inf. Syst. **13**(1), 233–264 (2004)
34. Peffers, K., Tuunanen, T., Rothenberger, M.A., Chatterjee, S.: A design science research methodology for information systems research. J. Manag. Inf. Syst. **24**(3), 45–77 (2007)
35. Penttinen, E., Kasslin, H., Asatiani, A.: How to choose between robotic process automation and back-end system automation? In: Proceedings of the 26th European Conference on Information Systems (ECIS), Portsmouth, pp. 1–14 (2018)
36. Ravn, R., Halberg, P., Gustafsson, J., Groes, J.: Get ready for robots: why planning makes the difference between success and disappointment (2016). http://eyfin ancialservicesthoughtgallery.ie/wp-content/uploads/2016/11/ey-get-ready-for-rob ots.pdf. Accessed 20 May 2020
37. Schmitz, M., Dietze, C., Czarnecki, C.: Enabling digital transformation through robotic process automation at Deutsche telekom. In: Urbach, N., Röglinger, M. (eds.) Digitalization Cases. MP, pp. 15–33. Springer, Cham (2019). https://doi. org/10.1007/978-3-319-95273-4_2
38. Schneider, M.: 3 Schritte für eine strategische robotic process automation (RPA) Einführung und Integration (2019). https://morethandigital.info/3-schritte-fuer-eine-strategische-robotic-process-automation-rpa-einfuehrung-und-integration/. Accessed 20 May 2020
39. Slaby, J.R.: Robotic automation emerges as a threat to traditional low-cost outsourcing. HfS Res. Ltd. **1**(1), 1–19 (2012)
40. Smeets, M., Erhard, R., Kaußler, T.: Robotic Process Automation (RPA) in der Finanzwirtschaft. Springer, Wiesbaden (2019). https://doi.org/10.1007/978-3-658-26564-9
41. Strauss, A., Corbin, J.: Grounded theory methodology. Handb. Qual. Res. **17**, 273–285 (1994)
42. Syed, R., et al.: Robotic process automation: contemporary themes and challenges. Comput. Ind. **115**, 1–15 (2020)

43. Wanner, J., Hofmann, A., Fischer, M., Imgrund, F., Janiesch, C., Geyer-Klingeberg, J.: Process selection in RPA projects: towards a quantifiable method of decision making. In: Proceedings of the 40th International Conference on Information Systems (ICIS), München, pp. 1–17 (2019)

44. Webster, J., Watson, R.T.: Analyzing the past to prepare for the future: writing a literature review. MIS Q. **26**(2), xiii–xxiii (2002)

45. Willcocks, L., Lacity, M., Craig, A.: Robotic process automation: Strategic transformation lever for global business services? J. Inf. Technol. Teach. Cases **7**(1), 17–28 (2017)

46. Willcocks, L.P., Lacity, M., Craig, A.: The IT function and robotic process automation. In: The Outsourcing Unit Working Research Paper Series, vol. 15, no. 5 (2015)

47. Willcocks, L.P., Lacity, M., Craig, A.: Robotic process automation at Xchanging. In: The Outsourcing Unit Working Research Paper Series, vol. 15, no. 3 (2015)

A Multi Perspective Framework for Enhanced Supply Chain Analytics

Owen Keates[✉], Moe Thandar Wynn, and Wasana Bandara

School of Information Systems, Queensland University of Technology, Brisbane, Australia
owen.keates@hdr.qut.edu.au, {m.wynn,w.bandara}@qut.edu.au

Abstract. Supply chain analytics, especially in the field of food supply has become a strategic business function. Monthly executive sales and operation planning meetings utilize supply chain analytics to inform strategic business decisions. Having identified gaps in the strategic management of food supply chains, a multi perspective supply chain analytics framework is developed incorporating process and data attributes to support decision making. Using Design Science as the research methodology, a novel framework with a supporting IT artefact is built and presented with early evaluation results.

The resulting multi perspective supply chain analytics framework equips practitioners to identify strategic issues, providing important decision support information. The case study further illustrates the framework has applicability across all integrated food supply chains. This research has highlighted gaps in the application of process science to the supply chain management domain, particularly in the area of simultaneous assessment of process and data. The outcomes contribute to research in this domain providing a framework that will enhance the significant reference modelling and operational management work that has occurred in this field.

Keywords: Multi perspective supply chain analytics · Food supply chains · Process and data analytics

1 Introduction

Food supply chain management is a matter of international and national strategic importance, this fact has been reinforced in the wake of the global disruption to food supply chain caused by events such as the Covid-19 pandemic [1]. Supply chain analytics, including data driven insights, allow for the assessment of a food chain's current state in real time, allowing for decisions to be made regarding alternative routing, sourcing and distribution [2]. It also allows for simulation to support scenario planning, further supporting short- and longer-term decision making [3].

Guided by a design science methodology [4] this research has initially focused on a single, revelatory case study [5], an integrated beef supply chain, to discover the challenges that the industry faces while simultaneously reviewing the adoption of process

© Springer Nature Switzerland AG 2020
D. Fahland et al. (Eds.): BPM 2020, LNCS 12168, pp. 489–504, 2020.
https://doi.org/10.1007/978-3-030-58666-9_28

science methodologies into the supply chain domain. We pose a research question, can process intelligence techniques solve complex supply chain problems? A proposition that a multi perspective process analytical approach will provide a new level of insight to managing and improving complex and dynamic supply chains is presented. These supply chain insights are used to drive the most strategic business decisions and are also used in the executive sales and operations planning meetings to drive operations [6]. To test the proposition, we have developed a framework, the **Multi Perspective Supply Chain Analytics Framework** (referred to as MPSCA), together with a supporting IT artefact and have evaluated it with several leading subject matter experts from practice.

The MPSCA framework was built and evaluated in a case study of a large integrated beef supply chain in Australia. The beef business was selected as it is one of the most integrated food supply chains extending from its breeding farms right through to packaged beef products on the retailer's shelf. This industry is subject to supply chain risk due to environmental factors (for example drought and flood) [7], as well as other factors such as trade tariffs and competition from other protein sources [8], making the ability to rapidly assess the supply chain from multiple perspectives and to evaluate alternative pathways to market, strategically important. The results and learnings are applicable to integrated food supply chain's globally.

Existing BPM tools and techniques are many and continue to grow [9]. Process mining techniques are proliferating with new approaches to support process discovery, conformance and enhancement. Across these three classes there has been a proliferation of solutions developed, both from an academic as well as commercial base [10]. However, most solutions are siloed into a single class and only few have been integrated for continuum across a process-management lifecycle. The intent of the MPSCA framework is to integrate a number of these technology solutions to support key analytical challenges across the entire end-to-end lifecycle of the food supply chain.

The objective of this research is to develop a data-driven multi perspective framework which will provide a new level of supply chain analytics contributing to the body of knowledge in this domain, while also addressing a real-world problem in managing vertically integrated food supply chains.

2   Related Work

In a literature review of big data in agriculture, Wolfert et al. [11] conclude that data analytics is influencing the entire supply chain and will have a major impact on efficiency as well as supply chain design, as the relationship between producer and consumer changes. Aramyan et al. [12] examine performance measures in agriculture food supply chains and propose a framework influenced by the SCOR[1] model, while Pham and Stack [13] present examples of how data analytics is redefining the competitive dynamics of agriculture production and supply. Wang et al. [14] in their extensive literature review of supply chain and big data analytics conclude these techniques should be treated as strategic assets applied holistically across a business, from strategy to operations.

---

[1] https://www.apics.org/apics-for-business/frameworks/scor.

Supply chain integration is essential to competitive advantage and viewed in some sectors as extended enterprises [15]. Analysis is currently centered on a process and control flow centric approach, with the Association of Supply Chain Management's SCOR™ model being one of the most widespread methodologies [16].

Supply chain management is still a young discipline and research in this field has largely focused on operational management areas [17]. The gap in the above methodology is that it approaches supply chain analytics from a single perspective which is the reference model and as a "static" methodology as opposed to a dynamic analytical process capable of interrogating event data; event data is execution data, produced as a side product when a task is executed. Supply chain by its very definition is a series of interconnected events. Analyzing the control flow aspects of a supply chain is one perspective, being able to co-currently analyze performance data will provide a new dimension of analytics not currently deployed in this domain. It is postulated that such a multi-perspective approach to supply chain analytics will enhance supply chain performance and can also further leverage the knowledge embedded in the SCOR™ model through advanced conformance checking.

Lapide [18] reinforces that supply chains are critical to market strategy, while Becker and Intoyoad [19] note that logistics can greatly benefit from process mining as the identification and tracking of goods involves many IT systems. Their work also focused on an area important to the meat and livestock value chain, namely, documentation. They focused on automated mining for process documentation by adding context information including frequency of occurrence of process and the cycle time of processes.

3 Method

This study applies a Design Science approach [4]. Below we present the methods applied for framework building and early evaluation outcomes presented herein.

3.1 Building the Framework

The framework building has three forms of input; insights from a literature analysis, case study data (from interviews and documents) and subject matter expert insights (collected in the form of interviews). The resultant framework is presented in Sect. 4 below.

Our earlier work [i.e. 20] in this domain provided a foundational basis. We also reviewed process mining literature to identify algorithms and solutions relevant to supply chain analytics and the beef supply chain [21]. Our earlier research work exposed us to several beef cattle businesses as well as indications that there were gaps in the analytics and insights available across the supply chain. Further literature research validated the gap, with lack of supply chain integration and data sharing identified as strategic risks [9, 22]. Research in other industries such as automotive component supply noted that logistics can greatly benefit from process mining approaches [23]. It was with this background that the concept of a supply chain analytics framework for food supply chain was created.

The case study chosen (Case A[2]) for this research is the largest vertically integrated beef supply chain in Australia. The case study is revelatory since other businesses are

---

[2] We use the pseudo-name 'Case A', in line with the anonymity and research ethics agreements.

less vertically integrated with a focus either on the cattle farming side, either breeding or backgrounding, the feedlotting or the processing component.

As depicted in Table 1, respondents from the case study and other selected subject matter experts from practice were identified to contribute to the design (and evaluation) of the framework. The interviewees were specifically selected in order to ensure a cross section of managers from C-suite Executives, in order to understand the strategic management requirements to Farm Managers, to understand the tactical management requirements. In addition to operations management, data managers and IT managers were selected to get insights into challenges in collection of data and accuracy. To obtain a broader industry perspective industry researchers from Meat and Livestock Australia[3] were also consulted. Each interview took 30–45 min.

Table 1. Interviewees and their contributions

Interviewee	Contribution to framework	Evaluation focus
C suite executive	Business value of improved decision making	Summative: high level review of case study data
Cattle business owner (small & medium)	Decisions required across the supply chain for improving business outcomes, current decision support solutions and their value	Formative: Initial review based on artificial data and digital twin simulation
Farm manager	Factors influencing on farm decision making, current sources and availability of data	Summative: high level review of case study data
Data manager	Current availability of data for decision making, data accuracy, accessibility of data, users of data	Summative: high level review of case study data
IT manager	Current systems for data capture, connectivity issues	Formative: initial review based on artificial data and digital twin simulation
Industry researcher × 2	Best practice in beef supply chains, adoption of best practice	Selected for phase 2 evaluation on different case study
Solution developer × 2	Technical advantages of their process analytics solution, specific questioning for a combined process and data perspective	Both formative and summative focused on their specific solutions

---

[3] See https://www.mla.com.au for further details.

3.2 Framework Evaluation

Venable et al.'s [24] FEDS framework was used for evaluation design. The FEDS framework covers both the functional purpose of evaluation as well as the type of evaluation. Our's was a summative approach with naturalistic criteria [24], and this required 'real' industrial data and an IT Artefact to evaluate the MPSCA framework, where the case study provided an opportunity to analyze data more readily across the supply chain. The IT Artefact consists of several process mining algorithms hosted on the open-source framework, ProM[4] with supporting data analytics solutions such as Power BI[5]. With the design risk of being technically orientated a Technical Risk and Efficacy Evaluation strategy was selected, allowing for an initial formative approach based on artificial data and simulations advancing through to a summative approach with naturalistic criteria.

The integrated beef supply chain extends from breeding farms through to the retailer as shown in Fig. 1. In analyzing the beef supply chain of Case A, the MPSCA Framework was followed and various process analytical solutions tested on the data. Interviewees were approached again at this stage (See Table 1). The IT Artefact was built focusing on the questions of interest that the interviewees had posed, as well as the cattle data that was made available to the researchers. The core focus of the case study was to validate the framework, with a key design principle being that the various data and process algorithms as well as visualization and simulation solutions used can be interchanged. The resulting (MPSCA) framework is presented in detail next.

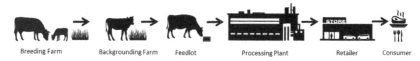

Breeding Farm   Backgrounding Farm   Feedlot   Processing Plant   Retailer   Consumer

Fig. 1. The integrated beef supply chain

4 Multi Perspective Supply Chain Analytics Framework

A conceptual framework from a synthesis of multiple data from the study was derived first, and this was then applied to Case A (as explained in Sect. 5).

The Multi Perspective Supply Chain Analytics Framework (referred to as MPSCA) combines process and data analytics while also factoring in the importance of effective visualization, simulation as well as an effective means of interaction with the user for decision support. At its core the framework is data driven. The key focus on a data driven approach resulted from both information received from the interviewees that the businesses were data rich, but information poor, as well as research that indicates much data is collected along a supply chain [25].

The MPSCA Framework consists of six stages, five of which we refer to as "views" to reflect the visualization that is provided to the processes and data:

---

[4] http://www.processmining.org/tools.
[5] https://powerbi.microsoft.com.

- Define Analysis Questions of Interest Stage
- Process Analytics Supply Chain View
- Data Analytics Performance View
- Multi Perspective Decisions View
- Simulation Analytics Scenario View
- Orchestration Prediction and Prescription View

The view all interact with the Data Extraction and Analysis Core as illustrated in Fig. 2 below.

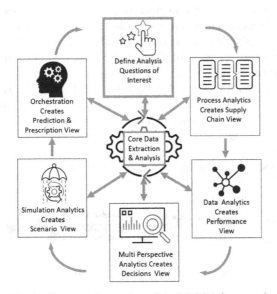

Fig. 2. Conceptual overview of the MPSCA framework

5 Applying the Framework to the Use Case

5.1 Define Analysis Questions of Interest

The key question of interest for the case study, as determined from the interviews is weight gain of the cattle through each stage of the supply chain. As cattle pass through the various stages of maturity: calf, weaner, backgrounder and feeder [26] they increasingly gain weight and it is farm management's role to ensure the cattle remain "on a rising plane of nutrition"[6]. While the key objective is to ensure that cattle always have enough edible pasture, this is not always the case with environmental factors playing a significant role, for example drought. Farmers must also carefully manage their stocking rates to ensure that pastures are not overgrazed, overgrazing can cause long term damage to

---

[6] Interview note from C Suite Executive large cattle business.

pasture and in extreme cases render them unsuitable for animals. With cattle weight the key criteria for determination of payment to farmers, the analysis questions of interest were posed as follows: "When do you move animals to the next stage of the supply chain?" Supporting questions being: "How much weight did each cow gain at each stage of the supply chain?" "How much did each cow weigh when it was transferred to the next stage of the supply chain?"

5.2 Core Data Analysis and Extraction

The business which participated in the case study made its cattle database available to the researchers for the purposes of building and evaluating the framework. The business began collecting and centralising individual cattle data since October 2018. In order to do this the business had to install RFID[7] readers and weighing systems together with cattle yard information gathering systems that are able to capture the data, on ruggedized laptops and later transmit the data to the headquarters central database, once the team conducing the cattle management process returned to an area with connectivity, which is normally the main farm house/office.

Due to the cost of installing the physical cattle management infrastructure and the sheer scale of operations, this process has been systematically rolled out over the past 18 months. The complete set of data since the beginning of the roll out was provided for the purposes of this research. The data set includes original testing data, this data was identified and excluded which reduced the data set to 390 834 records. New data attributes have been added to the cattle management system over the months as additional information requirements are identified. Currently the cattle management system captures 69 data attributes per animal all referenced to the animal RFID.

To understand the data attributes in more detail a summary data model was developed, see Table 2 below. The data model shows that key animal data is collected as well as location and supply chain history. Since recording and reporting the location of a specific animal is a mandatory regulatory requirement [27] it was hypothesised that this event data could well be used to extract the journey of the animal through its lifecycle using process analytics techniques. The location of the animal through each stage of its lifecycle together with its weight gain at each stage and location would provide good insights into how to improve the cattle supply chain for optimum yield such as weight gain.

5.3 Applying the Process Analytics Supply Chain View

Having assessed the cattle data next step in the MPSCA framework is apply process analytics to extract the supply chain view. As the extracted data set of 390834 records with 69 data attributes was considered too large for initial trial of process analytics techniques, it was decided to reduce the data attributes initially to weight only, aligning to the analysis question of interest. The key event data was classified as follows:

Case/Unique identifier: Individual animal RFID
Event name: CurrentPIC (Current Property/Farm Identification Code)

---

[7] Radio Frequency Identification.

Table 2. High level data model

	NLIS Register
PK	NLIS_id

	Cattle
PK	animal_id
FK	NLIS_id
	sex_id
	origin_id
	year_
	breed_id
	brand_id
	purpose_id
	weight_
	dentition_
	vaccinations_id
	diseases_id
	herdmob_id

	Breeding Property
PK	farm-id
FK	animal_id
FK	NLIS_id
FK	sex_id
FK	origin_id
FK	year_
FK	breed_id
FK	brand_id
FK	purpose_id
FK	weight_
FK	dentition_
FK	vaccinations_id
FK	diseases_id
	herdmob_id

	Backgrounding Property
PK	farm_id
FK	animal_id
FK	NLIS_id
FK	sex_id
FK	origin_id
FK	year_
FK	breed_id
FK	brand_id
FK	purpose_id
FK	weight_
FK	dentition_
FK	vaccinations_id
FK	diseases_id
	herdmob_id

	Breeding Paddock Book
PK	paddock_id
	biomass start_
	biomass finish_
	rainfall_
	temp_
	wind_
	ADG_
FK	herdmob_id

	Backgrounding Paddock Book
PK	paddock_id
	biomass start_
	biomass finish_
	rainfall_
	temp_
	wind_
	ADG_
FK	herdmob_id

Date and Time/Completion Time: Session Date
Data Attribute: Animal Weight

An initial process discovery analysis was conducted using the Inductive Visual Miner (IVM) algorithm [28]. The fitness of this model was checked and found to be unsatisfactory. A more suitable process mining algorithm was sought and after referencing Leemans et al. [29] the direct follows visual miner was used. The reason the Directly Follows Visual Miner, (DFVM), produced a better fit than the Inductive Visual Miner is due to nature of the cattle event logs. The sequential nature of supply chain is more suited to the type of algorithms deployed in the DFVM compared to the more complex algorithms of the IVM[8].

The discovered process model is shown in Fig. 3.

This view has discovered the individual supply chain of each animal as well as revealing several supply chain management issues which are discussed in Sect. 6.

5.4 Applying the Data Analytics Performance View

The Process Analytics Supply Chain View has highlighted several supply chain movements that do not appear to be optimal in order to satisfy the Analysis Question of

---

[8] Interview with Sander Leemans, developer of the IVM and DFVM algorithms.

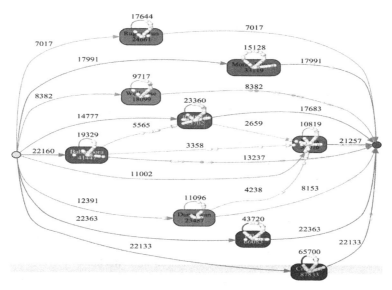

Fig. 3. Process analytics supply chain view

Interest. Animals are shown to be moved along the supply chain in paths that are not optimal. This observation led to the Process Analytics Supply Chain stage to be rerun focusing on Babbiloora, Dungowan, Redford and Niella (BDRN) supply chain in more detail.

After repeating the Process Analytics Supply Chain cycle several times on the BDRN supply chain and filtering out intra farm movements the Process Analytics Supply Chain View was able to detect that several animals were been returned to farms where they were being bred as well as directly to the finishing farm (Niella) bypassing the backgrounding farms. It was suspected that unusual environmental factors were the root cause and a check was made of rainfall and historical rainfall records[9]. These records showed that the region in which the BDRN farms were located had experienced extreme drought conditions over the period in which the cattle data was recorded.

The weight distributions on each farm were also extracted via Power BI, this data mining exercise shown in Fig. 4, further validated the observations from the Process Analytics Supply Chain View that extraordinary management practices were being applied. The holding of heavier animals on the breeding farm Babbiloora being an example.

These required steps corroborated the structure of the MPSCA framework and are discussed further in Sect. 6.

5.5 Applying Multi Perspective Decisions View

This view was included in the MPSCA Framework as the ability to create a data aware overlay to the supply chain perspective is of value, particularly in determining the impact

---

[9] http://www.bom.gov.au/qld.

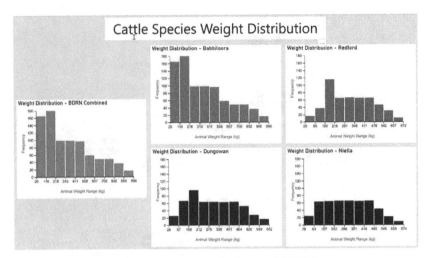

Fig. 4. Cattle weight distributions on BDRN farms

of data driven decision making along the supply chain. This perspective was tested on the case study data as follows.

Further literature research was conducted which led to the data-aware process mining work of de Leoni and van der Aalst [30]. Their work has focused on using conformance checking techniques to align an event log with data and a process model with decision points. Further development of this work has led to the development of the Multi-perspective process explorer [31]. This new algorithm factors in decisions that are not fully deterministic allowing for the discovery of overlapping decision rules. Due to the anomalies in the supply chain already discovered by the Process Analytics Supply Chain view as well as the lack of data across the cattle supply chain the decision making is clearly not deterministic and therefore the multi- perspective process explorer was selected to explore the data perspective.

Data attributes attached to events are used to analyse processes from other perspectives. With the significant amount of animal data now collected this perspective is most important in the analysis of the cattle supply chain. To discover this perspective the BDRN event log set was selected together with the BDRN petri net model and run through the multi-perspective process explorer. The results of the input model are shown in Fig. 5 below.

The data aware discovery algorithm was run on this input model based on the weight data attribute. Followed by the decision tree data discovery based on the weight algorithm. While the average fitness of the decision is relatively low at 59% the event logs are based on actual historical animal movements which we now know were determined by the drought. The output of this algorithm does however demonstrate that the influence of a key attribute such as animal weight can be discovered over a process model that represents the lifecycle of an animal. This result is most significant as it indicates that the proposed digital twin could utilise this functionality.

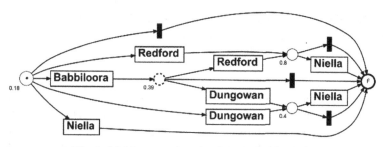

Fig. 5. Multi perspective view BRDN supply chain

5.6 Applying the Simulation Analytics Scenario View

The analysis in Sect. 5.3 has shown that while significant data is been captured per animal, it is not captured adequately across the supply chain. The hypothesis that a digital twin of both supply chain as well as a typical cow will be required to fill the data gaps therefore holds true. In order to create the Simulation Analytics view of the BDRN supply chain the discovered BDRN model was edited to exclude all edges that were as a result of abnormal factors. For the case study the simulation view requires the simulation of a cow with respect to its growth through its various stages of maturity. We have named the simulation the Digital Cow. In order to create a digital cow research had to be undertaken on typical growth patterns of a cow through the various lifecycle stages. Based on [32] an initial algorithm was developed to calculate the weight gain of a cow during the stages, calf, weaner, backgrounder and feeder. The initial algorithm considers weight gain when there is normal feed available to the animal. With further research the algorithm will be extended to account for weight gain in poor and good pasture conditions, ultimately linking to the available biomass modelling and measurements.

The output of the Digital Cow algorithm is shown in Fig. 6 below:

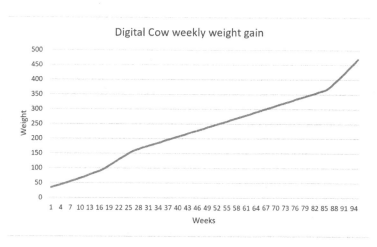

Fig. 6. Output of the digital cow algorithm

The Digital Cow algorithm was then used to develop synthetic event logs for the BDRN Digital Supply Chain which were then run through the multi perspective process explorer. The output further validates the MPSCA model as the data driven (weight) split of animals between Dungowan and Redford was 100% verifiable with the synthetic event logs.

Having proven that the combination of the digital twin of a supply chain as well as a digital cow can generate meaningful business data in circumstances where there are gaps in the actual supply chain data, our future research plan is to extend the digital supply chain to the entire integrated supply chain, using the digital cow to simulate data currently not available from the major breeding farms.

5.7 Orchestration Prediction and Prescription View

While each of the stages of the MPSCA Framework has shown to provide insights into management challenges and decisions along the supply chain, to be of value to business the framework must be able integrate and consolidate the insights for enhanced decision support. To identify an appropriate process orchestration engine several solutions were investigated. Camunda[10] has been rated by several studies [33, 34] as high in execution and operation criteria. While Camunda is a robust, BPMN 2.0 compliant workflow engine most suitable for commercial applications, the work of van der Aalst et al. [35] in developing RapidProM, an extension of the scientific workflow management solution RapidMiner[11], provides a solution specifically focused on process analytics. With RapidProM process mining analysis is repeatable and data and process mining combined, these features are considered core to the MPSCA Framework and has been used in this final stage.

The Orchestration Prediction and Prescription View was configured in RapidProM with several scientific workflows as follows:

1) Discover the cattle supply chain workflow: import supply chain event data > run visual miner > run conformance checker.
2) Run the multi-perspective process explorer workflow: import supply chain event data including special data attributes > run visual miner > run multi-perspective inductive miner.
3) Run the simulation analytics workflow digital twin - supply chain: import supply chain event data > import digital twin – supply chain petri net > run visual miner > run conformance checking.
4) Run the simulation analytics workflow digital twin – cow: import supply chain data generated by digital twin - cow > import actual supply chain petri net > run visual miner > run conformance checking.

6 Summary Discussion

As highlighted in the data model (Table 2) and the discovered process analytics supply chain view of Fig. 3, it is possible to discover and extract the complete supply chain

[10] https://camunda.com.

[11] https://rapidminer.com.

of an individual animal. This ability is most significant, not only for the deeper analytics that occur with this information (for example what were the environmental factors such as weather when the animal was on a farm), but also for provenance, a growing consumer requirement. By adjusting parameters in the 'directly follows visual miner' of the complete business cattle data, a group of farms (the BDRN group, as introduced in Sect. 5.5) was identified for deeper analysis. This group formed their own complete supply chain, illustrating that the MPSCA framework can "zoom-in" to areas of interest identified in the overall supply chain view.

Further focus on the BDRN group through filtering out of their intra – farm movements and focusing only on their inter-farm movements, highlighted several bidirectional animal transfers. Animals were returned to their previous property which is not best practice. Having observed in the data model (Table 2) that environmental data was not captured in the cattle data base, it was assumed that environmental factors were contributing to this supply chain behaviour. The framework's Data Analytics Performance view seeks to gain additional data to describe a supply chain action. Manual extraction of weather data for these farms was able to confirm that the farms were in severe drought during the observed supply chain events and animals had to be transferred between farms to ensure the animals had enough edible pasture.

The outputs from the process analytics on the BDRN group are significant, firstly, demonstrating that supply chain anomalies can be discovered with the 'directly follows visual miner' and reinforcing the need for scientific workflow as described in Sect. 5.7 within the framework. The scientific workflow should be extended to collect additional supply chain performance data, not captured in the event log for additional processing, for example in a decision model. The multi perspective process explorer was able to effectively detect the influence of the key data attribute, animal weight, on the decision to send animals to a farm. While the analysis question of interest for the case study, "When do you move animals to the next stage of the supply chain?" is dependent on more factors than animal weight alone, the fact that the animal weight dimension can be simultaneously analyzed with the control flow perspective adds significant value to the supply chain analytics.

Creation of the digital twin – farm was simplified through the ability to edit out unrequired "arcs" or supply chain connections from the discovered supply chain. The resultant petri net was then saved for later import into the 'directly follows visual miner' together with the real cattle event logs for compliance checking and highlighting of variations to the best practice supply chain. While the analysis shows that the BDRN supply chain had complete data, showing animals moving through their lifecycle and gaining weight through the various stages, the supply chain view of the farms (Fig. 3), shows that this is not the case for all. In discussing this observation with the business, it was noted that the large breeding properties supplying the cattle to these properties have not yet installed the cattle yard data capture systems. The first capture of all the historical data occurs when an animal reaches the backgrounding farm.

The above observation highlights the importance of the digital twin - cow in the Simulation Analytics view. Not only can the digital twin – cow algorithm produce event logs which can test various supply chain scenarios, it can also be used to produce event data, for example the typical weight gain of a calf and a weaner while it is on the breeding properties and close a key data gap. The digital twin - cow algorithm combined with the digital twin - supply chain can highlight where current cattle practices are deviating from best practice and alert cattle business owners especially those with large integrated cattle supply chains as to where the potential problem areas are. This information could be used to improve decision making regarding when to move animals to the next stage of the cattle supply chain in order to maximize weight gain and ultimately profit per animal.

The key challenge in this research has been the combination of process and data mining in order to solve the supply chain analytics gap, so critical to strategic management. Placing data extraction and analysis as the core of the framework has proven well suited, as a significant amount of data filtering and analysis occurred through the applied stages of the process. Testing the framework on significant amounts of real data has been most insightful, both in terms of the sorting and cleansing requirements when dealing with large quantities of industrial data as well as the gaps in data.

7   Conclusion

The study commenced with the research question: can process intelligence techniques solve complex supply chain problems and the proposition that, gaps in the strategic management of food supply chains could be addressed by a multi perspective supply chain analytics framework. A Multi Perspective Supply Chain Analytics (MPSCA) Framework was presented with empirical support, highlighting its ability to uniquely combine previously fragmented data and process mining methodologies to enable effective analysis of an integrated food supply chain. An IT Artefact was created and applied within the integrated beef supply chain of a revelatory case study (Case A), to demonstrate the applicability of the MPSCA Framework. This enabled evaluators to assess the framework from both formative and summative [24] perspectives. The core focus has been the development and evaluation of the framework and its design principles, while being agnostic to the various solutions used in each stage of the framework, as such an approach allows for a broader adoption of the framework. There has been a constant cycle of evaluation and feedback from domain specialists both within and external to the case study (Table 1) across the study phases, enabling the framework and its IT Artefact to be continuously improved.

The research and evaluation has shown that the proposition is true and that problems in strategic management of food supply chains can be addressed by a multi perspective supply chain analytics framework. The research question has been partially answered, in this case study a complex supply chain problem has been solved. Testing of the framework across a broader spectrum of supply chain problems is required to convincingly answer the question.

While the research has focused on a single integrated food supply chain, the size and scale of the case study as well as similarity to other food supply chains would suggest that there is an opportunity to apply the framework more broadly. We argue that the results and learnings from this integrated supply chain case study are applicable to integrated food supply chain's globally.

Having established the core scientific workflow for the MPSCA Framework, the next phase of research is to provide a workflow that will combine the decision support information. Learnings from this research can later be applied to beef supply chains with multiple business owners where the additional challenges of data ownership and transparency will need to be addressed. The researchers intend to validate the MPSCA in other areas (e.g. a horticulture business) in the next phase of evaluation. In combining event data as well as performance data in the MPSCA Framework, the opportunity to integrate the SCOR™ framework into MPSCA is also possible, both from a best practice reference perspective when conformance checking as well as from a performance data perspective. Such an inclusion will further drive adoption across food supply chains.

References

1. Behzadi, G., O'Sullivan, M.J., Olsen, T.L., Scrimgeour, F., Zhang, A.: Robust and resilient strategies for managing supply disruptions in an agribusiness supply chain. Int. J. Prod. Econ. **191**, 207–220 (2017). https://doi.org/10.1016/j.ijpe.2017.06.018
2. Plenert, G.: Supply Chain Optimization Through Segmentation and Analytics. CRC Press, Boca Raton (2014)
3. Sithole, B., Silva, S.G., Kavelj, M.: Supply chain optimization: enhancing end-to-end visibility. Procedia Eng. **159**, 12–18 (2016). https://doi.org/10.1016/j.proeng.2016.08.058
4. Hevner, A., March, S., Park, J., Ram, S.: Design science in information systems research. MIS Q. **28**(1), 75–105 (2004)
5. Yin, R.K.: Case Study Research: Design and Methods, 4th edn. Sage Publications, Thousand Oaks (2009)
6. Bowers, M., Petrie, A., Holcomb, M.: Unleashing the potential of supply chain. MIT Sloan Manag. Rev. **59**(1), 14–16 (2017). (1st edition)
7. Chen-Ritzo, C.-H., Ervolina, T., Harrison, T.P., Gupta, B.: Eur. J. Oper. Res. **205**(3), 604–614 (2010)
8. Boken, V., Cracknell, A., Heathcote, R.: Monitoring and Predicting Agricultural Drought: A Global Study. Oxford University Press, New York (2005)
9. Australian Meat Processor Corporation. http://www.ampc.com.au/uploads/pdf/strategic-plans/42161_AMPC_RiskDocumentvLR.pdf
10. van der Aalst, W.M.: Business process management: a comprehensive survey. ISRN Softw. Eng. **2013**(4), 4–5 (2013). https://doi.org/10.1155/2013/507984
11. Wolfert, S., Ge, L., Verdouw, C., Bogaardt, M.-J.: Big data in smart framing – a review. Agric. Syst. **153**, 69–80 (2017)
12. Aramyan, L.H., Oude Lansink, A.G.J.M., van der Vorst, J.G.A.J., van Kooten, O.: Performance measurement in agri-food supply chains: a case study. Supply Chain Manag. Int. J. **12**(4), 304–315 (2007)
13. Pham, X., Stack, M.: How data analytics is transforming agriculture. Bus. Horiz. **61**, 125–133 (2018)
14. Wang, G., Gunasekaran, A., Papadopoulos, T.: Big data analytics in logistics and supply chain management: certain investigations for research and applications. Int. J. Prod. Econ. **176**, 98–110 (2016)
15. Braziotis, C., Tannock, J.D.T., Bourlakis, M.: Strategic and operational considerations for the Extended Enterprise: insights from the aerospace industry. Prod. Plann. Control **28**(4), 267–280 (2017). https://doi.org/10.1080/09537287.2016.1268274
16. Delipinar, G.E., Kocaoglu, B.: Using SCOR model to gain competitive advantage: a literature review. Procedia Soc. Behav. Sci. **229**, 398–406 (2016). https://doi.org/10.1016/j.sbspro.2016.07.150

17. Stentoft, J., Rajkumar, C.: Balancing theoretical and practical relevance in supply chain management research. Int. J. Phys. Distrib. Logist. Manag. **48**(5), 504–523 (2018). https://doi.org/10.1108/IJPDLM-01-2018-0020

18. Lapide, L.: Competitive supply chains: excellence. Supply Chain Manag. Rev. **19**(4), 4–5 (2015)

19. Becker, T., Intoyoad, W.: Context aware process mining in logistics. Procedia CIRP **63**, 557–562 (2017)

20. Keates, O.: Integrating IoT with BPM to provide value to cattle farmers in Australia. In: Di Francescomarino, C., Dijkman, R., Zdun, U. (eds.) BPM 2019. LNBIP, vol. 362, pp. 119–129. Springer, Cham (2019). https://doi.org/10.1007/978-3-030-37453-2_11

21. Golini, R., Moretto, A., Caniato, F., Caridi, M., Kalchschmidt, M.: Developing sustainability in the italian meat supply chain: an empirical investigation. Int. J. Prod. Res. **55**(4), 1183–1209 (2017). https://doi.org/10.1080/00207543.2016.1234724

22. Simons, D., Francis, M., Bourlakis, M., Fearne, A.: Identifying the determinants of value in the U.K. red meat industry: a value chain analysis approach. J. Chain Netw. Sci. **3**(2), 109–121 (2008)

23. Gerke, K., Claus, A., Mendling, J.: Process mining of RFID-based supply chains. In: 2009 IEEE Conference on Commerce and Enterprise Computing, pp. 285–292. IEEE, Vienna (2009). https://doi.org/10.1109/cec.2009.72

24. Venable, J., Pries-Heje, J., Baskerville, R.: FEDS: a framework for evaluation in design science research. Eur. J. Inf. Syst. **25**(1), 77–89 (2016). https://doi.org/10.1057/ejis.2014.36

25. Verdouw, C.N., Beulens, A.J.M., Trienekens, J.H., Wolfert, J.: Process modelling in demand-driven supply chains: a reference model for the fruit industry. Comput. Electron. Agric. **73**(2), 174–187 (2010). https://doi.org/10.1016/j.compag.2010.05.005

26. https://www.mla.com.au/research-and-development/Genetics-and-breeding/

27. National Livestock Identification System. https://www.mla.com.au/meat-safety-and-traceability/red-meat-integrity-system/about-the-national-livestock-identification-system-2015/

28. Leemans, S.J.J., Fahland, D., van der Aalst, W.M.P.: Scalable process discovery and conformance checking. Softw. Syst. Model. **17**(2), 599–631 (2016). https://doi.org/10.1007/s10270-016-0545-x

29. Leemans, S., Poppe, E., Wynn, M.: Directly follows-based process mining: a tool. In: Burattin, A., van Zelst, S., Polyvyanyy, A. (eds.) Proceedings of the ICPM Demo Track 2019. CEUR Workshop Proceedings, vol. 2374, pp. 9–12. Sun SITE Central Europe (2019). http://www.ceur-ws.org/

30. de Leoni, M., van der Aalst, W.M.P.: Data-aware process mining: discovering decisions in processes using alignments. In: Proceedings of the 28th Annual ACM Symposium on Applied Computing, March 2013, pp. 1454–1461 (2013). https://doi.org/10.1145/2480362.2480633

31. Mannhardt, F., de Leoni, M., Reijers, H.A., van der Aalst, W.M.P.: Decision mining revisited - discovering overlapping rules. In: Nurcan, S., Soffer, P., Bajec, M., Eder, J. (eds.) CAiSE 2016. LNCS, vol. 9694, pp. 377–392. Springer, Cham (2016). https://doi.org/10.1007/978-3-319-39696-5_23

32. https://www.mla.com.au/news-and-events/industry-news/archived/2016/meeting-minimum-growth-rates-for-heifers/

33. Greiger, M., Harrer, S., Lenhard, J., Wirtz, G.: BPMN 2.0: the state of support and implementation. Future Gener. Comput. Syst. **80**, 250–262 (2018)

34. Median, A., Garcia-Garcia, J.A., Escalona, M.J., Ramos, I.: A survey on business process management suites. Comput. Stand. Interfaces **51**, 71–86 (2017)

35. van der Aalst, W., Bolt, A., van Zelst, S.: RapidProM: mine your processes and not just your data (2017)

Event Log Generation in a Health System: A Case Study

Simon Remy[1]($\boxtimes$), Luise Pufahl[2], Jan Philipp Sachs[1,3], Erwin Böttinger[1,3], and Mathias Weske[1]

[1] Hasso Plattner Institute, University of Potsdam, Potsdam, Germany
{simon.remy,jan-philipp.sachs,mathias.weske}@hpi.de
[2] Software and Business Engineering, Technische Universitaet Berlin, Berlin, Germany
luise.pufahl@tu-berlin.de
[3] Hasso Plattner Institute for Digital Health at Mount Sinai, Icahn School of Medicine at Mount Sinai, New York, NY 10029, USA
erwin.bottinger@mssm.edu

Abstract. Process mining has recently gained considerable attention as a family of methods and tools that aim at discovering and analyzing business process executions. Process mining starts with event logs, i.e., ordered lists of performed activities. Since event data is typically not stored in a process-oriented way, event logs have to be generated first. Experience shows that event log generation takes a substantial effort in process mining projects. This case study reports on the experiences made during the event log generation from the real-world data warehouse of a large U.S. health system. As the focal point, the case study looks at activities and processes that are related to the treatment of low back pain. Guided by the main phases of event log generation, i.e., extraction, correlation, and abstraction, we report on challenges faced, solutions found, and lessons learned. The paper concludes with future research directions that have been derived from the lessons learned from the case study.

Keywords: Process mining · Event log generation · Case study · Healthcare

1 Introduction

One of the main concerns of business process management is analyzing processes to find interesting aspects that require the attention of domain experts, for instance, to improve them. Process mining provides a rich set of algorithms and tools that work on event logs [2]. From an academic perspective, event logs are ordered lists of activities that have occurred during a business process [2]. With the increasing adoption of process mining in practice, the need for methods and techniques for generating event logs becomes apparent [3]. This is due to the fact that in real-world project environments, event data is not available

© Springer Nature Switzerland AG 2020
D. Fahland et al. (Eds.): BPM 2020, LNCS 12168, pp. 505–522, 2020.
https://doi.org/10.1007/978-3-030-58666-9_29

in event logs; instead, event data is stored in databases or data warehouses, so that event logs have to be generated first in order to use the process mining machinery for process analysis [10, 21]. Even though event log generation takes considerable effort in process mining projects [10], it is only marginally discussed in case studies [13].

This paper addresses the challenges and lessons learned from generating event logs in a complex healthcare environment. Patient data is stored in a data warehouse that was derived from the operational data of a large health system in the U.S. The data warehouse provides the raw data that has to be extracted, abstracted, and correlated to process instances. To scope the case study, activities and processes that are related to the treatment of low back pain are considered. Based on the methods and techniques for event log generation reported in the literature [10], the paper discusses the challenges faced and the solutions found. We also provide extensions, mainly to take advantage of medical ontologies and vocabularies. To illustrate the feasibility of the approach, one generated event log is fed into process mining algorithms for initial analysis discussed with three domain experts (two of which are co-authors and one is associate professor at the Icahn School of Medicine at Mount Sinai). Due to the strict data protection of the patient data, a non-disclosure agreement was applied to the case study. As a consequence of that, the raw data cannot be published.

The remainder of this paper is organized as follows. Section 2 discusses related work on event log generation and process mining in healthcare. The design of the case study and the methodology are described in Sect. 3. Section 4 reports on event log generation for the low back pain case, its challenges and solutions. The implementation, main results, the lessons learned, and the limitations of the case study are discussed in Sect. 5. Concluding remarks and future research directions that were derived from the lessons learned from the case study are given in Sect. 6.

2 Related Work

This work focuses on the event log generation in a complex healthcare environment, such that we discuss in the following related work on the event log generation, and process mining in healthcare.

2.1 Event Log Generation

Event log generation is an important activity in process mining projects. The PM^2 methodology [12] distinguishes between the following steps of a process mining project: (1) planning and (2) extraction, for defining the initial research questions and extracting the event data, (3) data processing, (4) mining & analysis, and (5) evaluation, through which the project might iterate several times, and finally, (6) process improvement. In this methodology, event log generation is split into two phases: extraction and data processing. Based on the process mining methodology, Emamjome et al. [13] reviewed 152 case studies on process mining for their "thoroughness" in conducting such a project in practice. They observed that the thoroughness for the event log extraction is "overall low and does not show much progress over the years", which means that often "data sources are introduced but there is no discussion on data characteristics and suitability to address research questions". They share similar observations for the data pre-processing phase. These results show that existing case studies report on the event log generation phase only to a limited extent, which stresses the relevance of the case study reported in this paper, focusing explicitly on insights into this phase.

Pérez-Castillo et al. [21] report on an approach for event log generation from non-process-aware systems. While their work provides interesting results, the data set, also from healthcare, investigated does not have the complexity nor the size of the one covered in this paper. Design decisions for the creation of an event log are discussed by [17], e.g., the selection of process instances. Further, a procedure for event log generation is proposed in [18]. A recent survey on event log generation by Diba et al. [10] organized the research approaches into three groups: techniques for event data extraction, correlation, and abstraction. Event log extraction is defined as the identification of "data elements that characterize events coming from heterogeneous data sources". This choice of data elements and sources should be driven by the research questions [3]. One approach to highlight here is the ontology-driven data extraction by Calvanese et al. [8] materializing an event log with an ontology developed by domain experts. This work shows the benefits of structured domain knowledge for the event log generation, whereby the focus is limited to the extraction phase – an ontology-based data access to extract the needed event log data. The second step, correlation, associates the event data extracted from data sources with process instance or cases, while abstraction transfers the event data to the needed granularity level [10]. Rather than developing a specific event log generation technique, this paper explores challenges and practical experiences in applying the event log generation pipeline in a complex, real-world healthcare environment.

2.2   Process Mining in Healthcare

Due to the relevance of clinical data in healthcare information systems (HIS), there is an increasing interest in applying process mining techniques to healthcare data [14,25].

In a recent literature survey on process mining in healthcare [14], 172 studies were identified from which 90% had a focus on process discovery. Further, Erdogan and Tarhan [14] highlight that currently the application is limited to processes of a single department in a single hospital, and observe as a gap the application of "process mining at larger scales."

Typical analysis questions for healthcare processes, such as "What are the most followed paths and what exceptional paths are followed?" or "Do we comply with internal and external guidelines?" and data challenges for process mining in healthcare are discussed by Mans et al. in [20].

Rojas et al. [25] report in their literature survey that most studies followed a direct implementation approach, where they manually generated an event log and used selected process mining tools and techniques. A minority of the selected studies (9%) in [25] used an integrated suite for data extraction and analysis. This might be due to the characteristics of healthcare data: Kumar et al. [19] discuss challenges of healthcare data, e.g. (1) clinical databases are often quite large, not only in the number of patients stored but also in terms of the data elements stored for them, (2) clinical data is incredibly variable, both semantically and numerically, (3) irregularity in healthcare data exists a lot, both as noisy and incomplete data. Gatta et al. [16] present a framework with an interface to flatten hierarchically organized healthcare data in an electronic health record to an event log. However, the proposed interface is limited with regards to the selection of cases, supports only one correlation mechanism of events to traces (i.e., patient-based), and has no abstraction mechanisms implemented, such that it only partially supports the event log generation from healthcare data.

Although process mining studies in healthcare reported on data preparation activities, this dimension is often not the centre of attention. Due to its complexity in data, this phase is very relevant for the success of a process mining project, such that we want to focus on and further explore it.

3   Research Methodology

As shown by the discussion of related work, the generation of an event log from a large data warehouse is not sufficiently researched. To provide a better understanding of the suitability of existing approaches and focus points for future research, we conducted a case study. According to Recker [24], a case study is a qualitative research method that explores phenomena in a natural setting to gain insights into new emerging topics. In a single case study, we explore the phenomena of event log generation, and want to answer the following research questions:

- RQ1: How to create a useful event log from a large, complex data warehouse for answering domain experts' questions?
- RQ2: How can standardized vocabularies and domain specific ontologies be used to improve this process?

A useful event log can help to answer the process analysis questions, which are usually defined in the planning phase of a process mining project [12], under the assumption that the quality of the available log can provide these insights. We selected a case from healthcare due to the availability of a large data warehouses with complex treatment data. Additionally, a rich set of standardized vocabularies for diseases, treatments, and medications can be found in that domain. This section continues with a description of the case, before the case study design and procedure is presented.

3.1   Case Description

This case is based on the clinical data collected at the Mount Sinai (MS) Health System in New York, U.S. Amongst the largest health systems in the United States, MS is approached by approximately 3.65 million patients per year. 42,000 employees –7,200 of which are physicians– are working in a total of eight major hospital campuses and more than 400 ambulatory practices[1].

Detailed health system-wide diagnostic and treatment data are available as Electronic Health Records (EHR) in a de-identified form in the Mount Sinai Data Warehouse (MSDW). This database has a total of 160 GB structured information from 8.4 million patients with around 137 million medical encounters and more than 50 billion data points. The underlying structure of the data warehouse is a star schema, consisting of multiple fact tables, which further reference numerous dimension tables. In total, it contains 39 tables and predefined views. Due to the sensible nature of EHR data, our work had to be approved by the Institutional Review Board (IRB)[2].

From the abundant clinical information in the MSDW, we chose to investigate the treatment processes of non-specific low back pain (LBP). It is amongst the most frequent complaints presented to health care professionals and responsible for a total direct and indirect costs of 87.6 billion U.S.-$ in the United States [11]. Both in the in- and outpatient settings, the treatment options for non-specific LBP are similar, i.e. there are no options exclusive to either of these. At the same time, this clinical entity has both a clinical guideline introduced shortly before major politically-enabled digitization efforts in healthcare (2007) and a very recent one (2017) [9,22]. As such, these guidelines are based on a systematic evaluation of available research on a specific area of disease and a consensus about how such evidence should be considered in daily routine, serving both as a blueprint of *how* and *in which order* screening, diagnosis and treatment should be carried out.

The analysis of *EHR* data warehouses requires the data to be stored in a structured, machine-readable format that can easily be translated into medical and domain-specific terms used by healthcare practitioners. Such translation is realized by vocabularies specific to each health system. In addition to these local vocabularies, resources mapping the relationships (e.g. hierarchy, context, and attributes) between the medical terms and concepts are needed to search, extract, and abstract the data. In our case, we tapped into the resources of the *International Classification of Diseases* (ICD) codes (Version 9/10) for describing diseases and disorders, the *Current Procedural Terminology* (CPT) in version 4 for diagnostic and therapeutic procedures, and *RxNorm* for any drug-related information. We used the ICD 10 code M54.5 (low back pain) for defining our patient cohort.

---

[1] https://www.mountsinai.org/about/facts (Accessed: 2020-03-10).
[2] IRB-19-02369.

3.2   Case Study Design and Procedure

By conducting the case study, we want to share experiences on how to approach the event log generation in a complex environment, the faced challenges, and solutions. During the case study, we collected different data, among which are (1) interviews with experts, (2) documentation of the event log generation steps and design decisions, (3) the prototypical implementation, and (4) the resulting event logs as well as the process mining results. The case study procedure is shown in Fig. 1.

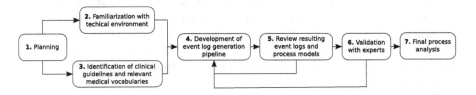

Fig. 1. Procedure used in the case study.

1. We conducted interviews with experts from MS on interesting scenarios for process mining. Thereby, the low back pain case was selected. Additionally, the driving questions for the process mining project were identified:
   - Q1: At which point during the treatment of low back pain are opioids applied?
   - Q2: Are LBP patients treated as proposed in the clinical guidelines?
   - Q3: Do different variations in the treatment procedure for the patients exist?
2. In the familiarization phase with the technical environment, the data warehouse was explained by the experts. Additionally, it was discussed how the patient cohort of low back pain can be identified.
3. The relevant clinical guidelines for the case were identified and translated into BPMN process models. Additionally, medical vocabularies were identified to bridge the gap between locally uses terms and standardized expressions.
4. The pipeline for the event log generation was developed.
5. Event logs were generated for the low back pain cohort. The traces and the resulting process models were reviewed.
6. The resulting event logs and process models were validated and discussed several times with experts both from the healthcare system as well as with two medical experts, one with and one without knowledge of business process modelling. Based on the feedback, we looped back into the development of the pipeline.
7. The resulting event log was used for the final process analysis to answer the questions by the experts.

4   Event Log Generation Pipeline for Low Back Pain

In this work, a general pipeline, as described in the literature, was adopted [10, 17]. With the three major steps, event extraction, event correlation, and event abstraction; it serves the goal of event log generation.

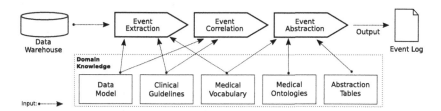

Fig. 2. As the product of multiple iterations with medical experts, we developed and applied the pipeline depicted above to generate an event log from the MSDW; it also shows the different types of domain knowledge as input for each step.

As depicted in Fig. 2, the pipeline has two kinds of inputs: structured data and domain knowledge. In this case study, the data warehouse was the only source of structured data. As one of the five types of domain knowledge inputs to the pipeline, a data warehouse schema was provided. The other four are clinical guidelines, standardized medical ontologies, locally used vocabulary and generated abstraction tables. All of them are healthcare-specific artefacts and will be explained in more detail later in this section. These additional inputs were evaluated with medical experts and used at different steps of the pipeline to support the corresponding tasks. The outcome of the pipeline is a single event log which, following the description of van der Aalst [2], consists of a set of events organized as cases. Each event refers to an activity (i.e., a particular step in a process) and has at least a name, a timestamp and a case identifier. If available, additional attributes, like resources or a department, were added. The resulting event log complies to the XES standard for event logs [1] and can be further processed by process mining tools. The approach faced challenges in each of the three steps, which will be explained in the following.

4.1   Event Extraction

Event extraction as the first activity in the pipeline aims to retrieve relevant events from the data warehouse, for which it has to be identified and located. To this end, knowledge about the underlying process and the structure of the data warehouse is required. For the latter, we had access to an existing database schema.

Relevant data can be split up into process-related and instance-related data. On the one hand, information about the general process, like activities and thus the notion of events is necessary. On the other hand, data for the relevant cases

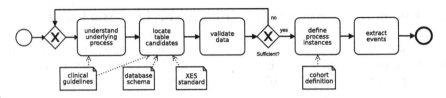

Fig. 3. Illustration of the steps taken to extract relevant event data. Due to the explorative nature of this task, it was necessary to locate and validate table candidates in the data warehouse, which let to an iterative approach, as shown by the loop.

need to be selected, i.e. data for process instances, which focuses on the handling of LBP patients. As a starting point to understand the underlying process clinical guidelines were used. As previously described, those guidelines have a normative character and describe how treatments should be performed. In a first step, BPMN process models, which reflect the treatment processes described in the guidelines, have been derived. Key activities in the resulting models were either performing a diagnostic or treatment task. Besides others, different diagnoses reflect decision points in the models, like the diagnose of acute or chronic low back pain and thus result in different treatment paths. Further, the guidelines distinguish between pharmacologic treatments, e.g. prescription of painkillers or opioids, and noninvasive, nonpharmacologic treatments, including exercise and massage. Based on this, different event notions for diagnosis, treatments and materials (i.e. medical drugs) have been derived.

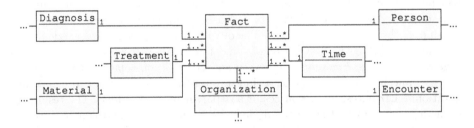

Fig. 4. Excerpt of the database schema with all case relevant dimensions. Based on the unique patient ids in the fact table, additional information can be related to single events in the pipeline.

Locating relevant event data in the warehouse is a challenging task. Even if the general structure of the data warehouse is known, the domain of each attribute stays hidden. That leads to the problem that potentially interesting table attributes turn out to be wrong or are not meaningful at all. This was the case especially for attributes, which occur multiple times in the data warehouse, like test results or temporal information. Also, the domains of some table attributes referred to abbreviations, like department identifiers, which are only internally used by the organization and thus was hard to interpret. To overcome these challenges, a mapping between medical vocabulary and internally used abbreviations were provided by domain experts. Since the temporal order of events is an important requirement of event logs [2], temporal information needed to be added to single events. As one step taken to de-identify the data, all absolute timestamps of the events were mapped to the age in days of the patient by MS. While this preserves the order of events of each patient, we aimed to recover the total ordering of events for the complete log. After consulting domain experts, we found a way to obtain this information from the data warehouse. Besides, we included general information about the patients, like age in days and gender as case attributes in this step. After completing the manual tasks of identifying all relevant dimensions and tables, as illustrated in Fig. 4, the implemented pipeline can automatically extract relevant events.

Concluding the first step of the pipeline, those challenges led to an iterative process in which potential dimension candidates got identified and validated. In the end, relevant event data was distributed over seven dimensions in the data warehouse, as shown in Fig. 4. Main challenges in this step were to select the correct events and their attributes. To extract data of the process instances, we filtered for patients with the LBP-specific ICD code M54.5. An example of the raw event data, extracted in this step, is given in Listing 1.1. However, the obtained data does not contain any case notion yet, which will be covered next.

```
<event>
  <id>8aa5c191-0ee6-4fbd-a4f4-6fbff4c17ae8</id>
  <patient-id>174799939184ABC</patient-id>
  <date-of-birth>1959-01-01</date-of-birth>
  <gender>gender</gender>
  <timestamp>2012-05-26T00:02:00.000Z</timestamp>
  <name>LOW BACK PAIN</name>
  <description>Low back pain</description>
  <context>ICD-10</context>
  <code>M54.5</code>
  <facility>12435</facility>
</event>
```

Listing 1.1. Example of one event, extracted form the data warehouse.

4.2 Event Correlation

After extracting the raw events from the data warehouse, events that correspond to the same process instance need to be correlated. Existing approaches, like [10], focus on the technical perspective of how to correlate events. To this end, a core assumption of this so-called correlation problem is that each event belongs to a single process instance [2]. In our study, we found that it is less a technical question of how to correlate events but, instead, what the most suitable notion of a case is.

Based on the structure of the data warehouse and medical evidence, three potential case notions were identified, (1) patient-based, (2) visit-based, and (3) encounter-based. The first type defines one case per patient, including all events that have ever occurred in any treatment. In this notion, events are correlated

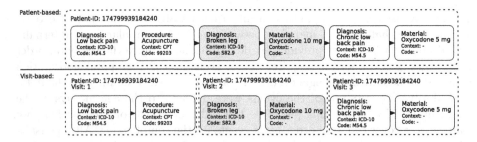

Fig. 5. Visualization of two possible case notions. Only events with a white background are related to a low back pain diagnosis or treatment. Applying the patient-based notion would assume a logical relation between all events in the case. In the visit-based approach, this trace would be excluded.

based on unique patient IDs. The second case notion are visits. A visit consists of events that are related via the fact table by a visit ID to a patient. A visit may cover a certain period, like multiple days, and can contain events created by different medical departments. Chaining up all visits related to one patient results in a patient-based case. The third possible case notion are encounters, which are a more fine-grained notion. Every visit consists of encounters, which again contain events. Based on an encounter ID, they can be matched with their corresponding visit.

Choosing the most suitable case notion was a challenging task. Each option has its advantages and limitations, as explained in the following. The advantage of the patient-based approach is that since the whole patient history is covered, all relations between relevant treatments and diagnoses are preserved. However, this assumes a logical relation between all available events, like the diagnosis of low back pain and the prescription of any following treatment. This might not always be true since a patient might undergo medical treatment related to, for instance, an accident. An example is given in Fig. 5, where the shaded events correspond to a broken leg that is not related to the LBP treatment of that patient. More concrete, the Oxycodone medication related to the broken leg might be associated with the treatment of low back pain. To summarize, using the patient ID for correlation might lead to misleading results in a future process analysis.

To overcome the disadvantage of the patient-based approach, the visit-based case notion was further investigated. Following this approach, several cases that belong to the same patient may exist in the event log. However, due to the higher granularity of this notion, unrelated cases could be filtered out in the next step. A case was considered unrelated if none of its events is related to the specific case. For this purpose, filters for diagnosis, treatments and medication are used. This way, noise in the data got reduced, but at the same time information about the relations between single visits got lost, as depicted in Fig. 5. That approach led to another challenge that was noticed only during the process mining analysis.

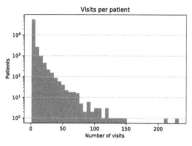

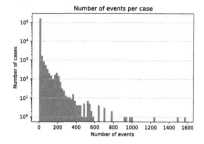

(a) Distribution of visits per patient.   (b) Distribution of events per case.

Fig. 6. Visualization of the number of cases (visits) per patient and the number of events per case on a logarithmic scale.

Since the treatment of a patient may require multiple visits, the resulting process model cannot distinguish between the very first visit and later visits. In other words, the resulting model cannot be properly aligned with the clinical guidelines any more. A similar problem occurred when investigating the third possible case notion. Since this would split the events into even smaller sets, the impact would be higher. Furthermore, since not all encounters could be mapped to existing visits, we decided to discard this case notion.

To summarize, the raw events are correlated according to one of the two case notions. Depending on the use case, the different notions can be specified as a parameter in our implemented pipeline. In the case study, we obtained 61,494 patient-based traces and 168,508 visit-based traces. As depicted in Fig. 6a, the majority of patients has less than ten visits. Further, there are 2.7 visits on average per patient. The patient with the most visits, however; has seen a doctor 232 times. Furthermore, there are six events on average per case, but about 21% of all cases only consists of a single event, as shown in Fig. 6b.

4.3 Event Abstraction

The last step in the pipeline covers event abstraction. This step is important, since data may differ in granularity. In our case, the term event abstraction is used as an umbrella term for several techniques, like aggregation, filtering and mapping, to bridge differences in the event data's granularities. As depicted in the event excerpt in Listing 1.1, the extracted events have several attributes, like medical context, code, timestamp, and description. Besides others, these attributes are used in the abstraction step, as shown in Fig. 7. Further, the event abstraction can be split into three tasks: (1) normalize event labels, (2) aggregate events to higher-level ones, and (3) merge temporal-related events, which will be described in the following.

The first task deals with different event labels that refer to the same activity. The root cause for this is that the raw event names base on a description

Fig. 7. To align different granularities in the event data, medical ontologies were used to normalize event labels. Further, low-level events were aggregated and identical events merged.

attribute, which can be entered in a free-text field in the HIS. To illustrate this, consider the two events *prescribe Oxycodone 10* mg and *prescribe Oxycodone 5* mg. Besides the name of the prescribed drug, the labels contain information about the dose, which results in different labels. To overcome this issue, the labels can semi-automatically be normalized based on the event's context, e.g. ICD, CPT, and RxNorm. For the given example, the RxNorm ontology was used and, the normalized event label is *prescribe Oxycodone*. In case no standardized medical context exists, an abstraction table was used to map event labels manually. In the second task, low-level events were aggregated to high-level events. Low-level events provide detailed information about an activity, which is not always required. For example, in the given case, several vital signs (e.g., blood pressure, pulse) were frequently measured. In this case, the domain experts suggested to aggregate these low-level events to the high-level event *check vital signs*, since they are not directly related to the treatment of LBP. This way, information about the high-level activity could be preserved, while the unnecessary details got reduced. As a result, the abstraction tables were extended by events that should be aggregated.

Lastly, identical events that directly follow each other in the same case get merged in the third task. Events are identical if they share the same label, attribute values, and timestamps. This behaviour was frequently observed for diagnoses and prescriptions. To sum up, event abstraction, as the last step in the pipeline, bridges differences in granularity and yields an event log that can be used for process mining.

5   Case Study Results

In this case study, an approach to generate event logs from a data warehouse in a health system was presented. In the following, the technical implementation and gained insights will be presented, followed by a summary of the lessons learned.

5.1   Technical Implementation and Process Analysis

Due to the strong data security requirements a dedicated infrastructure was set up. The technical setup consisted of a combination of a Linux virtual machine (VM) and an in-memory database. To further ensure security, both infrastructure components were hosted on a cloud platform, located in the U.S., and could

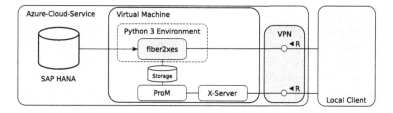

Fig. 8. Overview of the system architecture used in this case study. Due to strong data security requirements, the data had to be hosted in the U.S. in a private network.

only be accessed via VPN (see Fig. 8). On the VM, all services used to query the data warehouse, to extract the relevant data and to transform it into the XES format, ran within a Python 3 environment. Similarly, standard process mining software like ProM[3] was only installed on the VM and the graphical user interface forwarded to our local machines. The prototypical implementation[4] ("fiber2xes") of the pipeline is publicly available without containing any patient-related data and is independent of the presented case. Event logs for other healthcare processes can be generated if a cohort definition and abstraction tables are provided.

Based on the resulting event logs, we were able to answer the questions of medical domain experts, as stated in Sect. 3.2. As depicted in Fig. 9, one resulting process model discovered by a heuristic miner[5] reveals the complexity of the case. The model indicates that most treatment processes start with the *low back pain* diagnosis activity, mostly followed by non-pharmacological treatments or prescription of painkillers. In a minority of cases, opioids were prescribed right after the entry of the diagnosis. This complies, in general, with the clinical guidelines. However, these findings still have to be interpreted with caution, since multiple visits could belong together and, thus, the initial diagnosis could be stated in a previous visit already. Altogether, we could generate a useful event log with our pipeline as described in the previous section (*RQ1*). Notably, in the event extraction and abstraction steps, ontologies and medical knowledge were useful for the event log generation (*RQ2*). In the following, challenges during these phases and our solutions with and without medical ontologies are summarized.

5.2 Lessons Learned

As shown in Fig. 1, in the first three phases of the case study, it was necessary to understand the case and to collect necessary domain knowledge. Based on publicly available and standardized clinical guidelines and locally used medical vocabularies, this task was done without major challenges. Further, due to strict

---

[3] http://www.promtools.org/.
[4] https://github.com/bptlab/fiber2xes.
[5] https://pm4py.fit.fraunhofer.de/.

data protection regulations, a proper infrastructure had to be used. In the fourth phase of the project, the event log generation pipeline was developed, as presented in Fig. 2. The iterative nature of this process was caused by phases five and six, which required changes in the pipeline after validating and discussing intermediate results with domain experts. Those changes were caused by several challenges in the different steps, which we will elaborate on in the following. In comparison to the procedure proposed in [18], our study does not only provide suggestions about the general steps to follow to accomplish the task of event abstraction but also describes to what extent specific domain knowledge can be used to ease this process. An overview of the challenges, solutions and limitations is given in Table 1.

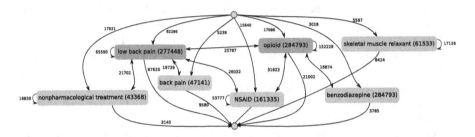

Fig. 9. Applying the heuristic miner yields a process model that depicts the complexity of the case. The model depicts the relations (edges) and their frequencies between activities (rectangles) in the treatment process.

For the event extraction questions about the notion of single events and how to extract them had to be answered. By translating the clinical guidelines to BPMN process models, key activities and related events could be identified. Inspired by related work [7,8], we used structured domain knowledge in this step. However, instead of relying on interviews with domain experts or individual domain models, we used existing and standardized domain knowledge, like clinical guidelines. Aligning the resulting process model and the existing database schema helped to select relevant dimensions and tables in the data warehouse. Further, to complete this task, medical vocabularies used in the guidelines and the data warehouse had to be mapped. Furthermore, parts of the event data had to be decoded into a human-readable description with the help of locally used vocabulary. As depicted in Fig. 3, the reliability of the data was discussed with the domain experts before the extraction. The quality of the data itself has not been considered yet. As described in literature [6] this is commonly addressed in a subsequent step after the event log generation. However, a common problem in health care is the quality of timestamps [4,15,20]. This can be due to inaccurate documentation and different granularities, depending on the origin of the data. The goal of the second step in the pipeline was to correlate events into cases. Based on medical evidence, multiple case notions have been explored. Domain experts agree that a suitable case notion highly depends on the specific questions. For instance, if the treatment of a specific disease is the main focus, the visit-based approach might be the better choice. Nonetheless, to enhance the visit-based notion, further research is necessary, for example, to identify visits that are related from a medical perspective. To this end, additional information, like billing cycles, clinical notes, or temporal properties could be used. In the abstraction step, differences in the granularity of the events had to be aligned. To overcome these challenges, related to [5], context information like medical ontologies have been used. The events in the example in Sect. 4.3 can be seen as a specialization of a higher-level activity based on their linguistic property, and can be easily abstracted. But the normalization also includes events where normalized labels can be derived from a shared context by converting different versions of the same context using an abstraction table. For example, the events "low back pain" (ICD-10) and "lumbago" (ICD-9) describe the same diagnostic event but for different versions of the ICD. In this case, one of the two contexts could be chosen as a reference, and all others converted accordingly. Lastly, by means of domain experts, further abstraction tables have been developed to aggregate low-level events.

So far, we reported case-specific challenges and discussed their solutions. In the following, we would like to point out general topics, related to this case study, that require further research. We successfully demonstrated how existing reference models, like guidelines, can be used to support the event log generation process. Since the healthcare domain has the advantage of existing standards and ontologies, we are convinced that some of the findings can be transferred to other medical cases but also to other domains, where reference models and ontologies are present. One example would be local administration and public law. The question is, to what extent such models can be used to support this task in general, and what requirements, except a normative character, they have to fulfil? A general methodology could help to guide this task and to prevent from missing out important information which may not be covered in the reference model. Further, we illustrated the application of abstraction tables, based on ontologies. This raises the question of how those could automatically be derived and in which case one should follow a bottom-up or top-down approach. Further, investigating the potential relationships between those ontologies might be helpful. Finally, we confirmed existing concerns on event correlation [23]. This remains a conceptual problem, which highly depends on the specific use case.

Table 1. Overview about the major challenges faced in each step of the case study, their solutions and limitations.

	Challenges	Solutions	Limitations
Event extraction (see Sect. 4.1)	Determine event notion	Clinical guidelines and analysis of the MSDW structure	Data warehouse specific
	Locate and validate relevant data	Use database schema and clinical guidelines	Manual and iterative task
	Decode event data	Map internally used medical vocabulary and public medical ontologies	May require feedback from domain experts
Event correlation (see Sect. 4.2)	Determine case notion	Focus on patient-based and visit-based case notion	Trade-off between loss of information and noise
Event abstraction (see Sect. 4.3)	Fine-grained event labels	Normalize event labels based on their contexts and medical standards	Requires context information for automation
	Low-level events	Aggregate low-level events into high-level events	Requires handcrafted abstraction tables
	Repetition of identical events	Group events based on temporal information	Potential loss of information

6   Conclusion

In this case study, we presented how clinical guidelines, standardized vocabulary, and domain-specific ontologies can be used to ease the event log generation process in a medical environment. This paper addresses the challenges and lessons learned, of the project and presents several solutions. The findings confirm conclusions from other related work on event log generation and add new insights, like the application of domain-specific ontologies.

However, looking only into one case limits the generalizability; in future, we plan to investigate further cases to elaborate the roles of reference models and ontologies in event log generation. Further, we would like to include more unstructured domain knowledge, like clinical notes or lab results, to improve our approach, e.g. the case notion. Lastly, the current approach lacks automation, as many steps in the pipeline require manual work.

Acknowledgement. We would like to thank Riccardo Miotto, Benjamin Glicksberg and Ismail Nabeel from the Icahn School of Medicine at Mount Sinai for their domain expertise. Further, we thank Arne Boockmeyer, Finn Klessascheck, Tom Lichtenstein, Martin Meier, Francois Peverali, and Simon Siegert from the Hasso Plattner Institute who contributed significantly to the technical implementation. Research reported in this paper was supported by the Office of Research Infrastructure of the National Institutes of Health under award numbers S10OD026880. The content is solely the responsibility of the authors and does not necessarily represent the official views of the National Institutes of Health.

References

1. IEEE standard for eXtensible event stream (XES) for achieving interoperability in event logs and event streams. IEEE Std 1849–2016, pp. 1–50 (2016)
2. van der Aalst, W.: Process Mining - Data Science in Action, 2nd edn. Springer, Heidelberg (2016). https://doi.org/10.1007/978-3-662-49851-4
3. van der Aalst, W., et al.: Process mining manifesto. In: Daniel, F., Barkaoui, K., Dustdar, S. (eds.) BPM 2011. LNBIP, vol. 99, pp. 169–194. Springer, Heidelberg (2012). https://doi.org/10.1007/978-3-642-28108-2_19
4. Andrews, R., et al.: Leveraging data quality to better prepare for process mining: an approach illustrated through analysing road trauma pre-hospital retrieval and transport processes in Queensland. Int. J. Environ. Res. Public Health **16**(7), 1138 (2019)
5. Baier, T., Mendling, J.: Bridging abstraction layers in process mining by automated matching of events and activities. In: Daniel, F., Wang, J., Weber, B. (eds.) BPM 2013. LNCS, vol. 8094, pp. 17–32. Springer, Heidelberg (2013). https://doi.org/10.1007/978-3-642-40176-3_4
6. Bozkaya, M., Gabriels, J., van der Werf, J.M.E.M.: Process diagnostics: a method based on process mining. In: International Conference on Information, Process, and Knowledge Management, pp. 22–27. IEEE Computer Society (2009)
7. Calvanese, D., Montali, M., Syamsiyah, A., van der Aalst, W.M.P.: Ontology-driven extraction of event logs from relational databases. In: Reichert, M., Reijers, H.A. (eds.) BPM 2015. LNBIP, vol. 256, pp. 140–153. Springer, Cham (2016). https://doi.org/10.1007/978-3-319-42887-1_12
8. Calvanese, D., Kalayci, T.E., Montali, M., Tinella, S.: Ontology-based data access for extracting event logs from legacy data: the onprom tool and methodology. In: Abramowicz, W. (ed.) BIS 2017. LNBIP, vol. 288, pp. 220–236. Springer, Cham (2017). https://doi.org/10.1007/978-3-319-59336-4_16
9. Chou, R., et al.: Diagnosis and treatment of low back pain: a joint clinical practice guideline from the American College of Physicians and the American Pain Society. Ann. Intern. Med. **147**(7), 478–91 (2007)
10. Diba, K., et al.: Extraction, correlation, and abstraction of event data for process mining. Wiley Interdiscip. Rev. Data Min. Knowl. Discov. **10**(3), e1346 (2020)
11. Dieleman, J.L., et al.: US spending on personal health care and public health, 1996–2013. JAMA **316**(24), 2627–2646 (2016)
12. van Eck, M.L., Lu, X., Leemans, S.J.J., van der Aalst, W.M.P.: PM^2: a process mining project methodology. In: Zdravkovic, J., Kirikova, M., Johannesson, P. (eds.) CAiSE 2015. LNCS, vol. 9097, pp. 297–313. Springer, Cham (2015). https://doi.org/10.1007/978-3-319-19069-3_19

13. Emamjome, F., Andrews, R., ter Hofstede, A.H.M.: A case study lens on process mining in practice. In: Panetto, H., Debruyne, C., Hepp, M., Lewis, D., Ardagna, C.A., Meersman, R. (eds.) OTM 2019. LNCS, vol. 11877, pp. 127–145. Springer, Cham (2019). https://doi.org/10.1007/978-3-030-33246-4_8

14. Erdogan, T., Tarhan, A.: Systematic mapping of process mining studies in healthcare. IEEE Access **6**, 24543–24567 (2018)

15. Fox, F., Aggarwal, V.R., Whelton, H., Johnson, O.: A data quality framework for process mining of electronic health record data. In: IEEE International Conference on Healthcare Informatics (ICHI), pp. 12–21. IEEE (2018)

16. Gatta, R., et al.: A framework for event log generation and knowledge representation for process mining in healthcare. In: International Conference on Tools with Artificial Intelligence (ICTAI), pp. 647–654. IEEE (2018)

17. Jans, M., Soffer, P.: From relational database to event log: decisions with quality impact. In: Teniente, E., Weidlich, M. (eds.) BPM 2017. LNBIP, vol. 308, pp. 588–599. Springer, Cham (2018). https://doi.org/10.1007/978-3-319-74030-0_46

18. Jans, M., Soffer, P., Jouck, T.: Building a valuable event log for process mining: an experimental exploration of a guided process. Enterp. IS **13**(5), 601–630 (2019)

19. Kumar, V., et al.: Exploring clinical care processes using visual and data analytics: challenges and opportunities. In: Knowledge Discovery and Data Mining KDD: Workshop on Data Science for Social Good, pp. 1–5 (2014)

20. Mans, R.S., van der Aalst, W.M.P., Vanwersch, R.J.B., Moleman, A.J.: Process mining in healthcare: data challenges when answering frequently posed questions. In: Lenz, R., Miksch, S., Peleg, M., Reichert, M., Riaño, D., ten Teije, A. (eds.) KR4HC/ProHealth -2012. LNCS (LNAI), vol. 7738, pp. 140–153. Springer, Heidelberg (2013). https://doi.org/10.1007/978-3-642-36438-9_10

21. Pérez-Castillo, R., et al.: Generating event logs from non-process-aware systems enabling business process mining. Enterp. IS **5**(3), 301–335 (2011)

22. Qaseem, A., et al.: Noninvasive treatments for acute, subacute, and chronic low back pain: a clinical practice guideline from the American College of Physicians. Ann. Intern. Med. **166**(7), 514–530 (2017)

23. Rebuge, Á., Ferreira, D.R.: Business process analysis in healthcare environments: a methodology based on process mining. Inf. Syst. **37**(2), 99–116 (2012)

24. Recker, J.: Scientific Research in Information Systems - A Beginner's Guide. Progress in IS. Springer, Heidelberg (2013). https://doi.org/10.1007/978-3-642-30048-6

25. Rojas, E., et al.: Process mining in healthcare: a literature review. J. Biomed. Inform. **61**, 224–236 (2016)

Author Index

Printed in the United States
By Bookmasters